Bibliography on Holocaust Literature

About the Book and Authors

A comprehensive and thorough work, this bibliography on Holocaust literature is the product of ten years of intensive research. Beginning their search with material written in the 1930s, the authors have included scholarly studies, contemporary newspaper reports, eyewitness testimonies, memoirs, and documentaries. Nearly 15,000 books, pamphlets, periodicals, and dissertations have been systematically researched and classified, many for the first time.

In addition to sources relating directly to the Nazi attempt to exterminate European Jewry, the authors have broadened their focus to include sections on Jewish life in prewar Europe, antisemitism, fascism and nazism, and the aftermath of the Holocaust. Important books and articles have been annotated, and introductory essays provide a guide for further study. Many of the citations are cross-referenced, and author and periodical indexes are included.

Abraham J. Edelheit, an instructor at Kingsborough Community College, New York, holds degrees from Yeshiva and Brandeis Universities in modern Jewish history. Hershel Edelheit, a Holocaust survivor who was incarcerated in a number of slave labor and concentration camps during World War II, is a student, researcher, and speaker on the Holocaust.

Bibliography on Holocaust Literature

Abraham J. Edelheit
and Hershel Edelheit

Westview Press / Boulder and London

Published in 1986 in the United States of America by Westview Press, Inc.; Frederick A. Praeger, Publisher; 5500 Central Avenue, Boulder, Colorado 80301

Library of Congress Cataloging in Publication Data
Bibliography on Holocaust literature.
Includes index.
1. Holocaust, Jewish (1939-1945)--Bibliography.
I. Edelheit, Abraham J. II. Edelheit, Hershel.
Z6374.H6B48 1986 016.94053'15'03924 86-9274
(D810.J4)
ISBN 0-8133-7233-X

Composition for this book was provided by the authors.

Printed and bound in the United States of America

The paper used in this publication meets the requirements of the American National Standard for Permanence of Paper for Printed Library Materials Z39.48-1984.

6 5 4 3 2 1

Dedicated to
Rabbi Abraham Jacob, Pesha Rachel, Zivia,
Mordechai, Pearl, Molly, and Shmuel Leib Edelheit
of Rymanov, Poland

Seven of the Six Million

Contents

PART II. THE PERPETRATORS

4 Fascism

5 The SS State

13 The Free World Reaction

19 Distorting the Holocaust

20 Historiography, Bibliographies and Guides

Preface

Ever since the end of World War II, when the truth about the near destruction of European Jewry surfaced in all its gruesomeness, thousands and perhaps hundreds of thousands of people from all walks of life - both survivors and those not directly touched by the incomprehensible events of the Holocaust - have brought up a similar question: How could a monstrous event like the Holocaust have happened in this day and age, during such an advanced stage in our society?

This question is at the core of many others that the serious scholar, the historian, and the student, as well as the layman, must ask. These questions deal with the causes and background of the Holocaust as well as the nature of the Holocaust itself and its aftermath.

Were the unfolding events of the Holocaust spontaneous in nature, as is the act of a riot or pogrom precipitated by a demagogue who arouses the prejudices and passions of people? Or were the events of the Holocaust a well-thought-out, well-planned, superbly executed affair?

How did Jews live in Europe before the war?

Was there a Jewish problem in Europe, or was the Jew used as a scapegoat for all the ills - both real and imagined - by bigot, priest, and politician alike?

Did the Jew, in fact, command such powers as to warrant his removal from Christian society?

Were the Holocaust and the emergence of National Socialism the outcome of swift and radical social change, depressed economic conditions, and the burden of defeat in World War I, or did the roots of hatred go much deeper?

Was antisemitism a modern problem or did it, in fact, have centuries-old historical roots?

As a result of World War I and the Allied victory many new states (especially in Eastern Europe) were created. Did the governments established in these nations act properly toward their minority populations?

What were the underlying causes of the outbreak of war in September, 1939? How was the war influenced by, and in turn how did it influence, the Jewish situation in Europe under the Nazis?

What precautions for long term security did European Jewry in general and Eastern European Jewry in particular take in order to prepare for the eventualities of war, Nazi conquest and the establishment of an antisemitic program?

How did the Nazis carry out their plan for a "New Order" in Europe, ruled by the One-Thousand-Year Reich?

To what extent did the citizens of occupied countries collaborate with the Germans, and how did occupation affect life in the occupied countries?

What was life like in the Nazi established ghettos of Eastern Europe? How did Jews fare in Western European countries under Nazi occupation and in the Axis Allied states?

How was the Judenrat, the Jewish Council, organized, and how did it function in the Nazi system and in the life of the ghettos?

How did the six Nazi death camps and the spiderweb of concentration and slave labor camps criss-crossing Europe actually operate?

Under what conditions, when, and to what degree did Jews resist their tormentors, and how did this resistance fit into the overall European underground struggle?

How did the Allies aid European and Jewish resistance?

What is the history of Jewish heroism during the war, on every battlefield, in every campaign, and in every arm of the Allied armies?

How did Jews and their gentile neighbors interact through the years of crisis?

Who were the Hasidei Umot Haolam, the Righteous Gentiles, and how did they uphold the bonds of humanity - even under the threat of death?

How did information on the unfolding danse macabre filter out to the West despite Nazi intentions to keep their Final Solution a secret?

How did the free world react to the ever-worsening situation in Nazi Germany during the "preparatory" stage (1933-1939)?

What was the Jewish reaction around the world as the events unfolded in Nazi Germany?

Did the Jews of the free world, in the United States and elsewhere, do enough in order to bring some relief to their beleagered, dying brethern?

What, if anything, did the international community do to alleviate the plight of the thousands of homeless and destitute refugees?

To what degree, if any at all, did the cold facts of the Nazi extermination program against the Jews of Europe influence the Allied war strategy?

What were the demographic, physical, psychological, and other effects of the Holocaust on the survivors and upon all of world Jewry?

How and to what extent did European Jewry rebuild itself after the trauma?

How did the Holocaust influence the rise of the State of Israel and the continuing struggle for Jewish freedom?

How have religious leaders, philosophers, and thinkers - Jewish and gentile - reacted to the Holocaust?

What role should the Holocaust play in the curricula of schools in the United States, Israel and the rest of the free World?

How have revisionist historians tried to rewrite history and in fact deny that the Holocaust ever occured?

Finally, in an era of nuclear proliferation, near-constant warfare, and the possible self-destruction of all humanity, has the world learned the lessons of the Holocaust?

SEARCHING FOR ANSWERS

We must search and sift if we hope to find some answers to these vexing questions. For that reason all sorts of individuals have taken up pen and paper to try to make sense out of the Holocaust. Consequently, the quantity of the relevant literature is staggering, and it increases annually. Seven thousand items exist on the subject of Auschwitz alone; as regards the literature on all cognate subtopics covering the period from 1933 to 1945, we must speak in the thousands or tens of thousands. Even when we limit ourself to works in English, a huge library exists: literature appearing before, during, and since the war and items ranging from newspaper reports to tomes heavy with footnotes and scholarly apparati, testimonies, memoirs, history books, and even novels.

Mindful of the fact that vital material exists in many languages, we have decided to focus only upon works written in English. This decision is not intended to denigrate the importance of such languages as Hebrew, Yiddish, Polish, French, and German. Thousands of important studies have been published in these and other languages. For students in the Anglo-American world, however, a basic knowledge of materials in English is crucial as a preparatory stage for further study.

Despite all efforts at comprehensiveness any bibliography is the result of a selection of materials. In making our selections we have followed a few simple rules. First, unsigned items shorter than a page were not included. Signed items of less than a page were included only when they were deemed of special interest or usefulness. Items of one or two page length not directly related to the Holocaust were also excluded. We have included a fairly comprehensive selection of periodicals, most of which originated in the United States or England; many others were unavailable and we could not review them. Still other periodicals were found to be in very poor physical condition, being fragments rather than pages; for obvious reasons these could not be included. As a rule the more recent the periodical, the more comprehensive our review. We did not, however, review the American Jewish press for the period after 1950 in any comprehensive fashion. Periodical citations can be considered complete to mid-1985, books to a slightly later point in time.

As regards citations of books, we actually saw most of the books listed. A number of booklets and some books were not available for review; booklets and pamphlets were only included when we were able to verify their existence. We did not, however, cite mimeographed or limited circulation materials, since these would largely be unavailable outside of few select research libraries. We have annotated a selection of the most important and interesting books. Articles were annotated only when the title was not sufficiently descriptive in and of itself. Space did not permit us to fully cross-reference books, some of which could fall into a number of categories. Some of our selections may seem arbitrary at first glance. Our early chapters are not by any means comprehensive, but are merely suggestions for further study.

The bibliographic references that follow give partial answers, from both Jewish and general perspectives, to the questions we have posed. We have grouped them into four parts: Before the Storm; The Perpetrators; The Crucible; and, finally, The Aftermath.

Abraham J. Edelheit
Hershel Edelheit

Acknowledgments

A project of this magnitude could not possibly have been undertaken without help rendered us by others. We therefore acknowledge the assistance of the following institutions and individuals.

The librarians and staff of the New York Public Library Jewish Division were extremely helpful in finding and making available to us the items we needed. The same may be said for the librarians at Yeshiva University's Landowne-Bloom, Gottesman, and Pollack Libraries. Although we cannot list their names individually we owe each of them a debt of gratitude.

Drs. Bernard Wasserstein and Charles Cutter of Brandeis University reviewed parts of the bibliography and made many valuable suggestions.

Rabbi and Mrs. Amos Edelheit have shown interest in every stage of the project, tracking down some of the citations and rendering other invaluable help. Special thanks to Goldie Wachsman for reading the manuscript versions of our essays. Her critical comments have been very helpful and incisive. To Mr. Allen Wollman who helped with the proofreading. To Mrs. Ann Edelheit, mother and wife, for her patience and encouragement.

Finally, we also thank the editors and staff of Westview Press who helped turn this project into reality. Nonetheless, all mistakes are ours and do not reflect upon the aforementioned individuals.

A.J.E.
H.E.

Index of Periodicals and Abbreviations

Central Conference of American Rabbis, Journal .... CCARJ
Central Conference of American Rabbis, Year Book .... CCAR/YB
Central European History .... CEH
Central European Observer .... CEO
Chicago Jewish Forum .... Ch J Forum
Christian Century .... Ch Century
Commentary .... Com
Committee Reporter .... Comm Reporter
Commonweal ....
Congress Bulletin .... CB
Congress Bi-Weekly .... CBW
Congress Monthly .... CM
Congress Weekly .... CW
Conservative Judaism .... Con Jud
Contemporary Jewish Record .... CJR
Contemporary Jewry .... C/J
Contemporary Review .... Cont Rev
Coronet ....
Cross Currents .... C/C
Current History .... Cur His
Current Jewish Record .... Cur J Rec
Czech Jewish Representative Committee/Bulletin .... CJRC/B

Davka ....
Dimensions ....
Dispersion ....
Dissent ....

East European Quarterly .... EEQ
English Historical Review .... EHR
Encounter ....
Eugenics Review .... Eugenics Rev
European Judaism .... Eur Jud
Explorations ....

Fascist Quarterly .... Fasc Q
Focus ....
Foreign Affairs .... F Affairs
Foreign Policy Report .... FPR
Fortnightly ....
Fortnightly Review .... FR
Forum ....
Fourth World Congress of Jewish Studies .... 4 WCJS
Free World .... FW
Furrows ....

Gesher ....
Ghetto Speaks .... GS

Hadar ....
Hadasah Monthly .... HM
Hamigdal ....
Harper´s Magazine .... Harper´s
Herzl Year Book .... Herzl YB
Historia Judaica .... HJ
The Historian ....
The Historical Journal .... Historical Jnl
History ....
History of the Second World War .... Hist/WWII
History Today ....
Horizon ....
Hungarian Jewish Studies .... HJS

Ideas ....
Inside Palestine .... IP
Institute of Jewish Affairs .... IJA
Institute of Jewish Affairs Research Report ..... IJA Res Rep
International Affairs .... Int Affairs
Israel Horizon .... IH

Jerusalem Quarterly .... Jer Q
Jewish Affairs .... J Affairs
Jewish Book Annual .... JBA
Jewish Combatant .... J Combat
Jewish Comment .... J Comment
Jewish Currents .... J Currents
Jewish Digest .... J Digest
Jewish Education .... J Ed
Jewish Forum .... J Fo
Jewish Frontier .... J Fr
Jewish Heritage .... JH
Jewish Horizon .... J Horizon
Jewish Journal of Sociology .... JJoS
Jewish Layman .... J Layman
Jewish Life .... J Life
Jewish Mirror .... J Mirror
Jewish Newsletter .... J Newsletter
Jewish Observer .... J Observer
Jewish Observer and Middle East Review .... JOMER
Jewish Outlook .... J Outlook
Jewish Press .... J Press
Jewish Quarterly .... JQ
Jewish Review .... J Rev
Jewish Social Service Quarterly .... JSSQ
Jewish Social Studies .... JSS

New York Times Magazine .... NY Times Mag
New Zealand Jewish Bulletin .... NZJB
Nineteenth Century and After .... 19th Century & After

Opinion ....
Ort Economic Bulletin .... Ort Eco Bul
Ort Economic Review .... Ort Eco Rev
Orthodox Jewish Life .... Ortho J Life

Palestine ....
Palestine Illustrated Newsletter..................... P.I.N.
Palestine Post Herald .... P/P Herald
Palestine Year Book .... PYB
Partisan Review .... Partisan Rev
Patterns of Prejudice .... PoP
Pedagogic Reporter .... P/Rep
Poland ....
Polish Fortnightly Review .... PFR
Polish Jew ....
Polish Review .... Polish Rev
Polish Western Affairs .... PWA
Political Science Quarterly .... Pol Sci Q
Present Tense .... PT
The Principal ....
Proceedings of the American Jewish Historical Society . PAJHS
Progressive ....
Psychiatric Quarterly .... Psych Q
Public Opinion Quarterly .... Pub Op Q
Publishers Weekly ....

Quarterly Review .... QR

Reader's Digest ....
Reconstructionist .... Recon
Rescue ....
Response ....
Review of Politics .... Rev of Politics

Saturday Evening Post .... SEP
Scribner's Magazine .... Scribner's
Sh'ma ....
Shoa ....
Shofar ....
Slavic Review ....
Slavonic and East European Review .... Slavonic/EER
Social Forces ....
Societas ....

Society ....
Soviet Jewish Affairs .... SJA
Soviet Studies ....
Studies in Zionism .... SiZ
Survey Graphic ....
Survey Midmonthly ....
Synagogue/Liberal Judaism .... Syn/LB

Today ....
Tradition ....
Twentieth Century .... 20th Century

Ukrainian Quarterly .... Uk Q

Viewpoints ....
Viewpoints Canadian Jewish Quarterly .... V CJQ
Voice Unconquered .... V/Unq

Wiener Library Bulletin .... WLB
World Jewish Congress/Australian Section Bulletin WJC/AS Bul
World Jewish Congress/British Section Report ..... WJC/BS Rep
World Jewry .... WJ

Yad Vashem Bulletin .... YVB
Yad Vashem News .... YVN
Yad Vashem Studies .... YVS
Yiddish ....
YIVO Annual ....
Young Judaean ....

Zion ....
Zionews ....
Zionist Quarterly .... Zionist Q

Table of Abbreviations Used for Edited Books

Yehuda Bauer: The Holocaust in Historical Perspective
Bauer: Perspective, #3406

Yehuda Bauer, A. Margaliot and Y. Gutman: Essays in Holocaust History
Bauer: Hol History, #8595

Yehuda Bauer and Nathan Rotenstreich (eds.): The Holocaust as Historical Experience
Bauer: Historical, #8596

Randolph L. Braham (ed.): Contemporary Views of the Holocaust
Braham: Contemporary, #3407

Randolph L. Braham (ed.): Jewish Leadership during the Nazi Era
Braham: Leadership, #5893

Randolph L. Braham (ed.): Perspectives on the Holocaust
Braham: Perspectives, #3408

Central Commission for Investigation of Nazi Crimes in Poland: German Crimes in Poland
Commission: GCIP, #3625

R. Chartock and J. Spencer (eds.): The Holocaust Years: Society on Trial
Chartock: Society, #3410

Conference on Manifestations of Jewish Resistance
Y/V: Resistance, #4189

A. T. Davies (ed.): Antisemitism and the Foundations of Christianity
Davies: Foundations, #420

Lucy S. Dawidowicz: The Jewish Presence
Dawidowicz: Presence, #7531

J. De Launay (ed,): European Resistance Movements, 1933-1945
De Launay: ERM, #4664

Joel E. Dimsdale (ed.): Survivors, Victims, and Perpetrators
Dimsdale: Survivors, #6907

L. Dinnerstein (ed.): Antisemitism in the United States
Dinnerstein: A/S, #605

M. Dobkowski and I. Walliman (eds.): Towards the Holocaust
Dobkowski: Toward, #965

Louis Falstein (ed.): The Martydom of Jewish Physicians in Poland
Falstein: Martyrdom, #8361

Joshua A. Fishman (ed.): Studies on Polish Jewry, 1919-1939
Fishman: Studies, #60

Eva Fleischner (ed.): Auschwitz the Beginning of a New Era?
Fleischner: Auschwitz, #7077

Josef Fraenkel (ed.): The Jews of Austria
Fraenkel: Austria, #62

Albert H. Friedlander (ed.): Out of the Whirlwind
Friedlander: Whirlwind, #3338

H. Friedlander and S. Milton (eds.): The Holocaust: Ideology, Buereaucracy, and Genocide
Friedlander: Ideology, #3416

Philip Friedman: Roads to Extinction: Essays on the Holocaust
Friedman: Roads, #3418

I. Graeber and S. H. Britt (eds.): Jews in a Gentile World
Graeber: JIG, #379

A. Grobman and D. Landes (eds.): Genocide: Critical Issues of the Holocaust
Grobman: Genocide, #3423

Y. Gutman and C. J. Haft (eds.): Patterns of Jewish Leadership in Nazi Europe, 1933-1945
G/H: Patterns, #2789

Y. Gutman and L. Rothkirchen (eds.): The Catastrophe of European Jewry
Gutman: Catastrophe, #3425

Y. Gutman and E. Zuroff (eds.): Rescue Attempts During the Holocaust
Gutman: Rescue, #5452

S. Hawes and R. White (eds.): Reststance in Europe, 1939-1945
Hawes: Resistance, #4675

R. S. Hirt and T. Kessner (eds.): Issues in Teaching the Holocaust — Hirt: Issues, #7435

Gerd Korman (ed.): Hunter and Hunted — Korman: Hunter, #3345

I. Kowalski (ed.): Anthology of Armed Jewish Resistance — Kowalski: Anthology, #4217

H. Krausnick et al: The Anatomy of the SS State — Krausnick: Anatomy, #1115

Max Kreutzberger (ed.): Studies of the Leo Baeck Institute — Kreutzberger: Studies, #104

Lyman H. Legters (ed): Western Society After the Holocaust — Legters: Western, #7551

Marcia S. Littell(ed.): Holocaust Education — Littell: Education, #7448

S. L. Luel and P. Marcus (eds.): Psychoanalytic Reflections on the Holocaust — Luel: Psycho, #6948

Abraham J. Peck (ed): Jews and Christians After the Holocaust — Peck: Jews/Chr, #7084

Judah Pilch (ed.): The Jewish Catastrophe in Europe — Pilch: Catastrophe, #3441

K. S. Pinson (ed.): Essays on Antisemitism — Pinson: Essays, #402

Jack N. Porter (ed.): Confronting History and Holocaust — Porter: Confronting, #3444

J. N. Porter (ed.): Genocide and Human Rights: A Global Anthology — Porter: Genocide, #1937

J. N. Porter (ed.): Jewish Partisans — Porter: JP, #4332

Michael D. Ryan (ed.): Human Responses to the Holocaust — Ryan: Responses, #3451

Leo W. Schwarz (ed.): The Root and the Bough — Schwarz: Root, #3375

B. L. Sherwin and S. G. Ament (eds.): Encountering the Holocaust — Sherwin: <u>Encountering</u>, #3453

E. Simmel (ed.): Antisemitism: A Social Disease — Simmel: <u>AS/SD</u>, #483

Society for the History of Czechoslovak Jews: The Jews of Czechoslovakia — Society: <u>JoCz</u>, #143

Yuri Suhl (ed.): They Fought Back — Suhl: <u>They</u>, #4231

B. Vago and G. L. Mosse (eds.): Jews and Non-Jews in Eastern Europe, 1919-1945 — Vago: <u>J/NJ</u>, #156

Pierre Van Passen and J. Wise (eds.): Nazism: An Assault on Civilization — PVP: <u>Nazism</u>. #1090

World Zionist Organization: Jewish Heroism in Modern Times — WZO: <u>Heroism</u>, #4237

Yad Vashem: Holocaust and Rebirth — Y/V: <u>Hol/Reb</u>, #6788

PART I

Before the Storm

Introduction

If it had not been for the terrible events that unfolded between 1933 and 1945, the Jews of Europe would have continued to live as they had for nearly a millenium. Jews had frequently been exposed to the storms of world history and were often perceived as an alien element in Europe. Jewish communities had to endure hatred, persecution, and, at times, almost daily violence. Jews were confined to designated areas called ghettos and were forced to wear distinctive marks upon their clothing. At times entire communities were obliterated by pogroms or expulsion.

Jewish history was not, however, only a history of tears. Judaism survived and even thrived, whenever it found fertile soil. A vibrant and varied social, political, and intellectual life developed in both ghettos and villages. Jewish institutions - <u>kehilot</u> (community councils), synagogues, <u>yeshivot</u> (academies), and <u>hevrot</u> (societies) - flourished as did the greatest of all Jewish institutions, the family. In the seventeenth and eighteenth centuries a series of crises, beginning with the Chmielnicki massacres in 1648-1649 and ending with the Shabbatean heresy of the late 1660s, very nearly rent asunder the Jewish community.

Although sorely tried, the autonomous Jewish community nevertheless weathered the storm. The Hasidic movement, which emphasized piety and articulated an optimistic world view, arose to fill the vacuum left by the crises. The Hasidic masters, the <u>tzadikim</u>, followed Israel ben Eliezer, the Baal-Shem-Tov, in laying emphasis upon <u>devekut</u> (devotion) and <u>hitlahavut</u> (joy) - both seen as important as, if not more important than, book learning. Hasidism's mystical piety and emphasis upon the cosmic importance of <u>Halacha</u> (Jewish Law) spoke to the Jewish everyman and soon spread from the steppes of the Ukraine to the foothills of the Carpathians even to central Poland and beyond.

Only in Lithuania did the Mitnagdim, those who opposed Hasidism, retain a foothold. The Mitnagdim were especially strong in and around Vilna, the "Jerusalem of Lithuania." Here the yeshivot reigned. For the further glory of Judaism, students spent days and nights studying Talmudic tomes replete with ancient law and lore. These Talmudic academies rivaled those of Babylonia and Eretz Yisrael, if they did not in fact surpass them. In Mir, Slobodka, Volozhin, Lublin, Vilna, and Brisk some of the greatest Jewish minds were honed to perfection.

THE HASKALA

Important changes occurred in Western Europe during the latter half of the eighteenth century. The development of absolutism and the nation-state as well as the Enlightenment led intellectuals to reconsider the status of the Jews. Because the nation-state could no longer tolerate autonomous entities within its borders, concerned thinkers proposed various plans for the "improvement" of the Jews. With the French Enlightenment this process quickened; a grand intellectual and political debate developed. The American Revolution added impetus to the European debate. The United States gave "bigotry no sanction," as President George Washington himself said, and its Constitution knew of no discrimination against Jews.

With the French Revolution (1789), the debate on Jewish status reached a crescendo. During the next century civil rights were granted to Jews in virtually all of Western Europe: in France (1791), Italy (1869), Great Britain (1858-1871), and Germany (1871). Tension often accompanied the emancipation, however, especially in France and Germany. Civil status was accorded to Jews as individuals, not to Jewish communities. In return for civil rights, Jews were thus asked to surrender their national identity and assimilate into the larger society.

In the Jewish world a new spirit was also kindled. Small numbers of Jews became aware of the "backwardness" of Jewish society and proposed remedies for all ills that kept Jews in what they saw as a cultural ghetto even while the walls of the physical ghetto were crumbling. The modernizers adopted the name of Maskilim (Enlighteners) and called their movement the Haskala (Enlightenment). Ideologically this group owed its background to the writings and teachings of Moses Mendelssohn, a German Jewish philosopher. The primary goal of the Haskala was to reeducate Jews so that they could fit into modern society. With the emancipation, the Maskilim, at least in Western Europe, led the way in creating "good" Jewish citizens. Thus, adaptation of Jewish mores to the larger society became the goal. "Be a Jew in your home and a man in the street" was their motto. Adaptation seemed to resolve the paradox of Jewish survival and also proved that Jews had made strides in "improving" themselves in order to become deserving citizens - Israelites of French, English, or German nationality. With the internalization by Jews of new liberal ideas, religious Judaism became more diverse. In Germany a number of Jews sought to reform Judaism in order to make it more compatible with modern society. A different group saw the need for some changes, but were only willing to make changes for which they found precedents in Jewish history. Yet a third group saw no need for changes in the tradition, although they too adopted a more modern worldview.

In Germany, England, and the United States, the most liberal group of the Maskilim, crystallized into the Reform movement, which was formulated by leaders such as Abraham Geiger, David Friedlander, and Samuel Holdheim. The middle group, under the guidance of luminaries including Zechariah Frankel and Solomon Schechter, became the Positive Historical school, better known as Conservative Judaism. The most traditional group, led by Rabbis Shimshon Raphael Hirsch, Isaac Breuer, and Azriel Hildesheimer, developed a neo-orthodoxy that combined a modern weltanschauung with strict adherence to Jewish law.

Closely related to the religious sphere is the development of modern Jewish studies. Applying modern historical principles to Judaism, the Wissenschaft des Judentums (Science of Judaism) offered both proofs for religious polemics and a more relevant way of understanding the Jews' role in society. In this way the liberal scholars, such as Geiger and Leopold Zunz, could meet traditionalists like Nachman Krochmal, Shlomo Yehuda Rapoport, and Shmuel David Luzzatto.

SEPHARDIC JEWRY

Jewish communities also flourished throughout the Mediterranean lands and in Southeast Europe. Among these communities perhaps the largest were those of the Sephardim, Jews who had been expelled from Spain in 1492. As was the case with Ashkenazi Jewry (Jews who had settled in the Germanic lands), the Sephardim and their offspring were able to rebound into a cohesive and well-organized community.

The Sephardim had spread far and wide. A majority of the exiles went east to the Ottoman Empire. Briefly, it seemed that the expulsion might lead to a renewed settlement in the Land of Israel. This possibility, in turn, led to renewed messianic speculation and the controversy surrounding the false messiah Shabbetai Zevi. Others from among the exiled of Spain came to the New World to establish what was to become the largest and richest Jewish community in history. Still other Sephardim sought refuge in the north, reestablishing Jewries in the Netherlands, England, and France. The largest concentration of Sephardim by far was in the Balkans. Their distinctive culture clearly identified them as originating in Spain, a fact that was later to play a role in their ability to survive under the Nazis.

EAST EUROPEAN JEWRY

By 1939, East European Jews and their descendants had spread worldwide, accounting for twelve million of the eighteen million Jews then alive. The great East European Jewish communities were thus the biological core of world Jewry. The communities in which these Jews lived were self-contained units. Every element of community life revolved around the _kahal_ (community council), which existed in every town, city, and _shtetl_ (village) where Jews lived. Most Jews in the _shtetlech_ lived in pressing poverty, barely eeking out a living.

The Wissenschaft des Judentums also bore fruit in Eastern Europe. Scholars trained in scientific historiography who made seminal contributions to Jewish scholarship included Meyer Balaban, Ignac Schipper, and Emanuel Ringelblum. Their dean was Simon Dubnow, the historian and political activist. Jewish literature also developed significantly with the likes of Haim Nahman Bialik, Saul Tchernikovsky, Isaac Leib Peretz, Judah Leib Gordon, Abraham Mapu, Mendele Mokher Seforim (S. J. Abramowitsch), and Shalom Aleichem (S. Rabinovitz), who depicted - in verse and prose - the life of a civilization.

East European Jewry faced harsher conditions than Jews in the West. In the East no emancipation movement ever developed. The majority of Jews in the East were therefore unassimilated and unassimilable. With the pogroms of 1881 a new turning point was reached as governments - especially Tsarist Russia - became even more malevolent. In reaction to the conditions, Jews turned inward; they offerred various solutions of their own to deal with their rapidly developing problems.

JEWISH NATIONALISM

Three different ideologies emerged. Folkism, or autonomism, argued that Jews should seek to preserve their ethnic identity through culture rather than politics. The Jewish nation was one of the spirit, according to Simon Dubnow. It needed no specific territory, but a renewed supracommunal organization to provide the kehilah with more flexibility in dealing with the daily needs of the community. The BUND (Algemeyner Yidisher Arbeter Bund), the Jewish socialist party founded in Russia in 1897, held a similar view but placed greater emphasis on the needs of Jewish workers. As it developed, the BUND stressed the need to establish true socialism throughout the world as the only way to guarantee Jewish rights.

At the same time modern Zionism came of age. In general the Zionists saw only one possible solution for the Jewish problem: self-emancipation and the consequent normalization of Jewish-gentile relations through the establishment of a Jewish national home, preferably in Eretz Yisrael. The establishment of Jewish sovereignty would, moreover, be likely to solve the problems of Judaism by infusing renewed vibrancy into a community suffering from too long an exile.

By the 1870s European Jewry was rapidly being drawn into the center of a storm of events only remotely of Jewish concern. Increasingly European power politics impinged upon the security of the Jews. In particular, the unification of Germany in 1870-1871 shook the foundations of the European balance of power. Hypernationalism, in a Volkish (populist) guise, was translated in Germany into an almost universal worship of the state, the nation, and, particularly, the German people.

ULTRANATIONALISM IN EUROPE

German Volkism was heavily influenced by romantic notions of nations and a belief in their organic nature. The nation was more than merely the sum of its citizens: It was a living organism. It followed then that all Germans had to unite under one banner and shun the decadence and philistinism of the West and that Germany was best off returning to its heroic past, to the period of Teutonic heroism. Of course, reality proved more banal. Chancellor Otto von Bismarck's Reich, for all the Volkish spirit, was but a part of the Teutonic world. There arose a group of "Germanic critics" - Paul de Legarde, Julius Langbehn, Moeller Van den Bruck, and Richard Wagner - who offered a new picture of what was wrong with Germany. For Germany to gain her "place in the sun" she first had to become pure. Foreign influences - democracy, liberty, constitutions - had to be done away with. So too, Germany had to purge itself of the inner enemy - the Jews. Even Christianity would undergo reform, it would develop into a new "Germanic" form. Although their ideas were not officially accepted, the critics, especially Wagner, exerted a good deal of influence. Even Bismarck stressed the "Germanic" way, as in his famous "Blood and Iron" speech.

The dislocation caused by the forcible unification of Germany, as well as French revanchism, added fuel to the fire. Germany's foreign relations became increasingly based upon mutual suspicion. Peace was based upon a system of alliances to maintain the balance of power as well as to neutralize France.

The same ultranationalist spirit had been developing in France. Whereas in 1789 nationalism had been a progressive movement, by 1848 ultranationalism had become a highly conservative and even reactionary force. Political theorists argued without a shudder that war could be a positive force in the world because violence was inherent in human nature. Not surprisingly, the French aristocracy - specifically, Count Arthur de Gobineau - originated the idea of the inequality of the races. The growing acceptance of racist theories and ultranationalist sentiment coincided with political and social unrest in France. The resounding defeat of the French by the Prussians in 1870 and the economic and social dislocations typified by the short-lived Paris commune (May 1871) further rent the nation asunder.

The blind wish for revenge, coupled with intense nationalism and worship of the army, led to a further French expression of this growing European phenomenon. In 1894 a French Jewish artillery captain, Alfred Dreyfus, was accused of espionage. Dreyfus was court-martialed and found guilty. Yet his exile was not considered a severe enough punishment, and nearly hysterical mobs came very close to a frenzy of anti-Jewish violence. Dreyfus was in fact an innocent victim. The Third Republic was almost brought down while the wheels of justice were grinding very slowly indeed. Moreover, Dreyfus's vindication was by no means the end of the affair.

An international system based on fear and suspicion could not work forever. By 1900 rival imperial claims in Africa and Asia, as well as economic and political competition in Europe, divided the continent into two armed camps - the Central Powers (Austria-Hungary, Germany, and Ottoman Turkey) and the Triple Entente (France, Great Britain, and Russia). Both entered an arms race of massive proportions, fearing that the other might gain the upper hand.

In the end it was the success of a fourth assassin's bullet - after three had tried and failed - that killed Archduke Francis Ferdinand in Sarajevo and brought the European national system crashing to its destruction. World War I was the largest European war since the days of Bonaparte. Fought not only on land but on the sea and in the air, it was the deadliest war of its time: Ten million soldiers perished in the trenches and battlefields of the world.

THE JEWISH PROBLEM

As Europe hurtled toward war, a Jewish problem developed in the minds of European antisemites. This Jew-hatred was the synthesis of three separate perspectives. First, the political, which harked back to the emancipation debates of the eighteenth century. Second, the quasiscientific, which was a decidedly nineteenth-century contribution - the result of racism and social Darwinism, which promoted and fed off of narrowly construed Volkish nationalism. Third, the diabolical, which had much deeper roots but took on increasingly ominous proportions. There had long been a belief in Jewish perversity, devil-worship, and conspiracy; the myth was merely updated.

One may legitimately question the novelty of the nineteenth century's Jewish problem. The phenomenon of antisemitism long predated use of the term, which was coined by Wilhelm Marr in 1879. Clearly, hatred, fear and dislike of Jews is as ancient as the Jewish people. Even in the relatively tolerant Greco-Roman world, Jew-hatred became a matter of public policy at times of economic and social upheaval. Nevertheless, pagan antisemitism arose primarily from a lack of a common cultural ground between Jew and non-Jew and ultimately led nowhere.

Christian antisemitism arose out of a different set of motives. Where paganism simply lacked a common religious ground with the Jews, Christianity rejected them. Judaism had been surpassed and was no longer relevant, and Jews were Deicides who had to pay for their sins. They could no longer even bear the title of Israel, for they were no longer the chosen people. Antisemitism, based upon the very foundations of Christian rejection of Judaism and the attempt to coopt the Bible for Christian purposes, could thus be seen as almost inherent in Christianity.

To be sure, a variety of factors - political, social, economic, and even intellectual - with different emphasis in different eras, insured that Judaism was never completely extirpated. Even the Catholic Church, although recommending pressuring the Jews, recognized their role in society. Under the so-called Doctrine of Testimony, Jews were to be downtrodden but not destroyed, eternal testimony for Divine justice.

To better understand the modern problem, the premodern background must be kept in mind. Beginning with the twelfth century, a diabolical view of the Jew emerged. It was widely believed that Jews knew the truth of Christianity, but stubbornly rejected salvation. In a superstitious world, this view of Jewish perversity and belief in the imminent, daily existence of Satan were soon linked. The Jews´ perversity was thus explained as a sign of Jewish cooperation with the Devil. Ultimately, Jews were seen as the Antichrist, whose sole purpose was to fight against the Divine order and to destroy all Christians. Of course, as the incarnation of pure evil, the Jews would stop at nothing to achieve their nefarious mission: Jews ritually slaughtered Christian children, drank Christian blood, desecrated the Host, murdered Christian patients, and poisoned wells. One need only to read the anti-Jewish rantings of Martin Luther to obtain a clear perception of the issue. The leading founder of Protestantism suggested his own solution to the Jewish problem in his work Concerning the Jews and Their Lies (1543). In a seven point program Luther called for the complete outlawing of Judaism. Expropriation of Jewish property, the burning down of their synagogues and prayer-books, and the reduction of Jews to slavery were key elements of this plan, as was the possibility of the expulsion of Jews from Germany.

The modern Jewish problem arose from slightly different origins. From the period of the enlightenment onward, it was no longer acceptable to hate Jews on religious grounds. Jews were no longer the "damned, rejected race" that Luther had fulminated against; their religion per se was no longer an issue. "Jew" or "Christian," they were still a problem, albeit for a host of new reasons: economic competition, disloyalty to the state, lack of cultural assimilation into the body of the nation, and racial differences. The Doctrine of Testimony, furthermore, which had guaranteed Jewish survival, was simply forgotten.

In the modern era the terminology became secularized. No longer was it a matter of religion, but of nationality or race. For the likes of Marr or Wagner the religious aspect of Judaism was insignificant; rather, one´s blood decided whether one was a man or an unmensch. Yet, the common denominator remained, as it had for 700 years, "Die Juden sind unser Unglueck!" (The Jews are our misfortune). Heinrich von Treitsche´s motto found an echo in almost every country in and outside of Europe. Jews are the root of all evil and, therefore, must be fought with every possible weapon. Moreover, the secularization of antisemitism meant that the last support system was lost: Jews could no longer have the option of conversion; there could no longer be any escape for the Jewish masses on any grounds. Antisemitism sought a Final Solution.

POST-WORLD WAR I UPHEAVALS

Still, these developments were kept in check as long as society remained relatively stable. World War I swept all such stability away. Three mighty empires - the Romanovs, the Habsburgs, and the Hohenzollerns - fell forever. In their place smaller successor states arose - less powerful, less secure, all trying to cope with the vacuum in the balance of power, massive debts, and demoralized populations. No economy was secure, no state safe from a putsch. Almost all turned to the right for solutions to their national problems.

In Russia a great upheaval led to the downfall of the Romanovs and the rise of communism. In a very short span of time history was "turned on its ear" as, for the first time, a state arose that called itself Marxist. This same state later gave the world the terms for modern dictatorship: Gulag (concentration camp), secret police, vaporization, nonperson, and mass terror.

This same upheaval also changed the status of Russian Jewry. The yoke of Tsarist oppression was cast off, and Jews were encouraged to Russify and drop their communal identity. To speed up the process of bolshevizing the Jewish community, a Jewish party apparatus, the Yevsektsia (Jewish section), was established. Antisemitism did not, however, disappear in Soviet Russia neither among the Bolsheviks nor among their foes. Given the totalitarian nature of the state, the Jewish community as such was placed in a precarious position.

THE SUCCESSOR STATES

New states arose out of the ashes of World War I. After a century of occupation, Poland was reborn, and Yugoslavia, Czechoslovakia, Latvia, Lithuania, and Estonia, all gained independence. All of these states shared common goals and problems. All were in favor of maintenance of the status quo through restoring the balance of power and collective security. All of these states had border disputes with their larger neighbors as well as with each other. All were saddled with huge national minorities problems, which presented the threat of foreign subversion through the "fifth column." Only in Czechoslovakia did democracy thrive. Yugoslavia, Poland, and Lithuania started on that path but, under the influence of the Nazis, changed to authoritarian regimes. The colonel´s cliques, the real power behind the state, dictated how their respective governments would act and behave.

In each of these states a Jewish problem existed to one degree or another. Violent antisemitism was most prevalent in Poland, which also had the largest Jewish population in Europe (3.5 million). Pogroms and random attacks were relatively common, as were political, religious, and economic excesses. In almost every sphere, the government and those behind it - be they of the Sanacja (the "colonel´s") or the National Democracy party, the Endecja (Narodowa Demokracja), better known as Endeks - were operating from a clear antisemitic program. Jewish economic life was systematically undercut; they were treated as second-class citizens; their political rights were ignored; and the minority treaties were reduced to a sham. Whether the issue was the anti-shechita (ritual slaughter) bill of 1937 or "Ghetto benches" in the universities, the Polish government pursued one policy: Rzeczypospolita Polska dla Polakow, Zydzi do Palestini (Poland for Poles, Jews to Palestine). Similar problems were encountered in Lithuania, although there the economic and social pressures made antisemitic sentiments less virulent.

In both Czechoslovakia and Yugoslavia, Jews found themselves caught between two rival ethnic groups vying for control of the state. The stability of Czech democracy and the personal goodwill of President Thomas G. Masaryk kept antisemitism in check. Antisemitic feelings did exist, however, being particularly strong in Slovakia. Jews were much less secure in Yugoslavia, where they were caught between Serbians and Croats. Both ethnic groups viewed Jews as an untrustworthy element, both were willing to eliminate their Jews at the proper moment.

WEIMAR GERMANY

In Germany´s case the problems of the postwar era were compounded by defeat and the onus of war guilt. The Weimar Republic began on a tenuous basis. Unable to pay its debts, particularly the reparations owed to the Allies, the Republic found itself forced to accept a French occupation of the Saar and Rhineland. The Republic also had been forced to accept a peace treaty - an unfair one in German eyes - signed at

Versailles. In this document Germany accepted blame for the war and surrendered its colonies, navy, and airforce. Territory was ceded in the East, and the army, the pride of the Prussian state, was limited to a mere 100,000 men - only enough for internal duties.

As long as the economy held stable, a certain degree of democracy flourished. Concurrently, tremors were felt as parties of both the left and right proceded to cut away the foundations of law and order. Increasingly the Republic turned to suppression in order to secure peace and quiet in the streets. Curiously, only the left was treated seriously. Judges often gave right-wing agitators token sentences for crimes that would bring communists under the headsman´s ax.

Similarly, rule by decree had to be used in order to govern the increasingly splintered Reichstag. The administration was rapidly collapsing under its own weight and was unable to sustain the day-to-day demands of governing a state.

Antisemitism, which had lain dormant during the war, returned with a passion in Weimar Germany. Parties of the right routinely denounced the Republic as a "Jew-republic." They accused communists, Jews, and liberals of having stabbed Germany in the back, of treachery and treason that led to defeat. Calls for action did not go unheeded. Individuals who were unhappy with the state of affairs in Weimar soon joined together into mass movements, especially during the inflation of 1923-1924. Soldaten verbande, roaming bands of rowdy and disenchanted veterans, arose as did dozens of private armies. Each offered the solution to Germany´s problems: Revenge for the disgrace of Versailles; justice against traitors, Jew and communist alike; and creation of a new Reich that would restore Germany to its rightful place in the sun.

On June 24, 1922, one of these groups assassinated Germany´s Jewish Foreign Minister Walter Rathenau. Such activities finally reached a crescendo in the Nationalsozialistiche Deutsche Arbeiter Partei´s (NSDAP) abortive "Beer Hall Putsch" of November 1923. As the problems waned with improvements to the economy and the passing of the inflation these groups grew weaker but were not uprooted.

Even the more secure Western states faced severe crisis and social dislocations. The United States, having briefly used its power on the world scene, now turned inward, isolating itself from all but the most immediate concerns. In France, demoralization on a mass scale set in and led to an inability to face Germany. France reacted only very slowly to the growing European crisis and, even then, only with outmoded solutions. War weariness also struck Great Britain, which preferred appeasement of every potential enemy to conflict.

In the final analysis European Jewry's long sojourn was to prove but a frail sukkah (tent). A new threat had emerged that soon would set the entire world ablaze. Unlike the dark times of the Spanish expulsion, when Jews still had the choice of conversion or securing a new place for a new start, the Jews now had few if any options: They could neither convert to nazism nor escape Hitler's reach.

Appropriate enough were the words of a popular Yiddish song of the time: Es brent, yidelech, es brent - unser urim shtetl nebich brent! (it's burning, brothers, it's burning - our poor village is engulfed by a consuming fire). These words proved to be a dire warning of the impending disaster.

1

Jewish Life in Prewar Europe

GENERAL HISTORIES

1. Ben-Sasson, Haim H. (ed.): A History of the Jewish People [Cambridge, MA: Harvard Univ. Press, 1976]

This volume, a collaborative effort by six Hebrew University professors, draws on years of research and teaching and represents the most comprehensive history of the Jewish people ever written. The Holocaust is reviewed in pp. 1017-1039.

2. Chazan, Robert and Marc L. Raphael (eds.): Modern Jewish History: A Source Reader [New York: Schocken, 1974]

3. Cohen, I.: Contemporary Jewry [London: Methuen, 1950]

4. Eban, Abba: Heritage: Civilization and the Jews [New York: Summit Books, 1984] * Text based on PBS TV series, profusely illustrated.

5. ___: My People: The Story of the Jews [New York: Behrman House, 1968]

6. Ehrman, Eliezer (ed.): Readings in Jewish History: From the American Revolution to the Present [New York: Ktav, 1981]

7. Elbogen, Ismar (M. Hadas, transl.): A Century of Jewish Life [Philadelphia: J. P. S., 1953]

8. Engelman, Uriah Z.: The Rise of the Jew in the Western World [New York: Behrman House, 1944]

9. Finkelstein, Louis (ed.): The Jews: Their History [New York: Schocken, 1970]

10. ___: The Jews: Their Religion and Culture [New York: Schocken, 1971]

11. ___: The Jews: Their Role in Civilization [New York: Schocken, 1971]

12. Goldmann, Nahum: Community of Fate: Jews in the Modern World [Jerusalem: Israel Univ. Press, 1977]

13. Goldscheider, Calvin and Alan S. Zuckerman: The Transformation of the Jews [Chicago: Univ. of Chicago Press, 1984]

14. Grayzel, Solomon: A History of the Jews [New York: New American Library, 1968]

15. Kedourie, Elie (ed.): The Jewish World: History and Culture of the Jewish People [New York: Abrams, 1979]

16. Keller, Werner (Richard and Clara Winston, transls.): Diaspora: The Post-Biblical History of the Jews [New York: Harcourt Brace & World, 1969]

17. Margolis, Max and Alexander Marx: A History of the Jewish People [New York: Atheneum, 1969]

18. Mendes-Flohr, Paul R. and Jehuda Reinharz (eds.): The Jews in the Modern World: A Documentary History [New York: Oxford Univ. Press, 1980]

19. Patai, Raphael: Tents of Jacob: The Diaspora Yesterday and Today [Englewood Cliffs, NJ: Prentice-Hall, 1971]

20. Potok, Chaim: Wanderings [New York: A. A. Knopf, 1978]

21. Roth, Cecil: A History of the Jews [New York: Schocken, 1961]

22. Sachar, Abram L.: Sufferance is the Badge: The Jews in the Contemporary World [New York: A. A. Knopf, 1939]

23. Sachar, Howard M.: The Course of Modern Jewish History [New York: Dell Pub., 1958]

Useful, though somewhat dated, single volume review of modern Jewish history. Social, political, and intellectual history are integrated. Chapters 20-21 deal with the Holocaust.

24. Schwarz, Leo W. (ed.): Great Ages and Ideas of the Jewish People [New York: Random House, 1956]

25. Seltzer, Robert M.: Jewish People, Jewish Thought: The Jewish Experience in History [New York: Macmillan, 1980]

Survey of Jewish history with emphasis on intellectual and social movements. In each section, however, the patterns of thought are put into specific historical context. The Holocaust is reviewed in pp. 661-671, post-Holocaust thought in pp. 757-766.

AREA AND TOPICAL STUDIES

26. Adler, H. G.: The Jews in Germany: From the Enlightenment to National Socialism [London: Univ. of Notre Dame Press, 1969]

Thematic history of German Jewry. Useful as a guide to general historical problems but otherwise superseded by later works.

27. Ain, Abraham: "Swilocz: Portrait of a Jewish Community in Eastern Europe." YIVO Annual, vol.4 (1949): 86-114.

28. Ainsztein, Reuben: "The Glory of Vilna That Was." JQ, vol.5 #3/4 (Sum., 1958): 56-60.

29. ___: "The Long March of Georgian Jewry." JOMER, vol.21 #46 (Nov. 17, 1972): 18-19; #47 (Nov. 24, 1972): 18-20.

30. Badt-Strauss, Bertha: "The World of Sholem Aleichem... in Pre-Nazi Germany." Recon, vol.12 #6 (May 3, 1946): 21-24.

31. Balla, Erzsebet: "Jews of Hungary: A Cultural Overview." HJS, vol.2 (1969): 85-136.

32. Bamberger, Ib Nathan: The Viking Jews: A History of the Jews in Denmark [New York: Shengold, 1983]

33. Barany, George: "Magyar Jew or Jewish Magyar? Reflections on the Question of Assimilation." Vago: J/NJ, pp. 51-98.

34. Barkai, A.: "The Austrian Social Democrats and the Jews." WLB, vol.24 #1 (Win., 1970): 32-40; #2 (Spr., 1970): 16-21.

35. Baron, Salo W.: "An Historical Critique of the Jewish Community." JSSQ, vol.12 #1 (Sept., 1931): 44-49.

36. ___: "Modern Capitalism and Jewish Fate." Menorah, vol. 30 #2 (July/Sept., 1942): 116-138.

37. ___: The Russian Jew Under Tsars and Soviets [New York: Macmillan, 1975]

Survey of Russian Jewish history. Social, political, and intellectual trends are reviewed, as are Jewish relations with the government. The Holocaust in Soviet Russia is dealt with in chapter 15.

38. Beller, Jacob: "The Jewish Community in Holland." Ortho J Life, vol.40 #1 (Jan., 1973): 32-40.

39. ___: "On Greek Shores." Ortho J Life, vol.34 #2 (Nov./ Dec., 1966): 43-50.

40. Ben-Moshe, M.: "Lithuanian Jewry, Its History in Pictures." J Affairs, vol.16 #12 (Dec., 1961): 22-25.

41. Bilgray, A. T.: "Jews in Holland." J Layman, vol.15 #5 (Jan., 1941): 8-10.

42. ___: "The Jews of Belgium." J Layman, vol.15 #6 (Feb., 1941): 3-5.

43. Blau, Bruno: "Nationality Among Czechoslovak Jewry." HJ, vol.10 #2 (Oct., 1948): 147-154.

44. Braham, Randolph L.: "Hungarian Jewry: An Historical Retrospect." JCEA, vol.20 #1 (April, 1960): 3-23.

45. Brugel, J.: "Jews in Political Life." Society: JoCz/II, pp.243-252.

46. Cahnman, Werner: "Two Maps on German-Jewish History." Ch J Forum, vol.2 #1 (Fall, 1943): 58-65.

47. Czekanowski, Jan: "Anthropological Structure of the Jewish People in the Light of Polish Analyses." JJoS, vol.2 #2 (Nov., 1960): 236-243.

48. Dawidowicz, Lucy S.(ed.): The Golden Tradition [Boston: Beacon Press, 1967]

49. Dicker, Herman: Piety and Perseverance: Jews from the Carpathian Mountains [New York: Hermon Press, 1981]

50. Dinaburg, Benzion: "Jerusalem in Lithuania." J Fr, vol. 11 #9 (Sept., 1944): 37-43.

51. Dinim, Samuel: "Lodz, City Built on Sand." Recon, vol.2 #16 (Dec. 11, 1936): 11-14.

52. Dobroszycki, Lucjan and Barbara Kirshenblatt-Gimblett: Images Before My Eyes: A Photographic History of Jewish Life in Poland, 1864-1939 [New York: Schocken, 1977]

Photographic history of Jewish life in interwar Poland. Based on award winning documentary film produced with pictures from the YIVO archive.

53. Elazar, Daniel J. and S. A. Cohen: The Jewish Polity: Jewish Political Organization from Biblical Times to the Present [Bloomington: Indiana Univ. Press, 1985]

54. ___ et al: The Balkan Jewish Communities [Washington, DC: Univ. Press of America, 1984]

55. ___ (ed.): Kinship and Consent: The Jewish Political Tradition and its Contemporary Uses [Ramat Gan, Israel: Turteldove Pub., 1981]

56. Embree, E. R.: "Jews on the Steppes." Survey Graphic, vol.24 #1 (Jan., 1936): 11-15.

57. Esformes, Maria: "Jewish Salonika." KP, vol.28 #3 (Jan., 1983): 7-9.

58. Feuchtwanger, L.: "The Rise and Fall of German Jewry." J Mirror, vol.1 #1 (Aug., 1942): 45-49.

59. Fischer, Alfred J.: "The Rise and Fall of Greek Jewry." J Affairs, vol.8 #8 (Aug., 1953): 23-29.

60. Fishman, Joshua A. (ed.): Studies on Polish Jewry 1919-1939 English/Yiddish [New York: YIVO, 1974]

61. Fleischman, Gustav: "The Religious Congregation, 1918-1938." Society: JoCz/I, pp.267-329.

62. Fraenkel, Josef (ed.): The Jews of Austria: Essays on Their Life, History and Destruction English/German [London: Valentine Mitchell, 1967] * Collection of essays examining a variety of sub-topics in the historical development of Austrian Jewry.

63. Freed, Clarence: "The Glory That Was Vilna." Lib Jud, vol.12 #7 (Nov., 1944): 6-14.

64. Freidenreich, Harriet P.: The Jews of Yugoslavia: A Quest for Community [Philadelphia: J. P. S., 1979]

65. Friedman, Mark: "The Kehilah in Lithuania, 1919-1926: A Study based upon Panevezys and Ukmerge (Vilkomir)." SJA, vol.6 #2 (Oct., 1976): 83-103.

66. Gelber, N. M.: "Jewish Life in Bulgaria." JSS, vol.8 #2 (April, 1946): 103-126.

67. Gergel, N.: "The Pogroms in the Ukraine, 1919-1921." YIVO Annual, vol.6 (1951): 237-252.

68. Gilbert, Martin: "Shtetlach of the Pripet Marshes." J Digest, vol.25 #6 (Feb., 1980): 42-48.

69. Glatt, J.: "Jews in Belgium." CJR, vol.3 #4 (July/Aug., 1940): 396-401.

70. Glicksman, William: "Polish Jewry." Yiddish, vol.4 #2 (Spr., 1980): 82-90.

71. Goldscheider, C. and A. S. Zuckerman: "The Formation of Jewish Political Movements in Europe." MJ, vol.4 #1 (Feb., 1984): 83-104.

72. Goshen, S.: "Zionist Students´ Organizations." Society: JoCz/II, pp.173-184.

73. Graupe, Heinz M. (J. Robinson, transl.): The Rise of Modern Judaism: An Intellectual History of German Jewry 1650-1942 [Melbourne, FL: R. E. Krieger, 1978]

74. Greenbaum, A. A.: "Soviet Nationality Policy and the Problem of the Fluid Nationalities." Vago: J/NJ, pp. 257-269.

75. Grilli, Marcel: "The Role of the Jews in Modern Italy." Menorah, vol.27 #3 (Oct./Dec., 1939): 260-280; vol.28 #1 (Jan./March, 1940): 60-81; #2 (April/June, 1940): 172-197.

76. Gringauz, S.: "Jewish National Autonomy in Lithuania (1918-1925)." JSS, vol.14 #3 (July, 1952): 225-246.

77. Hagen, William W.: Germans, Poles, and Jews [Chicago: Univ. of Chicago Press, 1980]

78. Halevi, H. S.: "The Demography of Jewish Communities in Eastern Europe." JJoS, vol.2 #1 (June, 1960): 103-109.

79. Hamerow, Theodore S.: "Cravat Jew and Caftan Jew." Com, vol.77 #5 (May, 1984): 29-38.

80. Handlin, O.: "Jews in the Culture of Middle Europe." Kreutzberger: Studies, pp.159-175.

81. Heller, Celia S.: On the Edge of Destruction: Jews of Poland between the Two World Wars [New York: Columbia Univ. Press, 1977]

Interesting socio-historical study of Polish-Jewish interactions during the interwar years. Heller richly documents both Polish antisemitism and Jewish self-defense efforts. The book suffers, however, from a dubious conceptualization, seeing Polish Jewry as a caste, rather than as a national minority.

82. ___: "Poles of Jewish Background: The Case of Assimilation without Integration in Interwar Poland." Fishman: Studies, pp.242-276.

83. Heschel, Abraham Joshua: "The Eastern European Era in Jewish History." J Sp, vol.12 #7 (May, 1947): 16-20.

84. Hostovsky, E.: "The Czech-Jewish Movement." Society: JoCz/II, pp.148-154.

85. Hughes, H. Stuart: Prisoners of Hope: The Silver Age of Italian Jews, 1924-1974 Cambridge, MA: Harvard Univ. Press, 1983]

86. Hyman, Paula: From Dreyfus to Vichy: The Remaking of French Jewry, 1906-1939 [New York: Columbia Univ. Press, 1979]

Social history dealing with the transformations wrought upon French Jewry by the immigration from Eastern Europe. Primary focus is on the internal and communal developments. Antisemitism and Fascism are dealt with only from the perspective of the Jewish community.

87. Israel, Gerald: Jews in Russia [New York: St. Martin´s Press, 1974]

88. Jacobson, Carol: "The Jews in the U.S.S.R." Am Rev/SU, vol.6 #4 (Aug., 1945): 50-68.

89. Jenks, Wm. J.: The Jews in Austria [New York: Columbia Univ. Press, 1960]

90. ___: "The Jews in the Habsburg Empire, 1879-1918." LBIYB, vol.16 (1971): 155-162.

91. Johnpoll, B.: The Politics of Futility: The General Jewish Workers Bund of Poland [Ithaca, NY: Cornell Univ. Press, 1967]

92. Kahler, E.: "The Jews and the Germans." Kreutzberger: Studies, pp.17-43.

93. Kastein, J. (D. Richardson, transl.): Jews in Germany [London: Cresset Press, 1934]

94. Katz, A.: "Bund: The Jewish Socialist Labor Party." Polish Rev, vol.10 #3 (Sum., 1965): 67-74.

95. Katz, Jacob: "German Culture and the Jews." Com, vol.77 #2 (Feb., 1984): 54-59.

96. ___: "The German-Jewish Utopia of Social Emancipation." Kreutzberger: Studies , pp.61-80.

97. ___: "The Uniqueness of Hungarian Jewry." Forum, #27 (1977): 45-53.

98. Katzburg, Nathaniel: "Hungarian Jewry in Modern Times: Political and Social Aspects." HJS, vol.1 (1966): 137-170.

99. ___: "The Jewish Question in Hungary during the Inter-war Period: Jewish Attitudes." Vago: J/NJ, pp.113-124.

100. Kestenberg-Gladstein, R.: "The Jews between Czechs and Germans in the Historic Lands." Society: JoCz/I, pp. 21-71.

101. Klepfisz, Heszel (Curt Leviant, transl.): Culture of Compassion: The Spirit of Polish Jewry from Hasidism to the Holocaust [New York: Ktav, 1983]

102. Kober, Adolf: "Jewish Communities in Germany from the Age of the Enlightenment to Their Destruction by the Nazis." JSS, vol.9 #3 (July, 1947): 195-238.

103. Kochan, Lionel (ed): The Jews in Soviet Russia Since 1917 [New York: Oxford Univ. Press, 1970]

104. Kreutzberger, Max (ed.): Studies of the Leo Baeck Institute [New York: Frederick Ungar, 1967]

105. Lador-Lederer, J.: "Jews in Austrian Law." EEQ, vol.12 #1 (Spr., 1978): 35-41; #2 (Sum, 1978): 129-142.

106. Laszlo, Erno: "Hungarian Jewry: Settlement and Demography." HJS, vol.1 (1966): 61-137.

107. Lestchinsky, Jacob: "Aspects of Jewish Sociology of Polish Jewry." JSS, vol.28 #4 (Oct., 1966): 195-211.

108. Lewin, Isaac: The Jewish Community in Poland [New York: Philosophical Library, 1985]

109. Liptzin, Solomon: Germany's Stepchildren: The Jews in Germany from Varnhagen to Zweig [Philadelphia: J. P. S., 1944]

110. Loewenthal, R.: "The Judeo-Tatars in the Caucasus." HJ, vol.14 #1 (April, 1952): 61-82.

111. Lowenthal, M.: "The First Jews in Germany." Menorah, vol.22 #2 (Oct./Dec., 1934): 147-158.

112. ___: The Jews of Germany: Story of Sixteen Centuries [Philadelphia: J. P. S., 1936]

113. Marcus, Jacob R.: Rise and Destiny of the German Jew [Cincinnati, OH: U. A. H. C., 1934]

Thematic survey of Jewish life in Germany from the earliest periods through National-Socialism. Covers all aspects of Jewish life: emancipation; economic and political activity; social, religious and cultural life; antisemitism. One third of the book is an analysis of the Nazi threat and possible Jewish responses.

114. Mark, Yudel: "The Shtetl: It was a Concept and a Way of Life." J Digest, vol.9 #1 (Oct., 1963): 31-37.

115. Marton, Ernest: "The Family Tree of Hungarian Jewry: Outline of the History of the Jewish Settlement in Hungary." HJS, vol.1 (1966): 1-59.

116. Mendelsohn, Ezra: "The Dilemma of Jewish Politics in Poland: Four Responses." Vago: J/NJ, pp.203-219.

117. Meyer, Michael A.: "German Political Pressure and Jewish Religious Response in the 19th century." LBML #25 (1981).

118. Morgenthau, Hans J.: "The Tragedy of German Jewish Liberalism." LBML, #4 (1961). Also in Kreutzberger: Studies, pp.47-58.

119. Moritzen, Julius: "Denmark´s Jews." CJR, vol.3 #3 (May/June, 1940): 274-280.

120. Mosse, Werner E.: "The Conflict of Liberalism and Nationalism and its Effect on German Jewry." LBIYB, vol.15 (1970): 125-139

121. Papacosma, Victor: "The Sephardic Jews of Salonica." Mid, vol.24 #10 (Dec., 1978): 10-14.

122. Poppel, Stephen M.: "German Zionism and Jewish Identity." JJoS, vol.18 #2 (Dec., 1976): 115-122.

123. ___: "State Building and Jewish Community Organization in Germany." C/J, vol.5 #2 (Fall/Win., 1980): 13-26.

124. ___: Zionism in Germany, 1897-1933: The Shaping of a Jewish Identity [Philadelphia: J. P. S., 1976]

125. Rabinowicz, Aharon: "The Jewish Minority." Society: JoCz/I, pp.155-266.

126. ___: "The Jewish Party: A Struggle for National Recognition, Representation, and Autonomy." Society: JoCz/II, pp.253-346.

127. Rabinowicz, Harry M.: The Legacy of Polish Jewry 1919-1939 [New York: Thomas Yoseloff, 1965]

128. Rabinowicz, Oskar: "Czechoslovak Zionism: Analecta to a History." Society: JoCz/II, pp.19-136.

129. Reinharz, Jehuda: Fatherland or Promised Land: Dilemma of the German Jew, 1893-1914 [Ann Arbor, MI: Univ. of Michigan Press, 1975]

130. Rimalt, E. S.: "The Jews of Tyrol." Fraenkel: Austria, pp.375-384.

131. Rosenthal (Heller), Celia : "How the Polish Jew Saw His World." Com, vol.18 #1 (July, 1954): 70-75.

132. Rosenthal, Karl: "Reform Judaism in Germany." Lib Jud, vol.13 #1 (May, 1945): 9-17, 48; #2 (June, 1945): 24-30, 37.

133. Roskies, David G.: "Shtetl Society." J Sp, vol.42 #3 (Fall, 1977): 44-46.

134. Rossi, Mario: "Italian-Jewish History." Ch J Forum, vol.12 #2 (Win, 1953/1954): 80-85.

135. Rothenberg, Joshua: "Demythologizing the Shtetl." Mid, vol.27 #3 (March, 1981): 25-31.

136. Rothkirchen, Livia: "Slovakia: I. 1848-1918. II. 1918-1938." Society: JoCz/I, pp.72-84, 85-124.

137. Rubin, E.: 700 Years of Jewish Life in Poland [London: W. and G. Foyle, 1944]

138. Schwab, H. (I. Birnbaum, transl.): History of Orthodox Jewry in Germany [London: Mitre Press, 1950]

139. ___: Jewish Rural Communities in Germany [London: Cooper Books, 1957]

140. Schwarz, Moshe K.: "The Jews of Styria." Fraenkel: Austria, pp.391-394.

141. Schwarz, Solomon M.: The Jews in the Soviet Union [Syracuse, NY: Syracuse Univ. Press, 1951]

142. Seton-Watson, Hugh: "Two Contrasting Policies Toward Jews: Russia and Hungary." Vago: J/NJ, pp.99-112.

143. Society for the History of Czechoslovak Jews: The Jews of Czechoslovakia 2 vols. [Philadelphia: J. P. S., 1968/1971]

144. Sole, A.: "Subcarpathian Ruthenia." Society: JoCz/I, pp.125-154.

145. Steiner, Max: "The Rise and Fall of a Jewish Community in Bohemia." YIVO Annual, vol.12 (1958/1959): 247-258.

146. Stillschweig, Kurt: "The Jews of Germany as a National Minority." HJ, vol.11 #1 (April, 1949): 53-76.

147. ___: "Nationalism and Autonomy among Eastern European Jewry." HJ, vol.6 #1 (April, 1944): 27-68.

148. Stoessl, Silvio S.: "The Jews of Carinthia." Fraenkel: Austria, pp.385-389.

149. Stransky, Hugo: "The Religious Life in Slovakia and Subcarpathian Ruthenia." Society: JoCz/II, pp.347-392.

150. ___: "The Religious Life in the Historic Lands." Society: JoCz/I, pp.330-358.

151. Strauss, Max: "The Jewish Community of Aachen Half a Century Ago." YIVO Annual, vol.4 (1949): 115-122.

152. Szajkowski, Zosa: "The Growth of the Jewish Community in France." JSS, vol.8 #3 (July, 1946): 179-196; #4 (Oct., 1946): 297-318.

153. Tamir, Vicki: Bulgaria and Her Jews: The History of a Dubious Symbiosis [New York: Hermon Press, 1979]

Attempt to integrate the history of Bulgarian Jewry with that of the Bulgarian state. Deals mainly with the twentieth century.

154. Tint, A.: "The Jews of France (in the Last Half Century)." JJoS, vol.1 #1 (April, 1959): 127-131.

155. Tur-Sinai, N.: "Viennese Jewry." Fraenkel: Austria, pp.311-318.

156. Vago, Bela and George L. Mosse (eds.): Jews and Non-Jews in Eastern Europe, 1918-1945 [Jerusalem: Israel Univ. Press, 1974]

Collection of essays, based on a Haifa University seminar. Attempts to provide a comparative structure for understanding Jews in Eastern Europe between the World Wars.

157. Veghazi, I.: "The Role of Jewry in the Economic Life of Hungary." HJS, vol.2 (1969): 35-84.

158. Vishniac, Roman: Polish Jews: A Pictorial Record [New York: Schocken, 1968]

A photographic kalaidescope of Polish Jewry just before its destruction by the Nazis. These rare photos are accompanied by a introductory essay by Rabbi Abraham Joshua Heschel.

159. Weisz, A.: "The Jewish Press in Hungary." J Fo, vol.35 #3 (April, 1952): 41-43; #4 (May, 1952): 73-75.

160. Wistrich, Robert S.: Socialism and the Jew: The Dialectics of Emancipation in Germany and Austria-Hungary [Cranbury, NJ: Fairleigh Dickinson Univ. Press, 1981]

161. Zamoyski, Adam: "The Jews in Poland, 1264-1795/1795-1939." History Today, vol.26 #2 (Feb., 1976): 73-82, #3 (March, 1976): 194-200.

162. Zborowski, M. and E. Herzog: Life Is With the People: The Culture of the Shtetl [New York: Schocken, 1952]

A historical social study of ways of life in East European Jewish communities. Brings to life Jewish culture in the shtetl before World War II.

EUROPEAN JEWRY IN THE 1930s

Surveys

163. Ellenson, D.: "Jewish Religious Leadership in Germany: Its Cultural and Religious Outlook." Grobman: Genocide, pp.71-81.

164. Ettinger, Shmuel: "Jews and Non-Jews in Eastern and Central Europe between the Wars: An Outline." Vago: J/NJ, pp.1-19.

165. Gerber, Jane: "The Life and Culture of Sephardic Jews Before World War II." Grobman: Genocide, pp.39-42.

166. Janowsky, Oscar I.: People at Bay: The Jewish Problem in East-Central Europe [New York: Oxford Univ. Press, 1938]

167. Kiss, D.: "The Jews of Eastern Europe." F Affairs, vol.15 #2 (Jan., 1937): 330-339.

168. Kreutzberger, Max: "Problems and Programs for Central Europe." JSSQ, vol.12 #1 (Sept., 1935): 33-38.

169. Lestchinsky, J.: "The Jews of Central Europe." J Fr, vol.5 #6 (June, 1938): 13-16.

170. Lowenstein, S.: "Eastern European Jews Before World War II." Grobman: Genocide, pp.18-27.

171. ___: "Western European Jews Before World War II." Grobman: Genocide, pp.28-38.

172. Lvovich, David: "Problems and Programs in Eastern Europe." JSSQ, vol.12 #1 (Sept., 1935): 30-32.

173. Mendelsohn, Ezra: The Jews of East Central Europe Between the Two World Wars [Bloomington, IN: Indiana Univ. Press, 1983]

An illuminating comparative study of social, demographic, cultural, and political trends of East-Central European Jewry. The book focuses on the internal life of the Jewish communities as well as on the relations between Jews and gentiles in the highly nationalistic environment of Eastern Europe.

174. Polen, N.: "Aspects of Hasidic Life in Eastern Europe Before World War II." Grobman: Genocide, pp.63-71.

175. Seton-Watson, Hugh: "Government Policies Towards Jews in Pre-Communist Eastern Europe." Bul S/EEJA, #4 (Dec., 1969): 20-25.

176. Singer, I. B.: "Jewish Life in Eastern Europe before the Holocaust." CBW, vol.38 #13 (Dec. 10, 1971): 4-8.

177. Ury, Z.: "Impressions of Religious Life of the Shtetl Before World War II." Grobman: Genocide, pp.47-62.

178. Weinryb, B. D.: Jewish Emancipation Under Attack: Its Legal Recession Until the Present War [New York: Am. Jewish Committee, 1942]

Austria

179. Solow, Herbert: "Unrest in Austria." Menorah, vol.18 #2 (Feb., 1930): 137-147.

180. Wiesenthal, Herbert F.: "The Jews in Vienna Before the Anschluss." Ort Eco Bul, vol.1 #2 (March/April, 1940): 7-8.

Czechoslovakia

181. A. L.: "Masaryk and the Jews." J Sp, vol.2 #12 (Oct., 1937): 20-21, 38.

182. Baum, Oskar: "Jews of Czechoslovakia." J Fr, vol.3 #6 (June, 1936): 16-17.

France

183. "Decree Against Religious and Racial Incitement." CJR, vol.2 #3 (May/June, 1939): 66-68.

184. Hyman, Paula: "Challenge to Assimilation: French Jewish Youth Movement between the Wars." JJoS, vol.18 #2 (Dec., 1976): 105-114.

185. Weinberg, David: A Community on Trial: The Jews of Paris in the 1930s [Chicago: Univ. of Chicago Press, 1977]

Well written and important investigation into the mood of

Paris Jewry on the eve of World War II. Meticulously researched and documented the book is an excellent example of social history as applied to prewar European Jewry.

Germany

186. Edelheim, Margaret T.: "The Jews in Germany Before 1933." Ort Eco Bul, vol.1 #1 (Jan./Feb., 1940): 5-10.

187. Friedrich, Otto (ed.): Before the Deluge [New York: Harper & Row, 1973]

188. Niewyk, Donald: The Jews in Weimar Germany [Baton-Rouge: Louisiana State Univ. Press, 1980]

Study of Jewish aspects of Weimar´s short but turbulent history. Especially important in light of the rise of the Nazis this work fills the gap in our understanding of pre-Nazi German Jewry. Although Niewyk includes chapters on antisemitism and self-defense, he concentrates primarily on the internal developments within German Jewry.

189. Pierson, R.: "Embattled Veterans the ´Reichsbund Juedischer Front Soldaten´." LBIYB, vol.19 (1974): 139-154.

190. Rheins, C. J.: "The ´Verband Nationaldeutscher Juden´ 1921-1933." LBIYB, vol.25 (1980): 243-268.

Hungary

191. Cohen, I.: "The Jews in Hungary." Cont Rev, vol.156 #887 (Nov., 1939): 571-579.

192. Laszlo, Erno: "Hungary´s Jewry: A Demographic Overview 1918-1945." HJS, vol.2 (1969): 137-182.

Lithuania

193. Lestchinsky, J.: "The Jews in Lithuania." Ort Eco Bul, vol.1 #1 (Jan./Feb., 1949): 2-5.

Poland

194. Bacon, Gershon C.: "Religious Solidarity vs. Class Interest: The Case of Poaley Agudat Yisrael in Poland, 1922-1939." SJA, vol.13 #3 (May, 1983): 49-62.

195. Benedict, L.: "Polonaise: The Situation of the Jews in Poland." Menorah, vol.22 #1 (April/June, 1934): 19-26.

196. Bernson, E.: "Jewish Life in Poland." J Sp, vol.3 #2 (Dec., 1937): 24-26, 38.

197. Bronsztein, S.: "Jewish Population of Poland in 1931." JJoS, vol.6 #1 (July, 1964): 3-29.

198. Cang, J.: "The Opposition Parties in Poland and Their Attitude Towards the Jews and the Jewish Problem." JSS, vol.1 #1 (Jan., 1939): 241-257.

199. Castellan, Georges: "Remarks on the Social Structure of the Jewish Community in Poland between the Two World Wars." Vago: J/NJ, pp.187-202.

200. Ciolkosz, Adam: "The Spectre of Despair: Poland in the Interwar Years." JQ, vol.25 #4 (Win., 1977/78): 12-15.

201. Cohen, Israel: "The Jews in Poland." Cont Rev, vol.150 #852 (Dec., 1936): 716-723.

202. ___: "The Student Reign of Terror." Menorah, vol.25, #2 (April/June, 1937): 242-250.

203. ___: "3,000,000 Superfluous Jews." J Fr, vol.4 #2 (Feb., 1937): 8-11.

204. Duker, Abraham G.: The Situation of the Jews in Poland [New York: Am. Jewish Cong., 1936]

Socio-economic survey of Jewish status in post-Pilsudski Poland. Presented as a report to the American Jewish Congress. Contains important statistical material on Jewish economic life.

205. Glicksman, William M.: A Kehillah in Poland during the Interwar Years [Philadelphia: Advertisers Press, 1970]

206. Goldberg, Hillel: "Polish Jewry Before the Holocaust." J Sp, vol.44 #2 (Sum., 1979): 56-58.

207. Heller, Celia S.: "Assimilation: A Deviant Pattern Among the Jews of Inter-War Poland." JJoS, vol.15 #2 (Dec., 1973): 221-238.

208. Katz, M.: "The Crisis in Poland." J Life, vol.1 #3 (Oct., 1937): 7-12.

209. Lestchinsky, Jacob: "Bankruptcy in Poland." J Fr, vol. 4 #11 (Nov., 1937): 10-14.

210. ___: "Economic Aspects of Jewish Community Organization in Independent Poland." JSS, vol.9 #4 (Oct., 1947): 319-338.

211. ___: "The Industrial and Social Structure of the Jewish Population of Interbellum Poland." YIVO Annual, vol.11 (1956/1957): 243-269.

212. ___: "The Jews in the Cities of the Republic of Poland." YIVO Annual, vol.1 (1946): 156-177.

213. ___: "The Jews in Poland Before the War." Ort Eco Bul, vol.1 #3 (May/June, 1940): 12-16.

214. ___: "The Situation of the Jews in Poland." Recon, vol.3 #1 (Feb. 19, 1937): 7-13.

215. ___: "Terror in Polish Universities." J Fr, vol.6 #4 (April, 1939): 6-9.

216. Lurie, Zvi: "On the Eve of the Holocaust." IH, vol.7 #2 (Feb., 1959): 14-17.

217. Mahler, Raphael: "Jews in Public Service and the Liberal Professions in Poland 1918-1939." JSS, vol.6 #4 (Oct., 1944): 291-350.

218. Mendelsohn, E.: "Polish Zionism between the Two Wars." Dispersion, #17/18 (1973): 81-87.

219. ___: "The Politics of ´Agudas Yisroel´ in Inter-War Poland." SJA, vol.2 #2 (Oct., 1972): 47-60.

220. ___: Zionism in Poland [New Haven, CT: Yale Univ. Press, 1981]

221. Moskowitz, M.: "Anti-Shehitah Legislation in Poland." CJR, vol.2 #3 (May/June, 1939): 32-42.

222. ___: "Polish Public Opinion on the ´Getto Benches´." Menorah, vol.26 #1 (Jan./March, 1938): 94-102.

223. Rabinowicz, Harry M.: "Yeshivoth in Poland in the Interwar Years." Ortho J Life, vol.31 #4 (March/April, 1964): 53-59.

224. Reich, Nathan: "Towards a Solution of the Jewish Problem in Poland." Menorah, vol.26 #2 (April/June, 1938): 151-172.

225. Rosenthal, David: "Polish Jewry between the Wars." Mid, vol.30 #4 (April, 1984): 40-45.

226. Segal, Simon: The New Poland and the Jews [New York: Lee Furman, 1938]

227. Wynot, Edward D. Jr.: "A Necessary Cruelty: The Emergence of Official Antisemitism in Poland 1936-1939." AHR, vol.76 #4 (Oct., 1971): 1035-1058.

Rumania

228. Lorescu, A.: "The Jews of Rumania." Am J Times, vol.3 #1 (Sept., 1937): 108, 113, 116.

229. Starr, J.: "Jewish Citizenship in Rumania." JSS, vol.3 #1 (Jan., 1941): 57-80.

230. Vago, B.: "The Jewish Vote in Rumania between the Two World Wars." JJoS, vol.14 #2 (Dec., 1972): 229-244.

231. Zuckerman, William: "Can Rumanian Jewry Escape German Jewry´s Fate?" CJCh, vol.25 #37 (Feb. 4, 1938): 9, 16; #38 (Feb. 11, 1938): 5, 16.

Soviet Union

232. Koten, Bernard L.: "Jews Under the Soviets." J Survey, vol.1 #4 (Aug./Sept., 1941): 9-11.

233. Lestchinsky, Jacob: "The Jews in Soviet Russia." Ort Eco Bul, vol.2 #2 (March/April, 1941): 6-9; #3 (May/June, 1941): 8-12; #4/5 (July/Oct., 1941): 16-23.

234. ___: "Jews in the U.S.S.R." CJR, vol.3 #5 (Sept./Oct., 1940): 510-526; #6 (Nov./Dec., 1940): 607-621.

235. ___: "Jews Under the Soviets." CBW, vol.7 #3 (Nov. 29, 1940): 5-7.

2

Modern Europe: Seedbed for Destruction

MODERN EUROPEAN HISTORY

236. Arnal, Oscar L.: "Catholic Roots of Collaboration and Resistance in France in the 1930s." Can Jnl/His, vol. 17 #1 (April, 1982): 87-110.

237. "Baltic States." PFR, #23 (July 1, 1941): Whole Issue.

238. Barker, E. Austria, 1918-1972 [Coral Gables, FL: Univ. of Miami Press, 1973]

239. Berdahl, Robert M.: "New Thoughts on German Nationalism." AHR, vol.77 #1 (Feb., 1972): 65-80.

240. Bilmanis, Alfred: A History of Latvia [Westport, CT: Greenwood Press, 1957]

241. Boudin, L.: "The Economic Consequences of Versailles." Ort Eco Rev, vol.5 #1 (Sept., 1945): 39-66.

242. Broz, A.: "Minority Rights in the Czechoslovak State." F Affairs, vol.6 #1 (Oct., 1927): 158-160.

243. Buell, Raymond L. (ed.): New Governments in Europe: The Trend toward Dictatorship [New York: Nelson, 1934]

244. Burks, Richard V.: East European History: An Ethnic Approach [Chicago: Am. Historical Association, 1973]

245. Carr, E. H.: The Twenty Years Crisis, 1919-1939 [New York: St. Martin´s Press, 1966]

Introductory study of the international relations of the interwar period. Reviews the issues thematically not chronologically.

246. Dziewanowski, M. K.: Poland in the Twentieth Century [New York: Columbia Univ. Press, 1977]

247. Goodhart, Arthur L.: Poland and the Minority Races [New York: Arno Press, 1970]

Report of United States investigative committee on issue of Polish treatment of minorities, primarily Jews. An interesting primary source, although somewhat weak insofar as the committee reports the testimony of all witnesses as fact.

248. Halecki, Oscar (M. Gardner, transl.): A History of Poland [New York: Roy Pubs., 1943]

249. Hayes, Carlton J. H.: A Political and Cultural History of Modern Europe 2 vols. [New York: Macmillan, 1936]

250. Hertz, Alexander: "Social Background of the Pre-War Polish Political Structure." JCEA, vol.2 #2 (July, 1942): 145-161.

251. Herzog, Willhelm (W. Sorell, transl.): From Dreyfus to Petain: The Struggle of a Republic [New York: Creative Age Press, 1947]

252. Horak, S. M.: Eastern European National Minorities 1919-1980: A Handbook [Littleton, CO: Libraries Unlimited, 1985]

253. ___: Poland and Her National Minorities: 1919-1939 [New York: Vantage Press, 1961]

254. Hrushevsky, Michael: History of Ukraine [New Haven, CT: Yale Univ. Press, 1941]

255. Janowsky, O. I.: "Minorities: Pawns of Power." Survey Graphic, vol.28 #2 (Feb., 1939): 76-78, 162-165.

256. Jelavich, Barbara: History of the Balkans 2 vols. [Cambridge: Cambridge Univ. Press, 1983]

257. Macartney, C. A.: October Fifteenth: A History of Hungary, 1929-1945 [New York: F. A. Praeger, 1957]

258. Macdonald, Mary: The Republic of Austria, 1918-1934: A Study in the Failure of Democratic Government [New York: Oxford Univ. Press, 1946]

259. Mamatey, Victor S. and Radomir Luza (eds.): History of the Czechoslovak Republic, 1918-1948 [Princeton, NJ: Princeton Univ. Press, 1973]

260. Matley, Jan M.: Romania: A Profile [New York: F. A. Praeger, 1970]

261. Mikus, Joseph A. (K. D. Wyatt, transl.): Slovakia: A Political History, 1918-1950 [Milwakee: Marquette Univ. Press, 1963]

262. Miller, Herbert: "The Menace of Minorities." Annals, #175 (Sept., 1934): 60-64.

263. Miller, Kenneth: Government and Politics in Denmark [Boston: Houghton Mifflin, 1968]

264. Moody, Joseph N.: "Dreyfus and After." Bridge, vol.2 (1956): 160-190.

265. Page, Stanley W.: The Formation of the Baltic States: A Study of the Effects of Great Power Politics upon the Emergence of Lithuania, Latvia, and Estonia [Cambridge, MA: Harvard Univ. Press, 1959]

266. Pavlowitch, Stevan K.: Yugoslavia [New York: Frederick A. Praeger, 1971]

267. Pearson, R.: National Minorities in Eastern Europe, 1848-1945 [New York: St. Martin's Press, 1983]

268. Phillips, Cabell: From the Crash to the Blitz: 1929-1939 [New York: Macmillan/New York Times Books, 1969]

269. Polonsky, Antony: The Little Dictators: The History of Eastern Europe since 1918 [London: Routledge & Kegan Paul, 1975]

270. ___: Politics in Independent Poland, 1921-1939: The Crisis of Constitutional Government [New York: Oxford Univ. Press, 1972]

271. Raupach, Hans: "The Impact of the Great Depression on Eastern Europe." JCH, vol.4 #4 (Oct., 1969): 75-86.

272. Roberts, J. M.: Europe 1880-1945: A General History of Europe [New York: Holt, Rinehart and Winston, 1967]

273. Rothschild, Joseph: East Central Europe between the Two World Wars [Seattle: Univ. of Washington Press, 1974]

274. Roucek, Joseph et al: Central Eastern Europe: Crucible of World Wars [New York: Prentice-Hall, 1946]

275. Royal Institute of International Affairs: The Baltic States: Estonia, Latvia, Lithuania [London: The Institute, 1938]

276. Rundle, R. N.: International Affairs 1890-1939 [New York: Holmes & Meier, 1980]

277. Seton-Watson, Hugh R.: Eastern Europe betwen the Wars 1918-1941 [New York: Harper Torchbooks, 1967]

278. Seton-Watson, R.: A History of the Czechs and Slovaks [Hamden, CT: Archon Books, 1965]

279. Stromberg, Roland N.: Europe in the Twentieth Century [Englewood Cliffs, NJ: Prentice-Hall, 1980]

280. Super, D. E.: The Background of Polish-German Relations, in Charts and Figures [New York: Ellner, 1932]

281. Taylor, A. J. P.: From Sarajevo to Potsdam [New York: Harcourt, Brace & World, 1966]

282. Thomson, S. H.: Czechoslovakia in European History [Princeton, NJ: Princeton Univ. Press, 1953]

283. Wiskemann, E.: Europe of the Dictators, 1919-1945 [New York: Harper & Row, 1966]

284. Wynot, Edward D. Jr.: "The Polish Germans, 1919: A National Minority in a National State." Polish Rev, vol. 17 #1 (Win., 1972): 23-64.

285. ___: Polish Politics in Transition: The Camp of National Unity and the Struggle for Power, 1935-1939 [Athens: Univ. of Georgia Press, 1974]

Study of the transition of Polish politics during the period after Marshal Pilsudski´s death. Concentrates on the men and policies of the "camp of national unity", which Wynot sees as using fascist forms without their content. This national fascism, however, failed to unite the people and, in fact, increased dissension in the months before the Nazi onslaught. The government´s use of antisemitism as a way to cool national passions is well covered.

GERMANY IN THE MODERN ERA

286. Agus, Jacob B.: "The Problem of German Egotism." Ch J Forum, vol.1 #4 (Sum., 1943): 10-12.

287. Borg, Daniel R.: The Old Prussian Church and the Weimar Republic: A Study in Political Adjustment 1917-1927 [Worcester, MA: Clark University Press, 1984]

288. Bossenbrook, Wm. J.: The German Mind [Detroit: Wayne State Univ. Press, 1961]

289. Breitman, Richard: German Socialism and Weimar Democracy [New York: St. Martin´s Press, 1980]

Study integrating the history of the German Social Democratic Party and the Weimar Republic. The SPD is shown to have had conflicting loyalties, to Marxism and the Republic, which greatly weakened the party´s ability to control events.

290. Bridenthal, Renate: "Class Struggle around the Hearth: Women and Domestic Service in the Weimar Republic." Dobkowski: Toward, pp.243-264.

291. Campbell, F. Gregory: Confrontation in Central Europe: Weimar Germany and Czechoslovakia [Chicago: Univ. of Chicago Press, 1978]

292. Carr, E. H.: German-Soviet Relations between the Two World Wars [Baltimore, MD: Johns Hopkins Univ. Press, 1951]

Evaluatory essays on the tenor, purpose, and scope of relations between Germany and the Soviet Union in the interwar period. Special emphasis is placed on Russian efforts at subverting the Weimar Republic. The period of Nazi ascendency is dealt with in pp. 91-113, and the Molotov-Ribentrop pact in pp. 114-137.

293. Carr, William: A History of Germany 1815-1945 [New York: St. Martin´s Press, 1979]

294. Chickering, Roger P.: "The ´Reichsbanner´ and the Weimar Republic, 1924-1926." JMH, vol.40 #4 (Dec., 1968): 524-534.

295. Childs, David: Germany Since 1918 [New York: Harper & Row, 1971]

296. Craig, Gordon A.: Germany, Eighteen Sixty-Six to Nineteen Forty-Five [New York: Oxford Univ. Press, 1980]

297. ___: The Politics of the Prussian Army, 1640-1945 [New York: Oxford Univ. Press, 1975]

Surveys the role of the army in German history, and especially its role as catalyst for and inhibitor of political reform during the nineteenth century. Craig offers rich documentation, notably of the secret rearmament programs of the 1920s and the military´s role in the Nazi era.

298. Dahrendorf, R.: Society and Democracy in Germany [New York: W. W. Norton, 1979]

299. Diehl, J. M.: Paramilitary Politics in Weimar Germany [Bloomington: Indiana Univ. Press, 1977]

Well documented account of Nazi and Communist paramilitary groups during the Weimar Republic. Diehl argues that the battle of the streets waged by the various combat groups ultimately sapped the strength of the Republic and made the Nazi militarization of Germany that much easier.

300. Edmondson, Nelson: "The Fichte Society: A Chapter in Germany´s Conservative Revolution." JMH, vol.38 #2 (June, 1966): 161-180.

301. Eyck, Erich: History of the Weimar Republic 2 vols. [New York: Atheneum, 1970]

302. Fink, Carole: "Defender of Minorities: Germany in the League of Nations, 1926-1933." CEH, vol.5 #4 (Dec., 1972): 330-357.

303. ___: "Stresemann´s Minority Policies, 1924-1929." JCH, vol.14 #3 (July, 1979): 403-422.

304. Fromm, E.: Working Class in Weimar Germany: A Psychological and Sociological Study [Cambridge, MA: Harvard Univ. Press, 1984]

305. Gay, Peter: Weimar Culture: The Outsider as Insider [New York: Harper & Row, 1968]

306. Halperin, S. William: Germany Tried Democracy: A Political History of the Reich, 1918-1933 [New York: W. W. Norton, 1965]

307. Hiden, John: "The Weimar Republic and the Problem of the ´Auslandeutsche´." JCH, vol.12 #2 (April, 1977): 273-290.

308. Holborn, Hajo: A History of Modern Germany, 1840-1945 [New York: A. A. Knopf, 1969]

309. Jacobson, Jon: Locarno Diplomacy: Germany and the West 1925-1929 [Princeton, NJ: Princeton Univ. Press, 1972]

310. Jones, Larry E.: "The Dying Middle: Weimar Germany and the Fragmentation of Bourgeois Politics." CEH, vol.5 #1 (March, 1972): 23-54.

311. Kirchheimer, Otto: "The Growth and Decay of the Weimar Constitution." Cont Rev, vol.144 #815 (Nov., 1933): 559-567.

312. Komjathy, Anthony and R. Stockwell: German Minorities and the Third Reich: Ethnic Germans of East Central Europe between the Wars [New York: Holmes & Meier, 1980]

313. Kosok, P. and I. Ginsburg: Modern Germany: A Study of Conflicting Loyalties [Chicago: Univ. of Chicago Press, 1933]

314. Laqueur, Walter Z.: Young Germany: A History of the German Youth Movement [New York: Basic Books, 1962]

315. ___: Weimar: A Cultural History [New York: G. P. Putnam´s Sons, 1976]

316. Liang, Hsi-Huey: "The Berlin Police and the Weimar Republic." JCH, vol.4 #4 (Oct., 1969): 157-172.

317. Lorant, Stefan: Sieg Heil! An Illustrated History of Germany from Bismarck to Hitler [New York: W. W. Norton, 1974]

318. McKenzie, J. R.: Weimar Germany: 1918-1933 [Totowa, NJ: Rowman & Littlefield, 1971]

319. Mendelsohn-Bartholdy, A.: "The Political Dilemma in Germany." F Affairs, vol.8 #4 (July, 1930): 620-631.

320. Mosse, George L.: "National Cemeteries and National Revival: The Cult of Fallen Soldiers in Germany." JCH, vol.14 #1 (Jan., 1979): 1-20.

321. Passant, Ernest: Short History of Germany: 1815-1945 [New York: Cambridge Univ. Press, 1962]

322. Petzina, Dieter: "Germany and the Great Depression." JCH, vol.4 #4 (Oct., 1969): 59-74.

323. Pinson, Koppel S.: "Freedom Without Conscience: A History of the Weimar Republic." WLB, vol.12 #3/4 (1958): 23-30.

324. ___: Modern Germany: Its History and Civilization [New York: Macmillan, 1954]

Survey of German history from the eighteenth to the twentieth centuries. Primary focus is on political history, but social, intellectual, and economic currents are also detailed. There is also strong focus on German Jewry and antisemitism.

325. ___: Pietism As a Factor in the Rise of German Nationalism [New York: Columbia Univ. Press, 1934]

326. Reynolds, B. T.: Prelude to Hitler, a Personal Record of Ten Post-War Years in Germany [London: Cape, 1933]

327. Ringer, Fritz K.: The Decline of the German Mandarins: The German Academic Community, 1890-1933 [Cambridge, MA: Harvard Univ. Press, 1968]

328. Ritter, G.: "The Military and Politics in Germany." JCEA, vol.17 #3 (Oct., 1957): 251-271.

329. Ryder, A. J.: Twentieth-Century Germany [New York: Columbia Univ. Press, 1972]

330. Showalter, D.: "Letters to ´Der Sturmer´: The Mobilization of Hostility in the Weimar Republic." MJ, vol.3 #2 (May, 1983): 173-188.

331. ___: Little Man, What Now? Der Stuermer in the Weimar Republic [Hamden, CT: Archon Books, 1982]

Study which places Der Stuermer in its ideological context as the NSDAP´s party organ. Primary focus is on antisemitism and on the legal issues raised by an openly antidemocratic paper published in a democracy.

332. Snell, John L.: "Imperial Germany´s Tragic Era, 1888-1918: Threshold to Democracy or Foreground to Nazism?" JCEA, vol.18 #4 (Jan., 1959): 380-395; vol.19 #1 (April, 1959): 57-75.

333. Snyder, Louis L.: Basic History of Modern Germany [Melbourne, FL.: Krieger, 1980]

334. Stern, Fritz: The Failure of Illiberalism: Essays on the Political Culture of Modern Germany [Chicago: Univ. of Chicago Press, 1976]

335. ___: The Politics of Cultural Despair: A Study in the Rise of the Germanic Ideology [Los Angeles: Univ. of California Press, 1961]

Inquiry into the intellectual and emotional origins of National Socialism. Stern explores the nature and careers of a series of "Germanic critics" who arose in Wilhelmian Germany. The critics´ radical attack on modernity and their nihilism were the background of early Nazi ideology.

336. Tal, Uriel: "On Structures of Political Theology and Myth in Germany Prior to the Holocaust." Bauer: Historical, pp.43-74.

337. Vermeil, Edmond: Germany in the Twentieth Century: A Political and Cultural History of the Weimar Republic and the Third Reich [New York: F. A. Praeger, 1956]

338. Walker, D. P.: "The German Nationalist People´s Party: The Conservative Dilemma in the Weimar Republic." JCH, vol.14 #4 (Oct., 1979): 627-648.

339. Zorn, W.: "Student Politics in the Weimar Republic." JCH, vol.5 #1 (Jan., 1970): 128-143.

3

Antisemitism

ANTISEMITIC WORKS

340. Americanus: "The Judaic-Communist Movement in the United States." Fasc Q, vol.2 (1936): 89-100.

341. Chamberlain, Houston S. (J. Lees, transl.): The Foundations of the Nineteenth Century 2 vols. [New York: John Lane, 1911]

342. Clarke, John H.: England Under the Heel of the Jew [London: C. F. Roworth, 1918]

343. de Poncins, Leon: The Secret Powers Behind Revolution: Freemasonry and Judaism [London: Boswell, 1929]

344. Ford, Henry Sr.: Aspects of Jewish Power in the United States [Dearborn, MI: Dearborn Independent, 1922]

345. ___: The International Jew: The World´s Foremost Problem [Dearborn, MI: Dearborn Pub., 1920]

346. ___: Jewish Activities in the United States [Dearborn, MI: Dearborn Independent, 1922]

347. ___: Jewish Influences in American Life [Dearborn, MI: Dearborn Independent, 1921]

348. Fuller, J. F. C.: "The Cancer of Europe." Fasc Q, vol. 1 #1 (Jan., 1935): 66-81.

349. Hart, E. D.: "History of Usury." Fasc Q, vol.1 #3 (July, 1935): 315-326.

350. Joyce, William: "Analysis of Marxism." Fasc Q, vol.2 (1936): 530-542.

351. Luther, Martin: On the Jews and Their Lies in Luther´s Works vol.47 [St. Louis, MO: Fortress Press, 1958]

352. ___: On the Schem Hameforash in Luther´s Works vol.47 [St. Louis, MO: Fortress Press, 1958]

353. Nilus (Victor E. Marsden, ed. and transl.): The Protocols of the Learned Elders of Zion [New York: Gordon Press, 1977]

354. Spencer, Harold S.: Democracy or Shylocracy [London: C. F. Roworth, 1918]

355. Thompson, F.: America´s Ju-Deal [Woodhaven, NY: Community Press, 1935]

356. Thomson, A. Raven: "The Next Depression." Fasc Q, vol. 2 (1936): 289-301.

357. Wegg-Prosser, C.: "The Worker and the State." Fasc Q, vol.2 (1936): 255-266.

358. Weichardt, L.: "National Socialism in South Africa." Fasc Q, vol.2 (1936): 557-570.

STUDIES ON ANTISEMITISM

General Works

359. Arendt, Hannah: "Imperialism: Road to Suicide. The Political Origins and Use of Racism." Com, vol.1 #4 (Feb., 1946): 27-35.

360. ___: The Origins of Totalitarianism [New York: Harcourt, Brace & World, 1968]

Somewhat flawed factually but nonetheless a groundbreaking political and historical analysis of the role of antisemitism and imperialism in the foundations and politics of totalitarianism. The most important contribution Arendt made was integrating political and cultural trends, her integration of Jewish and European history, and her comparison of Nazi German and Soviet Russian totalitarianism.

361. Baron, Salo W.: "Changing Patterns of Antisemitism." JSS, vol.38 #1 (Win., 1976): 5-38.

362. Biddis, Michael D.: "European Racist Ideology, 1850-1945: Myths of Blood." PoP, vol.9 #5 (Sept./Oct., 1947): 11-19.

363. Boas, Franz: "Race and Race Prejudice." JSSQ, vol.14 #2 (Dec., 1937): 227-232.

364. Cahnman, Werner J.: "Theories of Antisemitism." Ch J Forum, vol.8 #1 (Fall, 1949): 50-53.

365. Chesterton, Arthur K. and Josepf Leftwich: The Tragedy of Antisemitism [London: R. Auscombe, 1948]

366. Cohen, Harry: A Panorama of Prejudice [New York: Bloch Pub., 1944]

367. Coudenhove-Calergi, Heinrich J. M. (A. S. Rappoport, transl.): Antisemitism Through the Ages [London: Hutchinson, 1935]

368. Daane, James: The Anatomy of Antisemitism [Grand Rapids, MI: Zondervan, 1965]

369. Dahlberg, Gunmar: Race, Reason and Rubbish: A Primer of Race Biology [New York: Columbia Univ. Press, 1942]

370. Dushaw, Amos I.: Antisemitism - the Voice of Folly and Fanaticism [Brooklyn, NY: Tolerance Press, 1943]

371. Ettinger, Shmuel: "Jew Hatred: An Historical View." J Digest, vol.26 #10 (June, 1981): 22-31.

372. Finot, Jean (F. Wade-Evans, transl.): Race Prejudice [New York: E. P. Dutton, 1965]

373. Flannery, E. H.: The Anguish of the Jews: Twenty-Three Centuries of Antisemitism [New York: Macmillan, 1965]
* Interesting, but somewhat apologetic, survey of antisemitism by an erudite Christian historian.

374. Funkenstein, Amos: "Anti-Jewish Propaganda: Pagan, Christian and Modern." Jer Q, #19 (Spr., 1981): 56-72.

375. Gade, Richard E.: A Historical Survey of Antisemitism [Grand Rapids, MI: Baker Book House, 1981]

376. Ginsberg, M.: "Antisemitism." WJC/BS Rep, #11 (May, 1944): 2-12.

377. Glassman, Samuel: Epic of Survival: Twenty-Five Centuries of Antisemitism [New York: Bloch Pub., 1981]

378. Golding, Louis: Hitler Through the Ages [London: Sovereign Books, 1939]

379. Graeber, Isacque and Stewart H. Britt (eds): Jews in a Gentile World: The Problem of Antisemitism [New York: Macmillan, 1942]

380. Halpern, Ben: "What is Antisemitism?" MJ, vol.1 #3 (Dec., 1981): 251-262.

381. Handlin, Oscar: "Prejudice and Capitalist Exploitation: Does Economics Explain Racism?" Com, vol.6 #1 (July, 1948): 79-85.

382. Hay, M.: Thy Brothers Blood [New York: Hart, 1975]

Survey of Church antisemitism by an eminent Catholic historian. Hay concludes that conscious Church policy was to denigrate, persecute, and hound Jews, keeping them in a state of abject slavery. Contains extensive documentation.

383. Hertzler, J.: "The Sociology of Antisemitism Through History." Graeber: JIG, pp.62-100.

384. Hogsben, L.: "Biology and Modern Race dogmas." CJR, vol.4 #1 (Feb., 1941): 3-12.

385. Hunterberg, Max: Tragedy of Ages: Antisemitism, the Root, Cause, and Cure [New York: Assoc. Press, 1937]

386. Kahler, Erich: "Forms and Features of Anti-Judaism." CJR, vol.3 #1 (Jan./Feb., 1940): 38-49.

387. Katz, J.: From Prejudice to Destruction: Antisemitism, 1700-1933 [Cambridge, MA: Harvard Univ. Press, 1980]

Extensive and detailed survey of the transformations in European attitudes towards Jews from 1700 to 1933. Special emphasis is placed on international developments and on the political activities of antisemitic parties in Germany, France, and Austria.

388. Leon, Abram: The Jewish Question: A Marxist Interpretation [New York: Path Press, 1971]

Poor attempt at a Marxist interpretation of Jewish history. The book is weak historically, the author relying too heavily on economic factors to explain antisemitism. Rejects Zionism as a solution to the Jewish problem, opting for neo-assimilationism.

389. Levinger, Lee J.: Antisemitism Yesterday and Tomorrow [New York: Macmillan, 1936]

390. Marrus, Michael R.: "The Theory and Practice of Antisemitism." Com, vol.74 #2 (Aug., 1982): 38-42.

391. Marx, Robert: "The New Antisemitism and the old." JRJ, vol.27 #2 (Spr., 1980): 1-11.

392. Montagu, F. A.: Man´s Most Dangerous Myth: The Fallacy of Race [New York: Columbia Univ. Press, 1945]

393. Morais, Vamberto: A Short History of Antisemitism [New York: W. W. Norton, 1976]

394. Oberman, H. (J. Porter, transl.): The Roots of Antisemitism in the Age of Renaissance and Reformation [Philadelphia: Fortress Press, 1983]

395. Parkes, James: An Enemy of the People: Antisemitism [New York: Penguin, 1946]

396. ___: Antisemitism: A New Analysis [Chicago: Quadrangle Books, 1964]

Short thematic survey, a world history of antisemitism. Incorporates much of the author´s earlier book, An Enemy of the People <see #395>. Primary focus is on psychological and political perspectives. Includes chapter on postwar Soviet and Arab antisemitism.

397. ___: The Jew and His Neighbour: A Study in the Causes of Antisemitism [London: Harper, 1930]

398. ___: "Unresolved Frictions." Lib Jud, vol.12 #1 (May, 1944): 18-27.

399. Patai, Raphael and J. Patai Wing: The Myth of the Jewish Race [New York: Charles Scribner's Sons, 1975]

Intriguing inquiry into the question of whether Jews do or do not actually constitute one race. The question is reviewed from historical, psychological, and genetic perspectives. Primary focus, however, is on physiognomy and the work is considerably weakened by the lack of one encompassing conclusion.

400. Patterson, Charles: Antisemitism: The Road to the Holocaust and Beyond [New York: Walker, 1982]

401. Pinson, K. S.: "Antisemitism in the Post-War World." Pinson: Essays/I, pp.3-16.

402. ___ (ed.): Essays on Antisemitism 2 vols. [New York: Conference on Jewish Social Studies, 1946]

403. Poliakov, Leon: The Aryan Myth: A History of Racist and Nationalist Ideas in Europe [New York: New American Library, 1977]

404. ___ (R. Howard, transl.): The History of Antisemitism: From the Time of Christ to the Court Jews vol.1 [New York: Vanguard Press, 1965]

405. ___ (N. Gerardi, transl.): The History of Antisemitism: From Mohamed to the Marranos vol.2 [New York: Vanguard Press, 1973]

406. ___ (M. Kochan, transl.): The History of Antisemitism: From Voltaire to Wagner vol.3 [New York: Vanguard Press, 1975]

Detailed survey of antisemitism, part of 4 volume set (last volume forthcoming). Includes theological, social, political and economic perspectives.

407. Prager, D. and J. Telushkin: Why the Jews? The Reasons for Antisemitism [New York: Simon and Schuster, 1983]

408. Radin, Paul: The Racial Myth [New York: Whittlessey House/McGraw-Hill, 1934]

409. Rosenthal, Ludwig (R. Elis, transl.): How Was it Possible? [Berkeley, CA: Magnes Memorial Museum, 1971]

410. Samuel, Maurice: *The Great Hatred* [New York: A. A. Knopf, 1948]

411. Tumin, Melvin M.: "What is Antisemitism?" Dinnerstein: *A/S*, pp.10-16.

412. Valentin, Hugo: *Antisemitism, Historically and Critically Examined* [New York: Viking Press, 1936]

413. World Congress for Jewish Studies: *From Hatred to Extermination* [Jerusalem: Yad Vashem, 1959] * Transcripts of seven lectures delivered at the Second World Congress for Jewish Studies Jerusalem, August 4,1957.

414. Zuckerman, Nathan: *The Wine of Violence: An Anthology of Antisemitism* [New York: Assoc. Press, 1947]

Origins

415. Berdiaev, Nikolai A. (V. B. Kanter, transl. with commentary and notes by A. A. Spears): *Christianity and Antisemitism* [New York: Philosophical Library, 1954]

416. Berliner, Bernard: "On Some Religious Motives of Antisemitism." Simmel: *AS/SD*, pp.79-84.

417. Bokser, Benzion: *Judaism and the Christian Predicament* [New York: A. A. Knopf, 1967]

418. Bratton, Fred G.: *The Crime of Christendom: The Theological Sources of Christian Antisemitism* [Boston: Beacon Press, 1969]

419. Brown, James: "Christian Teaching of Antisemitism: Scrutinizing Religious Texts." *Com*, vol.24 #6 (Dec., 1957): 494-501.

420. Davies, A. T. (ed.): *Antisemitism and the Foundations of Christianity* [Ramsey, NJ: Paulist Press, 1979]

421. Eckardt, A. Roy: *Christianity and the Children of Israel* [New York: King´s Crown Press, 1948]

422. ___: "Theological Approaches to Antisemitism." *JSS*, vol.33 #4 (Oct., 1971): 272-284.

423. Efroymson, D. P.: "The Patristic Connection." Davies: *Foundations*, pp.98-117.

424. Evans, C. D.: "The Church's False Witness against the Jews." Ch Century, vol.99 #16 (May 5, 1982): 530-533.

425. Feinberg, Abraham L.: "The Jews and the Crucifixion." J Sp, vol.17 #4 (April, 1952): 9-12.

426. Gager, John G.: The Origins of Antisemitism: Attitudes toward Judaism in Pagan and Christian Antiquity [New York: Oxford Univ. Press, 1983]

Investigation of the role antisemitism has played in Western civilization. His conclusions - that antisemitism in antiquity was rare and that its origins lay in the repudiation of Judaism - are methodologically sound and probably correct. More controversial is his assertion that Paul did not view Christ as abrogating or in any way changing Judaism. A useful and thought provoking work.

427. Gilbert, Arthur: "Lutherans and the Jews." Recon, vol. 30 #16 (Dec. 11, 1964): 7-12.

428. Glock, Charles Y. and Rodney Stark: Christian Beliefs and Antisemitism [New York: Harper & Row, 1969]

Survey of the role that Christian beliefs have played in the rise and continued strength of antisemitism. Relies heavily on psychological and sociological rather than historical methodology. Largely, but not exclusively, focused on antisemitism in the United States.

429. Hellwig, M. K.: "From the Jesus of Story to the Christ of Dogma." Davies: Foundations, pp.118-136.

430. Isaac, Jules (D. and J. Parkes, transls.): Has Antisemitism Roots in Christianity? [New York: Council of Christians and Jews, 1960]

431. ___ (S. Gizan, transl.): Jesus and Israel [New York: Holt, Rinehart and Winston, 1964]

432. ___ (H. Weaver, transl.): The Teaching of Contempt: Christian Roots of Antisemitism [New York: Holt, Rinehart and Winston, 1965]

433. Kisch, Guido: "The Jews in Medieval Law." Pinson: Essays/I, pp.57-66; Essays/II, pp.103-111.

434. ___: "The Yellow Badge in History." HJ, vol.4 #2 (Oct., 1942): 95-144.

435. Klein, Charlotte L.: Anti-Judaism in Christian Theology [Philadelphia: Fortress Press, 1977]

436. Langmuir, Gavin: "Medieval Antisemitism." Friedlander: Ideology, pp.27-36.

437. La Piana, G.: "The Church and the Jews." HJ, vol.11 #2 (Oct., 1949): 117-144.

438. Littell, F. H.: "Christian Antisemitism and the Holocaust." Braham: Perspectives, pp.41-56.

439. Maritain, Jacques: A Christian Looks at the Jewish Question [New York: Longmans, 1939]

440. Meagher, John C.: "As the Twig was Bent: Antisemitism in Greco-Roman and Earliest Christian Times." Davies: Foundations, pp.1-26.

441. Moehlman, C. H.: The Christian-Jewish Tragedy: A Study in Religious Prejudice [Rochester, NY: L. Hart, 1933]

442. Parkes, James: Conflict of the Church and Synagogue: A Study in the Origins of Antisemitism [New York: Atheneum, 1974]

443. ___: "The Jewish Case Through Gentile Eyes." J Fo, vol.28 #10 (Nov., 1945): 52-60.

444. Ravitch, Norman: "The Problem of Christian Antisemitism." Com, vol.73 #4 (April, 1982): 41-52.

445. Ruether, Rosemary R.: Faith and Fracticide: The Theological Roots of Antisemitism [New York: Seabury Press, 1974]

Investigation into the Christian roots of antisemitism by a professor of theology. Ruether seeks to place antisemitism in its proper context by asserting that it is "the left hand" of Christian theology rather than an accidental factor in Christian history. She proves her point admirably, making extensive use of evidence from the New Testament and the Patristic authors.

446. Runes, Dagobert D.: The Jew and the Cross [New York: Philosophical Library, 1967]

447. Sandmel, Samuel: Antisemitism in the New Testament [Philadelphia: Fortress Press, 1978]

448. Schoeps, Hans J. (D. E. Green, transl.): The Jewish-Christian Argument: A History of Theologies in Conflict [New York: Holt, Rinehart and Winston, 1963]

449. Sevenster, J. N.: The Roots of Pagan Antisemitism in the Ancient World [Leiden: E. J. Brill, 1975]

450. Sullivan, Kathryn: "Pro Perfidis Judaeis." Bridge, vol.2 (1956): 212-223.

451. Tal, Uriel: "Religious and Anti-Religious Roots of Modern Antisemitism." LBML #14 (1971).

452. Townsend, John T.: "The Gospel of John and the Jews." Davies: Foundations, pp.72-97.

453. Van Buren, P. M.: "The Theological Roots of Antisemitism: A Christian View." Grobman: Genocide, pp.86-90.

454. Wilken, Robert L.: John Chrysostom and the Jews: Rhetoric and Reality in the Late Fourth Century [Berkeley, CA: Univ. of California Press, 1984]

455. Winston, D.: "Pagan and Early-Christian Antisemitism." Friedlander: Ideology, pp.15-25.

Psychological Studies

456. Abel, Ernst L.: The Roots of Antisemitism [Cranbury, NJ: Fairleigh Dickinson Univ. Press, 1974]

Psycho-historical investigation into the origins of antisemitism. Abel posits the origins of antisemitism in the Hellenistic period, and sees them as being essentially psychological and social in nature. His primary conclusion is that antisemitism is the expression of "dislike of the unlike" on a mass scale. While the historical association of the origins of antisemitism with the so-called birth period of Western civilization is probably correct, the psychological underpinnings are less than convincing.

457. Ackerman, Nathan W. and Marie Jahoda: Antisemitism and Emotional Disorder: A Psychoanalytic Interpretation [New York: Harper & Row/ Am. Jewish Committee, 1950]

458. Allport, Gordon W.: "The Jew as Scapegoat." Chartock: Society, pp.89-93.

459. ___: The Nature of Prejudice [Cambridge, MA: Addison-Wesley Pub., 1954]

460. Bernstein, Peretz F. (D. Saraph, transl.): Jew-Hate as a Sociological Problem [New York: Philisophical Library, 1951]

461. Brown, J. F.: "The Origin of the Antisemitic Attitude." Graeber: JIG, pp.124-148.

462. Buk, Nicholas: "The Two Thousand Years´ Way: A Sociological Study of the Jewish Question." Judaism, vol.4 #1 (Win., 1955): 29-41.

463. Delos, Joseph T. et al: Race, Nation, Person: Social Aspects of the Race Problem [New York: Barnes & Noble, 1944]

464. Fenichel, Otto: "Elements of a Psychoanalytic Theory of Antisemitism." Simmel: AS/SD, pp.11-32.

465. ___: "Psychoanalysis of Antisemitism." Dinnerstein: A/S, pp.24-34.

466. ___: "A Psychoanalytic Approach to Antisemitism: The Unconscious Factors at the Root of Mass Aggression." Com, vol.2 #1 (July, 1946): 36-44.

467. Freeman, E.: "The Motivation of Jew-Gentile Relationship." Graeber: JIG, pp.149-178.

468. Frenkel-Brunswik, Else and R. N. Sanford: "The Antisemitic Personality: A Research Report." Simmel: AS/SD, pp.96-124.

469. Glicksberg, Ch. I.: "Psychoanalysis and Antisemitism." Ch J Forum, vol.11 #4 (Sum., 1953): 209-215.

470. Goldberg, David: Perish the Jew! A Clinical Treatment of Antisemitism [New York: Bloch Pub., 1939]

471. Grosser, Paul E. and E. C. Halperin: The Causes and Effects of Antisemitism: The Dimensions of a Prejudice [New York: Philosophical Library, 1977]

An encyclopaedia of antisemitism and antisemitic incidents, ideas, and personalities. The core of the book is a year by year chronicle of antisemitic incidents in the Western world from 70 C. E. until today. Antisemitism is then viewed from several perspectives with psychology given the most attention. Pages 367-389 deal with Islamic antisemitism from 600-1970. The book is extensively documented and useful as both a teaching text and resource guide.

472. Himelhoch, J.: "Is There a Bigot Personality?" Com, vol.3 #3 (March, 1947): 277-284.

473. Kressel, Neil J.: "Hating the Jews: A New View from Social Psychology." Judaism, vol.30 #3 (Sum., 1981): 269-275.

474. Levinger, Lee J.: "Antisemitism: A Sociological Approach." JSSQ, vol.13 #1 (Sept., 1936): 25-29.

475. Levinson, D. J.: "The Study of Antisemitic Ideology." Adorno: Authoritarian, pp.57-101.

476. Lipset, S. M.: "The Roots of Prejudice and Racism." J Digest, vol.23 #38 (April, 1978): 23-33.

477. Loewenstein, Rudolph (V. Damman, transl.): Christians and Jews: A Psychoanalytic Study [New York: International Univ. Press, 1951]

478. Orr, Douglas W.: "Antisemitism and the Psychopathology of Everyday Life." Simmel: AS/SD, pp.85-95.

479. Rapaport, Ernest A.: Anti-Judaism: A Psychohistory [Chicago: Perspective Press, 1976]

480. Rosenman, Stanley: "Psychoanalytic Reflections on Antisemitism." JP/J, vol.1 #2 (Spr., 1977): 3-23.

481. Sacher, Harry: "Revenge of the Prophets: A Psychoanalysis of Antisemitism." Menorah, vol.28 #3 (Oct./Dec., 1940): 243-253.

482. Simmel, E.: "Antisemitism and Mass Psychopathology." Simmel: AS/SD, pp.33-78.

483. ___: Antisemitism: A Social Disease [New York: International Univ. Press, 1946]

484. Slater, Eliot: "A Biological View of Antisemitism." JM, vol.1 #8 (Nov., 1947): 22-28.

485. Tenenbaum, Samuel: Why Men Hate [New York: Beechhurst Press, 1947]

486. Wechsler, I. S.: "Some Remarks on the Psychology of Antisemitism." Pinson: Essays/I, pp.167-174.

European Demonology

487. Bach, H. I.: "The Guilt Feeling in Antisemitism." PoP, vol.7 #4 (July/Aug., 1973): 24-31.

488. Bein, A.: "The Jewish Parasite. Notes on the Semantics of the Jewish Problem." LBIYB, vol.9 (1964): 3-40.

489. Bernstein, H.: The Truth About The Protocols of Zion: A Complete Exposure [New York: Covici-Friede, 1935]

490. Bokser, Benzion: "Talmudic Forgeries: A Case Study in Anti-Jewish Propaganda." CJR, vol.2 #4 (July/Aug., 1931): 6-22.

491. Charles, P. and W. G. Ryan: "The Learned Elders of Zion." Bridge, vol.1 (1955): 159-190.

492. Cohn, N.: "The Myth of the Jewish World Conspiracy: A Case Study in Collective Psychopathology." Com, vol.41 #5 (June, 1966): 35-42.

493. ___: Warrant for Genocide: The Myth of the Jewish World Conspiracy and the Protocols of the Elders of Zion [New York: Harper & Row, 1967]

Charts the spread, popularity, and political use of the myth of a Jewish world conspiracy as represented by The Protocols of the Elders of Zion. Heavy emphasis placed on textual and literary foundations.

494. Curtiss, John S.: An Appraisal of the Protocols of the Elders of Zion [New York: Columbia Univ. Press, 1942]

495. ___: "A Historian Analyzes the Protocols." CJR, vol.5 #1 (Feb., 1942): 51-70.

496. Franklyn, Julian: "Tabu and the Jews." Cont Rev, vol. 148 #840 (Dec., 1935): 713-720.

497. Jacobs, Melville: "Jewish Blood and Culure." Graeber: JIG, pp.38-55.

498. Kristol, Irving: "The Myth of the Supra-Human Jew: The Theological Stigma." Com, vol.4 #3 (Sept., 1947): 226- 233.

499. Nussbaum, Arthur: "The Ritual-Murder Trial of Pulna." HJ, vol.9 #1 (April, 1947): 57-74.

500. Segal, B. W.: The Protocols of the Elders of Zion: The Greatest Lie in History [New York: Bloch Pub., 1934]

501. Singerman, Robert: "The American Career of ´The Protocols of the Elders of Zion´." Am J His, vol.71 #1 Sept., 1981): 48-78.

502. Trachtenberg, Joshua: The Devil and the Jews : The Medieval Conception of the Jews and its Relation to Modern Antisemitism [New Haven, CT: Yale Univ. Press, 1944]

A chilling and important study of the diabolization of the Jews throughout the Middle Ages and into modern times. The Medieval concept of the Jews as Antichrist and devil is thoroughly presented with rich documentation, analysis, and illustration.

503. ___: Jewish Magic and Superstition: A Study in Folk Religion [New York: Atheneum, 1974] * An extensive study of the extent of truth behind the myth of Jewish sorcery.

504. Vishniak, Mark: "New Studies on the ´Elders of Zion´." YIVO Annual, vol.2/3 (1947/48): 140-145.

505. Weiss-Rosmarin, Trude: "The Christian Mythology and Deicide." J Sp, vol.33 #9 (Nov., 1968): 2-8, 31.

506. Wohlgelernter, M.: "Blood Libel - Fact and Fiction." Tradition, vol.8 #3 (Fall, 1966): 62-72.

507. Wolf, Lucien: The Myth of the Jewish Menace in World Affairs: The Truth About the Forged Protocols of the Elders of Zion [New York: Macmillan, 1921]

Germany/Austria

508. Aronsfeld, C. C.: "Prelude to Hitler." J Fr, vol.33 #9 (Nov., 1966): 9-12.

509. Bender, Charles: "From Luther to Hitler." CJCh, vol.33 #46 (April 3, 1936): 5-7, 51.

510. Bieber, Hugo: "Antisemitism in the First Years of the German Republic." YIVO Annual, vol.4 (1949): 123-145.

511. Braetz, Werner E.: "The Volkish Ideology and Antisemitism in Germany." YIVO Annual, vol.15 (1960): 166-187.

512. Davies, Alan T.: "Racism and German Protestant Theology: A Prelude to the Holocaust." Annals, #450 (July, 1980): 20-34.

513. Edwards, Mark U.: "Martin Luther: Is There a Holocaust Connection?" ADL Bul, vol.40 #9 (Nov., 1985): 11-13.

514. Esh, Shaul: "Designs for Anti-Jewish Policy in Germany Up to the Nazi Rule." YVS, vol.6 (1967): 83-120.

515. Field, Geoffrey G.: "Antisemitism and ´Welt Politik´." LBIYB, vol.18 (1973): 65-92.

516. ___: Evangelist of Race: The Germanic Vision of Houston Chamberlain [New York: Columbia Univ. Press, 1981]

517. Gilbert, Felix: "Bismarckian Society´s Image of the Jew." LBML #22 (1975).

518. Gurian, Waldemar: "Antisemitism in Modern Germany." Pinson: Essays/II, pp.218-265.

519. Gutteridge, Richard J.: Open Thy Mouth for the Dumb! The German Evangelical Church and the Jews: 1879-1950 [New York: Barnes & Noble, 1976]

Chronicles the dismal failure of the German Evangelical (Lutheran) Church to thwart the Nazi antisemitic campaign. By 1933 antisemitism had significantly infected most of the German Protestant Churches, thus silencing before it began any resistance to the Nazis.

520. Hagen, Paul: "Are the Germans Inherently Antisemitic?" J Fr, vol.11 #3 (March, 1944): 12-14.

521. Herz, Emil: Before the Fury: Jews and Germans Before Hitler [New York: Philosophical Library, 1966]

522. Jay, Martin: "Antisemitism and the Weimar Left." Mid, vol.20 #1 (Jan., 1974): 42-50.

523. Karbach, Oscar: "The Founder of Political Antisemitism Georg von Schoenerer." JSS, vol.7 #1 (Jan., 1945): 3-30.

524. Levin, S. M.: "Sombart, Prophet of Nazism." Menorah, vol.27 #1 (Jan./March, 1939): 110-119.

525. Liebschutz, Hans: "Treitschke and Momsen on Jewry and Judaism." LBIYB, vol.7 (1962): 153-182.

526. Low, Alfred: Jews in the Eyes of the Germans: From the Enlightenment to Imperial Germany [Philadelphia: Inst. for the Study of Human Issues, 1979]

527. Ludwig, Emil: "Is the German People Antisemitic?" J Fr, vol.11 #3 (March, 1944): 7-11.

528. Massing, Paul W.: Rehersal for Destruction: A Study of Political Antisemitism in Imperial Germany [New York: Harper, for the Am. Jewish Comm., 1949]

Inquiry into the rise and spread of political antisemitism in Imperial Germany. Primary focus is on the political and social conditions leading to the popularity of antisemitic parties. Also deals with racism and socialist antisemitism.

529. Mosse, G. L.: "Culture, Civilization, and German Antisemitism." Judaism, vol.7 #3 (Sum., 1958): 256-266.

530. ___: "German Socialists and the Jewish Question in the Weimar Republic." LBIYB, vol.16 (1971): 123-151.

531. ___: Germans and Jews: The Right, the Left and the Third Force in Pre-Nazi Germany [New York: Grosset and Dunlap, 1970]

532. ___: "The Influence of the Volkish Idea on German Jewry." Kreutzberger: Studies, pp.83-114.

533. ___: Towards the Final Solution: A History of European Racism [New York: Harper & Row, 1980]

Detailed and indispensible history of the development of both racism and social Darwinism in 19th century Europe. Intimately linked with Professor Mosse´s other books, he here charts the role that ideas, myths, and symbols played in radicalizing Germany´s Volkish national religion. Shows parallel developments throughout Europe and charts and assesses the role of demonological antisemitism in the murderous Nazi psychopathology.

534. Niewyk, Donald L.: Socialist, Antisemite and Jew: German Social Democracy Confronts the Problem of Antisemitism 1918-1933 [Baton Rouge: Louisiana State Univ. Press, 1971]

535. Pulzer, Peter G.: "The Development of Political Antisemitism in Austria." Fraenkel: Austria, pp.429-443.

536. ___: The Rise of Political Antisemitism in Germany and Austria [New York: John Wiley, 1964]

Groundbreaking study of the rise of political antisemitism in Central Europe. Posits that antisemitism arose from the political rejection of liberalism and the conservative war against modernity. Also covers the role and position of the Church on the issue of Jewish rights and antisemitism as a function of the national crisis and racialism. The perspective on the latter issue, however, is weakened by the author´s too general approach.

537. ___: "Why was There a Jewish Question in Imperial Germany." LBIYB, vol.25 (1980): 133-146.

538. Reichmann, Eva G.: Hostages of Civilisation: The Sources of National Socialist Antisemitism [London: Victor Gollancz, 1950]

539. Rosensaft, M. Z.: "Jews and Antisemites in Austria at the End of the Nineteenth Century." LBIYB, vol.21 (1976): 57-86.

540. Schorsch, Ismar: "German Antisemitism in the Light of Postwar Historiography." LBIYB, vol.19 (1974): 257-271.

541. Schwarz, R.: "Antisemitism and Socialism in Austria." Fraenkel: Austria, pp.445-466.

542. Stackelberg, Roderick J.: "Houston S. Chamberlain: From Monarchism to National Socialism." WLB, vol.31 #2 (1978): 118-125.

543. Stein, Leon: "The Antisemitism of Richard Wagner." Ch J Forum, vol.7 #3 (Spr., 1949): 244-247.

544. Stern-Taubler, Selma: "Hitler´s Ancestors." J Digest, vol.3 #4 (Jan., 1958): 59-67.

545. Tal, Uriel (N. Jacobs, transl.): Christians and Jews in Germany: Religion, Politics and Ideology in the Second Reich, 1870-1914 [Ithaca, NY: Cornell Univ. Press, 1975]

Attempt at integrating the political and religious history of the Second Reich with the development of German antisemitism from 1870-1914. Antisemitism is analyzed in both its Christian and non-Christian forms. Possibly the most useful work on the subject to date.

546. ___: "Liberal Protestanism and the Jews in the Second Reich, 1870-1914." JSS, vol.26 #1 (Jan., 1964): 23-41.

547. Weinzierl, Erika: "On the Pathogenesis of the Antisemitism of Sebastian Brunner (1814-1893)." YVS, vol. 10 (1974): 217-240.

548. Wiener, Peter F.: Martin Luther, Hitler´s Spiritual Ancestor [London: Hutchinson, 1945]

549. Wistrich, Robert S.: "Georg von Schoenerer and the Genesis of Modern Austrian Antisemitism." WLB, vol.29 #2 (1976): 20-28.

550. Zarchin, Michael M.: From Constantine to Hitler: An Historical Perspective of the Civil and Economic Rights of the Jews in Germany [San Francisco: United Council to Combat Antisemitism and Nazism, 1936]

France

551. Arendt, Hannah: "From the Dreyfus Affair to France Today." JSS, vol.4 #3 (July, 1942): 195-240.

552. Biddis, Michael D.: Father of Racist Ideology: The Social and Political Thought of Count Gobineau [New York: Weybright and Talley, 1970]

553. Byrnes, Robert: Antisemitism in Modern France: The Prologue to the Dreyfus Affair [New Brunswick, NJ: Rutgers Univ. Press, 1950]

554. ___: "Edouard Drumont and La France Juive." JSS, vol. 10 #2 (April, 1948): 165-184.

555. Chapman, Guy: The Dreyfus Case: A Reassessment [New York: Reynal, 1955]

556. Halasz, Nicholas: Captain Dreyfus: The Story of Mass Hysteria [New York: Simon and Schuster, 1955]

557. Hertzberg, Arthur A.: The French Enlightenment and the Jews [New York: Columbia Univ. Press, 1968]

Controversial history of Jewish emancipation and the enlightenment in France. Contrary to conventional opinion, Hertzberg concludes that it was the enlightenment which secularized and modernized antisemitism turning it into a political issue and thus leading the way for the "Jewish problem" that the Nazis attempted to solve.

558. Mehlman, Jeffrey: Legacies of Antisemitism in France [Minneapolis: Univ. of Minnesota Press, 1983]

559. Parkes, James: "Antisemitism as a Political Weapon in France. " J Digest, vol.12 #10 (July, 1967): 19-22.

560. Wilson, S.: Ideology and Experience: Antisemitism in France at the Time of the Dreyfus Affair [Rutherford, NJ: Fairleigh Dickinson Univ. Press, 1982]

561. ___: "The ´Ligue Antisemitique Francaise´, 1897." WLB, vol.25 #3/4 (Sum./Fall, 1972): 33-39.

Eastern Europe

562. Ainsztein, Reuben: "The Roots of Russian Antisemitism." JQ, vol.20 #3 (Aut., 1972): 3-20.

563. Alshanskiy, Naum: "Russian Antisemitism." JQ, vol.23 #4 (Win., 1975/1976): 33-36.

564. Grynberg, Henryk: "Is Polish Antisemitism Special?" Mid, vol.29 #7 (Aug./Sept., 1983): 19-23.

565. Korzec, Pawel: "Antisemitism in Poland as an Intellectual, Social and Political Movement." Fishman: Studies, pp.12-104.

566. Mahler, Raphael: "Antisemitism in Poland." Pinson: Essays/I, pp.111-142; Essays/II, pp.145-172.

567. Miller, Jack: "Kalinin and the Jews." SJA, vol.4 #1 (May, 1974): 61-65.

568. Moskowitz, Morris: "Totalitarianism and Antisemitism in Poland." CJR, vol.2 #1 (Jan., 1939): 16-25.

569. Poliakov, Leon: "Official Antisemitism in Old Russia: The Origins." Com, vol.22 #1 (July, 1956): 41-46.

570. Samuel, Maurice: Blood Accusation: The Strange History of the Beiliss Case [Philadelphia: J. P. S., 1966]

571. Shohat, Azriel: "The Beginnings of Antisemitism in Independent Lithuania." YVS, vol.2 (1958): 7-48.

572. Tager, A. B.: The Decay of Czarism: The Beilis Trial [Philadelphia: J. P. S., 1935]

573. Vishniak, Mark: "Antisemitism in Tsarist Russia: A Study in Government-Fostered Antisemitism." Pinson: Essays/I, pp.79-110; Essays/II, pp.121-144.

The "Jewish Problem"

574. Baron, Salo W.: "The Jewish Question in the 19th Century." JMH, vol.10 #1 (March, 1938): 51-65.

575. Beard, Miriam: "Antisemitism: Product of Economic Myths." Graeber: JIG, pp.362-401.

576. Bein, Alex: "The Jewish Question in Modern Antisemitic Literature. Prelude to the Final Solution." Dispersion, #4 (Win., 1964/65): 125-154.

577. ___: "Modern Antisemitism and its Effect on the Jewish Question." YVS, vol.3 (1959): 7-16.

578. Cassirer, Ernst: "Judaism and the Modern Political Myths." CJR, vol.7 #2 (April, 1944): 115-126.

579. Ettinger, Sh.: "The Origins of Modern Antisemitism." Dispersion, #9 (1969): 17-37.

580. Fried, John H. E.: "The Promotion of Antisemitism Through the Abuse of Democratic and Social Concepts." YVS, vol.3 (1959): 17-24.

581. Ginsberg, Morris: "The Jewish Problem." WJC/BS Rep, #4 (Feb., 1943): 1-14.

582. Golding, Louis: "The Jewish Problem." NJM, vol.53 #6 (Feb., 1939): 195-196, 201, 212-213; #7 (March, 1939): 228-229, 233, 236-237; #8 (April, 1939): 264-266.

583. Goodrich, N. H.: "Antisemitic Propaganda." CJR, vol.2 #6 (Nov./Dec., 1939): 20-26.

584. Gutman, Yisrael: "Why the Jew? Modern Antisemitism." Grobman: Genocide, pp.95-102.

585. Kallen, Horace M.: "Jewish Right, Christian Power." CJR, vol.6 #6 (Dec., 1943): 563-578.

586. Keenan, Alan: The Phoenix of the West: A Study in Pogrom [New York: Talpinger, 1961]

587. Lestchinsky, Jacob: "The Anti-Jewish Program: Tsarist Russia, the Third Reich, and the Independent Poland." JSS, vol.3 #2 (April, 1941): 141-158.

588. ___: "Factors in Modern Antisemitism." CW, vol.11 #15 (April 21, 1944): 9-11, 14.

589. Levine, Albert J.: "Antisemitism Without Illusions." J Sp, vol.5 #6 (April, 1940): 28-35.

590. Mayer, C.: "Religious and Political Aspects of Anti-Judaism." Graeber: JIG, pp.311-328.

591. Parkes, James: The Emergence of the Jewish Problem, 1878-1939 [New York: Oxford Univ. Press, 1946]

Paradoxical and insightful study into the development of the Jewish problem from 1878-1939. The paradox raises from the author´s efforts at being objective, thus his first section (on Mandatory Palestine) is "anti-Zionist", while the remainder of the work is "pro-Zionist". A thematic and topical study rather than a straight history.

592. Parsons, T.: "The Sociology of Modern Antisemitism." Graeber: JIG, pp.101-122.

593. Rennap, I.: Antisemitism and the Jewish Question [London: Lawrence & Wishart, 1942]

594. Sacks, G.: The Intelligent Man´s Guide to Jew-Baiting [London: Victor Gollancz, 1935]

595. Silberner, E.: "Two Studies on Modern Antisemitism." HJ, vol.14 #2 (Oct., 1952): 93-118.

596. Stonequist, Everett V.: "The Marginal Character of the Jews." Graeber: JIG, pp.296-310.

597. Straus, Raphael: "The Jewish Question as a Problem of Nationalism." HJ, vol.12 #1 (April, 1950): 3-20.

598. Vago, Bela: "The Attitude toward the Jews as a Criterion of the Left-Right Concept." Vago: J/NJ, pp.21-49.

599. Weinryb, B. D.: "The Economic and Social Background of Modern Antisemitism." Pinson: Essays/I, pp.145-166.

600. Zimmerman, Moshe: "From Radicalism to Antisemitism." Jer Q, #23 (Spr., 1982): 114-133.

Anglo-American

601. Baltzell, Digby: The Protestant Establihment [New York: Random House, 1966]

602. Belth, Nathan C.: A Promise to Keep: A Narrative of the American Encounter with Antisemitism [New York: A. D. L./New York Times Books, 1979]

603. Britt, George and Haywood Braun: Christians Only: A Study in Prejudice [New York: Vanguard Press, 1931]

604. Clymer, K. J.: "Antisemitism in the Late Nineteenth Century: The Case of John Hay." AJHQ, vol.60 #4 (June, 1971): 344-354.

605. Dinnerstein, Leonard (ed.): Antisemitism in the United States [New York: Holt, Rinehart and Winston, 1971]

606. Dobkowski, Michael N.: "Roots of U. S. Antisemitism." PoP, vol.9 #4 (July/Aug., 1975): 21-30.

607. ___: The Tarnished Dream: The Basis of American Antisemitism [Westport, CT: Greenwood Press, 1979]

In-depth analysis of antisemitism in America. Notes correctly that while Americans have always been ambivalent toward Jews only in times of great stress has antisemitism crystalized into a mass movement in the United States. An xcellent synthetic work, it also provides a useful conceptual framework for the study of antisemitism.

608. Friedman, Saul S.: The Incident at Masena: Antisemitic Hysteria in a Typical American Town [New York: Stein and Day, 1978]

609. Gorman, R. M.: "Racial Antisemitism in England: The Legacy of Arnold Leese." WLB, vol.30 #2 (1977): 65-73.

610. Handlin, Oscar: "American Views of the Jew at the Opening of the Twentieth Century." Dinnerstein: A/S, pp.48-57.

611. ___: "How U. S. Antisemitism Really Began: Its Grass-Roots Source in the 90´s." Com, vol.11 #6 (June, 1951): 541-548.

612. Highem, John: "American Antisemitism Historically Reconsidered." Dinnerstein: A/S, pp.63-77.

613. Hirshfield, Claire: "The British Left and the Jewish Conspiracy: A Case Study of Modern Antisemitism." JSS, vol.43 #2 (Spr., 1981): 95-112.

614. Holmes, Colin: Antisemitism in British Society, 1876-1939 [New York: Holmes & Meier, 1979]

615. Lebzelter, Gisela: Political Antisemitism in England, 1918-1939 [New York: Holmes & Meier, 1978]

Study which documents the rise and fall of political antisemitism in interwar Britain. The author also documents other manifestations of antisemitism in England at that time as well as the reaction of Anglo-Jewry. Lebzelter does not deal with the English response to the growing crisis in European Jewry and the Palestine issue except as they pertain to her study.

616. Lee, Albert: Henry Ford and the Jews [New York: Stein and Day, 1980]

Journalistic investigation into Ford's contribution to the antisemitic international and the connection between Ford, Father Coughlin, and Hitler.

617. Lestchinsky, Jacob: "The Position of the Jews in the Economic Life of America." Graeber: JIG, pp.402-416.

618. Maccoby, Hyam: "The Antisemitism of T. S. Eliot." Mid, vol.19 #5 (May, 1973): 68-79.

619. ___: "The Jew As Anti-Artist: The Antisemitism of Ezra Pound." Mid, vol.22 #3 (March, 1976): 59-71.

620. McWilliams, Carey: A Mask for Privilege: Antisemitism in America [Boston: Little, 1948]

621. Miller, Albert: "Canada's Fifth Column." CJR, vol.3 #4 (July/Aug., 1940): 388-395.

622. O'Brien, David J.: "American Catholics and Antisemitism in the 1930's." Dinnerstein: A/S, pp.109-115.

623. Ribuffo, P.: "Ford and the International Jew." Am J His, vol.69 #4 (June, 1980): 437-477.

624. Rome, David: Clouds in the Thirties: On Antisemitism in Canada, 1929-1939: A Chapter on Canadian Jewish History [Montreal: Canadian Jewish Congress, 1977/78]

Detailed account of antisemitism in Canada during the 1930s. Based upon extensive archival material the work offers an interesting parallel to the contemporary situation in England and America.

625. Sarna, J. D.: "Antisemitism and American History." Com, vol.71 #3 (March, 1981): 42-47.

626. Shapiro, Leo: "The Antisemitism of T. S. Eliot." Ch J Forum, vol.1 #3 (Spr., 1943): 23-29.

627. Stember, Charles (ed.): Jews in the Mind of America [New York: Basic Books, 1966]

628. Volkman, E.: A Legacy of Hate: Antisemitism in America [New York: Franklin Watts, 1982]

Varia

629. Andrew, Edward: "Marx and the Jews." Eur Jud, vol.3 #1 (Sum., 1968): 9-14.

630. Canepa, Andrew: "Reflections on Antisemitism in Liberal Italy." WLB, vol.31 #2 (1978): 194-210.

631. Carlebach, Julius: Karl Marx and the Radical Critique of Judaism [London: Routledge, Keegan & Paul, 1978]

632. Flowerman, S. H. and M. Jahoda: "Polls on Antisemitism: How Much Do They Tell Us?" Com, vol.1 #6 (April, 1946): 82-86.

633. Friedman, S. S.: "A Study in Comparative Antisemitism, Luther and Muhammad." PoP, vol.5 #2 (March/April, 1971): 6-11.

634. Geltman, Max: "On Socialist Antisemitism." Mid, vol.23 #3 (March, 1977): 20-30.

635. Gringauz, Samuel: "Antisemitism in Socialism." Com, vol.9 #4 (April, 1950): 371-373.

636. Hecht, Ben: A Child of the Century [New York: Simon and Schuster, 1954]

637. ___: A Guide to the Bedevilled [New York: Charles Scribner´s Sons, 1944]

638. Rose, Arnold: "Antisemitism´s Root in City Hatred: A Clue to the Jews Position as Scapegoat." Com, vol.6 #4 (Oct., 1948): 374-378.

639. Roth, Cecil: "Marranos and Racial Antisemitism." JSS, vol.2 #3 (July, 1940): 239-248.

640. Sartre, Jean-Paul (G. J. Becker, transl.): Antisemite and Jew [New York: Schocken, 1965]

641. ___: "Gentile and Jew." Com, vol.5 #6 (June, 1948): 522-531.

642. ___: "Portrait of the Inauthentic Jew." Com, vol.5 #5 (May, 1948): 389-397.

643. Silberner, Edmund: "Was Marx an Antisemite." HJ, vol. 11 #1 (April, 1949): 3-52.

644. Stepelevich, L. S.: "Marx and the Jews." Judaism, vol. 23 #2 (Spr., 1974): 150-160.

645. Wistrich, R. S.: "Antisemitism and the Origins of Jewish Nationalism. " Mid, vol.28 #9 (Nov., 1982): 10-15.

JEWISH REACTIONS TO ANTISEMITISM

646. Bachrach, W. Z.: "Jews in Confrontation with Racial Antisemitism 1879-1933." LBIYB, vol.25 (1980): 197-220.

647. Bergman, S.: "Some Methodological Errors in the Study of Antisemitism." JSS, vol.5 #1 (Jan., 1943): 43-60.

648. Bernstein, Hermann: The History of a Lie: 'The Protocols of the Wise Man of Zion'. A Study [New York: Ogilvie Pub., 1921]

649. Bettelheim, Bruno: "The Victim's Image of the Antisemite." Com, vol.5 #2 (Feb., 1948): 173-179.

650. Bolkowsky, Sidney: The Distorted Image: German-Jewish Perceptions of Germans and Germany, 1918-1935 [New York: Elsevier-North Holland Pub., 1975]

651. Carlebach, Julius: "German Jews and Antisemitism." JJoS, vol.23 #2 (Dec., 1981): 135-140.

652. Cohn, Bernard: "Two Jewish Responses to Antisemitism in Germany 1896 and 1907." JRJ, vol.28 #4 (Fall, 1981): 52-56.

653. Dawidowicz, Lucy S.: "Can Antisemitism be Measured." Com, vol.50 #1 (July, 1970): 36-43.

654. Diesendruck, Z.: "Antisemitism and Ourselves." JSS, vol.1 #4 (Oct., 1939): 399-408. Also in Pinson: Essays/I, pp.187-198; Essays/II, pp.41-48.

655. Fineberg, Solomon A.: "Can Antisemitism be Outlawed." CJR, vol.6 #6 (Dec., 1943): 619-631.

656. ___: "Checkmate for Rabble-Rousers: What to do When the Demagogue Comes." Com, vol.2 #3 (Sept., 1946): 220-226.

657. ___: Overcoming Antisemitism [New York: Harper, 1942]

658. Isaac, Jules: "Christian Teaching the Root of Antisemitism: A Plan for Ending Hatred of the Jew." J Digest, vol.10 #1 (Oct., 1964): 37-40.

659. Katz, Jacob: "Misreadings of Antisemitism." J Digest, vol.29 #5 (Jan., 1984): 39-47.

660. Kreppel, J.: "For the Protection of the Civil Rights of the Jews." Cur J Rec, vol.2 #4 (April, 1932): 33-35.

661. Kressel, Neil J.: "Studying Antisemitism: Is It Worthwhile?" Recon, vol.45 #1 (March, 1979): 20-25.

662. Lamberti, Marjorie: "The Attempt to Form a Jewish Bloc: Jewish Notables in Wilhelmian Germany." CEH, vol.3 #1/2 (March/June, 1970): 73-93.

663. ___: Jewish Activism in Imperial Germany: The Struggle for Civil Equality [New Haven, CT: Yale Univ. Press, 1978]

664. ___: "The Jewish Struggle for Legal Equality of Religions in Imperial Germany." LBIYB, vol.23 (1978): 101-116.

665. Lambroza, Shlomo: "Jewish Self-Defense during the Russian Pogroms of 1903-1906." JJoS, vol.23 #2 (Dec., 1981): 123-134.

666. Lazare, Bernard (H. L. Binsse, transl.): Job´s Dungheap [New York: Schocken, 1948]

667. Levy, R. S.: The Downfall of the Antisemitic Political Parties in Imperial Germany [New Haven, CT: Yale Univ. Press, 1975]

Important study catalogueing the failures of German antisemitic political parties before World War I. Levy argues cogently that the downfall of antisemitic parties in Germany had to do more with their own deficiencies than with the power of Jewish defense efforts. Further, the rebirth of antisemitism in Weimar Germany developed from a different, though related, orientation to nineteenth century political antisemitism.

668. Lewin, Kurt: "Self-Hatred Among Jews." CJR, vol.4 #3 (June, 1941): 219-232.

669. Maller, Allen S.: "Antisemitism and Jewish Historiography." Judaism, vol.21 #4 (Fall, 1972): 490-496.

670. Marcus, Jacob R.: "Defense Against Antisemitism." Pinson: Essays/I, pp.175-186; Essays/II, pp.49-58.

671. ___: "Jewish Defense Agencies: A Historical Perspective." Con Jud, vol.33 #3 (Spr., 1980): 63-73.

672. Marrus, Michael R.: "European Jewry and the Politics of Assimilation: Assessment and Reassessment." JMH, vol.49 #1 (March, 1977): 89-109.

673. ___: The Politics of Assimilation: A Study of the French Jewish Community at the Time of the Dreyfus Affair [New York: Oxford Univ. Press, 1971]

Controversial account of the role assimilation played in inhibiting Jewish defense efforts at the time of the Dreyfus trial. Marrus´ weakest point is his tendency to look at the Dreyfus affair backwards from the perspective of Vichy.

674. Paucker, Arnold: "Jewish Defense Against Nazism in the Weimar Republic." WLB, vol.26 #1/2 (Win./Spr., 1972): 21-31.

675. Pilzer, Jay (ed.): Antisemitism and Jewish Nationalism [Virginia Beach, VA: Donning, 1980]

676. Ragins, Sanford: Jewish Responses to Antisemitism in Germany, 1870-1914: A Study in the History of Ideas [Cincinnati, OH: Hebrew Union College Press, 1972]

677. Riff, Michael A.: "Czech Antisemitism and the Jewish Response before 1914." WLB, vol.29 #2 (1976): 8-19.

678. Rowe, Leonard: "Jewish Self-Defense: A Response to Violence." Fishman: *Studies*, pp.105-149.

679. Samuel, R. E.: "A Common Sense View of Antisemitism." *CJR*, vol.6 #3 (June, 1943): 254-260.

680. Schorsch, I.: *Jewish Reaction to German Antisemitism, 1870-1914* [New York: Columbia Univ. Press, 1972]

Ground breaking study on Jewish reactions to antisemitism from 1840 to World war I. Schorsch argues, with justification, that the very act of trying to defend Jewish rights and interests shows a high degree of political wisdom which belies the fact that Jews ultimately failed to defeat antisemitism in Germany.

681. ___: "On the History of the Political Judgement of the Jews." *LBML* #20 (1976).

682. Steinberg, Milton: "The Jew Faces Antisemitism: The Psychological Aspects." *Recon*, vol.2 #2 (March 6, 1936): 7-13.

683. ___: "The Jew Faces Antisemitism: Popular Panaceas." *Recon*, vol.2 #3 (March 20, 1936): 6-13.

684. ___: "The Jew Faces Antisemitism: The Realities." *Recon*, vol.2 #4 (April 3, 1936): 6-13.

685. Sterling, Eleonore: "Jewish Reactions to Jew-Hatred in the First Half of the 19th Century." *LBIYB*, vol.3 (1958): 103-121.

686. Strauss, Herbert A.: "Jewish Reactions to the Rise of Antisemitism in Germany." *AFJCE/CP*, (1969): 7-26.

687. Toury, J.: "Organizational Problems of German Jewry: Steps towards the Establishment of a Central Organization." *LBIYB*, vol.13 (1968): 57-90.

688. Volkov, Shulamith: "German Antisemitism and Jewish National Thought." *Jer Q*, #15 (Spr., 1980): 53-69.

689. Waton, Harry: *A Program for the Jews and an Answer to all Antisemites: A Program for Humanity* [New York: Committee for the Preservation of the Jews, 1939]

PART II

The Perpetrators

Introduction

The 1920s and 1930s saw a significant rise in right-wing political parties and movements in Europe. Although not all of these were Fascist, the most important ones were. It was the Fascist or quasi-Fascist right that attained power in Southern, Central, and Eastern Europe and plunged humanity into a new and more destructive world war.

In order to understand fascism, as well as nazism, it is necessary to recognize certain key principles. The core concept is that of the totalitarian state. The premise of any totalitarian movement is that the nation is an organic entity, more than just the sum of its individual parts; hence, the nation must be totally organized. Every aspect of national life must be directed by the national will. National will is not a conscious expression but a reflection of national character; only a few can possibly know what the nation must do. This elite must rule the country - not for self aggrandizement but for the greater good. Because most of the citizens, however, do not really know what they want and because democracy is inherently divisive and unstable, the party or movement need not worry about elections. The party must do whatever needs to be done to attain power, to establish its program, and to carry it out.

Because the national will cannot be easily fathomed, the leader who can do so is worthy of respect and perhaps even worship. At the same time, all national enemies must be uprooted, which necessitates the establishment, at least temporarily, of a police state. Finally, once the society has been transformed and brought into consonance with national character and national will, the nation may rightfully seek to expand its sphere of influence.

Clearly the preceding general scheme, with the possible exception of the last point, also fits the Soviet Union. Totalitarianism of all types - Nazi, Fascist, or Bolshevist - have similar characteristics. All of them flow from the premise that a party or movement must have total control over the society in order to achieve the millenium. Bolshevik totalitarianism differs from the Nazi and Fascist brands only insofar as it claims authority based upon creating a better, Marxist future, whereas the latter claim to be re-creating the glorious past of the Teutons or Romans.

In brief, fascism, nazism, and even communism base their political existence upon five points: (1) total control of all elements of society; (2) the remodeling of society in one way or another; (3) centrality of and worship for the leader; (4) a police state without specific rule of law; and (5) imperialism. An authoritarian state, such as a military dictatorship, controls only the political elements of the state, not all elements of society. It does not want to recast society at large; it does not establish a cult of the leader; it may or may not be a police state and may or may not be imperialist. Thus, not all dictatorships are totalitarian, although all totalitarian states are dictatorships.

THE RISE OF FASCISM

Within this context, although all right-wing totalitarian movements agreed on general principles, not all agreed on the way to achieve these principles. Few of the Fascist totalitarian parties even came to power in the same way. The Nazis came to power, at least "officially," by election. In Italy, Benito Mussolini came to power in a grand march on Rome, consciously aping Caesar´s crossing of the Rubicon. In Portugal, a coup d´etat put Alberto Salazar into power, and in Spain, a similar coup attempt by Generalissimo Francesco Franco led to a bloody civil war. Franco came to power only as a result of German and Italian intervention and a great international crisis, which in some ways prefigured World War II. In the Danubian region authoritarian governments arose out of the exigencies of royalism: Petty monarchs gave way to even pettier dictators, such as Hungary´s Miklos Horthy and Rumania´s Ion Antonescu.

In Poland, no Fascist movement ever actually gained power, the leaders preferring to exert their influence from behind the scenes. This was especially true after the death of Marshal Josef Pilsudski in 1935, when the colonel´s clique was in control, although the same may be said for the period after Pilsudski´s coup d´etat (March 1926). Yugoslavia, Greece, Finland, and the Baltic Republics had experiences similar to those of the Poles during the interwar era. Finally, the western Fascists never came to power, although they did deter a stronger anti-Nazi reaction, particularly in France during the 1930s.

Internally, the Fascist states differed widely. Some were more like the benevolent despotisms of an earlier era. Not all the Fascist states succeeded in becoming totalitarian. In Italy efforts to establish a unitary society were effectively checked by the resilience of social institutions, including the church and the family, as well as the underdeveloped state of much of the hinterland. Other Fascist states made no real effort at recasting society, but used Fascist and nationalist slogans as a justification for gangsterism. In the Nazi case, a true totalitarian state was established from the first moments of the Nazi takeover on January 20, 1933.

NAZI TOTALITARIANISM

In Adolf Hitler the Nationalsozialistische Deutsche Arbeiter Partei (NSDAP), as well as many of the roaming soldaten verbande, found their man. An Austrian by birth, Hitler mesmerized ever-widening segments of the population with his stirring, passionate speeches. In speech after speech Hitler called for restoration of German pride, revenge for the ignominy of Versailles, and the reinstatement of Germany´s place in the sun. He would be Germany´s Messiah, creating a new One-Thousand-Year Reich restoring that which properly was due to Germany and settling accounts with those who had betrayed Germany in 1918, especially the Jews. Hitler pictured a Germany secure, at peace, and powerful - a far cry from the rapidly disintegrating Weimar Rpublic. The Nazis seemed to offer Germany´s only hope for the future.

The Nazis were masters of psychological technique. Using triumphal marches, many held at night under the light of torches, the Nazis hoped to tap into the Volkish national spirit that had developed over the previous century. Everything the Nazis did was "German"; their very ideology called for a return to the glorious days of Teutonic heroism.

That which could not be gained by conversion of the masses could be gained by coercion. The NSDAP had its own private army, the Sturmabteilungen (SA), which rapidly wrested control of the streets from the Communists. In October 1929, when the bottom fell out of the world economy, the Nazis were catapulted to the forefront of German politics.

With the onset of economic depression, Germans from all strata turned to Hitler in hopes that he would prove to be the one man who could save Germany. Weimar´s political collapse now intensified. No party gained a clear victory in the elections of June 1932, although the Nazis received 40 percent of the vote. In the November elections, the NSDAP actually lost votes, although it was still Germany´s largest political party. Events moved rapidly. The Nazis began negotiations with a number of nonsocialist parties, and a coalition was finally established in January 1933. Thereafter the Nazis suppressed all opposition. The Reichstag fire, conveniently blamed upon the communists, gave Hitler his chance to use the Enabling Act to abolish parliament altogether. By March 23, 1933, Hitler totally controlled Germany.

Having attained power, the Nazis immediately began to establish their New Order. Nazi totalitarianism was based on a number of concepts, of which the most important were <u>Blut und Boden</u> (blood and soil), a quasipopulism; <u>Fuehrerprinzip</u> (worship of the leader); and <u>Gleichschaltung</u> (coordination). The last - and perhaps the most important - implied the centralization of all authority, political or otherwise, in the hands of the party. They aimed to create a completely new society, to fuse individual, family, state, and party into one entity, all sublimated to the existence and power of one man - Adolf Hitler.

NAZI INSTITUTIONS

Institutions also played a significant role in Nazi totalitarianism. Among the most important, of course, was the NSDAP itself. The party was the body that lent meaning to National Socialism. Of equal import were the Hitler Jugend and the Schutzstaffel (SS), the latter seeing itself as the corps d´elite of the party. The SS aimed to be the central institution of the One-Thousand-Year Reich and the key to the creation of the New Order.

The SS was more than that. Under the leadership of Reichsfuehrer SS Heinrich Himmler, the black-shirted SS developed from a minor organ of the party into a state within a state. The SS removed the SA during the blood purges known as "the Night of the Long Knives" (June 30, 1934). In this power struggle Himmler showed his tenacity, intelligence, and uninhibited lust for power. The SS - not the SA - displayed the total unwavering brutality that would terrorize all of Europe during the war.

Himmler organized his fiefdom into twelve main branches, with further subdivisions (amts) to carry out specific functions. The Reichsicherheithauptamt (RSHA) was charged with administrative control of Himmler's far-flung empire. The Wirtschafts und Verwaltungshauptamt (WVHA), which was the SS economic and administrative office, complemented the work of the RSHA. The Rasse-und-Siedlungshauptamt (RUSHA) served as the SS watchdog bureau for racial purity and resettlement. The Volksdeutsche Mittelstelle (VOMI) was responsible for the welfare of ethnic Germans in foreign lands. Finally, aiding in the racial reorganization of Europe was the Reichskommissar fuer die Festigung des Deutschen Volkstums (RKfDV), the Reich Commission for the Strengthening of the Germanic Peoples, established in 1939. Of these agencies the most important was probably the RSHA. Divided into seven departments, its offices were charged with all matters relating to national security. The RSHA maintained the SS police organs: Geheime Staatspolizei, or Gestapo (the Secret State Police); Kriminalpolizei, or Kripo (the Criminal Police); and Sicherheitspolizei, or Sipo (the Security Police), which combined both Gestapo and Kripo. RSHA also controlled the Reichsfuehrer's intelligence service, the Sicherheitsdienst (SD). Under the command of Reinhard Heydrich, and under Ernst Kaltenbrunner after Heydrich's assassination, the RSHA directed and oversaw the _Endloesung der Judenfrage_, the Final Solution, in cooperation with other SS organizations.

For internal security, as chief of the German Police (Chef der Deutschen Polizei), Himmler ruled in each region of the SS State through the Hoehrer SS-und Polizeifuehrer (HSSPF), the Senior SS and Police Commanders. Finally, he was the keeper of the largest and most sophisticated prison system in Western history - the concentration camps. The camps were in turn controlled by the Inspectorate of Concentration Camps, under Theodor Eicke, and guarded by members of the SS-Totenkopf-verbande.

In 1939, upon the outbreak of the war, Hitler ordered the recruitment of SS-Verfuegungstruppen, special duty troops under Himmler's exclusive command. Later still, these units were merged with the SS Leibstandarte Adolf Hitler and other units to form the Waffen-SS, which comprised the core of an independent army under Himmler's personal command. The SS Central Office controlled many other agencies, including a variety of business enterprises that employed slave labor from the camps. An SS press and communication service, operated in cooperation with the Propaganda Ministry of Josef Goebbels, published books and magazines (e. g., _Angriff_, _Das Schwarze Korps_, _Signal_) and produced a number of movies, for example _Der Ewige Jude_.

THE NEW ORDER

The purpose of the New Order was to create, or rather to re-create, a purely Teutonic civilization. The New Order would expurgate all Jewish influence, even in Christianity, and transmute all Western values. A key element in this New Order called for the reorganization of Europe. Most Western and Scandinavian countries would be nazified and coordinated. Barriers separating them would be destroyed. The Slavic Ostmensch, although retaining the status of "aryan," would be reduced to slavery and would do all the hard labor that their German masters required. In the words of Reinhard Heydrich, they would be reduced to "two-legged cattle."

A very different fate awaited the Jews. They, in fact, played a major role in the New Order: The removal of the Jew from the Earth was to signal the end of racial strife and announce the Messianic Era. The destruction of the "Jewish-vermin" was to be the first and most glorious phase of the Nazi Apocalypse. "Judea must perish that mankind may be saved" was the catchword.

The Nazi use of terror, however, extended beyond the Jews into almost every phase of life. Through the all-inclusiveness of the SS apparatus, the Nazis created a truly totalitarian state - the SS State. Virtually all institutions were gleichgeschalted. They nazified the labor unions, the schools, and universities. Even the army, the pride of the old Prussian Junkers, surrendered its independence, swearing an oath to the Fuehrer rather than to the state and thereby becoming accomplices in Nazi crimes. The SS State strictly regimented leisure time, as well as the everyday lives of youth and families. Nazism touched, tainted, and corrupted every element of German society. No one was safe. Random denunciations could easily land one in a concentration camp, as could even the most casual anti-Nazi remark. The crippled, infirm, and mentally retarded might have been consigned to a holocaust of their own, had public and Church resistance not stopped the Euthanasia program (Operation T4) after only a short duration. Still, approximately 275,000 mentally ill Germans were gassed to conform with Nazi eugenic dogma.

If this short review seems to paint a surrealist view of society, it is worth noting that Wagner´s composition Der Ring des Nibelungen, especially Gotterdammerung, was a particular favorite of the Nazis. The question does arise, however, as to how the Nazis could ever have attained power in Germany, a country considered by many to be the most rational one in Europe.

THE NAZI PERSONALITY

Seeking the answers to that question leads inevitably to the need to understand the Nazis themselves. In light of the wartime atrocities, they might seem to be a band of sadists who achieved almost sexual pleasure from seeing their victims tormented. Careful study shows exactly the opposite. With the possible exception of the Sturmabteilungen (SA), many of whose members were professional ruffians, most of the Nazis were of middle-class origin. Few were unusual before their nazification and few had previous police records. The Nazi system called upon a deep-seated core of violence that turned ordinary middle-class citizens into fanatical murderers.

The educated elite, it would seem, could not jump onto the Nazi bandwagon fast enough. Lawyers, doctors, historians, educators, scientists, and composers all lent a hand to Hitler´s grand undertaking. A case in point was Gerhard Kittel. Born in September 1889, he was the son of Rudolf Kittel, the Biblical scholar and author of _Biblia Hebraica_. Gerhard Kittel, a scholar in his own right, wrote _Die Probleme des Palestiner Spaetjudentums_ and was professor of theology at the University of Tubingen. Before the advent of the One-Thousand-Year Reich he frequently associated with Jewish scholars of the day. In 1933 he wrote a short book, _Die Judenfrage_ (The Jewish Question), in which he showed how the emancipation had been an error and ought to be undone. Later, during the period of extermination, Kittel used his knowledge of Judaism to justify the destruction of European Jewry.

Kittel, of course, was not an exception. "Hitler´s professors," some of them the best in their respective fields, were able to come up with precedents and antecedents to give legal sanction to the most brutal measures that any criminal state has ever undertaken.

The same holds true of the four original Einsatzgruppen commanders as well as their replacements: SS-Oberfuehrer Franz Stahlecker, Einsatzgruppe A; Arthur Nebe, Einsatzgruppe B; Oberfuehrer Otto Rasch, Einsatzgruppe C; SS-Brigadefuehrer Otto Ohlendorf, Einsatzgruppe D.

The four Einsatzgruppen, subdivided into smaller groups of commandos, murdered close to a million people during their first sweep from June 22 through December 1941. Stahlecker was head of Amt IVa (intelligence) of the RSHA; Nebe was chief of Amt V Reichskriminalpolizeiamt (Kripo) or Criminal Police; Rasch was an inspector in the Sicherheitspolizei (Sipo) or Security Police; while Ohlendorf was head of RSHA Amt III. The latter was a lawyer and economist, and all of them were educated men without criminal records.

The same was true of all the other major and minor Nazi leaders. Men such as Hans Frank (governor-general of Poland), Alfred Rosenberg (nazism's keenest racial theorist), and deputy Foreign Minister Martin Luther were all outwardly normal members of the middle class. Personally the majority of Nazi leaders could be characterized as plain, drab, and perhaps even banal. Only one figure in the Nazi hierarchy comes to mind in contradistinction to these bland bureaucrats - Reinhard Heydrich, who had been cashiered from the Reichswehr (army) for immorality.

THE WEHRMACHT

Even the army, the pride of Prussian conservatives, willingly played a role in the New Order. To be sure, many of the professional officers viewed Hitler with disdain as a mere upstart, an Austrian corporal who thought he could give them orders. But the generals who planned to use and control Hitler soon found themselves under his complete control. Those who attempted to show any independence were purged, embarrassed publicly, and neutralized. By the spring of 1934 the military had surrendered the last vestiges of its independence. Abandoning previous practice, the entire army - from the field marshals down to the lowest privates - swore an oath of allegiance to Hitler rather than to the state.

By 1939 the army had become a willing instrument in German aggression. Wehrmacht officers turned a blind eye to anti-Jewish excesses carried out by the SS. Often, military units - for example the Fieldgendarmerie (military police) - actively helped to carry out the Final Solution.

Only in 1943, when it became clear that the war was lost, did some officers of varied rank begin to express doubts about Hitler and the Nazi regime. At that point members of a conspiracy planned and tried to assassinate Hitler. Yet their attempt, code-named Operation Valkyrie, was a total failure. This late plot on the life of the Fuehrer, however, was not an exclusively Wehrmacht venture. Some members of the SS, among them Arthur Nebe, the former commander of Einsatzgruppe B, took part.

The Nazi regime even coopted medical science for their purposes. Nazi doctors committed numerous crimes in the name of science. Victor Brack, in the forefront of the nazification of German medicine, attempted to justify the gruesome "medical experiments" that were carried out on unwilling victims with often fatal results. Dozens of other doctors, all sworn by the Oath of Hippocrates to alleviate human suffering, also participated in the Nazi experiment, committing atrocious crimes on healthy human specimens: Injecting into their tormented bodies all kinds of poisonous chemicals; cutting out pieces of flesh without the benefit of anesthesia; and abandoning the subject to fight infections without anti-biotics. If the subject survived on his or her own initiative there would be more experiments. If not, it mattered little because plenty of other subjects were readily available.

None of these "doctors of doom" is more infamous than Joseph Mengele, the "purveyor of death" at Auschwitz, perhaps the most pernicious mass murderer of all time. The same Mengele almost single-handedly played god over millions of innocent souls, selecting arbitrarily those who should forfeit their lives and those who might stay alive, by his grace, a while longer. He was not, however, alone. In every extermination camp, a "Doctor Mengele" selected a few from the wretched masses of the ever-arriving transports to stay alive a while longer.

The same camp commanders, doctors, and officers who consigned millions to their deaths were also loving husbands and parents. Many of them were fond of animals, keeping pets in their homes. Quite a few were even vegetarians. What made them unique was that they could divorce murder, rape, and pillage from their personal lives. Their banality makes them even more frightening. Clearly, the National-Socialist rot had eaten deeply into the root of German society.

The end, of course, was Gotterdammerung. Nazism could not survive because it proved itself completely sterile. What else can be said of a movement whose only real accomplishment was the extermination of six million Jewish men, women, and children, as well as millions of others?

4

Fascism

COMPARATIVE STUDIES ON TOTALITARIANISM

690. Albert, E.: "Hitler and Mussolini." Cont Rev, vol. 159 #902 (Feb., 1941): 155-161.

691. Chamberlain, William: "Russia and Germany: Parallels and Contrasts." Atlantic, vol.156 #3 (Sept., 1935): 359-368.

692. Cobran, Alfred: Dictatorship: Its History and Theory [New York: Scribner, 1939]

693. Colton, E. T.: Four Patterns of Revolution: Communist USSR, Fascist Italy, Nazi Germany, New Deal America [New York: Assoc. Press, 1935]

694. Ebenstein, William: Today´s Isms: Communism, Fascism, Capitalism, Socialism [Englewood Cliffs, NJ: Prentice Hall, 1973]

695. Florinsky, Michael T.: Fascism and National Socialism [New York: Macmillan, 1936]

696. Fraenkel, Ernst: The Dual State [New York: Oxford Univ. Press, 1941]

697. Friedrich, Carl J. et al: Totalitarianism in Perspective: Three Views [New York: F. A. Praeger, 1969]

698. ___ (ed.): Totalitarianism [New York: Grosset & Dunlap, 1964]

699. ___ and Z. Brzezinski: Totalitarian Dictatorship and Autocracy [New York: F. A. Praeger, 1956]

Survey of totalitarianism as a form of government. After defining the characteristics of totalitarian regimes, the authors elucidate them by comparing Nazi Germany and the Soviet Union.

700. Garraty, John A.: "The New Deal, National Socialism, and the Great Depression." AHR, vol.78 #4 (Oct., 1973): 907-944.

701. Germani, Gino: Authoritarianism, Fascism and National Populism [New Brunswick, NJ: Transaction Books, 1978]

702. Gregor, A. James: Contemporary Radical Ideologies: Totalitarian Thought in the 20th Century [New York: Random House, 1968]

703. Haider, C.: "Pressure Groups in Italy and Germany." Annals, #179 (May, 1935): 158-166.

704. Heiman, E.: Communism, Fascism or Democracy? [New York: AMS Press, 1979] Rep. 1938 Ed.

705. Held, Joseph: The Cult of Power: Dictators in the 20th Century [New York: Columbia Univ. Press, 1983]

706. Lengyel, Emil: The New Deal in Europe [New York: Funk and Wagnalls, 1934]

707. Lubasz, Heinz (ed.): Fascism: Three Major Regimes [New York: J. Wiley & Sons, 1973]

708. Nolte, Ernst (L. Vennewitz, transl.): The Three Faces of Fascism: Action Francaise, Italian Fascism and National Socialism [New York: Dell Publishing, 1966]

Comparative history of Fascism in Western Europe. Compares the history, ideology, and political structures of Fascism in France, Italy, and Germany; also provides an overview of the fascist typology in radical politics.

709. Parmelee, M. F.: Bolshevism, Fascism and the Liberal-Democratic State [New York: J. Wiley & Sons, 1934]

710. Postal, Bernard: "Colored Shirts on Parade." NJM, vol. 48 #7 (April, 1934): 228-231, 250-252; #8 (May, 1934): 268-269, 287-291, 304; #9 (June, 1934): 316-317, 325, 333, 338, 348; #10 (July, 1934): 360-361, 380-381.

711. Ray, John: Hitler and Mussolini [Salem, NH: Heineman Educational Books, 1970]

712. Sauer, W.: "National Socialism: Totalitarianism or Fascism?" AHR, vol.73 #2 (Dec., 1967): 404-424.

713. Silone, Ignazio (W. Weaver, transl.): The School for Dictators [New York: Atheneum, 1963]

714. Talmon, Jacob L.: The Origins of Totalitarian Democracy [New York: F. A. Praeger, 1960]

A penetrating analysis of the roots of totalitarian democracy. Talmon defines totalitarian democracy as messianic in nature, ideologically motivated, egalitarian, and concerned with the broadest masses. These elements of thought came together in the eighteenth century to form the idea of general will and the patterns of collectivist thought which in turn led to both mass democracy and totalitarianism.

715. ___: Political Messianism: The Romantic Phase [New York: F. A. Praeger, 1960]

716. Thurlow, Richard C.: "Fascism and Nazism - No Siamese Twins." PoP, vol.14 #1 (Jan., 1980): 5-11; #2 (April, 1980): 15-23.

717. Utley, Freda: "Stalinism and Hitlerism." Cont Rev, vol.157 #889 (Jan., 1940): 40-48.

718. Wiskemann, Elizabeth: The Rome-Berlin Axis: A Study of the Relations Between Hitler and Mussolini [London: Collins, 1966]

GENERAL STUDIES

719. Allardyce, G. (ed.): The Place of Fascism in European History [Englewood Cliffs, NJ: Prentice-Hall, 1971]

720. ___: "What Fascism is Not: Thoughts on the Deflation of a Concept." AHR, vol.84 #2 (April, 1979): 367-398.

721. Ascoli, Max and Arthur Feiler: Fascism For Whom? [New York: W. W. Norton, 1938]

722. Beckett, J.: "Social Democracy in Decay." Fasc Q, vol. 1 #1 (Jan., 1935): 82-90.

723. Borgese, G: Goliath: The March of Fascism [New York: AMS Press, 1979] Rep. 1937 Ed.

724. Botz, G.: "Austro-Marxist Interpretation of Fascism." JCH, vol.11 #4 (Oct., 1976): 129-156.

725. Carsten, F. L.: The Rise of Fascism [Berkeley: Univ. of California Press, 1967]

Comparative survey of the origins and rise of fascism in central, eastern, and western Europe. Attempts to show why some European countries were susceptible to fascism, while others were immune to it. Carsten sees three factors as being vital: hyper-nationalism, racism, and antisemitism. In post World War I Europe these three elements combined to bring Fascism to power in Germany and Italy. The analysis of these movements is Carsten´s central concern.

726. De Felice, Renzo: Fascism: An Informal Introduction to its Theory and Practice [New Brunswick, NJ: Transaction Books, 1976]

727. ___ (B. H. Everett, transl.): Interpretations of Fascism [Cambridge, MA: Harvard Univ. Press, 1977]

728. Delzell, Ch. R. (ed.): Mediterranean Fascism 1919-1945 [New York: Macmillan, 1970]

729. Dutt, R. Palme: Fascism and Social Revolution [New York: International Pubs., 1935]

Communist political and economic analysis of fascism in the 1920s and 1930s. Also deals with the alleged treachery of Social Democrats who helped fascism develop. The anti-socialist polemic is interesting in light of the cooperation of the Comintern and KPD during the rise of Nazism in 1933 and in the Molotov-Ribbentrop agreement.

730. Einzig, Paul: The Economic Foundation of Fascism [New York: AMS Press, 1979] Rep. 1934 Ed.

731. Forman, James: Fascism: The Meaning and Experience of Reactionary Revolution [New York: Dell Pub., 1976]

732. Fuller, J. F. C.: "Fascism and War." Fasc Q, vol.1 #2 (April, 1935): 140-155.

733. Gentile, Giovanni: "The Philosophic Basis of Fascism." F Affairs, vol.6 #2 (Jan., 1928): 290-304.

734. Greene, N. (ed.): Fascism: An Anthology [Arlington Heights, IL: AHM Pub., 1968]

735. Gregor, A. James: The Fascist Persuasion in Radical Politics [Princeton, NJ: Princeton Univ. Press, 1974]

Thematic review of dictatorship and radical politics, seeking a comparative approach to all forms of totalitarian ideology. The author sees Fascism, National Socialism, and Bolshevism as developing out of the "new" radicalism and mass politics of the nineteenth century. Gregor shows the development of fascism from Marxist roots while setting it in what he considers its proper socio-political and economic context. A useful and thought provoking volume.

736. ___: The Ideology of Fascism: The Rationale of Totalitarianism [New York: Free Press, 1969]

737. ___: Interpretation of Fascism [Morristown, NJ: General Learning Press, 1974]

738. Guerin, Daniel (Francis Merrill, transl.): Fascism and Big Business [New York: Monad Press, 1973]

739. Hamilton, Alastair: The Appeal of Fascism: A Study of Intellectuals and Fascism, 1919-1945 [London: Anthony Blond, 1971]

740. Hayes, P. M.: Fascism [London: G. Allen & Unwin, 1973]

741. Joes, Anthony J.: Fascism in the Contemporary World [Boulder, CO: Westview Press, 1978]

Scholarly effort at placing Fascism in a historical and political context. Links the fascism of the 1920s and 1930s with postwar authoritarian regimes of the Third World. Italian fascism is dealt with in pp.17-74, Spanish fascism, pp.75-86, and Eastern European fascism, pp.87-96.

742. Kitchen, Martin: Fascism [Mystic, CT: L. Verry, 1977]

743. Laqueur, Walter Z. (ed.): Fascism: A Reader's Guide. Analyses, Interpretations, Bibliography [Berkeley, CA: Univ. of California Press, 1976]

Collection of essays offering a comparative history of Fascism, as well as a guide to Fascist ideology and praxis.

744. Larsen, Stein U. et al (eds.): Who Were the Fascists? Social Roots of European Fascism [Oslo: Universitetsforlaget, 1980]

745. Ledeen, M. A.: Universal Fascism: The Theory and Practice of the Fascist International 1928-1936 [New York: Howard Fertig, 1972]

Original study focussing on the importance of youth in the organization and operation of Italian fascism. In his comparison of nazism to Italian fascism the author broadly differentiates between the two.

746. Mitchell, O. C.: Fascism: An Introductory Perspective [Durham, NC: Moore Pub., 1978]

747. Mosley, Oswald: "Forward in Fascism." Fasc Q, vol.2 (1936): 30-33.

748. ___: "The Philosophy of Fascism." Fasc Q, vol.1 #1 (Jan., 1935): 35-46.

749. Mosse, G. L.: "The Genesis of Fascism." JCH, vol.1 #1 (Jan., 1966): 14-26.

750. ___: International Fascism: New Thoughts and New Approaches [New York: Sage Books, 1979]

751. Payne, S. G.: Fascism, a Comparative Approach Toward a Definition [Madison: Univ. of Wisconsin Press, 1980]

752. Pei, Mario A.: "Freedom Under Fascism." Annals, #180 (July, 1935): 9-13.

753. Reich, Wilhelm (V. R. Carfagno, transl.): The Mass Psychology of Fascism [New York: Noonday Press, 1970]

754. Rocco, A.: Political Doctrine of Fascism [New York: Carnegie Endowment for International Peace, 1926]

755. Rogger, H. and E. Weber (eds.): The European Right: A Historical Profile [Berkeley, CA: Univ. of California Press, 1965]

756. Schuddekopf, Otto: Revolution of Our Time: Fascism [New York: F. A. Praeger, 1973]

757. Seldes, George and Helen Seldes: Facts and Fascism [New York: In Fact, 1943]

758. Seton-Watson, Hugh: "Fascism, Left and Right." JCH, vol.1 #1 (Jan., 1966): 183-197.

759. Sillani, Tomaso (ed.): What is Fascism and Why? [New York: Macmillan, 1931]

760. Strachey, John: The Menace of Fascism [London: Victor Gollancz, 1933]

761. Thomson, A. R.: "Corporate Economics." Fasc Q, vol.1 #1 (Jan., 1935): 20-34.

762. ___: "Why Fascism?" Fasc Q, vol.1 #2 (April, 1935): 243-253.

763. Turner, Henry A. Jr.: Reappraisals in Fascism [New York: New Viewpoints, 1975]

Anthology focused on historiographical issues raised by the study of fascism. Includes essays working toward a comparative history of fascism in the 1920s and 1930s. Part of a series on problems of interpretation of European history.

764. Vajda, Mihaly: Fascism as a Mass Movement [New York: St. Martin´s Press, 1976]

765. Weber, Eugen: The Varieties of Fascism: Doctrines of Revolution in the Twentieth Century [Princeton, NJ: Van Nostrand, 1964]

Short well documented study of the history and ideology of fascist movements in Europe during the twentieth century. Reviews fascism country by country, including key documents representing the positions of the major fascist ideologues.

766. Weiss, John: The Fascist Tradition: Radical Rightwing Extremism in Modern Europe [New York: Harper & Row, 1967]

767. Winegarten, Renee: "The Temptations of Cultural Fascism." WLB, vol.23 #1 (Win., 1968/69): 34-40.

768. Woolf, Stuart J. (ed.): European Fascism [New York: Vintage Books, 1969]

769. ___ (ed.): The Nature of Fascism [New York: Vintage Books, 1969]

ITALIAN FASCISM

770. A Prato, Carlo: "Hitler's Roman Gau." FW, vol.1 #2 (Nov., 1941): 205-208.

771. Binchy, Daniel: Church and State in Fascist Italy [London: Oxford Univ. Press, 1941]

772. Borghi, Armando: Mussolini, Red and Black [New York: Haskell, 1974]

773. Cammett, J.: Italian Fascism: Its Origins and Nature [New York: Holt, Rinehart and Winston, 1969]

774. Cassels, A.: Fascist Italy [New York: Crowell, 1968]

775. Chabod, Federico (M. Grindrod, transl.): A History of Italian Fascism [New York: Howard Fertig, 1975]

776. Deakin, F. W.: The Brutal Friendship: Mussolini, Hitler, and the Fall of Italian Fascism [New York: Harper & Row, 1962]

777. De Grand, A. J.: "Curzio Malaparte: The Illusion of the Fascist Revolution." JCH, vol.7 #1/2 (Jan./April, 1972): 73-90.

778. Diggins, J. P.: Mussolini and Fascisms: The View from America [Princeton, NJ: Princeton Univ. Press, 1975]

779. Finer, H.: Mussolini's Italy [New York: Holt, 1935]

780. Gallo, Max (Charles L. Markham, transl.): Mussolini's Italy: Twenty Years of the Fascist Era [New York: Macmillan, 1973]

Surveys the twenty years of Italian fascist power from Mussolini's march on Rome to the collapse of the Fascist regime. Emphasizes the role of Mussolini in the development of Italian Fascism. Briefly describes fascist policy on the Jewish question.

781. Gentile, Emilio: "The Problem of the Party in Italian Fascism." JCH, vol.19 #2 (April, 1984): 251-274.

782. Gorgolini, Pietro: The Fascist Movement in Italian Life [New York: AMS Press, 1979] Rep. 1923 Ed.

783. Grandi, Dino: "The Foreign Policy of the Duce." F Affairs, vol.12 #4 (July, 1934): 553-566.

784. Gregor, A. J.: Italian Fascism and Development Dictatorship [Princeton, NJ: Princeton Univ. Press, 1979]

785. Hastie, Roy M.: The Day of the Lion: The Life and Death of Fascist Italy, 1922-1945 [London: Macdonald, 1963]

786. Lytteleton, Adrian: "Fascism in Italy: The Second Wave." JCH, vol.1 #1 (Jan., 1966): 75-100.

787. ___: Italian Fascism: From Pareto to Gentile [New York: Harper Torchbooks, 1973]

788. ___: The Seizure of Power: Fascism in Italy 1919-1921 [New York: Scribner, 1973]

789. Melograni, P.: "The Cult of the Duce in Mussolini´s Italy." JCH, vol.11 #4 (Oct., 1976): 221-237.

790. Mosca, Gaetano (H. Kahn, transl.): The Ruling Class [New York: McGraw-Hill, 1939]

791. Munro, Ion S.: Through Fascism to World Power: A History of the Revolution in Italy [New York: Arno Press, 1971] Rep. 1933 Ed.

792. Mussolini, Benito: The Political and Social Doctrine of Fascism [New York: Carnegie Endowment for International Peace, 1935]

793. Reale, E.: "The Italian Constitution under Fascism." F Affairs, vol.18 #1 (Oct., 1939): 153-157.

794. Roberts, David D.: The Syndicalist Tradition and Italian Fascism [Chapel Hill, NC: Univ. of North Carolina Press, 1979]

Well documented study into the origins of Italian Fascism. Focused on ideological developments and the development of syndicalism to Fascism. Roberts is especially interested in describing the transformation of a left-wing populist movement into a right-wing totalitarian government.

795. Roth, Jack J.: "The Roots of Italian Fascism: Sorel and Sorelismo." JMH, vol.39 #1 (March, 1967): 30-45.

796. Salvemini, Gaetano: The Fascist Dictatorship in Italy [New York: Howard Fertig, 1967]

797. ___: Under the Axe of Fascism [New York: Howard Fertig, 1970] Rep. 1936 Ed.

798. Sarti, Roland (ed.): The Ax Within: Italian Fascism in Action [New York: Watts, 1974]

799. ___: Fascism and the Industrial Leadership in Italy, 1919-1940: A Study in the Expansion of Private Power Under Fascism [Berkeley: Univ. of California Press, 1971]

800. Schmidt, C. T.: The Corporate State in Action: Italy under Fascism [New York: Russell, 1973] Rep. 1939 Ed.

801. ___: The Plough and the Sword [New York: AMS Press, 1966] Rep. 1938 Ed.

802. Schneider, Herbert: The Fascist Government in Italy [New York: Van Nostrand, 1936]

803. ___: Making the Fascist State [New York: Howard Fertig, 1968] Rep. 1928 Ed.

804. Settembrini, Domenico: "Mussolini and the Legacy of Revolutionary Socialism." JCH, vol.11 #4 (Oct., 1976): 239-268.

805. Sforza, Carlo: "The Fascist Decade." F Affairs, vol.11 #1 (Oct., 1932): 107-121.

806. Sturzo, Luigi (B. Carter, transl.): Italy and Fascism [London: Faber & Gweyer, 1966]

807. Tannenbaum, Edward: The Fascist Experience: Italian Society and Culture, 1922-1945 [New York: Basic Books, 1972]

808. Webster, Richard A.: The Cross and the Fasces: Christian Democracy and Fascism in Italy [Stanford, CA: Stanford University Press, 1960]

Inquiry into the history of the Christian Democratic Party in Italy. Focuses on the party's relations with the Fascists while placing those relations into the context of Vatican-Fascist relations in general.

809. Whealy, R.: "Mussolini's Ideological Diplomacy: An Unpublished Document." JMH, vol.39 #4 (Dec., 1967): 432-437.

OTHER FASCISMS

810. Kedward, H. R.: Fascism in Western Europe, 1900-1945 [New York: New York Univ. Press, 1980]

811. Patman, Wright: Fascism in Action: A Documented Study of Fascism in Europe [Washington, DC: Gov't Printing Office, 1947]

812. Sugar, P. F. (ed.): Native Fascism in the Successor State, 1918-1945 [Santa Barbara, CA: ABC-Clio, 1971]

Comparative history of fascism in East-Central Europe during the interwar years. Each country is dealt with separately. In each case the origins, history, and ideology of fascist or quasi-fascist movements are charted.

Austria

813. Jedlicka, Ludwig: "The Austrian Heimwehr." JCH, vol.1 #1 (Jan., 1966): 127-144.

814. Pauley, Bruce F.: "Fascism and the Fuhrerprinzip: The Austrian Example." CEH, vol.12 #3 (Sept., 1979): 272-296.

815. Wistrich, Robert S.: "Fascist Movements in Austria." WLB, vol.30 #2 (1977): 60-64.

Belgium

816. Callender, Harold: "Fascism in Belgium." F Affairs, vol.15 #3 (April, 1937): 554-563.

817. Carpinelli, Giovanni: "The Flemish Variant in Belgian Fascism." WLB, vol.26 #3/4 (Sum./Aut., 1972): 20-28.

Britain

818. Benewick, R.: Political Violence and Public Order. A Study of British Fascism [London: Allen Lane, 1969]

819. Blackney, R. B. D.: "British Fascism." 19th Century & After, vol.97 #575 (Jan., 1925): 132-141.

820. Gordon-Canning, R.: "Some Aims and Principles of British Fascism in the Conduct of Imperial and Foreign Affairs." Fasc Q, vol.2 (1936): 68-80.

821. Morris, James: "Fascist Ideas in English Literature." PoP, vol.13 #3 (July/Aug., 1979): 22-30; #4 (Sept./Oct., 1979): 25-34.

822. Mosley, Oswald: "The World Alternative." Fasc Q, vol. 2 #3 (1936): 377-395.

823. Thurlow, R.: "Destiny and Doom: Spengler, Hitler and British Fascism." PoP, vol.15 #4 (Oct., 1981): 17-33.

824. Webber, G. C.: "Patterns of Membership and Support for the British Union of Fascist." JCH, vol.19 #4 (Oct., 1984): 575-606.

France

825. Allardyce, Gilbert D.: "The Political Transition of Jacques Doriot." JCH, vol.1 #1 (Jan., 1966): 56-74.

826. Douglas, Allen: "Violence and Fascism: The Case of the Faisceau." JCH, vol.19 #4 (Oct., 1984): 689-712.

827. Duelffer, Jost: "Bonapartism, Fascism and National Socialism." JCH, vol.11 #4 (Oct., 1976): 109-128.

828. Mueller, Klaus-Juergen: "French Fascism and Modernization." JCH, vol.11 #4 (Oct., 1976): 75-107.

829. Soucy, Robert J: "Centrist Fascism: The Jeunesses Patriotes." JCH, vol.16 #2 (April, 1981): 349-368.

830. ___: Fascism in France: The Case of Maurice Barres [Berkeley, CA: Univ. of California Press, 1979]

831. ___: "The Nature of Fascism in France." JCH, vol.1 #1 (Jan., 1966): 27-55.

832. Weber, Eugen: Action Francaise [Stanford, CA: Stanford Univ. Press, 1962]

Intensive study of the French Radical Royalist movement from its foundation in 1899 through World War II. A year by year review of the party and its ideology. Includes a discussion of the successes and failures of Action Francaise, including the organization´s role during the Nazi occupation.

833. Werth, Alexander: "French Fascism." F Affairs, vol.15 #1 (Oct., 1936): 141-154.

834. Winston, C. M.: "The Proletarian Carlist Road to Fascism: Sindicalismo Libre." JCH, vol.17 #4 (Oct., 1982): 557-586.

Rumania

835. Van Til, William: The Danube Flows Through Fascism [New York: Charles Scribner´s Sons, 1938]

Russia

836. Oberlander, Erwin: "The All-Russian Fascist Party." JCH, vol.1 #1 (Jan., 1966): 158-173.

837. Stephan, John J.: The Russian Fascists: Tragedy and Farce in Exile, 1925-1945 [New York: Harper & Row, 1978]

Investigation into the ideology and psychology of the Russian Fascist movement. Deals mainly with Russian emigres who formed the core of the movement. Does not deal directly with collaborationist groups in the Soviet Union during the war.

838. Weber, Eugen: "The Men of the Archangel." JCH, vol.1 #1 (Jan., 1966): 101-126.

Spain/Portugal

839. Gallo, Max (J. Stewart, transl.): Spain Under Franco: A History [New York: E. P. Dutton, 1974]

840. Not Used.

841. Nogales, Manuel Ch.: "Franco´s Spain." Fortnightly, #862 (Oct., 1938): 412-423.

842. Payne, Stanley G.: Falange: A History of Spanish Fascism [Stanford, CA: Stanford Univ. Press, 1961]

843. Yglesias, Jose: The Franco Years [Indianapolis, IN: Bobbs-Merrill, 1977]

JEWS UNDER FASCISM

General Studies

844. "Antisemitism: Stigmata of Fascism." J Fr, vol.2 #6 (April, 1935): 3-4.

845. Busi, F.: "The Jew in 20th Century French Thinking, the Impact of Fascism." PoP, vol.8 #1 (Jan./Feb., 1974): 9-16.

846. Cohen, Israel: "Antisemitism and Treachery." J Sp, vol.8 #1 (Nov., 1941): 25-26.

Italy

847. Adorno, T. W.: "Antisemitism and Fascist Propaganda." Simmel: AS/SD, pp.125-137.

848. Agronsky, Martin: "Racism in Italy." F Affairs, vol.17 #3 (Jan., 1939): 391-401.

849. Bernardini, G.: "The Origins and Development of Racial Antisemitism in Fascist Italy." JMH, vol.49 #3 (Sept., 1977): 431-453.

850. Brand E.: "The Attitude of the Italians Towards the Jews in the Occupied Territories." YVB, #6/7 (June, 1960): 17-18.

851. Carpi, Daniel: "The Catholic Church and Italian Jewry under the Fascists (to the Death of Pius XI)." *YVS*, vol.4 (1960): 43-56.

852. ___: "The Origins and Development of Fascist Antisemitism in Italy (1922-1945)." Gutman: *Catastrophe*, pp. 283-298.

853. ___: "The Rescue of Jews in the Italian Zone of Occupied Croatia." Gutman: *Rescue*, pp.465-525.

854. "Digest of Public Opinion: Racist Policy in Italy." *CJR*, vol.1 #2 (Nov., 1938): 55-64.

855. Franklin, Harold: "Jews in Far Off Italy." *J Layman*, vol.8 #2 (Oct., 1933): 3, 8; #3 (Nov., 1933): 6-7; #5 (Jan., 1934): 3-4.

856. Goodman, Paul: "Judaism Under Fascist Italy." *Cur J Rec*, vol.2 #6 (June, 1932): 54-58.

857. Gordon, H. L.: "Development of the Anti-Jewish Policy in Italy." *CJR*, vol.1 #2 (Nov., 1938): 37-43.

858. Harris, Leon: "Mussolini in Hitler´s Footsteps." *J Life*, vol.2 #9 (Sept., 1938): 15-19.

859. Herzer, Ivo: "How Italians Saved Jews." *Mid*, vol.29 #6 (June/July, 1983): 35-38.

860. "Italian Racial Legislation." *CJR*, vol.2 #3 (May/June, 1939): 68-86.

861. "The Jewish Question in Italy." *Am J Ch*, vol.1 #7 (Feb. 15, 1940): 9-10.

862. J. L.: "The Jews in Italy." *Ort Eco Bul*, vol.1 #3 (May/June, 1940): 5-6.

863. Josephs, Joseph: "Italy Risks All. Economic Desperation Is the Cause of Its Antisemitism." *NJM*, vol.53 #2 (Oct., 1938): 78-79.

864. Kleinlerer, Edward: "Ersatz Antisemitism in Italy." *CW*, vol.9 #33 (Nov. 6, 1942): 9-10.

865. ___: "Jews in Italy´s History." *J Mirror*, vol.1 #2 (Sept., 1942): 46-49.

866. ___: "A Year of Racialism in Italy." CJR, vol.2 #4 (July/Aug., 1939): 30-43.

867. Ledeen, Michael: "The Evolution of Italian Fascist Antisemitism." JSS, vol.37 #1 (Jan., 1975): 3-17.

868. ___: "Italian Jews and Fascism." Judaism, vol.18 #3 (Sum., 1969): 277-298.

869. ___: "Jews Under Italian Fascism." J Digest, vol.16 #3 (Dec., 1970): 31-37; #4 (Jan., 1971): 41-47.

870. Levin, Alexander: "Caesar´s and Mussolini´s Jews." J Sp, vol.4 #3 (Jan., 1939): 18-19, 41.

871. Michaelis, M.: Mussolini and the Jews: German-Italian Relations and the Jewish Question in Italy, 1922-1945 [London: Institute of Jewish Affairs, 1978]

Detailed study on the influence of Nazism on the development of Fascist Italy´s Jewish policy. Primary focus is on Il Duce, Benito Mussolini, and the decline of his relations with Italian Jewry from 1938-1943.

872. ___: "On the Jewish Question in Fascist Italy: The Attitude of the Fascist Regime to the Jews in Italy." YVS, vol.4 (1960): 7-42.

873. Pedatella, Anthony: "Italians and Jews." J Sp, vol.48 #3 (Fall, 1983): 17-21.

874. ___: "Italy During the Holocaust." J Sp, vol.50 #2 (Sum., 1985): 55-57.

875. Poliakov, Leon: "Mussolini and the Extermination of the Jews." JSS, vol.11 #3 (July, 1949): 249-258.

876. ___ and J. Sabille: Jews Under the Italian Occupation [Paris: Editions du Centre, 1955]

Collection of documents relating to Italian policy against Jews in France, Croatia, and Greece. Taken primarily from the archives of the RSHA the documents trace the development of Italian attitudes toward Jews, 1940-1943, and prove the involvement of Italian military governors in those territories in attempting to thwart the Final Solution.

877. Postal, Bernard: "Mussolini Changes His Political Shirt." CJCh, vol.26 #12 (Aug. 12, 1938): 5, 16.

878. "Racial Legislation in the Schools." CJR, vol.1 #2 (Nov., 1938): 12-15.

879. "Racism in Italy." CJR, vol.1 #1 (Sept., 1938): 10-12.

880. "Racism in Italy." CJR, vol.2 #1 (Jan., 1939): 77-82.

881. Ravin, Selma: "Italian Persecution of the Jews." J Sp, vol.4 #1 (Nov., 1938): 13, 43.

882. Research Dept. of the Am. Jewish Congress: "Nuremberg Laws in Italy." CW, vol.8 #6 (Feb. 7, 1941): 12-13.

883. Runes, Dagobert D.: "What do you Think of the Plan to Settle Jews under Italian Rule in Ethiopia?" CJCh, vol.26 #39 (Feb. 10, 1939): 7, 15.

884. Silone, I.: "Italian Antisemitism." New Republic, vol. 97 #1251 (Nov. 23, 1938): 67-69.

885. Slousch, Nahum: "Italy Comprehends Value of Jewish Homeland in Palestine: Eretz Israel and Mussolini's Politics." CJCh, vol.22 #11 (Aug. 3, 1934): 9, 16.

886. Starr, Joshua: "Italy's Antisemites." JSS, vol.1 #1 (Jan., 1938): 105-124.

887. Stigliani, N. A. and A. Marzotto: "Fascist Antisemitism and the Italian Jews." WLB, vol.28 #2 (1975): 41-49.

888. Trakatsch, Josef: "Fascist Gratitude. Italian Jewry is Crushed in Spite of All Its Loyalty to Mussolini." NJM, vol.53 #4 (Dec., 1948): 142-143.

889. Zevi, T.: "How Mussolini Aped the Nazis." J Digest, vol. 25 #5 (Jan., 1980): 36-38.

Spain/Portugal

890. Alvarez del Vayo, J.: "Franco as Friend of the Jews." CW, vol.16 #7 (Feb. 14, 1949): 5-7.

891. Avni, Haim (E. Shimoni, transl.): Spain, the Jews and Franco [Philadelphia: J. P. S., 1981]

Study of Sephardic Jewry. The author attempts to assess the role played by Fascist Spain, especially its leader Generalissimo Franco, during the Holocaust. Seperating fact from fiction, Avni evaluates Spain´s actual contribution to saving Jewish lives, as well as the ambivalent attitude that the Spanish have had towards Jews since 1492.

892. Ezratti, H. A.: "When Spain Rescued Jews from Hitler: A Forgotten Episode in Jewish History." J Digest, vol. 7 #8 (May, 1962): 9-11.

893. "Franco Learns from Hitler: Antisemitism in the Rebel Press." J Fr, vol.4 #9 (Sept., 1937): 14-15.

894. Kahanoff, J.: "Spain and the Sephardim." HM, vol.46 #4 (Dec., 1964): 10, 24-25.

895. Kogan, Michael S.: "The Jews and General Franco." Ideas, vol.1 #2 (Win., 1968/69): 35-43.

896. Leshem, Perez: "Rescue Efforts in the Iberian Peninsula." LBIYB, vol.14 (1969): 231-256.

897. Lipschitz, Chaim U.: Franco, Spain, the Jews, and the Holocaust [New York: Ktav, 1983]

Highly polemic and apologetic survey of Spanish rescue activities in World War II. Clearly biased toward Franco the book offers no new documentation and exaggerates both Spanish policies and their actual results.

898. Robinson, Nehemiah: The Spain of Franco and its Policies Toward the Jews [New York: Institute of Jewish Affairs, 1944]

899. Weyl, N.: "Israel and Francisco Franco." Mid, vol.28 #2 (Feb., 1982): 11-16.

900. Wigoder, Geoffrey: "Franco and the Jews." Mid, vol.24 #1 (Jan., 1978): 27-32.

The Danubian States

901. Braham, Randolph L.: "The Rightists, Horthy, and the Germans: Factors Underlying the destruction of Hungarian Jewry." Vago: J/NJ, pp.137-156.

902. Chary, Frederick: "The Bulgarian Writers´ Protest of October 1940 Against the Introduction of Antisemitic Legislation into the Kingdom of Bulgaria." EEQ, vol.4 #1 (March, 1970): 88-93.

903. Fischer-Galati, Stephen: "Fascism, Communism, and the Jewish Question in Rumania." Vago: J/NJ, pp.157-175.

904. Macartney, C. A.: "Hungarian Foreign Policy during the Inter-War Period, with special Reference to the Jewish Question." Vago: J/NJ, pp.125-136.

905. Mevorah, N.: "Bulgaria Shields its Jews." J Life, vol. 1 #10 (Aug., 1947): 11-13.

906. Rothkirchen, Livia: "Hungary: An Asylum for the Refugees of Europe." YVS, vol.7 (1968): 127-146.

907. Vago, Bela: "Political and Diplomatic Activities for the Rescue of the Jews of Northern Transylvania, June 1944 - February 1945." YVS, vol.6 (1967): 155-173.

BIOGRAPHIES

Galeazzo Ciano

908. Ciano, G. (Hugh Wilson, ed. and transl.): The Ciano Diaries, 1939-1943 [Garden City, NY: Doubleday, 1946]

909. ___ (A. Mayor, transl.): Ciano´s Hidden Diary, 1937-1938 [New York: Dutton, 1953]

Miklos Horthy

910. Lengyel, E.: "Hungary´s Amazing Horthy." Am Mercury, vol.50 #198 (June, 1940): 176-183.

Oswald Mosley

911. Aronsfeld, C. C.: "Old Fascism Writ Large." PoP, vol. 2 #6 (Nov./Dec., 1968): 17-20.

912. Bach, Julian S.: "Little Hitler." Survey Graphic, vol. 26 #3 (March, 1937): 129-131.

913. Chesterton, A. K.: Apotheosis of the Jew [London: B. U. F. Publishers, 1937]

914. ___: Oswald Mosley, Portrait of a Leader [London: B. U. F. Publishers, 1937]

915. Cohen, Joseph L.: "Fascist Interlude in England." Menorah, vol.25 #1 (Jan./March, 1937): 101-110.

Benito Mussolini

916. de Fiori, V. E. (M. Pei, transl.): Mussolini, the Man of Destiny [New York: AMS Press, 1979] Rep. 1928 Ed.

917. Fermi, Laura: Mussolini [Chicago: Univ. of Chicago Press, 1966]

918. Gregor, A. J.: Young Mussolini and the Intellectual Origins of Fascism [Berkeley, CA: Univ. of California Press, 1979]

919. Halperin, Samuel W.: Mussolini and Italian Fascism [Princeton, NJ: Van Nostrand, 1964]

920. Kemenchy, L. (M. Vamos, transl.): Il Duce: The Life and Work of Benito Mussolini [New York: Williams and Norgate, 1930]

921. Kirkpatrik, Ivone: Mussolini: A Study in Power [New York: Hawthorn Books, 1964]

922. Kleinlerer, Edward D.: "Hitler´s Gauleiter in Italy." CW, vol.8 #26 (July 11, 1941): 6-7.

923. Monelli, Paolo (B. Maxwell, transl.): Mussolini: The Intimate Life of a Demagogue [New York: Vanguard Press, 1954]

924. Mussolini, Benito (Max Ascoli, ed.): The Fall of Mussolini: His Own Story [Westport, CT: Greenwood Press, 1975] Rep. 1948 Ed.

925. Seldes, George: Sawdust Ceasar: The Untold Story of Mussolini and Fascism [New York: Harper, 1935]

5

The SS State

THE NAZI RISE TO POWER

Contemporary Views

926. An Observer: "A Bloodless Revolution." Cont Rev, vol. 143 #808 (April, 1933): 402-410.

927. Baynes, Helton G.: Germany Possessed [New York: AMS Press, 1978] Rep. 1941 Ed.

928. Bodin, J. W.: "Hitler: Prussianism's Final Gamble." CEO, vol.18 #7 (April 4, 1941): 76-77.

929. Brandt, Karl: "Junkers To the Fore Again." F Affairs, vol.14 #1 (Oct., 1935): 120-134.

930. Creel, George: "German Lies About Versailles." Am Mercury, vol.56 #229 (Jan., 1943): 54-62.

931. Fay, Sidney B.: "Nazis Consolidate Their Power." Cur His, vol.38 #6 (June, 1933): 358-362.

932. Heberle, R.: From Democracy to Nazism: A Regional Case Study on Political Parties in Germany [Baton Rouge: Louisiana State Univ. Press, 1945]

933. Hoover, Calvin: Germany Enters the Third Reich [New York: Macmillan, 1933]

934. King, Joseph: The German Revolution: Its Meaning and Menace [London: Williams and Norgate, 1933]

935. Klotz, Helmut (ed.): The Berlin Diaries May 30, 1932-January 30, 1933 [New York: AMS Press, 1979] Rep. 1934 Ed.

936. Mowrer, Edgar A.: Germany Puts the Clock Back [New York: M. Morrow, 1933]

937. Oberfohren, Ernst: "The Nazis Burned the Reichstag." New Republic, vol.76 #977 (Aug. 23, 1933): 36-38.

938. Pensieroso: "The Defeat of Democracy in Germany." Cont Rev, vol.145 #822 (June, 1934): 679-687.

939. Petrov, Piotr and I. Petrov: The Secret of Hitler´s Victory [London: Woolf, 1934]

940. Simon, Heinrich: "German Class Lines Crumble." Cur His, vol.37 #3 (March, 1933): 649-655.

941. Steed, Henry W.: Hitler, Whence and Whither [London: Nisbet & Co., 1934]

942. Thompson, Dorothy: "Back to Blood and Iron: Germany Goes German Again." SEP, vol.205 (May 6, 1933): 3-4, 67, 70-71, 74.

943. Van Passen, Pierre: "Hitler Rehearses." Cur J Rec, vol.1 #2 (Dec., 1931): 33-37.

944. von Lowenstein-Scharffeneck, Hubertus: The Tragedy of a Nation: Germany, 1918-1934 [London: Faber & Faber, 1934]

945. Watkins, F. M.: The Failure of Constitutional Emergency Powers Under the German Republic [Cambridge, MA: Harvard Univ. Press, 1939]

946. Wertheimer, Mildred S.: "Forces Underlying the Nazi Revolution." FPR, vol.9 (July 14, 1933): 106-116.

947. Wheeler-Bennett, J. W.: "The German Political Situation." Int Affairs, vol.11 #4 (July, 1932): 460-472.

948. ___: "The New Regime in Germany." Int Affairs, vol.12 #3 (May/June, 1933): 313-326.

949. Wiskemann, E.: "Prospects in Germany." Cont Rev, vol. 143 #806 (Feb., 1933): 155-163.

950. Wolfers, Arnold: "The Crisis of the Democratic Regime in Germany." Int Affairs, vol.11 #6 (Nov., 1932): 757-783.

951. World Committee for the Victims of German Fascism: The Brown Book of the Hitler Terror and the Burning of the Reichstag [New York: Alfred A. Knopf, 1933]

952. ___: The Reichstag Fire Trial: The Second Brown Book of the Hitler Terror [London: J. Lane, 1934]

Historical Studies

953. Abel, Theodore: The Nazi Movement: Why Hitler Came to Power [New York: Atherton Press, 1966]

954. Abraham, David: Collapse of the Weimar Republic: Political Economy and Crisis [Princeton, NJ: Princeton Univ. Press, 1981]

955. Allen, William S.: The Nazi Seizure of Power: The Experience of a Single German Town, 1930-1935 [Chicago: Univ. of Chicago Press, 1965]

Intimate study on the experience of one town during the Nazi machtergreifung (power grabbing). Based upon in-depth interviews and documentation, Allen shows how Nazi totalitarianism filtered down from the party to the masses.

956. Almond, Gabriel L. (ed.): The Struggle for Democracy in Germany [Chapel Hill: Univ. of North Carolina Press, 1949]

957. Bessel, Richard: Political Violence and the Rise of Nazism: The Storm Troopers in Eastern Germany, 1925-1934 [New Haven, CT: Yale University Press, 1984]

Study on the Nazi machtergreifung with emphasis on the composition and activities of the SA in Eastern Germany from 1932 until 1934. Bessel is particularly interested in political violence and the SA´s use of street warfare in gaining power for the NSDAP.

958. ___: "The Potempa Murder." CEH, vol.10 #3 (Sept., 1977): 241-254.

959. Brady, Robert A.: Spirit and Structure of German Fascism [Secaucus, NJ: Citadel Press, 1971]

960. Braunthal, G.: "The German Free Trade Unions During the Rise of Nazism." JCEA, vol.15 #4 (Jan., 1956): 339-353.

961. Breitman, R.: "Nazism in the Eyes of German Social Democracy." Dobkowski: Toward, pp.197-212.

962. Burden, Hamilton T.: The Nuremberg Party Rallies: 1923-1939 [New York: F. A. Praeger, 1967]

963. Childers, Thomas: The Nazi Voter: The Social Foundations of Fascism in Germany, 1919-1933 [Chapel Hill: Univ. of North Carolina Press, 1983]

964. ___: "The Social Bases of the National Socialist Vote." JCH, vol.11 #4 (Oct., 1976): 17-42.

965. Dobkowski, Michael and I. Walliman (eds.): Towards the Holocaust: The Social and Economic Collapse of the Weimar Republic [Westport, CT: Greenwood Press, 1983]

966. Dornberg, John: Munich 1923: The Story of Hitler´s First Grab for Power [New York: Harper & Row, 1982]

967. Earley, George and R. Earley: "Bavarian Prelude, 1923: A Model for Nazism." WLB, vol.30 #2 (1976): 53-59.

968. Epstein, Klaus: "The Nazi Consolidation of Power." JMH, vol.34 #1 (March, 1962): 74-80.

969. Faris, Ellsworth: "Takeoff Point of the National Socialist Party: The Landtag Elections in Baden, 1929." CEH, vol.8 #2 (June, 1975): 140-171.

970. Farquaharson, J.: "The NSDAP in Hanover and Lower Saxony, 1921-1926." JCH, vol.8 #4 (Oct., 1973): 103-120

971. Feis, Herbert: 1933: Characters in Crisis [Boston: Little, Brown and Company, 1966]

972. Feldman, Gerald: "Big Business and the Kapp Putsch." CEH, vol.4 #2 (June, 1971): 99-130.

973. Felix, David: "Walter Rathenau: German Foreign Minister in 1922." History Today, vol.20 #9 (Sept., 1970): 638-647.

974. Fischer, C.: "The SA and the NSDAP: Social Background and Ideology of the Rank and File in the Early 1930s." JCH, vol.17 #4 (Oct., 1982): 651-670.

975. Gates, Robert A.: "German Socialism and the Crisis of 1929-1933." CEH, vol.7 #4 (Dec., 1974): 332-359.

976. Geary, R.: "The Failure of German Labor in the Weimar Republic." Dobkowski: Toward, pp.177-196.

977. Gellately, Robert: "German Shopkeepers and the Rise of National Socialism." WLB, vol.28 #2 (1975): 31-40.

978. Gordon, Harold J.: Hitler and the Beer Hall Putsch [Princeton, NJ: Princeton Univ. Press, 1972]

979. ___: The Reichswehr and the German Republic 1919-1926 [Princeton, NJ: Princeton Univ. Press, 1957]

980. Grill, J. H.: "The Nazi Party's Rural Propaganda Before 1928." CEH, vol.15 #2 (June, 1982): 149-165.

981. Hamilton, Richard: Who Voted for Hitler? [Princeton, NJ: Princeton Univ. Press, 1982]

982. Hanser, R.: Prelude to Terror: The Rise of Hitler, 1919-1923 [London: Rupert Hart-Davis, 1971]

983. Hehn, Paul N.: "The Collapse of the Weimar Republic and the National Socialist Revolution, 1923-1933: The View from Warsaw and Moscow." Polish Rev, vol.25 #3/4 (Sept./Dec., 1980): 28-48.

984. Hoerster-Philipps, Ulrike: "Conservative Concepts of Dictatorship in the Final Phase of the Weimar Republic: The Government of Franz von Papen." Dobkowski: Toward, pp.115-130.

985. Hofer, W. and C. Graf: "The reichstag Fire of 27 February, 1933." WLB, vol.28 #2 (1975): 21-30.

986. Holborn, Hajo (ed.): Republic to Reich: The Making of the Nazi Revolution [New York: Pantheon Books, 1972]

987. Jones, Larry: "Between the Fronts: The German National Union of Commercial Employees from 1928 to 1933." JMH, vol.48 #3 (Sept., 1976): 462-482.

988. ___: "Inflation, Revaluation and the Crisis of Middle Class Politics: A Study in the Dissolution of the German Party System." CEH, vol.12 #2 (June, 1979): 143-168.

989. Jorge, A.: The Weimar Chronicle: Prelude to Hitler [New York: Paddington Press, 1978]

990. Kuhnl, Reinhard: "The Rise of Fascism in Germany and Its Causes." Dobkowski: Toward, pp.93-114.

991. Layton, Roland V. Jr.: "The ´Volkischer Beobachter´ 1920-1933: The Nazi Party Newspaper in the Weimar Era." CEH, vol.3 #4 (Dec., 1970): 533-582.

992. Lyttleton, Adrian: The Seizure of Power [New York: Charles Scribner´s Sons, 1973]

993. Maisky, I. (A. Rothstein, transl.): Who Helped Hitler? [London: Hutchinson, 1964]

994. Maste, Ernst: "Walter Rathenau." WLB, vol.26 #3/4 (1972/73): 46-51.

995. Morris, Warren B. Jr.: The Weimar Republic and Nazi Germany [Chicago: Nelson-Hall, 1982]

996. Mosse, George L.: The Crisis of German Ideology [New York: Grosset & Dunlap, 1964]

997. ___ and Steven Lampert: "Weimar Intellectuals and the Rise of National Socialism." Dimsdale: Survivors, pp. 79-105.

998. Nelson, Otto M.: "´Simplicissimus´ and the Rise of National Socialism." The Historian, vol.40 #3 (May, 1978): 441-462.

999. Nicholls, Anthony J. (Ch. Thorne, ed): Weimar and the Rise of Hitler [New York: St. Martin´s Press, 1969]

Short Survey of the decline of the Weimar Republic and the rise of the Nazis. Mentions antisemitism only in passing. The book contains an extensive chronological table and bibliography. Part of a series on the making of the twentieth century.

1000. ___ and E. Matthias (eds.): German Democracy and the Triumph of Hitler: Essays in Recent German History [London: G. Allen & Unwin, 1971]

1001. Noakes, Jeremy: Nazi Party in Lower Saxony, 1921-1933 [New York: Oxford Univ. Press, 1971]

1002. Orlow, D.: "The Conversion of Myths Into Political Power: The Case of the Nazi Party, 1925-1926." AHR, vol.72 #3 (April, 1967): 906-924.

1003. Petzina, Dietmar (I. Stumberger, transl.): "Problems in the Social and Economic Development of the Weimar Republic." Dobkowski: Toward, pp.37-59.

1004. Plummer, Thomas G. et al (eds.): Film and Politics in the Weimar Republic [New York: Holmes & Meier, 1984]

1005. Pool, James and S. Pool: Who Financed Hitler? The Secret Funding of Hitler's Rise to Power, 1919-1933 [New York: Dial Press, 1979]

1006. Pridham, Geoffrey: Hitler's Rise to Power: The Nazi Movement in Bavaria, 1923-1933 [New York: Harper Torchbooks, 1973]

1007. Rauschning, Hermann (E. Dickes, transl.): The Revolution of Nihilism: Warning to the West [New York: AMS Press, 1978] Rep. 1939 Ed.

1008. Reed, Douglas: The Burning of the Reichstag [New York: Covici, 1934]

1009. Rosenhaft, Eve: Beating the Fascists? The German Communists and Political Violence, 1929-1933 [New York: Cambridge Univ. Press, 1983]

Studies the street violence during the Nazi grab for power. Interesting in its perspective, the book is a useful addition to the studies on the collapse of Weimar.

1010. Snell, John L. (ed): The Nazi Revolution: Germany's Guilt or Germany's Fate? [Lexington, MA.: Heath and Company, 1973]

1011. Snyder, L. S.: German Nationalism: The Tragedy of the People. Extremism Contra Liberalism in Modern German History [Port Washington, NY: Kennikat Press, 1969]

1012. Stachura, Peter D.: Gregor Strasser and the Rise of Nazism [London: Allen & Unwin, 1983]

1013. ___: "The NSDAP and the German Working Class, 1925-1933." Dobkowski: Toward, pp.131-153.

1014. ___ (ed.): The Nazi Machtergreifung [London: George Allen & Unwin, 1983]

1015. Stackelberg, R.: Idealism Debased: From Voelkisch Ideology to National Socialism [Kent, OH: Kent State Univ. Press, 1981]

1016. Stark, Gary D.: Entrepreneurs of Ideology: Neo Conservative Publishers in Germany, 1890-1933 [Chapel Hill: Univ. of North Carolina Press, 1981]

1017. Steinberg, Michael S.: Sabers and Brown Shirts: The German Students´ Path to National Socialism 1918-1935 [Chicago: Univ. of Chicago Press, 1977]

1018. Stern, Fritz et al (J. Conway, transl.): The Path of Dictatorship 1918-1933: Ten Essays by German Scholars [New York: Anchor Books, 1966]

1019. Tilton, Timothy A.: "The Social Origins of Nazism: The Rural Dimensions." Dobkowski: Toward, pp.61-74.

1020. Tobias, Fritz (A. Pomerans, transl.): The Reichstag Fire [New York: G. P. Putnam´s Sons, 1964]

1021. Tobin, E. H.: "Revolution and Alienation: The Foundations of Weimar." Dobkowski: Toward, pp.155-176.

1022. Turner, Henry A. Jr.: "Big Business and the Rise of Hitler." AHR, vol.75 #1 (Oct., 1969): 56-70.

1023. ___: German Big Business and the Rise of Hitler [New York: Oxford Univ. Press, 1985]

1024. ___: "Hitler´s Secret Pamphlet for Industrialists, 1927." JMH, vol.40 #3 (Sept., 1968): 348-374.

1025. Waite, Robert G.: Vanguard of Nazism: The Free Corps Movement in Post-War Germany, 1918-1923 [Cambridge, MA: Harvard Univ. Press, 1952]

1026. Ward, James J.: "Smash the Fascists: German Communist Efforts to Counter the Nazis, 1930-1931." CEH, vol.14 #1 (March, 1981): 30-62.

1027. Wheaton, Eliot B.: Prelude to Calamity: The Nazi Revolution 1933-1935, with a Background Survey of the Weimar Era [New York: Anchor Press, 1969]

1028. Winkler, H.: "German Society, Hitler and the Illusion of Restoration 1930-33." JCH, vol.11 #4 (Oct., 1976): 1-16.

Reflective Works

1029. Adler-Rudel, S.: "Lest We Forget 1933." Zion, vol.3 #4 (Feb., 1953): 11-17.

1030. Aronsfeld, C. C.: "25 Years Since the Day of Infamy." J Affairs, vol.13 #4 (April, 1958): 9-11.

1031. Draper, Theodore: "The Specter of Weimar." Com, vol. 52 #6 (Dec., 1971): 43-49.

1032. Meinecke, F.: The German Catastrophe [Magnolia, MA: Peter Smith, 1963]

GENERAL STUDIES ON NAZISM

Nazi Philosophy and Ideology

1033. Aycaberry, Pierre (R. Hurley, transl.): The Nazi Question: An Essay on the Interpretations of National Socialism [New York: Pantheon Books, 1981]

Historiographical guide to the literature about and the issues raised by National Socialism. The author is intimately aquainted with all relevant texts, and attempts an interpretative organization of them. He begins with Nazi and Fascist historians and covers the varied interpreters up through today´s social scientists and their efforts to make sense of the senseless.

1034. Baum, Rainer C.: The Holocaust and the German Elite: Genocide and National Suicide in Germany, 1871-1945 [Totowa, NJ: Rowman and Littlefield, 1981]

1035. Binion, Rudolph: Hitler Among the Germans [Amsterdam: Elsevier, 1976]

1036. Brady, Robert A.: The Spirit and Structure of German Fascism [New York: Howard Fertig, 1969]

1037. Brown, Harrison: "Hitler´s Age of Heroism." Cont Rev, vol.143 #809 (May, 1933): 532-541.

1038. Butler, R. D´Olier: The Roots of National Socialism, 1783-1933 [New York: AMS Press, 1979] Rep. 1941 Ed.

1039. Cohen, Israel: "The Nazi World Conspiracy." CJR, vol. 4 #6 (Dec., 1941): 625-636.

1040. Drennan, James: "The Nazi Movement in Perspective." Fasc Q, vol.1 #1 (Jan., 1935): 47-58.

1041. Epstein, Klaus: The Genesis of German Conservatism [Princeton, NJ: Princeton Univ. Press, 1966]

1042. Fodor, M. W.: "The Austrian Roots of Hitlerism." F Affairs, vol.14 #4 (July, 1936): 685-691.

1043. Forman, James: Nazism [New York: Dell Pub., 1980]

Easy to read primer of Nazi ideology and the history of the Third Reich. Primarily aimed at high school students but useful for adults as well.

1044. Not Used.

1045. Friedlander, Saul: Reflections of Nazism [New York: Harper & Row, 1984]

1046. Gasman, Daniel: The Scientific Origins of National Socialism [London: Macdonald, 1971]

1047. Gavit, John: "Nationalism on the Rampage." Survey Graphic, vol.22 #5 (May, 1933): 270-271, 276-277.

1048. Glaser, Hermann (Ernest Menze, transl., with notes): The Cultural Roots of National Socialism (Spiesser-ideologie) [Austin: Univ. of Texas Press, 1978]

1049. Gordon, Harold J. Jr. (H. F. Freniere, transl.): The Hitler Trial Before the Peoples Court in Munich 3 vols. [Arlington, VA: Univ. Pub. of America, 1976]

1050. Heiden, Konrad: A History of National Socialism [New York: A. A. Knopf, 1935]

1051. Herf, Jeffrey: Reactionary Modernism: Technology, Culture and Politics in Weimar and the Third Reich [New York: Cambridge Univ. Press, 1984]

1052. Herzstein, Robert E.: Adolf Hitler and the German Trauma, 1913-1945: An Interpretation of the Nazi Phenomenon [New York: G. P. Putnam´s Sons, 1974]

1053. Heyl, John D.: "Hitler´s Economic Thought: A Reappraisal." CEH, vol.6 #1 (March, 1973): 83-96.

1054. Holborn, Hajo: "Origins and Political Character of Nazi Ideology." Pol Sci Q, vol.79 #4 (Dec., 1964): 542-554.

1055. Hook, Sidney: "Hitlerism: A Non-Metaphysical View." CJR, vol.7 #2 (April, 1944): 146-155.

1056. Jackel, Eberhard (H. Arnold, transl.): Hitler´s Weltanschauung: A Blueprint for Power [Middletown, CT: Wesleyan Univ. Press, 1972]

1057. Kresge, Elijah E.: Toward an Understanding of Nazism and its Threat to Democracy [Lancaster, PA: Franklin and Marshall, 1943]

1058. Krieger, Leonard: "Nazism: Highway or Byway." CEH, vol.11 #1 (March, 1978): 3-22.

1059. Lane, Barbara M.: "Nazi Ideology: Some Unfinished Business." CEH, vol.7 #1 (March, 1974): 3-30.

1060. ___ and L. J. Rupp (eds.): Nazi Ideology Before 1933: A Documentation [Austin: Univ. of Texas Press, 1978]

1061. McGovern, Wm.: From Luther to Hitler: The History of Fascist-Nazi Political Philosophy [Boston: Houghton Mifflin, 1941]

1062. Mosse, George L.: "On Nazism." Society, vol.14 #4 (May/June, 1977): 69-73.

1063. Neumann, S.: Permanent Revolution: The Total State in a World at War [New York: Harper, 1942]

1064. Raab, Earl: The Anatomy of Nazism [New York: Anti-Defamation League of Bnai Brith, 1961]

1065. Shuster, George N.: Strong Man Rules: An Interpretation of Germany Today [New York: D. Appleton-Century, 1934]

1066. Snyder, Louis S.: Roots of German Nationalism [Bloomington: Indiana Univ. Press, 1978]

1067. Sollohub, N.: "Forerunners of the Third Reich." Cont Rev, vol.156 #883 (July, 1939): 54-63.

1068. Steel, Johannes: Hitler as Frankenstein [London: Wishart and Company, 1933]

1069. Von Dewall, Wolf: "The National Socialist Movement in Germany." Int Affairs, vol.10 #1 (Jan., 1931): 4-20.

1070. Weiss, John (ed.): Nazis and Fascists in Europe [Chicago: New Viewpoints, 1969]

1071. Whiteside, A. G.: "The Nature and Origins of National Socialism." JCEA, vol.17 #1 (April, 1957): 48-73.

Issues in Nazi Weltanschauung

1072. Baird, Jay W.: "Goebbels, Horst Wessel, and the Myth of Resurrection and Return." JCH, vol.17 #4 (Oct., 1982): 633-650.

1073. Bodin, J. W.: "Forerunners of Hitler´s ´New Order´." CEO, vol.18 #1 (Jan. 3, 1941): 7-9.

1074. Brown, W. Norman: The Swastika, a Study of the Nazi Claims of its Aryan Origin [New York: Emerson Books, 1933]

1075. Herf, Jeffrey: "The Engineer as Ideologue: Reactionary Modernists in Weimar and Nazi Germany." JCH, vol. 19 #4 (Oct., 1984): 631-648.

1076. Mosse, George L.: The Nationalization of the Masses: Political Symbolism and Mass Movements in Germany from the Napoleonic Wars Through the Third Reich [New York: Howard Fertig, 1971]

1077. Nyomarkay, J.: Charisma and Factionalism in the Nazi Party [Minneapolis: Univ. of Minnesota Press, 1967]

Argues that Nazi totalitarianism rested primarily on Hitler´s personal charisma, rather than on ideology. He analyzes the causes, attitudes, and motivations which led to conflicts within the party from 1924 to 1935.

1078. Stackelberg, R.: "Voelkisch Idealism and National Socialism: The Case of Friedrich Lienhard." WLB, vol. 29 #2 (1976): 34-40.

1079. Tal, Uriel: "Nazism as a Political Faith." Jer Q, #15 (Spr., 1980): 70-90.

1080. von Maltitz, H.: The Evolution of Hitler´s Germany: The Ideology, the Personality, the Moment [New York: McGraw-Hill, 1973]

1081. Wise, James W.: Swastika, the Nazi Terror [New York: Harrison Smith and Robert Haas, 1933]

1082. Wolff, F.: "Hitler and ´the Ring´." Cont Rev, vol.163 #927 (March, 1943): 176-179.

The Nazi Revolution

1083. Bartlett, Vernon: Nazi Germany Explained [London: Victor Gollancz, 1933]

1084. Braun, R. (M. Davidson, transl.): Fascism, Make or Break? German Experience Since the June Days [New York: International Pubs., 1935]

1085. Brown, Harrison: "Germany in Revolution." FR, vol.139 (April 1, 1933): 441-452.

1086. H. P. G.: "The National-Socialist Revolution." Cont Rev, vol.144 #811 (July, 1933): 31-38.

1087. Lewisohn, Ludwig: "The German Revolt Against Civilization." Harper´s, vol.167 (Aug., 1933): 275-283.

1088. Schoenbaum, D.: Hitler´s Social Revolution: Class and Status in Nazi Germany, 1933-1939 [Garden City, NY: Doubleday, 1967]

1089. Tracey, Donald R.: "The Development of the National Socialist Party in Thuringia." CEH, vol.8 #1 (March, 1975): 23-50.

1090. Van Passen, Pierre and James Wise (eds.): Nazism: An Assault on Civilization [New York: Harrison Smith and Robrt Haas, 1934]

ANATOMIES OF THE SS STATE

Histories of the Third Reich

1091. Alexander, H. G.: "Whither Germany? Whither Europe?" Cont Rev, vol.144 #816 (Dec., 1933): 662-672.

1092. Armstrong, Hamilton F: Hitler´s Reich: The First Phase [New York: Macmillan, 1933]

1093. Baumont, Maurice et al (eds.): The Third Reich [New York: F. A. Praeger, 1955]

1094. Berwick, M.: Third Reich [New York: Putnam´s, 1972]

1095. Bracher, Karl D. (J. Steinberg, transl.): The German Dictatorship: The Origins, Structure and Effects of National Socialism [New York: F. A. Praeger, 1970]

Authoritative survey of Nazi Germany´s history which examines and evaluates all the issues, organizations, and personalities of the Third Reich.

1096. Brady, Robert A.: The Spirit and Structure of German Fascism [New York: Viking Press, 1937]

1097. Broszat, M. (K. Rosenbaum and I. P. Boehm, transls.): German National Socialism, 1919-1945 [Santa Barbara, CA: ABC-Clio Press, 1966]

1098. ___ (John W. Hiden, transl.): The Hitler State: The Foundation and Development of the Internal Structure of the Third Reich [London: Longman, 1981]

1099. Buchheim, Hans: The Third Reich: Its Beginnings, its Development, its End [London: O. Wolff, 1961]

1100. Carr, Albert H.: Juggernaut: The Path of Dictatorship [New York: AMS Press, 1978] Rep. 1939 Ed.

1101. Cunningham, C.: Germany Today and Tomorrow [New York: AMS Press, 1978] Rep. 1936 Ed.

1102. Dell, Robert E.: Germany Unmasked [London: Hopkinson, 1934]

1103. Ebenstein, William: The Nazi State [New York: Farrar, 1943]

1104. Edwards, Tony: Hitler and Germany 1919-1939 [Salem, NH: Heinemann Educational Books, 1972]

1105. Ermarth, Fritz: The New Germany: National Socialist Government in Theory and Practice [Washington, DC: Digest Press, 1936]

1106. Feder, Gottfried: Hitler's Official Programme [New York: Howard Fertig, 1971]

1107. Fry, M.: Hitler's Wonderland [London: Murray, 1934]

1108. Gangulee, N. (ed.): The Mind and Face of Nazi Germany: An Anthology [London: John Murray, 1942]

1109. Green, Margaret: Eyes Right! A Left-Wing Glance at the New Germany [London: Christophers, 1935]

1110. Grunberger, Richard: The 12-Year Reich: A Social History of Nazi Germany, 1933-1945 [New York: Holt, Rinehart & Winston, 1971]

Thematically organized social history of Nazi Germany. The thirty chapters of the book deal with such diverse topics as the Party, the civil service, education, and leisure. The impact of Nazism on every aspect of life is carefully detailed as is the persecution of the Jews and the German reaction thereto.

1111. Herzstein, R. E. et al: The Nazis [Chicago: Life-Time, 1980]

1112. Hildebrand K. (P. S. Falla, transl.): The Third Reich [London: George Allen & Unwin, 1984]

Comprehensive survey of Hitler's Germany. Gives the history of the Third Reich from the machtergreifung of 1933 to the gotterdamerung of 1945. The author's main interest is in stating the historiographical questions that have grown out of the study of Nazism and the Third Reich. A useful primer in Nazi history and the historiography on the Nazi regime; contains almost nothing on Nazi racial policies and little on the Holocaust.

1113. Holmes, John: "The Threat to Freedom." PVP: Nazism, pp.127-142.

1114. Jarman, Thomas L.: The Rise and Fall of Nazi Germany [New York: New York Univ. Press, 1956]

1115. Krausnick, Helmut et al (R. Barry et al, transls): The Anatomy of the SS State [New York: Walker and Co., 1968]

Authoritative review of the inner workings of the SS state, based on background evidence given at the Auschwitz trial of 1963.

1116. Leiser, Erwin: A Pictorial History of Nazi Germany [Harmondsworth, England: Penguin Books, 1962]

1117. Lichtenberger, Henri (K. S. Pinson, transl.): Third Reich [New York: The Greystone Press, 1937]

1118. Loewenstein, Karl: Hitler´s Germany [New York: Arno Press, 1972] Rep. 1940 Ed.

1119. Lyons, E.: "Hitler´s Blueprint for a Slave World." Am Mercury, vol.50 #200 (Aug., 1940): 391-400.

1120. Mitchell, Otis C. (ed.): Nazism and the Common Man: Essays in German History [Washington, DC.: Univ. Press of America, 1981]

1121. Neumann, Franz L.: Behemoth: The Structure and Practice of National Socialism, 1933-1944 [New York: Harper & Row, 1966]

Marxist interpretation of Nazism. Strong on political and economic issues, but weak on Nazi racism and ideology.

1122. Newmann, Robert: The Pictorial History of the Third Reich [New York: Bantam, 1962]

1123. Noakes, Jeremy and Geoffrey Pridham (eds.): Documents on Nazism, 1919-1945 [New York: Viking Press, 1975]

1124. Noar, Gertrude: "The Third Reich in Perspective." Chartock: Society, pp.103-111.

1125. Oliver, D. and F. Newmann: Nazi Germany [Washington, DC: US Dept. of Health, Education and Welfare, 1971]

1126. Pascal, Roy: The Nazi Dictatorship [London: Routledge & Sons, 1934]

1127. Peterson, Edward N.: The Limits of Hitler´s Power [Princeton, NJ: Princeton Univ. Press, 1969]

1128. Phillips, Peter: The Tragedy of Nazi Germany [London: Routledge & Kegan Paul, 1969]

1129. Procktor, Richard: Nazi Germany: The Origins and Collapse of the Third Reich [New York: Holt, Rinehart and Winston, 1974]

1130. Remak, Joachim (ed.): The Nazi Years: A Documentary History [Englewood Cliffs, NJ: Prentice-Hall, 1969]

1131. Roberts, Stephen H.: The House that Hitler Built [New York: Methuen, 1937]

1132. Schuman, Frederick L.: The Nazi Dictatorship: A Study in Social Pathology and the Politics of Fascism [New York: A. A. Knopf, 1936]

1133. Shirer, William L.: The Rise and Fall of the Third Reich: A History of Nazi Germany [New York: Simon and Schuster, 1960]

Synthetic history of Nazi Germany from the Weimar era, through the rise of Nazism, to the war and ultimate defeat of Hitler´s One-Thousand-Year Reich. Attempts to report and also explain the horrors that National Socialism unleashed.

1134. Snyder, Louis I.: Hitler and Nazism [New York: Bantam Books, 1971]

1135. ___: Hitler´s Third Reich: A Documentary History [Chicago: Nelson-Hall, 1981]

1136. Stachura, Peter D. (ed.): The Shaping of the Nazi State [New York: Harper & Row, 1978]

1137. Stern, J. P.: Hitler: The Fuehrer and the People [London: Fontana/Collins, 1975]

1138. Turner, Henry A. Jr.: Nazism and the Third Reich [New York: New Viewpoints, 1973]

1139. Von Maltitz, Horst: The Evolution of Hitler Germany [New York: McGraw-Hill, 1973]

1140. Weinstein, Fred: The Dynamics of Nazism: Leadership, Ideology and the Holocaust [New York: Academic Press, 1980]

A novel and interesting reinterpretation of Nazi ideology. Attempts to explain the Nazi program of systematic mass murder within the context of the subjective goals of the Nazi leadership. Tries to explain why the Final Solution was seen as a viable and honorable program despite its negation of all common morality.

The Third Reich: Political Organs

1141. Apfel, Alfred: Behind the Scenes of German Justice [London: Bodley Head, 1935]

1142. Fearnside, W. Ward: "Three Innovations of National Socialist Jurisprudence." JCEA, vol.16 #2 (July, 1956): 146-155.

1143. Jones, J. W.: The Nazi Conception of Law [New York: Farrar and Rinehart, 1939]

1144. Kahler, Erich: "Nihilism and the Rule of Technics." Menorah, vol.31 #2 (July/Sept., 1943): 176-192.

1145. Klausner, Joseph: "Where There Is No God." J Layman, vol.19 #8 (May, 1945): 6-10.

1146. Marx, Fritz: Government in the Third Reich [New York: McGraw-Hill, 1936]

1147. "The National-Socialist Conception of Law." PFR, #40 (March 15, 1942): Whole Issue.

1148. Noakes, Jeremy (ed.): Government, Party and People in Nazi Germany [Exeter, Eng.: Exeter Univ. Press, 1980]

1149. Pelcovits, Nathan: "The Social Honor Courts of Nazi Germany." Pol Sci Q, vol.53 #3 (Sept., 1938): 350-374

1150. Peterson, E. N.: "The Bureaucracy and the Nazi Party." Rev of Politics, vol.28 #2 (April, 1966): 172-192.

1151. Picton, Harold: "Justice in Nazi Germany." Cont Rev, vol.156 #886 (Oct., 1939): 447-452.

1152. Not Used.

1153. Roper, Edith and Clara Leiser: Skeleton of Justice: System of Terror and Perversion of Justice [New York: E. P. Dutton, 1941]

1154. Sinclair, Thronton: "The Nazi Party at Nuremberg." Pub Op Q, vol.2 #4 (Oct., 1938): 570-583.

Nazi Culture

1155. Angebert, J. and M. Angebert (L. Sumberg, transl.): The Occult and the Third Reich: The Mystical Origins of Nazism and the Search for the Holy Grail [New York: McGraw-Hill Paperbacks, 1975]

1156. Beard, Charles A.: "Education Under the Nazis." F Affairs, vol.14 #3 (April, 1936): 437-452.

1157. Beyerchen, A.: "The Physical Sciences." Friedlander: Ideology, pp.151-163.

1158. ___: Scientists Under Hitler: Politics and the Physics Community in the Third Reich [New Haven, CT: Yale Univ. Press, 1977]

1159. Blackburn, Gilmer W.: Education in the Third Reich: Race and History in Nazi Textbooks [Albany, NY: SUNY Press, 1984]

Study of the process of Nazification of the German school system. Main focus is on the reorientation of textbooks to raise boys and girls in Nazi ideology. Special emphasis is put on the part race played in the Nazi textbooks.

1160. Boozer, Jack S.: "Children of Hippocrates: Doctors in Nazi Germany." Annals, #450 (July, 1980): 83-97.

1161. Bridenthal, Renate et al (eds.): When Biology Became Destiny: Women in Weimar and Nazi Germany [New York: Monthly Review Press, 1985]

1162. Brieger, Gert: "The Medical Profession." Friedlander: Ideology, pp.141-150.

1163. Cocks, Geoffrey: Psychotherapy in the Third Reich [New York: Oxford Univ. Press, 1985]

Details the use and abuse of psychology in Nazi Germany. Cocks evaluates the Goering Institute in a positive light, seeing its work as advancing psychotherapy, in spite of its obviously totalitarian nature. The author does not, however, hide the racist and ultra-nationalist overtones of the Institute´s work. Cocks sees the anti-Freudian bias as a positive step in the overall development of psychotherapy. One asks whether these developments were worth the price paid.

1164. Friedlander, Henry: "The Manipulation of Language." Friedlander: Ideology, pp.103-113.

1165. Hamilton, Alice: "The Enslavement of Women." PVP: Nazism, pp.76-87.

1166. Hartshorne, Edward Y.: The German Universities and National Socialism [New York: AMS Press, 1979] Rep. 1937 Ed.

1167. Hegemann, Werner: "The Debasement of the Professions." PVP: Nazism, pp.59-75.

1168. Hermand, Jost: "All Power to the Women: Nazi Concepts of Matriarchy." JCH, vol.19 #4 (Oct., 1984): 649-668.

1169. Hinz, Berthold: Art in the Third Reich [New York: Pantheon Books, 1979]

1170. Hirschmann, Ira A.: "The Degredation of Culture." PVP: Nazism, pp.88-107.

1171. Hughes, Thomas: "Technology." Friedlander: Ideology, pp.165-181.

1172. Hull, David S.: Film in the Third Reich: A Study of the German Cinema, 1933-1945 [New York: Simon and Schuster, 1973]

1173. Josephson, Matthew: Nazi Germany: The Brown Darkness Over Germany [New York: The John Day Co., 1933]

1174. Kamenetsky, Ch.: Children's Literature in Hitler's Germany: The Cultural Policy of National Socialism [Athens, OH: Ohio Univ. Press, 1984]

Surveys the manipulation of children's literature in the Third Reich. Shows the Nazi development of programs to instill its ideology in the next generations. Does not, however, attempt to assess how successful the Nazi education program really was.

1175. Kater, Michael H.: "The Reich Vocational Contest and Students of Higher Learning in Nazi Germany." CEH, vol.7 #3 (Sept., 1974): 225-261.

1176. Kneller, George F.: The Educational Philosophy of National Socialism [New Haven, CT: Yale Univ. Press, 1941]

1177. Kohn, Hans: The Mind of Germany: The Education of a Nation [New York: Charles Scribner's Sons, 1960]

1178. Leiser, E.: Nazi Cinema [New York: Macmillan, 1975]

1179. Lewisohn, Ludwig: "The Revolt Against Civilization." PVP: Nazism, pp.143-160.

1180. Lorch, J.: "The Nazi Misuse of Mendel." WLB, vol.23 #1 (Winter, 1968/69): 29-33.

1181. Meyer, M.: "The Nazi Musicologist as Myth Maker in the Third Reich." JCH, vol.10 #4 (Oct., 1975): 649-666.

1182. Mosse, George L.: Nazi Culture: Intellectual, Cultural and Social Life in the Third Reich [New York: Grosset & Dunlap, 1968]

Documentary charting of what life was like in Nazi Germany, 1933-1945. Illuminates Germany by using official German documents on such topics as youth, movies, marriage and family life, psychoanalysis, racism and antisemitism, art, and education. Shows how Nazi concepts pervaded almost every sector of German life.

1183. Ringer, Fritz K.: "The Perversion of Ideas in Weimar Universities." Friedlander: Ideology, pp.53-62.

1184. Ritchie, James M.: German Literature Under National Socialism [Totowa, NJ: Barnes and Noble, 1983]

1185. Rowan-Robinson, A.: "The Training of the Nazi Leaders of the Future." Int Affairs, vol.17 #2 (March/April, 1938): 233-250.

1186. Schutz, William: Pens Under the Swastika: A Study in Recent German Writing [Toronto: Macmillan, 1946]

1187. Sklar, Dusty: Gods and Beasts: The Nazis and the Occult [New York: Crowell, 1977]

1188. Steiner, John M.: Power Politics and Social Change in Nationalist Socialist Germany: A Process of Escalation into Mass Destruction [Atlantic Highlands, NJ: Humanities Press, 1975]

1189. Stephenson, Jill: Women in Nazi Society [New York: Barnes & Noble Books, 1975]

1190. Taylor, Telford: "The Legal Profession." Friedlander: Ideology, pp.133-140.

1191. Thomas, Katherine: Women in Nazi Germany [New York: AMS Press, 1979] Rep. 1943 Ed.

1192. Thompson, D.: "Culture under the Nazis." F Affairs, vol.14 #3 (April, 1936): 407-423.

1193. Ziemer, Gregor: Education for Death: The Making of the Nazi [New York: Oxford Univ. Press, 1941]

The NSDAP and Its Organs

1194. Farwell, George: "The Soul of Hitler Germany." P/P Herald, vol.3 #1/2 (Jan./Feb., 1934): 17-20.

1195. Gerth, H.: "The Nazi Party: Its Leadership and Composition." Am Jnl Soc, vol.45 #4 (Fall, 1940): 517-541.

1196. Hoffmann, P.: "Hitler´s Personal Security." JCH, vol. 8 #2 (April, 1973): 25-46.

1197. Horn, Daniel: "The National Socialist 'Schuler Bund' and the Hitler Youth, 1929-1933." CEH, vol.11 #4 (Dec., 1978): 355-375.

1198. Koch, Hans J. W.: Hitler Youth [New York: Stein and Day, 1976]

1199. Mckale, Donald M.: The Nazi Party Courts: Hitler's Management of Conflict in His Movement, 1921-1945 [Lawrence, KS: Regents Press of Kansas, 1974]

Study of conflict within the NSDAP and of the means that the Nazi hierarchy used to control such conflict. The work deals also with the perversion of justice under the National Socialist regime.

1200. Nagle, John: "Composition and Evolution of the Nazi Elite." Dobkowski: Toward, pp.75-91.

1201. Noakes, Jeremy: "Conflict and Development in the NSDAP, 1924-1927." JCH, vol.1 #4 (Oct., 1966): 3-36.

1202. ___: The Nazi Party in Lower Saxony [New York: Oxford Univ. Press, 1971]

1203. Orlow, Dietrich: A History of the Nazi Party 1919-1933 2 vols. [Pittsburgh: Univ. of Pittsburgh Press, 1969/73]

1204. ___: "The Organizational History and Structure of the NSDAP 1919-1923." JMH, vol.37 #2 (June, 1965): 208-226.

1205. Stachura, Peter D.: "The Ideology of the Hitler Youth in the 'Kampfzeit'." JCH, vol.8 #3 (July, 1973): 155-167.

1206. Wolfe, Burton H.: Hitler and the Nazis [New York: G. P. Putnam's Sons, 1970]

The SS: Institutions and Activities

1207. Aronson, S.: The Beginnings of the Gestapo System: The Bavarian Model in 1933 [Jerusalem: Keter, 1970]

1208. Baxter, R.: Women of the Gestapo [London: Quality Press, 1943]

1209. Bramstedt, E. K.: Dictatorship and Political Police: The Technique of Control By Fear [London: Kegan Paul, 1945]

1210. Buchheim, Hans (R. Barry, transl.): "Command and Compliance." Krausnick: Anatomy, pp.303-396.

1211. ___ (R. Barry, Transl.): "The SS: Instrument of Domination." Krausnick: Anatomy, pp.127-301.

1212. Butler, Rupert: The Black Angels: A History of the Waffen-SS [New York: St. Martin´s Press, 1979]

1213. Crankshaw, Edward: Gestapo: Instrument of Tyranny [New York: Viking Press, 1956]

1214. Delarue, Jacques (M. Savill, transl.): The Gestapo: A History of Horror [New York: William Morrow, 1964]

Perhaps the most in-depth history of the agencies which terrorized Europe from 1933-1945. Dealing with the SS in general, the main focus of the book is the RSHA and the Gestapo. The author was a member of the French police before World War II and worked for the Maquis during the Nazi occupation.

1215. Dukes, Paul: An Epic of the Gestapo [London: Cassell, 1940]

1216. Fischer, Conan: "The SA of the NSDAP: Social Background and Ideology of the Rank and File in the Early 1930´s." JCH, vol.17 #4 (Oct., 1982): 651-670.

1217. ___: Stormtroopers: A Social, Economic and Ideological Analysis, 1929-1935 [London: George Allen & Unwin, 1983]

Extensively researched and well documented study on the SA. Revises many of the standard conclusions about SA membership. Fischer argues that the majority of stormtroopers were not members of the lower middle class but young and unemployed workers. These lacked any real understanding of the principles of Nazism, but saw National Socialism as the only way to equalize the economic unfairness of the liberal state.

1218. Friedlander, Henry: "The SS and Police." Grobman: Genocide, pp.150-154.

1219. Gallo, Max: The Night of the Long Knives [New York: Harper & Row, 1972]

1220. "Gestapo: The Terror of Europe." Hist/WWII, #64 (1973): 1772-1773.

1221. Giles, O. C.: The Gestapo [Oxford: Clarendon Press, 1940]

1222. Graber, G. S.: The History of the SS [New York: Charter Books, 1978]

Popularized history of the SS. Well written, though undocumented. Includes material on the Warsaw ghetto.

1223. Grunberger, R.: Hitler´s SS [New York: Dell, 1970]

1224. Hohne, Heinz: The Order of the Death´s Head: The Story of Hitler´s SS [New York: Coward-McCann, 1969]

1225. Keegan, John: "Waffen-SS." Hist/WWII, #107 (1974): 2969-2975.

1226. Kirst, H. (M. Brownjohn, transl.): Night of the Long Knives [New York: Coward Press, 1976]

1227. Koehl, Robert: The Black Corps [Madison, WI: Univ. of Wisconsin Press, 1983]

Useful synthetic history of the SS and its organs. Succeeds in showing the centrality of the SS in the Nazi State. The SS was constantly expanding its power base until it rivaled even the NSDAP as the authoritative source of ideology.

1228. ___: "The Character of the Nazi SS." JMH, vol.34 #3 (Sept., 1962): 275-283.

1229. Koehler, Hansjurgen: Inside the Gestapo: Hitler´s Shadow Over the World [London: Pallas, 1940]

1230. Manvell, Roger and Heinrich Fraenkel: SS and Gestapo: Rule by Terror [New York: Ballantine Books, 1969]

Short survey of the history of the SS and of the SS-state.

The authors trace the history of the most evil organization ever to oppress humanity. They end with the disturbing question of whether this past has been vanquished, or if its seeds are merely lying dormant.

1231. Merkl, Peter H.: The Making of a Storm Trooper [Princeton, NJ: Princeton Univ. Press, 1979]

1232. ___: Political Violence Under the Swastika: 581 Early Nazis [Princeton, NJ: Princeton Univ. Press, 1975]

Integrated history attempting to elucidate the role that street violence played in the rise of the Nazis. Merkl is especially interested in the motivations of individual SA troopers. Their psyche can be compared to the activities of other paramilitary organizations of both the right and left.

1233. Reider, Frederic: The Order of the SS: How Did It Happen? [Tuscon, AZ: Aztex, 1975]

1234. Reitlinger, Gerald: The SS: Alibi of a Nation, 1922-1945 [Englewood Cliffs, NJ: Prentice-Hall, 1981]

History of the SS based on intensive German documentation. Tracing the SS from its origins until 1945 Reitlinger shows the steady increase in SS power and the virtual reorganization of the state around the SS during the war. Also discussed is the role the SS played in the Final Solution.

1235. Rosinski, H.: "Hitler´s Stormtroopers." Am Mercury, vol.58 #246 (June, 1944): 661-666.

1236. Speer, Albert (J. Naugroschel, transl.): The Slave State: Heinrich Himmler´s Masterplan for SS Supremacy [London: Weidenfeld & Nicolson, 1981] Also published as Infiltration [New York: Macmillan, 1981]

1237. Stein, George H.: The Waffen SS 1939-1945: Hitler´s Elite Guard at War [Ithaca, NY: Cornell Univ. Press, 1966]

1238. Steven, Hugh: Night of the Long Knives [Ventura, CA: Regal Books, 1972]

1239. Sydnor, Charles W. Jr.: "The History of the SS ´Totenkopf´ Division and the Postwar Mythology of the Waffen SS." CEH, vol.6 #4 (Dec., 1973): 339-362.

1240. ___: Soldiers of Destruction: The SS Death´s Head Division, 1933-1945 [Princeton, NJ: Princeton Univ. Press, 1977]

Important study of the Third SS Panzer (Totenkopf) Division from inception to destruction in 1945. The history of Totenkopf Division is more that just a military chronicle and is related to the development of the concentration camps as well as to the unfolding Nazi war crimes.

1241. Tolstoi, Nikolai: Night of the Long Knives [New York: Ballantine Books, 1972]

Account of the blood purges which began on June 30, 1934 and ended with the virtual destruction of the SA. Also explores Hitler´s relations with Ernst Roehm, commander of the SA, from 1923 to the machtergreifung.

1242. Vogel, Traugott: Under the SS Shadow [New York: Bantam Books, 1978]

1243. Walton-Kerr, Philip: Gestapo [London: Hale, 1939]

1244. Weingartner, James J.: Hitler´s Guard: The Story of the Leibstandarte SS Adolf Hitler, 1933-1945 [Carbondale: Southern Illinois Univ. Press, 1974]

1245. ___: "Sepp Dietrich, Heinrich Himmler and the ´Leibstandarte´ SS Adolf Hitler, 1933-1938." CEH, vol.1 #3 (Sept., 1968): 264-284.

The Army

1246. Boeninger, H.: "Hitler and the German Generals, 1934-1938." JCEA, vol.14 #1 (April, 1954): 19-37.

1247. Cooper, M.: The German Army, 1933-1945: Its Political and Military Failure [London: Macdonald/Jane´s, 1978]

1248. Davies, W. J. K.: German Army Handbook: 1939-1945 [New York: Arco Pub., 1973]

Encyclopaedic survey of the German army in World War II. Deals mainly with technical information and equipment used by the German ground forces. Appendix 3, on the Waffen SS, is somewhat apologetic, especially in relation to their commission of atrocities.

1249. Deutsch, Harold Ch.: Hitler and His Generals: The Hidden Crisis, January-June 1938 [Minneapolis: Univ. of Minnesota Press, 1974]

1250. Fried, Hans: The Guilt of the German Army [New York: Macmillan, 1942]

1251. Goerlitz, Walter (B. Battershaw, transl.): History of the German General Staff, 1657-1945 [New York: F. A. Praeger, 1953]

Traces the history of the high command of the Prussian-German army from the seventeenth century through World War II. Heavy emphasis on the Nazi period and on the interplay of the party, Hitler, and the generals.

1252. Hottle, Wilhelm (R. H. Stevens, transl.): The Secret Front: The Story of Political Espionage [New York: F. A. Praeger, 1954]

1253. Kahn, David: Hitler's Spies: German Military Intelligence in World War II [New York: Macmillan, 1978]

1254. O'Neill, Robert J.: The German Army and the Nazi Party, 1933-1939 [New York: Heineman, 1966]

Study of the process by which the German army was nazified during the period before World War II. The author, however, tends to under-emphasize the pre-Nazi militarism of the German officer corps as well as the degree of antisemitism in both the pre-and post-Nazi Wehrmacht.

1255. Wheeler-Bennett, John W.: The Nemesis of Power: The German Army in Politics, 1918-1945 [New York: St. Martin's Press, 1964]

The Economy of Nazi Germany

1256. De Witt, Thomas E. J.: "The Economics and Politics of Welfare in the Third Reich." CEH, vol.11 #3 (Sept., 1978): 256-278.

1257. Einzig, Paul: Germany's Default: The Economics of Hitlerism [London: Macmillan, 1934]

1258. Farquharson, John E.: Plough and the Swastika: The NSDAP and Agriculture in Germany 1928-1945 [New York: Sage Books, 1977]

1259. Gerschenkorn, A.: Bread and Democracy in Germany [Los Angeles: Univ. of California Press, 1943]

1260. Green, William: "The Attack on Labor." PVP: Nazism, pp.280-283.

1261. Heyl, John D.: "The Construction of the Westwall, 1938: An Exemplar for National Socialist Policy Making." CEH, vol.14 #1 (March, 1981): 63-78.

1262. Holmes, K.: "The Forsaken Past: Agrarian Conservatism and National Socialism in Germany." JCH, vol.17 #4 (Oct., 1982): 671-688.

1263. Kele, Max H.: Nazis and Workers: National Socialist Appeals to German Labor 1919-1933 [Chapel Hill: Univ. of North Carolina Press, 1972]

1264. Lore, Ludwig: "The Rate of the Worker." PVP: Nazism, pp.108-126.

1265. Manchester, Wm.: The Arms of Krupp [Boston: Little, Brown and Company, 1968]

1266. Nathan, Otto and Milton Fried: The Nazi Economic System: Germany's Mobilization for War [Durham, NC: Duke Univ. Press, 1944]

1267. Palyi, Melchior: "Economic Foundations of the German Totalitarian State." Am Jnl Soc, vol.46 #4 (Jan., 1941): 469-486.

1268. Rabinbach, Anson: "The Aesthetics of Production in the Third Reich." JCH, vol.11 #4 (Oct., 1976): 43-74.

1269. Rudolf, F.: "German Agriculture and the National Socialist Government." Fasc Q, vol.2 (1936): 500-511.

1270. Schweitzer, Arthur: Big Business in the Third Reich [Bloomington: Indiana Univ. Press, 1964]

1271. Shaud, James: "The 'Reichsautobahn': Symbol of the Third Reich." JCH, vol.19 #2 (April, 1984): 189-200.

1272. Simpson, Amos E.: "The Struggle for Control of the German Economy, 1936-1937." JMH, vol.31 #1 (March, 1959): 37-45.

1273. Stephenson, Jill: "Women´s Labor Service in Nazi Germany." CEH, vol.15 #3 (Sept., 1982): 241-265.

1274. Taylor, Robert R.: The World in Stone: The Role of Agriculture in the Nationalist Socialist Ideology [Berkeley, CA: Univ. of California Press, 1974]

1275. Thomas, Norman: "Labor Under the Nazis." F Affairs, vol.14 #3 (April, 1936): 424-436.

1276. Winkler, Heinrich A.: "From Social Protectionism to National Socialism: The German Small Business Movement in Comparative Perspective." JMH, vol.48 #1 (March, 1976): 1-18.

1277. Winkler, Max: "Nazi Economic Policy." PVP: Nazism, pp.161-177.

NAZI RACISM AND ANTISEMITISM

1278. Abramowitz, Isidore: "Scapegoats of Hate: The Anti-Jewish Section." J Fr, vol.3 #4 (April, 1936): 12-15.

1279. Adler, Morris: "Nazism and the Jewish Doctrine of Election." Recon, vol.1 #4 (Feb. 22, 1935): 6-11.

1280. Ainsztein, Reuben: "Final Solution of the Slav Problem: Colonisation with Assassination." WLB, vol.13 #3/4 (1959): 36, 38.

1281. "Antisemitism and German Morale." J Comment, vol.1 #8 (June 25, 1943): 1-4.

1282. Berenger, Henry: "Hitler and Israel." WJ, vol.1 #15 (Aug. 10, 1934): 341-342.

1283. Blau, Bruno: "The Jew as Sexual Criminal." JSS, vol. 13 #4 (Oct., 1951): 321-324.

1284. Boder, David P.: "Nazi Science." Ch J Forum, vol.1 #1 (Fall, 1942): 23-29.

1285. Brown, Harrison: "The Boomerang of Persecution." FR, vol.140 (Dec., 1933): 684-694.

1286. Clough, Nathaniel P.: "´The Eternal Jew´ in Vienna." J Fo, vol.22 #4 (May, 1939): 51-52, 64.

1287. Cohen, J. P.: "The New Antisemitism." J Rev, #5 (June/Sept., 1933): 83-94.

1288. de Haas, Jacob: "Drops of Jewish Blood." Menorah, vol.22 #2 (Oct./Dec., 1934): 159-163.

1289. Friedman, Martin: "The Philosophic, Social and Religious Implications of the Newer Antisemitism in Germany." CCAR/YB, vol.44 (1934): 242-264.

1290. Friedman, Philip: "The Jewish Badge and the Yellow Star in the Nazi Era." HJ, vol.17 #1 (April, 1955): 41-70. Also in Friedman: Roads, pp.11-33.

1291. Fvans, I.: "The Magnitude of Intolerance." J Affairs, vol.16 #6 (June, 1961): 18-21.

1292. Glasgow, G.: "The Germanic Race." Cont Rev, vol.150 150 #848 (Aug., 1936): 229-240.

1293. Goldberg, Abraham: "Motives of German Jew-Hatred." J Sp, vol.5 #3 (Jan., 1940): 12-14; #4 (Feb., 1940): 33-34.

1294. Goldstein, Jeffrey A.: "On Racism and Antisemitism in Occultism and Nazism." YVS, vol.13 (1979): 53-72.

1295. Green, Warren P.: "The Nazi Racial Policy Towards the Karaites." SJA, vol.8 #2 (Oct., 1978): 36-44.

1296. Grunberger, Richard: "Lebensborn: Himmler´s Selective Breeding Establishment." WLB, vol.16 #3 (Sum., 1962): 52-53.

1297. ___: "The Lebensborn Movement." Chartock: Society, pp.136-138.

1298. Hausheer, Herman: "The Socio-Economic Background of Nazi Antisemitism." Social Forces, vol.14 #3 (March, 1936): 241-354

1299. Hertz, Richard: "The Torahs the Nazis Collected." J Digest, vol.18 #4 (Jan., 1973): 16-18.

1300. Hillel, Marc and C. Henry (E. Mossbacher, transl.): Of Pure Blood: The Never Before Told Story Behind Hitler´s Secret Program to Breed the Master Race [New York: McGraw-Hill, 1977]

Well documented study into the history of the Lebensborn organization. Lebensborn was responsible for the Nazi breeding the aryan super race. Methods used included the providing of maternity care for German women, especially those who were unmarried, and the selective kidnapping of aryan-looking children in occupied Eastern Europe.

1301. Janowsky, Oscar L. and Melvin Fagen: International Aspects of German Racial Policies [New York: Oxford Univ. Press, 1937]

1302. Kerr, Alfred: "A Preface to German Cartoons of Jews." J Fr, vol.3 #1 (Jan., 1936): 14-15.

1303. Knoebel, E. E.: Racial Illusion and Military Necessity [Boulder: Univ. of Colorado Press, 1965]

1304. Koehl, Robert L.: RKFVD: German Resettlement and Population Policy, 1939-1945: A History of the Reich Commission for the Strengthening of Germandom [Cambridge, MA: Harvard Univ. Press, 1957]

1305. Komjathy, Anthony and R. Stockwell: German Minorities and the Third Reich: Ethnic Germans of East Central Europe between the Wars [New York: Holmes & Meier, 1984]

1306. Lowenthal, Marvin: "The Cup and the Sword." Menorah, vol.28 #1 (Jan./March, 1940): 1-8.

1307. Mahler, Ella: "The Half-Jews of Nazi Germany." IH, vol.10 #9 (Nov., 1962): 13-17.

1308. Marcus, Jacob R.: "Hitlerism Without Hitler." NJM, vol.49 #10 (July, 1935): 356-357, 367, 372-373.

1309. Meyer, Isidore: "History into Propaganda: How Nazi ´Scholars´ are Rewriting Jewish History." Menorah, vol.26 #1 (Jan./March, 1938): 51-74.

1310. Needler, Martin: "Hitler´s Antisemitism: A Political Appraisal." Pub Op Q, vol.24 #4 (Win., 1960): 665-669.

1311. Opler, Morris E.: "The Bio-Social Basis of Thought in the Third Reich." Am Soc Rev, vol.10 #4 (Dec., 1945): 776-786.

1312. Pois, R.: "Jewish Treason Against the Laws of Life: Nazi Religiosity and Burgeois Fantasy." Dobkowski: Toward, pp.343-376.

1313. Sarolea, Charles: "The Religion of Race." Menorah, vol.24 #1 (Jan./March, 1936): 1-7.

1314. Seidler, Fritz: The Bloodless Pogrom [London: Victor Gollancz, 1934]

1315. Stein, Leo: The Racial Thinking of Richard Wagner [New York: Philosophical Library, 1950]

1316. Tal, Uriel: "Violence and the Jew in Nazi Ideology." in Salo W. Baron and George S. Wise (eds.): Violence and Defense in the Jewish Experience [Philadelphia: J. P. S., 1977]: 205-223.

1317. Tenenbaum, Joseph: Race and Reich: The Story of the Epoch [New York: Twayne Pubs., 1956] * Examines the racial policies of Nazi Germany.

1318. ___: Races, Nations and Jews [New York: Bloch, 1934]

Investigation into the concepts of race and nation, as they relate to the Nazi generated Jewish problem. Concludes that Jews are not a race but a spiritual nation.

1319. Thompson, Larry V.: "´Lebensborn´ and the Eugenics Policy of the Reichsfuhrer SS." CEH, vol.4 #1 (March, 1971): 54-77.

1320. Von Ossietzky, Carl: "These Literary Antisemites." Menorah, vol.26 #1 (Jan./March, 1938): 105-113.

1321. Weingartner, James J.: "The SS Race and Settlement Main Office: Towards an Orden of Blood and Soil." The Historian, vol.34 #1 (Nov., 1971): 62-77.

1322. Weinryb, B. D.: "Nazification of Jewish Learning." J Rev, vol.13 #1 (April, 1945): 25-54. Part I.

1323. ___: "Political Judeology in Nazi Germany (Nazification of Jewish Learning)." J Rev, vol.3 #2 (July, 1945): 107-123. Part II.

1324. ___: "Nazification of Science and Research in Nazi Germany." JCEA, vol.3 #4 (Jan., 1944): 373-400.

GERMAN FOREIGN POLICY

General Studies

1325. Bischoff, R. F.: Nazi Conquest Through German Culture [Cambridge, MA: Harvard Univ. Press, 1942]

1326. Bodin, J.: "Towards Hitler's New Order." CEO, vol.18 #2 (Jan. 17, 1941): 18-19; #3 (Feb. 3, 1941): 28-29.

1327. Borkin, Joseph and Charles A. Welsh: Germany's Master Plan: A Story of Industrial Offensive [New York: Duell, Sloan & Pearce, 1943]

1328. Browning, Christopher: "'Understaatssekretar' Martin Luther and the Ribbentrop Foreign Office." JCH, vol. 12 #2 (April, 1977): 313-344.

1329. Ciechanowski, M. Jean: "German-Polish Relations." Int Affairs, vol.12 #3 (May/June, 1933): 366-386.

1330. De Jong, Louis (C. Geyl, transl.): The German Fifth Column in the Second World War [New York: Howard Fertig, 1973] Rep. 1956 Ed.

1331. Documents on German Foreign Policy, 1918-1945. Series D, 1937-1945 [Washington, DC: U. S. Department of State, 1947]

1332. "Geopolitics as an Instrument of German Aggression." PFR, #74 (Aug. 15, 1943): Whole Issue.

1333. Gisevius, Hans: To the Bitter End [Boston: Houghton Mifflin, 1947]

1334. Guttman, Werner: "What is the Fifth Column?" Survey Graphic, vol.29 #10 (Oct., 1940): 503-508.

1335. Hauner, Milan: "Did Hitler Want a World Dominion?" JCH, vol.13 #1 (Jan., 1978): 15-32.

1336. Henri, E. (M. Davidson, transl.): Hitler Over Europe? [London: Dent, 1934]

1337. Herz, John H.: "The National Socialist Doctrine of International Law and the Problems of International Organization." Pol Sci Q, vol.54 #4 (Dec., 1939): 536-554.

1338. Hildebrand, Klaus: Foreign Policy of the Third Reich [Berkeley, CA: Univ. of California Press, 1974]

1339. Jarausch, Konrad H.: "From Second to Third Reich: The Problem of Continuity in German Foreign Policy." CEH, vol.12 #1 (March, 1979): 68-82.

1340. Lengyel, E.: "The Brown International." PVP: Nazism, pp.178-201.

1341. Mairr-Hultschin, J. C.: "Hitler's Success Among Germans Outside the Reich." Cont Rev, vol.158 #895 (July, 1940): 70-78.

1342. Mandell, R. D.: The Nazi Olympics [London: Souvernir Press, 1972]

1343. Mckale, Donald M.: The Swastika Outside Germany [Kent, OH: Kent State Univ. Press, 1977]

Investigation into the organization and activities of the Auslands-Organisation (A-O), the NSDAP organ for furthering the spread of Nazism throughout the world. Interestingly, while the A-O activities were much greater than commonly realized, the successes of the A-O were in fact minimal. This, however, does not minimize the importance of the Nazi International.

1344. Murphy, Raymond E. et al (eds.): National Socialism: Basic Principles, their Application by the Nazi Party's Foreign Organization, and the Use of Germans Abroad for Nazi Aims [Washington, DC: Gov't Printing Office, 1943]

1345. Poole, DeWitt C.: "Light on Nazi Foreign Policy." F Affairs, vol.25 #1 (Oct., 1946): 130-154.

1346. Postal, Bernard: "Nazis and the 1936 Olympic Games." Ch J Forum, vol.23 #1 (Fall, 1964): 7-11. Also in J Digest, vol.14 #2 (Nov., 1968): 73-80.

1347. Rich, Norman: Hitler's War Aims: Ideology, the Nazi State and the Course of Expansion vol.1 [New York: W. W. Norton, 1973]

1348. ___: The Establishment of the New Order vol.2 [New York: W. W. Norton, 1974]

1349. Schellenberg, W.: Hitler´s Secret Service [New York: Pyramid Pubs., 1974]

1350. Schuman, Frederick: "The Conduct of German Foreign Affairs." Annals, #176 (Nov., 1934): 185-221.

1351. Schwarz, W.: "Germany and the League of Nations." Int Affairs, vol.10 #2 (March, 1931): 197-207.

1352. Seabury, Paul: The Wilhelmstrasse: A Study of German Diplomats under the Nazi Regime [Berkeley, CA: Univ. of California Press, 1954]

1353. Smith, Rennie: "Europe As a Nazi Colony." CEO, vol.18 #11 (May 30, 1941): 131-132.

1354. ___: "Revolutionary Germany and its Foreign Relations." Cont Rev, vol.144 #812 (Aug., 1933): 144-151.

1355. Steel, J.: "Germany´s Dreams of Expansion." Nation, vol.138 #3585 (March 21, 1934): 324-326.

1356. Steigerhof, A.: "German Expansion Boxes the Compass." CEO, vol.18 #15 (July 25, 1941): 197-198.

1357. Townsend, Mary E.: "The German Colonies and the Third Reich." Pol Sci Q, vol.53 #2 (June, 1938): 186-206.

1358. Toynbee, A.: Disarmament and Security: The National Socialist Germany and Her Neighbors. The Historical Background of the ´Third Reich´ [London: Survey of International Affairs, 1934]

1359. Van Passen, Pierre: "The Danger to World Peace." PVP: Nazism, pp.212-226.

1360. Von Dirksen, Herbert: Moscow, Tokyo, London: Twenty Years of German Foreign Policy [Norman, OK: Univ. of Oklahoma Press, 1952]

1361. Walter, G. B.: "Does Germany Need More Living Space?" CEO, vol.17 #18 (Oct. 16, 1940): 167-168.

1362. Watt, Donald C.: "The German Diplomats and the Nazi Leaders." JCEA, vol.15 #2 (July, 1955): 148-160.

1363. Weinberg, Gerhard L.: The Foreign Policy of Hitler Germany: Diplomatic Revolution in Europe, 1933-1936 [Chicago: University of Chicago Press, 1971]

1364. Wolfe, Henry C.: The German Octopus: Hitler Bids for World Power [Garden City, NY: Doubleday, 1938]

1365. World Committee for the Victims of German Fascism: The Brown Network: The Activities of the Nazis in Foreign Countries [New York: Knight Pub., 1936]

The Export of Antisemitism

1366. "American Prisoners of War." J Comment, vol.2 #13 (April 28, 1944): 3-4. * Nazi antisemitic and racial indoctrination.

1367. Aronsfeld, C. C.: "British Jewry as Seen Through Nazi Eyes." JM, vol.1 #2 (June, 1947): 46-52.

1368. ___: "A Nazi Historian of British Jewry." J Fr, vol. 45 #10 (Dec., 1978): 19-22.

1369. Bernhard, Georg: "Poison with and without Gas." CW, vol.9 #22 (June 12, 1942): 6-7.

1370. Brandt, Albert A.: "Banzai Antisemitism: Hitler's Gift to Japan." Menorah, vol.32 #1 (April/June, 1944): 113-121.

1371. Krents, M. E. and M. Ehrlich: "Radiokrieg Against America." CJR, vol.3 #6 (Nov./Dec., 1940): 587-594.

1372. Michaelis, Meir: "Rosenberg's Foreign Policy Office and 'Jewish Influence' in the Soviet Union, 1940: A Documentary Note." SJA, vol.4 #1 (May, 1974): 66-72.

1373. Miller, Clyde: "Germany's Campaign to Place the War-Guilt on the Jews." CJR, vol.2 #6 (Nov./Dec., 1939): 16-19.

1374. "The New Reich Plan for Refugees." CJR, vol.2 #2 (March/April, 1939): 77-78.

1375. Viton, Albert: "The Exile of the 16,000." NJM, vol.53 #6 (Feb., 1939): 192-194, 213. * On the deportation of Polish Jews.

Eastern Europe

1376. Brown, MacAlister: "The Third Reich's Mobilization of the German Fifth Column in Eastern Europe." JCEA, vol.19 #2 (July, 1959): 128-148.

1377. Budurowycz, Bohdan B.: "Poland and Hitler's Offers of Alliance." Polish Rev, vol.3 #4 (Aut., 1958): 16-29.

1378. Dean, Vera: "Pan-Germanism Redivivus." New Republic, vol.96 #1244 (Oct. 12, 1938): 259-260.

1379. Gasiorowski, Z. J.: "The German-Polish Nonaggression Pact of 1934." JCEA, vol.15 #1 (April, 1955): 4-29.

1380. Haferkorn, Reinard: "Danzig and the Polish Corridor." Int Affairs, vol.12 #2 (March/April, 1933): 224-234.

1381. Henlin, K.: "The German Minority in Czechoslovakia." Int Affairs, vol.15 #4 (July/Aug., 1936): 561-572.

1382. Hitchens, Marilynn: Germany, Russia, and the Balkans: Prelude to the Nazi-Soviet Non-Aggression Pact [New York: Columbia Univ. Press, 1983]

1383. Jackh, Ernst: "The German Drive in the Balkans." Int Affairs, vol.18 #6 (Nov./Dec., 1939): 763-783.

1384. Knaust, E.: "Goebbels Framed the Hitler-Stalin Pact." Am Mercury, vol.49 #194 (Feb., 1940): 135-142.

1385. Leonhardt, Hans L.: Nazi Conquest of Danzig [Chicago: Univ. of Chicago Press, 1942]

1386. Levine, Herbert S.: Hitler's Free City: A History of the Nazi Party in Danzig, 1925-1939 [Chicago: Univ. of Chicago Press, 1973]

Detailed well documented study of the Nazi Party in Danzig. Places the Danzig crisis in context, especially in terms of Nazi goals and methods. Contains considerable information on the destruction of Danzig Jewry.

1387. Lumans, V.: "The Ethnic German Minority in Slovakia and the Third Reich, 1938-1945." CEH, vol.15 #3 (Sept., 1982): 266-296.

1388. Lundin, C. L.: "The Nazification of the Baltic German Minorities." JCEA, vol.7 #1 (April, 1947): 1-28.

1389. Mason, John B.: The Danzig Dilemma: A Study in Peacemaking by Compromise [Stanford, CA: Stanford Univ. Press, 1946]

1390. Michaelis, M.: "The Third Reich and Russian 'National Socialism', 1933: A Documentary Note." SJA, vol.5 #1 (May, 1975): 88-94.

1391. "Nazi Anti-Polish Propaganda." PFR, #61 (Feb. 1, 1943): 5-8.

1392. Orlow, Dietrich: The Nazis in the Balkans: A Case Study of Totalitarian Politics [Pittsburgh, PA: Univ. of Pittsburgh Press, 1968]

Case study in Nazi foreign policy, focused on the activities of the Sudosteuropa-Gesselschaft. Orlow charts the aims and failures of Nazi policy in the Balkans. He concludes that expectations of victory postponed rational foreign policy aims and led to failure in the long run.

1393. Pressiesen, Ernst: "Prelude to Barbarossa: Germany and the Balkans, 1940-1941." JMH, vol.32 #4 (Dec., 1960): 359-370.

1394. Prokop, Myroslav: "Ukraine in Germany's World War II Plans." Uk Q, vol.11 #2 (Sept., 1955): 134-144.

1395. Rose, W. J.: "The German-Polish Pact of 1934 as a Factor in Shaping the Relations of Two Neighboring Peoples." Int Affairs, vol.13 #6 (Nov./Dec., 1934): 792-814.

1396. Smelser, Ronald: "The Betrayal of a Myth: National Socialism and the Financing of Middle-Class Socialism in the Sudetenland." CEH, vol.5 #3 (Sept., 1978): 256-277.

1397. ___: The Sudeten Problem, 1933-1938: Volkstumpolitik and the Formulation of Nazi Foreign Policy [Middletown, CT: Wesleyan Univ. Press, 1975]

1398. Soloveytchik, George: "Germany and Russia." Cont Rev, vol.150 #852 (Dec., 1936): 665-674.

1399. Steed, Henry W.: "The Anti-Bolshevist Front." Int Affairs, vol.16 #2 (March/April, 1937): 179-200.

1400. Thaler, K. B.: "Germany's New Balkan Plans." CEO, vol.18 #19 (Sept. 19, 1941): 257-258.

1401. "The Ukrainian Question in German Politics." PFR, #20 (May 15, 1941): Whole Issue.

1402. Walter, G. B.: "Germany's Outlook in the Balkans." CEO, vol.17 #20 (Nov. 16, 1940): 188-190.

1403. Weinberg, Gerhard: Germany and the Soviet Union 1939-1941 [Leiden: E. J. Brill, 1954]

1404. ___: "Secret Hitler-Benes Negotiations in 1936-1937." JCEA, vol.19 #4 (Jan., 1960): 366-374.

1405. Wiskemann, E.: "The 'Drang Nach Osten' Continues." F Affairs, vol.17 #4 (July, 1939): 764-773.

Western Europe

1406. Araquistain, L.: "Hitler and Spain." CEO, vol.20 #6 (March 19, 1943): 83-85.

1407. Beck, Peter: "England vs. Germany 1938: Football as Propaganda." History Today, vol.32 #6 (June, 1982): 29-34.

1408. Epstein, Fritz: "National Socialism and French Colonialism." JCEA, vol.3 #1 (April, 1943): 52-64.

1409. Hillgruber, A.: "England's Place in Hitler's Plans for World Dominion." JCH, vol.9 #1 (Jan., 1974): 5-22.

1410. Joesten, J.: "The Nazis in Scandinavia." F Affairs, vol.15 #4 (July, 1937): 720-728.

1411. Kloss, G.: "The Image of Britain and the British in the German National Socialist Press." WLB, vol.24 #3 (Summer, 1970): 21-28.

1412. Olberg, Paul: "Scandinavia and the Nazis." Cont Rev, vol.156 #883 (July, 1939): 27-34.

1413. Wiskemann, Elizabeth: "A Saar Close-Up." Cont Rev, vol.147 #831 (March, 1935): 296-304.

The Americas

1414. Artucio, Hugo F.: "Nazi Intrigue in Latin America." FW, vol.1 #1 (Oct., 1941): 99-102.

1415. Brandt, A.: "The Invasion of America." PVP: Nazism, pp.227-249.

1416. de Valdiva, J.: "The Technique of Nazi Penetration in Latin America." FW, vol.1 #3 (Dec., 1941): 287-294.

1417. Dickstein, Samuel: "Nazi Activities in the United States." J Fr, vol.5 #8 (Aug., 1938): 22-23.

1418. Freifeld, Sidney: "Nazi Press Agentry and the American Press." Pub Op Q, vol.6 #2 (Sum., 1942): 221-235.

1419. Frye, Alton: Nazi Germany and the American Hemisphere [New Haven, CT: Yale Univ. Press, 1967]

1420. Fuller, Hellen: "Nazism in Latin America." New Republic, vol.110 #5 (Jan. 31, 1944): 141-143.

1421. Goodman, Abram: "A Nazi Primer on America." Menorah, vol.27 #3 (Oct./Dec., 1939): 355-361.

1422. Goodrich, N. H.: "Nazi Interference in American Affairs." CJR, vol.3 #4 (July/Aug., 1940): 370-380.

1423. Graves, Harold N. Jr.: "Propaganda by Short Wave: Berlin Calling America." Pub Op Q, vol.4 #4 (Dec., 1940): 601-619.

1424. Habe, Hans: "America Through Goebbels´ Eyes." Am Mercury, vol.56 #230 (Feb., 1943): 166-173.

1425. Hilton, Stanley E.: Hitler´s Secret War in South America, 1939-1945 [New York: Ballantine Books, 1982]

1426. Hottle, Wilhelm (B. Creighton, transl.): Hitler´s Paper Weapon [St. Albans, England: Hart-Davis, 1955]

1427. Kris, Ernst and Hans Speier (eds.): German Radio Propaganda: Report on the Home Broadcasts during the War [New York: Oxford Univ. Press, 1944]

1428. Lang, Daniel: "Berlin Sends Radio Greetings." New Republic, vol.97 #1258 (Jan. 11, 1939): 279-281.

1429. Lore, Ludwig: "Nazi Politics in America." Nation, vol.137 #3569 (Nov. 29, 1933): 615-619.

1430. Martin, L. and S. Martin: "Nazi Intrigues in Central America." Am Mercury, vol.53 #21 (July, 1941): 66-73.

1431. May, Ernest: "Nazi Germany and the United States: A Review Essay." JMH, vol.41 #2 (June, 1969): 207-214.

1432. Padover, Saul K.: "How the Nazis Picture America." Pub Op Q, vol.3 #4 (Oct., 1939): 663-669.

1433. Pelcovits, Nathan A. and H. Schneiderman: "Respect for the American Passport." CJR, vol.4 #5 (Oct., 1941): 481-500.

1434. Priwer, Esther: "Nazi Exchange Students at the University of Missouri." Menorah, vol.26 #3 (Oct./Dec., 1938): 353-361

1435. Sayers, Michael and A. E. Kahn: Sabotage [New York: Harper & Bros., 1942]

1436. Smith, Arthur L. Jr.: "The 'Kameradschaft' USA." JMH, vol.34 #4 (Dec., 1962): 398-408.

1437. Sternfeld, W.: "Nazi Propaganda, Spying and Sabotage in the USA." CEO, vol.20 #1 (Jan. 8, 1943): 7-8.

1438. Trefousse, Hans L.: Germany and America: Essays on Problems of International Relations and Immigration [New York: Brooklyn College Press, 1981]

1439. ___: Germany and American Neutrality, 1939-1941 [New York: Octagon Press, 1969] Rep. 1951 Ed.

1440. Turner, Ewart: "German Influence in South Brazil." Pub Op Q, vol.6 #1 (Spr. 1942): 57-69.

1441. White, John B.: The Big Lie [New York: Crowell, 1956]

Propaganda Activities

1442. Albert, Ernst: "German Propaganda." Cont Rev, vol.157 #889 (Jan., 1940): 84-88.

1443. Baird, Jay W.: The Mythical World of Nazi War Propaganda, 1939-1945 [Minneapolis: Univ. of Minnesota Press, 1974]

1444. Balfour, M.: Propaganda in War, 1939-1945: Organisations, Policies and Publics in Britain and Germany [London: Routledge & Kegan Paul, 1979]

1445. Boelcke, Willi A.: The Secret Conferences of Dr. Goebbels [New York: E. P. Dutton, 1970]

1446. Bossowski, J.: "Documents of Polish Cruelty: Methods Used by Hitlerite Propaganda." Commission: GCIP/II, pp.163-168.

1447. Farwell, Gilbert: "The Great Conspiracy." P/P Herald, vol.3 #3/4 (March/April, 1934): 21-23.

1448. Freifeld, Sidney A.: "The War of Nerves in the News." CJR, vol.5 #1 (Feb., 1942): 11-40.

1449. "German Propaganda System in Europe." PFR, #73 (Aug. 1, 1943): Whole Issue.

1450. Habe, Hans: "The Smiling Nazi Soldier." FW, vol.1 #3 (Dec., 1941): 263-267.

1451. Harrison, Bernard: "The Propaganda War." Hist/WWII, #3 (1972): 63-66.

1452. "How to Protect Democracy Against Nazi Lies. A Symposium." J Fo, vol.22 #4 (May, 1939): 53-55; #5 (June, 1939): 67-68.

1453. Larson, Cedric: "The German Press Chamber." Pub Op Q, vol.1 #4 (Oct., 1937): 53-70.

1454. Marx, Fritz M.: "Criticism in a one-Party State." Pub Op Q, vol.1 #4 (Oct., 1937): 92-98.

1455. Nelson, Roger B.: "Hitler´s Propaganda Machine." Cur His, vol.38 #6 (June, 1933): 287-294.

1456. "The New Nazi Propaganda Offensive." J Comment, vol.1 #2 (May 21, 1943):1-3.

1457. Roetter, Charles: "The Propaganda War." Hist/WWII, #102 (1974): 2837-2846.

1458. Sington, Derrick and Arthur Weidenfeld: The Goebbels Experiment: A Study of the Nazi Propaganda Machine [New Haven, CT: Yale Univ. Press, 1943]

1459. Syrkin, Marie: "Spreading the Nazi Gospel." J Fr, vol.5 #12 (Dec., 1938): 12-15.

1460. Taylor, Edmond: The Strategy of Terror: Europe's Front [Boston: Houghton Mifflin, 1940]

1461. "Tons of Nazi Propaganda Mailed and Delivered Free." ADL Rev vol.2 #1 (Sept., 1940): 3-4.

1462. Weinryb, Bernard D.: "New Methods of Propaganda." CW, vol.8 #12 (March 21, 1941): 7-8.

1463. Welch, David: Propaganda and the German Cinema 1933-1945 [New York: Oxford Univ. Press, 1983]

1464. ___ (ed.): Nazi Propaganda: The Power and the Limitations [London: Croom Helm, 1983]

1465. Zeman, Z. A. B.: Nazi Propaganda [London: Wiener Library/Oxford Univ. Press, 1964]

Definitive study of the techniques used by the Nazi propaganda machine as well as of both the successes and failures of Nazi propaganda efforts. Both internal and external propaganda are examined. The role of antisemitism in Nazi propaganda, both internal and external, is covered although not systematically.

The Middle East

1466. Bennhaum, E. H.: "The Menace of Nazi Propaganda in the Near East." J Horizon, vol.2 #12 (Sept., 1939): 10-11.

1467. Boas, J.: "Nazi Travels to Palestine." History Today, vol.30 #1 (Jan., 1980): 33-38. * On Von Mildenstein's trip in support of Zionism in 1933.

1468. Cooper, Elias: "Nazi Policy in the Middle East, 1939-1945." Mid, vol.10 #6 (June, 1964): 61-75.

1469. Friedman, Saul S.: "Arab Complicity in the Holocaust." J Fr, vol.42 #4 (April, 1975): 9-15, 17.

1470. Hirszowicz, Lukasz: The Third Reich and the Arab East [Toronto: Univ. of Toronto Press, 1966]

Investigation of relations between Nazi Germany and the Arab world between 1936 and 1943. Viewed from the perspective of Nazi foreign policy, relations with the Arabs are placed in the context of the Palestine issue and of British policies in the Near East.

1471. Kanaan, Haviv: "The Nazi Fifth Column in Mandatory Palestine." JOMER, vol.14 #53 (Dec. 31, 1965): 17-19.

1472. Krug, Mark: "The Arabs and the War." Ch J Forum, vol.2 #4 (Sum., 1944): 221-226. Also in NJM, vol.58 #1 (July/Aug., 1944): 364-365.

1473. Marcus, Ernst: "The German Foreign Office and the Palestine Question in the Period 1933-1939." YVS, vol.2 (1958): 179-204.

1474. Melka, R. L.: "Max Freiherr von Oppenheim: Sixty Years of Scholarship and Political Intrigue in the Middle East." MES, vol.9 #1 (Jan., 1973): 81-94.

1475. ___: "Nazi Germany and the Palestine Question." MES, vol.5 #3 (Oct., 1969): 221-233.

1476. Nahmad, H. M.: "The Third Reich and the Arab East." WLB, vol.21 #2 (Spr., 1967): 26-29.

1477. Neumann, Emanuel: "Arab Alignments in the Near East." FW, vol.3 #3 (Aug., 1942): 219-225.

1478. Nicosia, Francis R.: "National Socialism and the Demise of the German-Christian Communities in Palestine during the Nineteen Thirties." Can Jnl/His, vol.14 #2 (Aug., 1979): 235-255.

1479. Schechtman, Joseph B.: "The Arab Pro-Nazi Record." CW, vol.13 #9 (March 1, 1946): 9-11.

1480. Schmidt, H. D.: "The Nazi Party in Palestine and the Levant 1932-9." Int Affairs, vol.28 #4 (Oct., 1952): 460-469.

1481. Yisraeli, David: "The Third Reich and Palestine." MES, vol.7 #3 (Oct., 1971): 343-353.

1482. ___: "The Third Reich and the Transfer Agreement." JCH, vol.6 #2 (April, 1971): 129-149.

The Mufti of Jerusalem

1483. Bar-Ai, M.: "I Saw the Mufti's Letters." J Horizon, vol.24 #4 (March/April, 1961): 13-15.

1484. Carmichael, Joel: "The Mufti as Myth." J Fr, vol.19 #12 (Dec., 1952): 16-20.

1485. Cooper, Elias: "Forgotten Palestinian - the Nazi Mufti." Am Zionist, vol.68 #4 (March/April, 1978): Special Issue.

1486. Hanan, Ben: "Mufti: The Missing Defendant." IH, vol.9 #2 (March/April, 1961): 23-24, 33.

1487. Nevo, Joseph: "Al-Haji Amin and the British in World War II." MES, vol.20 #1 (Jan., 1984): 3-16.

1488. Richards, B.: "The Mufti as War Criminal." CW, vol.12 #15 (April 27, 1945): 8-9.

1489. Schechtman, Joseph B.: The Mufti and the Fuehrer: The Rise and Fall of Haj Amin el-Husseini [New York: Thomas Yoseloff, 1965]

1490. ___: "The Mufti-Eichmann Team." CBW, vol.27 #16 (Nov. 7, 1960): 5-7.

1491. Waters, M. P. (Moshe Pearlman): "Mufti Over the Middle East." HM, vol.22 #6 (April, 1942): 6-9.

6

The Nazis

BIOGRAPHIES

Klaus Barbie

1492. Bower, Tom: Klaus Barbie: The Butcher of Lyons [New York: Pantheon Books, 1984]

1493. Murphy, Brenden: The Butcher of Lyon: The Story of Infamous Nazi Klaus Barbie [New York: Empire Books, 1983]

Martin Borman

1494. McGovern, James: Martin Borman [New York: A. Barker, 1968]

1495. von Lang, J. (C. Armstrong and P. White, transls.): The Secretary Martin Borman, the Man Who Manipulated Hitler [New York: Random House, 1979]

Wilhelm Canaris

1496. Amort, C. and M. Jedlicka: The Canaris File [London: Wingate, 1970]

1497. Hohne, Heinz (Maxwell Brounjohn, transl.): Canaris: A Biography [Garden City, NY: Doubleday, 1979]

1498. Sternfeld, W.: "Canaris: Chief of the German Intelligence Service." Cont Rev, vol.163 #929 (May, 1943): 296-299.

Houston S. Chamberlain

1499. Holmes, Colin: "Houston S. Chamberlain in Great Britain." WLB, vol.24 #2 (Spr., 1970): 31-36.

1500. Kaltenbrunner, Gerd K.: "Houston Stewart Chamberlain, the Most Germanic of Germans." WLB, vol.22 #1 (Win., 1967/68): 6-12.

Karl Doenitz

1501. Padfield, Peter: Doenitz: The Last Fuehrer [New York: Harper & Row, 1984]

The first full scale biographical study of Admiral of the Fleet Karl Doenitz. Uses the "life and times" approach to place Doenitz in context. Gives special attention to Doenitz´ position in the Nazi party and his eventual appointment as Fuehrer. Also includes material on the Final Solution.

Adolf Eichmann

1502. Clarke, Comer: Eichmann: The Man and His Crimes [New York: Ballantine Books, 1960]

1503. Dekonig, Ines: A Study of Adolf Eichmann (1906-1962) Adolf Hitler´s Expert in Jewish Affairs [Newton, MA: The Author, 1964]

1504. Donovan, John: Eichmann: Man of Slaughter [New York: Avon Books, 1960]

1505. Paneth, P.: Eichmann: Technician of Death [New York: Robert Speller & Sons, 1960]

1506. Reynolds, Quentin et al: Minister of Death: The Adolf Eichmann Story [New York: Viking Press, 1960]

Journalistic account of the Eichmann case. Written as the case unfolded. Has been largely superseded.

1507. Robinson, Nehemiah: Eichmann. Master of the Nazi Murder Machine [New York: World Jewish Congress, 1961]

1508. Schorsch, Emil: "Eichmann´s Education." J Sp, vol.26 #9 (Nov., 1961): 9-11.

1509. Wighton, Charles: Eichmann: His Career and Crimes [London: Odhams Press, 1961]

Josef Goebbels

1510. Bramsted, Ernest K.: Goebbels and National Socialist Propaganda, 1925-1945 [Lansing: Michigan State Univ. Press, 1965]

1511. Ebermayer, Erich and Hans-Otto Meissner: Evil Genius: The Story of Joseph Goebbels [London: Allan Wingate, 1953]

1512. Manvell, R. and H. Fraenkel: Dr. Goebbels: His Life and Death [New York: Simon and Schuster, 1960]

1513. Reimann, Viktor (S. Wendt, transl.): Goebbels [Garden City, NY: Doubleday, 1976]

1514. Riess, Curt: The Devil´s Advocate Joseph Goebbels: A Biography [Garden City, NY: Doubleday, 1948]

1515. Semmler, Rudolf: Goebbels, the Man Next to Hitler [New York: AMS Press, 1979] Rep. 1947 Ed.

1516. Stern-Rubarth, E.: "Goebbels, the Nazi Robespierre." Cont Rev, vol.159 #903 (March, 1941): 295-299

1517. Werner, Alfred: "Goebbels - Demonic Demagogue." CBW, vol.24 #15 (Oct. 24, 1960): 10-12

1518. ___: "Mephistopheles of Nazism." J Fo, vol.28 #11 (Nov., 1945): 272-274.

Hermann Goering

1519. Bewley, Charles H.: Hermann Goering and the Third Reich: A Biography Based on Family and Official Records [Old Greenwich, CT: Devin-Adair, 1962]

1520. Butler, Ewan and Gordon Young: Marshal Without Glory [London: Hodder & Stoughton, 1951]

1521. Frischauer, W.: The Rise and Fall of Hermann Goering [Boston: Houghton Mifflin, 1951]

1522. Lee, Asher: Goering: Air Leader [New York: Hippocrene Books, 1972]

1523. Manvell, Roger and H. Fraenkel: Goering: A Biography [New York: Simon and Schuster, 1962]

1524. Mosley, Leonard: The Reich Marshall [New York: Dell Pub., 1975] * Detailed biography of Hermann Goering from World War I to his suicide at Nuremberg.

1525. Singer, Kurt: Goering: Germany´s Most Dangerous Man [London: Hutchinson, 1940]

1526. Stern-Rubarth, Edgar: "Goering, the Nazi Would-be Bonaparte." Cont Rev, vol.159 #905 (May, 1941): 536-541

Rudolf Hess:

1527. Heiden, Konrad: "Hitler´s Better Half." F Affairs, vol.20 #1 (Oct., 1941): 73-86.

1528. Stern-Rubarth, Edgar: "Rudolf Hess." Cont Rev, vol. 159 #906 (June, 1941): 645-650.

1529. Thimmesch, N.: "Strange Saga of Rudolf Hess." SEP, vol.253 (March, 1981): 50-53.

Reinhard Heydrich

1530. Calic, Edouard: Reinhard Heydrich [New York: William Morrow, 1985]

1531. Deschner, Gunther: Reinhard Heydrich, a Biography [New York: Stein and Day, 1981] Also published as: Heydrich, the Pursuit of Total Power [London: Orbis, 1981]

1532. Graber, G. S.: The Life and Times of Reinhard Heydrich [New York: David McKay, 1980]

1533. Michaelis, Henry: "Reinhard Heydrich: Hangman of Europe." FW, vol.3 #1 (June, 1942): 36-39.

1534. Svaty, Ravel: "Heydrich, a Product of Prussian Militarism." CEO, vol.19 #12 (June 12, 1942): 183-184.

1535. Wighton, Ch.: Heydrich: Hitler´s Most Evil Henchman [Randor, PA: Chilton, 1962]

1536. Wykes, Alan: Heydrich [New York: Ballantine Books, 1973]

Biography of Hitler's heir-apparent. Focuses on Heydrich's activities in Bohemia-Moravia as well as on his assassination by members of British intelligence.

Heinrich Himmler

1537. Frischauer, Willi: Himmler: The Evil Genius of the Third Reich [Boston: Beacon Press, 1953]

1538. Manvell, Roger and Heinrich Fraenkel: Himmler [New York: G. P. Putnam's Sons, 1965]

1539. Smith, B. F.: Heinrich Himmler: A Nazi in the Making, 1900-1926 [Stanford, CA: Hoover Inst. Press, 1971]

1540. Stern-Rubarth, Edgar: "H. Himmler - Hitler's Fouche." Cont Rev, vol.158 #900 (Dec., 1940): 641-645.

1541. Werner, Alfred: "A Worm Goes to the Worms: A Portrait of Heinrich Himmler." Am Heb, vol.155 #8 (June 15, 1945): 10-11

Adolf Hitler

1542. Bezymenski, Lev: The Death of Adolf Hitler: Unknown Documents from Soviet Archives [New York: Harcourt, Brace and World, 1968]

1543. Boldt, Gerhard (S. Bance, transl.): Hitler: The Last Ten Days [New York: Coward, McCann & Geoghegan, 1973] Also published as: In the Shelter with Hitler [London: Citadel Press, 1948]

1544. Bullock, Alan: "The Death of Hitler." Hist/WWII, #87 (1974): 2411-2419.

1545. ___: Hitler: A Study in Tyranny [New York: Harper & Row, 1964]

Well written and thoroughly documented biography of Hitler, which attempts to assess Hitler's part in the history of the Third Reich. Still the standard to which other biographies of Hitler are compared, Bullock's work is based upon extensive documentary evidence which proves his primary contentions.

1546. Carr, William: Hitler: A Study in Personality and Politics [New York: St. Martin's Press, 1979]

1547. Churchill, Allen (ed.): Eyewitness: Hitler. The Nazi Fuehrer and His Times as Seen by Contemporaries [New York: Walker, 1979]

Collection of contemporary accounts which form a collective historical biography of Hitler as others saw him. The selections are from the magazine Liberty (New York) and cover virtually every aspect of Hitler's life. Most of the articles were written during the war and throw light on both Nazi lifestyles and western reactions thereto.

1548. Davidson, E.: The Making of Adolf Hitler: The Birth and Rise of Nazism [New York: Macmillan, 1978]

1549. Devaney, John: Hitler, Mad Dictator of World War II [New York: G. P. Putnam's Sons, 1978]

1550. Dolan, Edward F. Jr.: Adolf Hitler, a Portrait in Tyranny [New York: Dodd, Mead, and Co., 1981]

1551. Fest, Joachim C.: Hitler [New York: Harcourt, Brace & Jovanovich, 1974]

1552. Golfing, Francis: "What Manner of Man was Hitler?" Com, vol.15 #2 (Feb., 1953): 131-139.

1553. Haffner, Sebastian (E. Owens, transl.): The Meaning of Hitler: Hitler's Use of Power, His Successes and Failures [New York: Macmillan, 1979]

1554. Heiber, Helmut: Adolf Hitler: A Short Biography [London: Oswald Wolff, 1961]

1555. Heiden, Konrad (Winifred Ray, transl.): Der Fuehrer: Hitler's Rise to Power [Boston: Houghton Mifflin, 1969]

1556. ___: Hitler: A Biography [New York: AMS Press, 1975] Rep. 1936 Ed.

1557. Hoffman, H. (R. H. Stevens, transl.): Hitler Was My Friend [New York: AMS Press, 1979] Rep. 1955 Ed.

1558. Holden, M.: Hitler [New York: St. Martin's Press, 1975]

1559. Infield, Glen B.: Hitler´s Secret Life: The Mysteries of the Eagle´s Nest [New York: Stein and Day, 1979]

1560. Jacob, Walter: "Hitler and Christianity." J Sp, vol. 29 #8 (Oct., 1964): 19-23.

1561. Jaeger, Hugo and Albert Speer: "The Private World of Adolf Hitler." Life, vol.62 #14 (April 2, 1970): 45-58B.

1562. Jenks, William A.: Vienna and the Young Hitler [New York: Columbia Univ. Press, 1960]

1563. Jetzinger, Franz: Hitler´s Youth [Westport, CT: Greenwood Press, 1976] Rep. 1958 Ed.

1564. Jones, J. Dydney: Hitler in Vienna 1907-1913: Clues to the Future [New York: Stein and Day, 1983]

1565. Kater, M. H.: "Hitler in a Social Context." CEH, vol. 14 #3 (Sept., 1981): 243-272.

1566. Kellen, Konrad: "The Meaning of Hitler." Mid, vol.26 #8 (Oct., 1980): 48-54.

1567. Lande, Adolf (ed.): Chronology of Adolf Hitler´s Life [Washington, DC: Office of War Intelligence, 1944]

1568. Luethy, Herbert: "The Wretched Little Demon That Was Hitler: He Possessed the Mass Soul of the Third Reich." Com, vol.17 #2 (Feb., 1954): 129-138.

1569. Mann, H.: "Dictatorship of the Mind." F Affairs, vol. 12 #3 (April, 1934): 418-425.

1570. Maser, Werner: Hitler: Legend, Myth and Reality [New York: Harper & Row, 1973]

1571. Matanle, Ivor: Adolf Hitler: A Photographic Documentary [New York: Crescent Bks, 1983]

1572. Mckale, Donald M.: Hitler, the Survival Myth [New York: Stein and Day, 1980]

1573. McRandle, James H.: The Track of the Wolf: Essays on National Socialism and its Leader Adolf Hitler [Evanston, IL: Northwestern Univ. Press, 1965]

1574. Murphy, James: Adolf Hitler: The Drama of His Career [London: Chapman & Hall, 1934]

1575. Noakes, Jeremy: "Makers of the 20th Century: Hitler." History Today, vol.30 #7 (July, 1980): 22-27.

1576. O´Donnell, James P.: The Berlin Bunker [London: J. M. Dent & Sons, 1980]

1577. Olden, Rudolf (W. Ettinghausen, transl.): Hitler: The Pawn [New York: Covici-Friede, 1936]

1578. Payne, Robert: The Life and Death of Adolf Hitler [New York: F. A. Praeger, 1973]

1579. Picker, Henry et al (eds.): Hitler Close-Up [New York: Macmillan, 1973]

1580. Rubenstein, Joshua: Adolf Hitler [New York: Franklin Watts, 1982]

1581. Scheffer, Saul: "Hitler: Phenomenon and Portent." F Affairs, vol.10 #3 (April, 1932): 382-390.

1582. Schramm, Percy (D. S. Detwiler, transl.): Hitler: The Man and the Military Leader [Chicago: Watts, 1971]

1583. Shirer, W. L. The Rise and Fall of Adolf Hitler [New York: Random House, 1961]

1584. Smith, B. F.: Adolf Hitler: His Family, Childhood and Youth [Stanford, CA: Hoover Institute Press, 1967]

1585. Snodgrass, W. De Witt: The Fuehrer Bunker [Prockport, NY: Boa Editions, 1977]

1586. Steeh, Judith: The Rise and Fall of Adolf Hitler [New York: Galahad Books, 1980]

1587. Stein, George H. (ed.): Hitler [Englewood Cliffs, NJ: Prentice-Hall, 1968]

1588. Stierlin, Helm: Adolf Hitler: A Family Perspective [New York: Psychohistory Press, 1977]

1589. Stone, Norman: Hitler [London: Hodder and Stoughton, 1980]

1590. Strawson, J.: Hitler as Military Commander [Tuscon, AZ: Beachcomber Press, 1973]

1591. Suster, Gerald: Hitler, the Occult Messiah [New York: St. Martin´s Press, 1981]

1592. Toland, John: Adolf Hitler: The Pictorial Documentary of His Life [Garden City, NY: Doubleday, 1976]

1593. Trevor-Roper, Hugh R.: "Is Hitler Really Dead? A Historian Examines the Evidence." Com, vol.11 #2 (Feb., 1951): 120-130.

1594. ___: The Last Days of Hitler [New York: Macmillan, 1962]

Study of the circumstances surrounding Hitler´s death. Also gives a perceptive and interesting picture of the Nazi regime in its collapse. Originally written as a report for British intelligence.

1595. ___: "The ´Mystery´ of Hitler´s Death: The Facts Are Now In." Com, vol.22 #1 (July, 1956): 1-12.

1596. Turner, Henry A. (ed.) (R. Hein, transl.): Hitler: Memoirs of a Confidant [New Haven, CT: Yale Univ. Press, 1985]

1597. Varon, Benno W.: "Hitler - Anti-Jew, Anti-German." Mid, vol.26 #8 (Oct., 1980): 55-58.

1598. Waite, Robert G. L. (ed.): Hitler and Nazi Germany [New York: Holt, Rinehart and Winston, 1965.

1599. ___: "The Perpetrator: Hitler and the Holocaust." Ryan: Responses, pp.15-31.

1600. Waldman, M. D.: Sieg Heil! The Story of Adolf Hitler [Bobbs Ferry, NY: Oceana Pub., 1962]

1601. Wallach, Sidney: Hitler, Menace to Mankind [New York: Emerson Books, 1933]

1602. Wykes, Alan: Hitler [New York: Ballantine, 1976]

1603. Ziemer, Patzy: Two Thousand and Ten Days of Hitler [New York: Harper & Co., 1940]

Rudolf Hoess

1604. Field, Allan G.: "Criminals and Glory." J Sp, vol.25 #5 (May, 1960): 24, 26-27.

1605. Frankel, Theodore: "The Good German of Auschwitz." Mid, vol.6 #3 (Sum., 1960): 16-24.

1606. Hoess, Rudolf (C. FitzGibbon, transl.): Commandant of Auschwitz: The Autobiography of Rudolf Hoess [Cleveland, OH: World Book, 1960]

Memoir by the bloodiest of the Nazi hangmen, Rudolf Hoess, the Commandant of the Auschwitz death factory. Gives a unique picture of the psyche of Nazi war criminals.

1607. Poliakov, Leon: "Spiritual Automata." JM, vol.6 #2 (May, 1952): 90-99.

1608. Tenenbaum, Joseph: "Auschwitz in Retrospect: The Self Portrait of Rudolf Hoess, Commandant of Auschwitz." JSS, vol.15 #3/4 (July/Oct., 1953): 203-236.

1609. Werner, A.: "Self-Portrait of a Murderer." CBW, vol. 27 #6 (March 21, 1960): 15-17.

Carl Gustav Jung

1610. Haymond, Robert: "On Carl Gustav Jung: Psycho-Social Basis of Morality During the Nazi Era." JP/J, vol.6 #2 (Spr./Sum., 1982): 81-112.

1611. Kirsch, J.: "Carl Gustav Jung and the Jews: The Real Story." JP/J, vol.6 #2 (Spr./Sum., 1982): 113-143.

Ernst Kaltenbrunner

1612. Black, Peter R.: Ernst Kaltenbrunner: Ideological Soldier of the Third Reich [Princeton, NJ: Princeton Univ. Press, 1984]

Study of the life and thought of Reinhard Heydrich´s successor as chief of the RSHA upon the latter´s assassination in Prague. Argues in favor of the "Radical Evil" interpretation of Nazi psychology, as opposed to Hannah Arendt´s thesis about "the banality of evil". An extensively documented and valuable study.

Joseph Mengele

1613. Aziz, Philippe: "The Purveyor of Death." in P. Aziz: Joseph Mengele, the Evil Doctor pp.77-147 <see #3186>

1614. Lahola, A. "Angel of Death." J Sp, vol.29 #3 (March, 1964): 14-18.

1615. Lifton, Robert J: "What Made this Man? Mengele." NY Times Mag, (July 21, 1985): 16-25.

Franz von Papen

1616. Fischer, Alfred J.: "Papen the War Criminal." CEO, vol.22 #8 (April 27, 1945): 128-129.

1617. Koeves, Tibor: Satan in Top Hat: The Biography of Franz von Papen [New York: Alliance Book Corp., 1941]

Joachim von Ribbentrop

1618. Douglas-Hamilton, J.: "Ribbentrop and War." JCH, vol. 5 #4 (Oct., 1970): 45-64.

1619. Schwarz, Paul: This Man Ribbentrop: His Life and Times [New York: Julian Messner, 1943]

1620. Stern-Rubarth, Edgar: "Ribbentrop." Cont Rev, vol.157 #893 (May, 1940): 555-559.

1621. Straussman, Philip: "How Von Ribbentrop Repays His Jewish Friends." JVP, vol.4 #2/3 (March, 1941): 12, 22.

Alfred Rosenberg

1622. Cecil, Robert: The Myth of the Master Race: Alfred Rosenberg and Nazi Ideology [New York: Dodd, Mead, and Co., 1972]

1623. Chandler, Albert R.: Rosenberg´s Nazi Myth [Ithaca, NY: Cornell Univ. Press, 1945]

1624. Marinoff, I.: "Alfred Rosenberg." Cont Rev, vol.159 #902 (Feb., 1941): 184-189.

1625. Parry, A.: "Alfred Rosenberg: Hitler´s Jew-baiting Maniac." Mod Mon, vol.7 #9 (Sept., 1933): 461-467.

Hjalmar Schacht

1626. Peterson, Edward N.: Hjalmar Schacht For and Against Hitler: A Political-Economic Study of Germany, 1923-1945 [Boston: Christopher Pub. House, 1954]

1627. Werner, A.: "The Irrepressible Herr Schacht: Hitler´s Adviser Stages a Comeback." Com, vol.8 #1 (July, 1949): 58-61.

1628. ___: "Schacht Has One Plan and Seven Lives." J Fo, vol.33 #6 (June, 1950): 103-105, 110.

1629. ___: "Schacht, Merchant of Evil." CW, vol.20 #1 (Jan. 5, 1953): 5-7.

Albert Speer

1630. Dawidowicz, Lucy S.: "In Hitler´s Service: Albert Speer." Dawidowicz: Presence, pp.225-237.

1631. Hux, Samuel: "Nazi Albert Speer: Model of Culture and Morality?" Moment, vol.8 #8 (Sept., 1983): 53-58.

1632. Schmidt, Matthias: Albert Speer: The End of a Myth [New York: St. Martin´s Press, 1985]

1633. Werner, Alfred: "Devil´s Architect." Am Zionist, vol. 61 #4 (Dec., 1970): 10-13.

Franz Stangl

1634. Dawidowicz, L. S.: "An Obedient Killer: Franz Stangl, Commandant of Treblinka." Dawidowicz: Presence, pp. 238-246.

Julius Streicher

1635. Bondy, Louis: Racketeers of Hatred: Julius Streicher and the Jew-Baiters International [London: Newman, Wolsey, 1946]

1636. Bytwerk, Randall T.: Julius Streicher [New York: Stein and Day, 1983]

1637. ___: "Streicher and the Impact of Der Sturmer." WLB, vol.29 #2 (1976): 41-46.

1638. Riess, C.: "Streicher: Nazi Degenerate." Am Mercury, vol.56 #231 (March, 1943): 281-288.

Other Nazis

1639. Batty, Peter: The House of Krupp [New York: Stein and Day, 1967]

1640. Brett-Smith, Richard: Hitler's Generals [San Rafael, CA: Presidio Press, 1977]

1641. Cargill, M.: A Gallery of Nazis [Secaucus, NJ: Lyle Stuart, 1978]

1642. Dutch, Oswald (ed.): Hitler's Twelve Apostles [New York: Arno Press, 1940]

1643. Ericksen, Robert: "Theologian in the Third Reich: The Case of Gerhard Kittel." JCH, vol.12 #3 (July, 1977): 595-622.

1644. ___: Theologians Under Hitler: Gerhard Kittel, Paul Althaus and Emmanuel Hirsch [New Haven, CT: Yale Univ. Press, 1985]

1645. Fenton, Edwin and John Goode: "Seven Case Studies." Chartock: Society, pp.111-116.

1646. Fest, Joachim C. (M. Bullock, transl.) : The Face of the Third Reich: Portraits of the Nazi Leadership [New York: Pantheon Books, 1970]

Biographical survey of the Third Reich's leaders and bureaucrats. Not only retells the lives of Nazi leaders, but also gives a psychological and social explanation of their actions. Shows clearly the nature of the "totalitarian personality". Main emphasis is on the person and psyche of Hitler.

1647. Foley, Charles: Commando Extraordinary [New York: G. P. Putnam's Sons, 1955]

Biography of SS Colonel Otto Skorzeny, Hitler's favorite commando. Details the rise and fall of Skorzeny as a parallel to the decline of Germany in 1943-1945. Does not, however, deal with the issue of war crimes except as they relate to Skorzeny's unorthodox military operations.

1648. Friedlander, Henry: "The Perpetrators." Grobman: Genocide, pp.155-158.

1649. Grossmann, Kurt R.: "The Career of Otto Strasser." J Fr, vol.16 #6 (June, 1949): 20-25.

1650. Hart, W. E.: Hitler's Generals [New York: Arno Press, 1976] Rep. 1944 Ed.

1651. "Hermann Esser: Nazi with a Vengeance." WLB, vol.9 #5/6 (Sept./Dec., 1955): 50-51.

1652. Humble, Richard: Hitler's Generals [Garden City, NY: Doubleday, 1974]

1653. Infield, Glen: Skorzeny: Hitler's Commando [New York: St. Martin's Press, 1981]

1654. Katz, William L.: An Album of Nazism [New York: Franklin Watts, 1979]

1655. Keitel, Wilhelm and W. Gorlitz (D. Irving, transl.): In the Service of the Reich [New York: Stein and Day, 1979]

1656. Lennhoff, Eugene: Agents of Hell [London: Hutchinson, 1940]

1657. Neuman, Peter: The Black March: The Personal Story of an SS-Man [New York: Bantam Books, 1958]

1658. Norden, Albert: "Nazi Princes are War Criminals Too." FW, vol.10 #5 (Nov., 1945): 38-40.

1659. Reitlinger, Gerald: "The Doubts of Wilhelm Kube." WLB, vol.4 #5/6 (Sept./Nov., 1950): 33; vol.5 #1/2 (Jan./March, 1951): 8.

1660. Schellenberg, W. (L. Hagen, transl.): The Labyrinth [New York: Harper & Bros., 1956] Also published as: The Schellenberg Memoirs [London: Deutsch, 1956]

Memoir by the man who was chief of the SD after the assassination of Reinhard Heydrich. Involved with the SD from its beginnings Schellenberg was clearly Nazi Germany's chief spy. His memoirs give an intimate, insider's portrait of life in Nazi Germany.

1661. Strasser, Otto (G. David, transl.): Hitler and I [New York: AMS Press, 1979] Rep. 1940 Ed.

1662. ___ and Michael Stern: Flight From Terror [New York: R. M. McBride, 1943]

1663. Turner, Henry A. Jr.: "Emil Kirdorf and the Nazi Party." CEH, vol.1 #4 (Dec., 1968): 324-344.

1664. Werner, Alfred: "The Case of Veit Harlan." J Fr, vol. 18 #5 (May, 1951): 23-26.

1665. ___: "Knut Hamsun Versus Society." J Fr, vol.19 #3 (March, 1952): 24-27.

1666. Wistrich, R.: Who´s Who in Nazi Germany [New York: Bonanza Books, 1984]

1667. Zohn, H.: "The Case of Gerhart Hauptmann." J Sp, vol. 38 #8 (Oct., 1973): 22-25.

PSYCHOLOGICAL STUDIES

1668. Adler, Hans: "Berlin Apartment House: Clinical Notes on the Average German Mind." Com, vol.1 #7 (May, 1946): 54-56.

1669. Adorno, Theodor W. et al: The Authoritarian Personality [New York: Harper/Am. Jewish Comm., 1950]

1670. Alexander, Leo: "War Crimes and Their Motivation. The Socio-Psychological Structure of the SS and the Criminalization of a Society." Jnl/Crim Law/Criminology, vol.39 #3 (Sept./Oct., 1948): 298-326.

1671. ___: "War Crimes Their Social-Psychological Aspects." Am Jnl Psych, vol.105 #3 (Sept., 1948): 170-177.

1672. Bach, Julian Jr.: "Death of a Killer: Case History of the Nazi Mind." Com, vol.2 #4 (Oct., 1946): 317-319.

1673. Barnett, J.: "The Original Fascist Beast." WJ, vol.16 #2 (April, 1973): 13-16.

1674. Beradt, Charlote (A. Gottwald, transl.): The Third Reich of Dreams [Chicago: Quadrangle Books, 1968]

1675. Borofsky, G. L. and D. J. Brand: "Personality Organization and Psychological Functioning of the Nuremberg War Criminals: The Rorschach Data." Dimsdale: Survivors, pp.359-403.

1676. Bulka, R. P.: "Psychoanalyzing the Nazis." Tradition, vol.19 #2 (Sum., 1981): 171-181.

1677. Chakotin, Serge: The Rape of the Masses: The Psychology of Totalitarian Political Propaganda [New York: Haskell House, 1976]

1678. de Saussure, Raymond: "The Collective Neurosis of Germany." FW, vol.5 #2 (Feb., 1943): 121-126.

1679. ___: "Psychopathology of Adolf Hitler." FW, vol.3 #1 (June, 1942): 31-35.

1680. Dicks, Henry V.: Licensed Mass Murder: A Socio-Psychological Study of Some SS Killers [New York: Basic Books, 1972]

1681. Doblin, Ernest and Claire Pohly: "The Social Composition of the Nazi Leadership." Am Jnl Soc, vol.51 #1 (July, 1945): 42-49.

1682. Douglas, Donald M.: "The Parent Cell: Some Computer Notes on the Composition of the First Nazi Party Group in Munich, 1919-1921." CEH, vol.10 #1 (March, 1977): 55-72.

1683. Ebon, Martin: "Why Did Hitler Hate the Jews?" Mid, vol.25 #8 (Oct., 1979): 19-24.

1684. Gilbert, Gustave M.: "The Mentality of the SS Murderous Robots." YVS, vol.5 (1961): 35-42.

1685. ___: The Psychology of Dictatorship [New York: Ronald Press, 1950]

1686. Glazer, Nathan: "The Authoritarian Personality in Profile: Report on a Major Study of Race Hatred." Com, vol.9 #6 (June, 1950): 573-583.

1687. ___: "New Light on 'The Authoritarian Personality': A Survey of Recent Research and Criticism." Com, vol. 17 #3 (March, 1954): 289-297.

1688. Greenberg, Martin: "The Common Man and the Nazis: The Adversary that 'Anti-Fascism' Failed to See." Com, vol.2 #6 (Dec., 1946): 501-505.

1689. Haffner, Sebastian: The Meaning of Hitler [New York: Macmillan, 1980]

1690. Harrower, M.: "Were Hitler's Henchmen Mad?" Chartock: Society, pp.199-201.

1691. Hurwitz, S. J.: "Diagnosing the German Malady: The Events that Led Up to the Crime." Com, vol.4 #2 (Aug., 1947): 178-186.

1692. Kandel, Isaac L.: The Making of Nazis [Westport, CT: Greenwood Press, 1970] Rep. 1935 Ed.

1693. Kanter, Isaac: "The Psychopathology of Nazism." Am OSE Rev, vol.5 #3/4 (Sum./Fall, 1948): 15-19.

1694. Kater, Michael H.: The Nazi Party: A Social Profile of Members and Leaders, 1919-1945 [Cambridge, MA: Harvard Univ. Press, 1983]

1695. Klein, Mina C. and H. A. Klein: Hitler's Hangups [New York: E. P. Dutton, 1977]

1696. Koenigsberg, Richard A.: Hitler's Ideology: A Study in Psychoanalytic Sociology [New York: Library of Social Sciences, 1975]

1697. Kristol, Irving: "What the Nazi Autopsies Show: The Totalitarian Myth and the Nihilist Reality." Com, vol.6 #3 (Sept., 1948): 271-282.

1698. Kurth, G. M.: "The Complex Behind Hitler's Antisemitism: A Psychoanalytic Study in History." Com, vol.5 #1 (Jan., 1948): 77-82.

1699. Langer, Walter C.: The Hitler Source-Book: The Mind of Adolf Hitler [New York: Signet Books, 1972]

Psycho-biography of Hitler written by an eminent American psychologist. Originally published in 1943 as a report for the OSS. A useful contemporary document, especially for its interpretation of the role of Hitler's psyche in the Nazi regime.

1700. Lerner, D.: The Nazi Elite [Stanford, CA: Stanford Univ. Press, 1951]

1701. Lewis, Wyndham: Hitler Cult [New York: Gordon Press, 1972]

1702. Loewenberg, Peter: "The Psychohistorical Origins of the Nazi Youth Cohort." AHR, vol.76 #4 (Dec., 1971): 1457-1502.

1703. ___: "The Unsuccessful Adolescence of Heinrich Himmler." AHR, vol.76 #3 (June, 1971): 612-641.

1704. Madden, Paul: "Some Social Characteristics of Early Nazi Party Members 1919-1923." CEH, vol.15 #1 (March, 1982): 34-56.

1705. Miale, Florence and Michael Selzer: The Nuremberg Mind: The Psychology of the Nazi Leaders [Chicago: Quadrangle Books, 1975]

Attempts a psycho-biography of seventeen key Nazi figures. The text is based on the Rorschach Tests given to captured Nazis by the Allied Military Governments. The authors use the tests to argue against the school of thought that sees the Nazis as banal. Instead, they view the Nazis as diabolical sadists who suffered from inferiority and other complexes. Interesting but of little value to the layman.

1706. Milgram, Stanley: "The Compulsion to Do Evil. Obedience to Criminal Orders." PoP, vol.1 #6 (Nov./Dec., 1967): 3-7.

1707. ___: Obedience to Authority: An Experimental View [New York: Harper & Row, 1974]

1708. Muehlberger, Detlef: "The Sociology of the NSDAP: The Question of Working-Class Membership." JCH, vol.15 #3 (July, 1980): 493-512.

1709. Poliakov, Leon: "The Mind of the Mass Murderer: The Nazi Executioners - and Those Who Stood By." Com, vol.12 #5 (Nov., 1951): 451-459.

1710. Rubin, Gerald: The Evil that Men Do: The Story of the Nazis [New York: J. Messner, 1977]

1711. Sabini, J. P. and M. Silver: "Destroying the Innocent with a Clear Conscience: A Sociopsychology of the Holocaust." Dimsdale: Survivors, pp.329-358.

1712. Salomon, Albert: "The Historical German and the Perennial Nazi." J Fr, vol.10 #2 (Feb., 1943): 18-22.

1713. Steiner, John: "The SS Yesterday and Today: A Socio-Psychological View." Dimsdale: Survivors, pp.405-456.

1714. Viereck, Peter R. E.: Meta-Politik: The Roots of the Nazi Mind [New York: G. P. Putnam´s Sons, 1961]

1715. Waite, Robert G. L.: The Psychopathic God [New York: Basic Books, 1977] * On Hitler.

1716. Werner, Alfred: "German Education in the New World Order." Ch J Forum, vol.3 #4 (Sum., 1945): 235-342.

1717. ___: "Goebbels´ Jew-Complex." Ch J Forum, vol.7 #2 (Win., 1948/49): 117-121.

1718. Wulff, Wilhelm: Zodiac and Swastika: How Astrology Guided Hitler´s Germany [New York: Coward, McCann & Geoghean, 1973]

WORKS BY NAZIS

1719. Allen, William S. (ed. and transl.): The Infancy of Nazism: The Memoirs of Ex-Gauleiter Albert Krebs, 1923-1933 [New York: New Viewpoints, 1976]

1720. Angress, W. T. and B. F. Smith: "Diaries of Heinrich Himmler´s Early Years." JMH, vol.31 #3 (Sept., 1959): 206-224.

1721. Baynes, N. H. (ed.): The Speeches of Adolf Hitler, April 1922-August 1939 2 vols. [New York: Arno Press, 1969] Rep. 1942 Ed.

1722. Beard, Miriam: "Hitler Unexpurgated: Deletions from ´Mein Kampf´." PVP: Nazism, pp.257-279.

1723. Bramsted, E.: "What Goebbels Left Out: Some Significant Omissions in his Wartime Books." WLB, vol.9 #1/2 (Jan./April, 1955): 9, 15; #3/4 (May/Aug., 1955): 30, 34.

1724. Brennecke, Fritz (H. Childs, transl.): Nazi Primer: Official Handbook for Schooling the Hitler Youth [New York: AMS Press, 1972] Rep. 1938 Ed.

1725. Caspar, C.: "Mein Kampf - A Best Seller." JSS, vol.20 #1 (Jan., 1958): 3-16.

1726. Chernyshev, I.: "Murder, Inc." Am Heb, vol.153 #20 (March 17, 1944): 12-13. * Excerpts from a diary of a Nazi soldier.

1727. Coole, W. W. and M. F. Potter (eds.): Thus Speaks Germany [New York: Harper & Bros, 1941]

1728. "Document: Dr. Goebbels on the Jewish Question." J Rev, #6 (Sept./Dec., 1933): 102-104.

1729. "The Documents of Hitler´s Shame." Cur J Rec, vol.2 #2 (Feb., 1932): 33-37.

1730. Eberling, Julius: "I Was Stationed in Poland. From a Diary of a Wehrmacht Officer." Poland, #8/109 (1963): 30-31.

1731. Ensor, R. C.: "Mein Kampf and Europe." Int Affairs, vol.18 #4 (July/Aug., 1939): 478-496.

1732. "From the Diary of Professor Kremer." Poland, #1/125 (Jan., 1965): 18.

1733. "The Goebbels Diaries." Life, vol.24 #13 (March 29, 1948): 118-139.

1734. Goebbels, Josef: "Communism with the Mask Off." Fasc Q, vol.2 (1936): 167-183.

1735. ___ (H. Heiber, ed.): The Early Goebbels Diaries: The Journal of Josef Goebbels from 1925-1926 [New York: F. A. Praeger, 1962]

1736. ___: "What is Socialism?" Fasc Q, vol.1 #3 (July, 1935): 273-275.

1737. Goering, Hermann (H. Blood-Ryan, transl.): The Political Testament of Hermann Goering [New York: AMS Press, 1979] Rep. 1939 Ed.

1738. Goerlitz, Walter (ed.) (David Irving, transl.): The Memoirs of Field Marshal Keitel [New York: Stein and Day, 1966]

1739. Gritzbach, Erich (Gerald Griffin, transl.): Hermann Goering: The Man and His Work [New York: AMS Press, 1979] Rep. 1939 Ed.

1740. Hail, Hitler! The Nazi Speaks to the World [London: Christophers, 1934]

1741. Hitler, Adolf: "About the Jew." Chartock: Society, pp.130-131.

1742. ___ (Ralph Manheim, transl.): Mein Kampf [Boston: Houghton Mifflin, 1943]

1743. ___ (Raoul de Roussyde Sales, ed.): My New Order [New York: Octagon Books, 1973]

1744. Kremer, Hans H.: "From a Doctor's Diary." Chartock: Society, pp.146-147.

1745. Laing, Stuart: The Illustrated Hitler Diary 1917-1945 [New York: Galahad Books, 1980]

1746. Ley, Robert: "Strength Through Joy." Fasc Q, vol.2 (1936): 208-222.

1747. Lochner, Louis P. (ed.): The Goebbels Diaries, 1942-1943 [Garden City, NY: Doubleday, 1948]

1748. Ludecke, Kurt W.: I Knew Hitler: The Story of a Nazi who Escaped the Blood Purge [New York: Scribner's, 1937]

1749. Maser, W. (A. Pomerance, transl.): Hitler's Letters and Notes [New York: Harper & Row, 1974]

1750. ___ (R. H. Barry, transl.): Hitler's Mein Kampf: An Analysis [London: Faber, 1970]

1751. Moeller Van Den Bruck, Arthur (E. O. Lorimer, ed.): Germany's Third Empire [London: George Allen & Unwin, 1934]

1752. Piotrowski, Stanislaw (ed.): Hans Frank's Diary [Warsaw: Panstwowe Wydawnictwo Naukowe, 1961]

Documentation of Nazi war crimes in Poland, based on the personal archive (which he called his Diary) of Hans Frank, Governor General. Also includes a general review by the editor, a Polish lawyer. An important primary source vital to any study on Nazi policies in Poland.

1753. Rauschning, Hermann: The Voice of Destruction [New York: G.P. Putnam´s Sons, 1940]

1754. Reventlow, (Count) Ernest zu: "The Case for Antisemitism." Living Age, vol.344 (July, 1933): 426-430.

1755. Rosenberg, Alfred (Eric Posselt, transl.): Memoirs [Chicago: Ziff-Davis, 1949]

1756. ___ (Robert Pois, ed.) (J. Cape, transl.): Race and Race History and Other Essays [New York: Harper & Row, 1970]

1757. ___: "World Philosophy and Foreign Politics." Fasc Q, vol.1 #2 (April, 1935): 156-168.

1758. Santoro, Cesare: Hitler Germany as seen by a Foreigner [Berlin: Internationaler Verlag, 1938]

Pro-Nazi anatomy of the new German state. Covers every aspect of Nazism in great detail, and provides a different perspective on Nazi Germany.

1759. Schacht, Hjalmar: Account Settled [London: Weidenfeld and Nicolson, 1949]

1760. ___ (D. Pyke, transl.): Confessions of the Old Wizard [Boston: Houghton Mifflin, 1955]

1761. Sieburg, F. (W. Ray, transl.): Germany: My Country [London: J. Cape, 1933]

1762. Silfen, Paul H.: The Volkisch Ideology and the Roots of Nazism: The Early Writings of Arthur Moeller van den Bruck [Hicksville, NY: Exposition Press, 1973]

1763. Sinder, Henri: "Robert Ley´s Political Testament." CW, vol.12 #33 (Nov. 16, 1945): 8-10.

1764. Speer, Albert (R. and C. Winston, transls.): Inside the Third Reich: Memoirs [New York: Macmillan, 1970]

Highly controversial memoir by the chief Nazi architect. Speer downplays his role in National Socialism, especially in the Final Solution, to portray himself as an innocent man. Has almost no value as a historical document.

1765. ___ (Richard and Clara Winston, transls.): Spandau: The Secret Diaries [New York: Macmillan, 1976]

1766. Spengler, Oswald (Ch. F Atkinson, transl.): The Hour of Decision [New York: AMS Press, 1979] Rep. 1934 Ed.

1767. Staudinger, H. (P. M. Rutkoff and Wm. Scott, (eds): The Inner Nazi: A Critical Analysis of ´Mein Kampf´ [Baton Rouge, LA: Louisiana State Univ. Press, 1981]

1768. Strachey, Celia and John G. Werner (eds.): Fascist Germany Explains [New York: Covici Friede, 1934] * A Brief Anthology of Nazi statements.

1769. Taylor, F. (ed. and transl.): The Goebbels Diaries, 1939-1941 [New York: G. P. Putnam´s Sons, 1983]

1770. Trevor-Roper, Hugh R. (ed.): Final Entries 1945: The Diaries of Josef Goebbels [New York: Avon Books, 1978]

1771. ___ (ed.): The Goebbels Diaries [New York: G. P. Putnam´s Sons, 1978]

1772. von Hassell, Ulrich: The von Hassell Diaries, 1938-1944 [New York: AMS Press, 1979] Rep. 1947 Ed.

1773. von Papen, Franz (B. Connell, transl.): Memoirs [New York: AMS Press, 1979] Rep. 1953 Ed.

1774. von Ribbentrop, Joachim et al: Germany Speaks [New York: AMS Press, 1979] Rep. 1938 Ed.

1775. von Schirach, B. (R. Birch, transl.): "Young Germany Today." Fasc Q, vol.1 #4 (Oct., 1935): 410-21.

1776. von Weizsaecker, E. (J. Andrews, transl.): Memoirs of Ernst von Weizsaecker [London: Victor Gollancz, 1951]

1777. Warlimont, W. (R. H. Barry, transl.): Inside Hitler´s Headquarters, 1939-1945 [New York: F. A. Praeger, 1964]

PART III

The Crucible

Introduction

The Final Solution to the Jewish Problem was a well-organized, minutely planned, carefully executed campaign. Its sole purpose was Ausmerzung - complete eradication. Adolf Hitler stated in Mein Kampf: "Had 12,000 to 15,000 Hebrew enemies been gassed at the beginning of and during the First World War, the sacrifices of millions at the front would not have been in vain." Nazi policy, aimed at this goal, was carried out in four phases: incubation, formulation, preparation, and execution. Each phase set the stage for the next one, and successive phases presupposed those previously implemented.

PHASE I: INCUBATION

The incubation phase ran roughly from the Nazi accession to power in mid-January 1933 to September 1935. During this time German Jewry was besieged and, by and large, turned into a "leprous community" with which gentiles had no contact. Anti-Jewish violence was a sporadic and random affair, the level of violence varying according to place and time. The Nazi takeover immediately resulted in an increase of violence directed at Jews by the Sturmabteilungen, the brown-shirted SA. During this period, however, world opinion still carried some weight. Because responsible leaders found the anti-Jewish acts unacceptable, they were ended. Hitler did not, moreover, feel that attacks on single Jews really helped the cause. He sought a more inclusive and definitive solution. A general boycott of Jewish businesses began on April 1, 1933, under the auspices of Julius Streicher. Armed guards of the SA and SS posted at Jewish shops carried out orders to keep out all aryan customers, by whatever means. Jewish property was steadily aryanized while the country was rapidly nazified. Jews were removed from positions in the civil service and the army. The Nazis drummed poisonous antisemitic propaganda into the German citizenry to mark and isolate the Jewish community. To cement further the aryan culture of the state, the Nazis undertook a thorough purge of German-Jewish and anti-Nazi books, which culminated in a mass bonfire on May 10, 1933.

PHASE II: FORMULATION

The second phase, formulation, began with the Nuremberg party rallies in September 1935 and ended with the outbreak of war in 1939. The Nazi party rallies in Nuremberg were the occasion for the promulgation of a series of racial laws commonly known as the Nuremberg Laws. The statutes included clear racial definitions of who was a Jew, who was a German, and who belonged to the intermediate category of Mischlinge, persons of mixed ancestry. This Reich Law on Citizenship also defined the Reichsburger, citizens with full political rights, only Germans of pure blood, and the Staatsangehoeriger, subjects of the Reich, to which German Jewry was now reduced. The entire emancipation was undone. The Law for the Protection of German Blood and Honor was directed to the conservation of the purity of German blood. It made intermarriage a legal offense and created a new category of criminality for Nazi legal experts to ponder - Rassenschande (racial defilement). German Jewry was now thoroughly isolated, its economy almost completely aryanized.

The Nazis initiated similar measures upon their takeover in Austria on March 12, 1938, as well as during the occupation of Czechoslovakia as of March 16, 1939. Austrian Nazis greeted the Anschluss with anti-Jewish violence, especially in Vienna, where they forced Jews to scrub the streets with their bare hands. Upon the dismembering of Czechoslovakia, a similar fate befell Prague Jewry. The Nuremberg Laws placed all Jews outside the law: No Jew, therefore, would have any recourse within the established legal system, no matter what was done to him.

The Nazis at this time sought a solution to the Jewish problem through mass emigration. To facilitate the exodus a special emigration office was established within the Gestapo. Its head, Adolf Eichmann, used a carrot-and-stick approach to force Jews to leave. Despite all the difficulties in gaining admission to safe havens, some 315,000 Jews managed to escape the Grossreich (Greater Germany) before the outbreak of the war. Slightly less than half of those who left managed to enter Palestine, despite British demurral. The Yishuv, the Jewish community in Palestine, took in a large number of young people through its Youth Aliyah program. Another 60,000 immigrants entered Palestine under the _Haavara_, or transfer agreement. In August 1933 German Jewry was able to reach an agreement with the Gestapo, whereby any Jew who left Germany for Palestine would place a percentage of his capital into an account with the Palestine Jewish Trust Company (PALTREU). Upon his arrival in Palestine the immigrant received the equivalent of his deposit in German goods or services. The _Haavara_ agreement officially remained in existence until September 1939, although as Jews became more desperate to leave Germany, the Nazis allowed a smaller percentage of Jewish money to leave the country. Many Jewish organizations in both the United States and Europe opposed the agreement because the American Jewish Congress had declared a worldwide Jewish boycott of German goods in August 1934. They feared that the transfer of German goods to Jewish Palestine would undercut the boycott and render it worthless. These conflicting approaches to the Nazis were taken to the World Zionist Congress (WZC) in 1935. Approving the _Haavara_ by a wide majority, the WZC placed the deal under stricter national control by the Va´ad Leumi, which was, in effect, the sovereign government of the Yishuv. The _Haavara_´s single greatest contribution was the timely removal of some Jews and part of their capital from Nazi Germany.

Soon after the Nazi takeover, under the slogan "Wear the yellow badge with pride," members of almost all the factions of German Jewry united into a representative body comprising Zionists and non-Zionists, orthodox as well as assimilationists. Under the aegis of scholars such as Martin Buber, they formed a Kulturbund and attempted to reconstruct their lives by establishing Jewish cultural and social circles. "Say yes to our Judaism" became another battle cry. There were, however, still those who endeavored to remain "German" above all and who, under all circumstances, tried to accommodate the Nazis.

The Munich Agreement surrendering Czechoslovakia signaled to Hitler that England and France would not confront him. Munich was not, however, fated to bring peace. The Nazi´s territorial quest now turned toward the city of Danzig and the "Polish corridor," which they considered to be part of Greater German Pomerania. Germany had long sought _Lebensraum_ (living space) in the east. The Nazis added racial and messianic overtones to this expansionist ideology. Danzig and the Polish corridor was to be Germany´s final demand. Peace could still be maintained, Hitler declared, if only

Britain and France would cooperate. This time they refused: Prime Minister Neville Chamberlain was now, belatedly, ready to confront the Nazis. Previously, when Hitler publicly announced remilitarization and when Germany reoccupied the Saar and Rhineland, Britain and France had allowed the Nazis to do as they pleased. This time they felt that Hitler had gone too far. Both Britain and France pledged assistance to Poland if independence was threatened.

KRISTALLNACHT

The expansion of Germany's territory through bloodless conquests heightened Nazi hopes for a full solution to the Jewish question. They accelerated forced emigration and simply dumped thousands of East European Jews at border points between Germany and Poland. One case included some 17,000 former Polish Jews who were stripped of German citizenship and dumped on the Polish border at Zbaszyn on October 28, 1938. Not permitted to enter Polish territory, they endured harsh conditions, barely existing in the no man's land between the two states. Herschel Grynszpan, the son of one of the unfortunates, reacted by assassinating one of the German consular secretaries in Paris, Ernst von Rath.

Twenty-four hours later came the Nazi revenge - pogroms throughout Germany. That night, November 9 and 10, 1938, has become known as *Kristallnacht*, the Night of the Broken Glass. This night marked the beginning of further radicalization and violence, although the pogroms had actually been planned well in advance; the Nazis used the initial attack as a conveniently timed pretext. Following *Kristallnacht*, the Nazis rounded up perhaps as many as 30,000 German Jews and incarcerated them in various concentration camps. In addition, Reichsmarschal Hermann Goering saw fit to levy a collective fine on German Jewry of one billion Reichsmark to cover insurance company expenses for the Nazi destruction of Jewish property.

WORLD WAR II AND THE NEW ORDER

By dawn on September 1, 1939, the outlines of a more radical solution were becoming visible. Having secured a nonaggression treaty with the Soviet Union (the Ribbentrop-Molotov Pact, August 23, 1939), much to the surprise of the Western powers, Hitler now felt confident that he could pursue his blitz on Poland with impunity. The blitzkrieg soon enabled Germany to occupy most of Europe. Germany established an empire that stretched from the Atlantic to the fringes of the Black Sea.

Almost immediately the Nazis began to establish their New Order. In each country they introduced Nazi legislation and administration. However, according to Nazi dogma and interests, not every country or territory was to be treated in the same way. Western countries, such as Denmark, Norway, Belgium, and Holland, were to be treated kindly and eventually converted to the Nazi philosophy. The Nazis encouraged collaboration and fraternization and aimed to crush resistance to the regime, but with only the minimum force necessary. The same principle, to a degree, applied in occupied France, although resistance there would be treated more brutally. A nazified France that was not associated with German territorial aims (except for the reannexed territories of Alsace and Lorraine), could become a useful ally, and the Nazis made all efforts to encourage this development. They left southern France unoccupied (until November 1942) under the collaborationist government (Vichy) of Marshal Henri Petain and Pierre Laval.

In Czechoslovakia the same principle was applied: collaborationists were encouraged, resisters discouraged. To make such a policy feasible, Hitler divided Czechoslovakia into two parts: the Reichsprotektorat of Bohemia and Moravia, incorporated into the Grossreich, and the independent Slovakian republic, a thinly disguised puppet regime with only limited authority.

He implemented similar policies in Yugoslavia, exploiting ethnic rivalries between Croats and Serbs to cement Axis rule and weaken potential resistance. The Croat minority was granted self-determination in the guise of a puppet republic led by Ante Pavelic, whose Ustasa, the Fascist militia, was the principal perpetrator of all the crimes committed there, both against the Jews of Yugoslavia and others.

In every country collaborationists arose. These can be classified into three types: opportunists, who saw the Nazis as a vehicle for gaining power; ideologues, largely Fascist or quasi-Fascist parties; and ad hoc collaborators, the common folk, especially shopkeepers, who had little alternative but to accept the reality and do business with the Germans. The latter were usually the least committed to collaboration and the first to switch allegiance when the tide of war turned.

The collaborators moved by opportunism and ideology were largely one and the same. Men like Vidkun Quisling (Norway), Joseph Darnand (France), and Anton Mussert (Holland) and their associated parties saw fascism as the only solution to the problems of Europe. Working with Nazi Germany, especially in the anti-Bolshevik crusade, seemed to them the only way to save their countries. Many of these men ended up in the non-German volunteer legions of the Waffen-SS, which fought on the eastern front. The opportunists also included such men as Marshal Petain, the president of Vichy, and General Andrei Vlasov, a Russian renegade who threw in his lot with the Nazis, as well as thousands of anonymous Dutch, Latvians, Lithuanians, Ukrainians, Estonians, Cossacks, and others. We will probably never fully penetrate the psyche of the collaborators, who believed that nazism was the only way to save Europe. They were what we might term patriotic traitors, helping the enemy for what seemed to them to be the greater good of the nation.

A different fate awaited the Slavic countries, particularly the Poles and the Russians. Although the Nazis would allow some collaboration, their policy was not only to crush all resistance but also to reduce these Slavic groups to a state of abject slavery through the appropriation of property and cultural and political genocide. The Slavs were to lose their national and cultural identity, their political independence, and even their personal self-respect to become slaves for the master race - "two-legged cattle," in Reinhard Heydrich´s terminology. This, in turn, was to provide Germany with Lebensraum to expand its population to the fullest. In this manner the dream of the One-Thousand-Year Reich stretching from the foothills of the Urals to the Atlantic would be realized. The policy also would provide cheap labor and plentiful food for the Reich, which would insure Germany´s security in the future utopian era. Even the Slavs´ children could be taken from them. Under the concept of Lebensborn, Nazis could kidnap children younger than nine years old who possessed aryan features and, in fact, send them to special orphan´s homes to be brought up in the way of the Hitler Jugend.

PHASE III: PREPARATION

Formulation gave way to preparation, the third phase of the Final Solution. During the period between the occupation of Poland (September 1, 1939) and the invasion of Russia (June 22, 1941), Jews were systematically marked and registered, completely isolated, and hermetically sealed off from the rest of the world. But for what purpose?

At first the Nazis thought of exiling the Jews to the Island of Madagascar, to be kept there as prisoners under Nazi external administration. The Poles had proposed a similar plan in the mid-1930s, but the French had wanted no part of it. The Nazis faced no such problem because they controlled the French government. Even so, the plan fell through, obstensibly because of lack of adequate shipping to transport masses of Jews to Africa.

Another phantom solution was the so-called Lublin Reservation, a plot of land set aside in the Lublin-Nisko region of southeastern Poland. Jews from the Grossreich were to resettle there in similar fashion to American Indians on reservations. Many thousands of Jews were actually shipped to the region, only to find that no preparations had been made for them. Thousands died during the bitter cold of the winter of 1939-1940. Thereafter the effort lapsed, apparently because of lack of interest and difficulties in obtaining sufficient transport. By this time, furthermore, a more radical solution made all talk of resettlement moot.

The Jews saw this phase of the Nazi assault as a new challenge. Virtually all of European Jewry was joined under the heel of Nazi oppression. The Nazis had thoroughly reorganized Jewish life to fit their own ideology, plans, and needs. Thus began the process of deassimilation, the reversal of the previous century of European Jewish history.

In Poland, the Nazis incarcerated the Jews in ghettos. Some of the ghettos of the large cities were sealed with walls, barbed wire, and guard posts. Jews lived in appalling conditions in these closed ghettos. In Warsaw nearly half a million Jews resided in an area adequate for less than 100,000; similar conditions existed in Lodz, Cracow, Tarnow, and Lublin. The Nazis also redesignated some of the smaller communities as ghettos, although the Jews often remained in their homes without being, for the while, relocated. Living conditions were perhaps slightly better in the open ghettos. These were but temporary havens, however, because the open ghettos were the first to undergo Aussiedlung (deportation).

Even at this stage the Nazis sought a "natural" solution to the Jewish problem. Rations for Jews were barely 20 percent of the minimum daily nutritional requirements. Jews were denied even the most basic medicines, and sanitary conditions in the ghettos were inadequate. It is no wonder that epidemics took their ghastly toll. Nearly 100,000 Jews, 20 percent of the Jewish population in Warsaw, perished in that city during the winter of 1940-1941. The numbers were similar in other locations. In both open and closed ghettos Jews were systematically starved and worked to death.

Despite the obstacles, however, the Jews did not surrender their human dignity. They opened soup kitchens to feed the hungry and maintained clandestine schools, synagogues, and cultural activities to feed Jewish souls. The prewar Jewish political parties continued to operate in the underground, publishing a secret Jewish press and preparing the young members for the day of battle. In Warsaw a small group of young historians, led by Emanuel Ringelblum, set up a secret archive, code-named Oneg Shabbat, in which they painstakingly documented Jewish life and suffering. Dozens of others documented the torment of Jewish Europe in diaries and personal journals.

Indicative of the Jewish will to live were the ingenious methods Jewish children used to smuggle food and medicine into the ghettos. Jews were incarcerated like vermin; they were tired, cold, and hungry; they were hounded, hunted, and mistreated by almost everyone. Yet the suicide rate in the ghettos was almost nil. There were two sayings upon the lips of these eternally optimistic Jews: "Ein sho gelebt iz oich gelebt" (An hour of life is a lifetime); and "M´hot zei in drerd di rotzchim" (We shall yet live to see these murderers in their graves). Jews did not lose their sense of humor and even mocked their tormentors, waiting, hoping, and praying for the day of vengeance. Chaim Kaplan, one of the diarists of the Warsaw ghetto, quoted Victor Hugo, who summed up his feelings: "Daughter of Germany, blessed be he who picks your babe up and smashes its head upon the rocks."

THE JEWISH COUNCILS

Of course, there were also some Jewish collaborators, willing or otherwise. In every community, the Nazis selected the members for a Jewish council, called Judenrat, and appointed a Judenaelteste (Jewish elder) to run the council. The purpose of these institutions was to facilitate Germany´s Jewish policy on the local level. From the Nazi point of view the Judenrat had three main functions: to provide the Nazi authorities with updated lists of Jews and their possessions; to pay levies; and to provide Jewish laborers for Nazi-sponsored work projects. In almost every community the Nazis also established a Jewish auxiliary police, the Ordnungsdienst. Their role was to insure compliance with Nazi regulations and to help round up Jews for "relocation."

Initially the Jewish communities welcomed these entities. The councils and police seemed to reflect the possibility of accommodation and survival even under the Nazis. These institutions were, alas, to play a controversial role in the life of the ghettos. Objectively, the Judenrat did facilitate the Nazi extermination policy. We must, however, note that this was not the intent of the council members, elders, or policemen. They saw themselves in the unenviable position of having no recourse but to carry out Nazi orders. In their estimation it was likely that the Germans would have proceeded without their "help" and might have been infinitely more brutal without it. Moreover, they reasoned that if they acted properly, at least a remnant of their communities could be saved, although this would mean sacrificing some Jews to the Nazis. Not all the Judenaelteste were willing or able to bear the pressure. Adam Czerniakow, of Warsaw, refused to accommodate any further deportations when he discovered that what the Nazis termed "relocation" meant death in the gas chambers of Treblinka. Czerniakow took his own life rather than be party to the Nazi crimes. Other elders did not follow his example. Leaders such as Jacob Gens, of Vilna; Chaim Rumkowski, of Lodz; and Moses Merrin, of Sosnowiecz, developed into quasi-messianic figures. In their view survival made it necessary for Jews to work hard for the Nazis in order to become vital to the Nazi war machine; some sacrifice was unavoidable until the Allied victory would signal the liberation of at least part of the community.

Their tragedy was that they imputed some rationality to the Nazis. Would Germany exterminate even those who could be useful workers in the war industries? But the elders' hopes to mitigate the conditions under which Jews lived proved futile - as futile in the long-run as the social and cultural activities - for ultimately the Nazi Moloch would only be satisfied with a completely Judenrein Europe.

PHASE IV: EXECUTION

In the last phase, execution, the dance of death was played to its gruesome end. With the invasion of the Soviet Union on June 22, 1941, the Nazis began a massive campaign to slaughter the Jews of Europe. This campaign was known as Endloesung der Judenfrage, the Final Solution of the Jewish Problem. We cannot date the exact time and place of the decision to murder the Jews, but it seems likely that such a decision coincided with the orders to invade the Soviet Union, in the fall or winter of 1940.

By the spring of 1941 the decision to execute the Jews moved from theory to practice. The Einsatzgruppen, Flying Groups, of the SS were reassembled and given new orders. They were to follow the Wehrmacht into newly "liberated" territory, seeking out and destroying Jewish communities along the way. Throughout the Eastern front they took the same action. Before dawn,the men of the Einsatzkommando would surround a Jewish town, assisted by local volunteers, the Hilfswillinge (Hiwis), Wehrmacht Feldgendarmerie (military police), or both. They would assemble the Jews in an impromptu Umschlagplatz (loading place) and select some to form a "clean-up" unit. But they drove or marched the vast majority of the Jews out of town to prepared pits, anti-tank ditches, ravines, or other sites and then shoot them en masse. Occasionally the Nazis took no chances, tying their victims hands and shooting them in the back.

In the short time of their first sweep (June-December, 1941), the Einsatzgruppen performed their mission well, murdering close to one million Jews and numerous others. However, the men soon began to suffer from strain. Some took to drink, others became insubordinate, and their morale sank. Even HSSPF General Erich von dem Bach-Zelewski, one of the three overall commanders of the Einsatzgruppen, suffered a breakdown. Moreover, the process was neither fast enough nor secret enough for the murderers. It also could not be applied to other territories under Nazi control where life had, to a degree, been stabilized. In order to streamline the operation and to facilitate the completion of the Endloesung, the Reich's bureaucrats met in the Berlin suburb of Wannsee on January 20, 1942. They made practical plans and formulated a unified program. The Einsatzgruppen were to be sent out again, but this time they would be assisted by new mobile gas vans. To handle the masses of victims, including Jews from England and the United States, special camps, Ausrottungslagern, were to be set up for the sole purpose of murder.

After intense discussion the Nazis decided to deal first with Polish Jewry and to spread the Final Solution from there. Starting in the spring of 1942 they transported the majority of Polish Jews in closed cattle wagons to the newly established death camps. The number of Jews who were "resettled east" were staggering: Some 300,000 Jews were deported from Warsaw alone in the three months between June 22 and September 26, 1942. By then virtually every community had been decimated. A few Jews, primarily those needed as a labor force for war production, were given a respite and allowed to remain alive.

Jews in every country would face their turn at a railroad platform or at some impromptu Umschlagplatz. Aussiedlung became a byword for death. After Poland, the Grossreich was rendered Judenrein. The Jews of Holland, Belgium, and France became the hunters' next targets. Jews from Greece, Italy, Yugoslavia, and Czechoslovakia were next. Finally, the Jews of Rumania and Hungary were sonderbehandelt (specially dealt with). In all, some six million Jews were murdered by the Nazis and their henchmen.

THE CONCENTRATION CAMPS

Terror played a key role in Nazi rule. Routine seizures of hostages, summary executions, and imprisonment all kept occupied peoples in line. This system of applied terror operated through a spiderweb of camps established throughout Europe by the SS state.

As early as February 1933 the Gestapo rounded up political enemies into Schutzhaftlagern (protective-custody camps), the so-called "wild camps" that the SA had set up. When Himmler assumed the key internal security position in the Reich, he reorganized the entire camp system. Upon the outbreak of the war and the subsequent occupation of most of Europe, these SS camps expanded into a network of some 1,000 camps that criss-crossed the continent. The new camps were similar to the early camps, except that now the SS made the prisoners their chattel, renting them out as labor gangs to German industry. Cruelty was the order of the day in all the SS camps, although the unattached camps tended to be the worst. Through this terror, violence, and sadism, they aimed to break the human spirit of the victim - not to convert him or her to the Nazi way of thinking, but merely to dehumanize, to reduce the victim to human refuse. The Nazis sneeringly referred to their victims as Mussulman, a reference to a prisoner who had lost all will to live, literally squatting like a Muslim at prayer.

The Nazi concentration camp (KL) system, individual "wild camps" aside, was organized as follows.

Konzentrationslager(n) were concentration camps (KaZet in inmate language) created for the incarceration of political prisoners, convicts, asocials (homosexuals, prostitutes, and pimps), and some Jews. The latter were classified separately. In the camps, removed from society, the Nazis could wear down the inmates physically and mentally through hard labor and brutal treatment. Internally, the camps were run by the inmates themselves: Lageraelteste (usually a German or Austrian convict), chief camp prisoner appointed by and responsible to the SS; Blockaelteste, head prisoner of a barrack block; Stubenaelteste, chief room clerk, in charge of a number of Stubendienste, or room servants; Blockschreiber, clerk charged with keeping the block records; Oberkapo, chief overseer of the labor details; Kapo; Vorarbeiter (foreman under the command of the Kapo); and finally, Lagerpolizei, camp police, whose duty was to help the SS maintain order. Externally the camps were under the direct administration of the SS Inspectorate of Concentration Camps.

Each KL could, depending on the location and importance of the camp, be designated as a "mother" (base) camp for a number of subcamps - Ausenlagern. Each camp was surrounded by electrified barbed wire, augmented by guard towers, mounting searchlights, and machine guns. A KL, unlike its subcamps, contained a punishment block where inmates of a camp or subcamp were sent for disciplinary action; an execution site with a small gas chamber and crematorium; a central administrative building where all camp documents were kept; and a Gestapo office. Finally, in the Reviers of all the major KLs some medical experiments took place.

Zwangsarbeitslager(n) (ZAL) were forced-labor camps established by the Nazis after their conquest in Eastern Europe. The inmates in these camps, mostly Jews, were detained under the most horrible physical conditions. Hundreds of these camps existed, some with thousands of inmates and others with only a few dozen. Initially the SS rented out these camps to German or Ethnic German (Volksdeutsche) civilian businessmen who administered them. These camps were not a legal part of the KL system. In mid-1944, however, the Inspectorate of Concentration Camps siezed all remaining ZALs and integrated them into the KL system.

In the Judenlager(n), commonly known as Ju-lag, Jews were kept to await transport to the murder sites. If the conditions in the ZALs were bad, those in the Ju-lags were infinitely worse. Living, work, diet, sanitary, and health conditions quickly and cruelly took their daily toll. Most of the Ju-lags, unfortunately, were administered by a corrupt Jewish administration who sold favors to the highest bidder.

Rounding out the list of Nazi camps were: Zigeunerlager(n), camps for gypsies; Straflager(n), punitive camps; Schutzhaftlager(n), protective-custody camps; Krankenlager(n), hospital camps; Einsatzlager(n) camps for special construction projects; and a score or so of others. Together they formed the most extensive system of mass political incarceration in world history.

The Wannsee conference led to the establishment of yet another, even worse type of camp: the Ausrottungslager (extermination camp), or death factory. In most of these camps there was little labor. When a transport of Jews came to the camp (and they kept coming all the time, day and night) a small number of prisoners were selected to become the Sonderkommando (special detail). The rest were sent immediately, or almost immediately, to the gas chambers. The clean-up unit took the bodies, removing even the gold crowns from their teeth and anything else of value previously overlooked and moved them into giant crematoria where the bodies were burned. In most cases, after a short period of time the Sonderkommando too was disposed of and replaced by a newly selected group. Meanwhile, other crews - also potential candidates for the gas chamber - sorted, stored, and packed the victims´ personal belongings for shipment into the Reich.

PLANET AUSCHWITZ

Of all the camps none is more infamous than Auschwitz-Birkenau. A conglomorate of some forty subcamps, Auschwitz was home for prisoners-of-war, political prisoners, Polish and Czech intellectuals, convicted German and Austrian criminals, asocials, gypsies, and Jews. Most Jews brought there from all over occupied Europe hardly had time to become acquainted with the place; for them Auschwitz served only as an exit point via gas chamber and crematorium. As such they were never officially registered as camp arrivals in any of the well-kept records of the camp. Buna, industrial Auschwitz, where the large plants of I. G. Farbenindustrie, Deutsche Ausruestungswerke (DAW), Bunawerke, and others were situated, employed thousands in slave labor, and slave labor was also parcelled out from there by the thousands. Even though small in area (circa 40 square kilometers), Auschwitz is most likely the largest cemetery in the entire world. Almost four million human beings, including over two and a half million Jews, perished there. Auschwitz´s subcamps ranged from Peenemunde, the experimental rocket facility in German Pomerania, to an industrial complex within the Warsaw ghetto.

THE DEATH FACTORIES

The Auschwitz extermination center was unparalleled in human history, and at the same time, it was the largest industrial empire in Nazi Europe. Belzec, Chelmno (Kulmhof), Majdanek, Sobibor, and Treblinka were, on the other hand, strictly Ausrottungslagern - camps set up solely for the murder of Jews. For camouflage reasons, each camp had a few workshops, mainly repair shops to service the camp SS and their Ukrainian helpers. At least one and a half million Jews perished in these five extermination centers.

Each death factory used a different method, albeit all with the same ultimate goal: to eliminate as many Jews in the shortest, most economical way. In Auschwitz II (Birkenau) and Majdanek, once the victims were packed into the hermetically sealed gas chamber, an orderly dropped pellets of Zyklon B (manufactured by Degesch and supplied by Tesch und Stabenow, both German companies) into the air vent.

When it oxidized the chemical turned to gas. Depending on the level of humidity, all those in the gas chamber were killed within ten to twenty minutes. Death was due to suffocation and was accompanied by sensations of fear, diziness, and vomiting. In Treblinka the victims were asphyxiated by carbon monoxide pumped into the chamber from a captured Soviet tank located on the premises. In Belzec and Sobibor the victims were killed by carbon monoxide pumped into the chambers by diesel engines. In Chelmno, mobile gas vans took the victims from a reception building dubbed the "palace" on a ride to meet their heavenly Father.

In most of these camps no selection took place. All the members of a transport were sent straight down the Himmelstrasse, the heavenly road. In Auschwitz, some Jews were selected for labor - a chance for temporary survival. The Nazis made each victim pass singly before the SS doctor who decided who would go right, to the gas chamber, and who would go left, to work. The number of prisoners kept alive was very small, never more than one-third of a transport and often considerably less. Often those chosen to work were selected arbitrarily by a doctor who had never even looked at them.

The victims were transported to their final destination in various ways. Jews from Eastern Europe, including those from the General Government (Poland), were transported in closed freight cars - perhaps a hundred to a car - most of the time without any food or water. Passengers in these transports were deprived of all sanitary facilities. Many of the overcrowded, bolted cars were heavily lined with a residue of lime. By the time a given transport arrived at its destination and the bolted doors were opened for the first time, dozens of victims had already died. On the other hand, some of the victims from parts of the Grossreich and some Western countries were transported first-class. As a result, they were totally unprepared for what was in store for them.

The first sight that greeted the Jewish prisoners was a well-kept station, part of the Nazi ruse to lull the victims into a false sense of security. While the dark, low chimney stacks of the ever-burning crematoria constantly belched out a thick, smelly smoke, an orchestra made up of half starved musicians dressed in stripped pajamas played on. Depending on the location of the camp and temperament of the SS-Lagerfuehrer and his staff, once the "formal niceties" were over, the victims destined for the incinerator pile were stripped naked and led from station to station (hair cutting, final rectal examination for hidden gems or foreign currency, etc.). As the victims came nearer and nearer to the last station, the SS men dropped the camouflage completely. They lashed into the mass of prisoners, whipping them mercilessly and setting upon them specially trained dogs who tore into their naked flesh. In the less "sophisticated" death camps, such as Sobibor, the Ukrainian guards raised geese in order to mask the death-cries of those in the gas chambers.

In Nazi-occupied Western Europe, two additional types of camps were created. In the Durchsganglager (Dulag), or transit camp, Jews were held for a period - the length of time depending on transport availability - awaiting shipment to death factories. The Austauschlager played a lesser role, but nevertheless one of great importance to the Nazi high command. In these camps, certain important personalities, both gentile and Jewish, were held for exchange or to be used as political pawns with the Allied powers.

RESISTANCE: THE SECRET WAR

How did the victims, their European neighbors, and the free world react to these unfolding events? There is no simple answer. Unfortunately the issues have been made more complicated over the years by authors who have used history for the purpose of proving, disproving, or apologizing for any of a number of political positions. Praise or blame for those who did or did not "do enough" to save European Jewry does nothing to resurrect the dead. Political vituperation cannot alter the gruesome facts. Only a sensitive historical understanding of the whys and wherefores can perhaps help avoid a repetition of history.

Two wars were fought on the European continent during the Nazi occupation. One was the struggle for national independence and honor waged against the Nazi foe; the other was a desperate struggle for survival fought by European Jewry. Resistance in Europe has been elevated to the status of a myth, in which even the German masses (as opposed to the few bona fide anti-Nazi Germans) are considered resisters. Jews, however, have been seen as weak-willed fatalists, no better than a group of sheep. This trend has led, over the years, to accusations, debates, and apologias, few of which have helped to elucidate the history of Jewish resistance and heroism.

Whatever may be said about the extent of European resistance, one fact must be kept in mind. In every occupied country, stout-hearted men and women, for whom duty, honor, and country meant more than life itself, arose to fight the Nazis. Even some Germans looked forward to the demise of nazism, opposed everything fascism stood for, and readied themselves for the day of struggle. Some did lash out; others were caught before acting; all thirsted for the day of battle. Ultimately the altruists and visionaries, not the realists who collaborated with the Nazis, won the day. By their sacrifice the resisters proved that one does not have to surrender to evil, but that evil can be resisted and eventually defeated. Thousands of Europeans, from France to Russia and from Norway to North Africa and representing every political movement, answered the call of arms of the clandestine armies. Many brave souls gave their lives for liberty.

JEWISH RESISTANCE

Many Jews also participated in this struggle. The Jewish war, however, was fundamentally different. No other people faced Ausmerzung. The Nazis planned to enslave all of Europe, but never planned to murder all Europeans. Yet, National Socialism would accept nothing less than the total eradication of all Jews throughout the world. No quarter would be given.

The simple fact must be stated: The majority of European Jewry did not actively resist the Nazis. This does not, however, mean that Jews collaborated in their own destruction. The vast majority of Jews could not resist for a variety of reasons. Jews lacked military training, lacked weapons with which to fight, lacked a source of supplies, and lacked a suitable place to fight. They also tended to be law-abiding people and were taken in by the Nazi camouflage scheme. Most truly believed that deportation meant work. How could it be otherwise? Germany, after all, was the most rational, enlightened nation in Europe. A German might persecute, but would never stoop to murdering innocent women and children.

Despite these impediments to resistance, as well as other obstacles designed to keep Jews quiescent, Jews never surrendered. Even in death they walked with their pride intact. Lacking a state, Jews could not hope to fight for liberation. For European Jewry, resistance was a struggle to survive, a fight to choose the time and place of one´s death, a war to sell Jewish blood at a high price. The statement of the Jewish will to live and fight for survival was implicit in the Jewish struggle.

Jews rebelled in seventeen ghettos: Bendzin, Bialystok, Brody, Cracow, Czestochowa, Lwow, Lutsk, Minsk, Mir, Riga, Sielce, Sosnowica, Stryzow, Tarnopol, Tarnow, Vilna, and Warsaw. In April of 1943 the small Jewish fortress of Warsaw held out for twenty-eight days. The German plan had called for a three-day operation: The remains of the ghetto were to be burned to the ground, reduced to rubble, and pounded into dust by the SS with Wehrmacht and Luftwaffe (army and air force) as well as Ukrainian and Polish Blue Police assistance. The 1,000 Jewish defenders held out against nearly 3,000 Germans, despite a pitiful arsenal that comprised mostly pistols and Molotov bombs. That the Germans possessed all the accoutrements of modern warfare and still could not dislodge the Jewish resisters testifies to the resisters´ courage and audacity. Quite naturally the Warsaw ghetto uprising has become a modern symbol of Heroic struggle against insurmountable odds.

Jews also rose up in three death factories: Sobibor, Treblinka, and Auschwitz-Birkenau. Additional plots and small-scale fighting took place in dozens of towns, villages, and camps. In both east and west, bands of Jewish guerrillas arose. Some were integrated into general partisan brigades; others were all Jewish. In France, a 2,000-man Armee Juive (Jewish army) arose as an independent part of the Forces Frances de l´Interior (FFI).

The armed resistance that the Jews finally did effect received almost no aid from the Allies and, in Eastern Europe, little from their neighbors. They won a moral victory though, for, although doomed, they dared to declare that world Jewry was not yet ready to die - that it would live. The Jewish struggle in the war was a stage in the Jewish emergence from powerlessness. Ultimately the Jewish war that began in April 1943 ended in May 1948. The process begun by the resistance ended with the establishment of the State of Israel.

Hundreds of thousands of Jews outside the Nazi terror also resisted. They actively participated in the war against the new Haman, knowing that only thus could Jews live in peace. The Jews fielded an army over one and a half million strong, fighting on all battle fronts, in every campaign, in every corps and regiment.

Special mention must be made of the war effort of the Yishuv in Palestine. The members of the Va´ad Leumi of the Jewish Agency realized the need for Jewish participation in the anti-Nazi war. Nearly 50,000 Jews from the Yishuv served in the Royal Armed Forces, some in independent all-Jewish units, others in mixed ones. A Jewish Brigade was founded and fought courageously in Italy.

Jewish resistance was a reaffirmation of Jewish history. Throughout their long history the Jewish people had been attacked countless times merely for being born Jewish and for stubbornly adhering to their forefathers´ faith. They had to endure the early persecutions of the Catholic Church; the ravages of the Crusaders, desecration of the Host and blood libels; accusations of being the poisoners of wells and carriers of the Black Plague; the Inquisition; and the Cossak (Chmielnicki) massacres. They were tortured, burned at the stake, expelled, made to wander from place to place - always forced to rely on the whim of the ruling bishop or prince. Yet in many instances throughout their long journey, Jewish men and women defended themselves with whatever means available to them and acquitted themselves honorably. Despite the harsh reality, the Jews managed to survive. So too it was during the Holocaust. Reality declared that the Jews should not resist their murderers, nor survive them - but the Jews did both.

JEWS AND GENTILES UNDER THE NEW ORDER

How did the European peoples react to the murder of their neighbors? Although only a few in-depth studies of the subject exist, it is still possible to generalize about gentile behavior and the interaction between Jews and gentiles under the Nazi occupation. When we do so, one fact becomes apparent: There is a slight but perceptible difference between how Jews were treated in Eastern and in Western Europe. Obviously, such a difference would affect the chances a Jew would have to escape or evade the Nazis.

In Western Europe some gentiles were willing to help Jews. Accepted as citizens, Jews joined resistance forces, and gentiles helped and defended them when possible. More often than not in these countries, the clergy of various Christian churches helped Jews. In some limited cases collaborationists even helped in rescue operations. Western Europe was not without antisemites, but when help was possible it was usually available.

The single most systematic effort at rescue occured in Denmark. When the Nazis proposed solving the Jewish problem in Denmark they met considerable resistance. Decrees separating Jews from gentiles were ignored. When the yellow star identifying Jews was instituted, many Danes, among them King Christian X, likewise wore a yellow star as a sign of protest. In October 1943, as impending Nazi deportations became known to the King and his council, more drastic measures were called for. First, Jews were removed from their homes and hidden from the Nazis. Then small convoys were transported, right under the Nazis' eyes, by fishing boat to Sweden. All Danes, even collaborationist Danish police, participated in the rescue. In all 7,000 Jews were thus saved, thanks to the concerted efforts of all sectors of Danish society.

This was not the case in Eastern European countries. In

the Ukraine, Byelorussia, Lithuania, Latvia, Estonia, and parts of Poland, Jews initially feared their neighbors, more than the Germans as they were usually more brutal than even the Gestapo. In none of these countries, save Czechoslovakia, were Jews welcomed into the resistance. Jewish partisans often had to hide their Jewishness, not out of shame, but out of fear of their would-be "comrades."

Poland was typical of the Eastern European countries in regard to antisemitism. Prewar Poland had the most Jews of any European country and was the Nazi-chosen extermination site. The largest number of individual heroes in all Europe - more than three hundred Hasidei Umot Ha´olam (Righteous Gentiles) - arose in Poland. Antisemitism rose in Poland during the war, however, and most of the underground accepted the propriety of post-war limitations upon Jewish rights in a liberated Polish state. Most Poles remained apathetic to the Jews´ plight: some, in fact, were happy with the Nazi solution to the Jewish problem. Still others, such as the Oboz Narodowy Radicalny (ONR), the National Radical Camp, actively helped the Nazis, seeing Jews as the main threat to Poland.

Jews were never accepted into the resistance in Eastern Europe, except by Communist or Socialist undergrounds. The Armja Krajowa (AK), the underground home army, refused to give the assistance that would have allowed the Jews to defend themselves. Only a small number of weapons were transferred, and only begrudgingly. The general staff of the AK characterized any action on behalf of Jews as premature and contrary to Poland´s long-term interests. During the massive deportations of Jews, the underground had no reaction. When the Jews finally resisted, the underground made only a few half-hearted attempts to assist the Jewish fighters in their desperate last stand. During the height of the Warsaw Ghetto Uprising, Poles held Easter picnics outside the ghetto walls, watching and gawking as the Jews fought their last battle.

THE ATTITUDE OF THE CHURCH

How did the churches - both Protestant and Catholic - in their official capacities as shepherd of the people and the voice of morality, react to the slaughter of millions of innocent souls?

By and large the clergy´s attitude reflected that of their congregations. In places where gentiles made efforts to save their Jewish neighbors, the churches usually got involved in rescue efforts. The converse also held true. Here and there a priest, bishop, or even a cardinal spoke out in opposition to the Nazi treatment of the Jews. Unfortunately, like the Righteous Gentiles, they were few and far between. Most European representatives of the Roman Catholic Church adhered to the official Vatican position or, at best, were uncommitted.

The Vatican's attitude, unfortunately, was not very positive. The Holy See was unwilling to jeopardize its diplomatic status in Nazi Germany by doing anything to systematically help the Jews. The Pope was not even willing to mention Jews in his public denunciations of war crimes, again as part of his desire to maintain the status quo with Nazi Germany.

These facts do not denigrate the value of the heroic actions of the few who did try to help save Jews. Despite the dangers to themselves and their families, despite the general apathy toward Jews and antipathy to those who would help them, hundreds of men and women all over Europe did all that they could to save Jews. Some succeeded; others did not. In many cases the would-be rescuers and their charges were discovered (usually through betrayal) by the Gestapo and were murdered. Yet the actions of these few courageous men and women proved that even in the darkest of days the bonds of humanity had not completely broken.

REACTIONS OF THE FREE WORLD

As massive a system as that developed by the Nazis for the purpose of eradicating European Jewry could hardly have been kept secret for long. Try as they might, the Nazis could hardly have kept the murder of six million people from being discovered. Eventually some word would leak out to the free world. We might have thought that the Western Allies at war with Germany would have utilized all means at their disposal in order to end the massacres quickly and save at least a remnant of European Jewry.

But Allied reactions to Jewish suffering were slow. In the 1930s when the Nazis were trying to push Jews out of Germany, few countries were willing to offer Jews refuge. In 1938 Western nations met at Evian, France, to try to find a solution for the growing refugee problem. At no time was the word "Jew" ever mentioned by the participants, who preferred to deal with refugees in the abstract. Little in the way of rescue was achieved. No government - except Great Britain, which wanted to keep Jews out of Palestine - was willing to modify immigrant quotas.

In the end only one offer came from the conference. The Dominican Republic offered to allow 100,000 Jews to colonize the area near Santo Domingo (Sossua) in return for a large Jewish monetary contribution to insure that the refugees would not become a public charge. A small number of refugees actually were admitted, but by the late 1930s the money had dried up and the Dominican government, no longer subsidized by American Jewry, refused to admit even one more refugee.

With the outbreak of war, the refugee crisis became even more acute. The fear that spies might be infiltrated among refugees was cited as reason for continued obstruction of rescue. Similarly, the effort to win the war and not waste resources was touted as the only patriotic response to the Jewish catastrophe in Europe.

No single country was willing to become the Jews protectors. The Allies were not willing to divert any resources away from the war in order to defend the Jews, even in cases where targets had military significance, such as Auschwitz and its rail lines. Only in a few cases were radio messages beamed to Europe by the BBC, warning that what the Nazis termed "resettlement" in fact meant death. Even these broadcasts were stopped by the government so as not to create anti-Jewish resentment in the occupied countries by appearing to devote too much time to the Jews.

The attitude of the Allies toward the Jews was an apathetic one. Whereas the Nazis viewed killing Jews as a paramount goal of the war, the Allies never considered the Jewish question as a factor in the formulation of their war strategy; it was merely a side issue to be settled with the end of hostilities. The United States in particular had no sense of urgency to rescue Jews. Only when political pressure at home mounted during an election year did the administration act and even then only after Secretary of the Treasury Henry Morgenthau became involved. The creation of the War Refugee Board finally brought the rescue issue to the fore. The United States had been especially obstructionist in the previous decade, admitting almost one million fewer immigrants than immigration quotas allowed and refusing to consider changes in the quotas. The War Refugee Board was a case of too little too late.

Similarly obstructionist, although for very different reasons, was His Majesty´s Government. The British government feared that any act on behalf of Jews in Europe would aid the Zionists, and the Mandatory policy encapsulated in the 1939 White Paper undid Britain´s commitment to establish a Jewish National Home. The British government tried to ignore the Jewish problem for as long as possible, hoping it would go away.

It is interesting that with the exception of Sweden, whose government was willing to allow Jews to enter as long as it did not have to take any action, few of the democracies stood up to the test of the Holocaust. The Swiss answer, that the "life boat is full," was typical. Nor did any of the international charitable organizations come forward. The International Red Cross had conveniently declared Jews stateless and hence outside its sphere of activity, thus easing the way for the Nazis to carry out their designs. The International Red Cross inadvertently helped to spread Nazi propaganda by giving Terezin the air of respectability, even though it was merely an antechamber for Auschwitz. Having finally come to an agreement with the Nazis on the inspection of the concentration camps, the International Red Cross was willing to see only Nazi-selected sights. Of course, these sights had been carefully selected and prepared by the Germans. The International Red Cross refused to investigate anything they were not actually shown.

The various governments-in-exile also reflected the generally apathetic picture. They expressed sincere regrets at the Jews´ suffering; but with the exception of a few small-scale activities, the governments-in-exile were unable or unwilling to take concrete steps of any sort. Some, such as the Polish government-in exile, could not, or would not, curb antisemitic incidents among their own troops or censor openly anti-Jewish articles in newspapers under their own sponsorship. Almost all of the eastern European governments-in-exile had some sort of antisemitic law proposed in their legislative plans for the postliberation era.

Not even the Soviets, who were widely perceived by American Jews as being philosemitic, undertook any systematic efforts to save Jews. Although perfectly willing to use the Nazi threat to European Jewry for propaganda purposes - by means of the Jewish Anti-Fascist Committee, for example - the Soviets did no more than the Western powers to save European Jews.

In fact, Russian policy consistently placed Jews in an ambiguous and dangerous position. The Comintern had never paid much attention to Nazi antisemitism during the 1930s. The Soviet or Communist press did not cover anti-Jewish excesses. Russian Jews therefore never knew of the threat that rapidly approached them. To make matters worse, the Russians signed a nonagression pact with the Nazis in August 1939. At that point the Russian borders were closed to anti-Nazi refugees, and some agitators were handed over to the Gestapo by the NKVD, the Soviet secret police.

One might have expected that upon the German invasion this policy would change. In an ad hoc fashion, local Soviet authorities evacuated some Jews from the danger zone. By and large, however, they left Jews to their fate. The Supreme-Soviet was willing to make pronouncements but did as little or less than the Anglo-Americans.

FASCISMS AND THE JEWISH PROBLEM

Just before the outbreak of the war, some 25 percent of the European Jewish population found itself either under direct Nazi rule or under the influence of Nazi-oriented states. It is interesting to note the attitudes of the Fascist states to the Jewish problem.

While Il Duce, increasingly under Hitler's influence, was willing to sacrifice Jews to the Nazi Moloch, his lieutenants were less motivated to do so. The Italian occupation authorities in France and Yugoslavia played an especially prominent role in rescuing Jews. Ignoring Italy's officially anti-Jewish policies, the generals often warned Jews of impending danger, thus allowing at least some Jews to escape before the SS got them. Some officers and their men went a step further, actively rescuing Jews and giving or selling them weapons with which to defend themselves. In at least one case Italian troops in Russia used force, firing upon men of an Einsatzkommando, in order to save Jewish lives.

Even today these facts cause wonder and interest. How can we explain the actions of Nazi Germany's closest ally? We must look at two facts: There had been virtually no antisemitic movement of note in modern Italy, and, given the failure of totalitarianism in Fascist Italy, there was always some possibility of ignoring orders when morality and honor were at issue. This is not to deny the existence of a Jewish problem in Fascist Italy. In 1938 a series of very clearly antisemitic laws were published. Jews were virtually excluded from both the armed forces and the government aparatus. Yet, compared with the Endloesung, these laws were but trifles. Of all the European nations during the war, it can safely be said that only the Danes did more to help Jews.

In many ways the Balkan governments were the exact opposite of the Italians. Antisemitism had been a political issue in Rumania from the days of the Congress of Berlin (1878). Despite minority treaties, legislation in Rumanian Bukovina, Bessarabia, and Transylvania deprived Jews of their civil rights. Under the short-lived quasi-Fascist government of Octavian Goga (1938), more than one-third of Rumanian Jewry was stripped of its citizenship. Official discrimination against Jews in all branches of the government, the professions, and economic life was stronger in Rumania than in virtually any other East European country.

With the Nazi rise to power, the Iron Guard, Rumania's Fascist party, came to the forefront of political and social life. A rabidly antisemitic group, the Guard drew support from the Greek Orthodox Church as well as a variety of nationalist and chauvinist groups. Their slogan was "Rumania for the Rumanians." Upon gaining influence, the Guard proceeded to recreate nazism's Jewish policy on a smaller scale. They denied Jews citizenship, making it possible to discharge them from their jobs and to nationalize their businesses. Soon public manifestations of antisemitism became clearly discernable. Taking their cue from the Nazis, the Rumanian Fascists proved eager to help with the Final Solution. Bloodbaths ensued in every territory occupied by Rumanian troops during the Russian campaign. Large numbers of Jews were deported to Transnistria, where they were allowed to freeze or starve to death. Those who managed by some miracle to survive these travails were dealt with by Iron Guardmen's guns or in the crematoria of Auschwitz-Birkenau.

Fascism in Hungary played a similar, but more limited role. A Fascist party, the Arrow Cross, was organized and operated along Nazi lines. The Fascists played almost no role in the Hungarian state, however, until the war. The regent of Hungary, Miklos Horthy, refused to surrender the crown to the legitimate heir, but until 1939-1940 Horthy's power base lay outside the Fascist bloc. By 1941 Horthy had fallen under Hitler's influence and had begun to lead Hungary into the anti-Bolshevik and antisemitic crusade. During this period Jews in Hungary and Hungarian-occupied territory suffered much. Despite his antisemitic credentials, Horthy was never totally committed to any particular solution for the Jewish problem. Seeing the war as lost in 1944, Horthy tried to use the Jews as a way to contact the Allies and find an honorable way out of the war for Hungary. Unfortunately, the United States and England did not react quickly enough and allowed the Nazis time to recover. In the spring and early summer of 1944, the Germans unleashed the Arrow Cross and quickly deported most of the nearly one million Jews in Hungary to Auschwitz-Birkenau.

Although as antisemitic as any of the other governments, the Bulgarians wanted no part in mass murder. Seeking other solutions to the Jewish problem, the Bulgarian government stalled for time. Many Bulgarian Jews were thus able to escape deportation, although some 7,000 Bulgarian Jews perished as a result of government or Nazi action.

The situation was more complex in France. Despite the existence of Action Francaise, a Fascist party, and the collaborationist proclivities of Petain, Laval, and the Vichy apparatus, fascism per se played no role with regard to the Jewish question in wartime France. On one hand, nearly 100,000 French Jews were rounded up and "resettled East." Almost all of them were refugee Jews who had entered the country during the 1930s. Almost all of them were rounded up by the French Police, with little or no SS involvement.

Others found themselves in forced-labor camps in Vichy-controlled North Africa. On the other hand, neither Laval nor Petain wanted to surrender "French" Jews to the Nazis. Limit the Jews, get rid of the foreign elements, undo the emancipation: These were the goals of the French right, in many ways the final chapter to the Dreyfus affair. Despite the collaborationists, despite Nazi plans, nearly two-thirds of French Jewry survived thanks to the actions of the French people and the underground.

Franco and, to a lesser degree, Salazar, anticipated that by extending aid to Jews, even in a small way, they would enhance their own position in the postwar era. The Spanish hope to legitimize Fascist rule was, paradoxically, based upon the philosemitic use of antisemitism. They clearly believed the Jews to be in power in Washington, London, and Moscow. Furthermore, Franco may have had some Marrano blood in his family. Many Spaniards saw the expulsion of the Sephardim in 1492 as a national calamity and felt that now was the time to right that terrible wrong. Legislation was approved declaring Jews of Sephardi origin who could prove that their ancestors were exiles to be Spanish citizens. Because much leeway was provided for local consular officials as to what constituted proof, they saved a small number of Jews using this proviso. Others were allowed temporary refuge on Spanish soil. As long as they could prove that they would leave as soon as possible, no Jew, Sephardi or Ashkenazi, was turned away. Still others were saved literally from the clutches of death by members of the Spanish Blue Legion in Russia. Under the pretext that camp workers were needed to maintain their leaguers, dozens of Jews were thus saved and eventually smuggled to freedom.

The Fascist and quasi-Fascist parties in Great Britain and the United States were as intensely antisemitic as the Nazis themselves. Leaders such as Oswald Mosley, Father Coughlin, and Henry Ford spread racial and religious hatred for Jews on every possible level and by every conceivable medium. The Fascists never attained power in these countries, but they had a significant effect in the prewar era upon local politics and especially upon the attitudes of the local Jewish communities.

REACTIONS OF THE JEWISH WORLD

If the general apathy, callousness, and sloth of the free world can be considered problematic, the attitude of free-world Jewry can be considered no less so. Although deeply concerned by the events in Europe, Jews in the United States,

Britain, and Palestine were unable to effect a cogent rescue policy. Powerlessness, disunity, lack of clear policies, and lack of accurate information created this condition, but these factors worked differently in each community.

The Yishuv was in forefront of efforts involving the resettlement of refugees from Nazi Germany and elsewhere during the 1930s. During the ten years of the Fifth Aliyah (1929-1939), more than 250,000 Jews entered Palestine, including nearly 100,000 from Germany. The Yishuv, however, was saddled with a weak economy, Arab hostility, and the machinations of a British administration that tried to keep Jews out of Palestine while officially helping to create the Jewish National Home. Although officially committed to Zionism through the Balfour Declaration and the League of Nations Mandate, the British had come to the conclusion that imperial interests and Jewish interests no longer coincided. By the early 1930s the Mandatory government therefore sought to keep Jews out of the country, even if that meant liberalization of immigrant quotas to Britain itself.

In 1939 the split between the Yishuv and the Mandatory government became final. On May 17, 1939, the British issued a new White Paper that repudiated the Jewish National Home. Jewish immigration to Palestine was to be limited to 15,000 per annum for five years; thereafter further Jewish immigration would be contingent upon Arab approval. Similarly, Zionist land acquisition would be severly curtailed in nearly 90 percent of the territory of Western Palestine. To make matters worse, the Mandatory government declared its intention to create an independent Arab state in Palestine in 1949.

The outbreak of war in September forced the Zionists to cancel plans for a revolt and make a terrible decision on the issue of priorities. A truce was declared with the British in order to fight the greater threat. Zionist policymakers hoped to win a fairer solution for the Yishuv in postwar settlements. Meanwhile Zionist policy was, in the words of David Ben-Gurion, "to fight Hitler as if there were no White Paper and to fight the White Paper as if there were no Hitler." Given the Yishuv´s limited resources, it was not possible to do both. Even so, rescue efforts were made. The Jewish Agency launched a campaign for a public response by the Allied governments to the specifically Jewish issues raised by the war. Once information on the Nazi extermination policy became available in November 1942, the Agency stepped up this campaign. It demanded that the gates of Palestine be opened to Jews seeking refuge, requested that the Allies retaliate in order to stop the massacres, urged the governments to take other actions to stop or slow down the murder process, and urged the formation of a Jewish Army to fight against the murderers. The Yishuv in general and the Jewish Agency in particular sought recognition for their status as the sole legitimate spokesmen of world Jewry.

Unfortunately, the British did not see the issue through Zionist eyes. The British obstructed every opportunity for rescue work, fearing that a bold move to rescue Jews might suceed and create more potential candidates for immigrant certificates, thus creating pressure for a pro-Zionist solution to the Palestine impasse.

The Zionist establishment reacted by cooperating with the British on common issues, primarily relating to the war against the Nazis, while preparing for the eventual struggle with Britain or the Arabs. Meanwhile, the Zionist movement aimed to establish a postwar Jewish Commonwealth through the Biltmore Program of May 1942. More radical Zionists, especially the Revisionist-Zionist followers of Vladimir (Zeev) Jabotinsky, evaluated the situation in much the same manner as the Jewish Agency, opting for cooperation with the British while preparing for future revolt. The Revisionist-oriented underground, the Irgun Zvai Leumi (IZL), thus followed the Agency´s militia, the Haganah, in placing all resources into the anti-Nazi war effort. Not all Zionists agreed, however, that this path was the best one for Jews. A splinter group from IZL, led by Abraham Stern, came to exactly the opposite conclusion. Calling itself Lohame Herut Israel (LEHI), this group continued the armed struggle against the British throughout the war and even tried to contact and make a deal with the Nazis. Rebuffed and repudiated by the majority of thr Yishuv, LEHI took to assassinations and terrorism to achieve their goals. The Yishuv, however, was too weak to change the situation during the war. Diplomatic and military efforts notwithstanding, the situation in 1945 was exactly the same as it had been in 1939.

The most powerful Jewish community, however, was in the United States. Here, too, issues of Jewish interest met with failure. The government, as already noted, was less than enthusiastic about rescue. This very situation left American Jewry without an alternative and, in effect, without a policy. Moreover, those leaders who could see the parameters for a policy were largely without real power. Jews in positions of power were, to a large degree, unwilling to become involved. Unable to present a unified front on ideological grounds, American Jewry lacked one forceful leader to represent the entire communtiy. Furthermore, at no time did large numbers of Jews consider the problem from its political angle. So enamored of President Roosevlet were the masses of American Jews that voting against him was never a serious option that could have been used to force the rescue issue to the fore. A saying at the time was that American Jews "have three _velts_ (worlds): _dos velt_ (this world), _yene velt_ (the hereafter) and Roosevelt."

The tragedy was that in European Jewry's time of need, no one group arose with both the power and the interest in saving at least a _Shearit Hapleta_, a remnant of European Jewry. Powerless, the Jews both inside and outside Europe could only watch with horror at the unfolding Final Solution and prepare for the denoument of the Jewish war that Hitler had started.

7

World War II

THE CAUSES OF THE WAR

1778. Adamthwaite, Anthony: France and the Coming of the Second World War [Totowa, NJ: Frank Cass, 1977]

1779. Armstrong, H. Fish: "Armistice at Munich." F Affairs, vol.17 #2 (Jan., 1939): 197-296.

1780. Aster, Sidney: 1939: The Making of the Second World War [New York: Simon & Schuster, 1973]

1781. Beloff, M.: Foreign Policy of Soviet Russia 1936-1941 [London: Royal Inst. for International Affairs, 1949]

1782. Breitscheid, Rudolf: "The German Peril." Cont Rev, vol.149 #843 (March, 1936): 257-263.

1783. Bruegel, J. W.: Czechoslovakia before Munich: The German Minority Problem and British Appeasement Policy [Cambridge: Cambridge Univ. Press, 1973]

1784. Butterworth, Susan: "Daladier and the Munich Crisis: Reappraisal." JCH, vol.9 #3 (July, 1974): 191-216.

1785. Carr, E. H.: "From Munich to Moscow." Soviet Studies, vol.1 #1 (June, 1949): 3-7; #2 (Oct., 1949): 93-105.
* On the Molotov-Ribbentrop Pact.

1786. Chamberlain, Neville: In Search of Peace [New York: G. P. Putnams´ Sons, 1939]

1787. Cienciala, A. M.: "Poland and the Munich Crisis 1938: A Reappraisal." EEQ, vol.3 #2 (June, 1969): 201-219.

1788. ___: Poland and the Western Powers 1938-1939 [London: Routledge & Kegan Paul, 1968]

Study into the background of World War II as seen from Poland. Based on intensive study of documentary evidence the work's main focus is on the stormy relationship between Poland, the Western allies, and Nazi Germany; as well as on Polish-Russian relations.

1789. ___: "The Significance of the Declaration of Non-Agression of January 26, 1934, in Polish-German and International Relations: A Reappraisal." EEQ, vol.1 #1 (March, 1967): 1-30.

1790. Cowling, M.: The Impact of Hitler, British Politics and British Policy, 1933-1940 [Cambridge: Cambridge Univ. Press, 1975]

1791. Dallin, Alexander: "The Month of Decision: German-Soviet Diplomacy, July 22 - August 22, 1939." JCEA, vol.9 #1 (April, 1949): 1-31.

1792. "Digest of Public Opinion: The Yiddish Press on the German-Soviet Non-Aggression Pact." CJR, vol.2 #5 (Sept./Oct., 1939): 43-51.

1793. Edwardes, F.: "Memel." Fasc Q, vol.2 (1936): 81-88.

1794. Eimerl, Sarel: Hitler Over Europe: The Road to World War Two [Boston: Little, Brown & Co., 1972]

1795. Einzig, Paul: Appeasement Before, During and After the War [London: Macmillan, 1942]

1796. Elson, Robert T. and the Editors of Time-Life Books: Prelude to War [Alexandria, VA: Time-Life Books, 1976]

1797. Eubank, Keith (ed.): World War II: Roots and Causes [Lexington, MA: D. C. Heath, 1975]

Anthology of previously published articles illuminating the issue's relation to the outbreak of World War II. Part of a series on Problems of European Civilization. Quite useful, especially in the classroom.

1798. Foerster, Friedrich: Europe and the German Question [New York: AMS Press, 1978] Rep. 1940 Ed.

1799. Fuchser, Larry W.: Neville Chamberlain and Appeasement [New York: W. W. Norton, 1982]

Historiographical and intellectual study in the politics of appeasement. Argues that appeasement was not a mistake but a reasoned and reasonable policy for Britain to pursue.

1800. Gardiner, Rolf: "German Eastward Policy and the Baltic States." Cont Rev, vol.145 #819 (March, 1934): 324-331.

1801. Gedye, G. E. R.: Betrayal in Central Europe. Austria and Czechoslovakia: The Fallen Bastions [New York: Harper, 1939] Also published as: Fallen Bastions: The Central European Tragedy [London: Victor Gollancz, 1940]

1802. Gilbert, Martin: The Roots of Appeasement [New York: New American Library, 1966]

Studies the ideological, political, and social background of the policy of appeasement. Sees it as a post-World War I reaction to the carnage of the Western Front and a means to avoid a second world war. Gilbert concludes that appeasement was a failure but should not be seen as a silly or treacherous idea.

1803. ___ and R. Gott: The Appeasers [London: Weidenfeld & Nicolson, 1963]

1804. Gooch, G. P.: "The Background of the War." Cont Rev, vol.157 #892 (April, 1940): 393-403.

1805. Gorski, Ramon: "The Polish Corridor - Another Alsace Lorraine?" Annals, #174 (July, 1934): 126-133.

1806. Gunther, John: "The Rhineland Crisis." Nation, vol. 142 #3691 (April 1, 1936): 407-408.

1807. Hanc, Josef: "From Prague to Warsaw." JCEA, vol.1 #3 (Oct., 1941): 287-306.

1808. ___: "The Last Mile of Appeasement." JCEA, vol.1 #1 (April, 1941): 5-17.

1809. Herman, John: "Soviet Peace Efforts on the Eve of World War Two: A Review of the Soviet Documents." JCH, vol.15 #3 (July, 1980): 577-602.

1810. Hiden, John: Germany and Europe, 1919-1939 [New York: Longman, 1978]

1811. Hill, C. J.: "Great Britain and the Saar Plebiscite of 13 January 1935." JCH, vol.9 #2 (April, 1974): 121-142.

1812. Hill, Leonidas: "3 Crises, 1938-1939." JCH, vol.3 #1 (Jan., 1969): 113-144. * Author discusses Anschluss, Czechoslovakia, and Danzig.

1813. Hoptner, J. B.: Yugoslavia in Crisis, 1934-1941 [New York: Columbia Univ. Press, 1963]

1814. "The Ides of March 1939: March 15, 1939 in Documents." CEO, vol.17 #4 (March 15, 1940): 25-34.

1815. Joesten, Joachim: "Germany´s ´Bleeding´ Frontiers." Fortnightly, #862 (Oct., 1938): 407-411.

1816. Kee, Robert: 1939: In the Shadow of War [Boston: Little, Brown, 1984]

1817. Keith, Arthur B.: The Causes of the War [London: Thomas Nelson & Sons, 1940]

1818. Kennan, George: From Prague After Munich: Diplomatic Papers, 1938-1939 [Princeton, NJ: Princeton Univ. Press, 1968]

1819. Klooz, Marie et al: Events Leading Up to World War II: Chronological History of Certain Major International Events Leading up to and during World War II with the Ostensible Reasons Advanced for their Occurrence, 1931-1944 [Washington, DC: Government Printing Office, 1944]

1820 Korczynski, A. C. et al.: "Poland Between Germany and the USSR, 1926-1939: The Theory of Two Enemies." Polish Rev, vol.20 #1 (March, 1975): 3-64.

1821. Kulski, W.: "The Soviet Union, Germany and Poland." Polish Rev, vol.23 #1 (March, 1978): 18-57.

1822. Laffan, R. G. D. (revised by V. M. Toynbee and P. E. Baker): Survey of International Affairs, 1938: The Crisis over Czechoslovakia, January to December, 1938 [New York: Oxford Univ. Press, 1951]

1823. Lafore, Laurence: The End of Glory: A Interpretation of the Origins of World War II [Philadelphia: J. B. Lippincott, 1970]

1824. Litauer, Stefan: "The Role of Poland Between Germany and Russia." Int Affairs, vol.14 #5 (Sept./Oct., 1935): 654-673.

1825. Loewenheim, Francis L. (ed.): Peace or Appeasement? Hitler, Chamberlain, and the Munich Crisis [Boston: Houghton Mifflin, 1965]

1826. Lukacz, J. A.: The Great Powers and Eastern Europe [New York: American Book Co., 1953]

1827. Lukowitz, David: "George Lansbury´s Peace Mission to Hitler and Mussolini in 1937." Can Jnl/His, vol.15 #1 (April, 1980): 67-82.

1828. Matthews, H. P. S.: "Poland´s Foreign Relations." Fortnighhtly, #860 (Aug., 1938): 162-171.

1829. McSherry, James E.: Stalin, Hitler and Europe: The Origins of World War II vol.1 [Cleveland, OH: World Pub. Co., 1968]

1830. ___: Stalin, Hitler and Europe: The Imbalance of Power vol.2 [Cleveland, OH: World Pub. Co., 1970]

1831. Middlemas, Keith: The Strategy of Appeasement: The British Government and Germany, 1937-1939 [Chicago: Quadrangle Books, 1972]

1832. Ministry for Foreign Affairs: Official Documents Concerning Polish-German and Polish-Soviet Relations, 1933-1939 (Polish White Book) [London: The Polish Government-in-Exile, 1940]

1833. Mommsen, Wolfgang J. and Lothar Kettenacker (eds.): The Fascist Challenge and the Policy of Appeasement [London: George Allen & Unwin, 1983]

1834. Morrow, Jan F.: "Danzig: An International Problem." Cont Rev, vol.150 #849 (Sept., 1936): 303-311.

1835. Mosley, L.: On Borrowed Time: How World War II Began [New York: Random House, 1969]

1836. Namier, Lewis. B.: Diplomatic Prelude, 1938-1939 [New York: Macmillan, 1948]

1837. Offner, Arnold: American Appeasement: United States Policy and Germany [Cambridge, MA: Harvard Univ. Press, 1969]

1838. Oldson, William: "Rumania and the Munich Crisis." EEQ, vol.11 #2 (Sept., 1977): 177-190.

1839. Osusky, Stefan: "Why Czechoslovakia?" F Affairs, vol. 15 #3 (April, 1937): 455-471.

1840. Parker, Robert: "The Czech Crisis: The Background." Fortnightly, #862 (Oct., 1938): 398-406.

1841. Parkinson, R.: Peace For Our Time: Munich to Dunkirk the Inside Story [London: Rupert Hart-Davis, 1971]

1842. Rauschning, H.: "Hitler Could Not Stop." F Affairs, vol.18 #1 (Oct., 1939): 1-12.

1843. Remak, Joachim (ed.): Origins of the Second World War Englewood Cliffs, NJ: Prentice-Hall, 1976]

Collection of documents dealing with the outbreak of World War II covering the period from 1938 to 1941, as seen through the eyes of its participants and leaders.

1844. "The Rhineland Occupation in 1936: How the West was Bluffed." WLB, vol.10 #1/2 (1956): 4-6.

1845. Ripka, H. (Ida Sindelkova and E. P. Young, transls.): Munich: Before and After [New York: Howard Fertig, 1969] Rep. 1939 Ed.

1846. Robbins, Keith: Munich, 1938 [London: Cassell, 1968]

1847. Robertson, E.: Hitler´s Pre-War Policy and Military Plans, 1933-1939 [Secaucus, NJ: Citadel Press, 1967]

1848. ___ (ed.): The Origins of the Second World War [New York: Macmillan, 1971]

1849. Rocek, Joseph S. and J. Skvor: "Benes and Munich: A Reappraisal." EEQ, vol.10 #3 (Fall, 1976): 376-385.

1850. Rosenberg, Arthur: "The Soviet-German Pact and the Jews." J Fr, vol.6 #9 (Sept., 1939): 13-16.

1851. Rowse, Alfred L.: Appeasement: A Study in Political Decline, 1933-1939 [New York: W. W. Norton, 1961]

1852. Royal Institute of International Affairs (M. Curtis, ed.): Documents on International Affairs, 1938 [Oxford: Oxford Univ. Press, 1942/1943]

1853. Schuman, Frederick L.: "The Third Reich´s Road to War." Annals, #175 (Sept., 1934): 33-43.

1854. Secretary of State for Foreign Affairs: Documents Concerning German-Polish Relations and the Outbreak of Hostilities between Great Britain and Germany on Sept. 3, 1939 [London: HMSO, 1939]

1855. Seton-Watson, R. W.: From Munich to Danzig [London: Methuen, 1939]

1856. ___: "Munich and After." Fortnightly, #863 (Nov., 1938): 526-539.

1857. Shadow Over Europe: The Challenge of Nazi Germany [New York: Foreign Policy Assn., 1939]

1858. Snell, John L.(ed.): The Outbreak of the Second World War [Lexington, MA: Heath, 1962]

Anthology of readings on the outbreak of war in 1939. Designed as part of a series on Problems in European Civilization. Useful for high school or college history courses and especially important in teaching the critical analysis of source material.

1859. Somary, Felix: "The American and European Economic Depression and their political Consequences." Int Affairs, vol.10 #2 (March, 1931): 160-176.

1860. Sontag, R. J.: "The Origins of the Second World War." Rev of Politics, vol.25 #4 (Oct., 1963): 497-508.

1861. Steed, H. W.: "The Future of Europe." Int Affairs, vol.12 #6 (Nov./Dec., 1933): 744-762.

1862. Tarnowski, Adam: "Poland's Foreign Policy." Cont Rev, vol.145 #819 (March, 1934): 296-305.

1863. Taylor, A. J. P.: The Origins of the Second World War [London: Hamish Hamilton, 1961]

1864. Thompson, Laurence: The Greatest Treason: The Untold Story of Munich [New York: Wm. Morrow, 1968]

1865. Toynbee, A. J.: "After Munich: The World Outlook." Int Affairs, vol.18 #1 (Jan./Feb., 1939): 1-28.

1866. ___: "Peaceful Change or War? The Next Stage in the International Crisis." Int Affairs, vol.15 #1 (Jan./Feb., 1936): 26-56.

1867. ___ and Veronica Toynbee (eds.): The Eve of War 1939: Survey of International Affairs, 1939-1946 [New York: Oxford Univ. Press, 1958]

1868. Watt, Donald C.: "Before the Blitzkrieg." Hist/WWII, #1 (1972): 1-9.

1869. ___: "German Plans for the Reoccupation of the Rhineland: A Note." JCH, vol.1 #4 (Oct., 1966): 193-199.

1870. Weinberg, Gerhard L.: "A Proposed Compromise Over Danzig in 1939?" JCEA, vol.14 #4 (Jan., 1955): 334-338.

1871. Werth, Alexander: France and Munich [New York: Howard Fertig, 1969]

1872. Wheeler-Bennet, John W.: Munich: Prologue to Tragedy [New York: Duell, Sloan and Pearce, 1948]

Diplomatic history of the events leading to the Munich crisis of September 1938. Describes the Nazi rise to power, the "golden age" of appeasement, and the fate awaiting Czechoslovakia. Based mainly on Czech state documents as well as on German documents made public at Nuremberg.

1873. Wiskemann, E.: "Czechoslovakia and Her Future." Fortnightly, #859 (July, 1938): 57-65. * On the Sudeten problem.

COURSE AND EFFECTS OF WAR

Military Histories

1874. Anders, W.: Hitler's Defeat in Russia [Chicago: Regnery, 1953]

1875. Ansel, Walter: Hitler Confronts England [Durham, NC: Duke Univ. Press, 1960]

1876. Brower, Daniel R.: "The Soviet Union and the German Invasion of 1941: A New Soviet View." JMH, vol.41 #3 (Sept., 1969): 327-334.

1877. Bryant, Arthur: The Turn of the Tide [Garden City, NY: Doubleday, 1957]

History of the war, based on the war diary of Lord Alan Brooke, British Chief of Staff. Quotes extensively from the diary, but also contains much material by the author. Mentions Jews only once.

1878. Calvocoressi, Peter and G. Wint: Total War: The Story of World War II [New York: Pantheon Books, 1972]

Possibly the best written overall history of the war. Includes 34 maps by Martin Gilbert. Part III is on Europe under the Nazis, and includes a review of the persecution of the Jews in pp.220-241.

1879. Cecil, R.: Hitler's Decision to Invade Russia, 1941 [New York: David McKay, 1976]

1880-1885. Churchill, Sir Winston S.: The Second World War 6 vols. [Boston: Houghton Mifflin, 1948/1953]

1. The Gathering Storm (1948)
2. Their Finest Hour (1949)
3. The Grand Alliance (1951)
4. The Hinge of Fate (1950)
5. Closing the Ring (1951)
6. Triumph and Tragedy (1953)

Authoritative account of Britain at war by Britain's Prime Minister and chief architect of victory. Each volume contains much important material, including citations from the Premier's official war diary. Jews are mentioned in almost every volume.

1886. Clark, Alan: Barbarossa: The Russian-German Conflict, 1941-1945 [New York: William Morrow, 1965]

1887. Eisenhower, Dwight D.: Crusade in Europe [Garden City, NY: Doubleday, 1948]

Personal account by the Allied Supreme Commander of the Allied onslaught on Nazi Germany. Includes some information about Jews, both during and after the war.

1888. Gafencu, G. (E. Fletcher-Allen, transl.): Prelude to the Russian Campaign [London: Muller, 1945]

1889. Goldston, R. C.: The Life and Death of Nazi Germany [Indianapolis, IN: Bobbs-Merrill, 1967]

1890. Goralski, Robert: World War II Almanac 1939-1945 [New York: G. P. Putnam's Sons, 1981]

1891. Higgins, Trumbull: Hitler and Russia: The Third Reich in a Two-Front War, 1937-1943 [New York: Macmillan, 1966]

1892. Hoyle, Martha B.: A World in Flames: A History of World War II [New York: Atheneum, 1970]

1893. Irving, David J.: Hitler's War [New York: Viking Press, 1977]

1894. ___: The War Path: Hitler's Germany, 1933-1939 [New York: Viking Press, 1978] * Highly controversial revisionist histories of World War II.

1895. Korwin-Rhodes, Marta: The Mask of Warriors: The Siege of Warsaw, September 1939 [Roslyn Heights, NY: Libra Publishers, 1964]

1896. Michel, Henri: The Second World War [New York: F. A. Praeger, 1975]

1897. Pitt, Barrie: "The War: An Overview." Hist/WWII, #93 (1974): 2592-2597.

1898. Reilly, Henry J.: "Blitzkrieg." F Affairs, vol.18 #2 (Jan., 1940): 254-265. * On the conduct of war.

1899. Royal Institute of International Affairs: Chronology of the Second World War [London: The Institute, 1947]

1900. Saunders, Alan: The Invasion of Poland [New York: Franklin Watts, 1984]

1901. Schmidt, Paul K. (E. Osers, transl.): Hitler Moves East, 1941-1943 [Boston: Little, Brown, 1964]

1902. ___: Scorched Earth: The Russian-German War 1943-1944 [Boston: Little, Brown, 1970]

1903. Seaton, Albert: The Russo-German War, 1941-1945 [New York: F. A. Praeger, 1971]

1904. Snyder, L. S.: The War: A Concise History, 1939-1945 [New York: Simon & Schuster, 1960]

1905. Toland, John: The Last 100 Days [New York: Bantam Books, 1980]

1906. Trevor-Roper, Hugh R. (ed.): Blitzkrieg to Defeat: Hitler´s War Directives, 1939-1945 [New York: Holt, Rinehart & Winston, 1965]

1907. Van Creveld, Martin L.: Hitler´s Strategy 1940-1941: The Balkan Clue [Cambridge: Cambridge Univ. Press, 1973]

1908. Weinberg, Gerhard L.: World in the Balance: Behind the Scenes of World war II [Hanover, MA: Univ. Press of New England, 1982]

1909. Werth, Alexander: Russia at War, 1941-1945 [New York: E. P. Dutton, 1964]

1910. Whaley, Barton: Codeword Barbarossa [Cambridge, MA: MIT Press, 1973]

1911. Wiskemann, Elizabeth: "The Breaking of the Axis." Int Affairs, vol.22 #2 (April, 1946): 227-239.

1912. Wright, Gordon: Ordeal of Total War, 1939-1945 [New York: Harper & Row, 1968]

Military and political history of Europe in World War II. Deals comprehensively but concisely with most of the issues raised by the process of total warfare. Chapter Six deals with Nazi occupation policies in Europe including the Final Solution. Chapter Seven deals with resistance to Nazi tyranny.

1913. Addison, Paul: The Road to 1945: British Politics and the Second World War [London: Quartet Books, 1975]

1914. Allen, Louis: "Diplomacy." Hist/WWII, #114 (1974): 3165-3174.

1915. Bailey, Th. A. and P. B. Ryan: Hitler vs. Roosevelt [New York: Free Press, 1979]

1916. Bengtson, John: Nazi War Aims [Rock Island, IL: Augustana College Library, 1962]

1917. Carlyle, Margaret (ed.): Documents on International Affairs, 1939-1946: Hitler's Europe [New York: Oxford Univ. Press, 1954]

1918. Compton, James: The Swastika and the Eagle: Hitler, the United States, and the Origins of World War II [Boston: Houghton Mifflin, 1967]

1919. de Groot, Emile: "The Twilight of National Socialism in Germany, 1943-1945." Int Affairs, vol.23 #4 (Oct., 1947): 531-545.

1920. Friedlander, Saul: Prelude to Downfall: Hitler and the U. S. 1939-1941 [New York: A. A. Knopf, 1967]

1921. Hartshorne, Edward Y.: "Reactions to the Nazi Threat: A Study of Propaganda and Culture Conflict." Pub Op Q, vol.5 #4 (Win., 1941): 625-639.

1922. Jacobsen, Hans A. and A. L. Smith (eds.): World War II. Policy and Strategy: Selected Documents with Commentary [Santa Barbara, CA: ABC-Clio Press, 1979]

1923. Kantorowicz, Alfred: "The Strategy of Anti-Nazi Propaganda." FW, vol.2 #2 (March, 1942): 144-147.

1924. Koch, H. W.: "The Pocket Reich." Hist/WWII, #97 (1974): 2714-2716. * On the surrender of Germany.

1925. Lukas, R. C.: The Strange Alliance: The United States and Poland, 1941-1945 [Knoxville: Univ. of Tennessee Press, 1978]

1926. Mastny, Vojtech: "Stalin and the Prospects of a Separate Peace in World War II." AHR, vol.77 #5 (Dec., 1972): 1365-1388.

1927. McNeill, William H.: America, Britain and Russia: Their Co-operation and Conflict, 1941-1946 [New York: Johnson Reprint Corp., 1970]

1928. Orzell, Laurence: "Poland and Russia July 1941-April 1943: The Impossible Alliance." Polish Rev, vol.21 #4 (Dec., 1976): 35-58.

1929. Roetter, Charles: "The Clash of Propaganda." Hist/WWII, #42 (1973): 1162-1171.

1930. Rozek, Edward J.: Allied Wartime Diplomacy: A Pattern in Poland [New York: John Wiley & Sons, 1958]

1931. Schuman, F. L.: Night Over Europe: The Diplomacy of Nemesis, 1939-1940 [New York: A. A. Knopf, 1941]

1932. Sontag, Raymond J. and James Beddie (eds.): Nazi-Soviet Relations, 1939-1941: Documents from Archives of the German Foreign Office [Westport, CT: Greenwood Press, 1976]

WAR CRIMES, NON-JEWISH

General Surveys

1933. Drost, Peiter N.: The Crime of the State [Leyden: J. B. Brill, 1959]

1934. King, Christine E.: "Some Lesser-Known Victims of Totalitarian Persecution." PoP, vol.16 #2 (April, 1982): 15-26.

1935. Kinnard, Clark: This Must Not Happen Again! The Black Book of Fascist Horror [New York: Pilot Pen, 1945]

1936. Kuper, Leo: Genocide: Its Political Use in the Twentieth Century [New Haven, CT: Yale Univ. Press, 1981]

1937. Porter, Jack N. (ed.) Genocide and Human Rights: A Global Anthology [Washington, DC: Univ. Press of America, 1981]

Anthology of essays on genocide in the twentieth century. Forms the basis for a comparative history of the victimization of a variety of peoples in differing socio-political contexts. Part I is on the Holocaust.

1938. "Secret Nazi Instructions on Conquered Peoples: A Document." Am Mercury, vol.53 #212 (Aug., 1941): 144-149. * On orders concerning the behavior of German troops in countries occupied or to be occupied.

The Extermination of Gypsies

1939. Fein, H.: "Extermination of the Gypsies." Chartock: Society, pp.43-44.

1940. Ficowski, Jerzy (J. Rotblat, transl.): "The Fate of Polish Gypsies." Porter: Genocide, pp.166-177.

1941. Friedman, Philip: "The Extermination of the Gypsies: Nazi Genocide of an Aryan People." Friedman: Roads, pp.381-386. Also in Porter: Genocide, pp.151-157.

1942. Tyrnauer, Gabrielle: "Mastering the Past: Germans and Gypsies." Porter: Genocide, pp.178-192.

1943. Yates, Dora E.: "Hitler and the Gypsies: The Fate of Europe´s Oldest Aryans." Com, vol.8 #5 (Nov., 1949): 455-459. Also in Porter: Genocide, pp.158-165.

Racial and Ideological Crimes

1944. Batavia, S.: "Extermination of Patients with Mental Disorders." Commission: GCIP/II, pp.151-160.

1945. Fischer, Alfred J.: "Background of the German Kidnapping." CEO, vol.30 #19 (Sept. 13, 1946): 298-299. * On the Nazi concept of Lebensborn.

1946. Grunberger, Richard: "Euthanasia." Chartock: Society, pp.138-139.

1947. "The Judaeo-Masonic World Conspiracy: Nazi Persecution of the Lodges." WLB, vol.15 #2 (April, 1961): 36-37.

1948. Lunden, Sven G.: "The Anihilation of Freemasonry." Am Mercury, vol.52 #206 (Feb., 1941): 184-191.

1949. Rector, Frank: The Nazi Extermination of Homosexuals [New York: Stein and Day, 1981]

Crimes in Czechoslovakia

1950. Balint, Nicholas G. (ed.): Lidice Lives Forever [New York: Europa Books, 1942]

1951. Bradley, John: Lidice: Sacrificial Village [New York: Ballantine Books, 1972]

The story of the Nazi massacre of civilians in Czechoslovakia in revenge for the assassination of the Reichsprotektor, Reinhard Heydrich.

1952. Czechoslovak Ministry of Foreign Affairs: German Massacres in Occupied Czechoslovakia Following the Attack on Reinhard Heydrich [London: Wm. Lea, 1942]

1953. Hutak, J. B.: With Blood and with Iron [London: Hale, 1957]

1954. Kernan, William C.: "Lidice and the Jews." J Sp, vol. 8 #5 (March, 1943): 23-24.

1955. Lidice: A Tribute by Members of the International PEN [London: Allen and Unwin/Czechoslovak PEN, 1944]

1956. Wittlin, Th.: Time Stopped at 6:30 [Indianapolis, IN: Bobbs-Merrill, 1965]

1957. Zizka, V.: Lidice [London: Hutchinson, 1943]

Crimes in Poland

1958. Bartoszewski, W.: "German Crimes During the Warsaw Rising." Commission: GCIP/I, pp.187-231.

1959. ___: "Public Executions at Warsaw." Commission: GCIP/I, pp.171-183.

1960. Broniewska, Janina: "Hitlerite Crimes in Poland." CEO, vol.18 #25 (Dec. 12, 1941): 359-360.

1961. Czynska, S.: "Mass Executions in Poland in the Period 1939-1945." Commission: GCIP/II, pp.47-65. * Also deals with the extermination of Jews.

1962. "The German Mass Murder of the Polish People." PFR, #14 (Feb. 15, 1941): 6-8.

1963. Hudson, G. F.: "Who Is Guilty of the Katyn Massacre? The Truth at the Bottom of the Pit." Com, vol.13 #3 (March, 1952): 203-208.

1964. Klukowski, Z.: "How the Eviction of Poles by the Germans from the Area of Zamosc was Carried Out." Commission: GCIP/II, pp.69-85.

1965. The Persecution of the Catholic Church in German Occupied Poland [London: Burns, Oates, 1941]

1966. Starski, W. B.: "I was a German Hostage." FW, vol.3 #2 (July, 1942): 175-179.

1967. Wrzos-Glinka, Stanislaw et al: We Have Not Forgotten English/Polish/French [Warsaw: Polonia Pub. House, 1959]

Crimes in Russia

1968. Jacobsen, Hans-Adolf (D. Long, transl.): "The Kommissarbefehl and Mass Executions of Soviet Russian Prisoners of War." Krausnick: Anatomy, pp.505-535.

1969. New Soviet Documents on Nazi Atrocities [London: Hutchinson, 1943]

1970. Nikitin, M. N. and P. I. Vagin: The Crimes of the German Fascists in the Leningrad Region [London: Hutchinson, n. d.]

1971. Ploski, S.: "German Crimes Against Soviet Prisoners-of-War in Poland." Commission: GCIP/I, pp.261-268

1972. We Shall Not Forgive!: The Horrors of the German Invasion in Documents and Photographs [Moscow: Foreign Language Publishing House, 1942]

8

Europe Under Nazism

LIFE IN GERMANY UNDER THE NAZIS

Contemporary Views

1973. Balogh, Thomas: "The Economic Background in Germany." Int Affairs, vol.18 #2 (March/April, 1939): 227-248.

1974. Bayles, Wm.: "Living in Germany Today." Am Mercury, vol.52 #205 (Jan., 1941): 7-17. Also in J Sp, vol.6 #4 (Feb., 1941): 9-11.

1975. Book, Frederik (E. Sprigge and C. Napier, transls.): An Eyewitness in Germany [London: L. Dickson, 1933]

1976. Brandt, Albert A.: "The Situation Inside Germany: Hitler Prepares for German Civil War." Am Mercury, vol.55 #223 (July, 1942): 7-21.

1977. Breitschield, R.: "The Plight of Germany." Cont Rev, vol.146 #826 (Oct., 1934): 385-392.

1978. "A Decade of Decadence." NJM, vol.57 #5 (Jan., 1943): 152-155; #6 (Feb., 1943): 194-196; #7 (March, 1943): 228-230. * Ten years Nazi rule, a pictorial review.

1979. Dell, Robert E.: "The Future of Hitler." Nation, vol. 139 #3611 (Sept. 19, 1934): 320-322.

1980. ___: Germany Unmasked [London: M. Hopkins, 1934]

Critical examination of the policies and ideologies of

Nazism. Also views the causes of the rise of National Socialism and the implications of Nazism for Jews, Germany, and the world.

1981. Fromm, Bella: Blood and Banquets: A Berlin Social Diary [New York: Harper & Row, 1942]

1982. Gedye, G. E. R.: "Impressions of Hitler´s Germany." Cont Rev, vol.143 #810 (June, 1933): 669-676.

1983. "Germany´s Food Problem." PFR, #46 (June 15, 1942): Whole Issue.

1984. Gooch, G. P.: "The Terror in Germany." Cont Rev, vol. 146 #824 (Aug., 1934): 129-136.

1985. Greenwood, H. P.: Hitler´s First Year [London: Methuen, 1934]

1986. Grey, C. G.: "In Germany To-Day." Fasc Q, vol.2 (1936): 245-254.

1987. Grzesinski, Albert (A. Lipschitz, transl.): Inside Germany [New York: E. P. Dutton, 1939]

1988. Guillebaud, C. W.: The Social Policy of Nazi Germany [New York: Macmillan, 1942]

1989. Hamburger, Ludwig: "Labor Under Hitler." Am Mercury, vol.52 #210 (June, 1941): 730-736.

1990. Hamilton, A. L.: "Below the Surface." Survey Graphic, vol.22 #9 (Sept., 1933): 449-454.

1991. Johnson, Albin: "The State of German Morale Today." Am Mercury, vol.58 #244 (April, 1944): 391-395.

1992. Kurz, Fritz: "German Opinion and the Nazis." Cont Rev, vol.157 #890 (Feb., 1940): 195-201.

1993. Mann, Erika (Maurice Samuel, transl.): The Lights Go Down [New York: Farrar and Rinehart, 1940]

1994. Neuberger, Richard: "Germany Under the Chokebit." New Republic, vol.77 #989 (Nov. 15, 1933): 13-15.

1995. ___: "The New Germany." Nation, vol.137 #3561 (Oct. 4, 1933): 376-379.

1996. Peterson, Jan: Our Street: A Chronicle Written in Nazi Germany [London: Victor Gollancz, 1938]

1997. Phillips, H.: Germany Today and Tomorrow [New York: Dodd, Mead & Co., 1935]

1998. Pitlon, Harold: Nazis and Germans [London: Allen and Unwin, 1940]

1999. Schonfeld, Moses and H. Appelman (eds.): The Mark of the Swastika [New York: The Ad Press, 1941]

Collection of reports on the state of affairs in Nazi Germany culled from the reports of Ambassador Sir Neville Henderson. The authors also look at Hitler's ideology and how it was translated into practice. The text is in English and Yiddish.

2000. Schuman, Frederick L.: "Germany Prepares Fear." New Republic, vol.77 #1001 (Feb. 7, 1934): 353-355.

2001. Spivak, John L.: Europe Under the Terror [New York: Simon and Schuster, 1936]

2002. Thompson, Dorothy: "Nazi Rule of Terror Described." P/P Herald, vol.2 #1/6 (Special Issue, 1933): 21-32.

2003. Von Rauschenplat, Hellmut and Hilda Monte: "Government and People in Germany." Cont Rev, vol.157 #894 (June, 1940): 717-722.

2004. Wertheimer, Mildred: Germany Under Hitler [New York: Foreign Policy Association, 1935]

2005. Wilson, Duncan R.: Germany's New Order [Oxford: Clarendon Press, 1941]

2006. Wise, J. W.: "Nazi Program and Nazi Rule." P/P Herald vol.2 #1/6 (Special Issue, 1933): 18-21.

2007 Yahuda, A. S.: "The Nazi Menace to Liberty of Thought." WJ, vol.2 #38 (Jan. 25, 1934): 4, 6; #39 (Feb. 1, 1934): 6-7; #40 (Feb. 8, 1934): 6-7.

Historical Views

2008. Besser, O.: "The Nazis Rule Germany." Kowalski: Anthology/I, pp.80-84.

2009. Boehm, Erich H. (ed.): We Survived: 14 Histories of the Hidden and Hunted of Nazi Germany [New Haven, Yale Univ. Press, 1949]

2010. de Witt, Thomas E.: "The Struggle Against Hunger and Cold: Winter Relief in Nazi Germany, 1933-1939." Can Jnl/His, vol.12 #3 (Feb., 1978): 361-382.

2011. De Zaaijer, H. R.: "Law Enforcement." Annals, #245 (May, 1946): 9-18.

2012. Gilford, H.: The Reichstag Fire [New York: Franklin Watts, 1973]

2013. Grunfeld, Frederic: The Hitler File: A Social History of Germany and the Nazis, 1918-1945 [New York: Random House, 1974]

2014. Hagen, Paul: "Four Horsemen over Germany." Survey Graphic, vol.34 #11 (Nov., 1945): 434-437, 456-458.

2015. Hale, Oron: The Captive Press in the Third Reich [Princeton, NJ: Princeton Univ. Press, 1964]

Well documented study on the process of Gleichschaltung (coordination) with the German press from the Nazi takeover until 1945. By Supposedly legal means the German press was not only muzzled, but virtually absorbed into the NSDAP.

2016. Hans, D.: "The Legitimate Press." Annals, #245 (May, 1946): 113-117.

2017. Hauser, R.: True Tales of Hitler's Reich [London: Fawcett, Muller, 1964]

2018. Kershaw, Ian: Popular Opinion and Political Dissent in the Third Reich, Bavaria 1933-1945 [Oxford: Oxford Univ. Press, 1983]

Study of the workings of Nazi totalitarianism in Bavaria. Shows that despite repression and terror there was still room for popular dissent and complaint to and about the regime. Contains considerable information on the destruction of Bavarian Jewry. He concludes that for most Germans the Jewish question was of only minimal interest despite the availability of information on the Final Solution.

2019. Mayer, Milton S.: They Thought They Were Free: The Germans, 1933-1945 [Chicago: Univ. of Chicago Press, 1955]

2020. Posthumus, J. H.: "Order and Disorder." Annals, #245 (May, 1946): 1-8.

2021. Steinert, M. G. (T. E. de Witt, transl.): Hitler´s War and the Germans: Public Mood and Attitude during the Second World War [Athens: Ohio Univ. Press, 1977]

2022. Sydewitz, May: Civil Life in Wartime Germany: The Story of the Home Front [New York: Viking, 1945]

2023. Tartakower, Arieh: "Hitler´s Heritage." Dispersion, #5/6 (Spr., 1966): 77-138.

2024. "Where ´Gleichschaltung´ Failed: Nonconformity in the Third Reich." WLB, vol.13 #1/2 (1959): 9-11.

GERMAN JEWS UNDER THE NAZIS

Overviews

2025. "After the Olympics - What?" NJM, vol.50 #8 (May, 1936): 265, 271.

2026. Am. Jewish Committee: The Jewish Situation in Germany [New York: The Committee, 1934]

2027. ___: The Jews in Nazi Germany: A Handbook of Facts Regarding their Present Situation [New York: The Committee, 1935]

Handbook summarizng all Nazi anti-Jewish policies from 1933-1935. Outlines the development of German antisemitism and how it laid the groundwork for nazism. Contains useful statistical information.

2028. Am. Jewish Joint Distribution Comm.: Twelve Months Later: A Composite Report on the Situation of the Jews in Germany [New York: The Joint, 1934]

2029. Angress, Werner T.: "The German Jews, 1933-1939." Friedlander: Ideology, pp.69-82.

2030. Aron, Albert: "The Jews in Germany." CJR, vol.2 #2 (March/April, 1939): 6-14.

2031. Bender, Ch.: "Germany Fountain of Trouble." CJCh, vol.24 #15 (Aug. 28, 1936): 15, 18.

2032. Bentwich, Norman: "German Jews in 1936." NJM, vol.51 #9 (June, 1937): 292-293.

2033. ___: "German Jews Today." J Fr, vol.3 #5 (May, 1936): 11-12.

2034. ___: "Regeneration in Germany." J Fr, vol.3 #9/10 (Sept./Oct., 1936): 25-26.

2035. Bernays, Robert: "Nazis and the Jews." Cont Rev, vol. 144 #815 (Nov., 1933): 523-531.

2036. Bernstein, Philip: "Can Hitler be Trusted?" Nation, vol.137 #5373 (Dec. 27, 1933): 728-730.

2037. Blau, Bruno: "The Jewish Population of Germany, 1939-1945." JSS, vol.12 #2 (April, 1950): 161-172.

2038. ___: "The Jews of Germany, 1933-1945: Sources of Statistics." WLB, vol.6 #5/6 (Sept./Dec., 1952): 37.

2039. ___: "The Last Days of German Jewry in the Third Reich." YIVO Annual, vol.8 (1953): 197-204.

2040. Bolitho, G.: The Other Germany [New York: Appelton-Century, 1934] * A survey of early conditions in which German Jews had to live under the Nazi Regime.

2041. Carruthers, L. W.: "The fact Behind Hitler's Speech: Germany Plans New Frightfulness." JW, vol.2 #57 (June 7, 1935): 3, 6-7; #58 (June 14, 1935): 6, 16.

2042. "Chronology of Laws and Actions Directed Against Jews in Nazi Germany, 1933-1945." Chartock: Society, pp. 22-30.

2043. Cohen, Israel: "Jewish Tragedy." QR, vol.263 (Oct., 1934): 252-268. * Surveys anti-Jewish excesses in Nazi Germany and pro-Nazi movements around the globe.

2044. ___: "Jews in Germany." QR, vol.261 (July, 1933): 1-20.

2045. Dell, Robert E.: "The German Nightmare." Nation, vol. 137 #3563 (Oct. 18, 1933): 433-435.

2046. Elowitz, Mark H.: "The Friedberg Judenbad." JH, vol. 10 #4 (Spr., 1968): 11-12.

2047. Fay, Sidney B.: "Germany's Anti-Jewish Campaign." Cur His, vol.38 (May, 1933): 142-145.

2048. ___: "Nazi Treatment of the Jews." Cur His, vol.38 (June, 1933): 295-300.

2049. ___: "Plight of the German Jews." Cur His, vol.43 (Feb., 1936): 536-537.

2050. Fischer, Louis: "What I Saw in Germany." Nation, vol. 142 #3684 (Feb. 12, 1936): 176-178.

2051. Freeden, H.: "The Dance on the Volcano." J Digest, vol.10 #1 (Oct., 1964): 33-36.

2052. Fuss, O. R.: "The Plight of the Jews in Middle Europe." P/P Herald, vol.4 #1/3 (Jan./March, 1935): 16-17.

2053. "The Future of German Jewry." WJ, vol.2 #96 (March 13, 1936): 7, 24.

2054. Gennett, Isador J.: "Laying the Wreath and After." Menorah, vol.26 #3 (Oct./Dec., 1938): 291-315.

2055. "The German-Jewish Situation." J Rev, #6 (Sept./Dec., 1933): 23-25.

2056. "German Jewry in 1937." NJM, vol.52 #4 (Dec., 1937): 130-131, 146.

2057. "The German Situation." J Press, vol.4 #8 (May, 1933): 5-6.

2058. "The German Tragedy." J Rev, #5 (June/Sept., 1933): 4-22.

2059. "Germany: Notes." J Rev, #6 (Sept./Dec., 1933): 4-22.

2060. "Ghastly State of German Jewry. Whole Community Condemned to Die." CJCh, vol.23 #29 (Dec. 6, 1935): 12-13.

2061. Golden, S.: "Hitler´s New Wave of Terror." J Life, vol.2 #7 (July, 1938): 6-9.

2062. Gutman, L. L.: "The Yellow Spot." J Fr, vol.41 #1 (April, 1974): 20-22.

2063. Hamilton, Alice: "The Plight of the German Intellectuals." Harper´s, vol.168 (Jan., 1934): 159-169.

2064. Hertz, Anne: "Inside Germany. A Report." HM, vol.21 #8 (July/Aug., 1941): 11-13.

2065. High, Stanley: "The German Program of Antisemitism." Lit Digest, vol.116 #20 (Nov. 11, 1933): 13, 26-27.

2066. Hirsch, Felix E.: "The First Hundred Days of the Hitler Nightmare." NY Times Mag, (May 11, 1958): 14-15, 65-67. * On the 25th anniversary of the Nazi book burning. A recollection.

2067. "Hitler´s War of Extermination." J Fr, vol.2 #11 (Sept., 1935): 4-5.

2068. Institut zum Studium der Judenfrage: "The Jews in Germany." Fasc Q, vol.2 (1936): 302-309.

2069. Isserman, Ferdinand: "Doom of German Jewry Nearer." CJCh, vol.22 #18 (Sept. 21, 1934): 5, 12.

2070. ___: "I Revisit Nazi Germany." Am J Times, vol.1 #4 (July, 1936): 7, 10. Also in CJCh, vol.23 #26 (Nov. 15, 1935): 7, 14.

2071. ___: Sentenced to Death! The Jews in Germany: An Opinion Based on One Month´s Study in the Third Reich [St.Louis, MO: Modern View Pub., 1933]

2072. "The Jews in Germany." CJR, vol.1 #5 (Nov., 1938): 15-19.

2073. Kahn, Ernst: "Has German Jewry a Future?" Menorah, vol.23 #1 (April/June, 1935): 18-20.

2074. Kohenski, A. S.: "The ´Jewish Question´ in the Third Reich." Pilch: Catastrophe, pp.39-46.

2075. Krop, J. F.: "The Jews Under the Nazi Regime." Annals, #245 (May, 1946): 28-32.

2076. La Follette, S.: "´Goetterdaemmerung´." Scribner´s, vol.94 #1 (July, 1933): 13-16.

2077. Lestchinsky, Jacob: "The End of German Jewry." HM, vol.2 #7 (May/June, 1941): 10-11.

2078. Lewisohn Ludwig: "Germany´s Lowest Depths." Nation, vol.136 #3539 (May 3, 1933): 493-494.

2079. Lieberknecht, P.: "A German Student Speaks." Nation, vol.137 #3566 (Nov. 8, 1933) 534-535. * Eyewitness account of brutal treatment of Jews in Germany.

2080. Lore, Ludwig: "The Jews in Fascist Germany." New Republic, vol.74 #958 (April 12, 1933): 236-238.

2081. ___: "Nazi Revolution at Work." Nation, vol.136 #3537 (April 19, 1933): 440-443.

2082. Mann, Erika: "Postcards from Germany." NJM, vol.54 #2 (Oct., 1939): 45-46, 54-55.

2083. Mark, J.: "The Plight of the German Jew." J Layman, vol.8 #6 (Feb., 1934): 6-7.

2084. Montifiore, L. G.: The Jews in Germany [London: Anglo-Jewish Association, 1934/35] * A series of 3 pamphlets (Jan., 1934); (Sept., 1934); (Sept., 1935).

2085. Mowrer, Edgar A.: "Berlin: Civilization in Germany." Menorah, vol.21 #1 (April/June, 1933): 63-72.

2086. Nussbaum, Max: "How Jews Live in Germany Today." Ort Eco Bul, vol.1 #4/5 (July/Oct., 1940): 3-5.

2087. ___: "Life in Wartime Germany." CJR, vol.3 #6 (Nov./Dec., 1940): 577-586.

2088. Olden, Rudolph: "A Documentary Record of the Persecution of the Jews in Germany." J Rev, #8 (March/June, 1934): 81-87.

2089. Osborn, Max: "Jews of the Rhineland." CW, vol.12 #13 (April 13, 1945): 9-10.

2090. Ottenheimer, Hilde: "The Disappearance of Jewish Communities in Germany 1900-1938." JSS, vol.3 #2 (April, 1941): 189-206.

2091. "Outlawed and Without Protection. What Jews Suffer Today in Some of the Smaller Communities of Germany." NJM, vol.50 #2 (Nov., 1935): 45, 62-63; #3 (Dec., 1935): 78-79, 87.

2092. "The Outlawed Jews of Hesse: Judah, Get Out!" CJCh, vol.22 #36 (Jan. 25, 1935): 12-13.

2093. Pinson, K. S.: "The Jewish Spirit in Nazi Germany." Menorah, vol.24 #3 (Oct./Dec., 1936): 228-254.

2094. "The Record of Nazi Ruthlessness Against the Jews." Lit Digest, vol.116 #2 (July 8, 1933): 20-21.

2095. Rosenfeld, Kurt: "What Germany Does to the Jews." New Republic, vol.85 (Jan. 15, 1936): 275-277.

2096. Roth, Cecil: "The New Ghetto." FR, vol.144 (Nov., 1935): 593-599.

2097. Schleunes, Karl A.: The Twisted Road to Auschwitz: Nazi Policy Toward German Jews 1933-1939 [Urbana, IL: Univ. of Chicago Press, 1970]

Definitive study of Nazi Germany´s prewar Jewish policies. Schleunes points out that before 1938 there was no single Nazi policy on Jews but rather a plethora of competing and, at times, contradictory proposals. Only with the advent of war and the complete Nazi domination of Europe did Hitler feel secure enough to plan a "final" and total solution for the "Jewish problem".

2098. Schulz, Ernest: "The Hopeless State of German Jewry." NJM, vol.48 #2 (Nov., 1933): 54, 68-69.

2099. Schwab, Herman: "Germany, 1933. From a Diary." JQ, vol.1 #4 (Spr., 1954): 11-15.

2100. Silverman, Dore: "In Germany Now." NJM, vol.48 #6 (March, 1934): 184-185, 209-210.

2101. Simon, Erich M.: "The Plight of German Jewry." Ort Eco Bul, vol.2 #2 (March/April, 1941): 4-5.

2102. Smolar, Boris: "Grim Days Face German Jewry." CJCh, vol.22 #15 (Aug. 31, 1934): 5, 9.

2103. ___: "Nazis Starve 15,000 Professionals." CJCh, vol. 22 #19 (Sept. 28, 1934): 8, 13.

2104. Stone, Robert: "The Nazi War Against the Jew." CJCh, vol.20 #48 (April 21, 1933): 7, 15.

2105. "The Strategy of Hatred." Am Heb, vol.151 #11 (July 17, 1942): 8-9.

2106. Strauss, Walter (ed.): Signs of Life. Jews from Wuertemberg: Reports for the Period after 1933 in Letters and Description [New York: Ktav, 1982]

2107. Theilhaber, Felix A.: "Decline of the German Jews." Living Age, vol.349 (Sept., 1935): 58-60.

2108. Thompson, Dorothy: "National Socialism: Theory and Practice." F Affairs, vol.13 #4 (July, 1935): 557-573. * Study on the treatment of Jews.

2109. ___: "Record of Persecution." PVP: Nazism, pp.1-24.

2110. Trepp, Leo: "Of German Jewry." Con Jud, vol.3 #1 (Nov., 1946): 1-8.

2111. Viton, Albert: "The Nazi Throne Totters." NJM, vol.50 #1 (Oct., 1935): 13, 27-29. * Anti-Jewish acts are being planned very carefully in Nazi Germany.

2112. Warburg, Gustav O.: Six Years of Hitler: The Jews under the Nazi Regime [London: Allen and Unwin, 1939]

2113. Weinberg, S.: "East European Jews in Germany." NJM, vol.49 #6 (March, 1935): 196, 212.

2114. Weiss-Rosmarin, Trude: "Explaining the German Jew." J Sp, vol.2 #7 (May, 1937): 13-15, 40.

2115. Werner, A.: "In Defense of German Jewry." Judaism, vol.2 #2 (April, 1953): 170-176.

2116. Wertheimer, Mildred: "The Jews in the Third Reich." FPR, vol.9 (Oct. 11, 1933): 174-184. * Summary of anti-Jewish disabilities.

2117. "When ´Schrecklichkeit´ Reigns." CJCh, vol.26 #26 (Nov., 18, 1938): 5, 15.

2118. Wiesenfeld, Leon: "Blood, Sweat and Tears." JVP, vol. 4 #9/10 (Oct., 1941): 12-13, 21.

2119. Wise, S. S.: "The War Upon World Jewry." PVP: Nazism, pp.202-211.

2120. The Yellow Spot: The Extermination of the Jews in Germany [London: Gollancz, 1936]

Documentary account of the Nazi persecution of German Jewry from 1933 to 1936. Includes a large number of important documents.

2121. Zuckerman, Wm.: "Antisemitism Revives in Germany." Nation, vol.140 #3638 (March 27, 1935): 356-357.

2122. ___: "Can German Jewry be Saved? CJCh, vol.23 #11 (Aug. 2, 1935): 8, 12; #12 (Aug. 9, 1935): 5, 16.

2123. ___: "Nazis Without a Jewish Policy." FR, vol.144 (July, 1935): 86-94.

2124. ___: "Where the German Ghetto Leads." Nation, vol.142 #3683 (Feb. 5, 1936): 154-156.

Reorganization of Jewish Communal Life

2125. "The Age Distribution of German Jewry." J Rev, #6 (Sept./Dec., 1933): 44- 53.

2126. Ball-Kaduri, Kurt J.: "The National Representation of Jews in Germany: Obstacles and Accomplishments at its Establishment." YVS, vol.2 (1958): 159-178.

2127. Ben-Menachem, Michael: "Zionism in Germany." NJ, vol. 12 #4 (Jan., 1936): 53-55.

2128. "B´nai B´rith Crushed in Germany." NJM, vol.51 #8 (May, 1837): 252-253.

2129. Colodner, Solomon: Jewish Education in Germany Under the Nazis [New York: Jewish Ed. Comm. Press, 1964]

2130. Esh, Shaul: "The Establishment of the ´Reichsvereinigung der Juden in Deutschland´ and its Main Activities." YVS, vol.7 (1968): 19-38.

2131. Feinberg, Nathan: "The Activities of Central Jewish Organizations Following Hitler´s Rise to Power." YVS, vol.1 (1957): 67-84.

2132. Friedman, P.: "Aspects of the Jewish Communal Crisis in Germany, Austria, and Czechoslovakia during the Nazi Period." Friedman: Roads, pp.100-130.

2133. Grossman, Kurt R.: "Zionists and Non-Zionists under Nazi Rule in the 1930s." Herzl YB vol.4, (1961/62): 329-344.

2134. Gruenwald, Max: "The Beginning of the ´Reichsvertretung´." LBIYB, #1 (1956): 57-67.

2135. ___: "Who Are the Spokesman of German Jewry?" Recon, vol.7 #7 (May 16, 1941): 13-14.

2136. "The Hechalutz Movement in Germany." Hamigdal, vol.2 #6 (May, 1942): 7, 9.

2137. "The Jewish School Question in Germany." J Rev, #6 (Sept./Dec., 1933): 70-76.

2138. Karpf, Ruth: "Now it Can Be Told." NJM, vol.57 #6 (Feb., 1943): 198-199, 213. * On the desrtuction of the B´nai B´rith offices in Nuremberg.

2139. Kulka, Dov O.: "The ´Reichsvereinigung´ of the Jews in Germany." G/H: Patterns, pp.45-58.

2140. Margaliot, Abraham: "The Dispute Over the Leadership of German Jewry (1933-38)." YVS, vol.10 (1974): 129-148.

2141. ___: "The Struggle for Survival of the Jewish Community in Germany in the Face of Oppression" Y/V: Resistance, pp.100-111.

2142. Nusbaum, Max: "Zionism Under Hitler." CW, vol.9 #27 (Sept. 11, 1942): 12-15.

2143. "The Occupational Distribution of the German Jews." J Rev, #6 (Sept./Dec., 1933): 38-43.

2144. Prinz, J.: "B´nai B´rith Role in Germany." NJM, vol. 52 #5 (Jan., 1938): 164-165, 190.

2145. Rinott, Chanoch: "Major Trends in Jewish Youth Movements in Germany." LBIYB, vol.19 (1974): 77-96.

2146. Rosenstock, Werner: "The Jewish Youth Movement." LBIYB, vol.19 (1974): 97-106.

2147. Rosenthal, Erich: "Trends of the Jewish Population in Germany, 1910-1939." JSS, vol.16 #3 (July, 1944): 233-274.

2148. Rubinow, I. M.: "B´nai B´rith, as the Nazis See It." NJM, vol.50 #5 (Feb., 1936): 153, 164.

2149. "Transference to New Occupations." J Rev, #6 (Sept./Dec., 1933): 62-69.

Economic and Legal Restrictions

2150. American Jewish Committee: The Jews in Nazi Germany: The Factual Record of their Persecution by the National Socialists [New York: The Committee, 1933]

2151. "Denationalization of Emigrated German Jews." CJR, vol.5 #2 (April, 1942): 202-204.

2152. Deutsch, Bernard S: "The Disenfranchisement of the Jew." PVP: Nazism, pp.39-58.

2153. "The Economic Position of the German Jews." J Rev, #6 (Sept./Dec., 1933): 33-37.

2154. Garner, James W.: "Recent German Nationality Legislation." Am Jnl/International Law, vol.30 #1 (Jan., 1936): 96-99. * On the Nuremberg Laws.

2155. "Hitler Government Cuts Off Last Economic Retreat of Jews." CB, vol.1 #10 (March 15, 1935): 1, 4.

2156. Hoover, Calvin B.: "German Capitalism and the Nazis." Cur His, vol.38 (Aug., 1933): 533-540. * Study on forced elimination of Jewish businesses.

2157. "Jews in Professions." J Rev, #6 (Sept./Dec., 1933): 54-61.

2158. "Legal Status of Jews Defined in Orders Issued by Nazis." CB, vol.2 #4 (Nov.22, 1935): 1, 4.

2159. "Legal Terror in Germany." CJR, vol.2 #1 (Jan., 1939): 54-66.

2160. Lengyel, Emil: "German Publishers Under the Nazis." Publishers Weekly, vol.125 (Feb. 3, 1934): 569-572. * The elimination of Jews from the publishing field.

2161. McKale, D.: "A Case of Nazi Justice - The Punishment of Party Members Involved in the Kristallnacht 1938." JSS, vol.35 #3/4 (July/Oct., 1973): 228-238.

2162. "Nazi Registration Law Concerning Property of Jews." CJR, vol.1 #1 (Sept., 1938): 42-46.

2163. Pollock, James K. and H. Heneman (Comps.): The Hitler Decrees [Ann Arbor, MI: G. Wahr, 1934] * An anthology of Hitler´s speeches and Nazi enacted laws.

2164. Pozner, Vladinia: "Pogroms for Profit: Jewish Money for Nazi Trusts." Nation, vol.148 #2 (Jan. 7, 1939): 33-35

2165. Seidler, Fritz: The Bloodless Pogrom [London: Victor Gollancz, 1934]

2166. Starr, J. and E. W. Jelenko: The Economic Destruction of German Jewry by the Nazi Regime, 1933-1937 [New York: Am. Jewish Congress, 1937]

2167. Szanto, A.: "Economic Aid in the Nazi Era." LBIYB, #4 (1959): 208-219.

2168. Zukerman William.: "The Historic Russian Parallel." Menorah, vol.24 #2 (April/June, 1936): 160-168. * On the Nuremberg Laws.

Pogroms and Anti-Jewish Violence

2169. Ball-Kaduri, K. Y.: "The Central Jewish Organization in Berlin During the Pogrom of November 1938." YVS, vol.3 (1959): 261-282.

2170. "Digest of Public Opinion: The Nazi Pogroms." CJR, vol.2 #1 (Jan., 1939): 41-50.

2171. Freeden, Herbert: "Black Anniversary." CW, vol.25 #7 (March 31, 1958): 5-6. * On Nazi anti-Jewish boycott of April 1, 1933.

2172. ___: "A Day That Should Have Shaken the World: 30th Anniversary of Nazi Boycott of Jewish Shops." J Digest, vol.8 #11 (Aug., 1963): 33-36.

2173. ___: "The Day the War Began." CW, vol.30 #6 (March 18, 1963): 7-9. * On Nazi boycott.

2174. ___: "While Berlin Burned." CW, vol.25 #17 (Nov. 10, 1958): 8-9. * On Kristallnacht.

2175. Ginsberg, E.: "We Are all German Jews." Dimensions, vol.4 #1 (Fall, 1969): 38-40. * On Kristallnacht.

2176. Hahn-Cohn, Miriam: "Kristallnacht." J Sp, vol.36 #9 (Nov., 1971): 12-13.

2177. Halm, Peter: "At This Very Hour - The Lesson of the November Pogroms." Recon, vol.4 #19 (Jan. 27, 1939): 11-16.

2178. Kahn, Lothar: "The Jews in Germany, November 1938 - Night of Terror." HM, vol.50 #3 (Nov., 1968): 12, 28.

2179. Kantorowicz, Alfred: "The Burning of the Books." FW, vol.5 #5 (May, 1943): 421-425.

2180. Kober, Adolf: "The Fires on the Rhine." Am Heb, vol. 151 #29 (Nov. 20, 1942): 2, 14. * Eyewitness account of the burning of the Cologne synagogue.

2181. Kochan, Lionel: Pogrom: 10 November, 1938 [London: Deutsch, 1957]

2182. "Latest Nazi Wave of Terror." CJR, vol.1 #2 (Nov., 1938): 56a-56c.

2183. Lerner, David: "Was the Year of the Great Pogroms." CJCh, vol.27 #18 (Sept. 13, 1939): 8-9. * Review of events in Nazi Germany.

2184. Lewisohn, Ludwig: "The New Kultur." Nation, vol.136 #3546 (June 21, 1933): 695-696. * On book burning.

2185. Libau, M. I.: "That Bloody Day in November: A Personal Story of the Pogrom Made in Germany." CW, vol.9 #34 (Nov. 13, 1942): 5-7.

2186. Liepman, Heinz (E. Burns, transl.): Murder: Made in Germany [New York: Harper & Row, 1934]

2187. McLeith, K.: "The Nazi Terror in the University." Nation, vol.136 #3545 (June 14, 1933): 669-670.

2188. Murray, M.: The Crystal Nights [New York: Seabury Press, 1973]

2189. "The Night of the Broken Glass." Recon, vol.44 #7 (Nov., 1978): 5-6.

2190. "Pogrom in Berlin." J Fr, vol.2 #10 (Aug., 1935): 3-4.

2191. Rubashow (Shazar), Zalman: "The Burning of the Books. In Memoriam: May 10, 1933." J Fr, vol.2 #7 (May, 1935): 22-23.

2192. Thalmann, Rita and Emmanuel Feinermann (G. Cremonesi, transl.): Crystal Night 9-10 November 1938 [London: Thames and Hudson, 1974]

Meticulous study of the events surrounding the nation-wide pogrom in Germany known as Crystal Night. From the murder of Ernst von Rath by Herschel Grynszpan and the pogroms throughout Germany to the reaction of the world those terrible days in 1938 are carefully reconstructed. Sources were consulted from Germany, France, America, Britain, and Israel.

2193. Werner, Alfred: "Rehearsal for World Conquest." CW, vol.8 #36 (Nov. 7, 1941): 7-9.

2194. Zohn, Harry: "Twenty-five Years After the Book Burnings." J Affairs, vol.13 #7 (July, 1958): 14-17.

2195. Zurndorfer, Hannele: The Ninth of November [New York: Quartet Books, 1983]

Jewish Responses

2196. Bauer, Yehuda: "The ´Kristallnacht´ as Turning Point: Jewish Reactions to Nazi Policies." Legters: Western, pp.39-55. Comments and Rejoinder: Marie Syrkin, pp. 56-60; Erich H. Boehm, pp.60-65; Y. Bauer, pp.66-67.

2197. Bentwich, Norman: "Jew Into Israelite." NJM, vol.49 #2 (Nov., 1934): 46-47, 62. * Assimilated Jews are forced, by circumstances, to enter the mainstream of Judaism.

2198. Brugel, J. W.: "The Bernheim Petition: A Challenge to Nazi Germany." PoP, vol.17 #3 (July, 1983): 17-25.

2199. Colodner, Solomon: "Jewish Education under National Socialism." YVS, vol.3 (1959): 161-185.

2200. Edelsheim-Muehsam, Margaret T.: "The Jewish Press in Germany." LBIYB, vol.1 (1956): 163-176.

2201. ___: "Reactions of the Jewish Press to the Nazi Challenge." LBIYB, vol.5 (1960): 308-329.

2202. Edinger, Dora: "The German Jews Look at the Past." Recon, vol.4 #7 (May 20, 1938): 6-12.

2203. "Emigration from Germany." CJR, vol.4 #2 (April, 1941): 195-197.

2204. Freeden, Herbert: "A Jewish Theatre Under the Swastika." LBIYB, vol.1 (1956): 142-162.

2205. Fuchs, R.: "The ´Hochschule fuer die Wissenschaft des Judentums´ in the Period of Nazi Rule." LBIYB, vol.12 (1967): 3-31.

2206. Gaertner, H.: "Problems of Jewish Schools in Germany During the Hitler Regime." LBIYB, vol.1 (1956): 123-141

2207. "German Jewry Maintains Its Culture." NJM, vol.49 #1 (Oct., 1934): 16, 24.

2208. "German Jewry States Its Case." NJM, vol.48 #4 (Jan., 1934): 116-117, 142-143.

2209. Greenblum, Erika: "German Jews Under Nazism: Their Reaction to Oppression." JH, vol.4 #3 (Winter, 1961/1962): 32-37. * culled from Israelitisches Familienblatt.

2210. Harap, L.: "Lessons in Resistance: German Jewry Under Hitler." J Life, vol.4 #2 (Dec., 1949): 6-10.

2211. Helmreich, Ernst Ch.: "Jewish Education in the Third Reich." JCEA, vol.15 #2 (July, 1955): 134-147.

2212. Herzberg, A.: "Last Days of the German Jewish Press." CJR, vol.5 #2 (April, 1942): 145-153.

2213. "Jewish Relief Work in Germany." J Rev, #6 (Sept./Dec., 1933): 77-82.

2214. Lestchinsky, Jacob: "What German Jews Read." J Fr, vol.4 #3 (March, 1937): 26-27.

2215. Margaliot, A.: "The Reaction of the Jewish Public in Germany to the Nuremberg Laws." Bauer: Hol History, pp.39-71.

2216. Pineas, Herman: "The Jewish Hospital of Berlin in 1939-1943." Am OSE Rev, vol.4 #1 (Spr., 1947): 14-18.

2217. Pinl, Max and Lux Furtmueller: "Mathematicians Under Hitler." LBIYB, vol.18 (1973): 129-182.

2218. Poppel, Stephen M.: "Salman Schocken and the Schocken Verlag." LBIYB, vol.17 (1972): 93-113.

2219. "The Reaction of German Jewry." J Rev, #6 (Sept./Dec., 1933): 26-32.

2220. "Relief Work Outside of Germany." J Rev, #6 (Sept./Dec., 1933): 83-88.

2221. Rosenstock, Werner: "Exodus, 1933-1939: A Survey of Jewish Emigration from Germany." LBIYB, vol.1 (1956): 373-390.

2222. Schiratzki, S.: "The Rykestrasse School in Berlin - a Jewish Elementary School During the Hitler Period." LBIYB, vol.5 (1960): 299-307.

2223. Sichel, Frieda: "Jewish Welfare Work in Germany." J Affairs, vol.13 #9 (Sept., 1958): 36-37.

2224. Simon, E.: "Jewish Adult Education in Nazi Germany as Spiritual Resistance." LBIYB, vol.1 (1956): 68-104.

2225. ___: "The Spiritual Legacy of German Jewry." Judaism, vol.5 #3 (Summer, 1956): 217-224.

2226. Stahl, R.: "Vocational Retraining of Jews in Nazi Germany, 1935-1938." JSS, vol.1 #2 (April, 1939): 169-194.

2227. Strauss, Herbert A.: "Jewish Emigration from Germany. Nazi Policies and Jewish Responses." LBIYB, vol.25 (1980): 313-361.

2228. Walk, Joseph: "Jewish Education Under the Nazis: An Example of Resistance to the Totalitarian Regime." Y/V: Resistance, pp.123-131.

2229. Weltsch, Robert: "Wear the Yellow Badge with Pride." Friedlander: Whirlwind, pp. 119-123.

2230. Zahn, Lilian: "Jewish Art Surmounts Nazis." NJM, vol. 50 #4 (Jan., 1936): 114-115, 128, 130.

Personalities

2231. Baeck, Leo: "In Memory of Two of Our Dead." LBIYB, vol.1 (1956): 51-56. Also in Friedlander: Whirlwind, pp.124-132.

2232. Etzold, T. S.: "An American Jew in Germany: The Death of Helmut Hirsch." JSS, vol.35 #2 (April, 1973): 125-140.

2233. Goldstein, M.: "German Jewry's Dilemma: The Story of a Provocative Essay." LBIYB, vol.2 (1957): 236-254.

2234. Gruenwald, Max: "Critic of German Jewry: Ludwig Feuchtwanger and His 'Gemeindzeitung'." LBIYB, vol.17 (1972): 75-92.

2235. Nussbaum, Max: "Ministry Under Stress: Berlin Rabbis Under Hitler." WJ, vol.14 #4 (Oct., 1971): 14-18.

2236. Prinz, Joachim: "The Time was Midnight: Berlin Rabbis Under Hitler." WJ, vol.14 #4 (Oct., 1971): 10-14.

THE ANSCHLUSS: AUSTRIA 1938-1945

The Anschluss

2237. Anderson, P.: "Berlin: Vienna: Prague." Fortnightly, #853 (Jan., 1938): 83-91.

2238. Ball, Margaret: Post-War German-Austrian Relations: The 'Anschluss' Movement 1918-1936 [Palo Alto, CA: Stanford Univ. Press, 1937]

2239. Benedikt, E.: "The Situation in Austria." Cont Rev, vol.150 #847 (July, 1936): 20-27.

2240. Brailsford, H. N.: "Austria Confronts Fascism." New Republic, vol.76 #983 (Oct. 4, 1933): 202-204.

2241. Brook-Shepherd, G.: Anschluss [New York: Macmillan, 1963]

2242. ___: The Austrian Odyssey [New York: Macmillan, 1957]

2243. Carsten, Francis L.: Fascist Movements in Austria: From Schonerer to Hitler [Beverly Hills, CA: Sage, 1977]

2244. Danubius: "Austria's Struggle for Life." Cont Rev, vol.144 #811 (July, 1933): 24-30.

2245. Edmondson, C. E.: The Heimwehr and Austrian Politics, 1918-1936 [Athens, GA: Univ. of Georgia Press, 1978]

Political study of Austrian paramilitary organizations between 1918 and the Anschluss. The Heimwehr's ultimate failure was the inability of Austrian fascists to stear clear of Nazi Germany. By moving Austrian politics to the right they actually eased Hitler's path.

2246. Foerster, F. W.: "Germany and Austria: A European Crisis." F Affairs, vol.9 #4 (July, 1931): 617-623.

2247. Gedye, G. E. R.: "Austria - Below Ground and Above." Cont Rev, vol.149 #847 (May, 1936): 531-539. * On Austrian Nazis.

2248. Gehl, Juergen: Austria, Germany, and the Anschluss 1931-1938 [New York: Oxford Univ. Press, 1963]

2249. Gessner, R.: "The Future of Austria." Int Affairs, vol.15 #2 (March/April, 1936): 225-244.

2250. Gruber, Karl: "Austria Infelix." F Affairs, vol.15 #2 (Jan., 1947): 229-238.

2251. Gunther, John: "Will Austria Go Fascist?" Nation, vol.136 #3536 (April 12, 1933): 393-395.

2252. Holmes, B. R.: "Europe and the Habsburg Restoration in Austria, 1930-1931." EEQ, vol.9 #2 (Summer, 1975): 173-184.

2253. Hutton, G.: "Danubia Without Austria." Fortnightly #858 (June, 1938): 650-658.

2254. Maass, Walter B.: Assassination in Vienna [New York: Charles Scribner's Sons, 1972]

2255. Melville, C. F.: "The Austrian Tragedy." Fortnightly, #856 (April, 1938): 400-408.

2256. Pauley, Bruce F.: Hitler and the Forgotten Nazis, a History of Austrian National Socialism [Chapel Hill: The Univ. of North Carolina Press, 1981]

2257. Polanyi, Karl: "Austria and Germany." Int Affairs, vol.12 #5 (Sept./Oct., 1933): 575-592.

2258. Redlich, Joseph: "German Austria and Nazi Germany." F Affairs, vol.15 #1 (Oct., 1936): 179-186.

2259. Ritter, Harry: "Hermann Neubacher and the Austrian Anschluss Movement, 1918-1940." CEH, vol.8 #4 (Dec., 1975): 348-369.

2260. Selby, Walford: "Austria Before the Anschluss and a View of Her Future Prospects." Int Affairs, vol.21 #4 (Oct., 1945): 477-484.

2261. Seton-Watson, Robert W.: "Europe and the Austrian Problem." Int Affairs, vol.15 #3 (May/June, 1936): 327-350.

2262. Suval, Stanley: The Anschluss Question in the Weimar Era: A Study of Nationalism in Germany and Austria, 1918-1932 [Baltimore: John Hopkins Univ. Press, 1974]

2263. Von Schuschnigg, Kurt (F. von Hildebrand, transl.): Austrian Requiem [New York: Putnam's, 1946]

2264. Wagner, D. and G. Tomkowitz (G. Strachan, transl): Anschluss: The Week Hitler Seized Vienna [New York: St. Martin's Press, 1971]

2265. Weltsch, Felix: "Facing the Realities: On the Death of Austria." Menorah, vol.26 #2 (April/June, 1938): 230-233.

2266. Williams, M.: "Delusions of Grandeur: The Austrian National Socialists." Can Jnl/His, vol.14 #3 (Dec., 1979): 417-436.

2267. ___: "German Imperialism and Austria 1938." JCH, vol. 14 #1 (Jan., 1979): 139-154.

Life in Nazi Austria

2268. Bernstein, Victor H.: "Austria Under the Iron Heel." CJCh, vol.26 #3 (June 10, 1938): 5, 13.

2269. ___: "Nazi Victims or Collaborators?" HM, vol.48 #9 (May, 1967): 23-24.

2270. Bukey, Evan B.: "Hitler´s Hometown Under Nazi Rule: Linz, Austria 1938-1945." CEH, vol.16 #2 (June, 1983): 171-186.

2271. Fodor, M. W.: "What Happened to Vienna." Survey Graphic, vol.28 #2 (Feb., 1939): 69-71, 179-180.

2272. Maas, Walter B.: Country Without a Name: Austria Under Nazi Rule 1938-1945 [New York: F. Ungar, 1979]

2273. Williams, Maurice: "Aid Assistance and Advice: German Nazis and the Austrian Hilfswerk." CEH, vol.14 #3 (Sept., 1981): 230-242.

Jews in Austria Under the Nazis

2274. Berner, Georg: "Children in Vienna." J Fr, vol.6 #1 (Jan., 1939): 10-11.

2275. Bernstein, Victor H.: "Until Their Flesh Hung Raw." CJCh, vol.26 #5 (June 24, 1938): 5, 13.

2276. Botz, G.: "National Socialist Vienna: Antisemitism as a Housing Policy." WLB, vol.29 #2 (1976): 47-51.

2277. Brauner, E.: "The Situation of the Jews in Austria." J Life, vol.2 #5 (May, 1938): 17-18, 24.

2278. Drucker, Peter: "The Social Revolution in Austria." New Republic, vol.95 #1231 (July 6, 1938): 239-241.

2279. Karbach, O.: "The Liquidation of the Jewish Community of Vienna." JSS, vol.2 #3 (July, 1940): 255-278.

2280. Mahler, Raphael: "Setbacks in Jewish Emancipation." New Currents, vol.1 #3 (June, 1943): 25-27.

2281. Namier, L. B.: "On the Death of Austria: The Jews in Austria." Menorah, vol.26 #2 (April/June, 1938): 227-230.

2282. Pinot, Z. P.: "Hitler's Entry Into Vienna." YVB, #3 (April, 1958): 15-16.

2283. Revusky, Abraham: "Jew Baiting and the Social Revolution." J Fr, vol.5 #8 (Aug., 1938): 11-14.

2284. Rosenkranz, Herbert: "The Anschluss and the Tragedy of Austrian Jewry, 1934-1945." Fraenkel: Austria, pp. 479-546.

2285. Rothschild, K.: "Austrian Jewry: Between Forced Emigration and Deportation." G/H: Patterns, pp.65-74.

2286. Werner, Alfred: "Anniversary of a Black Thursday." J Layman, vol.16 #3 (Nov., 1941): 5-8.

2287. ___: "The End of Vienna's Jewry." J Sp, vol.9 #3 (Jan., 1944): 17-19.

2288. ___: "In Herzl's Vienna." HM, vol.21 #7 (May/June, 1941): 17-18.

2289. ___: "Prelude to Mass Murder: Terror in Vienna." CW, vol.25 #17 (Nov. 10, 1958): 5-7.

2290. ___: "The War Started in November 1938." J Sp, vol.9 #1 (Nov., 1943): 18-19.

LIFE IN THE AXIS-ALLIED STATES

Overviews

2291. Kirchwey, Freda: "The Puppet Axis." Nation, vol.154 #12 (March 21, 1942): 330-331.

2292. Nagy-Talavera, Nicholas M.: The Green Shirts and the Others: A History of Fascism in Hungary and Rumania [Stanford, CA: Hoover Institution Press, 1970]

Bulgaria

2293. Fischer A. J.:: "Bulgaria in Ferment." CEO, vol.19 #3 (Feb. 6, 1942): 39-40.

2294. Goldfarb, Jack: "Bulgaria." NJM, vol.77 #2 (Oct., 1962): 10-11.

2295. Miller, Marshall L.: Bulgaria During the Second World War [Stanford, CA: Stanford Univ. Press, 1975]

Using documentary material from five countries (America, England, Germany, Bulgaria, and Israel) Miller has placed Bulgarian governmental policies during World war II into their proper context. He notes that Bulgarian diplomacy was successful in resisting Nazi demands, including those for deporting Bulgarian Jews, while gaining German support for Bulgarian territorial demands. After 1943, however, Bulgarian diplomacy unraveled and at one point - in 1945 - was actually at war with both the Allies and the Axis.

Croatia

2296. Paris, Edmond (Lois Perkins, transl.): Genocide in Satelite Croatia, 1941-1945: A Record of Racial and Religious Persecutions and Massacres [Chicago: American Institute for Balkan Affairs, 1961]

Finland

2297. Lundin, C. Leonard: Finland in the Second World War [Bloomington, IN: Indiana Univ. Press, 1957]

Hungary

2298. Balaton, Paul: "Horthy´s Hitler Hungary." CEO, vol.19 #5 (March 6, 1942): 76-77.

2299. Bigler, Robert M.: "Heil Hitler und Heil Horthy." EEQ, vol.8 #3 (Fall, 1974): 251-272.

2300. Fenyo, Mario D.: Hitler, Horthy and Hungary: German-Hungarian Relations, 1941-1944 [New Haven, CT: Yale Univ. Press, 1972]

2301. ___: "The War Diary of the Chief of the Hungarian General Staff in 1944." EEQ, vol.2 #3 (Sept., 1968): 315-331.

2302. Floris, George A.: "Hungary Under Horthy." Cont Rev, vol.183 #1054 (Oct., 1953): 216-221.

2303. Horthy, Nicholas V. (F. G. Renier et al, transls.): Memoirs [London: Hutchinson, 1956]

2304. "Hungary Since the Occupation." CW, vol.11 #17 (May 5, 1944): 14-15.

2305. Kallay, Nicholas: Hungarian Premier [New York: Oxford Univ. Press, 1956]

2306. Kertesz, Stephen: Diplomacy in a Whirlpool: Hungary Between Nazi Germany and Soviet Russia [Notre Dame, IN: Univ. of Notre Dame Press, 1953]

2307. "Key Man in the Balkans." P.I.N., vol.8 #12 (March 23, 1940): 4-7. * On Horthy.

2308. Montgomery, John F.: Hungary, the Unwilling Satellite [New York: Devin-Adair, 1947]

2309. Nagy-Talavera, Nicholas M.: "The Second World War As Mirrored in the Hungarian Fascist Press." EEQ, vol.4 #2 (June, 1970): 179-208.

2310. Paloczy-Horvath, G.: In Darkest Hungary [London: Victor Gollancz, 1945]

2311. Schultz, Ignac: "Budapest´s Fake Mission." Nation, vol.153 #13 (Sept. 27, 1941): 276-277.

2312. Storrs, David: "Hungary: Germany´s Silent Partner." FW, vol.3 #3 (Aug., 1942): 264-267.

2313. Szinai, M. and L. Szucs (eds.): The Confidential Papers of Admiral Horthy [Toronto: Pannonia, 1965]

2314. Vambery, Rustem: The Hungarian Problem [New York: The Nation, 1942] * Critical review of the Horthy regime.

2315. ___: Hungary: To Be or Not to Be [New York: Frederick Ungar, 1946]

Rumania

2316. Arnold, John: "Swastika Over Rumania." J Life, vol.2 #2 (Feb., 1938): 7-11.

2317. Cretzianu, Alexandre: Lost Opportunity [London: Cape, 1957]

2318. Manning, Olivia: "Rumanian Coup D´Etat." Hist/WWII, #10 (1973): 253-255.

2319. Perlzweig, Maurice L.: "The Lesson of Rumania." CB, vol.7 #4 (Dec. 6, 1940): 8-9.

Slovakia

2320. Griffin, Joan: "Germany´s First Colony." Cont Rev, vol.157 #894 (June, 1940): 693-699.

2321. "Independent Slovakia." CEO, vol.17 #2 (Feb. 16, 1940): 9-10.

2322. Jelinek, Yeshayahu: The Parish Republic: Hlinka´s Slovak People´s Party, 1939-1945 [New York: Columbia Univ. Press, 1976]

Survey of collaboration in wartime Slovakia. Begins with the origin of Slovak nationalism and surveys the history of the Slovak People´s Party from founding (1905) to collapse (1945). Well written and richly documented. Includes sections on Slovakia´s Jewish policy and the murder of Slovakian Jewry.

2323. ___: "Slovakia´s Internal Policy and the Third Reich, August 1940 - February 1941." CEH, vol.4 #3 (Sept., 1971): 242-270. * Includes material on the Jewish situation.

2324. Machacek, Pavel: "Slovakia: A Mournful Anniversary." CEO, vol.18 #6 (March 15, 1941): 64-65.

2325. Steiner, Eugen: The Slovak Dilemma [Cambridge: At the Univ. Press, 1973]

Ukraine

2326. Armstrong, John: Ukrainian Nationalism: 1939-1945 [New York: Columbia Univ. Press, 1955]

Investigation of the struggles of Ukrainian nationalists. Surveys the background of Ukrainian nationalism concentrating on the wartime activities of the various factions. Emphasizes the nationalists reaction to the Nazi "liberation". Also reviews briefly Ukrainian-Jewish relations.

JEWS IN THE AXIS-ALLIED STATES

The Balkans

2327. "Expropriation and Corruption." J Comment, vol.1 #19 (Nov. 26, 1943): 2-4.

2328. Glass, Sylvia: "Spring in the Balkans." J Survey, vol.1 #2 (June, 1941): 18-19.

2329. "The Island of Pag." J Fr, vol.9 #11 (Nov., 1942): 34. * Croatia.

2330. Slavik, Juraj: "My Unsullied Compatriots." Lib Jud, vol.12 #2 (June, 1944): 5-7.

2331. Vital, H.: "The Jews of Bulgaria. A Survey of Jewish Ruin." CW, vol.8 #37 (Nov. 14, 1941): 12.

Baltic States

2332. "Latvia Following Example of Nazis in Curbs on Jews." CB, vol.2 #13 (Jan. 24, 1936): 3, 4.

2333. Lestchinsky, Jacob: "Jews in the Baltic States." J Fr, vol.5 #8 (Aug., 1938): 23-25.

2334. Nuremberg, Thelma: "Finland and Its Jewish Community." J Sp, vol.5 #4 (Feb., 1940): 25, 45.

Hungary

2335. Beller, Jacob: "Jews of Hungary." JVP, vol.8 #1 (Jan., 1945); 8-9, 12.

2336. Braham, Randolph L.: "The Jewish Question in German-Hungarian Relations during the Kallay Era." JSS, vol. 39 #3 (Sum., 1977): 183-208.

2337. ___: "Legitimism, Zionism and the Jewish Catastrophe in Hungary." Herzl YB, vol.6 (1965): 239-252.

2338. ___: "The Official Jewish Leadership of Wartime Hungary." G/H: Patterns, pp.267-285.

2339. ___: "The Role of the Jewish Council in Hungary: A Tentative Assessment." YVS, vol.10 (1974): 69-110.

2340. Faber, W. S.: Hungary's Alibi: Hungary's Anti-Jewish Policy Unmasked [London: Lincoln Prager, 1944]

2341. "Hungary on the Fence." J Comment, vol.1 #7 (June 18, 1943): 1-4.

2342. "Hungary Since the Occupation." J Comment, vol.2 #14 (May 5, 1944): 1-4.

2343. I. P. C.: "The Law Against the Jews in Hungary." J Life, vol.2 #6 (June, 1938): 22-24.

2344. Katzburg, Nathaniel: Hungary and the Jews: Policy and Legislation, 1920-1943 [Ramat Gan, Israel: Bar-Ilan Univ. Press, 1981]

Studies Hungarian Jewish policy from the 1920s to 1943. Katzburg focuses on Hungarian legislation regarding Jews. Attempts to place Hungarian policy into the broader context of radical right and antisemitic politics during the period concerned. Contains twelve key documents in English translation.

2345. Klein, Bernard: "Hungarian Politics and the Jewish Question in the Inter-War Period." JSS, vol.28 #2 (April, 1966): 78-98.

2346. Lestchinsky, Jacob: "The Tragedy of the Jews in Hungary." Ort Eco Bul, vol.1 #4/5 (July/Oct., 1940): 6-13.

2347. The Persecution of Hungarian Jewry. Six Years of German Pressure [London: Jewish Central Information Office, 1944]

2348. "Racism in Hungary." CJR, vol.2 #5 (Sept./Oct., 1939): 64-73.

2349. "Recent Anti-Jewish Legislation in Hungary." CJR, vol.1 #1 (Sept., 1938): 32-36.

2350. Rittenberg, Louis: "The Crisis in Hungary." CJR, vol. 2 #3 (May/June, 1939): 20-31.

2351. Schultz, Ignac: "Background to Pogroms." Am Heb, vol. 151 #8 (June 26, 1942): 9, 16.

2352. Stern, Samu: "A Race with Time: A Statement." HJS, vol.3 (1973): 1-48.

2353. The Tragedy of a People. Jews in Hungary [London: Kadimah Society, 1946]

2354. Ungar, Bela: "Surviving in Nazi Hungary." J Sp, vol. 34 #6 (June, 1969): 15-18.

2355. Union of Hungarian Jews: "Declaration of Protest Against the Introduction of the Occupational Restriction Law of May 1938." CJR, vol.1 #1 (Sept., 1938): 26-28.

2356. Vago, Bela: "Contrasting Jewish Leadership in Wartime Hungary and Rumania." Bauer: Historical, pp.133-152.

2357. ___: "Germany and the Jewish Policy of the Kallay Government." HJS, vol.2 (1969): 183-210.

2358. Vambery, Rustem: "The Jews in Hungary." V/Ung, vol.2 #5 (Aug., 1944): 1, 7.

Rumania

2359. "About Transnistria." CW, vol.11 #8 (Feb. 25, 1944): 15-17.

2360. Bickel, Alexander: "Bloodbath in Rumania." CW, vol.9 #28 (Oct. 2, 1942): 8-9.

2361. Bickel, Solomon: "Rumania's Scapegoat." CJR, vol.3 #1 (Jan./Feb., 1949): 26-37.

2362. "Cold Pogrom in Rumania." IJA, vol.1 #7 (Feb., 1942): 1-14.

2363. "Crisis in Rumania." CJR, vol.4 #5 (Oct., 1941): 529-540.

2364. "Discrimination and Extortion in Rumania." J Comment, vol.1 #15 (Oct. 29, 1943): 2-4.

2365. Easterman, Alexander L.: "Why Carol Turned Anti-semite." _J Fr_, vol.5 #4 (April, 1938): 22-23.

2366. Eichenthal, Herman: "Rumania - Classic Land of Anti-semitism." _J Fr_, vol.7 #8 (Aug., 1940): 15-17.

2367. Gourevitch, Boris: "Economic and Social Situation of the Jews in Roumania." _Ort Eco Bul_, vol.1 #2 (March/April, 1940): 3-6.

2368. "The Internees in Transnistria." _J Comment_, vol.2 #2 (Jan. 28, 1944): 1-2.

2369. Lavi, Theodore: "The Background to the Rescue of Romanian Jewry during the Period of the Holocaust." Vago: _J/NJ_, pp.177-186.

2370. Leonard, Oscar: "Carol Throws Jews to the Wolves." _J Fr_, vol.5 #2 (Feb., 1938): 8-10.

2371. ___: "Status of Jews in Rumania." _J Fr_, vol.5 #11 (Nov., 1938): 16-18.

2372. Lestchinsky, Jacob: "In Fascist Rumania." _J Fr_, vol.5 #9 (Sept., 1938): 17-18.

2373. Levin, Alexander: "The Jews of Rumania." _J Sp_, vol.5 #12 (Oct., 1940): 32-33, 42.

2374. Levin, Dov: "The Jews and the Inception of Soviet Rule in Bukovina." _SJA_, vol.6 #2 (Oct., 1976): 52-70.

2375. "Rumania on Trial." _J Comment_, vol.2 #20 (Sept. 1, 1944): 1-4.

2376. Schechtman, J. B.: "The Transnistria Reservation." _YIVO Annual_, vol.8 (1953): 178-196.

2377. Teich, Meir: "The Jewish Self-Administration in Ghetto Shargorod (Transnistria)." _YVS_, vol.2 (1958): 219-254.

2378. Vago, Bela: "The Ambiguity of Collaborationism: The Center of the Jews in Romania (1942-1944)." G/H: _Patterns_, pp.287-309.

Slovakia

2379. Conway, J. S.: "Churches, the Slovak State and the Jews, 1939-1945." Slavonic/EER, vol.52 (Jan., 1974): 85-112.

LIFE UNDER NAZI OCCUPATION

Overviews

2380. Armitage, John (ed.): Europe in Bondage [London: Drummond, 1943]

Country-by-country survey of the Nazi occupation and spoilation of Europe. Also discuses collaboration and resistance. Includes much information on the Jews.

2381. Basch, Antonin: "The New Order: A Study in Plunder." FW, vol.1 #1 (Oct., 1941): 70-78.

2382 Bayles, William D.: Ceasars in Goose Step [New York: Harper, 1940]

2383. Binder, Carroll: "Since September 1, 1939: European Canvas." Survey Graphic, vol.30 #11 (Nov., 1941): 560-563, 648-651.

2384. Bourne, G. H.: Starvation in Europe [London: Allen and Unwin, 1943]

2385. de Jaeger, Charles: The Linz File: Hitler´s Plunder of Europe´s Art [Exter, England: Webb & Bower, 1981]

2386. Deuel, Wallace R.: People Under Hitler [New York: Harcourt, Brace, 1962]

2387. Einzig, P.: Europe in Chains [Harmondsworth, England: Penguin Books, 1940]

2388. Hediger, Ernest S.: Nazi Exploitation of Occupied Europe [New York: Foreign Policy Association, 1942]

2389. Heiden, Konrad: "Europe Under the Master Race." Nation, vol.152 #12 (March 22, 1941): 334-337.

2390. Homze, Edward L.: Foreign Labor in Nazi Germany [Princeton, NJ: Princeton Univ. Press, 1966]

2391. Inter-Allied Information Committee: Conditions in Occupied Territories [London: HMSO, 1942]

2392. The International Labour Committee: The Exploitation of Foreign Labour by Germany [Montreal: ILO, 1945]

2393. Kalme, Albert: Total Terror [New York: Appleton-Century Crofts, 1951]

2394. Leale, J.: "Guernsey Under German Rule." Int Affairs, vol.22 #2 (April, 1946): 214-226.

2395. Lemkin, Raphael: Axis Rule in Occupied Europe: Laws of Occupation, Analysis of Government, Proposals for Redress [Washington, DC: Carnegie Endowment for International Peace, Div. of International Law, 1944]

Important study of German occupation policies. The book attempts to characterize the Nazi new order, for which purpose Lemkin coined the term Genocide. Includes a large number of documents. The text and documents cover all Nazi policies on a country by country basis.

2396. Lloyd, A. L. and Igor Vingradoff: Shadow of the Swastika [London: John Land the Bodley Head, 1940]

2397. Maranz, George: "Germany´s New Order." P.I.N., vol.10 #9 (Feb. 28, 1942): 1-2.

2398. Manvell, Roger and H. Fraenkel: "Hitler´s New Order." Hist/WWII, #16 (1973): 440-448.

2399. March, Anthony: Darkness Over Europe: First Person Accounts of Life in Europe during the War Years 1939-1945 [Chicago: Rand McNally, 1969]

2400. Mitchell, A.: "Polish, Dutch and French Elites Under the German Occupation." Friedlander: Ideology, pp. 231-241.

2401. Research Bureau of the Am. Jewish Congress: "Under the Swastika." CB, vol.7 #2 (Nov. 22, 1940): 11-13.

2402. Roxan, David and Ken Wanstall: The Rape of Art: The Story of Hitler´s Plunder of the Great Masterpieces of Europe [New York: Coward-McCann, 1964]

2403. Royal Institute of International Affairs: *Occupied Europe: German Exploitation and its Post-War Consequences* [London: The Institute, 1944]

2404. Soffner, Heinz: "Food for Freedom vs. Nazi Food Estate." *Survey Graphic*, vol.31 #5 (May, 1942): 249-253, 269-270.

2405. Taylor, Telford: *The March of Conquest: The German Victories in Western Europe 1940* [New York: Simon and Schuster, 1958]

2406. The Times Publishing Company: *Europe Under the Nazi Scourge* [London: The Times, 1940]

2407. Toynbee, Arnold J. and V. Toynbee (eds.): *Survey of International Affairs 1939-1946: Hitler's Europe* [New York: Oxford Univ. Press, 1954]

2408. The Underground Reporter: "France, Belgium, Russia." *FW*, vol.8 #1 (July, 1944): 57-61.

2409. ___: "(Untitled)." *FW*, vol.3 #4 (Sept., 1942): 377-380. * Overview of situation in occupied countries.

2410. "Under Hitler's Protection." *CEO*, vol.17 #1 (Feb. 1, 1940): 7; #2 (Feb. 16, 1940): 15; #3 (March 1, 1940): 23; #4 (March 15, 1940): 34-35.

2411. Winiewicz, J. M.: *Aims and Failures in the German New Order* [London: The Polish Research Centre, 1943]

2412. *A Worker's Day under German Occupation* [London: Liberty Publications, 1941]

2413. World Jewish Congress: "The Nazification of Europe." *CW*, vol.8 #16 (April 25, 1941): 12-13.

The Balkans

2414. Fotitch, Constantin: "What Southeastern Europe Expects." *FW*, vol.1 #2 (Nov., 1941): 149-153.

2415. La Farge, John: "Hitler's Criminal Onslaught Against Catholic Slovenia." *America*, vol.66 #21 (Feb. 28, 1942): 569-570.

2416. Tsatsou, I.: The Sword's Fierce Edge: A Journal of the Occupation of Greece by the Italians and Germans, 1940-1944 [New York: Vanderbilt Univ. Press, 1969]

2417. Zavalani, T.: "Albania: Four Years Under Fascist Oppression." CEO, vol.20 #8 (April 16, 1943): 117-118.

Bohemia-Moravia

2418. Basch, A.: "Germany's Economic Conquest of Czechoslovakia." CEO, vol.17 #5 (April 1, 1940): 39-41; #6 (April 16, 1940): 46-47; #7 (May 1, 1940): 57-58.

2419. Belina, Josef: Czech Labor Under Nazi Rule [London: Lincolns-Prager, 1943]

2420. "Black-Out in Bohemia." CEO, vol.17 #19 (Nov. 1, 1940): 177-178.

2421. Czechoslovakian Government-in-Exile: Two Years of German Oppression in Czechoslovakia [London: Czechoslovak Ministry of Foreign Affairs, 1941]

2422. Duff, Shiela G.: German Protectorate: The Czechs Under Nazi Rule [London: F. Cass, 1970]

2423. Erdely, E. V.: Prague Braved the Hangman [London: The Czechoslovak Independent Weekly, 1942]

2424. Hanc, Josef: "Czechs and Slovaks Since Munich." F Affairs, vol.18 #1 (Oct., 1939): 102-115.

2425. Jacoby, Gerhard: Racial State: The German Nationalities Policy in the Protectorate of Bohemia-Moravia [New York: The Institute of Jewish Affairs, 1944] * Chapter 13 deals with the Jews. See pp.233-247.

2426. Jelinek, Yeshayahu: "Bohemia-Moravia, Slovakia, and the Third Reich During the Second World War." EEQ, vol.3 #2 (June, 1969): 229-239.

2427. Kaasova, B.: "Czech Children in Wartime." CEO, vol.21 #8 (April 14, 1944): 118-119.

2428. Malik, J.: "Plundering Czechoslovakia." CEO, vol.17 #10 (June 15, 1940): 93-94.

2429. Masaryk, J.: Speaking to My Country [London: Lincoln-Prager, 1944]

2430. Moskowitz, M.: "Three Years of the Protectorate of Bohemia and Moravia." Pol Sci Q, vol.57 #3 (Sept., 1942): 353-375.

2431. "News from the Protectorate." CEO, vol.17 #8 (May 16, 1940): 70-71.

2432. Worsley, R. H. M.: "Bohemia Under Nazi Oppression." Cont Rev, vol.157 #889 (Jan., 1940): 49-54.

2433. ___: "Inside the Czech Protectorate." Cont Rev, vol. 156 #883 (July, 1939): 41-48.

2434. "A Year of Hitler´s Protection." CEO, vol.17 #5 (April 1, 1940): 37-38, 43.

France

2435. Allen, Jay: "Trouble with Hitler: Excerpts from a Correspondent´s Diary." FW, vol.1 #3 (Dec., 1941): 231-236.

2436. Berman, Harold: "The Barometer." J Fo, vol.26 #10 (Nov., 1943): 203-205.

2437. Chernoff, Victor: "The Riddle of the Fall of France." J Fr, vol.8 #8 (Aug., 1941): 13-18.

2438. Cobb, Richard: French and Germans, Germans and French [Waltham, MA: Tauber Institute, 1983]

Synthetic analysis of the Nazi occupation of France and the ways in which Germans and French interacted. An effort at social history, it pays little attention to institutions or administrations.

2439. Laroche, Herve: "The Aftermath in France." Hist/WWII, #8 (1973): 201, 204-205.

2440. ___: "Divided France." Hist/WWII, #42 (1973): 1149-1153.

2441. Lorraine, Jacques: The Germans in France [London: Hutchinson, n.d.]

2442. Pryce-Jones, David (M. Rand, Picture ed): Paris in the Third Reich: A History of the German Occupation, 1940-1944 [New York: Holt, Rinehart & Winston, 1981]

2443. R. L.: "The Underground Reporter: Repercussions in France." FW, vol.5 #3 (March, 1943): 276-278.

2444. Ragner, B.: "Paris Under the Germans." Am Mercury, vol.52 #206 (Feb., 1941): 135-143.

2445. Research Bureau of the Am. Jewish Congress: "In Nazi-Dominated France." CB, vol.7 #1 (Nov. 15, 1940): 11-13

2446. The Underground Reporter: "Paris: May 1, 1942." FW, vol.3 #3 (Aug., 1942): 278-281.

2447. ___: "The Tragic Face of Paris." FW, vol.6 #6 (Dec., 1943): 525-526.

2448. Van Passen, Pierre: "The Betrayal of France." CB, vol.7 #2 (Nov. 22, 1940): 5-8.

2449. Walter, Gerard (Tony White, transl.): Paris Under the Occupation [New York: Orion Press, 1960]

2450. Werth, Alexander: France 1940-1955 [London: Robert Hale, 1956]

2451. Wohl, Paul: "Hitler´s Biological War." FW, vol.2 #4 (May, 1942): 360-362.

Low Countries

2452. Ardenne, Robert: German Exploitation in Belgium [Washington, DC: Brookings Institute, 1942]

2453. Epstein, John (ed.): Belgium [Cambridge: Univ. Press, 1944]

2454. Goris, Jan-Albert: Belgium in Bondage [New York: Fischer, 1943]

2455. ___: (ed. and transl.): Belgium Under Occupation [New York: Belgian Government Information Center, 1947]

2456. Jelenko, E. W.: "The Lowlands under the Nazis." CB, vol.7 #3 (Nov. 29, 1940): 11-13.

2457. Kollewijn, R. D.: "The Dutch Universities Under Nazi Domination." Annals, #245 (May, 1946): 118-128.

2458. Maas, Walter B.: The Netherlands at War: 1940-1945 [New York: Abelard-Schuman, 1970]

2459. Marres, Juliette: "Nazi Overlords." Hist/WWII, #17 (1973): 450-459. * On Holland.

2460. Motz, Roger: Belgium Unvanquished [London: Drummond, 1942]

2461. Somerhausen, Anne: Written in Darkness: A Belgian Woman´s Record of the Occupation 1940-1945 [New York: A. A. Knopf, 1946]

2462. Warmbrunn, Werner: The Dutch Under German Occupation, 1940-1945 [Stanford, CA: Stanford, Univ. Press, 1963]

Poland

2463. Adamkiewicz, G.: "The Hammer and Sickle Over Poland." Cont Rev, vol.158 #895 (July, 1940): 63-69. * On the Soviet occupation of Eastern Poland.

2464. Aldor, Francis: Germany´s "Death Space": The Polish Tragedy [London: W. Aldor, 1940]

2465. Bartoszewski, Wladyslaw: "From the Chronicler´s Notebook: Days in Warsaw 1939-1945." Poland, #2/126 (Feb., 1965): 28B-30. * Includes material on Jews.

2466. ___: "Report from the Outer Brink of Life." Poland, #5/141 (May, 1966): 17-19.

2467. ___: Warsaw Death Ring 1939-1944 [Warsaw, Poland: Interpress Publishers, 1968]

2468. Bielecki, Tadeusz et al: Warsaw Aflame: The 1939-1945 Period [Los Angeles, CA: Polamerica Press, 1973]

2469. Brzeska, Maria: Through a Womans Eyes: Life in Poland Under the German Occupation [London: M. Love, 1944]

2470. Cyprian, T. and Jerzy Sawicki (E. Rothest, transl.): Nazi Rule in Poland, 1939-1945 [Warsaw: Polonia Pub., House, 1961]

2471. "The Destruction of Polish Culture." PFR, #49 (Aug. 1, 1942): Whole Issue.

2472. "The Destruction of the Catholic Church in Poland." J Mirror, vol.1 #3 (Oct., 1942): 86-89.

2473. "Documents from Poland: German Attempts to Murder a Nation." PFR, #47 (July 1, 1942): 1-7. * Includes material on Jews.

2474. Dobroszycki, Lucjan: "The Polish Language Press in German Occupied Poland 1939-1945." Polish Rev, vol.16 #1 (Win., 1971): 7-30.

2475. Dobrowska, Maria: "On a Beautiful Summer Morning." Poland, #4/56 (1959): 15-16, 25-28.

2476. Dmochowski, Leon: Food Conditions in Occupied Poland: Analysis of the German Food Rationing System in Poland [London: Polish Government-in-Exile, 1944]

2477. Dragomir, U.: It Started in Poland [London: Faber and Faber, 1941]

2478. "The Eastern Provinces of Poland Under Soviet Occupation." PFR, #9 (Nov. 15, 1940): Whole Issue.

2479. "The Economic Situation in Poland." PFR, #60 (Jan. 15, 1943): Whole Issue.

2480. Evans, Jon: The Nazi New Order in Poland London: Victor Gollancz, 1941]

2481. "An Experiment Against World Order." Poland, #3/149 (Jan., 1967): 3-7, 18.

2482. "The Fate of a Polish City: Lodz." PFR, #52 (Sept. 15, 1942): Whole Issue.

2483. "Four Years of German Economy in Poland." PFR, #76 (Sept. 15, 1943): 1-8.

2484. "The Gau Oberschlesien." PFR, #29 (Oct.1, 1941): 4-5.

2485. "German Crimes Arraigned." PFR, #48 (July 15, 1942): 1-3.

2486. "The German Economy in Poland." PFR, #15 (March 1, 1941): Whole Issue.

2487. "A German Fraud in Eastern Europe: Herr Rosenberg´s Land Reform." PFR, #42 (April 15, 1942): Whole Issue.

2488. "German Rule in Poland." PFR, #21 (June 1, 1941): Whole Issue. * Includes material on Jews.

2489. "The German War on Polish Children." PFR, #77 (Oct. 1, 1943): Whole Issue.

2490. "The Germanization of a People." PFR, #62 (Feb. 15, 1943): Whole Issue.

2491. "The Germans in Poland." PFR, #8 (Nov. 1, 1940): Whole Issue.

2492. Godden, Gertrude M.: Murder of a Nation: German Destruction of Polish Culture [London: B. Dates, 1943]

2493. "Governor Frank on Germany´s Aims in Poland." PFR, #5 (Sept. 15, 1940): 10-12.

2494. Gross, Jan T.: Polish Society Under German Occupation: The Generalgouvernment, 1939-1944 [Princeton, NJ: Princeton Univ. Press, 1979]

Masterful study on the workings of the Generalgouvernment and the results of the application of the "New Order" in Poland. Deals with collaboration and resistance as modes of accomodation with reality. Also views the underground as an alternative society, as a "underground state." Gross is brutally honest about Polish apathy to the extermination of the Jews and sees it as the culmination of pre-war antisemitism.

2495. Gumkowski, J. and K. Leszczynski: Poland Under Nazi Occupation [Warsaw, Poland: Polonia Pub. House, 1961]

2496. "Helots of the Herrenvolk." PFR, #65 (April 1, 1943): Whole Issue.

2497. Hirszfeld, Ludwik: "The City of Death: Excerpts from a Memoir." Poland, #1/65 (Jan., 1960): 27-30. * On occupied Warsaw.

2498. "How the Germans are Starving Poland." PFR, #58 (Dec. 15, 1942): Whole Issue. * Includes material on Jews.

2499. Junosza, J. P.: "Poland Under Nazi Rule." New Republic, vol.104 #13 (March 31, 1941): 426-428.

2500. Koehl, Robert L.: "The Deutsche Volksliste in Poland, 1939-1945." JCEA, vol.15 #4 (Jan., 1956): 354-366.

2501. Kolanczyk, K.: "German Law in Incorporated Territory." Commission: GCIP/I, pp.235-257.

2502. Lewak, Adam: "The Archives and Libraries of Warsaw During World War II." Polish Rev, vol.7 #2 (Spr., 1962): 3-40.

2503. Mead, James M.: "No Poles in Poland." Am Heb, vol.151 #16 (Aug. 21, 1942): 6, 18-19.

2504. Mikolajczyk, Stefan: "The German Terror in Poland." PFR, #48 (July 15, 1942): 4-6.

2505. Mikorska, Maria: Spring Held no Hope: The Facts of the German Occupation of Poland [London: Kolin, 1941]

2506. "Nazi Occupation of Poland in Light of Hans Frank´s Diary and Reports from the Cabinet Sittings of the General Government." Commission: GCIP/II, pp.11-43

2507. "Nazi Orgies in Poland." P.I.N., vol.7 #15 (April 13, 1940): 4-5.

2508. "The Nazi Party in Poland." PFR, #43 (May 1, 1942): Whole Issue.

2509. "The New German Colonization in Poland." PFR, #12 (Jan. 15, 1941): Whole Issue.

2510. "The Physical Destruction of the Polish Nation." PFR, #55 (Nov. 1, 1942): Whole Issue.

2511. "Poland After Two Years of German Occupation." PFR, #28 (Sept. 15, 1941): Whole Issue.

2512. "Poland Under the Nazi Heel: Eyewitness Stories of the Invasion." CJR, vol.3 #1 (Jan./Feb., 1940): 18-25.

2513. "Poland's Economic Plight Under the Germans." PFR, #37 (Feb. 1, 1942): Whole Issue.

2514. "The Policy of Germanization in Theory and Practice." PFR, #31 (Nov. 1, 1941): Whole Issue.

2515. Polish Ministry of Information: Bestiality [London: Polish Government-in-Exile, 1942]

2516. ___: The Black Book of Poland [New York: G. P. Putnam's Sons, 1942] Also published as: The German New Order in Poland [London: Hutchinson, 1942]

Detailed account of the Nazi-German "New Order" in Poland from the start of the occupation (September 1939) through June 1941. Based upon first hand documentation. Also covers Nazi persecution of Polish Jewry and life in the ghettos.

2517. ___: Poland After one Year of War [London: Allen and Unwin, 1940]

2518. ___: Polish White Book, German Occupation in Poland [New York: Greystone Press & Roj in Exile Pub., 1940]

2519. "The Polish Working Class Under the German New Order." PFR, #22 (June 15, 1941): 1-5.

2520. "The Real New Order: Terror." PFR, #32 (Nov. 15, 1941): Whole Issue. * Includes material on Jews.

2521. "Religion Under German Occupation." PFR, #83 (Jan. 1, 1944): 7-8.

2522. Rich, J. F.: "Aftermath in Poland." Survey Graphic, vol.28 #12 (Dec., 1939): 740-741.

2523. Schwarz, Maria: "A Record of Horror." CW, vol.9 #12 (March 20, 1942): 7-9.

2524. "Slaves of the Third Reich." PFR, #38 (Feb. 15, 1942): Whole Issue.

2525. Sobieski, Zygmunt: "Reminiscences from Lwow 1939-1946." JCEA, vol.6 #4 (Jan., 1947): 351-374.

2526. Sterzetelski, Stanislaw: Where the Storm Broke: Poland from Yesterday to Tomorrow [New York: Roy Slavonic Publications, 1942]

2527. Waligorski, Androzej: "Poland Under the Swastika." Cont Rev, vol.157 #894 (June, 1940): 678-685.

2528. Winiewicz, Jozef M.: Aims and Failures of the German New Order: A Study [Chicago: American Polish Council, 1943]

2529. Wirth, F.: "The Germans in Poland." Cont Rev, vol.156 #884 (Sept., 1939): 352-356.

2530. "The Work of Germanization in the General Gouvernement." PFR, #63 (March 1, 1943): Whole Issue.

2531 Wruk, Jozef and Helena Radomska-Strzemecka: "Occupation as Seen by Juveniles. Polish Children Accuse." Poland, #7/95 (July, 1962): 17-19.

Russia

2532. Clark, Alan: "Empires in the East." Hist/WWII, #107 (1974): 2976-2983.

2533. Dallin, Alexander: German Rule in Russia 1941-1945: A Study of Occupation Policies [New York: St. Martin´s Press, 1957]

Extensively documented history of the Nazi occupation of the Soviet Union. Covers the subject thematically, dealing extensively with each topic and theme. The Jewish problem is, unfortunately, dealt with in only a cursory way - a major gap in this otherwise superior example of World War II historiography.

2534. ___: Odessa, 1941-1944: A Case Study on Soviet Territory under Foreign Rule [Santa Monica, CA: Rand Corporation, 1957]

2535. Joesten, J.: "German Rule in Ostland." F Affairs, vol.22 #1 (Oct., 1943): 143-147.

2536. Kamenetsky, Ihor: Hitler´s Occupation of the Ukraine, 1941-1944 [Milwaukee: Marquette Univ. Press, 1956]

2537. ___: Secret Nazi Plans for Eastern Europe: A Study of Lebensraum Policies [New York: Bookman Assoc., 1961]

2538. Laskovsky, Nikolas: "Practicing Law in the Occupied Ukraine." Am Slavic/EER, vol.11 #2 (1952): 123-137.

2539. Reitlinger, Gerald: The House Built on Sand: The Conflicts of German Policy in Russia, 1939-1945 [New York: Viking Press, 1960]

Scandinavia

2540. Herung, John: "The Golden Rule in Denmark." Survey Graphic, vol.36 #2 (Feb., 1947): 152-155.

2541. Leistikow, Gunnar: "Denmark Under the Nazi Heel." F Affairs, vol.21 #2 (Jan., 1943): 340-353.

2542. ___: "Ruining Denmark." FW, vol.3 #1 (June, 1942): 70-73.

2543. Lyon, Katharine: "Norway's Secret Weapon." FW, vol.3 #1 (June, 1942): 49-53.

2544. "Norwegian Labor Under Nazi Rule." V/Unq, vol.1 #1 (March, 1943): 1, 6-7.

COLLABORATION

Overviews

2545. Armstrong, John A.: "Collaborationism in World War II: The Integral Nationalist Variant in Eastern Europe." JMH, vol.40 #3 (Sept., 1968): 396-410.

2546. "The Collaborationist Jitters." J Comment, vol.2 #6 (Feb. 25, 1944): 4-7.

2547. Dean, Clive: "The Little Entente of Quislings." CEO, vol.19 #8 (April 17, 1942): 124-125.

2548. Iain, Sproat: Wodehouse at War: The Extraordinary Truth About P. G. Wodenhouse's Broadcasts on Nazi Radio [New Haven, CT: Ticknor & Fields, 1981]

2549. Joesten, Joachim: "A Gallery of Quislings." Nation, vol.155 #10 (Sept. 5, 1942): 190-193.

2550. Littlejohn, D.: The Patriotic Traitors: A History of Collaboration in Europe, 1940-1945 [London: Heineman, 1971]

Idiosyncratic but nonetheless useful historical survey of

European collaboration. Special emphasis is placed on activities of the local fascists in the Foreign Legions of the SS during World War II as well as their role in the persecution of the Jews.

2551. Rings, Werner (M. Brownjohn, transl.): Life with the Enemy: Collaboration and Resistance in Hitler's Europe, 1939-1945 [Garden City, NY: Doubleday, 1982]

Carefully documented revisionist history of collaboration and resistance under the Nazis. Rings' main purpose is to demythologize both the heroic resistance and the cowardly collaborators. Based almost exclusively on secondary sources. Includes coverage of Jews.

2552. Soffner, Heinz: "Under What Flag..." Survey Graphic, vol.30 #12 (Dec., 1941): 693-697.

2553. Tschuppik, Walter: The Quislings: Hitler's Trojan Horses [London: Hutchinson, 1940]

2554. The Underground Reporter: "A Collaborationist Paper." FW, vol.7 #5 (May, 1944): 459-463.

Germany's Foreign Legions

2555. Ainsztein, Reuben: "Hitler's Generals and Vlasov's Volunteers." JQ, vol.24 #3 (Fall, 1976): 32-41.

2556. Dmytryshyn, B.: "The Nazis and the SS Volunteer Division 'Galicia'." Am Slavic/EER, vol.15 #1 (Feb., 1956): 1-10.

2557. Jelinek, Yeshayahu: "Stormtroopers in Slovakia: The Rodobrana and the Hlinka Guard." JCH, vol.6 #3 (July, 1971): 109-122.

2558. Joesten, Joachim: "Hitler's Shanghaied Volunteers." Nation, vol.157 #7 (Feb. 14, 1942): 191-193.

2559. Kleinfeld, G. R.: Hitler's Spanish Legion [Carbondale, IL: Southern Illinois Univ. Press, 1979]

2560. Koch, H. W.: "Hitler's Foreign Legions." Hist/WWII, #103 (1974): 2872-2881.

2561. ___: "The Renegade Armies." Hist/WWII, #78 (1974): 2168-2175.

2562. Ostry, Jan: "What is the Bander Gang?" CEO, vol.24 #17 (Sept. 19, 1947): 264-265.

2563. Thorwald, Juergen (Richard and C. Winston, transls.): The Illusion: Soviet Soldiers in Hitler´s Armies [New York: Harcourt, Brace Jovanovich, 1975]

Weakly executed study of German use of Russian collaborationists in the war against the Soviet Union. Argues that Nazi racial policy prevented their use in large numbers. Confuses the cases of some ethnic minorities (e.g. Ukrainians and Cossaks) with "White" Russians. Does, however, contain some insights.

Eastern Europe

2564. Harriman, Helga H.: "Slovenia as an Outpost of the Third Reich." EEQ, vol.5 #2 (June, 1971): 222-231.

2565. Polakewitch, Mosche: "The Polish Quisling." CW, vol.9 #10 (March 6, 1942): 8-9. * On former P. M. of Poland Leon Kozlowski.

Low Countries

2566. Burgher, John: "Hitler´s Quisling Dilemma in Holand." CEO, vol.19 #6 (March 20, 1942): 96.

2567. Hirschfeld, Gerhard: "Collaboration and Attentism in the Netherlands, 1940-1941." JCH, vol.16 #3 (July, 1981): 467-486.

2568. Marcq, Rene: "Collaboration Under Enemy Occupation." Annals, #247 (Sept., 1946): 69-72.

2569. Mason, Henry L.: The Purge of Dutch Quislings: Emergency Justice in the Netherlands [The Hague: Nijhoff, 1952]

2570. Schuvrsma, R.: "Dutch Fascists´ Share in Crime." WLB, vol.20 #2 (Spr., 1966): 34-37.

2571. Vermeylen, Pierre: "The Punishment of Collaborators." Annals, #247 (Sept., 1946): 73-77.

Norway

2572. Hayes, Paul M.: Quisling: The Career and Political Ideas of Vidkun Quisling, 1887-1945 [London: Newton Abbot, 1971]

2573. ___: "Quisling's Political Ideas." JCH, vol.1 #1 (Jan., 1966): 145-157.

2574. Hearst, E. A.: "Knut Hamsen: A Case of Intellectual Apostasy." WLB, vol.20 #3 (Sum., 1966): 37-39.

Vichy

2575. Ainsztein, Reuben: "New Judgment on Vichy: The Dilemma of Collaboration." WLB, vol.9 #5/6 (Sept./Dec., 1955): 46.

2576. Alperin, Aaron: "The Traitors of Vichy." CW, vol.8 #25 (June 27, 1941): 11-12.

2577. Aron, Robert: The Vichy Regime, 1930-1944 [New York: Macmillan, 1958]

Inquiry into the history of the French collaborationist regime from 1940-1944. Despite being a member of the resistance Aron views the Vichy regime quite objectively. Aron offers a detailed description of the politics of Vichy and the interaction of that regime with both the Allies and the Nazis.

2578. Cohen, Victor: "The Vichy Experiment." Cont Rev, vol. 188 #1075 (July, 1955): 24-26.

2579. Dank, M.: The French Against the French [Philadelphia: J. B. Lippincott, 1974]

2580. Dupont, P.: "The Underground's Indictment of Puchev." FW, vol.7 #4 (April, 1944): 361-364.

2581. Farmer, Paul: Vichy: Political Dilemma [New York: Columbia Univ. Press, 1955]

2582. Franck, Louis R.: "In Defeated France: The Forces of Collaboration." F Affairs, vol.21 #1 (Oct., 1942): 44-58.

2583. Hoffmann, Stanley: "Collaborationism in France during World War II." JMH, vol.40 #3 (Sept., 1968): 375-395.

2584. Hoover Institute, The (P. W. Whitcomb, transl.): France During the German Occupation, 1940-1944: A Collection of 292 Statements on the Government of Marechal Petain and Pierre Laval 3 vols. [Stanford, CA: Hoover Institution Press, 1957]

2585. Levy, Louis: "The Truth About France." CEO, vol.18 #5 (March 1, 1941): 54-55.

2586. Marchal, Leon: Vichy: Two Years of Deception [New York: Macmillan, 1943]

2587. Moch, Jules: "The Breakdown of Vichy." Nation, vol. 157 #23 (Dec. 4, 1943): 669-671.

2588. Osgood, Samuel M.: "The Antisemitism of the French Collaborationist Press." WLB, vol.23 #2/3 (Spr./Sum., 1968): 51-56.

2589. Paxton, Robert O.: Vichy France: Old Guard and New Order, 1940-1944 [New York: A. A. Knopf, 1972]

2590. Simone, A.: J´Accuse!: The Men Who Betrayed France [New York: Dial Press, 1940]

2591. Tillinger, Eugene: "I Escaped from France!" NJM, vol. 57 #3 (Nov., 1942): 90-91. * Eyewitness report, as told to author.

2592. Walter, Hilde: "German-French Cooperation." J Fo, vol.24 #6 (June, 1941): 98-99.

2593. Wiesenfeld, Leon: "The Vichy Clique Obeys Hitler´s Orders." JVP, vol.4 #4/5 (May, 1941): 4, 16.

2594. Wise, S. S.: "Tragedy of France Betrayed." CW, vol.8 #22 (June 6, 1941): 6-7.

Vichy: Pierre Laval

2595. Cole, Hubert: Laval: A Biography [London: Heinemann, 1963]

2596. Laval, Pierre: The Diary of Pierre Laval [New York: AMS Press, 1976] Rep. 1948 Ed.

2597. Poliakoff, S.: "The Real Laval." CW, vol.9 #30 (Oct. 16, 1942): 8-9.

2598. Smith, Rennie: "Gauleiter Laval: Smoking Volcano." CEO, vol.19 #9 (May 1, 1942): 133-134.

2599. Warner, Geoffrey: Pierre Laval and the Eclipse of France [New York: Macmillan, 1969]

Vichy: Henri Petain

2600. Ehrenburg, Ilya: "The Judas of France." Am Heb, vol. 155 #17 (Aug. 24, 1945): 8-9, 13.

2601. Fischer, Alfred J.: "Petain´s Responsibility." CEO, vol.20 #2 (Jan. 22, 1943): 21-22.

2602. Hoden, Marcel: "Petain: The End of a Legend." CEO, vol.18 #18 (Sept. 5, 1941): 242-243.

2603. Lottman, Herbert R.: Petain: Hero or Traitor. The Untold Story [New York: William Morrow, 1984]

2604. Paxton, Robert O.: Parades and Politics at Vichy: The French Officer Corps under Marshal Petain [Princeton, NJ: Princeton Univ. Press, 1966]

2605. Torres, H.: "Petain: Triumph of a Myth." Am Mercury, vol.54 #217 (Jan., 1942): 27-35.

2606. Winner, Percy: "The Shame of France." New Republic, vol.119 #18 (Nov. 1, 1948): 16-17.

JEWS UNDER NAZI OCCUPATION

Overviews

2607. Am. Jewish Committee: The Jewish Communities of Nazi Occupied Europe 2 vols. [New York: The Committee, 1944]

Authoritative wartime survey of the condition of European Jewry in 1942-1943. Written as a report to the American Jewish Committee.

2608. Bernstein, Edgar: "Jews in Conquered Europe: Conditions in Denmark, Holland and France." J Affairs, vol.1 #11 (April, 1942): 5, 11.

2609. ___: "Jews in Conquered Europe: The Position of Nazified Poland." J Affairs, vol.1 #10 (March, 1942): 3-4.

2610. Blumenthal, Nachman: "Magical Thinking Among the Jews During the Nazi Occupation." YVS, vol.5 (1961): 221-236.

2611. Comm. on European Cultural Reconstruction: Tentative List of Jewish Periodicals in Axis Occupied Countries [New York: Conference on Jewish Relations, 1947]

2612. "Death by Starvation: Nazi Weapon to Annihilate Europe´s Jews." J Affairs, vol.3 #2 (July, 1943): 3-4

2613. "The Diaspora: The Jewish Position in various Countries." NJ, vol.17 #1/2 (Oct./Nov., 1940): 15-17.

2614. Dworzecki, Meir: "The Day-to-Day Stand of the Jews." Gutman: Catastrophe, pp.367-399; Y/V: Resistance, pp. 152-181.

2615. Eck, Nathan: "The Place of the Jewish Political Parties in the Countries Under Nazi Rule." Y/V: Resistance, pp.132-147.

2616. Goldmann, Nahum: "The Jewish Situation in Europe and the War." J Sp, vol.5 #5 (March, 1940): 22-24.

2617. "The Halutzim Carry on in Europe." NP, vol.31 #24 (March 28, 1941): 7-8.

2618. Hilberg, R.: "Systematic Starvation." Korman: Hunter, pp.187-188.

2619. Institute of Jewish Affairs: Jews in Nazi Europe [Baltimore: Am. Jewish Conference, 1941]

Documented study of Nazi persecution of Jews. Based on extensive documentation. The text was written by Boris Shub.

2620. "The Jewish Religion in Axis Europe. Fortress Against Barbarism." IJA, vol.1 #11/13 (June/Aug., 1942): 1-23.

2621. Lvovitch, David: "Behind the Wall and Barbed Wire." Ort Eco Bul, vol.2 #2 (March/April, 1941): 1-2.

2622. "New Nazi Measures Against Jews." CJR, vol.3 #1 (Jan./Feb., 1940): 79-85.

2623. Shner, Zvi: "On Documentation Projects as an Expression of Jewish Steadfastness in the Holocaust." Y/V: Resistance, pp.191-201.

2624. Shub, Boris: Hitler´s Ten Year War on the Jews [New York: IJA/WJC, 1943]

2625. ___ and Zorach Warhaftig: Starvation Over Europe: A Documented Record [New York: IJA/WJC, 1943]

2626. Sonnabend, H.: "The Drama of East European Jewry." J Affairs, vol.1 #5 (Oct., 1941): 3-4.

2627. Starr, Joshua: "Jewish Cultural Property Under Nazi Control." JSS, vol.12 #1 (Jan., 1950): 27-48.

2628. Walk, Joseph: "The Religious Leadership During the Holocaust." G/H: Patterns, pp.377-391.

2629. Weinryb, Bernard D.: "Jewish History Nazified." CJR, vol.4 #2 (April, 1941): 148-167.

Belgium

2630. Marcus, Robert S.: "Jews in Belgium." CW, vol.13 #13 (March 29, 1946): 11-13.

2631. Steinberg, Maxime: "The Trap of Legality: The Association of the Jews of Belgium." G/H: Patterns, pp.353-376.

2632. Wiesenthal, Herbert F.: "The Belgian Jews." Ort Eco Bul, vol.1 #4/5 (July/Oct., 1940): 17.

Czechoslovakia

2633. "Antisemitism in Czechoslovakia." CJR, vol.2 #2 (March/April, 1939): 74-76.

2634. Baum, Karl: "Nazi Anti-Jewish Legislation in the Czech Protectorate: A Documentary Note." SJA, vol.2 #1 (May, 1972): 116-128.

2635. Brod, Max: "It Happened One Night." NJM, vol.53 #11 (July/Aug., 1939): 392-393, 400. * Last group of Jews to leave Czechoslovakia before Nazis close border.

2636. "Czechoslovakia's End Brings Alarm for Jews of Bohemia." NP, vol.29 #11 (March 17, 1939): 6.

2637. "Economic Legislation in Bohemia-Moravia." CJR, vol.3 #3 (May/June, 1940): 320-325.

2638. Goldelman, S.: "The Jews in the New Czechoslovakia." CJR, vol.2 #1 (Jan., 1939): 7-15.

2639. Holotik, Ludovit: "The 'Jewish Problem' in Slovakia." EEQ, vol.1 #1 (March, 1967): 31-37.

2640. Jacoby, Gerhard: The Common Fate of Czech and Jew: Czechoslovak Jewry Past and Future [New York: Inst. of Jewish Affairs, 1943]

2641. Maerz, Paul: "The Last Days of Zionist Activity in Czechoslovakia." CJRC/B #11 (April, 1944): 5-7.

2642. "Nuremberg Laws in Bohemia-Moravia." CJR, vol.3 #4 (July/Aug., 1940): 430.

2643. Rothkirchen, L.: "The Dual Role of the Jewish Center in Slovakia." G/H: Patterns, pp.219-227.

2644. Weltsch, Felix: "The Common Fate of Jews and Czechs." J Fr, vol.6 #7 (July, 1939): 21-23.

2645. Wiesenthal, Herbert F.: "Structure of the Jews in Czechoslovakia." Ort Eco Bul, vol.1 #3 (May/June, 1940): 6-7.

Denmark

2646. Adler, H. G.: "Danish Jewry Under German Occupation." WLB, vol.9 #1/2 (Jan/April, 1955): 12, 16.

2647. Moller, J. Ch.: "The Jews in Denmark." Am Heb, vol. 153 #6 (Dec. 10, 1943): 9.

2648. Yahil, Lenny: "Denmark Under the Occupation." WLB, vol.16 #4 (Oct., 1962): 73.

France

2649. Adelman, Seymour: "The Jews of France." J Sp, vol.6 #2 (Dec., 1940): 15-16.

2650. "Anti-Jewish Laws in the French Possessions." CJR, vol.5 #1 (Feb., 1942): 97-99.

2651. "Anti-Jewish Laws in Unoccupied France." CJR, vol.4 #6 (Dec., 1941): 673-679.

2652. Chomski, I. "Cafe Doctor." J Mirror, vol.1 #2 (Sept., 1942): 21-25. * Jewish doctors in occupied France.

2653. Cohen, Israel: "The Tragedy of the Jews in France." J Sp, vol.7 #12 (Oct., 1942): 10-13.

2654. Diamant, Zanvel: "Jewish Refugees on the French Riviera." YIVO Annual, vol.8 (1953): 264-280.

2655. "Health Conditions in France in 1943." Am OSE Rev, vol.3 #1 (Spr., 1944): 31-35.

2656. "Jews in the French Empire (1940-1941)." IJA, vol.1 #2 (Sept., 1941): 1-11.

2657. Kaplan, Jacob (J. M. Bernstein, transl.): "French Jewry Under the Occupation." AJYB, vol.47 (1945/1946): 71-118.

2658. Labin, Saniel: "What of Leon Blum?" Lib Jud, vol.12 #6 (Oct., 1944): 42-47, 63.

2659. "A Letter from Paris." J Sp, vol.9 #6 (April, 1944): 26-28.

2660. Levy, Claude and Paul Tillard: Betrayal at the Vel D'Hiv [New York: Hill & Wang, 1969]

Journalistic account of the deportation of Parisian Jews. The work is controversial because it tells the unpleasant truth that most French Jews were rounded up, confined, and deported without any direct involvement of the SS. Nearly all Parisian Jews were arrested by the French police.

2661. Marrus, Michael R. and Robert O. Paxton: Vichy France and the Jews [New York: Basic Books, 1981]

More aptly termed "Vichy on the Jews" the book attempts to assess the role of French collaborators in the Final Solution. French cooperation with the Germans on Jewish affairs is evaluated in light not only of French history, but also of the events in the rest of Europe. The conclusion, that French antisemitic collaboration was unparalleled, does not, however, seem to be supported by the survival of two-thirds of French Jewry as opposed, for example, to that of approximately ten percent of Polish Jewry.

2662. Maynard, John A. F.: "The Future of French Antisemitism." J Sp, vol.6 #3 (Jan., 1941): 16-17.

2663. Odic, Charles (H. N. Hall, transl.): Stepchildren of France [New York: Roy Pub., 1945]

2664. Oualid, W.: "Economic Recunstruction of French Jewry." Ort Eco Bul, vol.2 #2 (March/April, 1941): 2-4.

2665. Paskoff, Benjamin: "Dreyfus to Vichy." J Survey, vol. 1 #5 (Oct., 1941): 10-11.

2666. "Plight of Jewish Children in France." Am OSE Rev, vol.3 #1 (Spr., 1944): 36-37.

2667. Poliakoff, S.: "A Noteworthy Lesson: The Nature of Antisemitism in France." CW, vol.9 #23 (June 19, 1942): 7-8.

2668. ___: "Phantoms in France." CW, vol.8 #40 (Dec. 5, 1941): 8-9.

2669. Poliakov, Leon: "The Conflict Between the German Army and Secret Police over Bombings of Paris Synagogues." JSS, vol.16 #3 (July, 1954): 253-266.

2670. ___: "An Opinion Poll on Anti-Jewish Measures in Vichy France." JSS, vol.15 #2 (April, 1953): 113-134.

2671. Pozner, Vladimir: "France Fights Antisemitism." J Fr, vol.7 #11 (Nov., 1940): 652-653.

2672. "Racial Legislation in France." CJR, vol.3 #6 (Nov./ Dec., 1940): 652-653.

2673. "Racism in Occupied France." CJR, vol.4 #4 (Aug., 1941): 433-434.

2674. Rosmarin, Aaron: "The Destruction of Six Synagogues." J Sp, vol.7 #1 (Nov., 1941): 7-8, 11.

2675. Sender, Henri: "Lights and Shades of Jewish Life in France, 1940-1942." JSS, vol.5 #4 (Oct., 1943): 367-382

2676. Spire, Andre: "The Spirit of France." J Mirror, vol.1 #5 (Dec./Jan., 1942/43): 18-20. * French gentile expresses his indignation over Vichy treatment of Jews.

2677. Stein, Kalman: "The Fight for New Emancipation." CW, vol.9 #28 (Oct. 2, 1942): 6-8.

2678. Szajkowski, Zosa: Analytical Franco-Jewish Gazetteer, 1939-1945 [New York: Schulsinger Bros., 1966]

2679. ___: "The French Central Jewish Consistory During the Second World War." YVS, vol.3 (1959): 187-260.

2680. ___: "Glimpses of the History of Jews in Occupied France." YVS, vol.2 (1958): 133-158.

2681. ___: "The Organization of UGIF in Nazi-Controlled France." JSS, vol.9 (July, 1947): 239-256.

2682. Vishniac, Marc: "Jewish Fate in France After Her Collapse." Ort Eco Bul, vol.1 #6 (Nov./Dec., 1940): 4-8.

2683. Werner, Alfred: "Dreyfus and Present-Day France." J Sp, vol.7 #5 (March, 1942): 22-23, 34.

2684. Yahil, Leni: "The Jewish Leadership of France." G/H: Patterns, pp.317-333.

2685. Zermer, E. H. and Robert T. Bower: "German Occupation and Antisemitism in France." Pub Op Q, vol.12 #2 (Sum., 1948): 258-265.

French North Africa

2686. Arendt, H.: "Why the Cremieux Decree was Abrogated." CJR, vol.6 #2 (April, 1943): 115-123.

2687. Block, Armand: "African Portents." J Standard, vol.3 #42 (Jan. 29, 1943): 4, 8. * On anti-Jewish laws.

2688. Dluznowski, M.: "I Came from Morocco." NJM, vol.56 #7 (March, 1942): 218-219.

2689. Jung, Moses: "The Jews in Northern Africa." CJR, vol. 5 #6 (Dec., 1942): 618-675.

2690. Lyon, Mabel: "The Cremieux Law and its Author." J Mirror, vol.1 #6 (Feb./March, 1943): 52-55. * Deals with General Giraud´s edict on laws affecting Jews in Algeria.

2691. Peiser, Kurt: "Handicaps in North Africa." Lib Jud, vol.11 #6 (Oct., 1943): 47-50. * Report by the JDC.

2692. Roget, S. L.: "Giraud´s Jewish Policy." Lib Jud, vol. 11 #2 (June, 1943): 43-47.

2693. Torres, H.: "The Abrogation of the Cremieux Decree." FW, vol.5 #5 (May, 1943): 405-409.

2694. Zukerman, William: "The Darlan Incident and the Jews." Am Heb, vol.151 #32 (Dec. 11, 1942): 6.

Greece

2695. Abrahams, A.: "Voice That Cried in the Wilderness. The Lesson of Salonika." J Standard, vol.2 #2 (April 25, 1941): 4.

2696. Ben, Joseph: "Jewish Leadership in Greece during the Holocaust." G/H: Patterns, pp.335-352.

2697. Exintaris, George: "The Jews in Occupied Greece." J Layman, vol.18 #7 (April, 1944): 22-24.

2698. Kleinlerer, E. D.: "Sharing the Tragedy of Greece." CW, vol.8 #17 (May 2, 1941): 7-8.

2699. ___: "Thorns among the Roses." CW, vol.8 #14 (April 14, 1941): 7-8.

2700. Lagoudakis, Charilaos: "Jews of Greece." CW, vol.10 #22 (June 4, 1943): 9-11.

Holland

2701. de Jong, Louis: "Opening Remarks." G/H: Patterns, pp. 13-15.

2702. Gerbraudy, P. S.: "We Are Proud of the Dutch Jews." J Sp, vol.7 #5 (March, 1942): 13.

2703. Sijes, B. A.: "Several Observations Concerning the Position of the Jews in Occupied Holland During World War II." Gutman: Rescue, pp.527-553.

2704. Van Meister, Hendrik: "Out of the Desert, the Torch." Am Heb, vol.151 #5 (June 5, 1942): 5, 21-22.

2705. Van Tijn, G.: "Werkdorf Nieuwesluis." LBIYB, vol.14 (1969): 182-200. * On JDC school for German refugees.

Poland

2706. Cang, Joel: "Tragedy of the Polish Jews." CJCh, vol. 27 #23 (Oct. 20, 1939): 5, 13.

2707. Cohen, Israel: "Polish Jewry Under Nazi Tyranny." J Sp, vol.7 #7 (May, 1942): 13-17.

2708. Daniel, Howard: "Mass Murder in Poland." Nation, vol. 150 #4 (Jan. 27, 1940): 92-94.

2709. Engel, David: "An Early Account of Polish Jewry under Nazi and Soviet Occupation Presented to the Polish Government-In-Exile, February 1940." JSS, vol.45 #1 (Win., 1983): 1-16.

2710. Fodor, Renee: "The Impact of the Nazi Occupation of Poland on the Jewish Mother-Child Relations." YIVO Annual, vol.11 (1956/57): 270-285.

2711. Grodner, David: "In Soviet Poland and Lithuania." CJR, vol.4 #2 (April, 1941): 136-147.

2712. Itzhaki, Solomon: "Hitler's New 'Order' in Practice." CW, vol.9 #36 (Nov. 27, 1942): 5-6.

2713. Janowsky, Oscar I.: "More Minorities - More Pawns." Survey Graphic, vol.28 #11 (Nov., 1939): 669-672, 704.

2714. Jaszunski, G. and Ch. Rozenberg: "Jewish Polish Refugees in Lithuania." Ort Eco Bul, vol.1 #2 (March/April, 1940): 10-12. Also in: J Sp, vol.5 #7 (May, 1940): 24-25, 45.

2715. "A Jewish ´Reservation´." J Fr, vol.6 #11 (Nov., 1939): 5. * On Lublin-Nisko.

2716. Junosza, J. P.: "Jews in Poland." Ch J Forum, vol.11 #1 (Fall, 1942): 51-53.

2717. Karmi, A: "The Jewish Cemetery in Occupied Warsaw." YVB, #16 (Feb., 1965): 42-50.

2718. Kirchwey, Freda: "Jews in Hitler´s Poland." Nation, vol.150 #3 (Jan. 20, 1940): 61-62.

2719. Kogan, Shlomo: "The Long Road." Schwarz: Root, pp. 100-111. * Memoir of Eastern Poland under both Soviet and Nazi domination.

2720. Kuznetzki, Jacob: "Polish Jewry Under Nazi Rule." J Sp, vol.5 #4 (Feb., 1940): 36-37.

2721. Lestchinsky, J.: "The Catastrophe of Polish Jewry." J Fr, vol.6 #10 (Oct., 1939): 15-19.

2722. "Letters from Poland. Official Communication from the Jewish National Committee." J Fr, vol.11 #4 (April, 1944): 15-18.

2723. "Life in Nazi-Occupied Poland." CB, vol.7 #6 (Dec. 20, 1940): 9-10. * Culled from Gazeta Zydowska, official Polish language Jewish paper.

2724. Menes, A.: "How the Jews Live in Poland Today." Ort Eco Bul, vol.1 #6 (Nov./Dec., 1940): 8-11.

2725. My Name is Million: The Experiences of an Englishwoman in Poland [London: Faber and Faber, 1940] * Deals extensively with Nazi treatment of Jews.

2726. "Nazi Measures in Poland." CJR, vol.3 #3 (May/June, 1940): 313-320.

2727. "News from the ´Reservation´." J Fr, vol.7 #8 (Aug., 1940): 5. * Report based on the official German paper the Krakauer Zeitung.

2728. Pat, Jacob (Leo Steinberg, transl.): Ashes and Fire [New York: International Univ. Press, 1947]

Chronicle of Polish Jewry under Nazi occupation. Author includes a postwar overview.

2729. The Persecution of Jews in German-Occupied Poland [London: Free Europe Pamphlet #2, 1940]

2730. Revusky, Abraham: "Soviet Responsibility for Persecution of Polish Jews." J Fr, vol.6 #12 (Dec., 1939): 7-9.

2731. Rubin, Ruth: "Poland... Slaughterhouse of Europe." J Survey, vol.2 #6 (Oct./Nov., 1942): 8-10.

2732. Segal, Simon: The New Order in Poland [New York: A. A. Knopf, 1942]

Study for the Research Institute on Peace and Post-War Problems of the American Jewish Committee. The study covers extensively the situation of Polish Jewry under Nazi occupation.

2733. Shur, M.: "The ´New Order´ in Poland: The Ordeal and Resistance of Polish Jewry." J Affairs, vol.2 #5 (Oct., 1942): 7, 12.

2734. Spizman, Leib: "Jews and Poles Under the Nazis." J Fr, vol.10 #2 (Feb., 1943): 24-26.

2735. ___: "The Situation in Poland." J Fr, vol.8 #10 (Oct., 1941): 21-22.

2736. Tartakower, Aryeh: "Challenge to Death." HM, vol.23 #4 (Feb., 1943): 8-9.

2737. Tenenbaum, J.: "Nazi Rule in Poland and the Jewish Medical Profession." Falstein: Martyrdom, pp.125-298.

2738. "TOZ at Work." Am OSE Rev, vol.1 #3/4 (March/April, 1942): 15-19.

2739. Treist, Menachem: "Nazi Savagery in Poland." J Fr, vol.7 #3 (March, 1940): 7-9.

2740. Werner, Alfred: "Polish Jews Behind Barbed Wire." Polish Jew, vol.2 #4 (Jan., 1942): 3-5.

2741. World Jewish Congress: "Anti-Jewish Laws in Nazi Poland." CW, vol.8 #7 (Feb. 14, 1941): 10-12.

2742. ___: "The Jews in Present Day Poland." CW, vol.8 #10 (March 7, 1941): 11-13.

Soviet Union

2743. Adelman, Seymour: "The Jews of Russia." J Sp, vol.6 #10 (Aug., 1941): 11-13.

2744. Frank, M. Z. R.: "Jews in Occupied Russia." J Fr, vol.9 #12 (Dec., 1942): 20-22. * On their extermination by the Einsatzgruppen.

2745. "Jews Under Soviet Rule." J Sp, vol.6 #12 (Oct., 1941): 8-11, 20.

2746. Levin, Dov: "The Jews and the Election Campaigns in Lithuania, 1940-1941." SJA, vol.10 #1 (Feb., 1980): 39-51

2747. ___: "The Jews in the Soviet Lithuanian Establishment 1940-1941." SJA, vol.10 #2 (May, 1980): 21-38

2748. ___: "The Jews and the Sovietization of Latvia, 1940-1941." SJA, vol.5 #1 (May, 1975): 39-56.

2749. Redlich, S.: "The Jews in the Soviet Annexed Territories 1939-1941." SJA, vol.1 #1 (June, 1971): 81-90.

2750. Shochat, Azriel: "Jews, Lithuanians and Russians, 1939-1941." Vago: J/NJ, pp.301-314.

2751. World Jewish Congress: "Jews Under Soviet Rule." IJA, vol.1 #1 (Aug., 1941): 1-8.

Yugoslavia

2752. "How Yugoslav Jewry Died." J Layman, vol.18 #5 (Feb., 1944): 13.

2753. Jelenko, Edward W.: "Jews in Yugoslavia." CB, vol.7 #5 (Dec. 13, 1940): 11-13.

2754. Laitin, Ben: "The Old Synagogue of Dubrovnik." Ch J Forum, vol.23 #4 (Sum., 1965): 270-274.

2755. Vital, Haim: "A Community in Ruins: What Happened to Jews in Yugoslavia." CW, vol.9 #1 (Jan. 2, 1942): 8-10.

2756. Yovanovic, Slobodan: "The Jews in Yugoslavia." J Sp, vol.7 #11 (Sept., 1942): 33.

THE JEWISH GHETTOS

Life in the Ghettos

2757. Bryks, Rachmil (R. Soyer, transl.): "Writers in the Ghetto." Recon, vol.37 #7 (Oct. 15, 1971): 21-25.

2758. "Death by Starvation." CW, vol.10 #17 (April 30, 1942): 5-8. Also in: J Sp, vol.8 #8 (June, 1943): 21-24.

2759. Dworzecki, Mark: "Diseases in the Ghetto." Am OSE Rev, vol.4 #1 (Spr., 1947): 18-25.

2760. Eisenstein, Betty: "Women in the Nazi Ghettoes." J Sp, vol.20 #7 (Sept., 1955): 13-15.

2761. Friedman, Philip: "The Jewish Ghettos of the Nazi Era." JSS, vol.16 #1 (Jan., 1954): 61-88. Also in Friedman: Roads, pp.59-87.

2762. ___: "Social Conflicts in the Ghetto." Friedman: Roads, pp.131-152.

2763. "A Ghetto within a Ghetto." Am OSE Rev, vol.1 #1/2 (Jan./Feb., 1942): 4-5.

2764. Gringauz, Samuel: "Some Methodological Problems in the Study of the Ghetto." JSS, vol.12 #1 (Jan., 1950): 65-72.

2765. Gutman, Yisrael: "The Ghettos." Grobman: Genocide, pp.167-172.

2766. Heiman, Leo: "Jewish Doctors´ Immortal Work in Nazi-Made Ghettos." J Digest, vol.5 #6 (March, 1960): 25-29.

2767. Hilberg, Raul: "The Ghetto as a Form of Government." Annals, #450 (July, 1980): 98-112. Also in Bauer: Historical, pp.155-171.

2768. Kantorowich, N.: "Creative Powers in the Ghetto." CW, vol.9 #4 (April 10, 1942): 9-10.

2769. Kermish, Joseph: "Origins of the Education Problem in the Ghetto." YVB #12 (Dec., 1962): 28-34.

2770. Lestchinsky, Jacob: "Hitler as the Ghetto Provider." CW, vol.9 #5 (Jan. 30, 1942): 6-7.

2771. "Life in the Ghetto." WLB, vol.12 #5/6 (1958): 16.

2772. "The Political Aspects of the Jews in the Ghetto." GS, #3 (Sept. 1, 1943): 3.

2773. Ringelblum, Emanuel: Underground Cultural Work in the Jewish Ghettos in Poland [New York: YIVO, 1945]

2774. Sarakoff, Louis: "Ghetto Money." J Digest, vol.16 #11 (Aug., 1971): 62-64.

2775. Shalit, Levi: "Smugglers of the Ghetto." J Digest, vol.18 #6 (March, 1973): 70-75.

2776. Winick, Myron: "Hunger Disease." Shoa, vol.1 #3 (Win., 1979): 1-3.

2777. Zukerman, W.: "Meaning of the Nazi Ghetto." CW, vol.8 #20 (May 23, 1941): 8-10.

The Judenraete

2778. Bar-On, Z. A.: "Jewish Leadership: Policy and Responsibility." Y/V: Resistance, pp.227-244.

2779. Bauer, Yehuda: "Jewish Leadership Reactions to Nazi Policies." Bauer: Historical, pp.173-192.

2780. ___: "The Judenraete - Some Conclusions." G/H: Patterns, pp.393-405.

2781. Beem, Hartag: "The Jewish Council of the Province of Vriesland (Holland)." YVB, #17 (Dec., 1965): 21-23.

2782. Bloom, Solomon F.: "Toward the Ghetto Dictator." JSS, vol.12 #1 (Jan., 1950): 73-78.

2783. Boas, Henrietta: "Professor David Cohen Remembered." WLB, vol.21 #4 (Autumn, 1967): 5-7.

2784. Cholawsky, S.: "The Judenrat in Minsk." G/H: Patterns pp.113-132.

2785. Dobroszycki, Lucjan: "Jewish Elites Under German Rule." Friedlander: Ideology, pp.221-230.

2786. Feingold, H. L. et al: "Discussion: The Judenrat and the Jewish Response." Bauer: Historical, pp.223-271.

2787. Freiberg, M.: "The Question of the Judenraete." Com, vol.56 #1 (July, 1973): 61-63.

2788. Gutman, Yisrael: "The Concept of Labor in Judenrat Policy." G/H: Patterns, pp.151-180.

2789. ___ and Cynthia J. Haft (eds.): Patterns of Jewish Leadership in Nazi Europe, 1933-1945: Proceedings of the Third Yad Vashem International Historical Conference Jerusalem, April 4-7, 1977 [Jerusalem: Yad Vashem, 1979]

2790. Hilberg, R.: "The Judenrat: Conscious or Unconscious Tool." G/H: Patterns, pp.31-44.

2791. Klein, Bernard: "The Judenrat." JSS, vol.22 #1 (Jan., 1960): 67-84.

2792. Levin, Dov: "The Fighting Leadership of the Judenraete in the Small Communities of Poland." G/H: Patterns, pp.133-147.

2793. Michman, J.: "The Controversial Stand of the Joodse Rad in the Netherlands: Lodewijk Visser´s Struggle." YVS, vol.10 (1974): 9-68.

2794. ___: "The Controversy Surrounding the Jewish Council of Amsterdam." G/H: Patterns, pp.235-257.

2795. Taubes, Israel: "The Jewish Council of Amsterdam." YVB, #17 (Dec., 1965): 25-30.

2796. Trunk, Isaiah: "The Jewish Councils in Eastern Europe under Nazi Rule. (An Attempt at a Synthesis)." Societas, vol.2 #3 (Sum., 1972): 221-239.

2797. ___: Judenrat: The Jewish Councils in Eastern Europe Under Nazi Occupation [New York: Macmillan, 1972]

Definitive work on the Judenraete in Nazi occupied Eastern Europe. Extensively documented and using hundreds of Judenraete as examples. This is an extremely important work on the Jewish Councils and their activities.

2798. ___: "The Organizational Structure of the Jewish Councils in Eastern Europe." YVS, vol.7 (1968): 147-164.

2799. ___: "The Typology of the Judenraete in Eastern Europe." G/H: Patterns, pp.17-30.

2800. Wahlen, Verena: "Select Bibliography on Judenraete under Nazi Rule." YVS, vol.10 (1974): 277-294.

2801. Weiss, Aharon: "The Relations Between the Judenrat and the Jewish Police." G/H: Patterns, pp.201-217.

The Polish Ghettos

2802. Berger, L.: "Life in the Polish Ghetto." J Fr, vol.9 #5 (May, 1942): 13-15.

2803. Fass, Moshe: "Theatrical Activities in the Polish Ghettos During the Years 1939-1942." JSS, vol.38 #1 (Win., 1976): 54-72.

2804. "Ghettos in Poland." CJR, vol.6 #2 (April, 1943): 188-190.

2805. Katz, Alfred: Poland's Ghettos at War [Boston: Twayne Publishers, 1970]

Short but problematic survey of the ghettos in Poland from foundation to liquidation. Katz has an interesting structure for a comparative history. Unfortunately, the book is inadequately documented and full of factual errors.

2806. Mendelsohn, Shlomo: The Polish Jews Behind the Nazi Ghetto Walls [New York: YIVO, 1942]

2807. "The Nazis Gloat Over Ghetto Horror." J Standard, vol.2 #28 (Oct. 28, 1941): 2.

2808. Prokowsky, M.: Ghettos in Nazi Poland [New York: Background, 1942]

2809. Schupakevitch, L.: "Relief in the Polish Ghettos." CW, vol.8 #36 (Nov. 7, 1941): 5-7. * On help given by the American Joint Distribution Committee.

2810. Wulman, Leon: "Aid to the Polish Ghettos - When?" Am OSE Rev, vol.1 #5/7 (May/July, 1942): 6-9.

2811. ___: "Spread of Infectious Diseases Among Jews in Nazi Occupied Poland." Am OSE Rev, vol.2 #3/4 (March/April, 1943): 3-8.

Individual Ghettos

Bendzin

2812. Hava, L: "Bendzin." J Fr, vol.11 #11 (Nov., 1944): 22-26. * Last days in the life of the ghetto.

Bialystok

2813. Berman, Tzipora: "From the Bialystok Ghetto." J Sp, vol.36 #7 (Sept., 1971): 9-12.

2814. Blumenthal, N. (ed.): Conduct and Actions of a Judenrat: Documents from the Bialystok Ghetto Hebrew/Eng. abstract. [Jerusalem, Yad Vashem, 1962]

2815. Mark, Ber: "Portrait of a Ghetto Judenrat." J Life, vol.6 #6 (April, 1952): 6-9.

2816. Tenenbaum, Mordechai: "Three Letters from Bialystok." Com, vol.20 #6 (Dec., 1955): 560-562.

Cracow

2817. Pankiewicz, Tahdeusz: "The Eagle Pharmacy." Poland, #2/150 (Feb., 1967): 31-32.

Czernowicz

2818. Yavetz, Zvi: "Youth Movements in Czernowitz." JH, vol.14 (Spr., 1972): 9-18. Also in Korman: Hunter, pp.135-145. * Under Soviet and Nazi occupation.

Czestochowa

2819. Glicksman, William: "Daily Record Sheet of the Jewish Police (District I) in the Czestochowa Ghetto (1941-1942)." YVS, vol.6 (1967): 331-358.

2820. Glicksman, Wolf: "Silent Night, Holy Night (A Temple Burns)." J Fo, vol.30 #1 (Jan., 1947): 15-16.

2821. "The Liquidation of the Czestochowa Ghetto." J Fr, vol.12 #4 (April, 1945): 33-36.

Kolno

2822. Kolinsky, Harvey: "Kolno." J Sp, vol.36 #5 (May, 1971): 15-18.

Kovno

2823. Arad, Y.: "The Judenraete in the Lithuanian Ghettos of Kovno and Vilna." G/H: Patterns, pp.93-112.

2824. Gringauz, Samuel: "The Ghetto as an Experiment of Jewish Social Organization." JSS, vol.11 #1 (Jan., 1949): 3-20.

Lask

2825. Taube, Herman: "Purim 1940: A Defiant Rabbi Thwarts the Nazis." Kowalski: Anthology/I, pp.298-299.

Lodz

2826. Ainsztein, Reuben: "Life in Lodz 1942-1944: Wiener Library Collection of Ghetto Documents." WLB, vol.13 #1/2 (1959): 17.

2827. Bernet, Michael M.: "The Unknown Diarist of Lodz." HM, vol.51 #2 (Oct., 1969): 6-7, 37.

2828. Bryks, Rachmil: "Berele in the Ghetto." J Sp, vol.20 #2 (Feb., 1955): 15-18. Also in: JQ, vol.3 #2 (Aut., 1955): 32-35. * Story, based on personal experience.

2829. Dobroszycki, Lucjan (ed.)(R. Lourie et al, transls.): The Chronicle of the Lodz Ghetto, 1941-1944 [New Haven, CT: Yale Univ. Press, 1984]

A Unique and invaluable document on the Lodz ghetto, which also has more general implications for Jewish life in the Nazi ghettos. Based on the ghetto newspaper published in Lodz from 1941-1944 the volume includes useful introductory material and is thoroughly documented.

2830. ___: "The Untold Story of the Lodz Ghetto." NY Times Mag, (July 29, 1984): 13-18, 20, 57.

2831. Hershkovitch, Bendet: "The Ghetto in Litzmannstadt (Lodz)." YIVO Annual, vol.5 (1950): 85-122.

2832. Kranitz-Sanders, L.: Twelve Who Survived: An Oral History of the Jews of Lodz, Poland 1938-1954 [New York: Irvington Pub., 1984]

2833. Reines, Ch. W.: "The Jewish Attitude Toward Suicide." Judaism, vol.10 #2 (Spr., 1961): 160-170.

2834. Trunk, Isaiah: Ghetto Lodz: A Historical and Sociological Study Including Documents, Maps, and Tables Yiddish/English summary. [New York: YIVO, 1962]

Lodz: Mordechai Chaim Rumkowski

2835. Bloom, Solomon F.: "Dictator of Lodz Ghetto: The Strange History of Mordechai Chaim Rumkowski." Com, vol.7 #2 (Feb., 1949): 111-122.

2836. Checinski, Michael: "How Rumkowski Died." Com, vol.67 #5 (May, 1979): 63-65.

2837. Friedman, Philip: "Pseudo-Saviors in the Polish Ghettos: Mordechai Chaim Rumkowski of Lodz." Friedman: Roads, pp.333-352.

2838. Tushnet, Leonard: "King Chaim Rumkowski." Ch J Forum, vol.22 #1 (Fall, 1963): 2-10. Also in: J Digest, vol. 9 #9 (June, 1964): 41-52.

Lublin

2839. Moldawer, S: "The Road to Lublin." CJR, vol.3 #2 (March/April, 1940): 119-133.

Lwow

2840. Schoenfeld, J.: Holocaust Memoirs: Jews in the Lwow Ghetto and the Janowski Concentration Camp [New York: Ktav, 1985]

Documentary account of the suffering of the Jews of Galicia during the Nazi era. Also covers the deportation of Jews to Siberia by Soviet authorities.

Riga

2841. Rivosh, E. (S. J. Goldsmith, transl.): "Between Life and Death: Notes from the Riga Ghetto." J Digest, vol.9 #5 (Feb., 1964): 34-36.

2842. Schneider, Gertrude: Journey Into Terror: The Story of the Riga Ghetto [New York: Ark Home, 1979]

Attempts to give a social history of the Riga ghetto. Deals with both social and political issues, putting them in the context of the Nazi extermination of Riga Jewry. Gives special attention to the relations between native Latvian Jews and German Jews deported to Riga in 1941-1942. Includes fascimiles of documents and a list of survivors.

Salonica

2843. Eck, Nathan: "New Light on the Charges Against the Last Chief Rabbi of Salonica." YVB, #17 (Dec., 1965): 9-15; #19 (Oct., 1966): 28-35.

Sosnowiec

2844. Friedman, Philip: "The Messianic Complex of a Nazi Collaborator in a Ghetto: Moses Merin of Sosnowiec." Friedman: Roads, pp.353-364. * Biographical study of one of the most infamous ´ghetto dictators´. The study charts Merrin´s role in prewar Jewish politics as well as his collaboration with the Nazis.

Terezin

2845. Adler-Rudel, S.: "Alexandra Kollontai and the Jews of Theresienstadt." J Fr, vol.19 #9 (Sept., 1952): 17-19.

2846. Baeck, Leo: "Life in a Concentration Camp." J Sp, vol.11 #9 (July, 1946): 12-13.

2847. Bor, Josef (E. Pargeter, transl.): Terezin Requiem [New York: A. A. Knopf, 1963]

Novelized history of Theresienstadt. Though the stories that Bor tells are true, much of the dialogue is made up. The work´s highlight is a description of the Nazi-sponsored artistic endeavors to make Terezin, the ghetto/concentration camp,into a "respectable" place.

2848. Dawidowicz, Lucy S.: "Bleaching the Black Lie: The Case of Theresienstadt." Dawidowicz: Presence, pp. 247-268.

2849. Ehrmann, F. (ed.): Terezin 1941-1945 [London: Collet: 1965]

2850. Fischer, Alfred J.: "The 1,200 of Terezin." CEO, vol. 22 #7 (April 13, 1945): 111-112.

2851. Freeden, Herbert: "The Feuhrer Gives the Jews a Town." J Affairs, vol.15 #4 (April, 1960): 35-37.

2852. Gliksman, W.: "Baron Rudolf von Hirsch in Theresienstadt." J Fo, vol.29 #10 (Oct., 1946): 235-237.

2853. Jacobson, Jacob: Terezin: The Daily Life, 1943-1945 [London: Jewish Central Information Office, 1946]

2854. Karas, Joza: Music in Terezin, 1941-1945 [New York: Pendragon Press, 1985]

Examination of the role music played in the life of the Jews of Terezin. Surveys all types of musical activities at Theresienstadt. Includes a full list of existing compositions written and/or arranged in Terezin and biographical sketches of the Terezin musicians.

2855. ___: "The Use of Music as a Means of Education in Terezin." Shoa, vol.1 #2 (Fall, 1978): 8-9.

2856. Kobler, Franz: "History and Sociology of the Terezin Ghetto." HJ, vol.19 #1 (April, 1957): 67-73.

2857. "Last Days of Terezin." CEO, vol.22 #12 (June 29, 1945): 190-191.

2858. Lederer, Zdenek: Ghetto Theresienstadt [London: E. Goldston, 1953]

2859. Luft, Herbert G.: "Hitler Presents a Town to the Jews: A True Account." J Currents, vol.14 #11 (Dec., 1960): 12-14.

2860. Poliakov, Leon: "The Story of Theresienstadt." WLB, vol.10 #1/2 (1956): 5.

2861. Schmiedt, Shlomo: "Hehalutz in Theresienstadt - its Influence and Educational Activities." YVS, vol.7 (1968): 107-126

2862. Tal, Miriam: "Echoes from the Theresienstadt Ghetto." J Digest, vol.5 #12 (Sept., 1960): 38-40. * On exhibition of drawings by children in Terezin.

2863. Vogel, George: "The Fate of the Terezin Ghetto." CJRC/B, #18 (March, 1946): 4-6.

2864. Werner, Alfred: "Madhouse Theresienstadt." CW, vol.23 #13 (March 26, 1956): 13-15.

2865. ___: "Truths from Terezin." CBW, vol.35 #3 (Feb. 5, 1968): 18-19.

Vilna

2866. Abramowicz, Dina: "Yom Kippur, 1941-1945. Memories of the Vilna Ghetto." J Fr, vol.14 #1 (Jan., 1947): 18-22.

2867. Arad, Yitzhak: Ghetto in Flames: The Struggle and Destruction of the Jews in Vilna in the Holocaust [New York: Ktav, 1978]

Groundbreaking study of the Vilna Ghetto. The volume covers both the period of Soviet and German occupation and is a classic of Holocaust historiography.

2868. Dworzecki, Mark: "A day in the Vilna Ghetto." J Fr, vol.19 #5 (May, 1952): 7-12.

2869. ___: "Purim in the Vilna Ghetto." J Digest, vol.1 #5 (Feb., 1956): 9-10.

2870. Friedman, P.: "Jacob Gens: 'Commandant' of the Vilna Ghetto." Friedman: Roads, pp.365-380.

2871. Frimer, Norman: "Who is a Jew in the Vilna Ghetto?" Tradition, vol.17 #1 (Fall, 1977): 55-62.

2872. Kalmanovitch, Zelig: "A Diary of the Nazi Ghetto in Vilna." YIVO Annual, vol.8 (1953): 9-81.

2873. Kruk, Herman: "Diary of the Vilna Ghetto." YIVO Annual, vol.13 (1965): 9-78.

Warsaw

2874. Alperin, A.: "Passover in the Ghetto." CW, vol.11 #14 (April 7, 1944): 7-8.

2875. Banasiewicz, Czeslaw Z. (ed.): The Warsaw Ghetto [Cranbury, NJ: Thomas Yoseloff, 1968]

2876. Bartoszewski, W.: "The Living Stones." Poland, #6/94 (June, 1963): 13-15, 20.

2877. Berman, A.: "The Fate of the Children in the Warsaw Ghetto." Gutman: Catastrophe, pp.400-421.

2878. ___: "5 Portraits of Ghetto Heroes: Emanuel Ringelblum, Historian of the Ghetto; Yanush Kortchak, Lover of Children; Mordecai Anielevitch, Commander of the Uprising; Andzhei Schmidt and Joseph Levartovsky, Molders of Unity." J Currents, vol.12 #4 (April, 1958): 15-21, 33. * Mr. Berman, a participant in the Uprising recalls leading personalities of the Ghetto.

2879. Bialer, Tosha: "20,000 Christians in the Warsaw Ghetto. Survivor Reveals for the First time." NJM, vol.60 #2 (Oct., 1945): 50-51, 74-77.

2880. Ciolkosz, Adam: "Warsaw Ghetto, a Citadel of the Oppressed." Polish Jew, vol.3 #19 (Dec., 1943): 2-3.

2881. "Death of a Community." NJM, vol.55 #10 (June, 1941): 317-319. * Pictorial essay.

2882. Donat, Alexander: "Our Last Days in the Warsaw Ghetto." Com, vol.35 #5 (May, 1963): 378-389.

2883. ___: "Smugglers of the Ghetto." J Digest, vol.11 #10 (July, 1966): 49-54.

2884. Friedman, Kalman: "In the Warsaw Ghetto in its Dying Days." YVB, #13 (Oct., 1963): 24-30.

2885. Friedman, P. (ed.): Martyrs and Fighters: The Epic of the Warsaw Ghetto [New York: F. A. Praeger, 1954]

Anthology of short selections on the Warsaw ghetto uprising excerpted from a variety of eyewitness testimonies. The book is also a history of the ghetto and its sufferings.

2886. "Ghetto Walls in Warsaw." CB, vol.7 #4 (Dec. 6, 1940): 4-5.

2887. Gross, David C.: "Mother of the Ghetto." J Digest, vol.24 #2 (Oct., 1978): 14-15. * On Zivia Lubetkin.

2888. Grossman, Mendel (Zvi Shner and A. Sened, eds): With a Camera in the Ghetto [New York: Schocken, 1984]

2889. Gutman, Y. The Jews of Warsaw 1939-1943 [Bloomington, IN: Indiana Univ. Press, 1980]

The most up-to-date history of the Warsaw Ghetto. Based on all sources currently available. Can be considered definitive.

2890. Herman, E.: "Typhus Fever in the Warsaw Ghetto." Am OSE Rev, vol.4 #1 (Spr., 1947): 10-14.

2891. "Jews in Warsaw's Ghetto." CW, vol.8 #4 (Jan., 24, 1941): 11-14. * A report culled from Nazi sources.

2892. Kaplan, Chaim A. (Abraham I. Katsh, ed. and transl.): The Scroll of Agony [New York: Macmillan, 1965] Also published as: The Warsaw Diary of Chaim A. Kaplan [New York: Collier Books, 1973]

Compelling first-person account of life in the Warsaw ghetto. The latter edition contains new material made available to Professor Katsh by the Moreshet Institute in Israel.

2893. Kermisz, J.: "The Judenrat in Warsaw." G/H: Patterns, pp.75-90.

2894. ___: "The Testament of the Warsaw Ghetto." J Fr, vol. 18 #9 (Sept., 1951): 9-14.

2895. ___: "Warsaw Ghetto Intellectuals on Current Questions and Problems of Survival." YVB, #1 (April, 1957): 7-11.

2896. Kleinlerer, Edward D.: "A Fascist Views the Ghetto." CW, vol.8 #42 (Dec. 19, 1941): 11-12.

2897. Lachs, Manfred: The Ghetto of Warsaw [London: Dugdale Printing, 1942]

2898. Lenski, Mordecai: "Problems of Disease in the Warsaw Ghetto." YVS, vol.3 (1959): 283-294.

2899. "Life in the Warsaw Ghetto." GS, #18 (Dec. 1, 1941): 1-2.

2900. Lubetkin, Z.: "The Last Days of the Warsaw Ghetto." Com, vol.3 #5 (May, 1947): 401-411.

2901. Mark, Ber: "May Day in the Warsaw Ghetto." IH, vol.23 #6 (June, 1975): 17-19.

2902. Mazor, Michel: "The House Committees in the Warsaw Ghetto." Bauer: Historical, pp.95-108.

2903. Meed, Vladka (M. Spiegel and S. Meed, transls.): On Both Sides of the Wall: Memoirs from the Warsaw Ghetto [New York: Holocaust Library, 1979]

Early and still useful memoir of the Warsaw ghetto by one of the young smugglers who maintained contact between the ghetto and the Aryan side. Working for the Z. O. B. Vladka was personally responsible for smuggling weapons and ammunition into and messages and people out of the ghetto.

2904. Polish Government Report: "Liquidation of the Warsaw Ghetto: Jews Massacred in Cold Blood." Polish Jew, vol.3 #13/14 (Jan., 1943): 2-4.

2905. Ringelblum, E.: "Children of the Warsaw Ghetto." CW, vol.30 #7 (April 1, 1963): 13-17.

2906. ___ (Jacob Sloan, ed. and transl.): Notes from the Warsaw Ghetto: The Journal of Emmanuel Ringelblum [New York: McGraw-Hill, 1958]

Diary by the Warsaw ghetto's historian, creator of the secret "Oneg Shabbat" archives. His diary is an impressive day by day chronicle of the life and death of the Warsaw ghetto.

2907. ___: "Schachna Zagan, Ghetto Leader: Labor Zionist, a Force for Unity against the Judenrat and the Nazis." J Currents, vol.22 #4 (April, 1968): 9-13, 33-34.

2908. Rosenthal, D.: "The Unvanquished Sector of the Warsaw Ghetto: Its School System." J Fr, vol.46 #4 (April, 1979): 18-21.

2909. Samucha, M.: "Mother of the Ghetto: Tzivya Lubetkin." J Digest, vol.25 #7 (March, 1980): 30-34.

2910. Shainberg, M.: "Yom Kippur Warsaw, 1942." WJ, vol.15 #4 (Sept., 1972): 22-24.

2911. Spiesman, Leib: "In the Warsaw Ghetto." CJR, vol.4 #4 (Aug., 1941): 357-366.

2912. Szoszkes, Henry: "Affidavit on Conditions in Warsaw." CJR, vol.3 #2 (March/April, 1940): 202-204.

2913. Trunk, Isaiah: "Epidemics and Mortality in the Warsaw Ghetto 1939-1942." YIVO Annual, vol.8 (1953): 82-122.

2914. Tushnet, Leonard: The Uses of Adversity [New York: Thomas Yoseloff, 1966]

Chronicle of the heroic activities of the medical doctors of the Warsaw ghetto. Unable to improve the lot of those incarcerated in the ghetto, the doctors were able only to watch and describe. Tushnet´s book is based on the so-called Milikowski report written by the Ghetto doctors as they witnessed the events.

2915. "The Warsaw Ghetto." IJA, vol.1 #5 (Dec., 1941): 1-11.

2916. "The Warsaw Ghetto." Chartock: Society, pp.189-191.

2917. "Warsaw Jews Doomed to Extinction." Am OSE Rev, vol.1 #1/2 (Jan./Feb., 1942): 8-9.

2918. Weiss, A.: "In Nazi Warsaw." CJR, vol.3 #5 (Sept./Oct., 1940): 484-497.

2919. Ziemian, Joseph (D. Janina, transl.): The Cigarette Sellers of Three Crosses Square [Minneapolis, MN: Lerner Pub., 1975]

Personal account of the adventures of a small group of children living in the aryan section of Warsaw. They all worked as contacts and smugglers for the Z. O. B. and most fought in both the 1943 and 1944 uprisings.

2920. Zylberberg, Michael: "Assimilated Jews in Warsaw Ghetto." Am Heb, vol.159 #44 (Feb. 24, 1950): 9, 15.

2921. ___: A Warsaw Diary: 1939-1945 [London: Hartmore, 1969]

Warsaw: Adam Czerniakow

2922. Apenszlak, Jakob: "The Burgomaster of the Ghetto." Polish Jew, vol.2 #11/12 (Oct./Nov., 1942): 5.

2923. Blumenthal, N.: "A Martyr or a Hero? Reflections on the Diary of Adam Czerniakow." YVS, vol.7 (1968): 165-172.

2924. Ellenberg, Sh.: "My Meeting with Adam Czerniakow." YVB, #16 (Feb., 1965): 50-54.

2925. ___: "Warsaw Judenrat: One View of Adam Czerniakow." Korman: Hunter, pp.124-129. <see #2928>

2926. Gutman, Yisrael: "Adam Czerniakow - The Man and his Diary." Gutman: Catastrophe, pp.451-489.

2927. Hartglass, Apolinary: "How Did Cherniakow Become Head of the Warsaw Judenrat?" YVB, #15 (Aug., 1964): 4-7.

2928. ___: "Warsaw Judenrat: A Second View of Czerniakow." Korman: Hunter, pp.130-134. <see #2925>

2929. Hilberg, Raul, S. Staron, and J. Kermisz (eds): The Warsaw Diary of Adam Czerniakow: Prelude to Doom [New York: Stein and Day, 1979.

Compelling diary which gives an intimate portrait of the Judenrat leadership in Warsaw. The diary gives a clear portrait of the dire straits in which other council functionaries in other ghettos found themselves; they did not want the position but could not escape from their Nazi-given responsibilities.

2930. Tartakower, A. and K. R. Grossmann: "Adam Czerniakow the Man and his Supreme Sacrifice." YVS, vol.6 (1967): 55-67.

2931. Zylberberg, M.: "The Tragedy of Adam Czerniakow." WLB, vol.21 #4 (Aut., 1967): 2-5.

9

The Concentration Camp System

LIFE IN THE CAMPS AND SLAVE LABOR

Concentration Camps

2932. Alvarez, A.: "The Concentration Camp." Atlantic, vol. 210 #6 (Dec., 1962): 69-72.

2933. Arendt, Hannah: "The Concentration Camps." Partisan Rev, vol.15 #7 (July, 1948): 743-769.

2934. Broszat, M. (M. Jackson, transl.): "The Concentration Camps, 1933-45." Krausnick: Anatomy, pp. 397-504.

2935. Bruegel, F.: "Camouflaging the Concentration Camps." CEO, vol.22 #9 (May 16, 1945): 143.

2936. Dworzecki, Mark: Jewish Camps in Estonia, 1942-1944 Hebrew/Eng. summary. [Jerusalem: Yad Vashem, 1970]

2937. Faramus, Anthony Ch.: The Faramus Story [London: Wingate, 1954] * On Buchenwald and Mauthausen.

2938. Feig, Konnilyn: Hitler's Death Camps: The Sanity of Madness [New York: Holmes and Meier, 1981]

Synthetic review of the history of the concentration camp system. Primary focus is on the functioning of the camps within the context of the Final Solution. Also deals with other related topics such as: the role of women in Nazi ideology; the reaction of outside powers; the reactions of gentile neighbors; the attempts to resist. Includes useful appendices and extensive bibliography.

2939. Friedlander, Henry: "The Nazi Concentration Camps." Ryan: Responses, pp.33-69.

2940. Geta, Joseph: "Politics Inside Concentration Camps." CEO, vol.22 #12 (June 29, 1945): 195-196.

2941. Heger, Heinz (D. Fernbach, transl.): The Men with the Pink Triangle [Boston: Alyson Pubs., 1980]

2942. Kautsky, Benedikt: Devils and Damned [London: Brown and Watson, 1960]

2943. Kogon, Eugen (Heinz Norden, transl.): The Theory and Practice of Hell: The German Concentration Camps and the System Behind Them [New York: Farrar, Straus and Cudahy, 1950]

In-depth study of the concentration camp system and its place in the SS state. Using Buchenwald as an example Kogon was able to generalize about all the camps providing a vivid picture of life, and death, during the Nazi era.

2944. Manvell, Roger and H. Fraenkel: "Terror in Europe." Hist/WWII, #38 (1973): 1037-1043.

2945. Roditi, E.: "Living and Dying in the Concentration Camps." CBW, vol.34 #9 (May 8, 1967): 14-15.

2946. Roiter, Howard: Voices from the Holocaust: Testimonies from the Camps [New York: Frederich Press, 1980]

2947. Rousset, David (Ramon Guthrie, transl.): The Other Kingdom [New York: Reynal and Hitchock, 1947]

2948. Timmenga, A: "Concentration Camps in the Netherlands." Annals #245 (May, 1946): 19-27.

2949. Wallner, Peter: By Order of the Gestapo [London: Murray, 1941] * Graphic description of Dachau and Buchenwald.

Extermination Camps

2950. Borowski, Tadeusz (B. Vedeer, transl.): This Way for the Gas, Ladies and Gentlemen [New York: Viking Press, 1967]

2951. Czynska, S. and B. Kupsecz: "Extermination, Concentration and Labour Camps in Poland During the Years, 1939-1945." Commission: GCIP/I, pp.11-23.

2952. "Death Reigns in Poland." GS, #26 (June 1, 1944): 3-4.

2953. Korotynski, Henryk: "Never Again." Poland, #1/5 (1955): 6-7.

2954. Langer, Lawrence: "The Dilemma and Choice in the Death Camps." Centerpoint, vol.4 (Fall, 1980): 53-59.

2955. Lawrence, W.: "Nazi Mass Killing Laid Bare in Camp." Polish Jew, vol.4 #25 (Sept./Oct., 1944): 3-5, 22.

2956. "Murder Camps in Poland." J Standard, vol.3 #33 (Nov. 27, 1942): 1, 5.

2957. Simonov, Constantine: The Lublin Extermination Camp [Moscow: Foreign Languages Publication House, 1944]

Slave Labor

2958. Adler, Helmut G.: "The Jews in National-Socialist Compulsory Camps." World Congress for Jewish Studies, Jerusalem, vol.1 (1967): 27-34.

2959. Bernhard, Georg: "Slave Labor in Europe." CW, vol.9 #14 (April 10, 1942): 7-9.

2960. Bleiweiss, S.: "Seder in Stuttgart as slave laborer." HM, vol.51 #9 (May, 1970): 16, 29-30.

2961. Borkin, Joseph: The Crime and Punishment of I. G. Farben [New York: The Free Press/Macmillan, 1978]

Heavily documented account of the role of German industry played in the destruction of European Jewry as well as the indirect participation of many of the largest corporations in the free world in Nazi crimes.

2962. Clissold, Stephen: "The Power of the Slaves." CEO, vol.20 #15 (July 23, 1943): 235-236.

2963. Darvas, Iren: "Women in Nazi Munitions Factory." YVB, #21 (Nov., 1967): 28-34.

2964. Dubois, Josiah E.: The Devil´s Chemist [Boston: Beacon Press, 1952]

2965. Ferencz, Benjamin B.: Less Than Slaves: Jewish Forced Labor and the Quest for Compensation [Cambridge, MA: Harvard Univ. Press, 1979]

Study of slave labor in Nazi concentration camps and Jewish efforts to receive compensation. Written by an international lawyer, it focuses on the legal aspects of both forced labor and compensation requests.

2966. Fischer, Julius: "Death by Forced Labor." CW, vol.12 #20 (June 8, 1945): 10-12.

2967. Hronek, George: "An International of Slaves." CEO, vol.18 #13 (June 27, 1941): 165.

2968. "Jewish Forced Labor: Extract of Nazi Decree Establishing Jewish Forced Labor in Occupied Poland." IJA, vol.1 #8 (March, 1942): 1-7.

2969. Kalmer, Joseph: "Munition Factories in Nazi Camps." CEO, vol.19 #15 (July 24, 1942): 236.

2970. Koestler, Arthur: Scum of the Earth [New York: Macmillan, 1968]

2971. "Labor on Foreign Fronts." New Republic, vol.108 #2 (Jan. 11, 1943): 54-55.

2972. Michel, Jean and Louis Nucera (J. Kidd, transl.): Dora [New York: Holt, Rinehart and Winston, 1980]

Memoir of an inmate in the Dora-Nordhausen concentration camp where the Germans used slave labor to manufacture V-2 rockets. A member of the French resistance, Jean Michel was one of the survivors of the camp in which nearly 30,000 inmates died. Michel also condemns the expediency of the nations who adopted and used the Nazi rocket scientists, such as Werner von Braun, while shielding them from prosecution.

2973. Morris, Louis and Lowell Brickman: "German Industry´s Jewish Slaves." Focus, vol.3 #5/6 (Spr./Sum., 1980): 40-41.

2974. Nyquist, R. B.: "Slave Workers of Europe in Norway." CEO, vol.19 #19 (Sept. 18, 1942): 303-304.

2975. Rimer, A. B.: "Foreign Labour in Germany." Cont Rev, vol.164 #932 (Aug., 1943): 92-96.

2976. ___: "The Nazis´ Labour Slaves." CEO, vol.19 #6 (March 20, 1942): 88.

2977. Sasuli, Richard : I. G. Farben [New York: Boni and Gaer, 1947]

2978. Smith, Rennie: "European Labor and the Nazi War Machine." CEO, vol.19 #13 (June 26, 1942): 198.

2979. Soffner, Heinz: "Hitler´s Slave Legions." Nation, vol.154 #19 (May 9, 1942): 539-541.

2980. Sternberg, Fritz: "Collaboration - 3 Stages." Nation, vol.156 #25 (June 19, 1943): 863-864.

2981. Taborsky, E.: "Germany´s Deportation Policy in Europe." CEO, vol.20 #1 (Jan. 8, 1943): 5-6; #2 (Jan. 22, 1943): 27-28.

2982. Trunk, Isaiah: "Labor camps in Wartheland." Am OSE Rev, vol.5 #3/4 (Sum./Fall, 1948): 10-15.

2983. Von Klass, Gert (James Cleugh, transl.): Krupps: The Story of an Industrial Empire [London: Sidgwick and Jackson, 1954]

Life in the Camps

2984. Adler, David: "Pesach in the Death Camps: Even in Modern Slavery They Remembered." J Digest, vol.11 #7 (April, 1966): 67-71.

2985. Arnold-Forster, W.: "Germany´s Concentration Camps." 19th Century & After, vol.114 (Nov., 1933): 550-560. * Eyewitness description of the early "wild camps".

2986. Becher, Johannes R. et al: Murder in Camp Hohenstein, and Other Stories: A Cross-Current of the Hitler Regime [London: M. Lawrence, 1933]

2987. Becker, Jurek: Jacob the Liar [New York: Harcourt, Brace, Jovanovich, 1974]

2988. Billinger, Karl: Fatherland [New York: Farrar and Rinehart, 1935]

Personal account of life in Nazi Germany´s early concentration camps, written from a communist viewpoint. Includes information on Nazi persecution of German Jews.

2989. Bulka, Reuven P.: "Logotherapy as a Response to the Holocaust." Tradition, vol.15 #1/2 (Spr./Sum., 1975): 89-96.

2990. Cohen, Esther: "Women in the Camps." PT, vol.10 #4 (Sum., 1983): 10-11.

2991. Dworzecki, Mark: "A Yom Kippur Homily." J Fr, vol.13 #11 (Nov., 1946): 10-11.

2992. Friedlander, H.: "The Nazi Camps." Grobman: Genocide, pp.222-232.

2993. ___ and S. Milton: "Surviving." Grobman: Genocide, pp.233-235.

2994. Goldman, Gad: "Potatoes for Pesach." J Life, vol.41 #2 (Spr., 1974): 28-31.

2995. Halperin, Irving: "Victim, Fighter, Martyr: Literature of the Concentration Camps." Ch Century, vol.79 #30 (July 25, 1962): 907-910. <see #3006>

2996. Heilig, Bruno: Men Crucified [London: Eyre & Spottiswoode, 1941]

2997. Karmel-Wolfe, Henia: "Seder in a Concentration Camp." J Digest, vol.22 #7 (March, 1977): 35-37.

2998. Kisch, E.: "Under the Whip in Germany." New Republic, vol.74 #4 (April 26, 1933): 306-308. * Incarcerated Jews in the early concentration camps.

2999. Landes, Daniel: "Spiritual Responses in the Camps." Grobman: Genocide, pp.261-278.

3000. Langhoff, W. (Lilo Linke, transl.): Rubber Truncheon [New York: E. P. Dutton, 1935]

3001. Levi, P.: "If This is a Man." Friedlander: Whirlwind, pp.208-226.

3002. ___: "The Truce." Friedlander: Whirlwind, pp.425-433.

3003. Lingens-Reiner, Ella: Prisoners of Fear [London: V. Gollancz, 1948]

3004. Luft, Herbert G.: "Roll Call." J Sp, vol.19 #1 (Jan., 1954): 25-26.

3005. Martin, F.: "Marked for Death." J Digest, vol.2 #11 (Aug., 1957): 56-58.

3006. Means, Richard: "On the Socialization of Violence." Ch Century, vol.79 #46 (Nov. 14, 1962): 1392-1394. * A reply to Irving Halperin <see #2995>

3007. Munkacsi, Naomi W.: "Judaism in the Death Camps." J Digest, vol.14 #7 (April, 1969): 65-69.

3008. "Passover in the Concentration Camps: Celebration and a Mode of Resistance." M&R, vol.7 #4 (March/April, 1981): 13, 15.

3009. Pol, Heinz: "German Concentration Camps." Living Age, vol.350 (March, 1936): 30-32.

3010. "Polish Women in German Concentration Camps." PFR, #115 (May 1, 1945): Whole Issue.

3011. Poztawska, Wanda: "This is not History." Poland, #8/156 (Aug., 1967): 13-15, 32. * Eyewitness account by a non-Jewess.

3012. Robbin, Sheryl: "Life in the Camps: The Psychological Dimension." Grobman: Genocide, pp.236-242.

3013. Salvesen, Sylvia (Edward F. Russell, ed.): Forgive - but Do Not Forget [London: Hutchinson, 1958]

3014. Sandberg, Moshe: My Longest Year [Jerusalem: Yad Vashem, 1968]

3015. Seelav, Robert: "Number 1,000,000,1." Am Heb, vol.155 #50 (April 12, 1946): 28-29, 32-33.

3016. Spizman, Lieb: "Death and Resurrection: In the Concentration Camps." J Fr, vol.12 #8 (Aug., 1945): 7-10.

3017. Taube, Herman and Suzanne Taube (H. Frank, transl.): Remember [Baltimore: Nicholas & A. Gossman, 1951] *
A series of eight individual stories on life in the Nazi concentration camps.

3018. "Three Years of Slavery." CEO, vol.22 #15 (Aug. 24, 1945): 244-245.

3019. Triska, J. F.: "Work Redeems: Concentration Camp Labor and Nazi German Economy." JCEA, vol.19 #1 (April, 1959): 3-22.

3020. Varhaftig, Zorah: "Chalutzim in Concentration Camps." Hamigdal, vol.2 #3 (Jan., 1942): 12-13.

3021. Vrba, Rudolf and R. Manvell: "The Camps: An Inside View." Hist/WWII, #74 (1974): 2065-2072.

3022. Not Used.

3023. Winkler-Munkacsi, N.: "Jewish Religious Observance in Women's Death Camps in Germany." YVB, #20 (April, 1967): 35-38.

Studies on Camp Inmates

3024. Bloch, Herbert A.: "The Personality of Inmates of Concentration Camps." Am Jnl Soc, vol.32 #4 (Jan., 1947): 335-341.

3025. Bluhm, Hilde O.: "How Did They Survive? Mechanism of Defence in Nazi Concentration Camps." Am Jnl Psychotherapy, vol.2 #1 (Jan., 1948): 3-32.

3026. Cohen, Elie A. (M. Braaksma, transl.): Human Behavior in the Concentration Camp [New York: W. W. Norton and Company, 1953]

Remarkable and important psychological study into inmate and guard behaviour at Auschwitz. Includes a review of the camp organization and a detailed survey of Nazi medical experiments. Written without any emotional bias by a camp inmate who witnessed much of what he discusses.

3027. Des Pres, Terrence: The Survivor: An Anatomy of Life in the Death Camps [New York: Pocketbooks, 1976]

Psychological study of how survival is possible even in conditions within concentration camps. What emerges is the image of man's ability to cope and survive even the ultimate horror. Especially interesting is Des Pres' comparison of Nazi concentration camps and Soviet gulags.

3028. ___: "Victims and Survivors." Dissent, vol.23 (Win., 1976): 49-56.

3029. Frankl, Victor Emil: "The Decent and the Indecent." Chartock: Society, pp.175-176.

3030. ___: "Dehumanization and Starvation." Chartock: Society, pp.17-19.

3031. ___: "Experiences in a Concentration Camp." JH, vol. 11 #2 (Fall/Win., 1968): 5-7.

3032. Friedman, Paul: "Some Aspects of Concentration Camp Psychology." Am Jnl Psych, vol.105 #8 (Feb., 1949): 601-605.

3033. Glicksman, William: "Social Differentiation in the German Concentration Camps." YIVO Annual, vol.8 (1953): 123-150.

Incisive article probing the relationships among the different types of prisoners in concentration camps. Uses Auschwitz as its focus. Deals especially with the privileged few "organizers", prisoners who could get whatever they wanted despite incarceration. The majority of these "organizers" were, in fact, German criminals, most of whom treated Jews as badly as did the SS.

3034. Lehrer, Leibusch: "Concentration Camp: The Hangmen." J Fr, vol.20 #6 (June, 1953): 17-21.

3035. ___: "Concentration Camp: The Victim." J Fr, vol.20 #6 (June, 1953): 17-21.

3036. Luchterhand, Elmer: "Social Behavior of Concentration Camp Prisoners: Continuities and Discontinuities with Pre-and Postcamp Life." Dimsdale: Survivors, pp.259-282.

3037. Naumann, B.: "The Horrors of Daily Life." Chartock: Society, pp.7-9.

3038. Shirer, Wm.: "The Death House." Chartock: Society, pp.5-7.

3039. Tas, J.: "Psychical Disorders Among Inmates of Concentration Camps and Repatriates." Psych Q, vol.25 #3 (Oct., 1951): 679-690.

Vichy French Camps

3040. Bernard, Jean J. (E. O. March, transl.): The Camp of the Slow Death [London: Victor Gollancz, 1945]

3041. Feuchtwanger, Lion: The Devil in France [New York: Viking Press, 1941]

3042. Pol, Heinz: "Vichy Slave Battalions." Nation, vol.152 #18 (May 3, 1941): 527-529.

3043. Selke, Rudolf: "Trans-Saharan Inferno." FW, vol.2 #1 (Feb., 1942): 57-62. * On Jewish slave labor.

3044. "Starvation Problems (A Study of Starvation in the Camps of France)." Am OSE Rev, vol.2 #1/2 (Jan./Feb., 1943): 16-21; #3/4 (March/April, 1940): 20-24.

Individual Camps

Ampfing-Waldlager

3045. Gliksman, Wolf: "Life Behind Barbed Wire." J Fo, vol. 29 #9 (Sept., 1946): 189-190, 192.

Auschwitz

3046. Adamson, Jennie L.: The Camp of Death [London: Liberty Publications, 1944]

3047. Bedford, Sybille: "Worst That Ever Happened." SEP, vol.239 (Oct. 22, 1966): 29-33, 112.

3048. Berger, M. (A. Sinai, transl.): "Hanged but Alive." J Digest, vol.1 #3 (Dec., 1955): 35-36.

3049. Bezwinska, J.: Amid a Nightmare of Crime [Oswiecim, Poland: Panstwowe Muzeum w Oswiecimiu, 1973]

3050. Broad, Pery: KZ Auschwitz, Reminiscences: SS-Man in the Auschwitz Concentration Camp [Oswiecim, Poland: Panstwowe Muzeum w Oswiecimiu, 1965]

3051. Brycht, Andrzej: "An Excursion: Auschwitz-Birkenau." Poland, #7/131 (July, 1965): 28A-32. * Excerpt from his Polish memoir, translated by Christina Cenkalska.

3052. Central Commission for Investigation of Nazi Crimes in Poland: Concentation Camp Oswiecim [Warsaw: Wydawnictwo Prawnicze, 1955]

3053. "Daybreak at Auschwitz." J Horizon, vol.19 #4 (Dec., 1956): 18. * Entry from an unknown inmate of Auschwitz, translated by Aaron Schmuller.

3054. "Death Camp Oswiecim." GS, #31 (Nov. 1, 1944): 1.

3055. Delbo, Charlotte (John Githens, transl.): None of Us Will Return [New York: Grove Press, 1968] * Memoir of an Auschwitz inmate written as a prose-poem.

3056. Dewar, Diana: The Saint of Auschwitz: The Story of Maximillian Kolbe [New York: Harper & Row, 1982]

3057. Diament, F. E.: "We Are the Last Victims." J Sp, vol. 33 #4 (April, 1968): 9-12.

3058. Duncan, Ronald: Auschwitz [Welcombe, England: Rebel Press/Element Books, 1979]

3059. Fanelon, Fania: Playing for Time [New York: Atheneum, 1977]

3060. FitzGibbons, Constantine: "Auschwitz: A Portrait of Hell." New Leader, vol.43 #23 (June 6, 1960): 11-14.

3061. ___: "Auschwitz: A Portrait of Hell. The Insane World of the Nazi Concentration Camps." J Digest, vol.7 #2 (Nov., 1961): 41-51.

3062. ___: "Auschwitz: The Final Solution." New Leader, vol.43 #24 (June 30, 1960): 12-15.

3063. Friedrich, O.: "The Kingdom of Auschwitz." Atlantic, vol.248 #3 (Sept., 1981): 30-60.

3064. Heimler, Eugene: "Children of Auschwitz." in George Mikes (ed.): Prison [London: Routledge & Kegan Paul, 1963]: 1-24.

3065. ___ (Andre Ungar, transl.): Night of the Mist [New York: Vanguard Press, 1960] Also published as Concentration Camp [New York: Pyramid, 1961]

3066. Kalecka, Nelly: "A Day in Auschwitz." JM, vol.1 #5 (Aug., 1947): 29-32.

3067. Kaplan, Howard: "Escape!" Moment, vol.6 #2 (Jan./Feb., 1981): 42-47.

3068. Ka-Tzetnik 135633 (Pseudonym): Atrocity [Secaucus, NJ: Lyle Stuart, 1963]

Fictionalized account of life and death in Auschwitz. Yehiel de-Nur brings the horror of Auschwitz to light on every gripping page.

3069. ___: "Planet Auschwitz: A Witness from Hell on Earth." J Digest, vol.8 #7 (April, 1963): 61-86.

3070. Kessel, Sim (M. and D. Wallace, transls.): Hanged at Auschwitz [New York: Stein and Day, 1972]

3071. Kielar, Wieslaw: Anus Mundi [New York: New York Times Books, 1980]

Memoir of the Auschwitz concentration camp by a Polish inmate. The author was a member of the Polish underground, the Armia Krajowa. Mentions Jews inter-alia.

3072. Kozielewski, Ryszard: "Take a Deep Breath." Poland, #5/93 (May, 1962): 17-20.

3073. Kulka, Erich and Ota Kraus (Stephen Jolly, transl.): The Death Factory [New York: Pergamon Press, 1966]

3074. Lengyel, Olga (P. Weiss, transl.): Five Chimneys: The Story of Auschwitz [New York: Avon Pub., 1948]

3075. Levi, P. (S. Woolf, transl.): Survival in Auschwitz: The Nazi Assult on Humanity [New York: Collier Books, 1961] * Memoir of life and death in Auschwitz by the Italian-Jewish equivalent of Elie Wiesel.

3076. Lewinska, P. (A. Teichner, transl.): Twenty Months at Auschwitz [Secaucus, NJ: Lyle Stuart, 1968]

3077. Lewis, Theodore N.: "Auschwitz Revisited." J Sp, vol. 25 #2 (Feb., 1960): 19-22. * Historical and literary review of works on Auschwitz.

3078. Manvell, Roger and H. Fraenkel: "Factory for Extermination." Hist/WWII, #44 (1973): 1229-1232.

3079. Menasche, Albert: Birkenau-Auschwitz II: Memoirs of an Eyewitness, How 72,000 Greek Jews Perished [New York: I. Saltiel, 1947]

3080. Mueller, Filip (Susanne Flatauer, ed. and transl.): Eyewitness Auschwitz: Three Years in the Gas Chambers [New York: Stein and Day, 1979]

Diary of Auschwitz by one of the few Jewish members of the Sonderkommando to survive. Includes an account of the October 7, 1944 revolt by the Sonderkommando in crematoria 4.

3081. Nansen, O.: From Day to Day [New York: G. P. Putnam's Sons, 1949] Also published as: Day After Day [London: Putnam, 1949]

3082. Napora, P.: Auschwitz [San Antonio, TX: Naylor, 1967]

3083. National CID Relief Committee: The Camp of Disappearing Men [New York: Polish Labor Group, 1944]

3084. Naumann, Bernd: "Auschwitz: A Concentration Camp." Chartock: Society, pp.4-5.

3085. Newman, Judith: In the Hell of Auschwitz: The Wartime Memoirs [Hicksville, NY: Exposition Press, 1963]

3086. Nomberg-Przytyk, Sarah: Auschwitz: True Tales from a Grotesque Land [Chapel Hill: Univ. of North Carolina Press, 1985]

Vignettes of life and death in Auschwitz proving that decency, fortitude, and courage could still survive in hell on earth.

3087. Nowakowski, Tadeusz (N. Guterman, transl.): The Camp of all Saints [New York: St. Martin's Press, 1962]

3088. Nyiszli, Miklos (T. Kremer and R. Seaver, transls.): Auschwitz: A Doctor's Eywitness Account [New York: F. Fell, 1960]

3089. ___: "A Doctor for the Nazis Remembers." Chartock: Society, pp.143-145.

3090. Pawelczynska, Anna (C. S. Leach, transl.): Values and Violence in Auschwitz [Berkeley: Univ. of California Press, 1978]

Psychological study of Auschwitz inmates which proves the survival of moral and social values in extreme situations.

3091. Perl, Gisela: I Was a Doctor in Auschwitz [New York: International Univ. Press, 1948]

Eyewitness testimony by a Rumanian Jewish doctor of her experiences in Auschwitz and Bergen-Belsen.

3092. Sehn, J.: "Extermination Camp at Oswiecim." Commission: GCIP/I, pp.27-93.

3093. Shneiderman, S. L.: "Photos from the Auschwitz Hell." CBW, vol.32 #1 (Jan. 4, 1965): 5-7.

3094. Smolen, Kazimierz (ed.): Reminiscences of Former Auschwitz Prisoners [Oswiecim: Panstwowe Muzeum w Oswiecimu, 1963]

3095. Styron, W.: "Hell Reconsidered: Auschwitz." NY Rev of Books, vol.25 (June 29, 1975): 10-12.

3096. Szmaglewska, Seweryna: "Auschwitz." Poland, #2/6 (1955): 6-7.

3097. ___ (Jadwiga Rynas, transl.): Smoke Over Birkenau [New York: Rinehart and Winston, 1947]

3098. Tennyson, H.: "Protestant Heroine of Auschwitz." J Digest, vol.18 #3 (Dec., 1972): 50-52.

3099. Underground Reporter: "Oswiecim the Camp of Death." FW, vol.7 #3 (March, 1944): 271-284.

3100. Vrba, Rudolf: "Footnote to Auschwitz Report." J Currents, vol.20 #3 (March, 1944): 22-26.

3101. Wiesel, E.: "Arrival at Birkenau-Auschwitz." Korman: Hunter, pp.251-256.

3102. Zywulska, Krystyna (K. Cenkalska, transl.): I Came Back [New York: Roy Pub., 1951] * Graphic description of the horrors of daily life by a former inmate.

Belzec

3103. Perah (Blum), David: "At Belzec: Before it Became a Death Camp." YVB, #21 (Nov., 1967): 34-35.

3104. Szroj, T. E.: "Belzec Extermination Camp." Commission: GCIP/II, pp.89-96.

3105. Tregenza, Michael: "Belzec Death Camp." WLB, vol.30 #1 (1977): 8-24.

Bergen-Belsen

3106. Adler, H. G.: "Belsen." WLB, vol.16 #3 (Sum., 1962): 44, 56.

3107. Barton, Russell: "Belsen." Hist/WWII, #109 (1974): 3025-3029.

3108. Baumgarten, Shlomo: "A Belsen Diary." J Sp, vol.10 #11 (Oct., 1945): 26.

3109. Goldsmith, S. J.: "Belsen: Chamber of Incredible Horrors." J Digest, vol.2 #12 (Sept., 1957): 41-45.

3110. Levy-Hass, Hanna (R. Taylor, transl.): Inside Belsen [Totowa, NJ: Barnes & Noble, 1962]

3111. Napora, Paul: Death at Belsen [San Antonio, TX: Naylor, 1967]

3112. Playfair, Giles and Derrick Sington: The Offenders: Society and the Atrocious Crime [London: Secker and Warburg, 1957]

3113. Sington, Derrick and A. Weidenfeld: Belsen Uncovered [London: Duckworth, 1946]

3114. Weinberg, W.: "The Shame of Bergen-Belsen." JRJ, vol. 27 #2 (Spring, 1980): 81-83.

3115. Zimmerman-Wolf, Ruth: "Cain and Abel: A Belsen Camp Diary." WLB, vol.5 #5/6 (Sept./Nov., 1951): 28.

Buchenwald

3116. Burney, Christopher: The Dungeon Democracy [London: Heinemann, 1945]

Eyewitness testimony by a British prisoner of war in Buchenwald. Especially important for its views of the inner workings of the camps, and the author´s forthright approach to Jewish-gentile relations in the camps.

3117. ___: Solitary Confinement [New York: Macmillan, 1952]

3118. Carlebach, Emil: "The Buchenwald Story." J Life, vol. 3 #2 (Dec., 1948): 6-10.

3119. Castle, J.: The Password is Courage [New York: W. W. Norton, 1954]

3120. D´Harcourt, Pierre: The Real Enemy [New York: Charles Scribner´s Sons, 1967]

3121. Friedman, Philip: "The Buchenwald Era." J Fr, vol.18 #4 (April, 1951): 45-50.

3122. Friedman, Simon: "God in Buchenwald." J Sp, vol.34 #8 (Oct., 1969): 20-22.

3123. Gollancz, V.: What Buchenwald Really Means [London: Victor Gollancz, 1945]

3124. "The Horror that was Buchenwald." JOMER, vol.24 #16 (April 18, 1975): 10.

3125. Loren, Karl: Buchenwald [London: Brown, Watson, 1958]

3126. Robertson, E. H.: Paul Schneider, the Pastor of Buchenwald [London: S. C. M. Press, 1956]

3127. "That Hell-Hole Buchenwald." V/Unq, vol.3 #8/9 (Aug./Sept., 1945): 5, 9-10.

3128. Weinstock, Eugene (C. Ryan, transl.): Beyond the Last Path [New York: Boni and Gaer, 1947]

3129. Wiesel, Elie: "Agony at Buchenwald." Korman: Hunter, pp. 257-263.

Chelmno (Kulmhof)

3130. Bednarz, W.: "Extermination Camp at Chelmno." Commission: GCIP/I, pp.109-121.

Dachau

3131. Berben, Paul: Dachau [London: Norfolk Press, 1975]

3132. Blustein, Allan M.: "Dachau, the Devil's Domain." Ortho J Life, vol.38 #2 (Nov./Dec., 1970): 17-19.

3133. Cahnman, Werner J.: "In the Dachau Concentration Camp." Ch J Forum, vol.23 #1 (Fall, 1964): 18-23.

3134. "Death in Dachau." NJM, vol.53 #8 (April, 1939): 262-263.

3135. Hughes, Herman: "Christmas at Dachau, 1942." America, vol.119 #21 (Dec. 21, 1968): 643-644.

3136. Karst, Georg M.: The Beasts of the Earth [New York: A. Unger Pub., 1942]

3137. Kay, G. R. (comp.): Dachau: The Nazi Hell [London: Allen, 1939]

3138. Mayer, M.: "Suburb of Munich: Dachau." Progressive, vol.43 #2 (Feb., 1979): 34-37.

3139. Niemoeller, Martin: Dachau Sermons [London: Latimer House, 1947]

3140. "Pictures of Gruesome Dachau." V/Unq, vol.3 #12 (Dec., 1945): 3-5, 8. * A pictorial essay.

3141. "Prisoners of the Nazis." New Republic, vol.79 #1027 (Aug. 8, 1934): 337-339. * Dachau's early stages.

3142. Rothenberg, J.: "Dachau." Korman: Hunter, pp.275-278.

3143. Schowalter, H. P.: "This was Dachau." NJM, vol.81 #1 (Sept., 1966): 20-21, 40; #2 (Oct., 1966): 8-9, 11.

3144. Soc. for the Prevention of World War III: Dachau [New York: O. S. S. Section, U. S. Seventh Army, 1945]

3145. Werner, Alfred: "Infamous Dachau." Am Heb, vol.155 #6 (June 8, 1945): 6, 11.

3146. ___: "Inward Man at Dachau." J Fo, vol.31 #11 (Nov., 1948): 284-286.

Flossenbuerg

3147. "Flossenbuerg, the Story of One Concentration Camp. A Picture Feature." NJM, vol.60 #2 (Oct., 1945): 46-49.

3148. Rehyansky, J. A.: "Flossenbuerg." National Review, vol.28 (June 25, 1976): 678-679.

Janowska/Lublin

3149. Wells, Leon W.: The Death Brigade [New York: Holocaust Library, 1978] Also published as: The Janowska Road [New York: Macmillan, 1963] * Memoir of the Janowska concentration camp in Lwow.

Klooga

3150. Hersey, John: "Prisoner 339, Klooga." Life, vol.17 #18 (Oct. 30, 1944): 72-74, 76, 81-83. * On a Jew who managed to escape from Klooga.

Majdanek

3151. Davies, R. A. (as told to V. Bernstein): "I was at Majdanek Death-Camp." CJCh, vol.32 #28 (Nov.24, 1944): 5, 13.

3152. "Investigation of Crimes Committed by the Germans in Majdanek." Polish Jew, vol.5 #28 (April, 1945): 9-12.

Mauthausen

3153. Blustein, Allan M.: "Mauthausen Hill Into Hell!" Ortho Jew Life, vol.37 #3 (Jan./Feb., 1970): 53-56.

3154. Le Chene, E.: Mauthausen: The History of a Death Camp [London: Methuen, 1971]

3155. Wiesenthal, Simon: "Mauthausen. Steps Beyond the Grave." Korman: Hunter, pp.286-295.

Oranienburg

3156. Liepmann, Heinz: "Life in a Nazi Camp by a Prisoner." Living Age, vol.345 (Nov., 1933): 210-213.

3157. Seger, Gerhart H.: A Nation Terrorized [Chicago: Reilly and Lee, 1935]

Poniatow

3158. Fiszerowa, Ludwika: "The Camp at Poniatow." Am Heb, vol.153 #52 (Oct. 27, 1944): 10, 15.

Ravensbrueck

3159. Dufournier, Denise: Ravensbrueck: The Women's Camp of Death [London: G. Allen & Unwin, 1948]

3160. Maurel, Michelene: An Ordinary Camp [New York: Simon and Schuster, 1958] Also published as: Ravensbruck [London: Blond, 1958]

3161. Poltawska, Wanda: "Ravensbrueck Between Life and Death." Poland, #6/106 (1963): 17-19.

3162. Tillion, G. (G. Satterwhite, transl.): Ravensbrueck [New York: Anchor Press, 1975]

Eyewitness account by a French inmate of the infamous Nazi camp for women. The author was a member of the French resistance. Tillion makes some sound methodological points on the study of concentration camps. Also includes a chronology of the camp's history.

Sachsenhausen

3163. Heiman, Leo: "How Nazis Committed the World's Biggest Forgery." NJM, vol.74 #8 (May, 1960): 7-8. * On the forced production of counterfeit currency.

3164. Kruger, Bernhard: "I was the World's greatest Counterfeiter." J Digest, vol.4 #4 (Jan., 1959): 59-63.

3165. Lubienski, T.: "The Sachsenhausen University." Poland #8/108 (1963): 17-19. * On Polish intellectuals.

3166. Pigon, Stanislaw: "Reminiscences of the Sachsenhausen Concentration Camp." Poland, #3/151 (March, 1967): 21-23.

3167. Stein, Leo: "Rabbis in Sachsenhausen." NJM, vol.56 #5 (Jan., 1942): 154-155.

Sobibor

3168. Lukaszkiewicz, Z.: "Sobibor Extermination Camp." Commission: GCIP/II, pp.99-104.

3169. Novitch, Miriam (ed.): Sobibor: Martyrdom and Revolt [New York: Holocaust Library, 1980]

Collection of testimonies by 30 survivors of Sobibor. The culmination of the book is the heroic revolt of October 14, 1943 which is told by the participants who survived.

3170. Rutman, A. and S. Krasilshchik: "German Death Factory in Sobibor." Rescue, vol.1 #10 (Oct., 1944): 3-4.

Stutthof

3171. Lukaszkiewicz, Z.: "Stutthof Concentration Camp." Commission: GCIP/II, pp.107-124.

3172. Pickholz-Barnitsch, Olga: "The Evacuation of the Stutthof Concentration Camp, Jan-April, 1945." YVB, #17 (Dec., 1965): 34-49.

Treblinka

3173. Bartoszewski, W.: "The Story of Jankiel Wiernik." Poland, #10/122 (Oct., 1964): 54.

3174. Donat, Alexander (ed.): The Death Camp Treblinka: A Documentary [New York: Holocaust Library, 1979]

Documentary history of the Treblinka death factory, including excerpts from the trial of Treblinka guards held in Dusseldorf (1965). The revolt and resistance in Treblinka hold a special place in Donat's scroll of martyrdom and heroism.

3175. "I Escaped Treblinka." Rescue, vol.1 #2 (Feb., 1944): 5, 9.

3176. "Inside the Treblinka Death Camp." GS, #14 (Aug. 1, 1943): 2-4. Also in J Sp, vol.8 #11 (Sept., 1943): 24-25. * As reported by the Polish Telegraph Agency.

3177. "Inside the Treblinka Death Camp: A Report from Poland." Am Heb, vol.152 #14 (Aug. 6, 1943): 5, 12, 13.

3178. Lukaszkiewicz, Z.: "Extermination Camp at Treblinka." Commission: GCIP/I, pp.95-105.

3179. Steiner, Jean-F. (H. Weaver, transl.): Treblinka [New York: Simon and Schuster, 1967]

Novelized history of the revolt in the Treblinka death camp. Somewhat controversial in approach, the book´s main problem is the dubious authenticity of some of the facts that Steiner presents.

3180. "The Treblinka Slaughter House." Polish Jew, vol.3 #18 (Aug./Sept., 1943): 1

3181. Wiernik, Yankel: A Year in Treblinka [New York: Am. Rep. of the Jewish Workers Union of Poland, 1945]

Vernet

3182. Wolf, F.: Concentration Camp Vernet: Two Stories [Moscow: The International Book, 1942]

Westerbork

3183. Boas, J.: Boulevard des Miseries: The Story of Transit Camp Westerbork [Hamden, CT: Archon Books/Shoestring Press, 1985]

Illuminating study of the Westerbork durchgangslager. The book gives an insider´s view of the murder of Dutch Jewry. Reviews all aspects of life in the camp, culminating in the final "resettlement" to the death centers in the east. An important addition to the growing historical literature on the Nazi concentration camps.

3184. Mechanicus, Philip (I. R. Gibbons, transl.): Year of Fear: A Jewish Prisoner Waits for Auschwitz [New York: Hawthorn Books, 1968]

Diary of a Dutch journalist covering the time he spent in

Westerbork awaiting transport to Auschwitz. Mechanicus outlines the inner social and political life of the inmates as well as their reactions to the slow but steady realization that "resettlement" meant death.

MEDICAL CRIMES

3185-3188. Aziz, Phillipe (Edouard Bizub and P. Haentzler, transls.): Doctors of Death 4 vols. [Geneva: Ferni Pub. for Friends of History, 1976]

1. Karl Brandt, the Third Reich´s Man in White
2. Joseph Mengele, the Evil Doctor
3. When Man Became a Guinea Pig for Death
4. In the Beginning was the Master Race

Journalistic account of the lives and careers of the Nazi concentration camp doctors and the crimes they committed in the name of "science".

3189. Barram, A. S.: "Modern trends in Violence." Recon, vol.41 #3 (April, 1975): 7-18. * On German doctors who performed "medical experiments" using humans as guinea-pigs.

3190. Baruk, H.: "German Doctors and Criminal Medical Experiments." Am OSE Rev, vol.8 #1 (Fall, 1951): 3-10.

3191. Bernhard, Georg: "Jews as Guinea Pigs." CW, vol.9 #3 (Jan. 16, 1942): 10-11.

3192. Blacker, C. P.: "Eugenic Experiments Conducted by the Nazis on Human Subjects." Eugenics Rev, vol.44 #2 (April, 1952): 9-19; #4 (Oct., 1952): 125-126.

3193. Ford, Brian J.: "The New Dark Age." Hist/WWII, #37 (1973): 1031-1033.

3194. Friedman, Philip: "Crimes in the Name of Science." Friedman: Roads, pp.322-332.

3195. ___: "Medical Experiments on Concentration Camp Prisoners." Am OSE Rev, vol.5 #3/4 (Sum./Fall, 1948): 3-9.

3196. Herriot, Edouard: "Human Guinea Pigs." FW, vol.12 #3 (Oct., 1946): 21-23.

3197. Kepinski, Antoni: "A Psychiatrist´s Reflections on Auschwitz." Poland, #1/125 (Jan., 1965): 18-19.

3198. Michejda, K.: "Experimental Operations in the Ravensbrueck Concentration Camp." Commission: GCIP/II, pp. 133-148.

3199. Mitscherlich, Alexander and Fred Mielke (H. Norden, transl.): Doctors of Infamy: The Story of Nazi Medical Crimes [New York: Abelard-Schuman, 1949]

3200. Poller, Walter: Medical Block Buchenwald: The Personal Testimony of Inmate 996 Block # 36 [Secaucus, NJ: Lyle Stuart, 1961]

3201. Seman, Philip L.: "Experiment ´E´." Am Heb, vol.156 #14 (Aug. 2, 1946): 8-9, 12-14.

3202. Sereny, Gitta: Into That Darkness: From Mercy Killing to Mass Murder [New York: McGraw-Hill, 1974]

Intensive case study of the role that the euthanasia program played in laying the groundwork for the Endloesung. Based almost totally on oral-history sources, only contemporary documentation was not consulted.

3203. Sterling, Eleonore: "The Notorious Doctor (Willhelm) Grau." CW, vol.1 #2 (Jan. 9, 1956): 6-8.

3204. Szalet, L. (C. B. Williams, transl.): Experiment "E": A Report from an Extermination Laboratory [New York: Didier Pub., 1945]

Eyewitness testimony of the sufferings of Polish Jews interned at the Sachsenhausen concentration camp, by one of the survivors.

PRISONERS-OF-WAR AND THEIR TREATMENT

3205. Cohen, Bernard M. and Maurice Z. Cooper: A Follow-up Study of World War II Prisoners of War [Washington, DC: Government Printing Office, 1954]

3206. Collins, Douglas: P. O. W.: A Soldier´s Story of his Ten Escapes from Nazi Prison Camps [New York: W. W. Norton, 1968]

3207. Davis, Jerome: "Millions Behind Barbed Wire." Survey Graphic, vol.31 #8 (Aug., 1942): 345-348.

3208. Foreman, P. B.: "Buchenwald and Modern Prisoner-of-War Detention Policy." Social Forces, vol.37 (May, 1959): 289-298.

3209. Guri, J.: "Soviet Jewish Prisoners of War in German Captivity." YVB, #17 (Dec., 1965): 15-21.

3210. Gwiazdowski, A. P.: I Survived Hitler´s Hell [Boston: Meador Pub., 1954]

3211. Heiman, L.: "How 600 Jews Survived Four Years of Nazi Captivity: Joe Almogi, Incredible Hero of Stalag 8." J Digest, vol. 9 #11 (Aug., 1964): 36-40.

3212. "Jewish War Prisoners." Polish Jew, vol.3 #19 (Dec., 1943): 8.

3213. Majewski, W.: Six Months in a German Prison [London: Superior Printer, 1942]

3214. Melamet, A. M.: "The Man Behind the Barbed Wire: Intimate Stories of the Experiences of Jewish P.O.W.´s." J Affairs, vol.5 #4 (Sept., 1945): 7-9.

3215. Prouse, A. Robert: Ticket to Hell via Dieppe: From a Prisoner´s Wartime Log, 1942-1945 [Toronto: Van Nostrand Reinhold, 1982]

3216. "Six Months in a German Prison." PFR, #54 (Oct. 15, 1942): Whole Issue.

3217. "The ´Special Treatment´ of Jewish Prisoners of War." WLB, vol.18 #2 (April, 1964): 23.

3218. Strong, Tracy: "Prisoners of War." Survey Midmonthly, vol.80 #8 (Aug., 1944): 227-229.

3219. ___: We Prisoners of War: Sixteen British Officers and Soldiers Speak from a German Prison Camp [New York: Association Press, 1942]

3220. Winograd, Leonard: "Double Jeopardy." AJA, vol.28 #1 (April, 1976): 3-17. * On American Jewish POWs.

10

The Shoa

WARTIME LITERATURE

Overviews

3221. Abrahams, A.: "The Dam has Burst." J Standard, vol.3 #12 (July 3, 1942): 4.

3222. Berman, Harold: "Hitler´s Last Ten Years." CW, vol.10 #5 (Jan. 29, 1943): 10-12.

3223. Cohen, Israel: "The Doom of European Jewry." Cont Rev, vol.163 #926 (Feb., 1943): 77-81.

3224. Dijour, Ilja: Statistics of Extinction [New York: YIVO, 1944]

3225. Ehrenburg, Ilya: "The Murder of the Jewish People." J Sp, vol.8 #12 (Oct., 1943): 21-24, 30.

3226. Engelman, Uri Z.: "Facing the Spectre of Annihilation." J Fo, vol.26 #3 (April, 1943): 57-58, 66.

3227. Fry, V.: "The Massacre of the Jews." New Republic, vol.107 #25 (Dec. 21, 1942): 816-819.

3228. "Jews under the Axis, 1939-1942." J Fr, vol.9 #11 (Nov., 1942): Special Issue.

3229. Lestchinsky, Jacob: "Destruction of European Jewry: Where Hitler is Scoring his Greatest Victories." CW, vol.9 #27 (Sept. 11, 1942): 6-7.

3230. ___: "European Jewry After 3 Years of War." Am OSE Rev, vol.2 #1/2 (Jan./Feb., 1943): 10-15; #3/4 (March/April, 1943): 16-19.

3231. Marcus, Robert S.: "The Handiwork of Fascism." CW, vol.11 #33 (Nov. 17, 1944): 6-7.

3232. Parkes, James: "The Jewish World Since 1939." Int Affairs, vol.21 #1 (Jan., 1945): 87-99.

3233. Shoshkes, Henry (C. Riess, ed.): No Traveler Returns: The Story of Hitler´s Greatest Crime [Garden City, NY: Doubleday, 1945]

Eyewitness acconts and testimonies by members of the Polish underground detailing Nazi atrocities in Warsaw as well as the ghetto uprising.

3234. Shuster, Zachariah: "The Passion of a People: Anno MCMXLII (1942)." CJR, vol.6 #1 (Feb., 1943): 23-36.

3235. Shwartzman, B.: "The Collective Crime." Zionews, vol. 4 #23/24 (Feb. 28, 1943): 13-15, 21.

3236. Smith, Rennie: "Guilty Germany: The Extermination of European Peoples." CEO, vol.19 #17 (Aug. 21, 1942): 266-267.

3237. Szende, Stefan: The Promise Hitler Kept [New York: Roy Publishers, 1945]

Chronicles the experiences of Adolf Folkmann, a Polish Jew from Lwow, both under Russian and Nazi occupation. Folkmann managed to escape to Sweden in the latter part of 1943, where he told his story to the author.

Wartime Documentation

3238. American Council of Warsaw Jews: The Day-by Day Eye-witness Diary of a Polish Gentile: The Extermination of 500,000 Jews in the Warsaw Ghetto [New York: The Council and Friends, 1944]

3239. American Jewish Congress: Hitler´s Black Record: The Documented Story of Nazi Atrocities against the Jews [New York: Am. Jewish Congress, 1943]

3240. "An Eye-Witness Account from Poland." J Fr, vol.10 #3 (March, 1943): 15-17.

3241. "Annihilation of the Remnants of the Jews." GS, #30 (Oct. 15, 1944): 1-7.

3242. "An Unusual Document." GS, #26 (June 1, 1944): 6-7.

3243. "Authentic Report from Poland Describing the Wholesale Annihilation of Jews." GS, #8 (Feb. 1, 1943): 1-5.

3244. "Authentic Report from the Jewish Underground Movement of Poland to its American Representation." GS, #4 (Oct. 1, 1942): 1-2.

3245. "Bestial German Atrocities in Rumania." J Standard, vol.3 #14 (July 17, 1942): 2.

3246. "Blood Bath in Poland." J Standard, vol.3 #12 (July 3, 1942): 1-2.

3247. Cahman, Werner J.: "An Ethical Will and a Memorial Tribute. Documents from Europe." Recon, vol.9 #10 (June 25, 1943): 29-32.

3248. "Civil Death of Jews in Germany." CW, vol.10 #28 (Oct. 8, 1943): 12-13.

3249. "A Contribution to the History of the Annihilation of the Jews of Poland." GS, #16 (Oct. 1, 1943): 6-7.

3250. "Data on Party Members." GS, #31 (Nov. 1, 1944): 1-3.

3251. "Deportation and Death: Eyewitness Testimony." CW, vol.9 #37 (Dec. 4, 1942): 6-7.

3252. "Documents: German Government Decrees." J Rev, #5 (June/Sept., 1933): 105-113.

3253. "The Extermination Center. From a Document Received by the Polish Jewish Labor Party Bund." J Fr, vol.9 #11 (Nov., 1942): 15-16.

3254. "The Extermination of the Polish Jewry." PFR, #57 (Dec. 1, 1942): Whole Issue.

3255. "Eye-Witness Accounts of Intensified Terror and Torture of European Jews." V/Unq, vol.2 #6 (Sept., 1944): 3.

3256. "Eye-Witness Report of a Secret Courier Fresh from Poland: The Blackest Massacre of Jews in all Human History." V/Unq, vol.1 #1 (March, 1943): 5, 8.

3257. "Eyewitness Testimony on Massacres in Poland." CW, vol.10 #6 (Feb. 5, 1943): 2, 6, 12.

3258. "The Fate of European Jews: Oswiecim (Auschwitz) and Birkenau. A Document." CEO, vol.21 #15 (July 21, 1944): 226.

3259. "The Fate of Greek Jewry: How Over 50,000 Were Deported." J Survey, vol.4 #34 (Dec. 3, 1943): 5.

3260. "A Fearless Document on the Deportation of Holland's Jews." V/Unq, vol.1 #1 (March, 1943): 3.

3261. "Few Jews Survived Nazi Terror in Holland." V/Unq, vol.2 #9 (Dec., 1944): 1, 7.

3262. "First Pictures of the Big Nazi Antisemitic Exposition Held in Paris." NJM, vol.56 #6 (Feb., 1942): 181.

3263. "First Report of a Member of the Jewish Underground Youth Organization of Poland." GS, #19 Jan. 1, 1944): 4-5.

3264. "Five Million Personal Tragedies." Polish Jew, Vol.3 #13/14 (Jan., 1943): 7-8.

3265. "Foreign Jews in Poland Executed on the Sly." GS, #15 (Sept. 1, 1943): 4-5.

3266. "4,000 Jewish Children from Theresienstadt Gassed by Nazis." GS, #32 (Dec. 1, 1944): 2.

3267. "Germans Officially Describe the Annihilation of Jews in Pinsk." GS, #31 (Nov. 1, 1944): 5-6.

3268. Greenberg, Hayim: "The Plan of Destruction." J Fr, vol.9 #11 (Nov., 1942): 4-8.

3269. Gur-Ari, M.: "The Stages of Annihilation." J Fr, vol. 10 #9 (Sept., 1943): 8-11.

3270. Habas, Bracha: "How the Jewish Community of Radom Was Exterminated." J Fr, vol.10 #5 (May. 1943): 7-12.

3271. "Hear, O Israel!: A Report Describing the Massacre at Jassy, July 28, 29, 30, 1941." J Fr, vol.9 #11 (Nov., 1942): 30-31.

3272. "Holland's Jewish Population Deported by Nazis." V/Unq, vol.1 #5 (1943): 1.

3273. "How it was Done... The Annihilation of the Jews of Poland." GS, #15 (Sept. 1, 1943): 1-4.

3274. "Hundreds Slain as Nazis Burn Down Jewish Street." CJCh, vol.27 #35 (Jan. 5, 1940): 5.

3275. "The Indiscriminate Slaughter in Poland." Polish Jew, vol.3 #15 (Feb., 1943): 3-7.

3276. "In Nazi Poland: Eye-Witnesses Describe Nazi Mass Murder." Polish Jew, vol.3 #16 (April, 1943): 1, 6.

3277. Institute of Jewish Affairs: "Extermination of Jews in Rumania." CW, vol.9 #16 (Apr. 24, 1942): 12-13.

3278. ___: Jews in Nazi Europe, February 1933 to November 1941 [New York: IJA, 1941]

3279. "It Did Happen There." NJM, vol.57 #1 (Sept., 1942): 10-13.

3280. "Jewish Drama in Netherlands Drawing to an End." Am Heb, vol.153 #3 (Nov. 19, 1943): 8.

3281. "Jews in Greece under Nazi Occupation." GS, #22 (March 1, 1944): 3-5.

3282. Karski, Jan: "Polish Jewry's Martyrdom." Rescue, vol. 2 #1 (Jan., 1945): 1-2, 11.

3283. Krone, Moshe: "The Fate of Our European Movement." Hamigdal, vol.3 #6 (June, 1943): 6-8.

3284. Leftwich, Joseph: "Letters from London." NJM, vol.57 #11 (July/Aug., 1943): 347-348.

3285. Lest We Forget [New York: World Jewish Cong., 1943] * On the extermination of Polish Jewry.

3286. "Lidice Pales Beside Kossow!" CJCh, vol.31 #28 (Nov. 26, 1943): 2.

3287. "The Liquidation of the Jewish Hospital in Warsaw." Am OSE Rev, vol.2 #5/7 (May/July, 1943):21-22

3288. "Man Hunt: On the Anniversary of the Mass Deportations of French Jews." Am Heb, vol.152 #13 (July 30, 1943): 5, 12.

3289. "Mass Slaughter of Jews in Poland." GS, #2 (Aug. 5, 1942): 1-3.

3290. "The Massacres in Latvia." CW, vol.9 #37 (Dec. 4, 1942): 9-13.

3291. "Memorandum Concerning the Deportation of the Jews from Bukovina." CW, vol.10 #20 (May 21,1943): 13-14. Also in J Comment, vol.1 #2 (May 21, 1943): 3-4.

3292. "A Message from Poland." Am J Times, vol.5 #6 (March, 1940): 10, 15, 17.

3293. "Millions Facing Certain Death: Mass Murder of Jews in Poland." Polish Jew, vol.2 #11/12 (Oct./Nov., 1942): 3-4.

3294. "Murder in Poland." J Fr, vol.9 #9 (Sept., 1942): 28-29.

3295. "Nazi Barbarities in Poland: Accounts by Eyewitnesses." Polish Jew, vol.3 #17 (May/June, 1943): 3-8.

3296. "The Nazi Program." Chartock: Society, pp.132-136.

3297. "Nazis Destroyed Belgian Jewish Community." Comm Reporter, vol.1 #6 (Sept., 1944): 6.

3298. "The Nazis in Chelm. A Report Received by the United Relief Committee for Polish Jews in Tel-Aviv, Nov. 10, 1940." J Fr, vol.9 #11 (Nov., 1942): 13-14.

3299. "Nazis Speed up Extermination of Remaining Jews in Poland." V/Ung, vol.2 #7 (Oct., 1944): 1, 6, 7.

3300. "The Netherlands - Judenrein." J Comment, vol.1 #10 (July 9, 1943): 3-4. Also in CW, vol.10 #25 (July 16, 1943): 14-15.

3301. "The Ordeal of the Children in Poland." GS, #19 (Jan. 1, 1944): 1-2.

3302. "The People of the Warsaw Ghetto No Longer Among the Living: Their Homes, Their Institutions now Heaps of Ruin." V/Unq, vol.3 #2 (Feb., 1945): 4-5.

3303. "Pogroms in Poland." CW, vol.9 #37 (Dec., 4, 1942): 13-14.

3304. "Polish Underground Paper on German Problem." Polish Jew, vol.3 #18 (Aug/Sept., 1943): 7.

3305. "Report from Geneva, Dated August 5, 1942 Received on September 14, 1942." J Fr, vol.9 #11 (Nov., 1942): 33-34.

3306. "Report Nazi Campaign to Exterminate Jewish Children." V/Unq, vol.2 #1/2 (Feb., 1944): 1, 6.

3307. "Report on Extermination." Am Heb, vol.151 #31 (Dec. 4, 1944): 4.

3308. Ringelblum, Emmanuel: "A Report from Poland." New Currents, vol.2 #9 (Oct., 1944): 14-15, 28.

3309. Salpeter, Harry: "The Ordeal of Polish Jewry." J Fr, vol.12 #6 (June, 1945): 35-39.

3310. Schwartz, David: "The Month of Polish Jewry." Polish Jew, vol.2 #6/7 (March/April, 1942): 15-16, 19; #8/9 (May/June, 1942): 6-7.

3311. Shirer, William L.: "The Nazi Reign of Terror." Survey Graphic, vol.32 #4 (April, 1943): 121-122.

3312. "The Situation in Poland." J Comment, vol.2 #9 (March 17, 1944): 1-2.

3313. "Slaughter of the Jews in Poland." PFR, #71 (July 1, 1943): Whole Issue.

3314. "Special Underground Edition." Polish Jew, vol.4 #25 (Sept./Oct., 1944): Whole Issue.

3315. "Survey of Nazi Cruelty in Poland." J Survey, vol.4 #33 (Nov. 26, 1943): 2.

3316. "The Tragedy of European Jewry." J Mirror, vol.1 #5 (Dec./Jan., 1942/1943): 82-92.

3317. "Two Messages from the Warsaw Ghetto." Hamigdal, vol. 3 #2 (Jan., 1943): 10-11.

3318. "Underground Report from Poland on Massacres." Polish Jew, vol.2 #11/12 (Oct./Nov., 1942): 6, 9.

3319. "U. S. S. R. Report on German Atrocities in Lwow." Polish Jew, vol.5 #28 (April, 1945): 21-33.

3320. "The War Abroad." NJM, vol.56 #8 (April, 1942): 243-244.

3321. "War in Europe: The Lowest Depths." NJM, vol.56 #6 (Feb., 1942): 179-180; #7 (March, 1942): 211.

3322. "War in Europe: Massacres in the East." NJM, vol.56 #10 (June, 1942): 323-324.

3323. "War in Europe: The Murder of a People." NJM, vol.56 #9 (May, 1942): 292.

Documents and Anthologies

3324. Beit Lohamei Hagettaot: Extermination and Resistance: Historical Records and Source Material [Lohamei Hagettaot, Israel: Hakibbutz Hameuhad Pub. House, 1958]

3325. "The Black Book: The Silence is Broken." ADL Bul, vol.39 #4 (April, 1982): 7-8.

3326. Dawidowicz, Lucy S. (ed.): A Holocaust Reader [New York: Behrman House, 1976]

3327. Dingel, Erwin: "The Extermination of Two Ukrainian Communities: Testimony of a German Army Officer." YVS, vol.3 (1959): 303-320.

3328. Eck, Nathan (ed.): "An Official Nazi Report on the November (1938) Pogroms in Vienna." YVB, #2 (Dec., 1957): Endpage.

3329. ___: "Eichmann and His Creatures Discuss ´Evacuation´ of Jews." YVB, #6/7 (June, 1960): Endpage, 7.

3330. ___: "Hitler´s Political Testament." YVB, #10 (April, 1961): 12-19.

3331. Ehrenburg, Ilya and Vasily Grossman (eds.) (John Glad and J. S. Levine, transls.): The Black Book of Soviet Jewry [New York: Holocaust Publications, 1981]

Collection of testimonies and documents on the massacre of Soviet Jewry. The work was commissioned by the Jewish Anti-Fascist Committee, but was later suppressed by the Soviet government. The text was reconstructed from galley proofs that were smuggled out of Poland in 1980.

3332. "Eichmann and Poland." Atlas, vol.1 #1 (March, 1961): 72-73.

3333. Eisenberg, Azriel (ed.): Witness to the Holocaust [New York: Pilgrim Press, 1981]

Definitive anthology of testimonies on the Holocaust, most taken from previously published works. Very useful in both teaching and studying the subject.

3334. Eliach, Yaffa: Hasidic Tales of the Holocaust [New York: Oxford Univ. Press, 1982]

Collection of vignettes which attempts to show the Hasidic relation to the Holocaust. Gives glimses of life in Eastern European Communities under the threat of Nazism. It is, however, difficult if not impossible to sort out fact from fiction and to check the author´s sources.

3335. Engel, Joseph: "I Arranged the List of Candidates for ´Palestinian Exchanges´." YVB, #13 (Oct., 1963): 34-38.

3336. Esh, Shaul (ed.): From Hatred to Extermination [Jerusalem: Yad Vashem, 1957]

3337. "Four Letters from the Warsaw Ghetto." Com, vol.31 #6 (June, 1961): 486-492.

3338. Friedlander, Albert H. (ed.): Out of the Whirlwind: A Reader of Holocaust Literature [New York: UAHC, 1976]

Anthology of writings on the Holocaust, primarily designed for high schools, colleges, and adult education courses on the Holocaust. Its purpose is to inform and stimulate discussion on the issues raised. A teacher´s guide exist.

3339. Glatstein, Jacob et al (eds.): Anthology of Holocaust Literature [New York: Atheneum, 1976]

3340. Gutman, Yisrael et al (eds.): Documents on the Holocaust [New York: Ktav, 1981]

3341. Ha´shomer Ha´tza´ir: The Massacre of European Jewry: An Anthology [Kibbutz Merhavia, Israel: World Ha´shomer Ha´tza´ir, 1963]

3342. Hilberg, R. (ed.): Documents of Destruction: Germany and Jewry 1933-1945 [Chicago: Quadrangle, 1971]

3343. Hudson, G. F.: "Trains to Auschwitz." 20th Century, vol.154 #8 (Aug., 1953): 108-109.

3344. Katznelson, Yitzhak: The Song of the Murdered Jewish People [Tel-Aviv: Hakibbutz Hameuchad Pub. House, 1981]

3345. Korman, Gerd (ed.): Hunter and Hunted [New York: Viking Press, 1973]

3346. Krieger, Seymour (comp.): Documents: Nazi Germany´s War Against the Jews [New York: The American Jewish Conference, 1947]

A compilation of evidence provided by the Nuremberg war crimes trials concerning Nazi Germany´s war against the Jews and proposals by the American Jewish Conference to be included in the Allied (Western) peace treaty with post-war Germany.

3347. Lavi (Lowenstein), Theodor: "Documents on the Struggle of Rumanian Jewry for Their Rights during the Second World War." YVS, vol.4 (1960): 261-315.

3348. Levai, Jeno (ed.): Eichmann in Hungary: Documents [Budapest: Pannonia Press, 1961]

3349. "The Martyrdom of Lithuanian Jewry: Deeply Moving Accounts Written to relatives in South Africa." J Affairs, vol.5 #6 (Oct., 1945): 3-4.

3350. Meltzer, Milton (ed.): Never to Forget [New York: Harper & Row, 1976]

3351-3368. Mendelsohn, John (ed.): The Holocaust: Selected Documents in Eighteen Volumes [New York: Garland Pub., 1981]

1. Legalizing the Holocaust: The Early Phase, 1933-1939
2. Legalizing the Holocaust: The Later Phase, 1939-1943
3. The Crystal Night Pogrom
4. Propaganda and Aryanization, 1938-1944
5. Jewish Emigration from 1933 to the Evian Conference of 1938
6. Jewish Emigration 1938-1940, Rublee Negotiations and Intergovernmental Committee
7. Jewish Emigration: The SS St. Louis Affair and Other Cases
8. Deportation of the Jews to the East: Stetin 1940 to Hungary 1944
9. Medical Experiments on Jewish Inmates of Concentration Camps
10. The Einsatzgruppen or Murder Commandos
11. The Wansee Protocol and a 1944 Report on Auschwitz by the Office of Strategic Services
12. The "Final Solution" in the Extermination Camps and the Aftermath
13. The Judicial System and the Jews in Nazi Germany
14. Relief and Rescue of Jews from Nazi Oppression, 1943-1945
15. Relief in Hungary and the Failure of the Joel Brand Mission
16. Rescue to Switzerland: The Mussy and Saly Mayer Affairs
17. Punishing the Perpetrators of the Holocaust. The Brandt, Pohl, and Ohlendorf Cases
18. Punishing the Perpetrators of the Holocaust. The Ohlendorf and the von Weizsaecker Cases

Massive eighteen volume documentary collection with nearly 400 documents contained in about 5,000 pages. Documents included are primarily German, but also contains some American documents selected from the United States National Archives. The volumes are divided into four sections: 1. Preparation and Planning (7 volumes, 1845 pages, 152 documents) covering the period from 1933-1939; 2. The Killing of the Jews (6 volumes, 1553 pages, 174 documents); 3. Rescue Attempts (3 volumes, 828 pages, 19 documents); 4. Punishment (2 volumes, 550 pages, 26 documents). A number of the volumes have specially commissioned introductions:

vol.10 W. A. Fletcher, vol.11 R. Wolfe, vol.12 Henry Friedlander, vol.16 Sibyl Milton. Extremely useful for researchers and serious students of the Holocaust.

3369. Moczarski, K. (M. Fitzpatrick, ed.): Conversations with an Executioner [Englewood Cliffs, NJ: Prentice-Hall, 1981]

Transcript of a year-long discussion by the author and Jurgen Stroop, between the latter´s trial and execution. The conversations are unverifiable and hence of dubious value.

3370. Ringelblum, Emmanuel (Yuri Suhl, transl.): "How the Polish Yiddish Writers Perished." J Currents, vol.19 #4 (April, 1965): 7-10.

3371. ___: "In Memory of Janusz Korczak." J Currents, vol. 21 #7 (July/August, 1967): 26-29.

3372. Rothchild, Sylvia (ed.): Voices From the Holocaust [New York: New American Library, 1981]

3373. Rothkirchen, Livia (ed.): "Rescue Efforts with the Assistance of International Organizations: Documents from the Archives of Dr. A. Silberschein." YVS, vol.8 (1970): 69-79.

3374. Rubin, Maurice: "Lest We Forget." J Fo, vol.36 #7 (Aug., 1953): Front Cover, Cover 4; #9 (Oct., 1953): 153-154; #10 (Nov., 1953): 171-172; vol.37 #1 (Jan., 1954): 14.

3375. Schwarz, Leo W. (ed.): The Root and the Bough: The Epic of an Enduring People [New York: Rinehart, 1949]

Transcripts of interviews with some of the survivors in the Displaced Persons camps.

3376. Trunk, Isaiah: Jewish Responses to Nazi Persecution: Collective and Individual Behavior in Extremis [New York: Stein and Day, 1979]

Attempt to chart the day-to-day stand of the Jews in face of the Nazi persecution. Based largely on previously unpublished eyewitness testimonies from the Yivo Archive.

3377. "The Unknown Diarist of the Ghetto Lodz." YVN, #2 (1969/1970): 8-11.

3378. "The Unknown...The Nameless: One Hundred British Jews Gassed in Auschwitz Reveals Official Report." JQ, vol.14 #3 (Win., 1956/1957): 31.

3379. Zisenwine, D. W. (ed.): Antisemitism in Europe: Sources of the Holocaust [New York: Behrman House, 1976]

SURVEYS

The Origins of the Endloesung

3380. Blumenthal, Nachman: "About the Concept and Implementation of Annihilation." YVB, #10 (April, 1961): 9-11, 23.

3381. ___: "Concerning the Question: When Did the Idea of the ´Final Solution´ Originate in Hitler´s Germany." YVB, #20 (April, 1967): 6-10.

3382. Browning, Christopher R.: Fateful Months: Essays on the Emergence of the Final Solution, 1941-1942 [New York: Holmes and Meier, 1985]

Attempts to correct the Hitlerocentric view of the Final Solution by illuminating the attitudes of the lower bureaucracy towards the issue.

3383. ___: The Final Solution and the German Foreign Office: A Study of Referat D3 of Abteilung Deutschland 1940-1943 [New York: Holmes and Meier, 1978]

Authoritative and well documented study of the involvement of the German Foreign Office in the murder of European Jews. The study focuses on the activities of Martin Luther and the Foreign Ministry´s German office.

3384. ___: "The Government Experts." Friedlander: Ideology, pp.183-197.

3385. Eck, Nathan: "Were Hitler´s Political Actions Planned or Improvised?" YVS, vol.5 (1960): 333-370.

3386. "Euphemism for Murder: The Meaning of Special Treatment." WLB, vol.14 #1 (Jan., 1960): 13.

3387. Fleming, Gerald: Hitler and the Final Solution [Los Angeles: Univ. of California Press, 1984]

A meticulously documented attempt to assess the role Hitler played in the Final Solution. Fleming examines the network of authority as well as the decision making process that led to the Final Solution.

3388. Foster, Claude R. Jr.: "Historical Antecedents: Why the Holocaust?" Annals, #450 (July, 1980): 1-119.

3389. Friedlander, Saul: "On the Possibility of the Holocaust: An Approach to a Historical Synthesis." Bauer: Historical, pp.1-21.

3390. Goldhagen, Erich: "Albert Speer, Himmler, and the Secrecy of the Final Solution." Mid, vol.17 #8 (Oct., 1971): 43-50.

3391. ___: "The Mad Count: A Forgotten Portent of the Holocaust." Mid, vol.22 #2 (Feb., 1976): 61-63.

3392. ___: "Pragmatism, Function and Belief in Nazi Antisemitism." Mid, vol.18 #10 (Sept., 1972): 52-62

3393. Hilberg, R.: "German Motivation for the Destruction of the Jews." Mid, vol.11 #6 (June, 1965): 23-40.

3394. Horowitz, Irving: Genocide: State Power and Mass Murder [New Brunswick, NJ: Transaction Books, 1976]

3395. Katz, Jacob: "Was the Holocaust Predictable?" Bauer: Historical, pp.23-41.

3396. Kermish, J.: "When and by Whom was the Order for the Final Solution Given." YVB, #14 (March, 1964): 26-31.

3397. Kolakowski, L.: "Genocide and Ideology." Legters: Western, pp.7-23.

3398. Lasky, Melvin J.: "The First Glimmer of Extermination: Plate-Glass Pogrom and Aftermath." Com, vol.6 #2 (Aug., 1948): 157-160.

3399. Lenski, Mordecai: "Who Inspired Hitler´s Plans to Destroy the Jews?" YVB, #14 (March, 1964): 49-52.

3400. Rubenstein, Richard L.: "Reflections on Unemployment, Genocide, and Bureaucracy." Littell: Education, pp. 53-73.

3401. Not Used.

Historical Reviews and Texts

3402. Allen, Charles R., Jr.: "The Politics of Nazi Genocide and its Socio-Economic Base." M&R, vol.7 #4 (March/April, 1981): 7, 14; #5 (May/June, 1981): 3, 12; vol.8 #1 (Sept/Oct., 1981): 4, 6.

3403. Altschuler, David and Lucy S. Dawidowicz: Hitler's War Against the Jews: A Young Reader's Version of the War Against the Jews, 1933-1945 [New York: Behrman House, 1978] * School text <see #3412>.

3404. Baron, S. W.: "From a Historian's Notebook: European Jewry Before and After Hitler." AJYB vol.63 (1962): 3-53.

3405. Bauer, Yehuda: A History of the Holocaust [New York: Franklin Watts, 1982]

Up to date textbook for college courses on the Holocaust. Attempting to be comprehensive, Bauer includes information and deals with issues not previously touched on by other authors. An unsurpassed introductory study.

3406. ___: The Holocaust in Historical Perspective [Seattle: Univ. of Washington Press, 1978]

3407. Braham, Randolph L. (ed.): Contemporary Views of the Holocaust [Boston: Kluwer/Nijhoff Pub., 1983]

3408. ___: Perspectives on the Holocaust [Boston: Kluwer/Nijhoff Pub., 1983]

3409. Charny, Israel: How Can We Commit the Unthinkable? Genocide: The Human Cancer [Boulder, CO: Westview Press, 1982]

3410. Chartock, R. and Jack Spencer (eds.): The Holocaust Years: Society on Trial [New York: Bantam, 1978]

3411. Dawidowicz, L. S.: "The Final Solution of the Jewish Question." Chartock: Society, pp.9-12.

3412. ___: The War Against the Jews, 1933-1945 [New York: Holt, Rinehart & Winston, 1975]

Written as a corrective to Hilberg, especially in use of Jewish documentation. As such the volume is very useful, but is weak in a number of areas. Most important is the author's rather dubious assertion that World War II was waged solely to allow the Nazis to exterminate European Jewry.

3413. Fein, Helen: Accounting for Genocide: National Responses and Jewish Victimization during the Holocaust [New York: Free Press, 1979]

Important survey which combines sophisticated methodology with good historical insight to provide an overall explanation of both Jewish victimization and Jewish survival during the Holocaust.

3414. Friedlander, Albert H.: "The Scenes of the Holocaust." J Sp, vol.38 #6 (June, 1973): 21-23.

3415. Friedlander, Henry: "The Geography of the Holocaust." Grobman: Genocide, pp.106-108.

3416. ___ and Sybil Milton (eds.): The Holocaust: Ideology, Bureaucracy, and Genocide. The San Jose Papers [Millwood, NY: Kraus International Publications, 1981]

3417. Friedlander, Saul: "Some Aspects of the Historical Significance of the Holocaust." Jer Q, #1 (Fall, 1976): 36-59.

3418. Friedman, Philip (Ada J. Friedman, ed.): Roads to Extinction: Essays on the Holocaust [Philadelphia: J. P. S., 1980]

Collection of Friedman's historical essays, originally appearing in Yiddish, Hebrew and Polish, which cover almost every aspect of the Holocaust. The volume is divided into three sections covering 1933-1939, segregation and brutal discrimination; 1939-1945, extermination; and methodological problems. Especially important is the Appendix "Outline of Program for Holocaust Research" which is still useful today, despite being written in 1950, and can be used to gauge the gaps in our historical knowledge.

3419. Gilbert, Martin: The Final Journey: The Fate of the Jews in Nazi Europe [New York: Mayflower Books, 1979]

3420. ___: The Holocaust: A History of the Jews of Europe during the Second World War [New York: Holt, Rinehart and Winston, 1985]

3421. Goldhagen, Erich: "Obsession and ´Realpolitik´ in the Final Solution." Hirt: Issues, pp.39-68.

3422. Goldstein, Anatole: From Discrimination to Annihilation [New York: Institute of Jewish Affairs, 1952]

3423. Grobman, Alex and D. Landes (eds): Genocide: Critical Issues of the Holocaust. A Companion to the Film Genocide [Chappaqua, NY: Rossel Books for The Simon Wiesenthal Center, 1983]

Collection of some forty essays on a variety of topics all connected with and organized around the award winning documentary Genocide. Each subject is covered with scholarly dispassion, although the authors never lose sight of the human factor.

3424. Gutman, Yisrael: "The History of the Holocaust." Grobman: Genocide, pp.109-128.

3425. ___ and Livia Rothkirchen (eds.): The Catastrophe of European Jewry [Jerusalem: Yad Vashem, 1976]

Anthology of scholarly papers reprinted from Yad Vashem Studies. Divided into three sections: antecedents, history, and reflections. Unfortunately contains no papers on the issue of external responses to the Holocaust.

3426. Hilberg, Raul: "The Anatomy of the Holocaust." Friedlander: Ideology, pp.85-94.

3427. ___: The Destruction of the European Jews [Chicago: Quadrangle Books, 1961] 3 volume Revised New Edition [New York: Holmes and Meier, 1985]

Authoritative reconstruction of the Holocaust. Hilberg remains the standard text to which all others are compared. Hilberg´s primary focus is on the ways and means of the Nazi murder process. His strengths lie in the highly detailed account of the development of Nazi policy from its antecedents to its denouement. Much attention is given to the organizational and bureaucratic machinery of destruction. Weaker, however, is Hilberg´s controversial summary of the Jewish aspects and especially of his explanation of the lack of Jewish resistance. This classic work has recently been revised with much additional material.

3428. ___: "The Nature of the Process." Dimsdale: Survivors, pp.5-54.

3429. Jewish Black Book Committee: The Black Book: The Nazi Crime Against the Jewish People [New York: Duell, Sloan and Pearce, 1946]

Detailed chronicle of Nazi crimes against Jews written by a committee established under world wide Jewish auspices. Based primarily on Nazi documents and detailed first hand reports. Although superseded by later surveys, The Black Book still contains a wealth of useful material.

3430. Kaplan, Chaim A.: "Expulsion." Korman: Hunter, pp. 189-206.

3431. Keter Publishing House: Holocaust [Jerusalem: Israel Pocket Library, Keter Pub., 1975]

3432. Krakowski, Shmuel: "Chronological Table of Events, 1933-1945." Gutman: Catastrophe, pp.705-738.

3433. Krausnick, Helmut (D. Long, transl.): "The Persecution of the Jews." Krausnick: Anatomy, pp.1-124.

3434. Kren, George M. and Leon Rappoport: The Holocaust and the Crisis of Human Behavior [New York: Holmes and Meier, 1980]

3435. Levin, Nora: The Holocaust: The Destruction of European Jewry, 1933-1945 [New York: Schocken, 1975]

Survey/textbook organized both thematically and geographically on the history of the Holocaust. Levin´s first section "Preparation" is dubiously organized and its chapters do not fit well together. While not as useful as other similar volumes the book does contain some useful material, especially in the geographic section, Part II - "The Deportations".

3436. Lewis, Theodore N.: "The Pattern of Mass Murder." CW, vol.29 #11 (June 25, 1962): 11-13.

3437. Lipshutz, N.: Victory Through Darkness and Despair [New York: Vantage Press, 1960]

3438. Manvell, R. and H. Fraenkel: The Incomparable Crime: Mass Extermination in the Twentieth Century, the Legacy of Guilt [New York: G. P. Putnam's Sons, 1967]

Study of the mechanization, automation, and commercialization of genocide in Nazi Germany. Traces the search for a perfect method of extermination from its origins through to the death camps. Special emphasis is placed on the make-up and origins of the murderers.

3439. Musmanno, Michael A.: The Eichmann Kommandos [New York: Macfadden Books, 1962]

Penetrating analysis of Nazi crimes against Jews given originally as testimony by Justice Musmanno (who had previously presided at the Einsatzgruppen trials at Nuremberg) at the Eichmann trial. Based on trial documents and on other testimony. Main emphasis is on the activity of the Einsatzgruppen who are, however, incorrectly identified with Eichmann.

3440. Paneth, Philip: "From the Beginning to the End of the Greatest Tragedy." J Combat, vol.1 #2 (Fall, 1980): 6-7.

3441. Pilch, Judah (ed.): The Jewish Catastrophe in Europe [New York: Am. Assoc. for Jewish Education, 1968]

Text-book designed primarily for high school courses on Holocaust studies. Well written and profusely illustrated the book is still the best overall review available for use in schools.

3442. ___: "Years of Holocaust: The Factual Story." Pilch: Catastrophe, pp.47-86.

3443. Poliakov, Leon (M. Greenberg, ed., A. J. George, transl.): Harvest of Hate: The Nazi Program for the Destruction of the Jews of Europe [Syracuse, NY: Syracuse Univ. Press, 1954]

Chronicle of the extermination of European Jewry. Although Poliakov makes extensive use of offcial documents, he has not lost sight of the human dimensions of the tragedy. Perhaps the most well balanced account of the Holocaust.

3444. Porter, Jack N.: Confronting History and Holocaust: Collected Essays, 1972-1982 [Washington, DC: Univ. Press of America, 1983]

3445. Reitlinger, Gerald: The Final Solution: The Attempt to Exterminate the Jews of Europe, 1939-1945 [New York: Beechhurst Press, 1953]

Parallel to Hilberg and Poliakov, Reitlinger has a different perspective from either, being primarily a chronicler. Reitlinger's account is slightly marred by his overemphasis upon numbers and his lack of a contextual framework.

3446. Robinson, Jacob: "The Holocaust." in Encyclopaedia Judaica, (Geoffrey Wigoder, Editor in Chief) vol.8 [Jerusalem/New York: Keter/Macmillan, 1971]: columns 828-905. Also in Gutman: Catastrophe, pp.243-282.

3447. Rossel, Seymour: The Holocaust [New York: Franklin Watts, 1981]

Historical account of European Jewry, primarily for junior high and high school students. Makes extensive use of contemporary documents.

3448. Russell, Edward F. L.: The Scourge of the Swastika [New York: Ballantine Books, 1954]

3449. Rutherford, Ward: Genocide [New York: Ballantine Books, 1973]

Succint survey of the state of European Jewry under the Nazis. Covers the history of the Final Solution thematically rather than chronologically.

3450. Not Used.

3451. Ryan, Michael D. (ed.): Human Responses to the Holocaust: Perpertrators and Victims. Bystanders and Resisters [New York: The E. Mellen Press, 1981]

3452. Shanker, George: "The Holocaust: A Historical Overview." M&R, vol.10 #3 (Jan./Feb., 1984): 4, 16.

3453. Sherwin, B. L. and S. G. Ament (eds.): Encountering the Holocaust: An Interdisciplinary Survey [Chicago: Impact Press, 1979]

3454. Shoenberner, Gerhard (S. Sweet, transl.): The Yellow Star: The Persecution of the Jews in Europe [New York: Bantam Books, 1973]

3455. Stadtler, B. (M. D. Bial, ed.): The Holocaust: A History of Courage and Resistance [New York: Bantam Books, 1974]

3456. Tartakower, Arieh: "European Jewry: Summary of Disaster." HM, vol.25 #5 (Aug./Sept., 1945): 5, 24.

3457. Tsur, Muki and Nathan Yanai (eds): The Holocaust [New York: American Zionist Youth Foundation, 1970]

3458. Weinberg, David and Byron L. Sherwin: "The Holocaust: A Historical Overview." Sherwin: Encountering, pp. 12-22.

3459. Werner, Alfred: "Twelve Years and Twelve Weeks: The Gruesome History of Europe´s Jews under Fascism during which 6,000,000 Died in Greatest Tragedy of All Time." NJM, vol.60 #1 (Sept., 1945): 8-9, 17.

3460. Yad Vashem Remembrance Authority: The Holocaust [Jerusalem: Yad Vashem, 1977]

3461. ___: The Holocaust and Resistance: An Outline of Jewish History in Nazi Occupied Europe (1933-1945) [Jerusalem: Yad Vashem, 1972]

3462. Zuroff, Ephraim: "Timeline." Grobman: Genocide, pp. 134-140.

Demographic Surveys

3463. Duschinsky, Eugene: "Balance Sheet of a Decade." Ortho Jew Life, vol.24 #1 (Sept./Oct., 1956): 9-14.

3464. Fein, Helen: "Reviewing the Toll: Jewish Dead, Losses and Victims of the Holocaust." Shoa, vol.2 #2 (Spr., 1981): 20-26.

3465. Freeden, Herbert: "The Monstrous Harvest of the Past Decades." J Affairs, vol.14 #8 (Sept., 1959): 14-15.

3466. Grossman, Kurt R.: "What were the Jewish Losses." CW, vol.20 #26 (Oct. 12, 1953): 9-11.

3467. Guttmann, Josef: "The Fate of European Jewry in the Light of the Nuremberg Documents." YIVO Annual, vol. 2/3 (1947/48): 313-328.

3468. Lamm, Hans: "Note on the Number of Jewish Victims of National Socialism." JSS, vol.21 #2 (April, 1959): 132-134

3469. Lestchinsky, Jacob: "Balance Sheet of Extermination." IJA, vol.1 #1 (Feb., 1946): Whole Issue.; #12 (Nov., 1946): Whole Issue.

3470. ___: "The Catastrophe of European Jewry." JSSQ, vol. 24 #3 (March, 1948): 334-337.

3471. ___: Crisis, Catastrophe and Survival [New York: American Jewish Congress, 1948]

3472. ___: "The Demographic Fate of European Jewry." Am OSE Rev, vol.4 #2/3 (Sum./Fall, 1947): 21-23.

3473. ___: "For a Survey of the Jewish Tragedy." Ch J Forum, vol.4 #3 (Spr., 1946): 151-162.

3474. Shapiro, Leon and J. Starr: "Recent Population Data Regarding the Jews in Europe." JSS, vol.8 #2 (April, 1946): 75-86; #4 (Oct., 1946): 319-322.

AREA AND TOPICAL STUDIES

Phases of the Holocaust

3475. Bauer, Yehuda: "The Death Marches, Jan-May 1945." MJ, vol.3 #1 (Feb., 1983): 1-21.

3476. ___: "Genocide: Was it the Nazis´ Original Plan." Annals, #450 (July, 1980): 35-45.

3477. Blumenthal, Nachman: "Action." YVS, vol.4 (1960): 57-96.

3478. Browning, Christopher R.: "Deportations." Grobman: Genocide, pp.160-164.

3479. Cohen, Israel: "The Spiritual Desecration of European Jewry." NJ, vol.17 #9/10 (June/July, 1941): 145-148.

3480. Esh, Shaul: "Between Discrimination and Extermination: The Fateful Year 1938." YVS, vol.2 (1958): 79-93.

3481. Fischer, A. J.: "The History of the Star of David." CEO, vol.21 #22 (Oct. 27, 1944): 336-337.

3482. Friedman, Philip: "The Fate of the Jewish Book during the Nazi Era." JBA, vol.15 (1957/58): 3-13. Also in Friedman: Roads, pp.88-99.

3483. ___: "The Lublin Reservation and the Madagascar Plan: Two Aspects of Nazi Jewish Policy during the Second World War." YIVO Annual, vol.8 (1953): 151-177. Also in Friedman: Roads, pp.34-58.

3484. Hevesi, E.: "Hitler's Plan for Madagascar." CJR, vol. 4 #4 (Aug., 1941): 381-394.

3485. Hilberg, Raul: "The Einsatzgruppen." Societas, vol.2 #3 (Sum., 1972): 241-249. <see #3494>

3486. ___: "German Railroads - Jewish Souls." Society, vol. 14 #1 (Nov./Dec., 1976): 60-74.

3487. ___: "In Search of the Special Trains." Mid, vol.25 #8 (Oct., 1979): 32-38.

3488. Kahn, L.: "The Luncheon that Set the Holocaust in Motion." NJM, vol.86 #5 (January, 1972): 24-26.

3489. Kaiser-Blueth, Kurt: "Badges of Dishonor." J Digest, vol.3 #5 (Feb., 1958): 49-51.

3490. Keller, William: "Ledger of Death." Bridge, vol.1 (1955): 283-291.

3491. Kempner, Robert M.: "Blueprint for Murder." CW, vol. 17 #10 (March 6, 1950): 7-9.

3492. Lemkin, Raphael: "Genocide a Modern Crime." FW, vol.9 #4 (April, 1945): 39-43.

3493. Levin, Dov: "1939-1941: The Intermediate Period and its Implications for the Holocaust. The Jews of Eastern Europe under the Soviet Regime." Forum, #37 (1980): 103-116.

3494. Levine, H. S.: "Comments." Societas, vol.2 #3 (Sum., 1974): 271-278. * Response to Hilberg <see #3485>

3495. Littell, Franklin H.: "Defining the Holocaust." M&R, vol.10 #4 (March/April, 1984): 14-15.

3496. Pollack, F. W.: "Letters from the Ghetto: Philatelic Evidence of the Final Solution." JOMER, vol.10 #15 (April 14, 1961): 14, 16.

3497. Reitlinger, G.: "The Truth about Hitler's Commissar Order: The Guilt of the German Generals." Com, vol. 28 #1 (July, 1959): 7-18.

3498. Roth, John K.: "Holocaust Business: Some Reflections on Arbeit Macht Frei." Annals, #450 (July, 1980): 68-82.

3499. Rothkirchen, Livia: "The Final Solution in its Last Stages." YVS, vol.8 (1970): 7-30. Also in Gutman: Catastrophe, pp.319-345.

3500. Segalowitz, B.: "The Wehrmacht's Guilt." YVB, #21 (Nov., 1967): 10-18.

3501. Shneiderman, S. L.: "Prophets of the Catastrophe." CBW, vol.31 #13 (Oct. 26, 1964): 12-14.

3502. Shub, B. with Z. Warhaftig: "Starvation over Europe: Hunger as Hitler's War Weapon. Strategy of Jewish Extermination." WJC/BS Rep, #7 (Sept., 1943): 5-27.

3503. Snow, Edgar: "How the Nazi Butchers Wasted Nothing." SEP, vol.217 (October 28, 1944): 18-19, 96.

3504. Tenenbaum, Joseph: "The Crucial Year 1938." YVS, vol. 2 (1958): 49-78.

3505. ___: "The Einsatzgruppen." JSS, vol.17 #1 (January, 1955): 43-64.

Important review of the history of the SS mobile killing squads. Based almost exclusively on documentary sources. Proves the collusion of the SS, army, and Abwehr in the massacre of European Jewry. Also tells the fate of many of the Einsatzgruppen commanders after the war.

3506. ___: "Hitler's Jewish State in Madagascar." CW, vol. 21 #6 (Feb. 8, 1954): 11-12.

3507. Thalmann, Rita and E. Feinermann: "1938, the Decisive Year." Am Zionist, vol.65 #5 (Jan., 1975): 21-25.

3508. Werner, Alfred: "Where Hitler Planned Genocide." NJM, vol.66 #5 (Feb., 1952): 194-195, 200.

3509. Weyl, Nathaniel: "The Marx-Hitler-Holocaust Enigma." Mid, vol.29 #9 (Nov., 1983): 11-15.

3510. Yahil, L.: "Madagascar: Phantom of a Solution for the Jewish Problem." Vago: J/NJ, pp.315-334.

Implementors of the Final Solution

3511. Arad, Yitzhak: "Alfred Rosenberg and the Final Solution in the Occupied Soviet Territories." YVS, vol.13 (1979): 263-286.

3512. Bienstock, Victor: "Scholars Meet for an Examination of Hitler's Role in Final Solution." M&R, vol.11 #1 (Sept./Oct., 1984): 11, 14.

3513. Black, Peter R.: "Ernst Kaltenbrunner and the Final Solution." Braham: Contemporary, pp.183-199.

3514. Braham, Randolph L.: Eichmann and the Destruction of Hungarian Jewry [New York: Twayne Pub. for World Fed. of Hungarian Jews, 1961]

3515. Browning, Ch. R.: "The German Bureaucracy and the Holocaust." Grobman: Genocide, pp.145-149.

3516. Erdely, E.: "When Admiral Horthy was Taken in Tow." WLB, vol.14 #3 (July, 1960): 52.

3517. Karsai, Elek: "Edmund Veesenmeyer's Reports to Hitler on Hungary in 1943." NHQ, vol.5 (Aut., 1964): 146-153.

3518. Kermish, Joseph: "Eichmann's Role in the Destruction of Jews." YVB, #10 (April, 1961): 19-23.

3519. Poliakov, Leon: "Eichmann: Administrator of Extermination. 'The Definitive Solution of the Jewish Problem'." Com, vol.7 #5 (May, 1949): 439-446.

3520. Weinreich, Max: Hitler's Professors: The Part of Scholarship in Germany's Crimes Against the Jewish People [New York: YIVO, 1946]

Intensive bio-historical study into the role of scholars in the Nazi anti-Jewish program. Proves that the educated elite in Germany were perfectly willing to be good Nazis. It was they and not the rabble, mob, and/or professional thugs who planned and executed the greatest act of mass murder in human history.

The Victims

3521. Abrams, Alan: Special Treatment: The Untold Story of Hitler's Third Race [Secaucus, NJ: Lyle Stuart, 1985]

Highly speculative and melodramatic account of the Nazi treatment of Mischlinge as they termed mixed races.

3522. Brand, E.: "Jews who Found Refuge in Organization Todt." YVB, #18 (April, 1966): 11-16.

3523. "Document on the Grynszpan Trial Plans." WLB, vol.19 #2 (April, 1965): 26.

3524. Grossmann, K. R.: "The Trial Against World Jewry That Never Took Place." NJM, vol.73 #2 (Nov., 1958): 10, 23-27.

3525. Gutferstein, Joseph: "The Indestructible Dignity of Man: The Last 'Musar' Lecture in Slabodka." Judaism, vol.19 #3 (Sum., 1970): 262-263.

3526. Katz, Esther and J. M. Ringelheim (eds.): Women Surviving the Holocaust [New York: Inst. for Research in History, 1984]

3527. Kleinlerer, Edward L.: "Judeo-Bolshevik Hostages." CW, vol.9 #4 (Jan. 23, 1942): 5-6.

3528. Kohansky, M.: "Emanuel Ringelblum's Buried Archives." J Digest, vol.26 #3 (Nov., 1980): 50-55.

3529. Lengyel, Emil: "Jews in Fastnesses." Lib Jud, vol.16 #1 (June/July, 1948): 39-44.

3530. Lestchinsky, J.: "The Silent Martyrs." IJA Res Rep, vol.2 #6 (Jan., 1954): 1-3.

3531. Nalkowska, Zofia: "Beside a Railroad Track." Mid, vol.14 #4 (April, 1968): 59-61.

3532. Rosenthal, David: "Yizhok Katzenelson: His Premonition of the Holocaust." J Fr, vol.45 #4 (April, 1978): 8-11.

3533. Rosenthal, J.: "What Happened to Hershel Grynszpan?" J Digest, vol.20 #5 (Feb., 1975): 49-53.

3534. Schechtman, Joseph B.: "Jews and Gypsies." Am Heb, vol.156 #36 (Jan. 3, 1947): 4-5.

3535. Schwarz, Martin H.: "Europe´s Migrating Millions." FW, vol.5 #3 (March, 1943): 228-232.

3536. Schwarz, Stefan: "At the Hanging Place." J Fr, vol.15 #4 (April, 1948): 33-34.

3637. Strigler, M.: "Death of a Civilization." CW, vol.20 #13 (March 30, 1953): 10-12.

3538. Szner, Zvi: "The Records Kept by the Rabbi of Sanniki." Dispersion, #3 (Win., 1963/1964): 16-20.

3539. Zukerman, William: "Nazi Door-Slamming and the Jews." Am Heb, vol.153 #37 (July 14, 1944): 6.

The Children

3540. Abells, Chana B.: The Children we Remember: Photographs from the Archives of Yad Vashem [Rockville, MD: Kar-Ben Copies, 1983]

3541. Baron, Alexander: "The Anniversary." JQ, vol.1 #4 (Spr., 1954): 7-10.

3542. Bronsen, David: "Child of the Holocaust." Mid, vol.27 #4 (April, 1981): 50-56.

3543. D. B.: "The Children from Transnistria." J Fr, vol.11 #12 (Dec., 1944): 9-12.

3544. Ehrlich, B. J.: "Jewish Children in the Days of the Nazi Catastrophe." J Fo, vol.33 #6 (June, 1950): 102.

3545. Eisenberg, Azriel (ed.): The Lost Generation: Children of the Holocaust [New York: Pilgrim Press, 1982]

3546. Goldman, Solomon: "The Jewish Child during the Holocaust." J Ed, vol.46 #1 (Spr., 1978): 40-51.

3547. Justin, Dena: "Europe´s Children Cry Out." New Currents, vol.2 #10 (Dec., 1944): 7-9, 32.

3548. Lavi, Th.: "A Psychological Study of Jewish Children in Rumania during the Catastrophe." YVB, #12 (Dec., 1962): 45-49.

3549. Mahler, Ella: "About Jewish Children who Survived World War II on the Aryan Side." YVB, #12 (Dec., 1962): 49-56.

3550. ___: "The Fate of Jewish Children during the Holocaust." YVB, #15 (Aug., 1964): 48-59.

3551. Muszkat, Marion: "Research on the Problem of Youth during the Holocaust." YVB, #12 (Dec., 1962): 79-83.

3552. Rosenblum, Zofia: "Jewish Children in Ghettos, Camps and Woods - 1939-1945." Am OSE Rev, vol.4 #1 (Spr., 1947): 25-33.

3553. Ruziczka, A.: "Refugee Children from the Ghetto Struggle for their Lives." YVB, #13 (Oct., 1963): 59-63.

3554. Schwarberg, Gunther: The Murders at Bullenhauser Damm: The SS Doctor and the Children [Bloomington: Indiana Univ. Press, 1984]

Journalistic account of Nazi medical crimes using Jewish children. Also deals with the efforts to bring the doctor and others involved to trial.

3555. Zuieman-Zysman, J.: "Children Who Fled from the Ghetto." YVB, #12 (Dec., 1962): 5-10.

The Holocaust by Region

The Baltic Republics

3556. Arad, Y.: "Concentration of Refugees in Vilna on the Eve of the Holocaust." YVS, vol.9 (1973): 201-214.

3557. Gar, Joseph: "Jews in the Baltic Countries under German Occupation." in Gregor Aronson et al (eds.): Russian Jewry, 1917-1967 [New York: Thomas Yoseloff, 1969]

3558. Grinberg, Z.: "Nazi Extermination of Kovno Jews Revealed by Surviving Physician." V/Unq, vol.3 #6/7 (June/July, 1945): 1, 9-10.

3559. Lewis, Theodore N.: "Living by Jewish Law under the Nazis." J Sp, vol.41 #2 (Sum., 1976): 65-67.

3560. Minkin, Jacob S.: "The Tale of a City." CW, vol.11 #5 (Feb. 4, 1944): 8-9.

3561. Schneider, Gertrude: "The Jews of Riga." J Fr, vol.42 #3 (March, 1975): 15-20.

3562. Steinberg, Milton: "When I Think of Seraye." Recon, vol.12 #2 (March 8, 1946): 10-17.

Bulgaria

3563. Arditti, B.: "The Ordeal of the Jews in Bulgaria under the Hitlerite Regime." YVB, #6/7 (June, 1960): 18-19.

3564. Chary, Frederick B.: The Bulgarian Jews and the Final Solution [Pittsburgh, PA: Univ. of Pittsburgh Press, 1972]

Using German Foreign Ministry papers Chary has illuminated one of the least known aspects of the history of the Holocaust. As a result of Bulgarian vacillation a majority of Bulgarian Jews survived the war. This was due not to a lack of antisemitism within the Bulgarian government but to their unwillingness to become associated with murder.

3565. Oren, Nissan: "The Bulgarian Exception: A Reassesment of the Salvation of the Jewish Community." YVS, vol.7 (1968): 83-106.

Czechoslovakia

3566. Eichler, Benjamin: "Unforgettable Events in the Annihilation of Slovakian Jewry." M&R, vol.9 #2 (Nov./Dec., 1982): 9, 12.

3567. Federation of Czech Jews: The Persecution of the Jews in Nazi Slovakia [London: The Federation, 1942]

3568. Fraenkel, Josef: "The Miracle of the Alt-Neu-Schul." WJ, vol.16 #1 (Feb., 1973): 10-11.

3569. ___: "Slovakia's 70,000 Jewish Martyrs." J Fo, vol.39 #4 (April, 1956): 61.

3570. Jellinek, Yeshayahu: "Deportation from Slovakia." WLB, vol.16 #3 (Sum., 1962): 5.

3571. ___: "The Final Solution - the Slovak Version." EEQ, vol.4 #4 (Jan., 1971): 431-441.

3572. Lewisohn, L.: "Before Lidice and After." J Mirror, vol.1 #2 (Sept., 1942): 5-10.

3573. Neumann, Jeremiah O.: "The Destruction of Slovak Jewry." YVS, vol.5 (1960): 419-422.

3574. Ripka, H.: "Tribulations of Czechoslovakian Jewry." J Standard, vol.4 #40 (Jan. 14, 1944): 2.

France/North Africa

3575. Barnea, Arieh: "A Tragedy of North African Jewry: A Holocaust That No One Remembers." M&R, vol.10 #5 (May/June, 1984): 14, 16.

3576. Borsten, Joan: "Holocaust: The Libyan Chapter." HM, vol.64 #8 (April, 1983): 16-17, 30-31.

3577. Gerber, J.: "The Fate of Sephardic and Oriental Jews During the Holocaust." Grobman: Genocide, pp.129-133.

3578. Kleinlerer, Edward L.: "Fascist Policy in Libya." CB, vol.8 #1 (Jan. 3, 1941): 5-7.

3579. Levin, Meyer: "They Sent Away the Jews of Paris." CJCh, vol.32 #22 (Oct. 13, 1944): 8-9, 13.

3580. Wedeck, Harry E.: "The Last of the Jews of Provence." Am Heb, vol.151 #40 (Feb. 5, 1943): 6, 12.

Germany/Austria

3581. Ball-Kaduri, Kurt Y.: "Berlin is Purged of Jews: The Jews of Berlin in 1943." YVS, vol.5 (1963): 271-316.

3582. Bentwich, Norman: "The Destruction of the Jewish Community in Austria, 1938-1942." Fraenkel: Austria, pp. 467-478.

3583. Cahnman, Werner J.: "The Nazi Threat and the Centralverein - Recollection." AFJCE/CP, (1969): 27-36.

3584. Gordon, Sarah: Hitler, Germans, and the "Jewish Question" [Princeton, NJ: Princeton Univ. Press, 1984]

Controversial inquiry into the role of the German people in the extermination of the Jews. Her over-emphasis on Gestapo files and Nazi court sentences for Judenfreundschaft seems to place the entire blame for the extermination on the few real Nazis who forced all Germany to follow them. Trying to clarify the issues of responsibility and Jewish-Gentile relations, the work actually clouds them due to the conversion of a truism, that most gentiles neither approved nor disapproved of the murder of European Jews, to a central historical theory.

3585. Gross, Leonard: The Last Jews in Berlin [New York: Simon and Schuster, 1982]

3586. Henry, Frances: Victims and Neighbors: A Small Town in Germany Remembered [New York: Bergin and Garvey/ International Publication Group, 1984]

Interesting work on the destruction of the Jews in a single town - Sondberg, Germany. Primary focus is on how Jews and their neighbors interacted before, during, and after, the Nazi regime. Despite the author´s intimate personal involvement with the study she leaves unanswered a number of methodological questions. While excellent as social anthropology, the work is not quite history.

3587. Huttenbach, Henry R.: The Destruction of the Jewish Community of Worms 1933-1945 [New York: Sepher-Hermon Press, 1982]

3588. "The Jewish Community of Gleiwitz from 1933-1945." NZJB, vol.8 #5 (Nov., 1948): 10-11.

Greece

3589. Avni, Haim: "Spanish Nationals in Greece and their Fate during the Holocaust." YVS, vol.8 (1970): 31-68.

3590. Fischer, Alfred J.: "The End of Jewish Salonica." J Fr, vol.20 #8 (Aug., 1953): 19-21.

3591. Friedman, P.: "The Jews of Greece during the Second World War." in The Joshua Starr Memorial Volume: Studies in History and Philology [New York: Conference on Jewish Relations, 1953]: 241-248.

3592. Kominchowsky, L.: "The Liquidation of the Jews of Marcinkonis." YIVO Annual, vol.8 (1953): 205-223.

3593. Lengyel, Emil: "Tragedy of Salonika´s Jews." CW, vol. 16 #2 (Jan. 10, 1949): 11-13.

3594. Matkovski, Aleksander: "The Destruction of Macedonian Jewry in 1943." YVS, vol.3 (1959): 211-213.

3595. "Nazis Deported 48,000 Jews from Salonica to Extermination Camps in Poland." Rescue, vol.1 #5 (May, 1944): 7, 11.

3596. Roth, Cecil: "The Last Days of Jewish Salonica: What Happened to a 450-Year-Old Civilization." Com, vol.10 #1 (July, 1950): 49-55.

Hungary

3597. Balaton, Pal: "Tragedy of Hungarian Jewry." CEO, vol. 19 #15 (July 24, 1942): 239.

3598. Biss, Andre: A Million Jews to Save: Check to the Final Solution [Cranbury, NJ: A. S. Barnes, 1975]

Insider´s account of the negotiations between the Jewish Rescue Committee of Budapest and the Nazis for the ransom of Hungarian Jewry. Interesting account of a still unclear chapter of Jewish history under the Nazis.

3599. Braham, Randolph L.: The Destruction of Hungarian Jewry: A Documentary Account [New York: Pro Arte for World Federation of Hungarian Jews, 1963]

3600. ___: "The Holocaust in Hungary: An Historical Interpretation of the Role of the Hungarian Radical Right." Societas, vol.2 #3 (Sum., 1972): 195-220

3601. ___: "The Kamenets Podolsk and Delvidek Massacres: Prelude to the Holocaust in Hungary." YVS, vol.9 (1973): 133-156.

3602. ___: The Politics of Genocide: The Holocaust in Hungary 2 vols.[New York: Columbia Univ. Press, 1981]

Intensive study into the political, military, social, and economic conditions that led to the destruction of Hungarian Jewry. Includes a discussion of the international context and an in-depth analysis of the Kastner affair.

3603. ___: "The Rightist, Horthy, and the Germans: Factors Underlying the Destruction of Hungarian Jewry." Vago: J/NJ, pp.137-156.

3604. ___: "What Did They Know and When?" Bauer: Historical, pp.109-131.

3605. Fisher, Julius and Carol Klein: "Jews in Hungary." Am Heb, vol.153 #22 (March 31, 1944): 2, 14-15.

3606. Freudinger, Fulop (Philip) et al: "Report on Hungary: March 19-August 9, 1944." HJS, vol.3 (1973): 75-146.

3607. Handler, Andrew (ed.): The Holocaust in Hungary: An Anthology of Jewish Response [University: Univ. of Alabama Press, 1982]

Collection of personal accounts of the destruction of Hungarian Jewry. Some of the material was written at the time and slightly less than half was written afterwards. The most poignant fact revealed in the documents is the Magyar patriotism of Hungarian Jews, which makes their suffering under the Arrow Cross and the Nazis even more tragic.

3608. Lambert, Gilles (Robert Bullen and Rosette Letellier, transls.): Operation Hazalah [Indianapolis: Bobbs-Merrill, 1974]

Journalistic account of the efforts of the Hungarian Jewish underground to save Jews from the Nazis. Includes information on the Kastner-Brand-Eichman negotiations and on the activities of Raoul Wallenberg.

3609. Levai, Jeno (Lawrence P. Davis, ed.): Black Book on the Martyrdom of Hungarian Jewry [Zurich: Central European Times, 1948]

3610. ___: "The Deportations from Hungary, 1944: Did Horthy Order a Stop?" WLB, vol.17 #1 (Jan., 1963): 12-13

3611. ___: "The Hungarian Deportations in the Light of the Eichmann Trial." YVS, vol.5 (1963): 69-105.

3612. Zukerman, William: "The Eleventh Hour Murder of Hungarian Jews." Am Heb, vol.153 #52 (Oct. 27, 1944): 6.

Italy

3613. Katz, Robert: Black Sabbath: A Journey Through Crime Against Humanity [New York: Macmillan, 1969] * Journalistic account of the murder of Rome´s Jews by the SS.

3614. ___: Death in Rome [New York: Macmillan, 1966] * On Nazi reprisals against Rome´s Jews for an Italian partisan attack in which 156 Germans were killed.

Low Countries

3615. Boas, Henriette: "The Persecution and Destruction of Dutch Jewry, 1940-1945." YVS, vol.6 (1967): 359-372.

3616. De Jong, Louis: "The Destruction of Dutch Jewry." 4 WCJS, vol.1 (1967): 21-26.

3617. ___: "The Netherlands and Auschwitz." YVS, vol.7 (1968): 39-55. Also in Gutman: Catastrophe, pp.299-318.

3618. Presser, Jacob: Ashes in the Wind [London: Souvenir Press, 1968]

3619. ___ (Arnold Pomerans, transl.): The Destruction of the Dutch Jews [New York: E. P. Dutton, 1969]

One of only a handful of scholarly accounts on the extermination of West-European Jewry. Covers all aspects of Dutch Jewry under Nazi occupation. Well documented.

3620. Roe, Wellington: "Once There Were Jews in Holland." New Currents, vol.1 #6 (Sept., 1943): 10-11.

Poland

3621. Ainsztein, Reuben: "Need They Have Died? The Jews in Poland." 20th Century, vol.164 (Sept., 1958): 229-236. Discussion: vol.164 (Oct., 1958): 393-97, 481-88, 589-591; vol.165 (Jan., 1959): 85-88. <see #3624>

3622. Apenszlak, Jacob et al (eds.): The Black Book of Polish Jewry: An Account of Martyrdom of Polish Jewry under the Nazi Occupation [New York: Roy Pub. for Am. Federation of Polish Jews, 1944] * Documented account of life and death of Polish Jewry under Nazi occupation.

3623. Beckelman, Moses: "Polish Refugees Eastward Bound." JSSQ, vol.18 #1 (Sept., 1941): 50-54.

3624. Blit, L.: "They Did Not Die Alone." 20th Century, vol.164 (Oct., 1958): 387-392. * Reply to Reuben Ainsztein <see #3621>

3625. Central Commission for Investigation of Nazi Crimes in Poland: German Crimes in Poland 2 vols. New York: Howard Fertig, 1982]

Well documented collection of essays on a variety of subjects relating to the Nazi extermination of European Jewry in Poland. Originally published in 1946/47 by Wydawnictwo Prawnicze, Warsaw, a Polish government publishing house.

3626. Dangerfield, E.: "The Tale of Warsaw and Treblinka." Menorah, vol.31 #3 (Oct./Dec., 1943): 284-295.

3627. Eisenbach, Arthur: "Operation Reinhard: Mass Extermination of the Jewish Population in Poland." PWA, vol. vol.3 #1 (Jan., 1962): 80-124.

3628. Friedman, P.: "The Destruction of the Jews of Lwow, 1941-1944." Friedman: Roads, pp.244-321.

3629. ___: "Extermination of the Polish Jews." Commission: GCIP/I, pp.125-167.

3630. ___: "The Extermination of the Polish Jews during the German Occupation, 1939-1945." Friedman: Roads, pp. 211-243.

3631. Heiman, Leo: "The Truth about the Lemberg Massacres." J Digest, vol.5 #9 (June, 1960): 48-52.

3632. Hirshaut, Julien: Jewish Martyrs of Pawiak [New York: Holocaust Publications, 1982]

Memoir and history of the Pawiak prison in the Warsaw ghetto by an inmate who survived. Hirshaut also chronicles the terrifying experiences of those Jews who attempted to live on the aryan side.

3633. Kenner, Jacob: "The Jewish Culture Destroyed in Poland." J Fo, vol.27 #5 (May, 1944): 100-102.

3634. Krakowski, Shmuel.: "Policy of the Third Reich in Conquered Poland." YVS, vol.9 (1973): 225-245.

3635. Lestchinsky, Jacob: "Death of Polish Jewry." Ch J Forum, vol.3 #3 (Spr., 1945): 153-162.

3636. Mark, Ber: The Extermination and the Resistance of the Polish Jews during the Period, 1939-1945 [Warsaw: Jewish Historical Institute, 1955]

3637. Mozes, Mendel: "Nazis Massacre Jews in Polish Town: 800 Killed in Przemysl." CJCh, vol.27 #26 (Nov. 10, 1939): 6-7.

3638. ___: "1,500,000 Polish Jews Face Extinction under Nazis." CJCh, vol.27 #25 (Nov. 3, 1939): 7.

3639. ___ and B. Smolar: "Massacres of Jews Mount in Poland as Nazis Destroy whole Communities." CJCh, vol.27 #30 (Dec. 8, 1939): 6.

3640. Schwarzbart, I.: "The Crimes Committed by the Germans Against the Jewish Population in Poland." Polish Jew, vol.2 #10 (Sept., 1942): 3-4.

3641. ___: "The Disaster of Polish Jewry." J Sp, vol.10 #3 (Jan., 1945): 28.

3642. Sehn, J: "Liquidation of the Warsaw Ghetto in Light of German Documents." Commission: GCIP/II, pp.127-129

3643. Shulman, Abraham: The Case of Hotel Polski [New York: Holocaust Publications, 1982]

Investigation of one of the most puzzling questions to arise out of the destruction of the Jews of Warsaw. Was this, in fact, an opportunity for rescue that was lost, or was this merely another Nazi ploy, designed to lull Jews into passivity masterfully choreographed by the Gestapo?

3644. Simonov, K.: "Lublin Annihilation Camp." Polish Jew, vol.4 #25 (Sept./Oct., 1944): 6, 24-33; #26 (Nov./Dec., 1944): 4-9.

3645. W. J. C.: Extermination of Polish Jewry [New York: Inst. of Jewish Affairs, 1943]

3646. Woronowski, Izchak: "The Massacre of Lida - 40 Years Ago." Kowalski: Anthology/I, pp.562-573.

3647. Wulman, Leon: "Jewish Population Losses in Nazi-Poland." Am OSE Rev, vol.2 #5/7 (May/July, 1943): 3-10.

3648. ___: "Spread of Infectious Diseases Among Jews in Nazi-Occupied Poland." Polish Jew, vol.3 #18 (Aug./Sept., 1943): 5-7.

3649. X.: "Eywitness Report of the Annihilation of the Jews of Poland." GS, #9 (March 1, 1943): 1-5.

Rumania

3650. Carmilly-Weinberger, Moshe: "Jewish Education in Transylvania in the Days of the Holocaust." YVB, #21 (Nov., 1967): 21-27.

3651. ___: "The Tragedy of Transylvanian Jewry." YVB, #15 (Aug., 1964): 12-27.

3652. Fisher, Julius S.: "How Many Died in Transnistria?" JSS, vol.20 #2 (April, 1958): 95-101.

3653. ___: Transnistria: The Forgotten Cemetery [New York: A. S. Barnes & Co., 1969]

3654. Teich, Meyer: "Rumanian Jews in World War II." YVB, #18 (April, 1966): 46-49.

3655. Vago, Bela: "The Destruction of the Jews of Transylvania." HJS, vol.1 (1966): 171-221.

Scandinavia

3656. Abrahamsen, S.: "The Holocaust in Norway." Braham: Contemporary, pp.109-142.

Soviet Union

3657. Braham, Randolph L.: "The Destruction of the Jews of Carpatho-Russia." HJS, vol.1 (1966): 223-235.

3658. Friedman, Philip: "The Karaites Under Nazi Rule." Friedman: Roads, pp.153-175.

3659. Korey, William: "Forty Years ago at Babi Yar." PT, vol.9 #1 (Fall, 1981): 27-31.

3660. Kuznetsov, Anatoly (David Floyd, transl.): Babi Yar: A Documentary Novel [New York: Farrar, Straus and Giroux, 1970]

3661. Litani, Dora: "The Destruction of the Jews of Odessa in the Light of Rumanian Documents." YVS, vol.6 (1967): 135-154.

3662. Loewenthal, Rudolf: "The Extinction of the Krimchaks in World War II. " Am Slavic/EER, vol.10 #2 (1951): 130-136.

3663. Orbach, Wila: "The Destruction of the Jews in the Nazi-Occupied Territories of the USSR." SJA, vol.6 #2 (Oct., 1976): 14-51.

3664. St. George, J.: The Road to Babi Yar [London: Neville Spearman, 1967]

Yugoslavia

3665. Alkalay, David: "The Fate of the Jews of Yugoslavia." YVB, #4/5 (Oct., 1959): 19-21.

3666. Eck, N.: "The March of death from Serbia to Hungary (September 1944) and the Slaughter of Cservenka." YVS, vol.2 (1958): 255-294.

3667. Jelinek, Yeshayahu: "The Holocaust of Croatian Jewry: A Few Reflections." Shoa, vol.1 #4 (1979): 20-23.

3668. Palmieri-Billig, Lisa: "In Search of Yugoslav Jewry." Recon, vol.31 #17 (Dec. 24, 1965): 13-17.

3669. Romano, Jasa: Jews of Yugoslavia 1941-1945: Victims of Genocide and Freedom Fighters [Belgrade: Federation of Jewish Communities of Yugoslavia, 1982]

DIARIES AND TESTIMONIES

Diaries, Reviews

3670. Boyarin, J.: "During the Night, Deaths." Response, vol.12 #2 (Win., 1979/80): 55-63.

3671. Frank, Otto: "Has Germany Forgotten Anne Frank?" Coronet, vol.47 #4 (Feb., 1960): 48-54.

3672. Lewis, Theodore N.: "The Testimony of a Survivor." Recon, vol.30 #10 (June 26, 1964):23-26.

3673. Newman, Aryeh: "Moses Flinker: Anne Frank´s ´Double´ with a Difference." J Affairs, vol.15 #6 (June, 1960): 19-24.

3674. Shneiderman, S. L.: "The Last Testament of Emmanuel Ringelblum." Mid, vol.7 #2 (Spr., 1961): 39-53.

3675. Spintz, Joseph: "Two Diaries of Jewish Boys Killed in Poland." YVB, #12 (Dec., 1962): 11-16.

3676. Syrkin, M.: "Diaries of the Holocaust." Explorations, (1967): 73-98.

3677. ___: "Journal of Emmanuel Ringelblum." J Fr, vol.25 #7 (July, 1958): 13-16.

3678. ___ and R. Kunzer: "Holocaust Literature I: Diaries and Memoirs." Sherwin: Encountering, pp.226-266.

3679. Vago, Bela: "Budapest Jewry in the Summer of 1944: Otto Komoly´s Diaries." YVS, vol.8 (1970): 81-105.

3680. Wolff, Margo H.: "Anne Frank Lives On." HM, vol.38 #9 (May, 1959): 6.

Diaries/Journals

3681. Avinathan, J.: "My Friend David Sierakowiak and his Diary." YVB, #12 (Dec., 1962): 21-22.

3682. Berg, Mary: "Pages from a Warsaw Diary." CJR, vol.7 #5 (Oct., 1944): 497-510; #6 (Dec., 1944): 616-625

3683. ___ (Samson L. Shneiderman, ed.) (N. Guterman and S. Glass, transls.): Warsaw Ghetto Diary [New York: L. B. Fisher Pub., 1945]

3684. Berger, Zdena: Tell Me Another Morning [New York: Harper & Row, 1961]

3685. Berkowitz, Sara B.: Where Are My Brothers? From the Ghetto to the Gas Chamber [New York: Halios, 1965]

3686. Birenbaum, Halina: Hope is the Last to Die [Boston: Twayene Publishers, 1971]

3687. Borzykowski, Tuvia (M. Kohanski, transl): Between Tumbling Walls [Lohamei Haghettaot, Israel: Hakibbutz Hameuchad Pub. House, 1972]

Memoir of a member of ZOB in the Warsaw ghetto. Describes in detail the two stages of the revolt: the armed resistance of January, followed by the general uprising of April-May 1943. The author also chronicles the participation of Jews in the Polish uprising of August 1944.

3688. Cohen, Y. R.: "A Jewish Leader in Vichy France, 1940-1943: The Diary of Raymond-Raoul Lambert." JSS, vol. 43 #3/4 (Sum./Fall, 1981): 291-310.

3689. Davies, Raymond A.: Odyssey Through Hell [New York: Fischer, 1946] * Personal account of the devastation and destruction of East European Jewry.

3690. "Diary Reveals Appalling Nazi Atrocities." GS, #25 (May 1, 1944): 1-2.

3691. Dorian, Emil (Marguerita Dorian, ed.) (Mara S. Vamon, transl.): The Quality of Witness: A Romanian Diary, 1937-1944 [Philadelphia: J. P. S., 1983]

3692. Drenger, Gusta: "Justina´s Diary." Furrows, vol.4 #6 (May, 1946): 10-13.

3693. Eichel, Mietek: "Warsaw and After." Schwarz: Root, pp.284-293.

3694. "Extract from the Diary of Abraham Levin." YVS, vol.6 (1967): 315-330.

3695. Flinker, Moshe: Young Moshe´s Diary: The Spiritual Torment of a Jewish Boy in Nazi Europe [New York: Jewish Education Press, 1972]

3696. Frank, Anne (B. M. Mooyaart, transl.): The Diary of a Young Girl [Garden City, NY: Doubleday, 1952] * Excerpted in Com, vol.13 #5 (May, 1952): 419-432; #6 (June, 1952): 529-544; Chartock: Society, pp.174-175; Friedlander: Whirlwind, pp.26-34.

Possibly the best known Holocaust-related diary, written by a young Jewish girl hiding with her family in Nazi occupied Amsterdam. The translation of Anne´s words to stage and screen aroused a storm of controversy in the United States and Israel during the late 1950s.

3697. "From the Diary of Justina: A Story of the Jewish Underground." Com, vol.26 #7 (July, 1958): 63-65; #8 (Aug., 1958): 155-157.

3698. "From S. Szajnkinder´s Diary." YVS, vol.5 (1963): 255-269.

3699. Galnik, Werner: "Diary of a Ghetto Boy." J Life, vol. 6 #4 (April, 1947): 10-14.

3700. "Ghetto Uprising: From the Diary of Mordechai Tenenbaum." J Fr, vol.25 #4 (April, 1958): 6-7.

3701. Gimpel, Rene: Diary of an Art Dealer [New York: Farrar, Straus & Cudahy, 1966]

3702. Heimann, Eva: The Diary of Eva Heyman [Jerusalem: Yad Vashem, 1974]

3703. ___: "From a Diary of a Young Girl." YVB, #12 (Dec., 1962): 24-27.

3704. Heller, Paul: "A Concentration Camp Diary." Mid, vol. 26 #4 (April, 1980): 29-36.

3705. Herman, Josef: "The Diary of Dovidl Rubinovitch." JQ, vol.8 #1 (Win., 1960/1961): 19-22.

3706. Hillesum, Etty (A. Pomerans, transl.): Interrupted Life: Diaries of Etty Hillesum 1941-1943 [New York: Washington Square Press, 1983]

3707. Jarochowska, Maria: "The Diary of David Rubinowicz." J Digest, vol.6 #2 (Nov., 1960): 47-61.

3708. "Journey Into Limbo: From the Diary of Herman Piasker." Recon, vol.17 #18 (Jan. 11, 1952): 24-28. * Rumanian Jewry in 1940.

3709. Katznelson, Yitzhak: "Page from a Diary." J Sp, vol. 12 #4 (Feb., 1947): 22-25.

3710. ___ (Myer Cohen, transl.): Vittel Diary: 22-5-43/ 16-9-43 [Lohamei Haghettaot, Israel: Hakibbutz Hameuchad Pub. House, 1964]

3711. Kinsky, Helga et al: "Children of Terezin, Excerpts from Diaries." J Sp, vol.31 #1 (Jan., 1966): 15-20.

3712. Klonicki, A. (M. Hovev, ed., A. Tomaschoff, transl.): The Diary of Adam´s Father [Lohamei Haghettaot, Israel: Hakibbutz Hameuchad Pub. House, 1973]

3713. Komoly, Otto: "The Diary of Otto Komoly: August 21-September 16, 1944." HJS, vol.3 (1973): 147-250.

3714. Korczak, Janusz (J. Bachrach et al, transls.): Ghetto Diary [New York: Holocaust Library, 1978]

Diary of the friend of the children of the Warsaw ghetto. Korzak was a pediatrician in pre-war Poland. Although he could have saved his own life during the deportations he refused to do so preferring to perish with "his" children. Appended to the diary is "The Last Walk of Janusz Korzak", an essay by Aaron Zeitlin <see #3856>

3715. ___: The Warsaw Ghetto Memoirs of Janus Korczak [Washington, DC: Univ. Press of America, 1978]

3716. Langfus, Anna: The Whole Land Brimstone [New York: Pantheon Books, 1962]

3717. Lubetkin, Zivia: In Days of Destruction and Revolt [Lohamei Haghettaot, Israel: Hakibbutz Hameuchad Pub. House, 1980]

3718. Matenko, Percy (ed. and transl.): "Yitskhok Rudashevski´s Diary of the Vilna Ghetto." Yiddish, vol.1 #1 (Sum., 1973): 6-11.

3719. Melamed, Aliza: "From the Diary of a Young Fighter." IH, vol.15 #4 (April, 1967): 17-20. Also in J Digest, vol.15 #1 (Oct., 1969): 57-62.

3720. Newman, A.: "The Diary of Moses Flinker." J Horizon, vol.24 #1 (Sept./Oct., 1960): 7-10.

3721. Piasker, Hermann: "The Crystal Days of Bucharest." J Horizon, vol.17 #10 (June, 1955): 15-18.

3722. ___: "I Become a Fugitive and an Outlaw." Recon, vol. 19 #5 (April 17, 1953): 17-22.

3723. Rubinowicz, David (D. Bowman, transl.): The Diary of Dawid Rubinowicz [Edmonds, WA: Creative Options Pub., 1982]

3724. ___: "From a Diary of David Rubinowicz." YVB, #12 (Dec., 1962): 23-24.

3725. Rudashevski, Y.: "The Diary of the Vilna Ghetto." Young Judaean, vol.62 #4 (Feb., 1974): 6-8.

3726. Salomon, Charlotte: Charlotte: A Diary in Pictures [New York: Harcourt, Brace and World, 1963]

3727. Shneiderman, S. L.: "The Diary of Adam Czerniakow." HM, vol.47 #10 (June, 1966): 6, 20-21.

3728. Sierakowiak, David: "Exrtacts from the Diary of David Sierakowiak." YVB, #12 (Dec., 1962): 16-21.

3729. Sluyser, Meyer (A. Cohn, ed.): Before I Forget [New York: Thomas Yoseloff, 1962]

3730. Stanford, Julian C. (R. Fromer, ed., Eva Einstein, transl.): Reflections: The Diary of a German Jew in Hiding [Oakland, CA: Judah L. Magnes Memorial Museum, 1965]

3731. Van der Heide, Dirk (A. Deventer, transl.): My Sister and I: The Diary of a Dutch Boy Refugee [New York: Harcourt, 1941]

3732. Walk, Joseph: "The Diary of Gunther Marcuse. The Last Days of the Gross-Breesen Training Centre." YVS, vol. 8 (1970): 159-182.

3733. Zuker-Bujanowska, L.: Liliana´s Journal: Warsaw 1939-1945 [New York: Dial Press, 1980]

Testimonies

3734. Arad, Rachel (as told to Leo Heiman): "The Princess and the Captain: How a German Officer Saved me and my Daughter from the Nazis." J Digest, vol.7 #6 (March, 1962): 1-7.

3735. Ash, Sholem: "Exalted and Hallowed." J Fr, vol.9 #11 (Nov., 1942): 17-20, 25. * On Rabbi I. M. Rosenkranz of Praga (Poland), who chose death rather than to desecrate the Sabbath.

3736. Auerbach, Rachel: "Wax Candles." YVB, #1 (April, 1957): 17-18.

3737. Baeck, Leo: "I was a Witness." J Layman, vol.20 #6 (March, 1946): 5-6.

3738. Baerlin, Henry: "A Psychologist in a German Prison." CEO, vol.19 #22 (Oct. 30, 1942): 348.

3739. Bar-Tikva, Baruch: "From the Partisan Forests to the Bukharan Quarter of Jerusalem." YVB, #2 (Dec., 1957): 14-15.

3740. Boxerman, William I.: "He Saw It Happen." Am Heb, vol.151 #11 (July 17, 1942): 5, 16. * On fate of Yugoslavian Jewry, from an interview with the former chief rabbi of Yugoslavia.

3741. Burstyn, Daniel: "I Learned a Lot." Schwarz: Root, pp.272-276.

3742. Chaneles, Sol: Three Children of the Holocaust [New York: Avon Books, 1974]

3743. Deutsch, Henry: "Our Village Burns." Schwarz: Root, pp.300-303.

3744. Dworzecki, Mark: "Apologia of a Physician." Schwarz: Root, pp.232-240.

3745. Feigenbaum, M. J.: "Life in a Bunker." Schwarz: Root, pp.143-154.

3746. "The Final Solution in Action (Testimony)." Chartock: Society, pp.12-14.

3747. Fiszerowa, Ludwika: "Her Experiences in a Nazi Massacre Camp." GS, #31 (Nov. 1, 1944): 6-7.

3748. Frucht, Karl: "The Strange Case of Sarah E.: An Episode of Nazi Europe." Com, vol.4 #3 (Sept., 1947): 251-259.

3749. Glanz, Rudolf: "The Palace of the Rothschilds: Memoirs of a Jewish Emigre." J Fr, vol.9 #9 (Sept., 1942): 23-27.

3750. Glube, Samuel: "We Sang of Hope." Schwarz: Root, pp. 228-231.

3751. Goertz, Lisa: I Stepped into Freedom [London: Lutterworth Press, 1960]

3752. "The Graebe Memorandum." Chartock: Society, pp.14-17.

3753. Grin, Alexander: "From Belgrade." Korman: Hunter, pp. 172-175.

4754. Griner, M.: "Camp Child." Schwarz: Root, pp.294-296.

3755. Gross, N.: "Days and Nights in the Aryan Quarter." YVB, #4/5 (Oct., 1959): 12-13.

3756. Habas, Bracha: "In Warsaw It Got Worse and Worse." HM, vol.23 #7 (May/June, 1943): 9-10.

3757. Heszeles, Yanka: "As I Remember." Schwarz: Root, pp. 278-283.

3758. "I Was a Prisoner of the Gestapo." Polish Jew, vol.3 #13/14 (Jan., 1943): 9-11.

3759. Kahn, Jacob: "From Mannheim." Korman: Hunter, pp.156-171.

3760. Klajenan, Hanka (Nat Cohen, transl.): "To All Those Who Refuse to Believe." Today, vol.1 #10 (Oct., 1945): 2-4.

3761. Kleinman, Nathan: "The Road from Sandomir." Schwarz: Root, pp.241-247.

3762. Kolitz, Zvi: "A Gravedigger´s Tale." Am Heb, vol.153 #16 (Feb. 18, 1944): 6-7, 30-31.

3763. Korczak, Janusz: "Observations and Reflections." Poland, #6/94 (June, 1963): 16-20.

3764. Kovner, Abba: "A First Attempt to Tell." Bauer: Historical, pp.77-94.

3765. Landau, Ernest: "Men Versus Supermen." Schwarz: Root, pp.127-132.

3766. Lazar, Haya: "One Night of Many." YVB, #8/9 (March, 1961): 44.

3767. Lilienheim, Henry: "Mine Eyes Have Seen." Schwarz: Root pp.3-12.

3768. Mahler, Ella: "How Granny Saved Helenka from the Germans." YVB, #6/7 (June, 1960): 23-25.

3769. Mannheimer, Max: From Theresienstadt to Auschwitz [London: Jewish Central Information Office, 1945]

3770. Mendes-France, Pierre: "A French Trial in 1941." FW, vol.4 #2 (Nov., 1942): 157-164.

3771. ___: "Liberte, Liberte Cheri..." FW, vol.4 #1 (Oct., 1942): 69-73.

3772. Pawlowicz, Sala (with Kevin Klose): I Will Survive [New York: W. W. Norton, 1962]

3773. Peto, Erno (Ernst): "Statement." HJS, vol.3 (1973): 49-74. * On Nazi occupation of Hungary.

3774. Pinchewski, Rosa: "Rosa´s Journey." Schwarz: Root, pp.297-299.

3775. Polak, Jack: "High Holy Days Under the Nazis." J Digest, vol.22 #1 (Sept., 1976): 72-74.

3776. ___: "My Holy Days Under the Nazis." Sh´ma, vol.5 #96 (Sept. 5, 1975): 282-283.

3777. Pupko-Krinsky, Rachel: "Laurel Trees of Wiwulskiego." Schwarz: Root, pp.155-163.

3778. Rubinstein, S.: "Porick." Schwarz: Root, pp.180-183.

3779. Safran, Alexandre: "The Rulers of Fascist Rumania whom I had to Deal With." YVS, vol.6 (1967): 175-180.

3780. Schwab, Hermann: "Lest We Forget. The Last Jew from Halberstadt." JQ, vol.1 #1 (Spr., 1953): 89-90.

3781. Schwarz, Irene: "The Small Still Voice." Schwarz: Root, pp.189-200.

3782. Shtenkler, Ephraim: "What Happened to me in My Childhood: A Document of Modern History." Com, vol.9 #5 (May, 1950): 442-446.

3783. Soferr, B.: "Nightmare (N 9,´38)." Young Judaean, vol.62 #4 (Feb., 1974): 3-5.

3784. Stern, Elly: "Joy Cometh in the Morning." Schwarz: Root, pp.164-179.

3785. "The Story of a Jewish Boy from Lodz." GS, #20 (Feb. 1, 1944): 3-4.

3786. Warshawski, Edward: "My Two Years in the Warsaw Ghetto." Am Heb, vol.153 #9 (Dec. 31, 1943): 7.

3787. Wellers, George: "Three Portraits in Brown." Schwarz: Root, pp.248-262.

3788. Wells, Leon W.: "In the Name of Liberty." Schwarz: Root, pp.266-271.

3789. ___: "Recollections of a Witness." Mid, vol.26 #4 (April, 1980): 40-43.

3790. ___: "A Survivor´s Testimony." Ryan: Responses, pp. 71-77.

3791. Wiedermann, P.: "Conversation in Silesia." Schwarz: Root, pp.184-188.

3792. Wiesel, Elie: "An Evening Guest." Friedlander: Whirlwind, pp.3-9.

3793. ___: "Listen to Me!" Chartock: Society, pp.38-42.

Letters

3794. Blit, Lucjan: "A Fugitive from Warsaw Relates." GS, #19 (Jan. 1, 1944): 5-6.

3795. Eliashiv, Vera: "A Letter I Wrote in 1945." JQ, vol. 18 #2 (Summer, 1970): 23-27.

3796. "Escaping the German Hell." Nation, vol.136 #3538 (April 26, 1933): 471-471.

3797. "Inside Germany." GS, #5 (Nov. 1, 1942): 1-2.

3798. Kigel, N.: "Letters from Germany 1945." HM, vol.55 #10 (June, 1974): 15, 37-38.

3799. Slutzki, Yitzhok: "From Pinsk to Brooklyn, 1943: A Jewish Partisan near Pinsk writes to His Father in Brooklyn." J Currents, vol.19 #4 (April, 1965): 13-15.

Personal Narratives by Escapees

3800. Brod, Max: "My Escape from Prague." J Fr, vol.6 #5 (May, 1939): 5-7.

3801. "From the Valley of Death. By Three Who Escaped from Nazi Poland." J Sp, vol.9 #11 (Sept., 1944): 10-12.

3802. Glied, Bill: "To Freedom 55 Miles." Am Heb, vol.159 #24 (Oct.7, 1949): 4-5. * Author narates the episode of his successful escape to Switzerland.

3803. "I Escaped from a German Prison Camp." FW, vol.7 #4 (April, 1944): 319-321. * On Rawa-Ruska.

3804. Isolani, Gertrude: "One Family´s Flight to Freedom." J Digest, vol.13 #11 (Aug., 1968): 9-12.

3805. Jocum, H.: "Escape to Mozambique." J Digest, vol.25 #10 (June, 1980): 66-69. * As told to Suzy Green.

3806. Kaminska, Ida: "My Wartime Flight Through the Soviet Union." Mid, vol.19 #8 (Oct., 1973): 19-40.

3807. Noren, Catherine: "We Escaped from Hitler's Germany." Chartock: Society, pp.30-38.

3808. Spirro, Ch. A.: "Fleeing German Invasion." Ortho J Life, vol.40 #1 (Jan., 1973): 25-31.

3809. Stybel, A. J.: "From the Diary of a Refugee." J Sp, vol.10 #5 (March, 1945): 14-17.

3810. Unsdorfer, S. B.: "I Escaped the SS." Ortho J Life, vol.23 #1 (Sept./Oct., 1955): 21-24.

BIOGRAPHIES AND MEMOIRS

Biographies, Individuals

Tosya Alterman

3811. Biderman, I. M.: "Tosya Alterman 1910-1943: Heroine of the Warsaw Ghetto." J Fr, vol.34 #4 (April, 1967): 17-21.

Gabriel Ardosh

3812. Erez, D.: "Gabriel Ardosh - the Boy Poet." YVB, #12 (Dec., 1962): 27-28.

Leo Baeck

3813. Baker, Leonard: Days of Sorrow and Pain: Leo Baeck and the Berlin Jews [New York: Macmillan, 1978]

Biography of Leo Baeck including a positive assessment of his activities during World War II. Based on extensive written documentation and one hundred oral interviews.

3814. Ball-Kaduri, Kurt J.: "Leo Baeck and Contemporary History." YVS, vol.6 (1967): 121-130.

3815. Bieber, Hugo: "A Brave Liberal Voice." Lib Jud, vol. 11 #8 (Dec., 1943): 10-15.

3816. Gruenwald, Max: "Leo Baeck: Witness and Judge." Judaism, vol.6 #3 (Summer,1957): 195-201.

3817. Katz, Label A.: "Why Dr. Leo Baeck Refused U. S. Offer to Rescue Him from Nazis in 1939: A Footnote to History." NJM, vol.79 #2 (Oct., 1964): 7, 18.

3818. Meyer, Michael A.: "Leo Baeck - Upon His Tenth Anniversary." CCARJ, vol.13 #7 (Oct., 1966): 5-9.

3819. Shulman, Charles: "Leo Baeck." J Sp, vol.22 #1 (Jan., 1957): 13-16.

3820. Sichel, F.: "The Rabbi Who Stood Up to the Nazis." J Digest, vol.19 #6 (March, 1974): 76-80.

3821. Simon, Ernst: "Comments on the Article on the Late Rabbi Baeck." YVS, vol.6 (1967): 131-134.

Meier Balaban

3822. Bauminger, Arieh L.: "Meir Balaban: From Galicia to the Warsaw Ghetto." Forum, #30/31 (1978): 115-120.

3823. Zigler, F.: "In Memory of Professor Meyer Balaban." YVB, #2 (Dec., 1957): 15.

Andre Biss

3824. Heiman, Leo: "The Man Who Fooled Eichmann." NJM, vol. 75 #2 (Oct., 1960): 7, 11.

Leon Blum

3825. Gunther, John: "Leon Blum: A Man." Menorah, vol.25 #1 (Jan./March, 1937): 33-42.

3826. Joll, James: "Leon Blum." Recon, vol.24 #17 (Dec. 26, 1958): 6-14.

Martin Buber

3827. Simon, Ernst: "Martin Buber and German Jewry." LBIYB, vol.3 (1958): 13-39.

3828. Wolf, Ernest M.: "Martin Buber and German Jewry: Prophet and Teacher to a Generation in Catastrophe." Judaism, vol.1 #4 (Oct., 1952): 346-352.

Kadmi Isaac Cohen

3829. Szajkowski, Zosa: "Incident at Compiegne." Con Jud, vol.21 #2 (Win., 1967): 27-33.

Simon Dubnow

3830. Levenberg, S.: "Simon Dubnow: Historian of Russian Jewry." SJA, vol.12 #1 (Feb., 1982): 3-18.

3831. ___: "35 Years Since the Death of Simon Dubnow." J Fr, vol.43 #9 (Nov., 1976): 20-25.

3832. Rappaport, S.: "Dubnow: Historian, Thinker, Martyr." J Affairs, vol.15 #3 (March, 1960): 18-22.

Anne Frank

3833. de Jong, L.: "The Girl Who Was Anne Frank." Readers Digest, vol.74 #426 (Oct., 1957): 115-120.

3834. Puner, Morton: "The Mission of Otto Frank." ADL Bul, vol.16 #4 (April, 1954): 4-5.

3835. Schnabel, Ernst: "A Tragedy Revealed: Heroine´s Last Days." Life, vol.45 #7 (Aug. 18, 1958): 78-90.

Abraham Gepner

3836. Lichten, Joseph: "One of the Just: Abraham Gepner." Polish Rev, vol.14 #1 (Win., 1969): 40-52.

Uri Zvi Greenberg

3837. Alter, Robert: "A Poet of the Holocaust." Com, vol.56 #5 (Nov., 1973): 57-63.

Anna Ilukevitch

3838. Fuerst, Dorothy: "Anna Ilukevitch: Heroine in Riga." M&R, vol.8 #3 (Jan./Feb., 1982): 10.

Yitzhak Katzenelson

3839. Frank, M. Z.: "Yitzhak Katzenelson, Martyred Poet." J Fr, vol.30 #9 (Oct., 1963): 15-19.

A. Johanna Koenig

3840. Renbauld, Franziska: "Alma Johanna Koenig: Voice from the Holocaust." Eur Jud, vol.14 #2 (Win., 1980/1981): 14-19.

Janusz Korczak

3841. Arnon, J.: "The Passion of Janusz Korczak." Mid, vol. 19 #5 (May, 1973): 32-53.

3842. Czapska, Maria (A. Sinai, transl.): "The Doctor Who Died with the Ghetto Children: Janusz Korczak, Humanitarian, Teacher and Hero." J Digest, vol.8 #7 (April, 1963): 6-10.

3843. Frost, Shimon: "Janusz Korczak: Friend of Children and Martyr for Their Cause." The Principal, vol.24 #7 (March, 1979): 1-6.

3844. ___: "Janusz Korczak: His Life and Work." J Life, vol.33 #2 (Win., 1963): 89-96.

3845. Lichten, Joseph L.: "Defiant Martyr of the Warsaw Ghetto." ADL Bul, vol.20 #4 (April, 1963): 3, 7.

3846. Newerly, Igor (Ch. Cienkalska, transl.): "Crushed Lives." Poland, #9/133 (Sept., 1965): 28b-31.

3847. ___: "Janusz Korczak." Poland, #3-4/31-32 (1957): 24, 26.

3848. Perlis, Yitzhak: "Janusz Korczak." J Sp, vol.47 #4 (Win., 1982): 31, 34-37.

3849. Ringelblum, Emmanuel (Yuri Suhl, transl.): "Janusz Korczak - the Great Friend of Children." JQ, vol.9 #2 (Spr., 1962): 21-23.

3850. Rosensaft, Menahem Z.: "Janusz Korczak." Mid, vol.25 #5 (May, 1979): 53-57.

3851. Rosenthal, David: "Janusz Korczak: A Life of Ethical Nobility." J Fr, vol.45 #10 (Dec., 1978): 6-11.

3852. Samuel, Edwin: "Portrait of a Forgotten Hero: The Teacher who Outwitted the Gestapo." J Digest, vol.8 #11 (Aug., 1963): 75-80.

3853. Scharf, Rafael: "Janusz Korczak - The Man and His Time." JQ, vol.25 #2 (Sum., 1977): 36-42, 44.

3854. Stadtler, Bea: "Father of Orphans: Janusz Korczak." J Combat, vol.2 #3 (Spr., 1981): 18-19.

3855. Weingarten, Yerachmiel: "Janusz Korczak - Living Legend of Warsaw." CJCh, vol.32 #30 (Dec. 8, 1944): 9-14.

3856. Zeitlin, Aaron (H. Rosensaft and Gertrude Hirschler, transls.): "The Last Walk of Janusz Korczak." in Janusz Korczak: Ghetto Diary, pp.7-63 <see #3714>

Stefan Lux

3857. Levani, Moshe (A. Sinai, transl.) "The Suicide of the League of Nations." J Digest, vol.12 #2 (Nov., 1966): 16-20.

Nachum Remba

3858. Suhl, Yuri: "Nachum Remba Hero of the Warsaw Ghetto." Ch J Forum, vol.23 #3 (Spr., 1965): 193-194.

Emmanuel Ringelblum

3859. Glicksman, William: "Emmanuel Ringelblum - Chronicler of the Holocaust." JQ, vol.25 #3 (Aut., 1977): 37-40.

3860. Kozhen, M.: "Immanuel Ringelblum: Before and at the Beginning of the War." YVB, #6/7 (June, 1960): 21-23.

3861 Tenenbaum, Joseph: "Diarist of the Ghetto." CW, vol. 20 #13 (March 30, 1953): 13-15.

3862. Warhaftig H.: "Emmanuel Ringelblum: Hero as Teacher." M&R, vol.11 #2 (Nov./Dec., 1984): 7, 14.

Isaac Rubenstein

3863. Krell, I.: "A Hero of the Warsaw Ghetto." J Mirror, vol.1 #6 (Feb./March, 1943): 13-16.

Yitzhok Schipper

3864. Rosenthal, David: "Dr. Yitzhok Schipper." J Fr, vol. 41 #4 (April, 1974): 5-10.

Rabbi A. Shapira

3865. Rothkoff, Aaron: "The Last Rabbi of Kovno." Ortho J Life, vol.35 #4 (March/April, 1968): 35-40.

Wladislaw Szlengel

3866. Ringelblum, Emmanuel (Yuri Suhl, transl.): "Wladislaw Szlengel, the Poet of the Ghetto." J Currents, vol.17 #4 (April, 1963): 30-33.

Elchonon Wasserman

3867. Rothkoff, Aaron: "Rav Elchonon Wasserman." Ortho J Life, vol.39 #2 (April, 1972): 38-44. * On the Baranowicze Rosh Yeshiva, killed by the Nazis.

Michael Dov Wiesmandel

3868. Fuerst, D.: "The Heroic Story of Rabbi Weissmandel." M&R, vol.7 #4 (March/April, 1981): 6, 13.

Hillel Zeitlin

3869. Frimer, Norman: "A Vignette of Rabbi Hillel Zeitlin and the Holocaust." Tradition, vol.15 #1/2 (Spr./Sum., 1975): 80-88.

Menahem Ziemba

3870. Elfenbein, Israel: "Menahem Ziemba of Praga 1882-1943." Judaism, vol.7 #4 (Fall, 1958): 345-352.

3871. Rothkoff, Aaron: "Rabbi Menachem Ziemba of Warsaw." Ortho J Life, vol.37 #2 (Nov./Dec., 1969): 41-46.

Israel Zinberg

3872. Richards, Bernard G.: "A Tragic Footnote to History." CW, vol.10 #11 (March 12, 1943): 9-10.

Stefan Zweig

3873. Mann, Klaus: "Stefan Zweig." FW, vol.2 #3 (April, 1942): 274-276.

Biographies, Varia

3874. Alstat, Philip R.: "The Nun who Returned to Judaism." J Digest, vol.21 #9 (June, 1976): 63-65.

3875. Baebarash, Ernest E.: "A Holocaust Hero." Kowalski: Anthology/I, pp.437-438.

3876. Berkow, Ira: "Happy Ending." Kowalski: Anthology/I, pp.334-342.

3877. Brownlow, Donald G. and John E. du Pont: Hell was My Home: Arnold Shay, Survivor of the Holocaust [West Hanover, MA: Christopher Pub. House, 1983]

3878. Clare, George: Last Waltz in Vienna: The Rise and Destruction of a Family, 1842-1942 [New York: Holt, Rinehart & Winston, 1982]

3879. Finkelstone, Joseph: "Warsaw Ghetto Boy Found Alive." J Digest, vol.24 #9 (May, 1979): 14-17.

3880. Fischer, E.: "Seven Viennese Jewish Families: Form the Ghetto to the Holocaust and Beyond." JSS, vol.42 #3/4 (Sum./Fall, 1980): 345-360.

3881. Gurdus, Luba K.: "Last Moments of a Ghetto Fighter: Meeting of Yitzhok Zuckerman and Elie Wiesel." M&R, vol.8 #3 (Jan./Feb., 1982): 5, 8.

3882. Kagan, Raya: "Four Who Were Executed." YVB, #3 (April, 1958): 16-17.

3883. Leitner, Lisl: "The Germans and the Arab Princess." JM, vol.2 #3 (June, 1948): 167-171.

3884. Steg, Martin: "Three Years in an Extermination Camp and He Lives to Tell Tale!" Rescue, vol.2 #7/8 (July/Aug., 1945): 9-10.

3885. Werner, Alfred: "Martyred German-Jewish Writers." Ch J Forum, vol.18 #2 (Win.,1959/1960): 154-163.

3886. ___: "Masters and Martyrs: Jewish Artists Who Perished in the Nazi Holocaust." JQ, vol.17 #1 (Spr., 1969): 25-27.

Memoirs

3887. Adler, Stanislav: In the Warsaw Ghetto: The Memoirs of Stanislav Adler [Jerusalem: Yad Vashem, 1982]

3888. Apitz, Bruno: "We Found the Buchenwald Boy! How a Jewish Child Survived Naked Among the Wolves." J Currents, vol.18 #7 (July/Aug., 1964): 16-18.

3889. Arad, Yitzhak: The Partisan: From the Valley of Death to Mount Zion [New York: Holocaust Library, 1979]

3890. Aronsfeld, C. C.: "Refugee #562 Remembers." JQ, vol. 20 #4 (Win., 1973): 23-26.

3891. Auerbach, E. P.: "Amsterdam Yom Kippur, a Holocaust Memoir." Sh´ma, vol.11 #218 (Oct. 2, 1981): 137-138.

3892. Badt-Strauss, Bertha: "My World and How it Crashed." Menorah, vol.39 #1 (Spring, 1951): 90-100.

3893. Balshone, B.: Determined! [New York: Bloch, 1983]

3894. Barou, Noah: "Belsen Reminiscence." CW, vol.22 #15 (April 18, 1955): 4-6.

3895. Bass, Selma: "Memories of Hoppstaedten." J Sp, vol.40 #3 (Fall, 1975): 38-40.

3896. Behrend, Rahel: The Four Lives of Elsbeth Rosenfeld, as Told by her to the BBC [London: Victor Gollancz, 1964]

3897. Ben-Horin, A.: "Season of Our Liberation." J Sp, vol. 47 #1 (Spr., 1982): 23-24.

3898. Berczeller, Richard: Displaced Doctor [New York: Odyssey Press, 1964]

3899. Berger, Murray: "The Dreadful Hitler Era." Kowalski: Anthology/I, pp.552-555.

3900. Biber, Jacob: Survivors [New London, CT: Star Pub., 1982]

3901. Bitton Jackson, Livia E.: Elli: Coming of Age in the Holocaust [New York: Times Books, 1980]

3902. Breitowicz, Jacob: Through Hell to Life [New York: Shengold Pub., 1983]

3903. Buber-Neumann, M. (E. Fitzgerald, transl.): Under Two Dictators [New York: Dodd, Mead, 1949]

3904. Buch, Babette B.: Novembergeschichten. November Tales English/German [Frankfurt am Main: Ner-Tamid Verlag, 1963]

3905. Busi, Frederick: "In the Lair of the Fascist Beast." Mid, vol.19 #2 (Feb., 1973): 14-24.

3906. Charmandarian, M.: "Unforgettable Days." Con Jud, vol.28 #3 (Spr., 1974): 49-56.

3907. Chomski, Isaac: "Children in Exile." CJR, vol.4 #5 (Oct., 1941): 522-528.

3908. Cohen, Elie A.: The Abyss: A Confession [New York: W. W. Norton, 1973]

3909. Cohn, Vera: "The day I Met Anne Frank." ADL Bul, vol. 13 #6 (June, 1956): 7-8.

3910. Colebrook, Joan.: "August 1939 - a Memoir." Com, vol. 54 #1 (July, 1972): 75-85.

3911. Collis, R. and Han Hogerzeil: Straight On: Journey to Belsen and the Road Home [London, Methuen, 1947]

3912. David, Janina: A Square of Sky: The Recollection of Childhood [London: Hutchinson, 1968]

3913. Dobschiner, Johanna R.: Selected to Live: Memories [Glasgow: Pickering and Inglis, 1970]

3914. Donat, Alexander: The Holocaust Kingdom. A Memoir [New York: Holocaust Library, 1978] * Memoir of the Warsaw ghetto, including information on the revolt and Polish-Jewish relations.

3915. Donat, W. H.: "Memories of a Ghetto Child." KP, vol. 25 #2 (Dec., 1979): 18-19.

3916. Dribben, Judith S.: A Girl Called Judith Strick [New York: Cowles Press, 1970]

3917. Duncan, David D.: The Fragile Miracle of Martin Gray [New York: Abbeville Press, 1979]

3918. Dworzecki, Mark: "A Day in the Vilna Ghetto." J Sp, vol.11 #2 (Oct., 1946): 16-20.

3919. Eisner, Jack: The Survivor [New York: William Morrow, 1980] * Autobiographical account of life and death struggle in the Warsaw ghetto.

3920. Eldridge, Paul: The Homecoming: Chronicle of a Refugee Family [New York: Barnes, 1966]

3921. Engle, A.: "Through the Valey of Death." J Affairs, vol.14 #5 (May, 1959): 41-43.

3922. Feld, Merila: I Chose to Live [New York: Manor Books, 1979]

3923. Ferderber-Salz, Bertha: And the Sun Kept Shining [New York: Holocaust Library, 1980]

Memoir describing the destruction of the Jews of Galicia. The author survived and was liberated at Bergen-Belsen.

3924. Fox, R.: "The Odyssey of the Silver Torah." J Digest, vol.16 #4 (Jan., 1971): 19-22.

3925. Friedlander, Saul: "An Extraordinary Catholic Childhood." Com, vol.67 #4 (April, 1979): 57-66.

3926. ___ (H. R. Lane, transl.): When Memory Comes [New York: Farrar, Strauss & Giraux, 1979]

3927. Fryd, Norbert: "In the Anteroom of Hell." J Sp, vol. 31 #5 (May, 1966): 21-25.

3928. Gabor, Georgia M.: My Destiny: Survivor of the Holocaust [Arcadia, CA: Amen Pub., 1981]

3929. Gershon, Karen: "My Grandfather´s Death." Mid, vol.13 #10 (Oct., 1967): 33-43.

3930. ___ (ed.): We Came As Children: A Collective Autobiography [New York: Harcourt, Brace & World, 1966]

3931. Geve, Thomas: Youth in Chains [Jerusalem: Rubin Mass, 1958]

3932. Gluck, G.: "La Guardia's Sister, Eichmann's Hostage." Mid, vol.7 #1 (Win., 1961): 3-19.

3933. ___ (S. L. Shneiderman, ed.): My Story [New York: David McKay, 1961]

3934. Goldberg, I.: The Miracles Versus Tyranny [New York: Philosophical Library, 1978]

Curious but interesting memoir of the Holocaust. Interweaves the author's personal experiences, the war, and Nazi extermination policy with the author's philosophical and theological speculations.

3935. Goldberg, Michel: Namesake [New Haven, CT: Yale Univ. Press, 1982]

3936. Goldkorn, Dorka (N. Shapiro, transl.): "Memoirs of a Ghetto Fighter." J Life, vol.4 #6 (April, 1950):6-12.

3937. Goldstein, Bernard (L. Shatzkin, ed. and transl.): The Stars Bear Witness [New York: Viking Press, 1949] Also published as: Five Years in the Warsaw Ghetto [New York: Viking Press, 1961] * Chronicle of life and death of the Jewish community of Warsaw under Nazi occupation.

3938. Goldstein, Charles (E. Malkin, transl.): The Bunker [New York: Atheneum, 1973]

3939. Goldstein, H. I. (Max Rosenfeld, transl.): "Seven in a Bunker." JQ, vol.13 #1 (Spring, 1965): 35-40; #4 (Win., 1966): 36-40.

3940. Goodhill, Ruth M.: "Memoir of Yesterday." J Sp, vol. 47 #1 (Spr., 1982): 37-42.

3941. Gotfryd, B.: "Three Eggs." Mid, vol.31 #4 (April, 1985): 29-31.

3942. Grade, Chaim: "Vilna 1945 - Kol Nidre Among the Cobwebs." HM, vol.55 #2 (Oct., 1973): 8-9, 31.

3943. Gray, Martin with Max Gallo (A. White, transl.): For Those I Loved [Boston: Little, Brown & Co., 1972]

3944. Gross, N.: "Unlucky Clara." YVB, #15 (Aug., 1964): 55-60.

3945. Gruber, S. (Gertrude Hirshler, ed.): I Chose Life [New York: Shengold, 1978]

3946. Gruenwald, Max: "On the Eve of the Holocaust: Reminiscences of a German Rabbi." Con Jud, vol.32 #1 (Fall, 1975): 3-14.

3947. Grunwald, Joseph: "From the Depths of Suffering." J Sp, vol.15 #9 (Sept., 1950): 44-48.

3948. Grynberg, Henryk: Child of the Shadows [London: Vallentine, Mitchel, 1969]

3949. Guber, Rivka (comp.): Village of the Brothers: Memoirs of the Members of Kfar Ahim [New York: Shengold, 1979]

3950. Gurdus, Luba K.: The Death Train: A Personal Account of a Holocaust Survivor [New York: Holocaust Library, 1978]

Dramatic family saga of the Holocaust told in text and drawings done by the author - an eminent artist whose drawings form part of the permanent collection of the Yad Vashem museum in Jerusalem, Israel.

3951. Haas, Gerda: These I Do Remember: Fragments from the Holocaust [Freeport, ME: Cumberland Press, 1982]

3952. Hadar, Alizia with A. Kaufman: The Princess Elnusari [London: Heinemann, 1963]

3953. Hall, Mary H.: "The Nazi Doctor and His Jewish Patient." J Digest, vol.14 #2 (Nov., 1968): 39-40. * Article is based on an interview with Viktor Fraenkl.

3954. Not Used.

3955. Hart, Kitty: I Am Alive [New York: Coward-McCann, 1960]

3956. Hauer, Mordecai M.: "Reminiscences of a Survivor." JH, vol.6 #4 (Spr., 1964): 54-56. * On his meeting with Eichmann in Slovakia.

3957. Herman, I.: "Mother Finds Her Son Thrown Out of Transport." HM, vol.61 #7 (March, 1980): 38-42.

3958. Herzberg, Arno: "Thoughts of a Survivor." J Sp, vol. 32 #2 Feb., 1967): 10-11.

3959. Herzig, Jakub: The Wrecked Life: The War Story of a Physician [New York: Vantage Press, 1963]

3960. Hilsenrad, Helen: Brown Was the Danube: A Memoir of Hitler´s Vienna [New York: Thomas A. Yoseloff, 1966]

3961. Hoffman, Judy: Joseph and Me: In the Days of the Holocaust [New York: Ktav, 1979]

3962. Horbach, Michael (N. Watkins, transl.): Out of the Night [London: Vallentine, Mitchell, 1967]

3963. Hurwitz, Ruth S.: "The Emigres." Menorah, vol.44 #1/2 (Spr./Sum., 1956): 95-114.

3964. Hyams, J.: A Field of Buttercups [Engelwood Cliffs, NJ: Prentice-Hall, 1968]

3965. Itzkowitz, Nili: "An Event which Left a Profound Impression on Me." YVS, vol.12 (Dec., 1962): 70-71.

3966. Izbicki, John: The Naked Heroine: The Story of Lydia Lova [London: Spearman, 1963]

3967. Janta, Alexander: I Lied to Live: A Year as a German Family Slave [New York: Roy Pub., 1944]

3968. Jurman, Ezra: "A Survivor´s View." JQ, vol.14 #1 (Spr., 1966): 15-16.

3969. Kahn, Leon with Marjorie Morris: No Time to Mourn: A True Story of a Jewish Partisan Fighter [Vancouver: Laurelton Press, 1978]

3970. ___: "No Time to Mourn - Partisan, July-October, 1943." Kowalski: Anthology/I, pp.344-357.

3971. Kalnoky, Ingeborg with I. Herisko: The Guest House: The Witnesses at Nuremberg: A Memoir [Indianapolis, IN: Bobbs-Merrill, 1974]

3972. Kariv, Avraham: Lithuania Land of My Birth [New York: Herzl Press, 1967]

3973. Kats, Elizabeth: Child of the Holocaust [London: Collins, 1979]

3974. Katz, Josef (H. Reach, transl.): One Who Came Back: The Diary of a Jewish Survivor [New York: Herzl Press, 1973]

3975. Klein, Gerda W.: All But My Life [New York: Hill and Wang, 1957]

3976. Koehn, Ilse: Mischling, Second Degree [New York: Bantam Books, 1978]

3977. Kohn, Nahum and H. Roiter: A Voice from the Forest: Memoirs of a Jewish Partisan [New York: Holocaust Library, 1980]

Memoir of a Jewish partisan fighter in the forests of Volhynia. The author fought with the Medvedev unit of Soviet partisans near Kovno.

3978. Kohner, Hanna and Walter: Hanna and Walter: A Love Story [New York: Random House, 1984]

3979. Kolatch, Mollie: "A Chronicle for My Children." J Sp, vol.12 #5 (March, 1947): 29-30. * On the destruction of Jewish life in Krzeszow.

3980. Korczak, Ruszka: "A Hashomer Hatzair Pesach in Vilna Ghetto." IH, vol.21 #4/5 (May/June, 1973): 15-16.

3981. Korenblit, M and K. Janger: Until We Meet Again: A True Story of Love and War, Seperation and Reunion [New York: Putnam, 1983]

3982. Krantz, Morris with L. Auster: Hitler's Death March [New York: Zebra Books, 1978]

Memoir by a survivor who was hidden by Polish neighbors and eventually joined the partisans. Mr. Krantz, who witnessed the slaughter of his immediate family, rose to officer's rank in the Soviet Army. He now lives in the United States.

3983. Kressel, G.: "A Path Through a Sea of Tears." YVS, vol. 5 (1963): 371-386.

3984. Kronstadt, H. L.: "Sixteen Hlodno Street." J Sp, vol. 41 #2 (Sum., 1976): 49-52.

3985. Kubar, Z. S.: "I Survived." J Sp, vol.44 #3 (Fall, 1979): 18-20.

3986. Kuper, Jack: Child of the Holocaust [Garden City, NY: Doubleday, 1968]

3987. Kurzweil, A.: "The Secret Hidden in My Family Portrait." KP, vol.23 #12 (Oct., 1977): 6-8.

3988. Kvam, Ragnar (O. Reinert, transl.): "Among the Hundred Survivors from Auschwitz." Judaism, vol.28 #3 (Sum., 1979): 283-292.

3989. Kviatkovska, Reeva (M. Minders, transl.): "Between Two Rations (Memoirs of the Lodz Ghetto)." J Sp, vol. 13 #11 (Sept., 1948): 24-28.

3990. Lazar, Arnold: "Reminiscences from Fascist Slovakia." YVB, #18 (April, 1966): 17-25.

3991. Leitner, Isabella (I. A. Leitner, ed.): Fragments of Isabella: A Memoir of Auschwitz [New York: Thomas Y. Crowell, Pub., 1978]

3992. Lerner, Lily Gluck with Sandra L. Stuart: The Silence [Secaucus, NJ: Lyle Stuart, 1980]

3993. Lesnik, Celia: "A Child Alone in a World at War." Viewpoints, vol.8 #1 (Sum., 1973): 35-49.

3994. Level, Hildegard: "Memory of fear." Am Heb, vol.158 #16 (Aug. 13, 1948): 7.

3995. Levi, Primo: The Periodic Table [New York: Schocken, 1984]

3996. ___ (S. Woolf, transl.): The Reawakening [New York: Atlantic Monthly Press Book, 1963] Also published as: The Truce: A Survivor´s Journey Home from Auschwitz [London: The Bodley Head, 1963]

3997. Lichtiger, Joshua: The Odyssey of a Jew [New York: Vantage Press, 1979]

3998. Lind, Jakov: Counting My Steps: An Autobiography [New York: Macmillan, 1969]

3999. Lipson, Alfred: "The Blum Project." Mid, vol.29 #8 (Oct., 1983): 28-31.

4000. ___: "The Gamble that Saved Thirty-Five." Mid, vol.31 #4 (April, 1985): 31-35.

4001. Lubetkin, Zivia: "The Warsaw Ghetto's Final Hours." IH, vol.2 #4 (April, 1954): 8-10.

4002. Mandelstam, N. (M. Hayward, transl.): Hope Against Hope [New York: Atheneum, 1970]

4003. Margolius-Kovaly, Heda: "From Auschwitz to Prague - A Memoir." Com, vol.54 #6 (Dec., 1972): 47-53.

4004. Meier, Maurice (J. Kurtz, transl.): Refuge New York: W. W. Norton, 1962]

4005. Melchior, Marcus: A Rabbi Remembers [Secaucus, NJ: Lyle Stuart, 1968]

4006. Mermelstein, Mel: By Bread Alone: The Story of A-4685 [Los Angeles, CA: Crescent Pub., 1979]

4007. Michelson, Frida (Wolf Goodman, transl.): I Survived Rumbuli [New York: Holocaust Library, 1979]

Memoir-history of the destruction of Latvian Jewry under the Nazis. Focuses on life and death in the Rumbuli concentration camp which was located near Riga.

4008. Minco, Marga (Roy Edwards, transl.): Bitter Herbs: A Little Chronicle [New York: Oxford Univ. Press, 1960]

4009. ___: "My Mother's Village." J Affairs, vol.16 #11 (Nov., 1961): 30-35.

4010. Newman, J.: "I Remember Pressburg." J Sp, vol.29 #6 (June, 1964): 13-15.

4011. Nordon, Haskel: The Education of a Polish Jew: A Physician's War Memoirs [New York: Grossman Press, 1982]

4012. Pawlowicz, Sala with Kevin Klose: I Will Survive [New York: Norton Books, 1962]

4013. Pekier, Alter: From Kletzk to Siberia [Brooklyn, NY: Mesorah Publications, 1985]

4014. Petuchowski, Elizabeth: "Schooldays in Naziland." J Sp, vol.28 #4 (April, 1963): 21-23.

4015. Pilon, Juliana G.: Notes from the Other Side of Night [South Bend, IN: Regnery/Gateway, 1979]

4016. Pinkus, Oscar: The House of Ashes [New York: World Pub., 1964] * Details Nazi Atrocities and decries the apathetic stand of the Polish underground.

4017. Pisar, Samuel: Of Blood and Hope [Boston: Little, Brown and Co., 1981]

4018. Podhorizer-Sandel, E.: "A Book of Memories." Poland, #4/140 (April, 1966): 19-20.

4019. Postmantier, Harry: The Last of the Numbered Men: A Memoir of the Holocaust [New York: Vantage, 1984]

4020. Praeger, Moshe: "Five Yom Kippur Stories." ADL Bul, vol.35 #8 (Oct., 1978): 4-5.

4021. Putrament, J. (R. Ainsztein, transl.): "September." JQ, vol.2 #4 (Spr., 1955): 28-31. * On the September 1939 Nazi invasion of Poland.

4022. Radzivilover, M.: Now or Never: A Time for Survival [New York: F. Fell Pub., 1979]

4023. Ravel, A.: "My Sister´s Keeper." J Digest, vol.18 #1 (Oct., 1972): 35-42.

4024. Reiss, Johanna: The Upstairs Room [New York: Bantam Books, 1973]

4025. Rochman, Leyb: The Pit and the Trap: A Chronicle of Survival [New York: Holocaust Library, 1983] * Memoir of survival. The author, a journalist in Warsaw before the war, survived in hiding.

4026. Roosenburg, H.: The Walls Came Tumbling Down [London: Secker & Warburg, 1957]

4027. Rubinstein, Erna: "The Night the Prisoners Prayed." J Digest, vol.5 #9 (June, 1960): 67-68.

4028. ___: The Survivor in Us All: A Memoir of the Holocaust [Hamden, CT: Archon Books, 1983]

4029. Seedo, N. M.: In the Beginning Was Fear [London: Narod Press, 1964]

4030. Segal, L.: Other People's Houses [New York: Harcourt, Brace & World, 1964]

4031. Segre, Dan V.: "My Jewish-Fascist Childhood." Jer Q, #26 (Winter, 1983): 3-21.

4032. Seiden, Othniel J.: The Survivor of Babi Yar [Denver, CO: Stonehenge Books, 1981]

4033. Sender, Toni: "I Defied the Nazis." J Mirror, vol.1 #2 (Sept., 1942): 13-16.

4034. Shalit, Levi: "The Road from Dachau." J Affairs, vol. 10 #6 (June, 1955): 4-10; #7 (July, 1955): 4-11.

4035. Shatyn, Bruno (O. E. Swan, transl.): A Private War: Surviving in Poland on False Papers, 1941-1945 [Detroit: Wayne State Univ. Press, 1985]

Memoir of a Polish Jew from Cracow who survived on false (aryan) papers. The author was able to save not only himself but also other members of his family. Shatyn also gives thumbnail sketches of those around him - Jews, Poles, and Germans. An interesting and unique memoir.

4036. Siegal, Aranka: "Childhood Memories 1939-1944." ADL Bul, vol.39 #9 (Nov., 1982): 7, 9-11.

4037. ___: Upon the Head of a Goat: A Childhood in Hungary 1939-1944 [New York: Farrar, Strauss, Giroux, 1981]

4038. Starkopf, Adam: There is Always Time to Die [New York: Holocaust Library, 1981]

Memoir of Jews who survived with false papers and who, coincidentally, were hiding near Treblinka. The book's foreword is by Yehuda Bauer.

4039. Stein, Andre: Broken Silence: Dialogues from the Edge [Toronto: Lester and Orpen Dennys, 1984]

4040. Stiffel, Frank: The Tale of the Ring: A Kadish Wainscott, NY: Pushcart Press, 1984]

Memoir of the hope and horror of the Holocaust, written by a survivor of the Warsaw ghetto, Treblinka, and Auschwitz. The book is based on diaries the author kept during his captivity.

4041. Stone, A.: "The Last Years of German Jewry: One Man Reminisces." Recon, vol.45 #1 (March, 1979): 7-12.

4042. ___: "Reminiscences of the Last Years of German Jewry." J Digest, vol.25 #2 (Oct., 1979): 50-54.

4043. ___: "They Killed Dad in Auschwitz." Recon, vol.46 #3 (May, 1980): 21-24.

4044. Syrkin, Marie (ed.): "The Story of Helen (in her own words)." J Fr, vol.32 #5 (June, 1965): 12-17.

4045. Szenes, Katherine: "On the Threshold of Liberation - Reminiscences." YVS, vol.8 (1970): 197-126.

4046. Tec, Nechama: Dry Tears: The Story of a Lost Childhood [Westport, CT: Wildcat Pub., 1982]

4047. Temchin, Michael: The Witch Doctor: Memoirs of a Partisan [New York: Holocaust Library, 1983] Excerpted in Kowalski: Anthology/I, pp.202-217.

Memoir of Lt. Colonel Michael Temchin a medical doctor and one of the commanders of the Union of Jewish Partisans in Eastern Poland.

4048. Thorne, Leon: Out of the Ashes: The Story of a Survivor [New York: Rosebern Press, 1961]

4049. Torberg, Friedrich: "From Bacherach to Buchenwald." J Fr, vol.15 #3 (March, 1948): 52-54.

4050. Ungar, Andre: "Hungarian Memories." J Sp, vol.24 #6 (June, 1959): 10-14; #8 (Oct., 1959): 21-24.

4051. Unsdorfer, S. B.: "Tisha B´Av, 1942." Ortho J Life, vol.20 #6 (July/Aug., 1953): 22-23.

4052. ___: "When Eichmann Came: A Personal Experience." Ortho J Life, vol.28 #2 (Dec., 1960): 22-24.

4053. ___: The Yellow Star [New York: Th. Yoseloff, 1961]

Memoir of a survivor from Czechoslovakia. Includes first hand information on the Weismandel-Fleischman negotiations with Wisliczeni and other rescue efforts during the spring and summer of 1944.

4054. Vasileva, N. S.: "On the Catastrophe of the Thracian Jews: Recollection." YVS, vol.3 (1959): 295-302.

4055. Veffer, Sara: Hidden for a Thousand Days [Toronto: The Reyrson Press, 1960]

4056. Vida, Amy: "Sight of Dirty Dishes." J Digest, vol.11 #9 (June, 1966): 36-40.

4057. ___: "Sing-Jew-Sing." J Digest, vol.17 #5 (Jan., 1972): 28-30.

4058. Vrba, Rudolf and Alan Bestig: I Cannot Forgive [New York: Grove Press, 1964]

4059. Wander, Fred: "Joschko and His Brothers." J Sp, vol. 42 #4 (Winter, 1977): 26-29.

4060. Weinberg, W.: "A Vision of Bergen Belsen." JRJ, vol. 25 #4 (Fall, 1978): 25-27.

4061. ___: "Why I Did Not Leave Nazi Germany in Time." Ch Century, vol.99 #14 (April 21, 1982): 478-481

4062. Weinstein, Frida S.: Hidden Childhood [New York: Hill and Wang, 1985]

4063. Weinstein, Mala: "Memories from the Time of the Auschwitz Revolt." YVB, #17 (Dec., 1965): 53-55.

4064. Weinstock, Earl with Herbert Wilner: The Seven Years [New York: E. P. Dutton, 1959]

4065. Weiss, Reska: "I Was Buried Alive." J Affairs, vol.14 #4 (April, 1959): 35-39.

4066. ___: Journey Through Hell: A Woman´s Account of her Experiences at the Hands of the Nazis [London: Valentine-Mitchell, 1961]

4067. Werner, Alfred: "Before the Flood." J Fr, vol.27 #8 (Aug., 1960): 16-22.

4068. ___: "Ostjuden in Vienna." Polish Jew, vol.2 #5 (Feb., 1942): 4-5, 7.

4069. White-Beck, Valerie: "I Worked for Adolf Eichmann: A First Hand Report by a Czech Refugee." J Digest, vol. 7 #5 (Feb., 1962): 1-10.

4070. Wiechert, Ernst (Ursula Stechow, transl.): The Forest of the Dead [New York: Greenberg Publishers, 1947]

4071. Wiesel, Elie: "An Evening Guest." CBW, vol.33 #7 (April 4, 1966): 11-13.

4072. ___: "The Death of My Father." J Digest, vol.7 #4 (Jan., 1962): 68-80.

4073. ___: "My Teacher." Con Jud, vol.18 #4 (Sum., 1964): 63-66.

4074. ___ (S. Rodway, transl.): Night [New York: Hill and Wang, 1960]

Novelized autobiography of a young Hungarian Jew´s experiences at Auschwitz and Mauthausen. Wiesel was instrumental in bringing the Holocaust to the attention of audiences in the United States, Israel, and Europe.

4075. Wiesenthal, S. (C. Hutter, transl.): Max and Helen: A Remarkable True Love Story [New York: William Morrow, 1982]

4076. Winkler, Ernst: Four Years of Nazi Torture [New York: Appleton-Century, 1942]

4077. Wolf, Jacqueline: Take Care of Josette: A Memoir in Defense of Occupied France [New York: Franklin Watts, 1981]

4078. Zar, Rose: In the Mouth of the Wolf [Philadelphia: J. P. S., 1983]

4079. Zyskind, Sara: Stolen Years [Minneapolis, MN.: Lerner Publications, 1981]

11

Resistance

JEWISH RESISTANCE

The Question of Jewish Resistance

4080. Ainsztein, Reuben: "Jewish Cowardice." J Sp, vol.37 #8 (Oct., 1972): 7-10.

4081. ___: "The Sheep had Fangs." JOMER, vol.22 #12 (March 23, 1973): 18-19; #13 (March 30, 1973): 22-23; #14 (April 6, 1973): 18-21; #15 (April 13, 1973): 18-20; #16 (April 20, 1973): 14-15.

4082. Bettelheim, B.: "Did Anne Frank Die Needlessly? Were Concentration Camp Victims too Passive? J Digest, vol.6 #11 (Aug., 1961): 1-7.

4083. ___: "Freedom From Ghetto Thinking." Mid, vol.8 #2 (Spr., 1962): 16-25.

4084. ___: "The Ignored Lesson of Anne Frank." Harper´s, vol.221 #1326 (Nov., 1960): 45-50.

4085. Bick, Abraham: "Massada, Tel Hai, Warsaw." Hamigdal, vol.4 #5 (May, 1944): 8-9.

4086. Blumental, N.: "Accepted Ideas and Active Resistance to the Nazi Regime." YVB, #12 (Dec., 1962): 41-45.

4087. ___: "An Unwilling Reply." YVB, #2 (Dec., 1957): 6.

4088. ___: "Sources for the Study of Jewish Resistance." Y/V: Resistance, pp.46-59.

4089. Boetsch, J.: "Hide and Seek with Death." J Digest, vol.1 #4 (Jan., 1956): 62-64.

4090. Braun, A. Z. and Dov Levin: "Factors and Motivations in Jewish Resistance." YVB, #2 (Dec., 1957): 4-5. <see #4087>

4091. Daube, D.: Collaboration with Tyranny in Rabbinical Law [London: Oxford Univ. Press, 1965]

4092. Davies, Raymond A.: "Only Those Who Fought the Nazis Survived." Today, vol.1 #2 (Dec., 1944): 8-9.

4093. Dawidowicz, Lucy S.: "Resistance: A Doomed Struggle." Dawidowicz: Presence, pp.280-288.

4094. Donat, Alexander: Jewish Resistance [New York: Holt, Rinehart and Winston, 1965] Excerpted in Friedlander: Whirlwind, pp.50-67.

Somewhat apologetic review of the historiography of Jewish resistance. Attempts to answer the accusations made by authors such as Raul Hilberg, Bruno Bettelheim, and especially Hannah Arendt. Contains useful information.

4095. Edelheit, Abraham J.: "40 Years Later: Some Thoughts on Jewish Resistance During the Holocaust." Shofar, vol.2 #4 (Sum., 1984): 23-27.

4096. Efraykin, Israel: "Notes on Jewish Martyrdom." J Sp, vol.14 #6 (April, 1949): 15, 17, 19.

4097. Ehrenburg, Ilya: "Front Line or Ghetto." J Survey, vol.2 #3 (July, 1942): 28-29.

4098. Esh, Shaul: "The Dignity of the Destroyed: Towards a Definition of the Period of the Holocaust." Judaism, vol.12 #2 (Spr., 1962): 99-111. Also in Gutman: Catastrophe, pp.346-366.

Attempt to define the Jewish response to Nazi persecution. Especially important for Esh´s definitions of key terms such as resistance, Kiddush ha´Shem (martyrdom), and Kiddush ha´Hayim (sanctification of life).

4099. Feinberg, N.: "Jewish Political Activities Against the Nazi Regime in the Years 1933-1939." Y/V: Resistance, pp.74-94.

4100. Feingold, Henry L.: "Some Thoughts on the Resistance Question." Recon, vol.44 #14 (May, 1978): 7-11.

4101. Foxman, A. H.: "The Holocaust Years: Was There Jewish Resistance?" ADL Bul, vol.31 #4 (April, 1974): 1-2.

4102. ___: "On Resistance." Chartock: Society, pp.94-99.

4103. ___: "Resistance - The Few Against the Many." Pilch: Catastrophe, pp.87-142; Kowalski: Anthology/I, pp.86-105

4104. Friedman, Philip: "Jewish Reaction to Nazism." J Fr, vol.17 #9 (Sept., 1950): 20-24.

4105. ___: "Jewish Resistance to Nazism." Friedman: Roads, pp.387-408.

4106. ___: "Jewish Resistance to Nazism: Its Forms and Aspects." De Launay: ERM/I, pp.195-214.

4107. Goldmann, N.: "Jewish Heroism in Siege (Twenty Years After the Ghetto Revolts)." Dispersion, #3 (Winter, 1963/1964): 5-9.

4108. ___: "Jewish Heroism Under Siege." IH, vol.12 #4 (April, 1964): 11-14.

4109. Goldschmidt, J.: "Martyrdom and Heroism." Ortho J Life, vol.29 #1 (Oct., 1961): 38-46.

4110. Gottfarstein, Yosef: "Kiddush Hashem Over the Ages and its Uniqueness in the Holocaust Period." Y/V: Resistance, pp.453-482.

4111. Gottlieb, R. S. and M. Liebling: "Breaking the Silence: Need to Relate Jewish Resistance in the Holocaust." M&R, vol.7 #2 (Nov./Dec., 1980): 4, 6.

4112. Haft, Cynthia J.: "Dimensions of Heroism." M&R, vol.6 #1 (Sept./Oct., 1979): 10-11.

4113. ___: "The Other side of the Holocaust." Sh´ma, vol.5 #92 (April 18, 1975): 250-252.

4114. Halperin, Irving: "Spiritual Resistance in Holocaust Literature." YVS, vol.7 (1968): 75-82.

4115. Handlin, Oscar: "Jewish Resistance to the Nazis." Com, vol.34 #5 (Nov., 1962): 398-405.

4116. Hausner, Gideon: "Historic Miracle." Dimensions, vol.1 (Spr., 1967): 5-10.

4117. ___: "They Fought without Hope: New Light on the Jewish Resistance in Nazi Europe." J Digest, vol.13 #2 (Nov., 1967): 21-27.

4118. Hilberg, Raul: "Guerrilla Warfare." Korman: Hunter, pp.231-234.

4119. Holtz, Abraham: "Kiddush and Hillul Hashem." Judaism, vol.10 #4 (Fall, 1961): 360-367.

4120. Horowitz, L.: "Can We Judge the Victims?" Focus, vol. 3 #5/6 (Spr./Sum., 1980): 38-39, 41, 44.

4121. "How Jews Defied Their Persecutors: Conflicting Evidence." WLB, vol.16 #3 (Sum., 1962): 51.

4122. Jurman, Ezra: "A Survivor´s View." JQ, vol.14 #1 (Spr., 1966): 15-16.

4123. Kahn, Lothar: "The Holocaust: Missed Opportunities." J Sp, vol.48 #1 (Spr., 1983): 13-15 * Questions why Polish Jewry was so ill-prepared.

4124. Kaplan, S. D.: "Jews, Tradition and Resistance. A Discussion." J Currents, vol.16 #2 (Feb., 1962): 30-35; #4 (April,1962): 31-33; #5 (May,1962): 28-31; #6 (June, 1962): 29-32; #7 (July/Aug., 1962): 28-30; #8 (Sept., 1962): 31.

4125. Karpf, Ruth and Judson L. Teller: "The Jews Fight Back." Am Mercury, vol.58 #246 (June, 1944): 698-703.

4126. Korczak, Ruszka: "We Will Not Die Like Sheep: Flames Out of Ashes." IH, vol.15 #4 (April, 1967): 11-16.

4127. Krakowski, Shmuel: "The Opposition to the Judenraete by the Jewish Armed Resistance." G/H: Patterns, pp. 191-200.

4128. Kren, G. M. and Leon Rappaport: "Resistance to the Holocaust: Reflections on the Idea and the Act." Bauer: Historical, pp.193-221.

4129. Kubovy, A. L.: Criminal State Versus Moral Society: Bettelheim to Arendt´s Rescue [Jerusalem: Yad Vashem, 1963]

4130. Kwirt, Konrad: "Problems of Jewish Resistance Historiography." LBIYB, vol.24 (1979): 37-57.

4131. Landes, Daniel: "Spiritual Responses in the Ghettos." Grobman: Genocide, pp.196-211.

4132. Lang, Berel: "Why Didn´t they Resist?" Recon, vol.41 #10 (Jan., 1976): 7-12.

4133. Lestschinsky, Jacob: "The Silent Martyrs." CW, vol.21 #10 (March 8, 1954): 13-14.

4134. Levenberg, S.: "Did the Jews Fight?: Postcript to the Eichmann Trial." JOMER, vol.11 #2 (Jan. 12, 1962): 16-17. Also in: J Digest, vol.7 #10 (July, 1962): 53-56.

4135. Lewin, Kurt: "When Facing Danger." J Fr, vol.6 #9 (Sept., 1939): 18-22. * On the question of the victims reactions to Nazi brutality.

4136. Lewis, Th. N.: "Courage was Not Enough." J Sp, vol.29 #1 (Jan., 1964): 19-20.

4137. Mark, Ber: "Problems Related to the Study of the Jewish Resistance Movement in the Second World War." YVS, vol.3 (1959) 41-66.

4138. Michel, Ernest W.: "I Chose Life: A Survivor of Auschwitz Answers Dr. Bettelheim." J Digest, vol.6 #11 (Aug., 1961): 8-14.

4139. Michel, Henri: "Jewish Will to Live." Kowalski: Anthology/I, pp.416-418.

4140. Musmanno, Michael A.: "Did the 6,000,000 Kill Themselves?" NJM, vol.78 #1 (Sept., 1963): 11, 54.

4141. Ostow, M.: "The Jewish Response to Crisis." Con Jud, vol.33 #4 (Sum., 1980): 3-25.

4142. Paucker, Arnold and Lucien Steinberg: "Some Notes on Resistance." LBIYB, vol.16 (1971): 239-248.

4143. Perlzweig, Maurice: "Were the Jews to Blame? CW, vol. 32 #17 (Dec. 27, 1965): 6-8.

4144. Porter, Jack N.: "Why Didn´t the Jews Fight Back?" Porter: Genocide, pp.83-95.

4145. Prager, Moshe (Mordecai Schreiber,transl.): Sparks of Glory [New York: Shengold, 1974]

4146. Razor, I.: "Why the German Jews Did Not Resist Hitler." J Sp, vol.5 #5 (March, 1940): 38-40.

4147. Rosenberg, Bernhard H.: "They Went Like Sheep to the Slaughter and other fictions of the Holocaust." M&R, vol.10 #2 (Nov./Dec., 1983): 4, 16.

4148. Rosenthal, Maurice: "The Murdered Are Not Guilty!" J Sp, vol.27 #3 (March, 1962): 24-27. * Author takes Hilberg to task.

4149. Sabin, Arthur J.: "Jewish Powerlessness." J Sp, vol. 42 #1 (Spring, 1977): 12-13.

4150. Saperstein, Y.: "..Like Sheep?" J Observer, vol.11 #8 (June, 1976): 12-14.

4151. Schappes, M. U.: "Resistance is the Lesson." J Life, vol.2 #6 (April, 1948): 11-14.

4152. Shabbetai, Karl: As Sheep to the Slaughter [Tel Aviv: World Assc. of the Bergen-Belsen Survivors, 1963] * Apologetic answer to young Israeli´s accusations of Jewish passivity during World War II.

4153. ___: "The Legend of Cowardice." J Sp, vol.28 #2 (Feb., 1963): 7-9.

4154. Shenhabim, I.: "Kiddush Hashem: A Digest and Reevaluation on the Basis of Halakhah and Jewish Ethics." J Fo, vol.43 #6 (June, 1960): 96-97; #7 (July, 1960): 113-114; #8 (Aug., 1960): 123-124; #9 (Sept., 1960): 136-137; #10 (Oct., 1960): 173-174; vol.44 #2 (Feb., 1961): 23. * Traces martyrdom from Biblical times to the present.

4155. Shneiderman, S. L.: "They Never Stopped Fighting." CBW, vol.32 #12 (Sept. 20, 1965): 9-11.

4156. Slonim, R.: "Did Jews Go Like Lambs to Slaughter?" J Digest, vol.27 #2 (Oct., 1981): 20-29.

4157. Smoliar, Hersh: "The Lambs Were Legend, the Wolves Were Real: A New Look at the Charge of Jewish Passivity in the Ghettoes." J Currents, vol.13 #4 (April, 1959): 7-11.

4158. Spector, Shmuel: "The Convention of the Problems of Jewish Resistance during the Period of the Holocaust." YVS, vol.7 (1968): 193-196.

4159. Steckel, Charles W.: "The Agonizing Controversy." J Sp, vol.29 #1 (Jan., 1964): 10-11. * Explores the problem of responsibility for the Holocaust.

4160. ___: "Courage and Cowardice." J Sp, vol.27 #1 (Jan., 1962): 7-10.

4161. Suhl, Yuri: "The Evidence." Suhl: They, pp.144-147.

4162. ___: "They Fought Back!" JH, vol.9 #3 (Win., 1966/67): 26-31.

4163. Trunk, Isaiah: "The Attitude of the Judenrats to the Problems of Armed Resistance Against the Nazis." Y/V: Resistance, pp.202-227; Gutman: Catastrophe, pp. 422-450.

4164. ___: "Note: Why Was There No Armed Resistance Against the Nazis in the Lodz Ghetto?" JSS, vol.43 #3/4 (Sum./Fall, 1981): 329-334.

4165. Unsdorfer, S. B.: "Resistance." Ortho J Life, vol.31 #4 (March/April, 1964): 20-25.

4166. Weiss-Rosmarin, Trude: "Heroism and Martyrdom." J Sp, Vol.38 #3 (March, 1973): 2-4.

4167. ___: "Strategist of Hindsight." J Sp, vol.28 #6 (June, 1963): 3-6. * Critique of Bettelheim.

4168. ___: "Survival and Guilt." J Sp, vol.27 #1 (Jan., 1962): 3-4. * Responsibility is that of Nazis, not the victims; a refutation of Hilberg.

4169. Werner, Alfred: "The Trial of the Jewish Soul." CW, vol.10 #6 (Feb. 5, 1943): 7-9. * Psychological reaction of Jews under Nazis.

4170. Wiesel, Elie: "Why So Little Resistance?" Chartock: Society, pp.197-199.

4171. Yahil, Leni: "Jewish Resistance - An Examination of Active and Passive Forms of Jewish Survival in the Holocaust Period." Y/V: Resistance, pp.35-46.

4172. Yefroikin, Israel (A. Sinai, transl.): "The Lie of Jewish Cowardice." J Digest, vol.2 #6 (March, 1957): 17-20.

4173. Zuker, Shimon (Gertrude Hirschler, ed. and transl.): The Unconquerable Spirit [New York: Mesorah, 1980]

Survey of Jewish spiritual resistance during the Nazi era. Based primarily on vignettes of how religious Jews related to Nazi persecution.

Overviews

4174. Ainsztein, Reuben: Jewish Resistance in Nazi-Occupied Eastern Europe, with a Historical Survey of the Jew as a Fighter and Soldier in the Diaspora [New York: Barnes & Noble, 1974]

Massively documented study giving the lie to the idea of Jewish cowardice. The book is marred, however, by errors of methodology and research which weaken the author's arguments. The section on the Warsaw Ghetto has also been published seperately <see #4376>

4175. Arad, Yitzhak: "Jewish Armed Resistance in Eastern Europe: Its Characteristics and Problems." Gutman: Catastrophe, pp.490-517.

4176. Arendt, Hannah: "New Leaders Arise in Europe." New Currents, vol.2 #4 (April, 1944): 13-14.

4177. Barkai, Meyer (ed. and transl.): The Fighting Ghettos [Philadelphia: J. B. Lippincott, 1962] * Authorized translation and abridgement of Y. Zuckerman et al (ed.) Sefer Milhamot Hagetaot.

4178. Bauer, Y.: "The Facts About the Jewish Resistance." J Digest, vol.15 #4 (Jan., 1970): 65-70.

4179. ___: "Jewish Resistance: Fact or Fiction." JH, vol.10 #4 (Spring, 1968): 13-21.

4180. ___: "Resistance During the Holocaust." J Sp, vol.47 #2 (Summer, 1982): 44-48.

4181. ___: "They Chose Life: By Force of Arms." Kowalski: Anthology/I, pp.44-52.

4182. ___: They Chose Life: Jewish Resistance in the Holocaust [New York: Am. Jewish Comm., 1973] Excerpted in J Digest, vol.19 #6 (March, 1974): 14-20.

4183. Ben-Shlomo, Z. and D. Sonin: "Resistance in World War II: The Forgotten Army." HM, vol.62 #7 (March, 1981): 6-7, 34-35, 37-39.

4184. "The Bitter Saga of the Jewish Partisans." IH, vol.12 #5 (May, 1964): 8-16; #6 (June/July, 1964): 22-25.

4185. Blumenthal, N.: "Jewish Resistance Under the Nazis." YVB, #22 (May, 1968): 8-13.

4186. "Chalutzim in Europe Go Underground." Hamigdal, vol.1 #6 (May, 1941): 7-8.

4187. Cholawski, S.: "The Jewish Partisan." WZO: Heroism, pp.1-44.

4188. ___: "Jewish Partisans: Objective and Subjective Difficulties." Y/V: Resistance, pp.323-334.

4189. Conference on Manifestation of Jewish Resistance During the Holocaust: Proceedings [Jerusalem: Yad Vashem, 1971]

Papers from First Yad Vashem Historical Conference, held in Jerusalem on April 7-11, 1968. Because of the lack of a unified and systematic history of Jewish resistance the essays in the book are especially useful and interesting.

4190. Cowan, Lore: Children of the Resistance [Des Moines, IA: Meredith Press, 1969]

4191. Dobkin, Eliyahu: "Fallen Jews and Fighting Zionists." Furrows, vol.3 #2 (Dec., 1944): 16-19.

4192. Edelheit, Abraham J.: "Jewish Resistance During the Holocaust." Focus, vol.6 #3 (Spr., 1983): 31-32.

4193. Ehrenburg, I.: "Our Place." Porter: JP/I, pp.222-223.

4194. Elkins, Michael: Forged in Fury [New York: Ballantine Books, 1971]

4195. Fischer, A. J.: "Jews in the Fight Against Hitler." J Sp, vol.9 #7 (May, 1944): 23-24.

4196. Foxman, Abraham: "Resistance in the Concentration Camps." Chartock: Society, pp.192-197.

4197. ___: "Resistance within the Ghetto Walls." J Combat, vol.1 #1 (Spr., 1980): 25-28.

4198. Gallin, Martin: "Ish Hayil, the Jewish Fighting Man." J Combat, vol.1 #1 (Spr., 1980): 4-6.

4199. Glicksman, William: "Jewish Resistance in Historical Perspective." JQ, vol.23 #3 (Aut., 1975): 35-40.

4200. Goldsmith, S. J.: "The Book in the Box: A Jewish Epic of the Resistance." J Digest, vol.14 #2 (Nov., 1968): 9-12.

4201. Grobman, Alex: "Attempts at Resistance in the Camps." Grobman: Genocide, pp.243-255.

4202. "Guerrillas Worthy of the Name: The Untold Story of Jewish Resistance." JOMER, vol.23 #3 (Jan. 18, 1974): 22-24.

4203. Gutman, Y.: "The Battles of the Ghettos." Grobman: Genocide, pp.191-195.

4204. ___: "The Holocaust: Twenty Years After the Ghetto Revolts." Dispersion, #3 (Winter, 1963/1964): 27-34.

4205. ___: "Rebellions in the Camps: Three Revolts in the Face of Death." Grobman: Genocide, pp.256-260.

4206. ___: "Youth Movements in the Underground and the Ghetto Revolts." Y/V: Resistance, pp.260-284.

4207. Heiman, Leo: "The Jewish Partisans of World War II." JH, vol.5 #1 (Sum., 1962): 53-56.

4208. ___: "When Jews Fought Nazis: The Story of Jewish Partisans in World War II." J Digest, vol.8 #7 (April, 1963): 27-30.

4209. Herman, J.: "Who Were Those Soldiers Without Hope." JQ, vol.9 #2 (Spr., 1962): 10-14.

4210. Hexter, Larry: "The Fighting Jew." CW, vol.10 #2 (Jan. 8, 1943): 4-6.

4211. "Hiding with the Underground." J Comment, vol.2 #2 (Jan. 28, 1944): 4-6. Also in: CW, vol.11 #5 (Feb. 4, 1944): 10-12.

4212. Holevsky, Sh.: "In the Ghettoes and in the Forests." IH, vol.7 #4 (April, 1959): 8-13.

4213. Not Used.

4214. Justin, Dena: "How the Jews Fought Back in the Very Jaws of Death." Today, vol.1 #10 (Oct., 1945): 19-21, 32.

4215. Kermish, Joseph: "The Place of the Ghetto Revolts in the Struggle Against the Occupier." Y/V: Resistance, pp.306-323.

4216. Konischuk, Nikolai: "They Were Many." Porter: JP/I, pp.203-206.

4217. Kowalski, Isaac (ed.): Anthology on Armed Jewish Resistance, 1939-1945 [New York: Jewish Combatants Pub. House, 1984]

4218. Laska, Vera (ed.): Women in the Resistance and in the Holocaust: The Voice of Eyewitnesses [Westport, CT: Greenwood Press, 1983]

4219. Levin, Dov: "Eastern European Jews in the Partisan Ranks During World War II." Grobman: Genocide, pp. 213-217.

4220. ___: "Life and Death of Jewish Partisans." YVB, #18 (April, 1966): 41-46.

4221. Levin, Nora: "Rescue and Resistance by Jewish Youth During the Holocaust." Kowalski: Anthology/I, pp.111-124.

4222. Levine, Burton: "Jewish Partisans." J Sp, vol.48 #1 (Spr., 1983): 56-58.

4223. Michel, Henri: "Jewish Resistance." WJ, vol.16 #1 (Feb., 1973): 12-13.

4224. Poliakov, Leon: "Jewish Resistance in the West." Y/V: Resistance, pp.284-291.

4225. Porter, Jack N.: "Jewish Women in the Resistance." Kowalski: Anthology/I, pp.290-295.

4226. "Resistance." J Comment, vol.1 #6 (June 11, 1943): 1-4.

4227. Serebrenik, R.: "The Saga of Jewish Resistance." CW, vol.23 #13 (March 26, 1956): 11-12.

4228. Steinberg, Lucien (M. Hunter, transl.): Not As a Lamb [Farnborough: Saxon House, 1974] Also published as: Jews Against Hitler [New York: Gordon-Cremonesi, 1978]

Country by country survey of Jewish resistance which tries, and largely succeeds, to give lie to the canard of "sheep to the slaughter".

4229. Stone, Reca R.: Revolt in the Ghetto [Sydney, Aust.: United Emergency Committee for European Jewry, 1944]

4230. Suhl, Yuri: "Jewish Resistance With the Pen: How Jewish Writers Fought the Nazi Terror." J Currents, vol.19 #8 (Sept., 1965): 17-19.

4231. ___ (ed.): They Fought Back [New York: Crown Pub., 1967]

Anthology of studies on Jewish resistance. Some of the chapters are scholarly works, others are memoirs, still others are simple stories. All are interesting, albeit of unequal quality. Many of the essays have an apologetic air.

4232. Syrkin, Marie: Blessed is the Match: The Story of Jewish Resistance [Philadelphia: J. P. S., 1947]

Early account of the Jewish resistance against Nazism. Syrkin's is a chronicle of the horror endured and the heroism shown by European Jewry. Neither accuser nor apologist this is a classic account of the Jewish underground struggle during and immediately after World War II.

4233. Trunk, I.: "Uprising in the Camps." Barkai: Fighting, pp.193-200.

4234. Unger, Menashe: "The Jews of Europe Fight Back." New Currents, vol.2 #3 (March, 1944): 10-11, 33.

4235. Weissbrod, A.: "Partisans." Kowalski: Anthology/I, pp.576-578.

4236. Werner, Alfred: "Hitlerism's Lost Battle." CW, vol.10 #8 (Feb. 19, 1943): 7-9.

4237. World Zionist Organization: Jewish Heroism in Modern Times: A Hanukah Anthology [Jerusalem: WZO, 1966]

4238. Zbanatzki, Y.: "Talking of Friends." Porter: JP/I, pp.196-202.

Jewish and European Resistance

4239. Blumenthal, Nachman: "The Jews Fought Alone." YVB, #4/5 (Oct., 1959): 2-4.

4240. ___: "The Plight of the Jewish Partisans." YVB, #1 (April, 1957): 4-7.

4241. Borwicz, Michael: "Factors Influencing the Relations Between the General Polish Underground and the Jewish Underground." Y/V: Resistance, pp.343-351.

4242. Eck, N.: "Jewish and European Resistance." YVB, #8/9 (March, 1961): 2-5. Also in: J Sp, vol.27 #2 (Feb., 1962): 14-18.

4243. Klurman, A.: "Stages in the Organization of the Partisan Fighting." Kowalski: Anthology/I, pp.548-550.

4244. Lipscher, L.: "Jewish Participation in the Slovak Resistance Movement." SJA, vol.7 #2 (Oct.,1977):40-52.

4245. Lubetkin, Zivia: "The Polish Uprising." Kowalski: Anthology/I, pp.151-160.

4246. Michel, Henri: "Jewish Resistance and the European Resistance Movement." YVS, vol.7 (1968): 7-16. Also in Y/V: Resistance, pp.365-375.

Jewish Resistance by Country

Belgium

4247. Gutfriend, Jacob: "The Jewish Resistance Movement in Belgium." Suhl: They, pp.304-311.

4248. Steinberg, L.: "Jewish Rescue Activities in Belgium and France." Gutman: Rescue, pp. 603-615.

Bulgaria

4249. Nizani, Yaacov: "Fighter of the Jewish Underground in Bulgaria." YVB, #8/9 (1961): 35-36.

4250. Oren, Uri: "A Town Called Monastir: The Heros." Kowalski: Anthology, pp.484-489.

4251. Yulzari, Matei: "The Bulgarian Jews in the Resistance Movement." Suhl: They, pp.275-281.

Czechoslovakia

4252. Knieza, Emil F. (J. Markovic, transl.): "The Resistance of the Slovak Jews." Suhl: They, pp.176-181.

4253. Rothkirchen, Livia: "Activities of the Jewish Underground in Slovakia." YVB, #8/9 (March, 1961): 28-30.

France

4254. Ariel, J.: "French-Jewish Resistance to the Nazis." Judaism, vol.18 #3 (Sum., 1969): 299-312.

4255. ___: "Jewish Self-Defence and Resistance in France during World War II." YVS, vol.6 (1967): 221-250.

4256. Avni, Haim: "The Zionist Underground in Holland and France and the Escape to Spain." Gutman: Rescue, pp. 555-590.

4257. Garel, Georges: "The Miraculous Rescue of Children: The OSE Under the German Occupation in France, 1940-1944." Am OSE Rev, vol.5 #1/2 (Win./Spr., 1948): 30-39.

4258. Gryn, Nathaniel (A. Sinai, transl.): "Jewish Heroes of the French Underground: A Personal Account." J Digest, vol.10 #11 (Aug., 1965): 55-59.

4259. Hartanau, Charles: "Castor´s Idea." Schwarz: Root, pp.122-126.

4260. Kieval, Hillel J.: "Legality and Resistance in Vichy France: The Rescue of Jewish Children." Proceedings of the American Philosophical Society, vol.124 #5 (Oct., 1980): 339-366.

4261. Latour, A. (I. R. Ilton, transl.): Jewish Resistance in France (1940-1944) [New York: Holocaust Library, 1981]

Anecdotal history of the Jewish resistance in France. Particular focus is on the Zionist-oriented Armee Juive which fielded some 2,000 maquis in 1943-1944.

4262. Lazarus, Jacques: "The Jewish Resistance in France." Dispersion, #5/6 (Spr., 1966): 178-183.

4263. Lerner, Bernard: "Jews Led French Maquis." CJCh, vol. 33 #31 (Dec. 15, 1944): 6.

4264. Levin, Leo: "With the Maquis in France." J Horizon, vol.9 #1 (Oct., 1945): 11-15.

4265. Lissner, Abraham: "Diary of a Jewish Partisan in Paris." Suhl: They, pp.285-297.

4266. Marcus, Robert S.: "French Jews Did Their Best." CW, vol.13 #5 (Feb. 1, 1946): 8-10.

4267 Poliakov, Leon: "Jewish Resistance in France." YIVO Annual, vol.8 (1953): 252-263.

4268. Raisky, Abraham: "We Fought Back in France: A Chapter in Resistance History." Com, vol.1 #4 (Feb., 1946): 60-65.

4269. "The Resistance of the Tunisian Jews." J Comment, vol.1 #13 (Oct. 8, 1943): 3-4.

4270. Stock, Ernest: "The Maquis in Action: How 200 Jewish Boy Scouts Helped Free France." NJM, vol.60 #1 (Sept., 1945): 12.

Germany

4271. Ball-Kaduri, Kurt J.: "Did the Jews of Germany Resist." YVB, #8/9 (March, 1961): 31-32.

4272. Eschwege, Helmut: "Resistance of German Jews against the Nazi Regime." LBIYB, vol.15 (1970): 143-182.

4273. "Jews´ Defiance in Berlin. The Baum Group." WLB, vol. 15 #3 (July, 1961): 52.

4274. Josephson, Leon: "Jewish Heroes of the Pre-War Underground." J Life, vol.1 #12 (Oct., 1947): 13-15.

4275. Keller, Julius: German Jews Fought Back [New York: Vantage Press, 1979]

4276. Mark, Ber: "The Herbert Baum Group: Jewish Resistance in Germany in the Years 1937-1942." Suhl: They, pp. 55-68.

Greece

4277. Jaffe, Jean: "Greek Jews Fight On." NJM, vol.55 #7 (March, 1941): 211.

4278. Kabeli, Isaac: "Jews in the Greek Underground." Dispersion, #3 (Win., 1963/64): 21-26.

4279. ___: "The Resistance of the Greek Jews." YIVO Annual, vol.8 (1953): 281-288.

4280. Koniuchowski, Leyb: "The Revolt of the Jews of Marcinkonis." Suhl: They, pp.160-164.

Italy

4281. "Jewish Resistance in Italy." Kowalski: Anthology/I, pp.430-435.

4282. Vitale, Masimo A.: "The Destruction and Resistance of the Jews in Italy." Suhl: They, pp.298-303.

Poland

4283. "The Activities of Our Movement." GS, #30 (Oct. 15, 1944): 7-9.

4284. Alperin, Aaron: "Chapters of Glory: The Heroic Story of the Jews in Poland." Polish Jew, vol.4 #25 (Sept./ Oct., 1944): 2, 9-24 center columns.

4285. Apenszlak, Jacob and Isaac Polakiewicz: Armed Resistance by the Jews of Poland [New York: Am. Federation of Polish Jews, 1944]

4286. ___: "The Polish Jews Fight Back: The Story of the Armed Resistance of the Jews in Poland." Polish Jew, vol.4 #22 (April, 1944): 3-50.

4287. "Armed Resistance of Polish Jews." GS, #11 (May 1, 1943): 1-2.

4288. Bauminger, Aryeh: "´Chazit Dor Bnei Midbar´ Zionist Youth Movement in the Lodz Ghetto." YVB, #1 (April, 1957): 29-31.

4289. "The Fighting Hechalutz." Furrows, vol.2 #5 (March, 1944): 21-24.

4290. "The Final Struggle in the Polish Ghettos." CW, vol. 11 #12 (March 23, 1944): 5-7.

4291. Gruber, Samuel: "Memories of a Soldier." Kowalski: Anthology/I, pp.240-248.

4292. "Headquarters of the Jewish Labor Underground of Poland Reports." GS, #24 (April 15, 1944): 1-4.

4293. "The Jewish Armed Resistance Organization." GS, #29 (Oct. 1, 1944): 2-8.

4294. "The Jewish Underground Movement at Work." GS, #1 (Aug. 1, 1942): 1-2.

4295. Kantorowicz, Moshe: "Underground Work in Poland." CW, vol.9 #32 (Oct. 30, 1942): 5-6.

4296. ___: "The Uprising in the Polish Ghettos against the Nazis." J Fr, vol.35 #4 (April, 1968): 10-12.

4297. Kowarski, George: "The Jewish Underground Movement in Poland." Polish Jew, vol.3 #18 (Aug./Sept., 1943): 2-3.

4298. Krakowski, S.: The War of the Doomed: Jewish Armed Resistance in Poland, 1942-1944 [New York: Holmes and Meier, 1984]

Authoritative history of Jewish resistance in Poland. Surveys the issues from political, social, and military perspectives. Also deals with the interactions, some positive but mostly negative, between the Jewish and Polish underground movements. Extensively documented. Krakowski concludes that Jewish armed resistance was considerably larger than heretofore presumed.

4299. Kurland, Samuel: "Heroes of the Ghetto." Furrows, vol.2 #5 (March, 1944): 17-21.

4300. Lampell, Miliard: "Heroines of the Ghetto: Jewish Women Fighters of the Polish Underground." J Digest, vol.8 #7 (April, 1963): 41-54.

4301. Luderstein, M.: "No More Retreats." Barkai: Fighting, pp.156-164. * Details Jewish partisan activity around Lublin.

4302. "Manifestation of Resistance by Jewish Communities in Poland During Their Liquidation by the Nazis." G/H: Patterns, pp.148-149.

4303. Nirenstein, Albert (ed.) (D. Neiman and M. Savill, transls.): A Tower From the Enemy: Contributions to a History of Jewish Resistance in Poland [New York: Orion Press, 1959]

4304. Praeger, Moshe: "A Chasidic Underground in the Polish Ghettos." YVB, #6/7 (June, 1960): 10-12.

4305. Salsitz, Norman and Mania Salsitz: "Jews saved Cracow the Pope´s City." Kowalski: Anthology/I, pp.220-238.

4306. Sternovlitz, Motel: "What Happened Around Lublin." Barkai: Fighting, 151-155.

4307. Suhl, Yuri: "We Cannot Build on Tears: Jewish Partisan from Poland Tells of Struggle for his People." Am Heb, vol.156 #19 (Sept. 6, 1946): 4-5, 14.

4308. Tenenbaum, Joseph L.: Underground: The Story of a People [New York: Philosophical Library, 1952]

Early and now largely superseded work on the destruction and resistance of Polish Jewry. Still contains a good deal of useful material on conditions of life and resistance in the Polish ghettos.

4309. Tushnet, Leonard: "Two Doctors." J Currents, vol.16 #3 (March, 1962): 14-15.

Rumania

4310. Artzi, A.: "The Underground Activities of the Pioneer Movements in Rumania during World War II." YVB, #12 (1962): 34-41.

4311. Litani, Dora: "´Courier´, an Underground Newspaper in Transnistria: April-September 1943." YVB, #14 (March, 1964): 44-48.

4312. ___: "Halutzim of the Rumanian Hashomer Hatzair during the War." YVB, #8/9 (1961): 33-35.

Russia

4313. Arad, Yitzhak: "Jewish Family Camps in the Forests - An Original Means of Rescue." Gutman: Rescue, pp.333-353.

4314. Bar-On, Zvi: "The Jews in the Soviet Partisan Movement." YVS, vol.4 (1960): 167-190.

4315. ___: "On the Position of the Jewish Partisan in the Soviet Partisan Movement." De Launay: ERM/I, pp.215-247.

4316. Belsky, Tuvia: "Brigade in Action." Schwarz: Root, pp.112-114.

4317. ___: "Jews of the Forest." Barkai: Fighting, pp.170-183.

4318. Brand, Emmanuel: "The Forest Ablaze: A Jewish Partisan Group in the Kovpak Division." YVB, #2 (Dec., 1957): 16, 21.

4319. Eckman, Lester S. and Chaim Lazar: The Jewish Resistance [New York: Shengold, 1977]

History of Jewish resistance in Lithuania and the Western Soviet Union. Concentrates on Jewish partisan activities. The book attempts to retell and explain the story of Jewish resistance. Also includes a large number of eyewitness testimonies collected in the last 100 pages of the book. The book is part of a projected three volume series on Jewish resistance, but no other titles have appeared to date.

4320. Feodorov, A. P.: "Partis Friendship." Porter: JP/I, pp.86-92.

4321. Gaman, Shirka: "Without Fire." Porter: JP/I, pp.83-85

4322. Gildenman, M.: "We Attack a German Garrison." Barkai: Fighting, pp.184-189. * On Diada Misha.

4323. Kahanovich, Moshe: "Why No Separate Jewish Partisan Movement Was Established During World War II." YVS, vol.1 (1957): 153-168.

4324. Kaplan, Israel: "The Partisan Movement in Lithuania." J Sp, vol.31 #8 (Oct., 1966): 18-22.

4325. Kowalski, Isaac: A Secret Press in Nazi Europe: The Story of a Jewish United Partisan Organization [New York: Shengold, 1978]

Memoir-history of the United Partisan Organization of the Vilna ghetto. Also documents Jewish resistance activities. The book suffers from idiosyncratic organization but is, nonetheless, engrossing reading.

4326. Levin, Dov: Fighting Back: Lithuanian Jewry's Armed Resistance to the Nazis [New York: Holmes and Meier, 1984]

4327. Meierson, Moses: "No Surrender." Schwarz: Root, pp. 95-99.

4328. National Jewish Committee: "Resistance in Ponyatov and Trabnik." Barkai: Fighting, pp.230-231.

4329. Neshamit, Sarah: "Rescue in Lithuania During the Nazi Occupation (June 1941-August 1944)." Gutman: Rescue, pp.289-331.

4330. Osland, H.: "Remember!" Porter: JP/I, pp.61-63.

4331. "The Partisan Oath." Porter: JP/I, pp.70-71.

4332. Porter, J. N. (ed.): Jewish Partisans: A Documentary of Jewish Resistance in the Soviet Union during World War II [Lanham, MD: Univ. Press of America, 1982]

4333. Singer, L.: "Soviet Jews During and After the War of the Fatherland." Porter: JP/I, pp.220-221.

4334. Stonov, D.: "Friendship." Porter: JP/I, pp.72-82.

4335. Vershigora, Pavlo: "A Civilian Camp in the Forest." Porter: JP/I, pp.133-134.

Yugoslavia

4336. Albala, Pauline: "Our Jewish Sisters of Yugoslavia." CW, vol.10 #30 (Nov. 5, 1943): 18.

4337. Herzog, Milan L.: "Jews as Yugoslav Guerrillas." CW, vol.9 #14 (April 10, 1942): 6-7. Also in J Standard, vol.3 #11 (June 26, 1942): 6.

4338. ___: "Two Jewish Heroes of Yugoslavia." CW, vol.9 #17 (May 1, 1942): 11.

4339. Steckel, Ch. W.: "Survivors and Partisans." Kowalski: Anthology/I, pp.472-477.

The Warsaw Ghetto Uprising

Contemporary Documentation

4340. "The Battle of Ghettograd." CJCh, vol.31 #48 (April 13, 1944): 5.

4341. "The Battle of Warsaw Ghetto." Polish Jew, vol.3 #19 (Dec., 1943): 3-6.

4342. "The Battle of the Warsaw Ghetto." CW, vol.11 #1 (Jan. 7, 1944): 6-8.

4343. "The Battle of the Ghetto of Warsaw as Viewed by Polsh Clandestine Publications." GS, #17 (Nov. 1, 1943): 1-4.

4344. Bernfes, Alexander B. (ed.): The Warsaw Ghetto No Longer Exists [New York: Marshall Cavendish, 1973]

4345. Blit, Lucjan: "Who are the Heroes of the Armed Resistance in the Ghetto of Warsaw." GS, #15 (Sept. 1, 1943): 6-7.

4346. "Jews Die Proudly." J Sp, vol.9 #1 (Nov., 1943): 25-27.

4347. Karsavina, Jean: "Hostages to the Future." New Currents, vol.2 #4 (April, 1944): 4-7.

4348. "The Last Passover: The Heroes of the Battle of Warsaw." J Standard, vol.4 #52 (April 7, 1944): 4-5.

4349. "The Martyrs of the Warsaw Ghetto." Recon, vol.21 #5 (April 15, 1955): 4-5.

4350. Milton, Sybil and A. Worth (eds. and transls): The Stroop Report: The Jewish Quarter of Warsaw is No More! [New York: Pantheon Books, 1979]

4351. "On the Agenda: Death. A Document of the Jewish Resistance." Com, vol.8 #2 (Aug., 1949): 105-109.

4352. "Polish Fascist Describes the Battle of the Warsaw Ghetto." GS, #16 (Oct. 1, 1943): 2-5.

4353. "Polish Jews Continue Desperate Last Ditch Struggle Against Nazis." V/Unq, vol.1 #4 (June, 1943): 1, 7.

4354. "Revisionists in the Warsaw Ghetto Revolt." J Standard, vol.6 #38 (Dec. 28, 1945): 3.

4355. Ringelblum, Emmanuel: "The Jews Fought Back." Polish Jew, vol.5 #28 (April, 1945): 2-4.

4356. Schwarzbart, Ignacy: "Heroes of the Warsaw Ghetto." CW, vol.11 #18 (May 12, 1944): 17.

4357. "Warsaw Fights Again." GS, #28 (Sept. 1, 1944): 1-2.

4358. Wise, Stephen S.: "Jewish Heros of Warsaw." CW, vol. 10 #24 (June 25, 1943): 10-11.

4359. Zukerman, Wm.: "Aftermath of the Revolt." Lib Jud, vol.11 #3 (July, 1943): 27-32.

Historiography

4360. Blumenthal, Nachman: "New Books on the Warsaw Ghetto Uprising." YVB, #16 (Feb., 1965): 36-42.

4361. ___: "The Stroop Report, a Reliable Historical Source Despite its Distortions." YVB, #13 (Oct., 1963): 21-24.

4362. Dawidowicz, L. S.: "The Epic of the Warsaw Ghetto." Menorah, vol.38 #1 (Winter, 1950): 88-103.

4363. E. B.: "The Warsaw Ghetto Uprising Caused Anxiety among the Germans in Lodz." YVB, #13 (Oct., 1963): 39-41.

4364. Hilberg, Raul: "How They Smashed the Warsaw Ghetto Revolt: The Epic of Heroism as the Nazis Saw it." J Digest, vol.8 #7 (April, 1963): 33-37.

4365. Kermish, Joseph: "The Land of Israel in the Life of the Ghetto as Reflected in the Illegal Warsaw Ghetto Press." YVS, vol.5 (1961): 105-132.

4366. ___: "New Jewish Sources for the History of the Warsaw Ghetto Uprising." YVB, #15 (Aug., 1964): 27-33.

4367. ___: "The Oneg Shabbat Archives." YVB, #16 (Feb., 1965): 16-25.

4368. ___: "On the Underground Press in the Warsaw Ghetto." YVS, vol.1 (1957): 85-124.

4369. ___: "The Role of the Underground Press in the Warsaw Ghetto in Preparing the Ground for Armed Resistance." YVB, #8/9 (March, 1961): 9-11.

4370. ___: "The Warsaw Ghetto Uprising in the Light of a Hitherto Unpublished Official German Report." YVS, vol.9 (1973): 7-28. Also in Gutman: Catastrophe, pp. 559-581.

4371. Mark, Ber: "The Warsaw Ghetto Uprising in War and Post-War Literature." JQ, vol.5 #4/5 (Sum., 1958): 52-54.

4372. Shneiderman, S. L.: "A New Look at the Warsaw Ghetto Uprising." J Digest, vol.22 #7 (March, 1977): 22-29.

4373. Suhl, Yuri: "Falsehoods about the Warsaw Ghetto." J Currents, vol.22 #7 (July, 1968): 16-17. * A reply to charges made by Kurier Polski.

4374. Trunk, I.: "Sources of the Warsaw Ghetto Uprising." Polish Rev, vol.9 #1 (Win., 1964): 87-93.

Histories of the Uprising

4375. Ainsztein, R.: "Conquered and Betrayed: Tragedy in Warsaw´s Ghetto Battle." WLB, vol.12 #1/2 (1958): 11

4376. ___: The Warsaw Ghetto Revolt [New York: Holocaust Library, 1979] * Seperate excerpt from his Jewish Resistance <see #4174>

4377. ___: "The Warsaw Ghetto Uprising and the Poles." Mid, vol.9 #2 (June, 1963): 20-38.

4378. Bozikowski, T. (Max Rosenfeld, transl.): "Amid Crumbling Walls." J Life, vol.9 #6 (April, 1955): 7-12.

4379. ___: "April." Barkai: Fighting, pp.47-58.

4380. ___: "April 19, 1943: The Glorious, Terrible Hour." IH, vol.1 #6 (April, 1953): 15-17.

4381. Edelman, Marek: The Ghetto Fights [New York: Am. Rep. General Jewish Workers Union of Poland, 1946]

One of the earliest accounts of the Jewish resistance in Warsaw. Published in Yiddish in 1945, this edition is an official English translation. Has heavy Bundist leaning.

4382. ___: "The Last Stand." Schwarz: Root, pp.58-65.

4383. Fast, Howard: Never to Forget the Battle of the Warsaw Ghetto [New York: Jewish People´s Fraternal Book League, 1946]

4384. Felberbaum, M.: "It was Jan. 18, 1943." M&R, vol.9 #3 (Jan./Feb., 1983): 7, 9.

4385. ___: "When the Warsaw Ghetto Burned." M&R, vol.11 #4 (March/April, 1985): 6, 11.

4386. Friedman, Philip: "The Epic of the Warsaw Ghetto." ADL Bul, vol.11 #3 (March, 1954): 1-2, 7-8.

4387. Goldstein, Bernard: "Girding Our Strength." Schwarz: Root, pp.16-43.

4388. Goodman, Philip: The Warsaw Ghetto Uprising [New York: National Jewish Welfare Board, 1963]

4389. Grayek, Shalom: "Fighting At the Workshops." Schwarz: Root, pp.54-57.

4390. ___: "Remnants of the Warsaw Ghetto in the Revolt of the Poles in Warsaw." YVB, #8/9 (March, 1961): 18-19.

4391. ___: "The Teben-Schultz Section." Barkai: Fighting, pp.59-63

4392. Gutman, Yisrael: "The Genesis of the Resistance in the Warsaw Ghetto." YVS, vol.9 (1973): 29-70. Also in Bauer: Hol History, pp.72-113.

4393. ___: "Warsaw Ghetto: The Uprising Begins." IH, vol.16 #4 (April, 1968): 8-13.

4394. Halperin, A.: "Betar´s Role in the Warsaw Ghetto Uprising." Gutman: Catastrophe, pp.549-558.

4395. Hirshaut, H.: "The Sun Sets in Blood on Mila Street." M&R, vol.5 #4 (March/April, 1979): 6.

4396. Hirshaut, Julian: "Paviak Memories: The Giant of Revenge." Kowalski: Anthology/I, pp.162-170.

4397. Katzman, Jacob: The Battle of the Warsaw Ghetto [New York: Farband-Labor Zionist Order, n.d.]

4398. Kermish, Joseph: "Arms Used by the Warsaw Ghetto Fighters." YVB, #2 (April, 1958): 5-9.

4399. ___: "First Stirrings." Korman: Hunter, pp.209-230.

4400. ___: "The Ghetto's Two-Front Struggle: Prelude to the Ghetto Rising, September 1942-April 1943." YVB, #13 (Oct., 1963): 12-20.

4401. ___: "The Poles and the Warsaw Ghetto Uprising." YVB, #22 (May, 1968): 13-18.

4402. ___: "Who Organized the Revolt?" YVB, #4/5 (Oct., 1959): 4-7.

4403. Kurzman, Dan: The Bravest Battle: The Twenty-Eight Days of the Warsaw Ghetto Uprising [New York: G. P. Putnam's Sons, 1976]

4404. ___: "The Last Days of Mila 18." NJM, vol.90 #4 (Dec., 1976): 24-26.

4405. Lazar (Litai), Chaim: Muranowska 7: The Warsaw Ghetto Rising [Tel Aviv: Massada Press, 1966]

4406. Lubetkin, Z.: "How the Warsaw Ghetto Revolt Began: An Eyewitness Account by one of Its Leaders." J Digest, vol.8 #7 (April, 1963): 1-5.

4407. ___: "The Last Days of the Warsaw Ghetto." Barkai: Fighting, pp.64-87.

4408. ___: "Warsaw: The January 1943 Uprising." Barkai: Fighting, pp.32-40.

4409. Malkin, Jacob with Leo Heiman: "I Led the Sewer Rats of the Warsaw Ghetto: A Chapter from an Epic in Heroism." J Digest, vol.10 #1 (Oct., 1964): 62-68.

4410. Mark, Ber: "The Ghetto Uprising." Poland, #4/20 (1956): 20-21.

4411. ___: "How Unity Was Forged." J Life, vol.8 #6 (April, 1954): 13-15.

4412. ___: "Rubble Fighters of the Ghetto: The Uprising Did Not End with the May Battles but Continued for Weeks." J Life, vol.10 #6 (April, 1956): 16-20, 32-34.

4413. ___: "Strategy for Survival." J Life, vol.1 #6 (April, 1947): 8-9.

4414. ___: "The Unvanquished." J Life, vol.3 #6 (April, 1949): 9-12.

4415. ___ (Gershon Friedlin, transl.): The Uprising of the Warsaw Ghetto [New York: Schocken, 1975] Excerpted in Suhl: They, pp.92-127.

Account of the uprising by a Polish-Jewish communist historian. Earlier editions (in Yiddish) were quite tendentious and very pro-Soviet Union. In this edition Communist propaganda has been significantly toned down and equal credit is given to all parties in the resistance. Some propaganda still remains - for example, calling the ZZW and its supporters "fascists" - but by and large the survey is accurate. Includes a selection of eighty-four documents.

4416. Meed, V.: "Smuggling Arms." Kowalski: Anthology/I, pp.143-149.

4417. Mendelsohn, Shlomo: The Battle of the Warsaw Ghetto [New York: YIVO, 1944] Also in: Menorah, vol.32 #1 (April/June, 1944): 5-25.

Early account attempting to piece together the history of the ghetto resistance. Useful as a primary source but superseded by later accounts.

4418. ___: "Heroism of Warsaw Ghetto." Am Heb, vol.153 #25 (April 21, 1944): 9, 12.

4419. Peltel, Vladka: "Smuggling Weapons Into the Ghetto." Barkai: Fighting, pp.41-46. <see #2903>

4420. Plonski, D.: "Two Uprisings." Poland, #8/48 (1958): 6-9. * On the Ghetto and the Polish Uprising of August 1944.

4421. Polakiewicz, Moshe: "On the Ghetto Barricades." CW, vol.10 #37 (Dec. 24, 1943): 7-9.

4422. Rosenthal, A. M.: "Forgive Them Not, For They Knew What They Did: Warsaw Ghetto." NY Times Mag, (Oct. 24, 1965): 50-51; Discussion (Nov. 7, 1965): 22.

4423. Rudnicki, Adolf (R. Ainsztein, transl.): "Easter." JQ, vol.2 #4 (Spr., 1955): 31-34.

4424. Schwarzbart, Isaac I.: "The Revolt in the Ghetto." CW, vol.15 #14 (April 9, 1948): 12-14.

4425. ___: The Story of the Warsaw Ghetto Uprising. Its Meaning and Message [New York: W. J. C., 1953]

Analysis of the ghetto uprising written by the former Zionist representative at the Polish Government-in-Exile. Primarily an elegy for the rebels and an analysis of their importance in modern Jewish history.

4426. Shneiderman, S. L.: "Life, Death and Resistance in the Warsaw Ghetto." CM, vol.50 #3 (April/May, 1983): 10-12.

4427. ___: "The Warsaw Ghetto Struggle." J Digest, vol.24 #8 (April, 1979): 68-77.

4428. Silver, E.: "The Warsaw Ghetto Uprising." Hist/WWII, #49 (1973): 1360-1363.

4429. Syrkin, Marie: "The Flag on the Ghetto Wall." J Fr, vol.10 #7 (July, 1943): 10-13.

4430. ___: "The Flag On the Ghetto Wall: The Epic of Warsaw Jewry." J Affairs, vol.3 #5 (Oct., 1943): 4-5.

4431. Tenenbaum, Joseph: "The Battle of the Ghetto." J Sp, vol.18 #4 (April, 1953): 7-9.

4432. "They Rose in Arms." Furrows, vol.3 #6 (April, 1945): 9-16.

4433. Tushnet, Leonard: To Die with Honor: The Uprising of the Jews in the Warsaw Ghetto [New York: Citadel Press, 1965]

4434. Wdowinski, David: And We Are Not Saved [New York: Philosophical Library, 1963] * Historical reflections on the Holocaust.

4435. ___: "Warsaw Ghetto Recollections." Kowalski: Anthology/I, pp.127-138.

4436. Werstein, Irving: The Uprising in the Warsaw Ghetto [New York: W. W. Norton, 1968] * History of the ghetto and resistance in Warsaw primarily aimed at teen-agers.

4437. Zuckerman, Izhak: "The Jewish Fighting Organization - Z. O. B. - Its Establishment and Activities." Gutman: Catastrophe, pp.518-548.

4438. ___: "The Jewish Revolt." Barkai: Fighting, pp.19-31.

Implications/Commemorations

4439. Abelson, Alter: "War in the Warsaw Ghetto." J Fo, vol.29 #11 (Nov., 1946): 267-268, 270.

4440. Ainsztein, R.: "Lest We Forget. What Did They Fight and Die For?" JQ, vol.2 #1 (Sum., 1954): 9-16.

4441. ___: "Thirty Years After: Reassessment of the Warsaw Ghetto Uprising in 1943." JQ, vol.21 #1/2 (Sum./Fall, 1973): 23-30.

4442. "Big Warsaw Ghetto Commemoration." JIEE, vol.2 #2 (May, 1963): 72-73.

4443. Blumenthal, N.: "16 Years After the Ghetto Rising." YVB, #6/7 (June, 1960): 13-15.

4444. Borzykowski, Tuvia: "Warsaw Ghetto Revolt Plus Twenty Years." NJM, vol.77 #8 (April, 1963): 6-7.

4445. Budish, J. M. (ed.): Warsaw Ghetto Uprising [New York: United Committee to Commemorate the Tenth Anniversary of the Warsaw Ghetto, 1953] Part I: English, pp.3-53.

4446. Feron, J.: "At the Wall in Warsaw, 30 Years Later." NY Times Mag, (April 15, 1973): 68-69, 84-86.

4447. "Forthcoming Ghetto Rising Anniversary." JIEE, vol.2 #1 (Dec., 1962): 53-54.

4448. Frimer, Hayim: "The Day of the Revolt." JQ, vol.6 #3/4 (Sum., 1959): 6-8.

4449. Gillon, Adam: "Testament of Lost Men." CW, vol.20 #13 (March 30, 1953): 16-18.

4450. Glatstein, J.: "This Night Was Different." CW, vol.24 #15 (April 15, 1957): 5-6. Also in J Digest, vol.5 #7 (April, 1960): 1-4.

4451. Harap, Louis: "Warsaw Ghetto Uprising: Fourteenth Anniversary April 19. Fourteen Years Later." J Life, vol.11 #6 (April, 1957): 8-11.

4452. Hausner, Gideon: "Warsaw Revisited." NJM, vol.78 #1 (Sept., 1963): 14-15.

4453. Herman, Josef: "The Warsaw Ghetto Exhibition: An Appreciation." JQ, vol.8 #4 (Aut., 1961): 26-27.

4454. "The Heroes of Warsaw's Ghetto." NY Times Mag, (April 21, 1963): 22, 112-113.

4455. Hodes, D. A.: "The Warsaw Ghetto Revisited 30 Years After the Uprising." J Fr, vol.40 #8 (Oct., 1973): 7-10.

4456. Johnson, Hawlett: "Thoughts at the Warsaw Ghetto." J Life, vol.5 #7 (May, 1951): 20-21.

4457. Kallen, Horace: "The Meaning of the Warsaw Ghetto." IH, vol.18 #4 (April, 1970): 17-20.

4458. Kennedy, John F.: "The Warsaw Ghetto Uprising." CBW, vol.30 #7 (April 1, 1962): 1. * Text of a Presidential proclamation.

4459. Kovner, Abba: "It Was Not the Last of the Ghettos." IH, vol.1 #6 (April, 1953): 17-18.

4460. Kugler, Israel and Kalman Sultanik: "The 40th Anniversary of the Warsaw Ghetto Uprising: Two Views." Mid, vol.29 #7 (Aug./Sept., 1983): 42-46.

4461. Kulka, E.: "40th Anniversary of Heroic Resistance." M&R, vol.11 #3 (Jan./Feb., 1985): 5, 6; #4 (March/April, 1985): 11.

4462. Lenowicz-Gordin, Aleksander: "Legacy of the Warsaw Ghetto." J Life, vol.5 #8 (June, 1951): 25-27. * Address by the attache at the Polish Consulate in New York.

4463. Levenberg, S.: "April the Nineteenth, 1943: Revolt of the Warsaw Ghetto." J Observer, vol.17 #15 (April 12, 1968): 11-13.

4464. ___: "Remembering Warsaw." J Observer, vol.26 #16 (April 21, 1977): 12-13.

4465. Lichten, J. L.: "The Uprising of the Warsaw Ghetto: The Legend of Yesterday and the Reality of Today." Polish Rev, vol.13 #2 (Spr., 1968): 47-57.

4466. ___: "Warsaw Ghetto Uprising: Legend and Reality." Polish Rev, vol.8 #3 (Sum., 1963): 61-69.

4467. Lipski, J. J.: "The Warsaw Ghetto Uprising. A Tribute from a Catholic Pole." Mid, vol.30 #4 (April, 1984): 31-32.

4468. Lubetkin, Z.: "Then and Now. 20 Years After the Ghetto Revolts." Dispersion, #3 (Win., 1963/64): 10-15.

4469. Manuhin, Yehudi: "1943 Twentieth Anniversary of the Ghetto Uprising 1963: They Served Humanity." JQ, vol. 10 #1 (Spr., 1963): 3-4.

4470. Mark, Ber: "Uprising in the Warsaw Ghetto: Uotbreak of Rebellion." Mid, vol.21 #4 (April, 1975): 32-37.

4471. Minsky-Sender, Ruth: "The Cage. A Memorial to the Warsaw Ghetto Fighters." HM, vol.49 #9 (May, 1968): 4, 30.

4472. Mirski, Michael and Hersh Smolar: "Commemoration of the Warsaw Ghetto Uprising: Reminiscences." SJA, vol. 3 #1 (May, 1973): 98-103.

4473. North, Joseph: "Noblest of Deeds in All of Time." J Life, vol.1 #6 (April, 1947): 5-7.

4474. Piorkowski, J.: "The Truth." Poland, #7/107 (1963): 6-7, 16-17.

4475. Poteranski, Waclaw: The Warsaw Ghetto. On the Twenty-Fifth Anniversary of the Armed Uprising in 1943 [Warsaw: Interpress Publishers, 1968]

4476. Proskauer, J. M.: "The Battle of the Warsaw Ghetto: A Heroic Symbol." Am Heb, vol.153 #25 (April 21, 1944): 15.

4477. Rosenthal, David: "Commemorating Warsaw Jewry." J Fr, vol.44 #4 (April, 1977): 6-10.

4478. Schwarzbart, Isaac L.: "The Spirit of Heroism and Faith." CW, vol.30 #7 (April 1, 1963): 10-12.

4479. ___: "What They Fought For." CW, vol.20 #13 (March 30, 1953): 4-7.

4480. Serebrenik, Robert: "The Warsaw Ghetto Revolt." J Sp, vol.23 #4 (April, 1958): 12-15.

4481. Shneiderman, S. L.: "The Warsaw Ghetto Revolt." CW, vol.30 #7 (April 1, 1963): 4-9.

4482. ___: "The Warsaw Ghetto Struggle." Mid, vol.24 #6 (June/July, 1978): 18-27.

4483. Sultanik, Kalman: "The Warsaw Ghetto Uprising." Mid, vol.25 #5 (May, 1979): 49-52.

4484. Sunntag, Jacob: "The Warsaw Anniversary." JOMER, vol. 12 #17 (April 26, 1963): 13-14.

4485. "The Torch of the Revolt in the Warsaw Ghetto." J Digest, vol.2 #2 (Nov., 1956): 17-18.

4486. "They Fought Back." JQ, vol.16 #1 (Spring, 1968): 1-3, 26. * 25th anniversary.

4487. "They Have Not Died. Tribute to the Jews of Warsaw." V/Unq, vol.1 #6 (Nov., 1943): 2-3.

4488. Uris, Leon: "The Most Heroic Story of Our Country." Coronet, vol.49 #1 (Nov., 1960): 170-178. Also in J Digest, vol.6 #7 (April, 1961): 1-6.

4489. The Warsaw Ghetto Uprising [New York: Congress for Jewish Culture, 1974]

4490. The Warsaw Ghetto Uprising and Its Historical Significance [New York: W. J. C., 1968] * Twenty-Fifth anniversary publication.

4491. "The Warsaw Ghetto Uprising: April 19, 1943." J Currents, vol.37 #4 (April, 1983): 8-9.

4492. Weiss, Burton: "Meditations on the Warsaw Ghetto Uprising." Response, vol.5 #3 (Win., 1971/72): 105-113.

4493. Wiesel, Elie: "Warsaw ´43." HM, vol.54 #8 (April, 1973): 10, 46.

4494. Winocour, Jack (ed.): The Jewish Resistance: On the Twenty-Fifth Anniversary of the Warsaw Ghetto Uprising [London: W. J. C., 1968]

4495. Zuckerman, Y.: "Twenty-Five Years After the Warsaw Ghetto Revolt." Y/V: Resistance, pp.23-34.

Other Uprisings

Auschwitz/Birkenau

4496. Halivni, Tzipora H.: "The Birkenau Revolt: Poles Prevent a Timely Insurrection." JSS, vol.41 #2 (Spr., 1979): 123-154.

Interesting investigation of the circumstances surrounding the October 1944 revolt of the Sonderkommando at Auschwitz. Argues convincingly that the revolt might have occured earlier and have had a greater impact, perhaps even saving Jewish lives, had the Polish underground in the camp given more aid. Hager-Halivni concludes that it was the Polish underground which, ultimately, prevented the revolt.

4497. Korman, Yudel: "The Ten Commandments Arrive in Auschwitz: Recollections of an Underground Leader." J Currents, vol.25 #4 (April, 1971): 7-12.

4498. Kraus, Ota and Erich Kulka: "The Day of Armed Revolt at Auschwitz Death Camps." JQ, vol.13 #4 (Win., 1966): 33-35.

4499. Kulka, E.: "Five Escapes from Auschwitz." Suhl: They, pp.196-218.

4500. Silber, G.: "Revolt of the Auschwitz ´Sonderkommando´ is Recalled by Survivor 36 Years Later." M&R, vol.7 #1 (Sept./Oct., 1980): 5.

4501. Suhl, Yuri: "Underground Assignment in Auschwitz." Suhl: They, pp.189-195.

Bialystok

4502. Ainsztein, Reuben: "The Bialystok Ghetto Revolt." Suhl: They, pp.136-143.

4503. ___: "Jewish Tragedy and Martyrdom. The Bialystok Uprising in 1943." JQ, vol.3 #4 (Spr., 1956): 17-20.

4504. Birman, Tzipora: "From the Bialystok Ghetto." J Sp, vol.36 #7 (Sept., 1971): 9-12.

4505. ___: "Grodna and Bialystok." Barkai: Fighting, pp. 107-111.

4506. Blumenthal, Nahman: "German Document on the Bialystok Ghetto Revolt." YVB, #14 (March, 1964): 19-25.

4507. Datner, Szymon: The Fight and Annihilation of the Bialystok Ghetto [Lodz: Central Jewish Historical Commission, 1946]

4508. Grossman, Chaika: "The Day of the Uprising." Barkai: Fighting, pp.112-128.

4509. Klibanski, Bronia: "The Bialystok Underground." J Sp, vol.34 #9 (Nov., 1969): 8-12.

4510. ___: "The Underground Archives in the Bialystok Ghetto founded by Zevi Mersik and Mordecai Tenenbaum." YVS, vol.2 (1958): 295-330.

4511. "Preparation for the Revolt." Barkai: Fighting, pp. 96-106.

Kovno

4512. Spector, S.: "History of the Jewish Underground in Kovno." YVB, #13 (Oct., 1963): 54-56.

4513. Yellin, M. and D. Galperin: "The Partisans of the Kovno Ghetto." Porter: JP/I, pp.180-195.

Minsk

4514. Cholawski, Shalom: "Resistance and Survival." JQ, vol.9 #2 (Spr., 1962): 18-20, 38.

4515. Chorny, A.: "The Avengers of the Minsk Ghetto." Porter: JP/I, pp.93-100.

4516. Eckman, L. and Chaim Lazar: "The Jewish Resistance in the Ghetto of Minsk." Kowalski: Anthology/I, pp.314-332.

4517. Greenstein, Jacob: "Children - Couriers in the Ghetto of Minsk." Suhl: <u>They</u>, pp.241-245.

4518. Smoliar, Hersh (H. Lewbin, transl.): "How the Minsk Ghetto Resisted the Nazis." <u>J Life</u>, vol.2 #6 (April, 1948): 21-23.

4519. ___ (Henry Lewbin, transl.): <u>Resistance in Minsk</u> [Oakland, CA: J. L. Magnes Memorial Museum, 1966]

4520. Suhl, Yuri: "The Resistance Movement in the Ghetto of Minsk." Suhl: <u>They</u>, pp.231-240.

<u>Sobibor</u>

4521. Ainsztein, Reuben: "Jewish Underground Resistance: The Story of the Sobibor Uprising." <u>JOMER</u>, vol.14 #17 (April 23, 1965): 16-21.

4522. Ehrenburg, Ilya: "Witness Against the Nazi Beast." <u>CJCh</u>, vol.32 #19 (Sept. 22, 1944): 5, 13.

4523. Pechersky, Alexander: "The Outbreak in Sobibor." Barkai: <u>Fighters</u>, pp.205-226.

4524. ___: "Revolt in Sobibor." Suhl: <u>They</u>, pp.9-50.

4525. Rashke, R.: <u>Escape From Sobibor</u> [Boston: Houghton Mifflin, 1982]

Admirable attempt to reconstruct the desperate revolt in the Sobibor death camp. The accuracy of dialogue quoted is, however, questionable.

4526. Sorin, Gerald: "Resistance in Sobibor." <u>J Currents</u>, vol.38 #8 (Sept., 1984): 24-27.

<u>Treblinka</u>

4527. Donat, Alex.: "The Death Camp Treblinka: The Rebels." Kowalski: <u>Anthology/I</u>, pp.186-198.

4528. Mark, B.: "The Risisng in Treblinka: The Ghetto Fight Inspired Jews to Resist in a Death Camp." <u>J Life</u>, vol.11 #6 (April, 1957): 15-17.

4529. Rajzman, Samuel: "Uprising in Treblinka." Suhl: <u>They</u>, pp.129-135.

4530. Wiernik, Yankel: "The Revolt in Treblinka." Barkai: Fighting, pp.201-204.

4531. ___: "Uprising in Treblinka." Schwarz: Root, pp.115-121.

4532. Willenberg, S.: "Revolt at Treblinka." YVB, #8/9 (March, 1961): 39-40, 51.

Vilna

4533. Foxman, A. H.: "The Resistance Movement in the Vilna Ghetto." Suhl: They, pp.148-159.

4534. Kovner, Abba: "Easy Revenge." Kowalski: Anthology/I, pp.523-525; Barkai: Fighting, pp. 148-150.

4535. Sutzkever, Abraham: "Heroic Jewish Guerrillas." Lib Jud, vol.12 #7 (Nov., 1944): 35-38.

4536. ___: "Jewish Guerrillas." Am Heb, vol.154 #1 (Nov. 3, 1944): 9, 12.

4537. ___: "Never Say This Is the Last Road." Schwarz: Root, pp.66-92.

4538. ___: "The Secret Town." JQ, vol.1 #3 (Win., 1954): 55-57.

Varia

4539. Aaronson, Yehoshua: "The Burning of the Konin Camp." Barkai: Fighting, pp.227-229.

4540. Alpert, Nakhum: "The 51st Jewish Partisan Group from Slonim." Kowalski: Anthology/I, pp.600-603.

4541. Andreyev, V. A.: "In the Forests of Bryansk." Porter: JP/I, pp.102-120.

4542. Bauminger, Aryeh: "The Rising of the Cracow Ghetto." YVB, #8/9 (March, 1961): 22-25.

4543. Brand, E.: "Underground Activities of the Halutz Group in Lwow Ghetto." YVB, #8/9 (March, 1961): 20-22.

4544. Brinsky, A. P.: "Meetings and Events." Kowalski: Anthology/I, pp.614-625.

4545. Cholawski, Shalom: Soldiers from the Ghetto [New York: The Herzl Press, 1980]

4546. "Escape to the Partisans." Kowalski: Anthology/I, pp. 527-528.

4547. Foxman, Joseph M.: "The Escape from Koldyczewo Camp." Suhl: They, pp.172-175.

4548. Glicksman, William: "The Story of Jewish Resistance in the Ghetto of Czestochowa." Suhl: They, pp.69-76.

4549. Green, Boris: "Wilejka Near Vilna." Kowalski: Anthology/I, pp.538-545.

4550. Green, Joe: "Untold Glory, 1943." Kowalski: Anthology/I, pp.610-611.

4551. Izraelevitch, N.: "With the Partisans in the Vicinity of Kletzk." Kowalski: Anthology/I, pp.534-536.

4552. Mann, Mendel: "The Revolt in the Tuczyn Ghetto." Suhl: They, pp.168-171.

4553. Mayne, W. G.: "Juda the Maccabee." Ch J Forum, vol.3 #3 (Spr., 1945): 174-179.

4554. Persov, Shmuel: "In the Tunnels of Odessa." Porter: JP/I, pp.207-212.

4555. Schworin, Aaron et al: "Revolt in Lachwa." Suhl: They, pp.165-167.

4556. Shulman, Moyshe: "Among Partisans." Kowalski: Anthology/I, pp.530-531.

4557. Spinc, Joseph: "Survivors of the Bodzentyn Ghetto Fought in the Forest." YVB, #13 (Oct., 1963): 42-44.

4558. Wermuth, Joshua: "The Jewish Partisans of Horodenka." Suhl: They, pp.226-230.

4559. Weyler, Shmuel: "The Jewish Resistance Movement in Brodi." Barkai: Fighting, pp.88-95.

4560. "Yizkor Elokim." Hamigdal, vol.4 #3 (Feb., 1944): 10-11 * On Bendin.

Personalities

4561. Amipaz-Silber, Gitta: "Yitzhak ´Antek´ Zuckerman: One Less Survivor." IH, vol.29 #5 (Nov./Dec., 1981): 6-7.

4562. Aron, Isaac: "Fallen Leaves." Kowalski: Anthology/I, pp.302-312.

4563. Benkler, R.: "Haviva Reik: Heroine without Heroics." IH, vol.12 #10 (Dec., 1964): 15-19.

4564. Berkin, S.: "Sonya Gutina." Porter: JP/I, pp.213-214.

4565. Blumenthal, Nahman: "Exemplary Heroism." YVB, #8/9 (March, 1961): 5-6, 19. * On the Draengers.

4566. Brinsky, A. P.: "Meetings and Events." Porter: JP/I, pp.121-132. * On "Dadya Petya".

4567. Chaver Paver (Psd.): "Jewish Partisans of the Woods." J Life, vol.7 #2 (Dec., 1952): 18-20.

4568. Cohen, Haskel: "Herschyl Grynszpan´s Childhood." NJM, vol.56 #1 (Sept., 1941): 12-13.

4569. Eckman, Lester and Ch. Lazar: "Dr. Yehezkiel Atlas." J Combat, vol.1 #2 (Fall, 1980): 8-13.

4570. Eisenstadt, Mira: "The Davidovich Family." Porter: JP/I, pp.215-218.

4571. Feiginov, Shimon: "Shoots 28 Germans." Kowalski: Anthology/I, pp.282-283.

4572. Freund, A. (A. Sinai, transl.): "Herschel Grynszpan - Man or Phantom?" J Digest, vol.6 #12 (Sept., 1961): 65-71.

4573. Fuerst, Dorothy: "An Uncommon Martyrdom Revealed in the Story of Gisela Fleischmann." M&R, vol.7 #3 (Jan./Feb., 1981): 5, 9.

4574. Fyodorov, A.: "Yakov Zusserman, Soviet Partisan Fighter." J Life, vol.5 #3 (Jan., 1951): 19-22.

4575. Galitzki, J.: "Partisan Memoirs." Kowalski: Anthology/I, pp.580-598.

4576. Gildenman, Misha: "Diadia Mischa and His Partisans: The Attack." Suhl: They, pp.268-270.

4577. ___: "Diadia Misha (Uncle Misha) and His Partisans: The Blowing Up of the Soldiers´ Home." Suhl: They, pp.261-267.

4578. ___: "Diadia Misha and His Partisans: David of Yarevitch." Suhl: They, pp.271-273.

4579. Granatstein, J. and Moshe Kahanovich: "Dr. Ezekiel Atlas, Doctor and Partisan Leader." YVB, #8/9 (March, 1961): 41-43.

4580. Greenstein, Jacob: "The Story of the Amazing (Shmuel) Rufeisen." Suhl: They, pp.246-252.

4581. Grossman, Chayke: "My Memory of Mordechai Anilewicz." IH, vol.10 #4 (April, 1962): 7-10.

4582. Guri, J.: "Ilya Ehrenburg Among Jewish Partisans." YVB, #16 (Feb., 1965): 14-16.

4583. Gutman, Y.: "Joseph Kaplan: Profile of a Fighter." YVB, #8/9 (March, 1961): 16-18.

4584. Heiman, Leo: "The First Jewish Avenger." CBW, vol.28 #6 (March 13, 1961): 5-7. * On David Frankfurter.

4585. ___: "He Struck the First Blow Against Hitler: The Forgotten Jewish Avenger." J Digest, vol.8 #7 (April, 1963): 57-60.

4586. Kahanovitch, M.: "Moshe Gildenman, Partisan Commander of the Yevgrupa." YVB, #3 (April, 1958): 13-14.

4587. ___: "Organizers and Commanders." Barkai: Fighting, pp.134-147. * On Dr. Yehezkel Atlas.

4588. Klibanski, B.: "Rivkaleh." J Sp, vol.45 #1 (Spr., 1980): 14-16.

4589. "The Legend of the Jailbird." Kowalski: Anthology/I, pp.478-482.

4590. Liebesmann, M.: "Arthur Safrin, a Hero from the Stanislawow Ghetto." YVB, #14 (March, 1964): 64-66.

4591. Linkov, Gregory: "David Kaimach." Porter: JP/I, pp. 170-179.

4592. ___: "The Partisan Mine and Abraham Hirschfeld, the Watchmaker." Porter: JP/I, pp.64-68.

4593. ___: "Women Spies." Porter: JP/I, pp.164-167.

4594. Ludwig, E.: The Davos Murder [London: Methuen, 1937]

4595. ___: "The Man who Killed Gustloff." Am Heb, vol.155 #36 (Jan. 4, 1946): 4-5, 8-9. * On David Frankfurter.

4596. Mark, Esther: "A Brave Fighter of the Anti-Nazi Underground: A Wartime Photograph of Zofia Yamaika." JQ, vol.14 #1 (Spr., 1966): 38-40.

4597. ___: "Zofia Yamaika." Suhl: They, pp.77-81.

4598. Miedzyrzecki (Meed), W.: "The Underground." Schwarz: Root, pp.44-53.

4599. Popkin, Zelda: "A Warsaw Fighter in Israel: A Visit with Antek." Com, vol.13 #1 (Jan., 1952): 34-37.

4600. Richter, J. H.: "Forgotten Resistance Leader: Herbert Baum, Martyr of Nazism." J Digest, vol.7 #5 (Feb., 1962): 15-16.

4601. Ringelblum, Emmanuel (Yuri Suhl, transl.): "Comrade Mordechai. Mordechai Anielewicz - Commander of the Warsaw Ghetto Uprising." J Currents, vol.16 #4 (April, 1962): 14-22. Also in Suhl: They, pp.85-91.

4602. ___: "Mordechai Anielewicz of Hashomer Hatzair." IH, vol.11 #4 (April, 1963): 9-12.

4603. Rosen, Donia: The Forest, My Friend [New York: Bergen Belsen Memorial Press, 1971]

4604. Saphire, William B.: "Moshe Pijade - Aid to Tito." CJCh, vol.31 #33 (Dec. 31, 1943): 7.

4605. Savitch, A.: "The Partisan Filmmaker." Porter: JP/I, pp.152-163.

4606. Shneiderman, S. L.: "Hero of the Underground. New Polish Consul in U. S." NJM, vol.60 #8 (April, 1946): 270-271. * On Jan Galewicz, Warsaw ghetto resister.

4607. Stadtler, Bea: "A Machine Gun Named Lisa." J Digest, vol.23 #8 (April, 1978): 73-75.

4608. Starr, Peggy: "An Underground Emissary." Lib Jud, vol.13 #5 (Sept., 1945): 50-51. * An interview with Mylech Topiol, leader of the Jewish partisans in France.

4609. Suhl, Yuri: "Chief Physician Remba." Suhl: They, pp. 82-84.

4610. ___: "Little Wanda with the Braids." Suhl: They, pp. 51-54.

4611. ___: "Rosa Robota, Heroine of the Auschwitz Underground." Suhl: They, pp.219-225. Also in: HM, vol.48 #2 (Oct., 1966): 6-7.

4612. ___: Uncle Misha´s Partisans [New York: Four Winds Press, 1973]

4613. ___: "Wanda, a True Story." NJM, vol.80 #7 (March, 1966): 26, 34.

4614. Syrkin, Marie: "Zivia - the Passing of a Heroine." Mid, vol.24 #8 (Oct., 1978): 56-59.

4615. Tushnet, Leonard: "The Little Doctor: A Resistance Hero." J Currents, vol.15 #7 (July/Aug., 1961): 9-14. Also in Suhl: They, pp.253-259. * On Dr. Yehezkel Atlas.

4616. Udkofsky, B.: "Unaish - the Jewish Partisan." Barkai: Fighting, pp.165-169.

4617. Weisblum, Giza: "The Escape and death of the Runner´ Mala Zimetbaum." Suhl: They, pp.182-188.

4618. Werner, A.: "Not the Murderer is guilty! In Memorian Herschel Grynszpan." Polish Jew, vol.2 #6/7 (March/ April, 1942): 11-12, 19.

4619. A Witness: "Partisan Alexander Abugov." Porter: JP/I, pp.135-151.

Testimonies

4620. Amiel. M.: "Hashomer Ha´tsair and Betar in a United Front." YVB, #22 (May, 1968): 56.

4621. Auerbach, Rachel (ed.): "Testimonies by Fighters and their Relatives: Introduction." YVB, #22 (May, 1968): 19-23.

4622. Avni, S.: "Rescue and Defense in Rumania During the Holocaust." YVB, #22 (May, 1968): 50-51.

4623. Benvenisti, M.: "Jewish Partisans in Bulgaria." YVB, #22 (May, 1968): 56-57.

4624. Berkowicz, E.: "We Dug a Tunnel and Escaped from the Camp." YVB, #22 (May, 1968): 42.

4625. Bernsztejn, P.: "I Stood Beside my Husband as he Fell in the Wilna Ghetto Battle." YVB, #22 (May, 1968): 39.

4626. Cohen-Solal, S.: "With the French Maquis." YVB, #22 (May, 1968): 58

4627. Damaszek, M.: "On the Day of Liquidation We Fired at the Germans and Set our Little Town Ablaze." YVB, #22 (May, 1968): 42-43.

4628. Eisinger, G.: "I Brought Down German Planes." YVB, #22 (May, 1968): 48.

4629. Eldar, A.: "Smuggling Annihilation-Bound Fugitives into Rumania." YVB, #22 (May, 1968): 52-53.

4630. Frankfurter, D.: "I Kill a Nazi Gauleiter: Memoir of a Jewish Assassin." Com, vol.9 #2 (Feb., 1950): 133-141.

4631. Glatjtman-Putermilch, M.: "The Story of Melech Perlmman." YVB, #22 (May, 1968): 31, 33.

4632. Gruen, M.: "From Czech Army to Jewish Brigade and Haganah." YVB, #22 (May, 1968): 47.

4633. Gur-Grosz, D.: "We Evaded the Murderers in Fascist Budapest." YVB, #22 (May, 1968): 48-49.

4634. Hayun, E.: "With Tito's Partisans." YVB, #22 (May, 1968): 54-55.

4635. Kadmon, E.: "In Disguise of International Red Cross Officials." YVB, #22 (May, 1968): 49.

4636. Meed, Vladka: "Survivors of the Ghetto Take Part in the Polish Uprising." YVB, #22 (May, 1968): 34-35.

4637. ___: "Underground Activity on the Aryan Side of Warsaw." YVB, #22 (May, 1968): 24-25.

4638. Neuer, M.: "The Fighting Doctor." YVB, #22 (May, 1968): 47.

4639. Pechner, A.: "Lt. Stimm and Machine-Gunner R. Hirsz Zawada in the Kosciusko Division." YVB, #22 (May, 1968): 44.

4640. Porter, Jack N.: "Zalonka: An Interview with a Jewish Partisan Leader." Davka, vol.3 #2/3 (Win./Spr., 1973): 14-20.

4641. Putermilch, B. J.: "Street Battles in the Warsaw Ghetto." YVB, #22 (May, 1968): 29, 31.

4642. Rosenberg, J. and A. Gutman: "We Looted German Arms." YVB, #4/5 (Oct., 1959): 10-12.

4643. Rosenberg, R.: "5 to 6 Thousand People were Rescued this Way." YVB, #22 (May, 1968): 53.

4644. Rotem-Rathajzer, S.: "The Battles in the Area of the Brush Factory." YVB, #22 (May, 1968): 26-29.

4645. Rubanov, R.: "My Sister Mati Rubanov." YVB, #22 (May, 1968): 57.

4646. Segalczyk, J.: "Attack on the Germans and their Collaborators in Dolhinow." YVB, #22 (May, 1968): 43-44.

4647. Shaeftel, A.: "Volunteer in the Free French Forces." YVB, #22 (May, 1968): 58-60.

4648. Singer, E.: "Disguised Jews in the Polish Underground." YVB, #22 (May, 1968): 33-34.

4649. Steiner, G.: "In the Free Czechoslovak Forces and in the Banska-Bystryca Uprising." YVB, #22 (May, 1968): 45-46.

4650. Teichman, E.: "Jews in Nyilas Uniforms." YVB, #22 (May, 1968): 49.

4651. Tenzer, P.: "Shoulder to Shoulder with the Red Army." YVB, #22 (May, 1968): 46.

4652. Werber, A.: "Jewish Resistance in Belgium." YVB, #22 (May, 1968): 60-61.

4653. Wertheim, A.: "The Family Camp of the Fighter Senion Zorin." YVB, #22 (May, 1968): 44.

4654. Wilner, G.: "My Brother Lulek (Aryeh)." YVB, #22 (May, 1968): 35-37.

4655. Wilner, J.: "My Son Aryeh." YVB, #22 (May, 1968): 35.

4656. Zdrojewicz, M.: "I was One of the Three Fighting Girls Captured and Photographed by General Stroop´s Men." YVB, #22 (May, 1968): 37-39.

4657. Zelwer, L.: "Battle of the Czestochowa Ghetto." YVB, #22 (May, 1968): 40-41.

EUROPEAN RESISTANCE

Surveys

4658. Bailey, Ronald and The Eds. of Time-Life: Partisans and Guerrillas [Alexandria, VA: Time-Life, 1978]

4659. Brome, Vincent: Europe´s Free Press [London: Feature Books, n.d.]

4660. Carse, R.: The Unconquered [New York: McBride, 1942]

4661. Chapman, B.: "The German Counter-Resistance." Hawes: Resistance, pp.170-185.

4662. Charles, Jean-Leon: "Build Up for D-Day: Europe´s Secret Armies." Hist/WWII, #64 (1974): 1765-1769, 1774-1776.

4663. Churchill, Peter: The Spirit in the Cage [London: Hodder and Stoughton, 1954]

4664. De Launay, J. (ed.): European Resistance Movements, 1939-1945: In English, French and German 2 vols. [London: Pergamon Press, 1960/64] * First and second international conference on the history of the resistance movements.

4665. Dolivet, Louis: "Political War: Forces of World Rebirth." FW, vol.1 #4 (Jan., 1942): 365-368.

4666. Dupont, Pierre: "Powder Magazine of the Balkans." FW, vol.6 #2 (Aug., 1943): 180-183.

4667. ___: "The Weapon of Humor." FW, vol.5 #4 (April, 1943): 371-375.

4668. Foot, M. R. D.: Resistance: An Analysis of European Resistance to the Nazis [New York: Macmillan, 1977]

In depth survey of European resistance history, this is an excellent primer on the methods, technicalities, and operations of European resistance to Nazism. Foot deals with the organizations, personalities, and activities of every resistance movement, including Jewish undergrounds, from the Urals to the Atlantic and from Norway to North Africa, as well as their relations with official directing staffs from England, the United States, and Russia.

4669. ___: Six Faces of Courage [London: Magnum Books, 1980] * Biographical sketches of six European resisters.

4670. ___: "What Good Did Resistance Do?" Hawes: Resistance, pp.204-220.

4671. G. K.: "The Underground Reporter: A Year of Resistance." FW, vol.4 #1 (Oct., 1942): 83-90; #2 (Nov., 1942): 179-183.

4672. Gerber, John W. and A. Kantorowicz: "Europe Against Hitler." Nation, vol.156 #18 (May 1, 1943): 631-634; #19 (May 8, 1943): 666-669; #20 (May 15, 1943): 704-706.

4673. Gross, Feliks: "Some Sociological Considerations on Underground Movements." Polish Rev, vol.2 #2/3 (Spr./Summer, 1957): 33-56.

4674. Haestrup, J.: Europe Ablaze: An Analysis of the History of the European Resistance Movement, 1939-1945 [Copenhagen, Denmark: Odense Univ. Press, 1978]

4675. Hawes, Stephen and Ralph White (eds.): Resistance in Europe: 1939-1945 [London: Allen Lane, 1975]

4676. Hegt Noordhoek, W. F.: "The Resistance of the Medical Profession." Annals, #245 (May, 1946): 162-168.

4677. Heilbrunn, Otto: Partisan Warfare [New York: F. A. Praeger, 1962; London: George Allen & Unwin, 1962]

4678. Heimler, Eugene (ed.): Resistance Against Tyranny [London: Routledge, 1966]

4679. "Inside Fortress Europe: The Allies´ Secret Weapon." FW, vol.8 #1 (July, 1944): 31-33.

4680. Kraus, Rene: Europe in Revolt [New York: Macmillan, 1942]

4681. Lipgens, Walter: "European Federation in the Political Thought of Resistance Movements During World War II." CEH, vol.1 #1 (March, 1968): 5-19.

4682. Macksey, Kenneth: The Partisans of Europe in the Second World War [New York: Stein and Day, 1975]

4683. Michel, Henri: "The Shadow States." Hist/WWII, #37 (1973): 1034-1036.

4684. ___ (R. Barry, transl.): The Shadow War: European Resistance, 1939-1945 [New York: Harper & Row, 1973]

Detailed and sensitive account of European resistance by the dean of European resistance historians. Particular emphasis is placed on the different stages in the development of European resistance movements during World War II. Includes information on Jewish resistance, and a historian´s evaluation of its importance.

4685. Milward, Alan: "The Economic and Strategic Effectiveness of Resistance." Hawes: Resistance, pp.186-203.

4686. Montgomery, M.: "Resistance in the Baltic States." Hist/WWII, #108 (1974): 3013-3015.

4687. Mountfield, David: The Partisans [London: Hamlyn Pub. Group, 1979]

4688. Nover, Barnet: "Occupied Europe Fights Back." Am Mercury, vol.53 #214 (Oct., 1941): 415-424.

4689. Ponomarev, B.: The Peoples of Europe Versus Hitler [Moscow: Foreign Languages Pub. House, 1942]

4690. Ries, Curt: Underground Europe [New York: Dial Press, 1942]

4691. Seth, Ronald: The Undaunted: The Story of Resistance in Western Europe [New York: Philosophical Library, 1956]

4692. Stokesbury, James L.: "The European Resistance Movement." Kowalski: Anthology/I, pp.54-72.

4693. The Underground Reporter: "Belgian Resistance and the Polish Village." FW, vol.5 #5 (May, 1943): 465-470.

4694. ___: "On France, Hungary and Portugal." FW, vol.1 #4 (Jan., 1942): 398-405.

4695. ___: "On Italy, Czechoslovakia and Rumania." FW, vol.1 #3 (Dec., 1941): 298-305.

4696. ___: "On Poland, France and Spain." FW, vol.1 #2 (Nov., 1941): 209-215.

4697. ___: "Resistance." FW, vol.3 #1 (July, 1943): 76-81.

4698. ___: "Somewhere in Europe, April 1942." FW, vol.2 #4 (May, 1942): 368, 370-371.

4699. ___: "Somewhere in Europe, February 1942." FW, vol.2 #2 (March, 1942): 185-189.

4700. ___: "Somewhere in Europe, July 1942." FW, vol.3 #2 (July, 1942): 180-184.

4701. ___: "Somewhere in Europe, March 1942." FW, vol.2 #3 (April, 1942): 285-287.

4702. Valtin, Jan: Out of the Night [New York: Alliance Book, 1941]

4703. Visson, Andre: "The Danger in the Resistance Forces." Am Mercury, vol.60 #254 (Feb., 1945): 156-165.

4704. Wachsman, Zvi: Trail Blazers for Invasion [New York: York: Frederick Ungar Pub., 1943]

4705. White, Ralph: "The Unity and Diversity of European Resistance." Hawes: Resistance, pp.7-23.

4706. Woodman, Dorothy: Europe Rises [London: V. Gollancz, 1943]

4707. Wordley, D.: The Third Front [London: Hammond, 1943]

4708. Yarham, C. R.: "Europe´s Secret Freedom Press." FW, vol.5 #6 (June, 1943): 561-565.

Resistance by Country

Belgium

4709. "Belgium Fights Back." Am Heb, vol.151 #15 (Aug. 14, 1942): 9, 20.

4710. Ehrenburg, Ilya: "Belgium." Am Heb, vol.154 #10 (Jan. 12, 1945): 4, 9.

4711. Fast, H.: "A Clandestine Paper ´La Libre Belgique´." CEO, vol.18 #19 (Sept. 19, 1941): 260.

4712. Scheyven, Raymond: "Belgian Underground Was Financed by Loans Floated Among Patriots." V/Unq, vol.3 #6/7 (Jan./July, 1945): 4, 11.

4713. The Underground Press in Belgium [London: The Belgian Government-In-Exile, 1944]

Czechoslovakia

4714. Clementis, Vladimir: "The Slovak Uprising." CEO, vol. 21 #19 (Sept. 15, 1944): 273-275.

4715. Czechoslovakian Government-in-Exile: Czechoslovakia Fights Back: A Document [Washington, DC: Am. Council on Public Affairs, 1943]

4716. ___: Four Fighting Years [London: Hutchinson, 1943]

4717. Duncan, Ivor: "The Czechs´ War with the Germans." CEO, vol.18 #21 (Oct. 17, 1941): 287-288.

4718. Fucik, Julius: Report from the Gallows [London: Fore Publications, 1951]

4719. Ivanov, Miroslav (P. O´Brien, transl.): The Assassination of Heydrich [London: Hart-Davis, MacGibbon, 1974]

4720. Kratky, Karel and A. Snejdarek: "The Slovak Rising." Hist/WWII, #78 (1974): 2157-2166.

4721. Kybal, Milic: "Czechoslovakia Fights Back." FW, vol.5 #1 (Jan., 1943): 85-87.

4722. Luza, Radomir: "The Communist Party of Czechoslovakia and the Czech Resistance, 1939-1945." Slavic Review, vol.28 #4 (Dec., 1969): 561-576.

4723. Macworth, Cecily: Czechoslovakia Fights Back [London: Drummond, 1942]

4724. Mastny, V.: The Czechs Under Nazi Rule: The Failure of National Resistance, 1939-1943 [New York: Columbia Univ. Press, 1971]

Well documented evaluation of the concepts of terror, collaboration, and resistance as they were developed in Nazi occupied Czechoslovakia. Focuses on the Czech lands, that is the Nazi-created Protectorate of Bohemia-Moravia. Notes that despite post-war mythology, civilian resistance was an almost total failure in the Protectorate. Mentions Jews inter-alia.

4725. Muller, Edwin: "The Indigestible Czechs." Survey Graphic, vol.29 #1 (Jan., 1940): 18-20. * On passive resistance.

4726. Ripka, H.: "The Significance of the Slovak Rising." CEO, vol.21 # 21 (Oct. 13, 1944): 309-311.

4727. Wiener, Jan G.: The Assassination of Heydrich [New York: Pyramid Pub., 1969]

Denmark

4728. Haestrup, J.: "Denmark´s Connection with the Allied Powers during the Occupation." De Launay: ERM/II, pp. 282-297.

4729. ___: Secret Alliance: A Study of the Danish Resistance Movement 1940-1945 [Denmark: Odense Univ. Press, 1978]

4730. Leistikow, Gunnar: "Denmark: A Nation Underground." Am Mercury, vol.60 #253 (Jan., 1945): 74-80.

4731. Roussell, Aage: The Museum of the Danish Resistance Movement, 1940-1945 [Copenhagen: National Museum, 1970]

4732. Thomas, John: The Giant-Killers: The Danish Resistance Movement 1940-1945 [New York: Talpinger, 1976]

4733. The Underground Reporter: "Danes Say No to Hitler." FW, vol.6 #4 (Oct., 1943): 370-372.

France

4734. Allen, Louis: "Resistance and the Catholic Church in France." Hawes: Resistance, pp.77-93.

4735. Benenson, Mira: "The ´Illegal´ Press of France." CEO, vol.19 #25 (Dec. 11, 1942): 395-396.

4736. Clarck, Michael K.: "The Plot that Took Algiers." Nation, vol.157 #1 (July 3, 1943): 13-14.

4737. Dolivet, Louis: "Underground in France." Nation, vol. 152 #19 (May 10, 1941): 554-556.

4738. ___: "Volcano Under Vichy." Nation, vol.153 #4 (July 26, 1941): 67-69.

4739. Ehrlich, B.: The French Resistance [London: Chapman and Hall, 1966]

4740. Foot, M. R. D.: "The Triumph of the Resistance." Hist/WWII, #72 (1974): 1989-1995.

4741. Fourcade, Marie M.: Noah´s Ark: The Secret Underground [New York: Zebra Books, 1974]

4742. Gerbault, Jean: "What the French Resistance Wants." FW, vol.7 #5 (May, 1944): 440-444.

4743. Hawes, Stephen: "The Individual and the Resistance Community in France." Hawes: Resistance, pp.117-134.

4744. Kedward, H. R.: "Behind the Polemics: French Communists and Resistance 1939-41." Hawes: Resistance, pp. 94-116.

4745. ___: Resistance in Vichy France: A Study of Ideas and Motivation in the Southern Zone, 1940-1942 [New York: Oxford University Press, 1978]

Very useful history of the early days of the French resistance. Unlike other histories this work emphasizes the uncertainties, lack of organization, and problems of the early resistance. Lays out the stages of development of opposition to Vichy and to the Nazis, noting that resistance was not the most obvious response to defeat. Only by 1942 was the underground set up in an organized fashion, ready to oppose the Nazis and aid the Allies.

4746. King, Jonathan H.: "Emanuel D´Astier and the Nature of the French Resistance." JCH, vol.8 #4 (Oct., 1973): 25-46.

4747. Knight, F.: The French Resistance [New York: Beekman Pubs., 1976]

4748. Laugier, Henri (H. Lipman, tr.): "The Struggle for Free France." FW, vol.3 #2 (July, 1942): 170-174.

4749. Leslie, Peter: The Liberation of the Riviera: The Resistance to the Nazis in the South of France and the Story of its Heroic Leader Ange-Marie Miniconi [New York: Wyndham Books, 1980]

4750. Marchand, Lucienne: "A Woman of the Maquis, Personal Story." FW, vol.10 #3 (Sept., 1945): 62-64.

4751. Millar, George: Maquis [London: Heinemann, 1945]

4752. Novick, Peter: The Resistance Versus Vichy: The Purge of Collaborators in Liberated France [London: Chatto and Windus, 1968]

4753. Pearson, M.: Tears of Glory: The Heroes of Vercors, 1944 [Garden City, NY: Doubleday, 1979]

4754. Perrin, Jean: "Unchanging French Spirit." FW, vol.2 #1 (Feb., 1942): 28-33.

4755. Schoenbrun, David: Soldiers of the Night: The Story of the French Resistance [New York: Dutton, 1979]

Comprehensive history of the French resistance. Tends to be anecdotal in its discussion of individual heroism, but integrates these anecdotes into the larger organizational history. Does not take sides with any faction, but gives credit where due. Also recounts the contribution of Jews to the resistance, including that of the Armee Juive.

4756. Shiber, Etta with Anne and Paul Dupre: Paris Underground [New York: Charles Scribner´s Sons, 1943]

4757. Simon, Paul: One Enemy Only - the Invader: A Record of French Resistance [London: Hodder and Stoughton, 1943]

4758. Sweets, John F.: The Politics of Resistance in France 1940-1944: A History of the Mouvements Unis De la Resistance [Chicago: Northern Illinois Univ. Press, 1976]

Study of the organizational history of the Mouvements Unis de la Resistance in the Vichy zone. Puts the activities, both military and political, of the MUR into context. Discusses the relations between the MUR, De Gaulle, and the communists. Mentions antisemitism in the context of Vichy, but says nothing about Jewish resistance.

4759. Torres, Henry: "The Coming French Revolution." Am Mercury, vol.53 #215 (Nov., 1941): 519-526.

4760. The Underground Reporter: "They Took to the Maquis." FW, vol.8 #2 (Aug., 1944): 134-138.

4761. ___: "Two Letters from Paris." FW, vol.4 #3 (Dec., 1942): 268-272.

4762. Vinde, Victor: "In Defeated France: The Spirit of Resistance." F Affairs, vol.21 #1 (Oct., 1942): 59-70.

4763. Wright, Gordon: "Reflections on the French Resistance (1940-1944)." Pol Sci Q, vol.77 #3 (Sept., 1962): 336-349.

Germany/Austria

4764. Andreas, F. and Ruth Andreas (B. Mussey, transl.): Berlin Underground, 1938-1945 [New York: Holt, Rinehart and Winston, 1945]

4765. Balfour, Michael and J. Frisby: Helmuth von Moltke: A Leader Against Hitler [London: Macmillan, 1972]

4766. Deutsch, Harold C.: The Conspiracy Against Hitler in the Twilight War [Bloomington: Univ. of Minnesota Press, 1968]

Overblown account of the German resistance in the early months of World War II. Claims that the German underground could have removed Hitler. The author is, however, aware of the total failure of the German resistance. Also attempts to vindicate the activities of the Pope. A disappointing book which places the peak of German resistance some three years too early.

4767. ___: "The German Resistance: Answered and Unanswered Questions." CEH, vol.14 #4 (Dec., 1981): 322-331.

4768. Donohoe, J.: Hitler´s Conservative Opponents in Bavaria, 1930-1945: A Consideration of Catholic, Monarchist and Seperatist Anti-Nazi Activities [Leiden: E. J. Brill, 1961]

4769. Dulles, Allen W.: Germany´s Underground [New York: Macmillan, 1947]

4770. Enfel-Janosi, Friedrich: "Remarks on the Austrian Resistance, 1938-1945." JCEA, vol.13 #2 (July, 1953): 105-122.

4771. FitzGibbon, Constantine: 20 July [New York: W. W. Norton, 1956] Also published as: The Shirt of Nessus [London: Cassel, 1956]

4772. Fraenkel, Heinrich: German People Versus Hitler [New York: W. W. Norton, 1941]

4773. Friedman, P.: "The German Resistance to the Nazis." J Sp, vol.46 #1 (Spr., 1981): 26-30.

4774. Galante, Pierre (Mark Hawson and C. Ryan, transls.): Operation Valkyrie: The German Generals Plot Against Hitler [New York: Harper & Row, 1981]

Definitive account of the attempt to kill Hitler and the military coup that followed. Well documented, including reports of those involved in the plot. The book focuses exclusively on the German military resistance, detailing the indecision and bad luck that constantly plagued the anti-Hitler forces.

4775. Gallin, Mary A.: German Resistance to Hitler: Ethical and Religious Factors [Washington, DC: The Catholic of America Univ. Press,1961]

4776. Graml, Hermann et al: The German Resistance to Hitler [London: Batsford, 1970]

4777. Haag, J.: "The Spann Circle and the Jewish Question." LBIYB, vol.18 (1973): 93-126.

4778. Hauser, Richard: The Revolt of the Munich Students Against Hitler [New York: P. G. Putnam´s Sons, 1979]

4779. Heinemann, G. W.: "Protestant Witness: Documents of Christian Resistance, 1933-1945." WLB, vol.5 #3/4 (May/July, 1951): 18.

4780. Hill, L. F.: "Towards a New History of German Resistance to Hitler." CEH, vol.14 #4 (Dec., 1981): 369-399.

4781. Hoffmann, Peter (R. Barry, transl.): The History of the German Resistance, 1933-1945 [Cambridge: Harvard Univ. Press, 1977]

4782. ___: "Ludwick Beck: Loyalty and Resistance." CEH, vol.14 #4 (Dec., 1981): 332-350.

4783. Jansen, John B. and Stefan Weyl: The Silent War: The Underground Movement in Germany [Philadelphia: J. B. Lippincott, 1943]

4784. Kantorowicz, Alfred: "´Free Germany´ in Moscow." FW, vol.7 #2 (Feb., 1944): 149-156.

4785. ___: "The Third Front: A Report on the German Underground." FW, vol.5 #2 (Feb.,1943): 127-133.

4786. Kater, Michael H.: "Anti-Fascist Intellectuals in the Third Reich." Can Jnl/His, vol.16 #2 (Aug., 1981): 263-277.

4787. Krammer, A.: "Germans Against Hitler: The Thaelmann Brigade." JCH, vol.4 #2 (April, 1969): 65-84.

4788. Leber, A. et al (eds.): Conscience in Revolt: Sixty-Four Stories of Resistance in Germany 1939-1945 [Westport, CT: Associated Book Sellers, 1957]

4789. Lend, Evelyn: The Underground Struggle in Germany [New York: League for Industrial Democracy, 1939]

4790. Lengyel, Emil: "Germany's Fifth Column." Nation, vol. 149 #16 (Oct. 19, 1939): 404-406.

4791. Lestchinsky, Jacob: "Not Nazis but Germans." CW, vol. 11 #4 (Jan. 28, 1944): 8-10.

4792. Liepmann, Heinz (R. T. Clark, tr.): Fires Underground [Philadelphia: J. B. Lippincott, 1936] * Early study of anti-Nazi underground activity in the Third Reich.

4793. Littell, Franklin H.: The German Phoenix [Garden City, NY: Doubleday, 1960]

4794. Lukens, N.: "Adam Von Trott: Resistance and Contemplation Work Ethic in Nazi Germany." Ryan: Responses, pp.169-201.

4795. Manvell, Roger and H. Fraenkel: "The Bomb Plot." Hist/WWII, #68 (1974): 1877-1885, 1888-1889.

4796. ___: The Canaris Conspiracy: The Secret Resistance to Hitler in the German Army [New York: D. McKay, 1969]

4797. Mason, H. M., Jr.: To Kill the Devil: The Attempt on the Life of Adolf Hitler [New York: W. W. Norton, 1978]

4798. Molden, F.: Exploding Stars: A Young Austrian Against Hitler [New York: William Morrow, 1979]

4799. Paxton, Robert O.: "The German Opposition to Hitler: A Non-Germanist's View." CEH, vol.14 #4 (Dec., 1981): 362-368.

4800. Prittie, Terence: Germans Against Hitler [London: Hutchinson, 1964]

4801. Ritter, G. (ed.) (R. T. Clark, transl.): The German Resistance: Carl Goerdler's Struggle Against Tyranny [New York: Arno Press, 1958]

4802. Romoser, G. K.: The Crisis of Political Direction in the German Resistance to Nazism [Urbana, Ill.: Univ. of Chicago Press, 1958]

4803. Rothfels, H. (L. Wilson, tr.): The German Opposition to Hitler: An Appraisal [Chicago: H. Regnery, 1962]

4804. ___: "The Intellectual Resistance." Friedlander: Ideology, pp.207-218.

4805. Schlamm, Willi: "Is There Another Germany?" J Fr, vol.7 #4 (April, 1940): 12-16

4806. Scholl, Inge (A. R. Schultz, tr.): Students Against Tyranny: The Resistance of the White Rose Munich 1942-1943 [Middletown, CT: Wesleyan University Press, 1970]

4807. Spangenthal, Max: "The Jewish Question and the German Resistance Movement." YVB, #19 (Oct., 1966): 60-63.

4808. Sykes, Christopher: Tormented Loyalty: The Story of a German Aristocrat who Defied Hitler [New York: Harper & Row, 1969]

4809. Van Roon, G. (P. Ludlow, tr.): German Resistance to Hitler: Count von Moltke and the Kreisau Circle [New York: Van Nostrand Reinhold Co., 1971]

4810. von Klemperer, Klemens: "Adam von Trott zu Solz and Resistance Foreign Policy." CEH, vol.14 #4 (Dec., 1981): 351-361.

4811. von Schlabrendorff, Fabian (H. Simon, tr): The Secret War Against Hitler [London: Hodder & Stoughton, 1966]

4812. von Schramm, W. (R. T. Clark, tr.): Conspiracy Among Generals [New York: Charles Scribner's Sons, 1957]

4813. Werner, Alfred: "Germans Against Hitler." Ch J Forum, vol.8 #4 (Summer, 1950): 223-227.

4814. ___: "The Junker Plot to Kill Hitler: The Dying Gesture of a Class." Com, vol.4 #1 (July, 1947): 36-42.

4815. Williams, Anthony: "Resistance and Opposition Amongst Germans." Hawes: Resistance, pp.135-169.

4816. Zassenhaus, Hiltgunt: Walls: Resisting the Third Reich. One Woman's Story [Boston: Beacon Press, 1976]

4817. Zeller, E. (R. P. Heller and D. Masters, transls.): The Flame of Freedom: The German Struggle Against Hitler [London: Wolff, 1967]

Greece

4818. Dupont, Pierre: "Greece Prepares for Invasion." FW, vol.6 #3 (Sept., 1943): 273-276.

4819. Rodinus, P.: The Fight in Greece [London: The New Europe Publishing Co., 1943]

4820. Vlavianos, Basil: "The Greek United Front." Nation, vol.157 #19 (Nov. 6, 1943): 527-528.

4821. Wason, Betty: Miracle in Hellas: The Greeks Fight On [London: Museum Press, 1943]

4822. Woodhouse, C. M.: "The Greek Resistance, 1942-1944." De Launay: ERM/I, pp.374-390.

Holland

4823. Boas, H. J.: Religious Resistance in Holland [London: George Allen and Unwin, 1945]

4824. Boolen, J. J. and J. C. Van Der Does: Five Years of Occupation: The Resistance of the Dutch Against Hitler Terrorism and Nazi-Robbery [Holland: Secret Press of D.A.V.I.D., n.d.]

4825. De Jong, Louis: "Anti-Nazi Resistance in the Netherlands." De Launay: ERM/I, pp.137-149.

4826. ___: "The Dutch Resistance Movement and the Allies, 1940-1945." De Launay: ERM/II, pp.340-365.

4827. ___: Holland Fights the Nazis [London: Drummond, n.d]

4828. ___ and Joseph W. F. Stoppelman: The Lion Rampant: The Story of Holland´s Resistance to the Nazis [New York: Querido, 1943]

4829. Ford, Herbert: Flee the Captor: The Story of the Dutch-Paris Underground and the Compassionate Leader John Henry Weidner [Nashville, TN: Southern Pub. Association, 1966]

4830. Romein, J. M.: "The Spirit of the Dutch People During the Occupation." Annals, #245 (May, 1946): 169-180.

4831. Van Duren, Theo: Orange Above [London: Staples Press, 1956]

Italy

4832. Delzell, Charles R.: Mussolini´s Enemies: The Italian Anti-Fascist Resistance [Princeton, NJ: Princeton Univ. Press, 1961]

Survey of anti-Fascist resistance activities in Italy from the March on Rome (1926) to the fall of Il Duce (1943). The climax of the book is a description of the operations of the partisans who fought in Northern Italy until the final liberation of the country by the Allied armies.

4833. Dresner, Julio: "Fermentation in Italy. The Memory of anti-Fascist Resistance." PoP, vol.4 # 4 (July/Aug., 1970): 9-11.

4834. Parri, F. and F. Venturi: "The Italian Resistance and the Allies." De Launay: ERM/II, pp.xiii-xliii.

4835. Pesce, Giovanni (F. M. Shaine, transl.): And No Quarter: An Italian Partisan in World War II [Athens, OH: Ohio Univ. Press, 1972]

4836. Rosengarten, Frank: The Italian Anti-Fascist Press, 1919-1945: From the Legal Opposition Press to the Underground Newspapers of World War II [Cleveland, OH: Press of Case Western Reserve Univ., 1968]

4837. Tilman, H. W.: When Men and Mountain Meet [Cambridge: Cambridge Univ. Press, 1946]

Norway

4838. Astrup, H. and B. L. Jacot de Boinod: Oslo Intrigue: A Woman´s Memoir of the Norwegian Resistance [New York: McGraw-Hill, 1954]

4839. Berg, P.: "Rebirth of a Nation." FW, vol.10 #4 (Oct., 1945): 65-69.

4840. Harriman (Mrs.), J. Borden: Norway Does Not Yield: The Story of the First Year [New York: Am. Friends of German Freedom, 1941]

4841. Kjelstadli, S.: "The Resistance Movement in Norway and the Allies 1940-1945." De Launay: ERM/II, pp.324-339.

4842. Mikes, G.: The Epic of Lofoten [London: Hutchinson, 1941]

4843. Moen, Peter (B. Koefoed, transl.): Peter Moen´s Diary [London: Faber & Faber, 1951]

4844. Riste, Olav and Besit Nokleby: Norway, 1940-1945: The Resistance Movement. [Oslo: International Pub., 1970]

4845. Walker, Roy: A People Who Loved Peace: The Norwegian Struggle Against Nazism [London: Victor Gollancz, 1946]

Poland

4846. Bor-Komorowski, Tadeusz: The Secret Army [New York: Macmillan, 1951]

4847. "Continued Service." Poland, #8/120 (Aug., 1964): 4-5. * On the Warsaw uprising, August 1944.

4848. Cyrankiewicz, J.: "Resistance in Auschwitz." Poland, #1/125 (Jan., 1965): 16-17, 20.

4849. Czeszko, Bohdan (Ch. Cenkalska, transl.): "Threnody." Poland, #7/143 (July, 1966): 17-19.

4850. Garlinski, Josef: Fighting Auschwitz [New York: Fawcet Publications, 1976]

Definitive study of the Polish political underground in Auschwitz. Although extensively documented, the author´s discussion of the Jews is inadequate and his version of the October 1944 Sonderkommando revolt is tendentious.

4851. ___: "The Polish Underground State (1939-1945)." JCH, vol.10 #2 (April, 1975): 219-260.

4852. ___: "The Underground Movement in Auschwitz Concentration Camp." Hawes: Resistance, pp.55-76.

4853. Grunspan, Roman: The Uprising of the Death Box of Warsaw [New York: Vantage Press, 1978]

4854. Hauptmann, Jerzy: "The Warsaw Uprising of 1944 in the American Press." Polish Rev, vol.4 #4 (Aut., 1959): 46-56.

4855. Hochfeld, J.: "The Social Aspects of the 1944 Warsaw Uprising." JCEA, vol.5 #1 (April, 1945): 36-44.

4856. Iranek-Osmacki, Kazimierz (ed. and transl.): The Unseen and the Silent: Adventures from the Underground Movement Narrated by the Paratroops of the Polish Home Army [London: Sheed & Ward, 1954]

4857. ___: "Warsaw Rising." Hist/WWII, #74 (1974): 2054-2063.

4858. Karski, Jan: "The Polish Underground State." PFR, #82 (Dec. 15, 1942): 1-8.

4859. ___: Story of a Secret State [Boston: Riverside Press, 1944]

Personal narrative of the Polish underground state as described by the home army´s most important emissary to the West. Deals inter-alia with Jews in Poland.

4860. Korbonski, S. (F. B. Czarnomski, transl.): Fighting Warsaw: The Story of the Polish Underground State 1939-1945 [New York: Funk & Wagnalls, 1956]

4861. ___ (Marta Erdman, transl.): The Polish Underground State: A Guide to the Underground, 1939-1945 [New York: Columbia Univ. Press, 1969]

An almost encyclopaedic history of the Polish underground, this work represents a highly detailed and intricate history of the activities of the Armia Krajowa (AK). Somewhat apologetic, especially when relating to Jewish issues, the book is, nevertheless, a well written and authoritative survey of resistance in Poland.

4862. Kulski, Julian E.: Dying, We Live [New York: Holt, Rinehart and Winston, 1979]

4863. Malinowski, W. R.: "Underground in Poland." Nation, vol.153 #14 (Oct. 4, 1941): 304-306.

4864. Nagorski, Zygmunt: "The Polish Underground Army." PFR, #84 (Jan. 15, 1944): 1-8.

4865. Nowak, Jan: Courier from Warsaw [Detroit: Wayne State Univ. Press, 1982] * Eyewitness report of secret courier for the Polish underground movement in World War II.

4866. Orlowski, Leopold: "The Insurrection of Warsaw." JCEA, vol.7 #2 (July, 1947): 133-142.

4867. Orska, Irena (Marta Erdman, transl.): Silent is the Vistula: The Story of the Warsaw Uprising [New York: Longmans, 1946]

4868. Segal, Simon: "Poland Fights Back." CJR, vol.5 #2 (April, 1942): 171-186.

4869. Zamoyski, Adam: "The Underground Factory: Poland in 1939-1945." History Today, vol.24 #12 (Dec., 1974): 868-873.

4870. Zawodny, J. K.: Nothing But Honor: The Story of the Warsaw Uprising, 1944 [Stamford, CA: Hoover Inst. Press, 1978]

Chronicle of the Polish Warsaw uprising of August, 1944. Places the revolt in the context of inter-Allied relations, as well as of internal Polish politics. Little mention is made of the Jews.

Soviet Union

4871. Armstrong, John A.: Organization and Control of the Partisan Movement [Maxwell Air Force Base, AL: Human Resource Research Institute, 1954]

4872. ___: The Soviet Partisan Movement in World War II [Madison: Univ. of Wisconsin Press, 1964]

4873. Baritz, J. J.: "The Phantom War." Hist/WWII, #49 (1973): 1365-1372.

4874. ___: "The War of the Rails." Hist/WWII, #103 (1974): 2858-2865.

4875. Cooper, Matthew: The Nazi War Against Soviet Partisans, 1941-1944 [New York: Stein and Day, 1979]

4876. Dallin, Alexander: The Kaminsky Brigade: 1941-1944 [Cambridge: Russian Research Center, Harvard Univ. Press, 1956]

4877. Dupont, Pierre: "Behind Enemy Lines in White Russia." FW, vol.7 #2 (Feb., 1944): 166-169.

4878. Heiman, Leo: I Was a Soviet Guerrilla [London: Brown and Watson, 1959]

4879. Howell, Edgar M.: The Soviet Partisan Movement, 1941-1944 [Washington, DC: Deptartment of the Army, United States Printing Office, 1956]

4880. Mavrogodato, Ralph and E. Ziemke: The Partisan Movement in the Polotsk Lowland [Maxwell Air Force Base, AL: Human Resources Research Institute, 1954]

4881. Snow, Edgar: "Guerrilla Tactics in Soviet Defense." Am Rev/SU, vol.4 #4 (Oct/Nov., 1941): 3-10.

4882. Utley, Freda: "The Limits of Russian Resistance." Am Mercury, vol.53 #213 (Sept., 1941): 292-300.

4883. von Luttichau, Charles V. P.: Guerrilla and Counter-Guerrilla Warfare in Russia during World War Two [Washington, DC: Office of the Chief of Military History, Dept. of the Army, 1963]

Yugoslavia

4884. Auty, Phyllis: "The Rise of Tito." Hist/WWII, #50 (1973): 1392-1400.

4885. Clissold, Stephen: "The Guerillas of Yugoslavia as Seen Through Fascist Eyes." CEO, vol.20 #3 (Feb. 5, 1943): 41-42.

4886. Davidson, Basil: Scenes from the Anti-Nazi War [New York: Monthly Review Press, 1980]

4887. Dedijer, Vladimir: "Partisan: The Yugoslav View." Hist/WWII, #108 (1974): 3001-3002.

4888. Lessner, Erwin: "The Fight of the Chetniks." FW, vol. 2 #4 (May, 1942): 299-302.

4889. Maclean, Fitzroy: "Tito´s HQ as I Saw It." Hist/WWII, #108 (1974): 3004-3005.

4890. Pomeranz, Frank: "Fall of the Cetniks." Hist/WWII, #54 (1973): 1508-1512.

4891. Radista, Bogdan: "Tito´s Partisans." Nation, vol.157 #14 (Oct. 2, 1943): 380-382.

4892. Tito, Josip B.: "The Yugoslav Peoples Fight to Live." FW, vol.7 #6 (June, 1944): 491-509.

THE ALLIES AND THE RESISTANCE

Allied Aid to European Resistance

4893. Alvarez Del Vayo, J.: "Undermining the Underground." Nation, vol.156 #20 (May 15, 1943): 701-702.

4894. Auty, Phyllis and R. Clogg (eds.): British Policy Towards Wartime Resistance in Yugoslavia and Greece [London: Macmillan, 1975]

4895. Barry, R. H.: "Helping the Resistance." Hist/WWII, #64 (1974): 1777, 1780-1783.

4896. ___: "Resistance: Aid from Outside." Hist/WWII, #17 (1973): 467-468.

4897. Brown, Anthony C.: Bodyguard of Lies 2 vols. [New York: Harper & Row, 1975]

History of the secret war for Europe in World War II, based on the Allied attempts to deceive the Nazis as to where the Overlord operation would take place. Also deals with several other aspects of espionage in World War II. Brown has trouble, however, dealing with documents and often lapses into inplausibility thus limiting the works usefulness.

4898. Buckmaster, Maurice J.: Specially Employed [London: The Batchworth Press, 1952]

4899. Deakin, F. W.: "Great Britain and European Resistance." De Launey: ERM/II, pp.98-119.

4900. De Weerd, H. A.: "Guns for Europe´s Guerrillas." Nation, vol.154 #8 (Feb. 21, 1942): 217-219.

4901. Fishman, Jack: And the Walls Came Tumbling Down [New York: Macmillan, 1982]

On the RAF bombing of the Amiens prison in 1944 which freed a large number of captured French resistance fighters. Obliquely raises questions about the possible use of similar techniques to bomb the gas chambers at Auschwitz.

4902. Foot, M. R. D.: SOE: An Outline History of the Special Operations Executive 1940-1946 [London: British Broadcasting Corporation, 1984]

Outline history of the activities and operations of the British Special Operations Executive, which was charged with aiding European anti-Nazi resistance movements. Foot makes a well balanced assessment of the importance of the SOE and its activities.

4903. ___: "Was SOE Any Good?" JCH, vol.16 #1 (Jan., 1981): 167-182.

4904. ___ and J. M. Langley: MI 9: Escape and Evasion [Boston: Little, Brown & Company, 1979]

Detailed account of the activities of the office within the British and American military intelligence services whose resposibility was to care for and otherwise assist Allied troops to escape Nazi hands.

4905. Gardiner, Muriel: Code Name Mary: Memoirs of an American Woman in the Austrian Underground [New Haven, CT: Yale Univ. Press, 1983]

4906. Garlinski, Josef (P. Stevenson, transl.): Poland, SOE and the Allies [London: G. Allen and Unwin, 1969]

4907. Gubbins, Colin M.: The Art of Guerrilla Warfare [San Francisco, CA: Interservice Press, 1981] * Classic technical manual written by the foremost of SOE´s military commanders.

4908. ___: Partisan Leaders Handbook [San Francisco, CA: Interservice Press, 1981] * Technical manual for resistance leaders, covering the how-to of guerrilla warfare.

4909. Hohne, Heinz: Codeword: Direktor [New York: Coward, McCann, and Geoghegan, 1971]

An intensive but one-sided account of the activities of Leyb (Leopold) Trepper´s "Red Orchestra", a communist oriented espionage cell in Nazi Germany and occupied Western Europe. Details Trepper´s activities but curiously omits that many of his agents were Jews. Hohne is especially apologetic about the fact that many Germans sought to resist Hitler´s tyranny by working for the communists. It is, nonetheless, a useful work.

4910. Howarth, Patrick: Undercover: The Men and Women of the Special Operations Executive [London: Routledge & Kegan, 1980]

4911. Kogan, Norman: "American Policies Towards European Resistance Movements." De Launay: ERM/II, pp.72-97.

4912. Lorain, Pierre (D. Kahn, transl.): Clandestine Operations: The Arms and Techniques of the Resistance, 1941-1944 [New York: Macmillan, 1983]

Technical history of SOE operational equipment. Discusses the weapons and materials sent by the SOE to the French Maquis. Lorain evaluates the importance of SOE help given to the French underground, and assesses the work of the brave men and women who fought against Hitler´s tyranny.

4913. Marshall, B.: The White Rabbit [London: Evans, 1952]

4914. Michel, Henri: "The Allies and the Resistance." YVS, vol.5 (1963): 317-332.

4915. Paul, Oscar (O. Pollak): Underground Europe Calling [London: Victor Gollancz, 1942]

4916. Perrault, Gilles: The Red Orchestra [New York: Simon and Schuster, 1969]

4917. Persico, Joseph E.: Piercing the Reich [New York: Viking Press, 1979]

Definitive study of the infiltration of Germany by the OSS. Based on extensive documentation only recently declassified. Includes two chapters related to Jews - Chapter 13 on the incredible heroism of Frederick Mayer, a Jewish agent who penetrated the German army, and Chapter 16 on the experience of agent Fritz Molden in the Mauthausen concentration camp.

4918. Ree, Harry: "Agents, Resisters and the Local Population." Hawes: Resistance, pp.24-54.

4919. Stafford, David: Britain and European Resistance, 1940-1945: A Survey of the Special Operations Executive with Documents [Toronto: Univ. of Totonto Press, 1980]

4920. ___: "Britain Looks at Europe, 1940: Some Origins of SOE." Can Jnl/His, vol.10 #2 (Aug., 1975): 231-248.

4921. ___: "The Detonator Concept: British Strategy, SOE and European Resistance after the Fall of France." JCH, vol.10 #2 (April, 1975): 185-217.

4922. West, Nigel: MI 6: British Secret Intelligence Service Operations 1900-45 [New York: Random House, 1983]

The definitive history of the British secret intelligence service before and during World War II. Based on secret documents none of which can be made public. Deals inter-alia with the Jews, including some novel interpretations of British immigration policy to Palestine during the 1920s.

4923. Wheeler, Mark: "The SOE Phenomenon." JCH, vol.16 #3 (July, 1981): 513-520.

Jews in the Secret War

4924. Ainsztein, Reuben: "Leyb Trepper´s War." JOMER, vol. 21 #7 (Feb. 18, 1972): 20-27.

4925. Bar-Adon, Dorothy and Pesach Bar-Adon: Seven Who Fell Tel Aviv: Lion the Printer, 1947]

4926. Bondy, Ruth (S. Katz, transl.): The Emisary: A Life of Enzo Sereni [Boston: Little, Brown and Co., 1977]

Chronicles the life of a hero of the twentieth century, one of 32 Palestinian parachutists sent to Europe by the British in 1944. Without exaggeration or undue praise, Bondy has accurately portrayed the man who was Enzo Sereni.

4927. Halpern, Ben: "Enzo." Furrows, vol.4 #2 (Dec., 1945): 14-18.

4928. Leasor, James: Code Name Nimrod [Boston: Houghton Mifflin, 1981]

Novelized history of X-Troop #10 Inter-Allied Commando. Based on archival material. Names, dates, and dialogue have been changed to protect the identity of the men involved. Most of the personnel of #10 CDO, especially of X-Troop, were Jews.

4929. Levin, Mayer: "Of Hannah Szenes and Other Secret Agents." Menorah, vol.34 #1 (April/June, 1946): 122-132.

4930. Masters, Anthony: The Summer That Bled: The Biography of Hannah Senesh [New York: St. Martin´s Press, 1972]

4931. Persico, Joseph: "Mission Green Up." NJM, vol.93 #6 (Feb., 1979): 26-37.

4932. "The Red Orchestra." Kowalski: Anthology/I pp.285-288

4933. Rothkirchen, Livia: "The Legacy of Hannah Szenes - A Documentary Legend." YVB, #13 (Oct., 1963): 66-69.

4934. Senesh, Cathrine: "The Death of Hannah Senesh." Mid, vol.4 #4 (Aut., 1958): 57-65.

4935. Senesh, Hannah (M. Cohn, transl.): Hannah Senesh: Her Life and Diary [New York: Schocken Books, 1972]

4936. Stadtler, Bea: "Rescue from the Sky." J Combat, vol.2 #3 (Spr., 1981): 20-23. * On Enzo Sereni.

4937. ___: Saviour from the Skies: The Life of Enzo Sereni [London: Valentine, Mitchell, 1972]

4938. Syrkin, Marie: "The Parachutists from Palestine: A Chapter in the European Resistance Movement." Com, vol.1 #7 (May, 1946): 30-38.

4939. Ungar, Andre: "Hannah Szenes." J Sp, vol.38 #10 (Dec., 1973): 23-24.

4940. Urquhalt, Clara and Peter L. Brent: Enzo Sereni: Hero of Our Time [London: Hale, 1967]

4941. Vago, Bela: "The Intelligence Aspects of the Joel Brand Mission." YVS, vol.10 (1974): 111-128.

THE JEWS IN THE ALLIED ARMIES

Surveys

4942. Barr, Emil N.: "The Jewish Participation in the Present War." J Fo, vol.25 #2 (Feb., 1942): 23, 30.

4943. Bentwich, N.: "Fighting Their Fatherland's Crooked Cross." Am Heb, Vol.152 #14 (Aug. 6, 1943): 7, 11. * On German Jewish refugees in the Allied armies.

4944. Biben, Joseph H.: "Jews at War." Am Heb, vol.151 #51 (April 23, 1943): 7, 14; #52 (April 30, 1943): 8, 12, 13. * Battle record of American and British Jews.

4945. Blumenthal, Nachman and J. Kermish: "Jews in the War Against the Nazis." J Combat, vol.2 #4 (Sum., 1981): 5-12.

4946. Bokser, Benzion: "The Jews and War." Recon, vol.6 #14 (Nov. 15, 1940): 7-11, 16. * Historical review.

4947. Cohen, Israel: "Jews in the Allied War Effort." CJR, vol.5 #4 (Aug., 1942): 373-389.

4948. ___: The Jews in the War [London: F. Muller, 1942]

4949. Darsie, Hugh D.: "The War and the Jew." J Fo, vol.25 #2 (Feb., 1942): 19-21.

4950. Davis, Mac: Jews Fight Too! [New York: Jordan Pub., 1945]

Survey of Jewish military service and heroism during World War II. The book is an answer to the antisemitic canard that Jews are cowards and shirkers. Composed mainly of vignettes of individual and collective Jewish heroism. Contains many interesting stories.

4951. Heinze, Howard: "Jews are Valiant Combatants." JVP, vol.5 #3/4 (April/May, 1942): 10-11, 20.

4952. The Jews and the War [Melbourne, Aust.: Jew. Council to Combat Fascism and Antisemitism, 1943]

4953. Klinov, J.: "How Jews Fight for Freedom." J Sp, vol.7 #10 (Aug., 1942): 25-27.

4954. ___: "The War Effort of the Jewish People in 5702." P.I.N., vol.10 #37 (Sept. 12, 1942): 3, 4.

4955. Learsi, Rufus: The Jew in Battle [New York: American Zionist Youth Commission, n.d.]

4956. Mead, James M.: "Why We Fight." Opinion, vol.12 #9 (July, 1942): 11-13.

4957. M. M.: "A Jewish Soldier Against the Nazi Enemy." YVB, #13 (Oct., 1963): 56-59.

4958. Numberg, Ralph: The Fighting Jews [New York: Creative Age Press, 1945]

4959. Silver, Abba Hillel: "The Army of Jewish Liberation." Hamigdal, vol.6 #1 (Nov., 1945): 2.

4960. Steinberg, L.: "The Participation of Jews in the Allied Armies." Y/V: Resistance, pp.379-391.

4961. Tenenbaum, Joseph: "The United Jewish War Effort." CW, vol.10 #2 (Jan. 8, 1943): 9-10.

4962. Weil, Frank L.: "We Do Our Share: The Story of Jewish Service in World War II." Opinion, vol.14 #8 (June, 1944): 8-9.

4963. Freeden, Herbert: "V Day Ten Years Ago." CW, vol.22 #18 (May 9, 1955): 5-7.

4964. Gallin, Martin: "American Jews in World War II." Kowalski: Anthology/I, pp.38-41.

4965. ___: "The Lord is my Rock." J Combat, vol.1 #2 (Fall, 1980): 30-31.

4966. Gordon, F.: "Victim of Nazi Treachery." Lib Jud, vol. 13 #1 (May, 1945): 53-55. * On the murder of Major General Maurice Rose.

4967. Kaufman, I.: "American Jews in World War II: Inside Germany." Kowalski: Anthology/I, pp.442-466.

4968. ___: American Jews in World War Two: The Story of 550,000 Fighters for Freedom (2 vols.) [New York: Dial Press, 1947]

4969. "Keeping a Record of Jewish War Service." CJR, vol.6 #5 (Oct., 1943): 521-524. * On difficulty of keeping records.

4970. Kohs, Samuel C.: "Jews in America´s Armed Forces." CW, vol.12 #1 (Jan. 5, 1945): 8-9.

4971. ___: "Jewish War Records of World War II." AJYB, vol. 47 (1945/1946): 153-172.

4972. McCormack, John W.: "Their Names will Live." Am Heb, vol. 151 #19 (Sept. 11, 1942): 8-9.

4973. National Jewish Welfare Board: Compiling Jewish War Records During World War Two [New York: NJWB, 1946]

4974. ___: Fighting for America: A Record of the Participation of Jewish Men and Women in the Armed Forces During 1944 [New York: NJWB, 1944]

4975. ___: In the Nation´s Service [New York: NJWB, 1942]

4976. Oblas, Irving: "The First Jew Over Berlin." Opinion, vol.14 #3 (Jan., 1944): 9-11.

4977. Ribalow, Harold U.: "The American Jewish Soldier." CW, vol.10 #20 (May 21, 1943): 9-10.

4978. ___: "Portrait: Four Soldiers." CW, vol.10 #15 (Apr. 9, 1943): 12-13.

4979. ___: "Three Old Soldiers." CW, vol.11 #2 (Jan. 14, 1944): 10-11, 14.

4980. Rontch, Isaac E.(ed.): Jewish Youth at War: Letters from American Soldiers [New York: Marstin Press, 1945]

4981. Saundrow, Edward: "Jews in the Army - A Short Social Study." Recon, vol.10 #3 (Mar. 17, 1944): 10-17.

4982. Smedley, Clarence G.: "Jews Seek Armed Service." NJM, vol. 57 #5 (Jan., 1943): 156-157.

4983. Talpalar, Morris: "Antisemitism in the Army." Am Heb, vol.154 #18 (Mar. 2, 1945): 4-5, 10.

4984. Title, Julius M.: :"The Jewish American Soldier: What is He Fighting For?" Am Heb, vol.153 #44 (Sept. 1, 1944): 7, 14.

4985. Weill, Milton: "Jews in Action." Opinion, vol.12 #9 (July, 1942): 6-8.

4986. ___: "Our Military Record: The First Year." CJR, vol. 5 #6 (Dec., 1942): 567-577.

Canada

4987. Canadian Jewry and the War Effort [Montreal: Canadian Jewish Congress, 1943]

4988. Canadian Jews in World War II [Montreal: Canadian Jewish Congress, 1947/1948]

4989. Frank, M. Z.: "Canadian Jewry in the War." CW, vol.9 #4 (Jan. 23, 1942): 6-9.

4990. Jewish War Heroes [Montreal: Canadian Jewish Congress, 1946]

4991. Wincett, Louis A.: "Canadian Jewry's War Effort." CW, vol.11 #1 (Jan. 7, 1944): 11-12.

Czechoslovakia

4992. Kulka, Erich: "Czechoslovak Jews in the ´Svoboda Army´." JQ, vol.23 #4 (Wint., 1975/76): 29-32.

4993. ___ (ed.): Collection of Testimonies and Documents on the Participation of Czechoslovak Jews in the Second World War Against Nazi Germany Heb/Eng [Jerusalem: Yad Vashem, 1976]

France

4994. Dluznowski, M.: "Jews Fought for France." Am Heb, vol.151 #19 (Sept. 11, 1942): 14, 55.

4995. Szajkowski, Zosa: Jews and the French Foreign Legion [New York: Ktav, 1975]

Polemical account of the drafting and mistreating of Jews in the French Foreign Legion during two wars. Service in the FFL almost exclusively fell to "foreign" Jews and to a great degree was a forerunner of the mistreatment of Jews by the Vichy government.

4996. ___: "Jews in the Foreign Legion." Con Jud, vol.21 #4 (Sum., 1967): 22-34.

4997. ___: "The Soldiers France Forgot." CJR, vol.5 #6 (Dec., 1942): 589-596.

Great Britain

4998. Annenberg, Jerrold: "Jewish Officers in His Majesty´s Forces." J Standard, vol.4 #10 (June 18, 1943): 2, 6.

4999. ___: "Jews in the R. A. F." J Standard, vol.4 #14 (July 16, 1943): 6, 5.

5000. ___: "Jews in the Royal Navy." J Standard, vol.4 #30 (Nov. 5, 1943): 2, 6.

5001. Bentwich, Norman: I Understand the Risks [London: V. Gollancz, 1950] * On Jewish refugees who volunteered their services to the Royal army.

5002. Brodie, I.: "British and Palestinian Jews in World War II." AJYB, vol.48 (1946/1947): 51-72.

5003. Krug, Mark: "Brigadier Kisch of the Eighth Army." CJR, vol.8 #3 (June, 1945): 282-289.

5004. Werner, Alfred: "Refugees Fight for Allies." NJM, vol.56 #8 (April, 1942): 246-247.

Greece

5005. Dombalis, C. N.: "Frizis, Greece´s Beloved Jewish Hero." J Digest, vol.15 #10 (July, 1970): 78-80.

5006. ___: "The Jewish Colonel: Mordecai Frizis, Greece´s Beloved Hero." J Digest, vol.9 #1 (Oct., 1963): 15-17.

Poland

5007. "Jews in the Polish Army." J Comment, vol.2 #13 (April 28, 1944): 1-2.

5008. Nussbaum, Klemens: "Jews in the Polish Army in the USSR, 1943-1944." SJA, vol.2 #1 (May, 1972): 94-104.

5009. Redlich, Shimon: "Jews in General Anders´ Army in the Soviet Union, 1941-1942." SJA, vol.1 #2 (Nov., 1971): 90-98.

5010. Shainberg, Maurice: "With the Polish Army in Battle." Kowalski: Anthology/I, pp.252-261.

5011. Stein, Kalman: "Jews in the Polish Army." J Fr, vol. 11 #5 (May, 1944): 17-19.

5012. Not Used.

5013. "The Story of a Jewish Boy from Lodz." GS, #20 (Feb. 1, 1944): 3-4.

5014. "The Trial of Jewish Soldiers of the Polish Army." GS, #26 (June 1, 1944): 1-3.

Russia

5015. Abarbanel, David: "Scourge of the Supermen." Lib Jud, vol.12 #4 (Aug., 1944): 20-21.

5016. Ainsztein, Reuben: "The Forgotten Jew of Stalingrad." JOMER, vol.11 #50 (Dec. 14, 1962): 12-13, 15.

5017. ___: "The Jew Who Helped Save Stalingrad: Vainrub, Russia's Forgotten Military Genius." J Digest, vol.9 #1 (Oct., 1963): 60-64.

5018. ___: "Jews Who Fought to Save Moscow." JOMER, vol.16 #17 (April 28, 1967): 11-13.

5019. ___: "Soviet Jewry's Unsung Heros." JOMER, vol.18 #14 (April 2, 1969): 16-19.

5020. ___: "War Record of Soviet Jewry." JSS, vol.28 #1 (Jan., 1966): 3-24.

5021. Feffer, Itzig: "Hitler Forgot One Little Thing: Our Courage." Today, vol.1 #2 (Dec., 1944): 14-15, 31.

5022. ___: "Not Back to the Ghetto: Forward to Battle." Am Heb, vol.150 #20 (Sept. 18, 1942): 10, 14.

5023. Gruber, Samuel: "Memories of a Soldier." J Combat, vol.1 #1 (Spr., 1980): 21-23.

5024. Guri, Joseph: "Jewish Fighters in the Red Army." Dispersion, #5/6 (Spr., 1966): 172-177.

5025. ___: "Jewish Heroes of the Soviet Union." YVB, #19 (Oct., 1966): 45-52.

5026. ___: "Jewish Participation in the Red Army in World War II." YVB, #16 (Feb., 1965): 6-13.

5027. Isaacs, S.: "Jewish Heroes on Russian Front." CW, vol.9 #2 (Jan. 9, 1942): 11-12.

5028. Levin, Dov: "Facts and Problems in the Study of the Fighting of the Jews of the Soviet Union in World War Two." Y/V: Resistance, pp.392-402.

5029. ___: "Jews in Soviet Lithuanian Forces in World War II: The Nationality Factor." SJA, vol.3 #1 (May, 1973): 57-64.

5030. ___: "Participation of the Lithuanian Jews in the Second World War." J Combat, vol.2 #4 (Spr., 1981): 21-26. Also in Kowalski: Anthology/I, pp. 264-278.

5031. Levin, K.: "A Bridge at Midnight." Lib Jud, vol.13 #3 (July, 1945): 51-52.

5032. Parrish, Michael: "General G. M. Shtern: A Biographical Inquiry." SJA, vol.5 #1 (May, 1975): 73-76.

5033. The Russian Jews in the War [London: Jewish Fund for Soviet Russia, 1943]

5034. Saphire, William B.: "Soviet Forces Have Their Jewish Heroes." CJCh, vol.32 #52 (May 11, 1945): 5, 12.

5035. Sonin, David and Z. Ben-Sholmo: "Jewish Heroism in Red Army: For Our Fathers and Mothers." HM, vol.61 #6 (Feb., 1980): 12-13, 35-36, 38-39.

5036. Spector, Sh.: "The Pen is Mightier than the Sword." YVB, #18 (April, 1966): 50-52. * On Soviet Jewish war correspondents.

5037. Wedeck, Harry E.: "Jewish Heroes in Russia." Am Heb, vol.151 #19 (Sept. 11, 1942): 11, 18, 58.

THE STRUGGLE FOR A JEWISH ARMY

5038. Angel, Norman: "Your Foe is Our Foe." NP, vol.31 #5 (Nov. 15, 1940): 7-8.

5039. Benari, I.: "David Raziel: Hero and Soldier of Zion." J Standard, vol.2 #9 (June 13, 1941): 4.

5040. Ben-Gurion, David: "The Arrest of the 43." JOMER, vol.12 #45 (Nov. 8, 1963): 16-19.

5041. ___: "The Birth of the Jewish Brigade." JOMER, vol.13 #2 (Jan. 10, 1964): 18-21.

5042. ___: "Churchill Makes a Promise." JOMER, vol.13 #1 (Jan 3, 1964): 16-19.

5043. ___: "The First Days of the Jewish Brigade." JOMER, vol.13 #3 (Jan. 17, 1964): 14-17.

5044. ___: "Ironside Supports a Jewish Army." JOMER, vol.12 #46 (Nov. 15, 1963): 18-22.

5045. ___: "Why We Fought for Britain." JOMER, vol.12 #47 (Nov. 22, 1963): 15-18.

5046. ___: "The Yishuv Goes to War." JOMER, vol.12 #44 (Nov. 1, 1963): 20-23.

5047. ___: "The Yishuv Joins Up." JOMER, vol.12 #51 (Dec. 20, 1963): 18-20. * Series of articles on the Yishuv in World War Two written by Israel´s First Prime Minister.

5048. Ben-Horin, Eliahu: "A Jewish Army." Am J Ch, vol.1 #14/15 (Jan. 20, 1940):: 12-14.

5049. Boukstein, M. M.: "Palestine at War." CJR, vol.3 #6 (Nov./Dec., 1940): 595-604.

5050. Cohen, Israel: Britain´s Nameless Ally [London: W. A. Allen, 1942]

5051. ___: "The Jewish Issue of the War." J Sp, vol.8 #5 (March, 1941): 24-26.

5052. ___: "Palestine, the Jews, and the War." J Sp, vol.7 #9 (July, 1942): 10-12.

5053. Cohen, Renato: "Palestine At War." J Standard, vol.3 #18 (Aug. 14, 1942): 7; #19 (Aug. 21, 1942): 10; #21 (Sept. 4, 1942): 5; #23 (Sept. 18, 1942): 3.

5054. Dougdale, Blanche: "Palestine and the War." Cont Rev, vol.158 #899 (Nov., 1940): 524-527.

5055. Errey, Eric D.: "The Forgotten Ally." CJCh, vol.32 #18 (Sept. 15, 1944): 27-28.

5056. Ginsburg, Elias: "Why a Jewish Army?" J Fo, vol.25 #2 (Feb., 1942): 24-25.

5057. Goldmann, Nahum: "Jewish Palestine." FW, vol.9 #1 (Jan., 1945): 47-50. * Contributions to the Allies.

5058. "The Government and a Jewish Fighting Force." NJ, vol.18 #2/3 (Nov./Dec., 1941): 23-27.

5059. Heinze, Howard J.: "The Heroic Fighters of the Jewish Legion." JVP, vol.6 #1/2 (Jan./Feb., 1943): 4-5.

5060. Itzhaki, Solomon: "Palestine Jewry´s War Effort." CW, vol.12 #22 (June 22, 1945): 8-10.

5061. ___: "Soldiers of the Jewish People." CW, vol.10 #21 (May 28, 1943): 8-10, 20.

5062. ___: "Soldiers of Our People." JVP, vol.6 #7/8 (Oct./ Nov., 1943): 8-9, 41.

5063. Jabotinsky, Vladimir: "A B C of the Jewish Army." Am J Ch, vol.1 #14/15 (June 20, 1940): 11-12.

5064. ___: The War and the Jew [New York: Dial Press, 1943]

Discussion of the goals and aims Jews must set themselves with the outbreak of World War II. Jabotinsky, the founder and first leader of the Revisionist wing of Zionism, covers a wide range of related topics. His conclusion is that in the short range Jews must be treated as an allied nation, while in the long range only a Jewish state will solve world Jewry's problems.

5065. "Jewish Commandos in Action." NP, vol.33 #12 (April 16, 1943): 9-10.

5066. "Jewish Palestine's War Effort." PYB, #2 (1945/1946): 363-379.

5067. "The Jewish War Effort in Palestine." NJ, vol.17 #12 (Sept., 1941): 184-185.

5068. Joseph, Bernard: "Jewish Palestine Fights." HM, vol. 21 #5 (March, 1941): 6-9.

5069. Kleinlerer, Edward D.: "Jewish Epic in Cyrenaica." CW, vol.9 #6 (Feb. 6, 1942): 10-11.

5070. ___: "Jewish Heroism at Tobruk." CW, vol.9 #24 (June 26, 1942): 7-8.

5071. Leftwich, Joseph: "How the Jewish Army Plans Were Sabotaged." J Sp, vol.7 #7 (May, 1942): 20-22.

5072. Levenberg, S.: "Fighting Under the Star of David." JOMER, vol.23 #41 (Oct. 11, 1974): 14-15. Also in: J Digest, vol.20 #4 (Jan., 1975): 74-76.

5073. Levin, Harry: "Prelude to a Jewish Army." NP, vol.31 #25 (April 4, 1941): 9-10.

5074. Levinthal, Louis E.: "Needed: A Jewish Army." J Sp, vol.7 #3 (Jan., 1942): 6-7.

5075. Lipsky, Louis: "No More Anonymity." CB, vol.7 #1 (Nov. 15, 1940): 6-7.

5076. ___: "The Unnamed Ally of the United Nations." FW, vol.3 #4 (Sept., 1942): 361-365.

5077. Nadich, J.: "The Jewish Brigade and Ulm." J Combat, vol.2 #4 (Spr., 1981): 13-16.

5078. "Palestine in the War Zone." NJ, vol.16 #9 (June, 1940): 140-143.

5079. "Palestine Jews Train to Defend Their Country." NJM, vol.56 #10 (June, 1942): 329-330.

5080. "A Palestine Regiment - Seperate Jewish and Arab Battalions: Statement by the Secretary of State for War." NJ, vol.18 #11/12 (Aug./Sept., 1942): 163-171.

5081. Penkower, Monty N.: "The Struggle for an Allied Jewish Fighting Force During World II." Braham: Contemporary, pp.47-75.

5082. Rabinowitz, Louis: "In the Royal Navy." HM, vol.24 #2 (Dec., 1943): 6-7.

5083. ___: Soldiers from Judea: Palestinian Jewish Units in the Middle East 1941-1943 [New York: American Zionist Emergency Council, 1945]

Short regiment-by-regiment survey of the Yishuv´s war effort and of Rabinowitz´ experiences as senior chaplain of the British Eighth Army.

5084. ___: "They Served the Eighth Army." J Sp, vol.9 #4 (Feb., 1944): 24-25, 27.

5085. ___: "With the Jewish Fighting Units." HM, vol.23 #3 (Dec., 1942/Jan., 1943): 6-7.

5086. "Recruitment of Jews in Palestine: Debate in the House of Lords." NJ, vol.18 #8/9 (May/June, 1942): 122-130.

5087. Revusky, Abraham: "Why a Jewish Army?" J Fr, vol.8 #11 (Nov., 1941): 12-15.

5088. Rosmarin, Aaron: "A Zionist Army?" J Sp, vol.7 #5 (March, 1942): 11-13.

5089. Schwartz, Shulamith: "Britain and the Jewish Brigade." Palestine, vol.1 #10 (Oct., 1944): 5-8.

5090. Shertok (Sharett), Moshe: "The Palestine Jewish Units in Italy." J Fr, vol.11 #7 (July, 1944): 19-21.

5091. ___: "The Yishuv´s Army of Freedom: Lib Jud, vol.11 #1 (May, 1943): 52-58.

5092. Shir, Miriam: "Palestine´s Women Soldiers." HM, vol. 23 #1 (Sept./Oct., 1942): 14-16.

5093. Sterling, Yates Jr.: "A Jewish Army in Palestine." JVP, vol.5 #3/4 (April/May, 1942): 6-7, 36. * Admiral Sterling proposes that a Jewish army would defend the Holy Land with honor and courage.

5094. Test Case for Democracy: The American Press and the Jewish Army [Washington, DC: Comm. for a Jewish Army of Palestinian and Stateless Jews, 1942]

5095. "The Unknown Hero." Zionews, vol.3 #16 (June 4, 1941): 2-3. * On David Raziel.

5096. "The War and Palestine." CJR, vol.2 #5 (Sept./Oct., 1939): 62-63.

5097. "The War Situation: Palestine." CJR, vol.2 #6 (Nov./Dec., 1939): 52-54.

5098. Weiner, Albert: "Palestine´s Jews in the War." Today, vol.1 #3 (Jan., 1945): 12-15.

5099. Weizmann, Vera: "We Shall Fight..." HM, vol.21 #8 (July/Aug., 1941): 8-9.

5100. World Jew. Congress: "The Problem of a Jewish Army." IJA, vol.1 #3 (Oct., 1941): 1-10.

12

The Bystanders

JEWISH-GENTILE RELATIONS

Overviews

5101. Agar, Herbert: "Christians Who Dared Death to Save Jews: How Thousands of Jews Escaped Nazis." J Digest, vol.6 #8 (May, 1961): 17-20.

5102. Bauer, Yehuda: "Christian Behaviour During the Holocaust." J Sp, vol.43 #3 (Fall, 1978): 17-21.

5103. Bernier, Linda: "Saviors Revisited." HM, vol.64 #5 (Jan., 1983): 10-11, 28.

5104. Federman, Simon: "New Light on Resistance History: The Record of Non-Jews who Saved Jews from Nazis." J Currents, vol.13 #5 (May, 1959): 31-33.

5105. Fried, H. and Z. Shuster: "Conquered Europe Resists Antisemitism." CJR, vol.4 #1 (Feb., 1941): 31-43.

5106. Friedman, Philip: "Battle of the Badge." J Digest, vol.4 #3 (Dec., 1958): 33-40.

5107. Friedman, Theodore: "Judaism and Christianity - Fact and Fiction." Recon, vol.10 #8 (May 26, 1944): 21-23.

5108. Itzhaki, Solomon: "Christians Against Antisemitism." CW, vol.9 #28 (Oct. 2, 1942): 9-10.

5109. Kennedy, Raymond: "The Background of Jewish-Gentile Relations." J Fo, vol.26 #3 (April, 1943): 53-54; #4 (May, 1943): 85-86.

5110. Schulweis, Harold M.: "Remember the Righteous Redeemers: A Proposal." J Digest, vol.9 #1 (Oct., 1963): 65-69. * Calls for a memorial for Christians who saved Jews.

5111. Schwartz, David: "Antisemitic ´Blitz´ Bogs Down." CW, vol.8 #32 (Oct. 3, 1941): 11-12.

5112. Zukerman, William: "Auguries of a New Europe." CJR, vol.6 #1 (Feb., 1943): 37-48.

5113. ___: "The Christian World Did Not Forsake the Jews." J Newsletter, vol.17 #13 (June 26, 1961): 1-2.

Eastern Europe

5114. Ainsztein, Reuben: "The Polish Jews Need Not Have Died." Mid, vol.4 #4 (Aut., 1958): 2-4, 101-103.

5115. Alcalai, David: "Tito´s Record Toward the Jews." J Fr, vol.20 #1 (Jan., 1953): 20-23.

5116. Apenszlak, Jacob: "The Problem of Polish-Jewish Relations." Polish Jew, vol.1 #3 (Dec., 1941): 1-3.

5117. Bartoszewski, Wladislaw: The Blood Shed United Us: Pages from the History of Help to Jews in Occupied Poland [Warsaw: Interpress Publications, 1970]

5118. Bauer, Yehuda: "Rescue Operations Through Vilna." YVS, vol.9 (1973): 215-223.

5119. Berenstein, Tatana and Adam Rutkowski (E. Rothert, transl.): Assistance to the Jews in Poland [Warsaw: Polonia Press, 1963]

5120. Ciolkosz, Adam: "Polish Labor vs. Antisemitism." CW, vol.9 #34 (Nov. 13, 1942): 8-9.

5121. Edin, M.: "The PPR and Ghetto Resistance." J Life, vol.5 #6 (54) (April, 1951): 12-15.

5122. Friedman, Philip: "Ukrainian-Jewish Relations during the Nazi Occupation." Friedman: Roads, pp.176-208.

5123. Frost, Shimon: "Reclaiming the Past of the Jews in Poland." CM, vol.50 #7 (Sept./Oct., 1983): 6-7.

5124. G. K.: "Fascists of the Polish Underground." FW, vol. 5 #3 (March, 1943): 280-281.

5125. Gross, Feliks: "The Polish Democratic Front." CW, vol.8 #33 (Oct. 17, 1941): 6-8.

5126. Gutman, Yisrael: "The Attitude of the Poles to the Mass Deportations of Jews from the Warsaw Ghetto in the Summer of 1942." Gutman: Rescue, pp.399-422.

5127. ___: "Polish Responses to the Liquidation of Warsaw Jewry." Jer Q, #17 (Fall, 1980): 40-55.

5128. Heiman, Leo: "They Saved Jews: Ukrainian Patriots Defied Nazis." Uk Q, vol.17 #4 (Win., 1961): 320-332.

5129. ___: "Ukrainians and the Jews." Uk Q, vol.17 #2 (Sum, 1961): 107-116.

5130. "In Face of a Common Foe: Poles and Jews during the Occupation." WLB, vol.15 #1 (Jan., 1961): 10.

5131. Itzhaki, Solomon: "Lights and Shadows in Balkans." CW, vol.9 #22 (Jun. 12, 1942): 9-10.

5132. Karski, Jan: "My Visit to the Warsaw Ghetto." Am Mercury, vol.59 #251 (Nov., 1944): 567-575.

5133. ___: "Polish-Jewish Collaboration in Underground Poland." J Fo, vol.27 #8 (Aug., 1944): 160, 170.

5134. Kermish, Joseph: "The Activities of the Council for Aid to Jews ('Zegota') in Occupied Poland." Gutman: Rescue, pp.367-398.

5135. Kosciesza, Bogumil: "And All of You Say: Amen, Nisan 5703." Commonweal, vol.106 (April 27, 1979): 240-241. * Memoir by gentile witness of Warsaw Ghetto revolt.

5136. Krug, Mark: "The Poles, a Time for Healing." Sh'ma, vol.3 #56 (Sept. 7, 1973): 124-126.

5137. Lauterbach, Richard: "Sunday in Poland." Life, vol.17 #12 (Sept. 18, 1944): 17-18. * First hand account of Majdanek.

5138. Lednicki, Waclaw: "Poles and Jews Before and After the War." J Fo, vol.27 #8 (Aug., 1944): 151-153.

5139. Lichten, Joseph L.: "Did Polish Jews Die Forsaken?" Polish Rev, vol.4 #1/2 (Win./Spr., 1959): 119-126.

5140. Modras, R.: "Jews and Poles: A Relationship Reconsidered." America, vol.146 #1 (Jan. 2/9, 1982): 5-8.

5141. Oren, Uri (M. Segal, transl.): A Town Called Monastir [Tel Aviv: Dror, 1951] * On Bulgaria.

5142. "The Polish Underground Labor Movement Fights Antisemitism." GS, #20 (Feb. 1, 1944): 2-3.

5143. Rothkirchen, Livia: "Czech Attitudes Towards the Jews during the Nazi Regime." YVS, vol.13 (1979): 287-320.

5144. ___: "The Role of the Czech and Slovak Jewish Leadership in the Field of Rescue Work. Gutman: Rescue, pp. 423-434.

5145. Tartakower, Aryieh: "Poland´s Underground." CW, vol.8 #42 (Dec. 19, 1941): 12-13.

5146. Tenenbaum, Joseph: "I Am a Polish Jew." CW, vol.8 #19 (May 16, 1941): 6-7.

5147. Wasita, Ryszard: "The Wall Did Not Divide the City." Poland, #6/154 (June, 1967): 14-15.

5148. Weigler, Zvi: "Two Polish Villages Razed for Extending Help to Jews." YVB, #1 (April, 1957): 18-20.

5149. Zachariash, S.: "The Ghetto Was Not Alone." J Life, vol.5 #6 (April, 1951): 10-12.

Western Europe

5150. Arnold, Elliot: "A Night of Rescue: 25 Years Ago in Denmark." HM, vol.50 #2 (Oct., 1968): 15, 33.

5151. Atchildi, Asaf: "Rescue of Jews of Bukharian, Iranian and Afghan Origin in Occupied France (1940 - 1944)." YVS, vol.6 (1967): 257-282.

5152. Baron, Joseph L.: "In the Danish Tradition." Lib Jud, vol.12 #2 (June, 1944): 8-13, 18.

5153. Beller, Jacob: "Holland: A Bright Star in an Overcast Horizon." JVP, vol.9 #2/3 (April/May, 1946): 20-22, 40-41.

5154. Bendix, Hans: "Denmark: Oasis of Decency." Com, vol.4 #3 (Sept., 1947): 246-250.

5155. Bertelson, Aage (M. Lindholm and W. Agtby, tranls.): October ´43 [New York: G. P. Putnam´s Sons, 1954]

Inside account of the rescue of Danish Jewry by one of the organizers of Danish resistance. The book is both a chronicle of and a tribute to the heroism and human decency of the Danes. Shows the vital role that saving Jews played in broadening the base of the Danish underground.

5156. Borchenius, Paul: "Aspects of the Rescue of Danish Jews." WLB, vol.22 #4 (Aut., 1968): 36-40. Also in: J Sp, vol.34 #6 (June, 1969): 7-10.

5157. Cohen, David: "How Holland Helped the Jews during the Occupation." V/Unq, vol.3 #10/11 (Oct./Nov., 1945): 10.

5158. "The Danish Case: A Summary." J Comment, vol.2 #3 (Feb. 4, 1944): 4-7.

5159. De Jong, Pieter: "Responses of the Churches in the Netherlands to the Nazi Occupation." Ryan: Responses, pp.121-143.

5160. "Denmark and Sweden Point the Way." J Comment, vol.1 #14 (Oct. 15, 1943): 1-2.

5161. Duquesne, Jacques: "Defensor Judaeorum - The French Episcopate, 1940-1944." WLB, vol.21 #2 (Spr., 1967): 15-20.

5162. Eligulashvili, Levi: "How the Jews of Gruziya in Occupied France were Saved." YVS, vol.6 (1967): 251-255.

5163. Fisher, Samuel: "Not All of France is Vichy." JVP, vol.4 #9/10 (Oct., 1941): 20-21.

5164. Flender, Harold: "The Magnificent Danes." ADL Bul, vol.18 #8 (Oct., 1961): 4-5, 8.

5165. ___: Rescue in Denmark [New York: Simon & Schuster, 1963] Excerpted in Friedlander: Whirlwind, pp.353-370

Chronicle of the single most systematic effort to rescue Jews. Flender has written a true adventure story, which, because the events are true, is all the more dramatic.

5166. Foxman, Abraham H.: "The Righteous Danes." Chartock: Society, pp.166-167.

5167. "From the Belgian Underground: Practical Measures to aid the Jewish Population." Am Heb, vol.152 #11 (July 16, 1943): 2, 21.

5168. Gerber, George: "The Voice of the True France." J Sp, vol.7 #12 (Oct., 1942): 13-14, 25.

5169. Glenthoj, Jorgen: "The Little Dunkerque: The Danish Rescue of Jews in October, 1943." Ryan: Responses, pp.93-119.

5170. Goris, Jan Albert: "Belgians Fight Antisemitism." CW, vol.10 #2 (Jan. 8, 1943): 8-9.

5171. "Greek Underground Saves Thousands of Jews." GS, #25 (May 1, 1944): 3-4.

5172. Hallie, Philip P.: Lest Innocent Blood Be Shed: The Story of the Village of La Chambon and how Goodness Happened There [New York: Harper & Row, 1978]

Chronicles the activities of a village of French Huguenots who saved Jews from the Nazis. For Hallie their activities prove that good can defeat evil.

5173. Katz, Franz: "Israel´s Nordic Champions." CJR, vol. 7 #1 (Feb., 1944): 52-62. * On Denmark.

5174. Langodakis, C.: "The Story of a Gallant People: How the People in Greece fought the introduction of Anti-semitism Under the Terror Occupation of the Nazis." JVP, vol.7 #4 (Oct., 1944): 23, 28.

5175. Levin, M.: "The Epic of Children´s Rescue." Rescue, vol.2 #2 (Feb., 1945): 9-12. * In France.

5176. Moller, J. Christmas: "Denmark´s Attitude." J Layman, vol.18 #4 (Jan., 1944): 12-13.

5177. "Protection Given to Jews by Belgium's Underground." GS, #32 (Dec. 1, 1944): 4-6.

5178. "Protests Against Vichy's Treatment of Jews." CJR, vol.6 #6 (Dec., 1942): 645-649.

5179. Ramati, A.: The Assisi Underground: The Priests Who Rescued Jews [New York: Stein and Day, 1978]

Journalistic account of the efforts of some Itialian townsfolk to save 300 Jews. These efforts were organized by Friar Rufino Niccacci, the spiritual leader of the town. The Assisi underground proved that Jewish lives could be saved by those with the will to do so.

5180. Robinson, J.: "Report from Le Chambon: The Power of Nonviolence." PT, vol.7 #4 (Sum., 1980): 18-20.

5181. Sapir, Boris: "I was a Jew in Occupied Holland." J Mirror, vol.1 #4 (Nov., 1942): 47-49.

5182. Sauvage, Pierre: "A Most Persistent Haven: Le Chambon Sur-Lignon." Momemt, vol.8 #9 (Oct., 1983): 30-35.

5183. Schwarzbart, Isaac I.: "Denmark's Heroic Rescue of Jews." CW, vol.21 #31 (Nov. 22, 1954): 5-6. Also in J Affairs, vol.10 #2 (feb., 1955): 24-26.

5184. Singer, Kurt: "A Danish Anniversary." Lib Jud, vol.12 #7 (Nov., 1944): 33-34.

5185. Stoppelman, Joseph: "The Dutch Defy Hitler." CW, vol. 9 #25 (July 10, 1942): 6-8.

5186. Vignaux, Paul: "Christian Trade Unions Fought Antisemitism Throughout Period of France's Occupation." V/Unq, vol.3 #3 (March, 1945): 3, 6.

5187. Werner, Alfred: "The 'Dunkirk' of Danish Jewry." NJM, vol.73 #6 (March, 1959): 9-10, 20-21.

5188. ___: "Norway - Faithful to Freedom." CW, vol.9 #33 (Nov. 6, 1942): 7-8.

5189. Not Used.

5190. Yahil, L.: The Rescue of Danish Jewry [Philadelphia: J. P. S., 1969]

Authoritative historical account of the dramatic events of October, 1943. Yahil reviewed all the pertinent archival sources, as well as making use of oral testimonies. Yahil also places the Danish actions into the context of the Nazi occupation as well as the Final Solution.

5191. ___: "The Uniqueness of the Rescue of Danish Jewry." Gutman: Rescue, pp.617-625.

Germany

5192. Aronsfeld, C. C.: "Not All Germans Are Guilty." J Sp, vol.20 #2 (Feb., 1955): 9-11.

5193. Friedman, Philip: "Was There an Other Germany during the Nazi Period?" YIVO Annual, vol.10 (1955): 82-127. Also in Friedman: Roads, pp.422-464.

5194. Gay, R.: "Outwitting the Final Solution: Jews in Berlin." Horizon, vol.19 #1 (Jan., 1977): 42-47.

5195. Janowitz, Morris: "German Reactions to Nazi Atrocities." Am Jnl Soc, vol.52 (Sept., 1946): 141-145.

5196. Kulka, Otto D.: "Public Opinion in Nazi Germany and the Jewish Question." Jer Q, #25 (Fall, 1982): 121-144.; #26 (Win., 1983): 34-45. * Research into the German attitude toward the Final Solution of the Jewish question in the Third Reich.

5197. Stokes, Lawrence D.: "The German People and the Destruction of the European Jews." CEH, vol.6 #2 (June, 1973): 167-191.

HASIDEI UMOT HA´OLAM

Surveys

5198. Bartoszewski, Wladyslaw and Zofia Lewin (eds.): The Samaritans: Heroes of the Holocaust [New York: Twayne Publishers, 1970]

Somewhat propagandistic and apologetic but nevertheless useful account of the assistance given to Jews by some of the 300 Polish righteous. Also includes information on the "Zegota Council" which attempted to extend aid to Jews throughout Poland.

5199. Bauminger, Aryeh L.: Roll of Honor [Tel Aviv: Menora, 1971]

Biographical history of twenty of the Hasidei Umot Ha´olam (Righteous Gentiles). Every country in Europe is represented. Also tells the stories of Charles Coward, a British POW who helped save Jews at Auschwitz, and Raul Wallenberg, the Swedish diplomat who saved nearly 100,000 Hungarian Jews. Includes the list of 300 receipients of Yad Vashem´s heroism award.

5200. Bejski, Moshe: "The ´Righteous´ Among the Nations and Their Part in the Rescue of Jews." Gutman: Rescue, pp.627-647; Gutman: Catastrophe, pp.582-607.

5201. Berman, Adolf: "He Who Rescues One Life Saves the World." Poland, #6/154 (June, 1967): 17-19.

5202. Felberbaum, Marysia: "Remembering Those Who Helped." M&R, vol.11 #3 (Jan./Feb., 1985): 14, 16.

5203. Friedman, Philip: "Righteous Gentiles in the Nazi Era." Friedman: Roads, pp.409-421.

5204. ___: Their Brothers´ Keepers [New York: Holocaust Library, 1979] * Bio-history of the European gentiles who risked their lives to help save Jews.

5205. Halperin, Michael: "He Who Saves One Life." Moment, vol.6 #7 (July/Aug., 1981): 37-41.

5206. Hellman, Peter: Avenue of the Righteous [New York: Bantam Books, 1981]

5207. Huntley, Chet: "The Righteous Gentiles." HM, vol.43 #6 (Feb., 1963): 9, 15.

5208. Iranek-Osmacki, Kazimierz: He Who Saves One Life [New York: Crown Pub., 1971]

5209. Landau, Moshe: "Hasidei Umot Ha´olam: The Righteous of the Nations of the World." HM, vol.50 #1 (Sept., 1968): 12, 46.

5210. Lestchinsky, Jacob: "An Item of Good News." CW, vol.8 #25 (June 27, 1941): 10-11.

5211. Littell, Franklin H.: "Righteous Gentiles: Praise for the Just. Laments that There Were So Few of Them." M&R, vol.10 #3 (Jan./Feb., 1984): 7, 13.

5212. Milton, S.: "The Righteous Who Helped Jews." Grobman: Genocide, pp.282-287.

5213. Oliner, Samuel P.: "The Need to Recognize the Heroes of the Nazi Era." Recon, vol.28 #4 (June, 1942): 7-14.

5214. Pritchard, Marion: "It Came to Pass in Those Days..." Sh´ma, vol.14 #273 (April 27, 1984): 97-102.

5215. Tartakower, Aryeh: "The Planting Ceremony at the Avenue of the Just in Honour of Hermann Langbein." Y/V: Resistance, pp.403-406.

Raoul Wallenberg

5216. Anger, Per (D. M. Paul and M. Paul, transls.,): With Raoul Wallenberg in Budapest: Memories of the War Years in Hungary [New York: Holocaust Library, 1981]

Intimate portrait and description of Raoul Wallenberg´s activities in Hungary. Written by Wallenberg´s closest compatriot in Budapest.

5217. Bierman, John: Righteous Gentile: The Story of Raoul Wallenberg Missing Hero of the Holocaust [New York: Viking Press, 1981]

5218. Edelman, Lily: "The Case of Raoul Wallenberg." J Digest, vol.26 #2 (Oct., 1980): 12-14.

5219. Freeden, Herbert: "The Wallenberg Mystery." CW, vol. 23 #10 (March 5, 1956): 7-8. Also in: J Affairs, vol. 11 #3 (March, 1956): 36-38.

5220. Goldman, Lynda: "The Wallenberg File." J Digest, vol. 25 #4 (Dec., 1979): 7-13.

5221. Hechinger, Grace B.: "Raoul Wallenberg: Hidden Hero." Recon, vol.24 #1 (Feb. 21, 1958): 18-21.

5222. Kovach, Kim: "In Search of the Hero of Budapest: The Disappearance of Raoul Wallenberg." IH, vol.28 #3/4 (March/April, 1980): 11-13, 26-28.

5223. Lester, Elenore: Wallenberg: The Man in the Iron Web [Englewood Cliffs, NJ: Prentice-Hall, 1982]

5224. Lichten, Joseph L.: "The Mystery of a War Hero." ADL Bul, vol.13 #5 (May, 1956): 1-2.

5225. ___: "The Unsolved Mystery of a War Hero." J Digest, vol.2 #4 (Jan., 1957): 9-12.

5226. Marton, K.: Wallenberg [New York: Random House, 1982]

5227. Raoul Wallenberg Fighter for Humanity [Stockholm: Fredens Foerlag, 1947]

5228. Wallace, Ralph: "Raoul Wallenberg, Hero Of Budapest." Readers Digest, vol.64 #303 (July, 1947): 96-100.

5229. ___: Unforgotten Hero." NJM, vol.68 #10 (June, 1954): 12, 34-38.

5230. Werbell, Frederick E. and Thurston Clarke: Lost Hero: The Mystery of Raoul Wallenberg [New York: McGraw-Hill, 1981]

The Righteous

5231. Ben-Horin, Eliahu: "Kolodjik vs. Eichmann." Recon, vol.28 #6 (May 4, 1962): 19-21.

5232. "Bernhard Lichtenberg, Prelate." Chartock: Society, pp.149-151.

5233. Blumenthal, Nachman: "Spinka, the Shabbes-Goy." YVB, #18 (April, 1966): 30-33.

5234. Dvorjetski, M. "The Anti-Nazi Sergeant of the Vilna Ghetto." J Digest, vol.5 #8 (May, 1960): 68-70.

5235. ___: "Anton Schmidt: Anti-Nazi Sergeant in the Vilna Ghetto." YVB, #3 (April, 1958): 18-19, 29.

5236. Friedman, Philip: "She Saved Lives with a Gun and a Flower." ADL Bul, vol.14 #8 (Oct., 1957): 4-5.

5237. Grossmann, Kurt R.: "He Cheated Hitler." J Digest, vol.5 #4 (Jan., 1960): 7-11. * On Oscar Schindler.

5238. Gruber Michaelis, Ruth: "The Pole Who Saved 32 Jews." HM, vol.50 #4 (Dec., 1968): 21, 36.

5239. Harden, Norbert: "In Memory of King Christian X of Denmark." JVP, vol.10 #34 (Sept./Oct., 1947): 14-15.

5240. Heard, Raymond: "He Cheated the Nazis of Fifty Lives: A Wartime Rescue in Rumania." J Digest, vol.14 #9 (June, 1969): 49-57. * On Jeffrey Joffre.

5241. Jacob, Ernest I.: "The Unknown Martyr." Lib Jud, vol. 12 #4 (Aug., 1944): 24-29. * On Aime Palliere.

5242. Keneally, Thomas: Schindler's List [New York: Simon and Schuster, 1982]

Novelized account of Oskar Schindler, a German industrialist who used his personal fortune and position in Nazi occupied Poland to save thousands of Jews from the Nazi death camps.

5243. Korwin, Y.: "Paying Homage to Anne and Piotr Rawicz." M&R, vol.9 #2 (Nov./Dec., 1982): 5, 11.

5244. Labin, Samiel: "French Foe of Fascism." Lib Jud, vol. 13 #10 (Feb. 1946): 53-56. * On Bernard Lecache.

5245. Lamm, Hans: "Portrait of Three Germans." Ch J Forum, vol.11 #2 (Win., 1952/1953): 119-123.

5246. Lazar-Litai, H.: "The Professor and the Nun." YVB, #2 (Dec., 1957): 10-11.

5247. Liebesmann-Mikulsky, A.: "A German Who Saved Jews in the Stanislawow Ghetto." YVB, #15 (Feb., 1965): 54-59.

5248. Lipman, E. J.: "Lamedvavnik of Heidelberg." NJM, vol. 65 #5 (Feb., 1951): 186, 202-205. * On Hermann Maas.

5249. Lynne, Edward: "Heroine from Holland. The Dutch Woman Who Rescued 10,000 Jewish Children." J Digest, vol.13 #3 (Dec., 1967): 39-40.

5250. Magnes, David: "Pineau and Block 36: French Statesman Saved Jews at Buchenwald." J Digest, vol.5 #6 (March, 1960): 23-24.

5251. Meyer, Ernie: "A Christian Actress´ Role as Righteous Gentile." J Digest, vol.26 #11 (July, 1981): 62-65.

5252. ___: "A German Who Saved Jews: Oskar Schindler." J Digest, vol.20 #3 (Dec., 1974): 32-35.

5253. O´Brien, John A.: "The Good Companion." ADL Bul, vol. 17 #10 (Dec., 1960): 4-5. * On P. Marie-Benoit.

5254. "The Reminiscences of Victor Kugler, the ´Mr. Kraber´ of Anne Frank´s Diary." YVS, vol.13 (1979): 353-385. * As told to Eda Shapiro.

5255. Rorty, James: "Father Benoit: Ambassador of the Jews. An Untold Chapter of the Underground." Com, vol.2 #6 (Dec., 1946): 507-513.

5256. Rosen, Dunia: "Joop Westerweel and His Group." YVB, #12 (Nov., 1967): 59-61.

5257. ___: "Professor Pawel Horbaczewski." YVB, #20 (April, 1967): 39-40.

5258. ___: "The Woman Who Saved my Life." YVB, #19 (Oct., 1966): 63-65.

5259. Rubenstein, Richard L.: "A Visit with Dean Grueber." Recon, vol.28 #12 (Oct. 19, 1962): 12-19.

5260. "The Story of Wladyslaw Kowalski." YVN, #3 (June, 1970/June, 1971): 35-36.

5261. Werner, Alfred: "A Saintly German Pastor." CW, vol.19 #26 (Oct. 27, 1952): 5-7. * On Hermann Maas.

5262. "Witness of Righteousness: The Work and Faith of Dean Grueber." WLB, vol.16 #1 (Jan., 1962): 9.

THE CHURCHES, NAZIS, AND THE JEWS

Overviews

5263. Cain, Seymour: "The Holocaust and Christian Responsibility." Mid, vol.28 #4 (April, 1982): 20-27.

5264. Clinchy, Everett R.: "The Church and Freedom." Survey Graphic, vol.28 #2 (Feb., 1939): 139-140.

5265. Conway, J. S.: "The Churches." Friedlander: Ideology, pp.199-206.

5266. Israel, Edward L.: "The Catholic Problem." Recon, vol.7 #6 (May 2, 1941): 6-10.

5267. Pawlikowski, John T.: "The Holocaust: Failure in Christian Leadership?" Grobman: Genocide, pp.288-297.

5268. Von Fulhaber, Michael (G. Smith, transl.): Judaism, Christianity and Germany [New York: Macmillan, 1934]

5269. Wall, Bernard: Report on the Vatican [London: Weidenfeld and Nicholson, 1956]

5270. Zahn, Gordon Ch.: Christian Responsibility and Race [London: Centre for Biblical & Jewish Studies, 1965]

The Churches and the Nazis

5271. Borgese, G. A.: "Pius XII and the Axis." Nation, vol. 148 #11 (March 11, 1939): 285-288.

5272. ___: "The Pope´s Neutrality." Nation, vol.154 #22 (May 30, 1942): 621-623.

5273. Conway, John S.: "The Vatican, Great Britain, and Relations with Germany 1938-1940." Historical Jnl, vol. 16 #1 (March, 1973): 147-167.

5274. Douglas, P. F.: God Among the Germans [Philadelphia: Univ. of Pennsylvania Press, 1935]

5275. Fabian, Bela: "Mindszenty and the Nazis." America, vol.80 #21 (Feb. 26, 1949): 569-570.

5276. Graham, Robert A.: "Pius XII and the Nazis: An Analysis of the Latest Charges that the Pope was a Friend of the Axis." America, vol.111 #23 (Dec. 5, 1964): 742-743.

5277. Holmes, I. D.: The Papacy in the Modern World, 1914-1978 [London: Burns & Oates, 1981]

5278. Hunt, James C.: "Between the Ghetto and the Nation: Catholics in the Weimar Republic." Dobkowski: Toward, pp.213-226.

5279. Kent, George O.: "Pius XII and Germany: Some Aspects of German-Vatican Relations 1933-1943." AHR, vol.70 #1 (Oct., 1964): 59-78.

5280. Kleinlerer, E. D.: "Pope's Challenge to Hitlerism." CW, vol.9 #1 (Jan. 2, 1942): 7-8.

5281. Lewy, Gunther: The Catholic Church and Nazi Germany [New York: McGraw-Hill, 1964]

Examination of involvement of the German Catholic Church with Nazism from the Weimar era to 1945. Authoritatively documented, Lewy demonstrates the general agreement on some goals between the Churches and the NSDAP before 1933. He then portrays the ever widening entrapment of the Church in Nazi policies and the failure of the Churches to encourage resistance movements.

5282. Matheson, Peter (ed.): The Third Reich and the Christian Churches [Grand Rapid, MI: W. B. Eerdmans, 1981]

5283. McCabe, Joseph: The Vatican and the Nazis [London: Watts, 1942]

5284. Moeller-Dostali, Rudolf: "Nazi Diplomacy and the Vatican." CEO, vol.20 #11 (May 28, 1943): 167-168.

5285. Schorsch, Emil: "Christianity and the Nazis." J Sp, vol.12 #1 (Nov., 1946): 16-17.

5286. Schuetz, W.: "The Pope and European Dictatorship." Cont Rev, vol.157 #889 (Jan., 1940): 61-66.

5287. Sforza, Carlo: "The Vatican and the War." FW, vol.1 #1 (Oct., 1941): 50-54.

5288. Sheehan, James J.: "The Catholic Church and National Socialism." WLB, vol.19 #1 (Jan., 1965): 1-2.

5289. Simon, Maurice: "Nazis and Christians." J Rev, #7 (Dec./March, 1934): 39-46.

5290. Spectator: "National Socialism and the Church." Cont Rev, vol.156 #886 (Oct., 1939): 474-484.

5291. Spotts, Frederick: The Churches and Politics in Germany [Middletown, CT: Wesleyan Univ. Press, 1973]

5292. Stehlin, Stewart A.: Weimar and the Vatican 1919-1933 [Princeton, NJ: Princeton Univ. Press, 1983]

5293. Walker, Lawrence D.: Hitler Youth and Catholic Youth, 1933-1936 [Washington, DC: Catholic Univ. Press, 1971]

5294. Zabel, James A.: Nazism and the Pastors [Chico, CA: Scholars Press, 1976]

5295. Zahn, Gordon Ch.: German Catholics and Hitler´s War [New York: Sheed & Ward, 1962]

The German Church Struggle

5296. Beazley, Raymond: "Christianity in Germany Today." Cont Rev, vol.150 #848 (Aug., 1936): 156-163.

5297. Brandt, Albert: "Hitlerism versus Catholicism." Cath World, vol.137 #822 (Sept., 1933): 641-651.

5298. "The Church and the Resistance Movement in Germany." WLB, vol.11 #3/4 (1957): 21-23.

5299. Conway, John S.: "The German Church Struggle and its Aftermath." Peck: Jews/Chr pp.39-52.

5300. ___: The Nazi Persecution of the Churches, 1933-1945 [New York: Macmillan, 1969]

Review of the Church struggle in Nazi Germany. Treats the subject chronologically not thematically. Attempts to cover all Christian denominations, but focuses on the Catholic and the Evangelical (Lutheran) Churches and their relations with Hitler and Nazism. The author, however, puts too much emphasis on Church opposition to Nazism, and their consequent persecution, and does not mention that both the highest Church authorities (e.g. the Vatican) and most Germans supported Hitler, to some degree, to the very end.

5301. Gurian, Waldemar: "Hitler´s Undeclared War on the Catholic Church." F Affairs, vol.16 #2 (Jan. 1, 1938): 260-271.

5302. Helmreich, Ernst C.: "The Arrest and Freeing of the Protestant Bishop of Wuerttemberg and Bavaria, Sept.-Oct. 1934." CEH, vol.2 #2 (June, 1969): 159-169.

5303. ___: The German Churches Under Hitler: Background, Struggle and Epilogue [Detroit, MI: Wayne State Univ. Press, 1978]

5304. High, Stanley: "The War on Religious Freedom." PVP: Nazism, pp.25-38.

5305. King, C. E.: "Strategies for Survival: An Examination of the History of Five Christian Sects in Germany, 1933-1945." JCH, vol.14 #2 (April, 1979): 211-234.

5306. Leiper, Henry: Churchmen Who Defy Hitler [New York: National Conference of Christians and Jews, 1942]

5307. Lengyel, Emil: "The Catholic War on Hitler." Nation, vol.141 #3670 (Nov. 6, 1935): 532-534.

5308. The Persecution of the Catholic Church in the Third Reich [London: Burns Oates, 1940]

5309. Reed, D. L.: "The German Church Conflict." F Affairs, vol.13 #3 (April, 1935): 483-498.

5310. Shuster, George N.: Like a Mighty Army: Hitler Versus Established Religion [New York: D. Appleton-Century, 1935]

5311. Stein, Leo: "The German Church Goes Underground." NJM, vol.58 #7 (March, 1944): 220-221; #8 (April, 1944): 252-253, 258.

5312. ___: "Niemoeller Speaks!" NJM, vol.55 #9 (May, 1941): 284-285, 301-303.

The Nazi Church

5313. Macfarland, Ch.: The New Church and the New Germany: A Study of Church and State [New York: Macmillan, 1934]

5314. "Religion, Irreligion and Pseudo-Religion: The Lesson of Germany." WLB, vol.1 #5 (July, 1947): 17, 22.

5315. Russell, Bertrand: "They are Beating the Cross into a Swastika in Germany." CJCh, vol.21 #45 (March 30, 1934): 25, 34.

5316. Sarolea, Charles: "Religion of the Blood." Cont Rev, vol.148 #837 (Oct., 1935): 424-430.

5317. "Schicklgruber Und Gott: What the Nazis Are Doing to Christianity Today." NJM, vol.56 #7 (March, 1942): 212-215. * A pictorial essay.

5318. Smith, P. (ed. and transl.): The Bishop of Muenster and the Nazis: The Documents in the Case [London: Burns, 1943]

5319. von Redwitz (Baron), Hans: "The Religious Situation in Germany." Fasc Q, vol.1 #3 (July, 1935): 299-314.

5320. Weiss-Rosmarin, Trude: "The Nazis Turn Heathen." NJM, vol.49 #11 (Aug./Sept., 1935): 394, 406-407.

5321. Wiskemann, Elizabeth: "Germany´s Second Reformation." Cont Rev, vol.145 #817 (Jan., 1934): 32-40.

The Vatican and the Jews

5322. Berard, Leo: "Pope Pius XII and the Jews." J Sp, vol. 29 #2 (Feb., 1964): 13-17.

5323. Conway, John S.: "Silence of Pope Pius XII." Review of Politics, vol.27 (Jan., 1965): 105-131.

5324. Dietrich, Donald: "Historical Judgement and Eternal Verities." Society, vol.20 #3 (March/April, 1983): 31-35.

5325. Flannery, Edward H.: "Vatican Diplomacy during the Holocaust." Con Jud, vol.33 #4 (Sum., 1980): 84-88.

5326. Friedlander, Saul: Pius XII and the Third Reich: A Documentation [New York: A. A. Knopf, 1966]

Relatively early but nonetheless useful documentation of Vatican-Nazi Germany relations from 1933-1945. Integrates the Vatican position on the war and the Nazi administration with the Jewish question. Barring further research in the Vatican archives this seems to be the definitive work on the subject.

5327. Graham, Robert A.: "The Latest Charges Against Pius XII." America, vol.114 #21 (May 21, 1966): 733-736.

5328. ___: Pope Pius XII and the Jews of Hungary in 1944 [New York: U. S. Catholic Historical Society, 1964]

5329. Grayzel, Solomon: "The Ties that Bind Synagogue and Church." Recon, vol.33 #4 (April 14, 1967): 22-36.

5330. Hochuth, Rolf: "The Vatican and the Jews." Society, vol.20 #3 (March/April, 1983): 4-20.

5331. Katz, Fred E.: "Old Wounds and New Lessons." Society, vol.20 #3 (March/April, 1983): 27-30.

5332. Kubovy, Aryeh L.: "The Silence of Pope Pius XII and the Beginnings of the ´Jewish Document´." YVS, vol.6 (1967): 7-26.

5333. Lahav, E.: "Vatican´s Concern for Slovak Jewry: New Light on Holocaust Diplomacy." JOMER, vol.16 #39 (Sept. 29, 1967): 13-15.

5334. Lavi, Theodore: "The Vatican Endeavors on Behalf of Rumanian Jewry During the Second World War." YVS, vol.5 (1963): 405-418.

5335. Not Used.

5336. Lehman, Leo H.: Vatican Policy in the Second World War [New York: Agora Pub., 1945]

5337. Levai, Jeno (J. R. Foster, transl.): Hungarian Jewry and the Papacy [London: Sands & Co., 1968]

5338. Lewy, Gunther: "Pius XII, the Jews, and the German Catholic Church." Com, vol.37 #2 (Feb., 1964): 32-35.

5339. Lichten, J. L.: "Pope Pius XII and the Jews." ADL Bul, vol.15 #8 (Oct., 1958): 4-5.

5340. ___: A Question of Judgment: Pius XII and the Jews [Washington, DC: National Catholic Welfare Conference, 1963]

5341. Lipstadt, Deborah E.: "Moral Bystanders." Society, vol.20 #3 (March/April, 1983): 21-26.

5342. Mashberg, M.: "The Unpublished Encyclicals of Pope Pius XI." NJM, vol.92 #8 (April, 1978): 40-42, 44-46.

5343. McCabe, Joseph: The Vatican and the Nazis [London, Watt, 1942]

5344. Morley, John: Vatican Diplomacy and the Jews During the Holocaust, 1939-1943 [New York: Ktav, 1980]

Well documented study of the efforts of the Vatican in Jewish affairs during World war II. Surveys the Jewish condition and Vatican relations on a country-by-country basis. Proves that the Vatican was well informed about the Final Solution. Concludes that the Vatican could have done more to save Jews but, for a variety of reasons, failed to do so.

5345. Nichols, P.: The Politics of the Vatican [New York: F. A. Praeger, 1968]

5346. Poliakov, Leon: "Pope Pius XII and the Nazis." J Fr, vol.31 #3 (April, 1964): 7-13.

5347. ___: "The Vatican and the Jewish Question: The Record of the Hitler Period - and After." Com, vol.10 #5 (Nov., 1950): 439-449.

5348. Randall, Alex: The Pope, the Jews, and the Nazis [London: Catholic Truth Society, 1963]

5349. Rhodes, Anthony: The Vatican in the Age of the Dictators, 1922-1945 [New York: Holt, Rinehart & Winston, 1975]

5350. Rothkirchen, Livia: "Vatican Policy and the Jewish Problem in Independent Slovakia (1939-1945): YVS, vol.6 (1967): 27-53.

5351. Schwartz, Barry D.: "The Vatican and the Holocaust." Con Jud, vol.18 #4 (Sum., 1964): 27-50.

5352. Shneiderman, S. L.: "Guilt and Absolution at the Vatican." CBW, vol.31 #16 (Dec. 7, 1964): 5-7.

5353. ___: "A J'Accuse against Pope Pius XII." CW, vol.30 #11 (June 24, 1963): 18-21.

5354. ___: "The Silence of Pope Pius XII." CBW, vol.31 #4 (Feb. 24, 1964): 5-7.

5355. Spiro, Jack D.: "All God's Deputies." J Sp, vol.29 #6 (June, 1964): 7-9.

National Churches and the Jews

5356. Barnett, Victoria: "For the Soul of the People: Reflecting on Germany's Confessing Church." Ch Century, vol.97 #17 (May 7, 1980): 514-517.

5357. Bereczky, Albert: Hungarian Protestanism and the Persecution of the Jews [Budapest: Sylvester, 1946]

5358. Cavert, Samuel M.: "Hitler and the German Churches." Ch Century, vol.50 #21 (May 24, 1933): 683-685.

5359. Jelinek, Y.: "The Vatican, the Catholic Church, the Catholics and the Persecution of the Jews During World War II: The Case of Slovakia." Vago: J/NJ, pp. 221-255.

5360. Littell, Franklin H. and Hubert G. Locke (eds.): The German Church Struggle and the Holocaust [Detroit, MI: Wayne State University Press, 1974]

5361. Snoek, J. M.: "Did the Non-Catholic Churches Keep Silent?" YVB, #20 (April, 1967): 30-34.

5362. Touw, H. C.: "The Resistance and the Netherlands Churches." Annals, #245 (May, 1946): 149-161.

13

The Free World Reaction

MEDIA AND INFORMATION ON THE HOLOCAUST

Prewar Literature

5363. "Digest of Editorial Opinion: The Evian Conference." CJR, vol.1 #1 (Sept., 1938): 47-56.

5364. "Digest of Public Opinion: The German-American Bund Meeting." CJR, vol.2 #2 (March/April, 1939): 53-58.

5365. Isserman, F. M.: "Personal Contacts with German Refugees." CJCh, vol.23 #27 (Nov. 22, 1935): 5, 13.

5366. "A List of Events in 5694 (1933-1934)." AJYB, vol.36 (1934/35): 121-246.

5367. Mevaker: "5694 - Review of Events." WJ, vol.1 #19 (Sept. 7, 1934): 434-435.

5368. Postal, B.: "The Black Year: Review of Year 5698." Am J Times, vol.4 #1 (Sept., 1938): 14-15, 28, 34-35, 68-69, 82-83, 86-87.

5369. Schneiderman, Harry: "Review of the Year." AJYB, vol. 34 (1932/33): 56-76; vol.35 (1933/34): 21-69; vol.37 (1935/36): 135-215; vol.38 (1936/37): 175-394; vol.39 (1937/38): 205-502; vol.40 (1938/39): 87-349.

5370. Smolar, Boris: "Another Year in Germany." Am J Times, vol.3 #1 (Sept., 1937): 17, 47.

5371. Adlerstein, Fanny: "Assistance to Overseas Communities." AJYB, vol.43 (1941/42): 88-97.

5372. "American Press Comments on the Massacre of Jews." CW, vol.9 #38 (Dec. 11, 1942): 8-11.

5373. Benedict, Libby: "Reaction to Events Overseas." AJYB, vol.45 (1943/44): 191-198.

5374. Braunstein, Baruch: "Highlights of the Year 5703." CW, vol.10 #27 (Sept. 24, 1943): 18-21.

5375. Brill, F.: "The Close of an Unhappy Year." J Layman, vol.16 #1 (Sept., 1941): 19-20.

5376. ___: "Finale to a Dark Year." J Layman, vol.15 #1 (Sept., 1940): 13-15.

5377. "The Crucifiction of a People." FW, vol.6 #3 (Sept., 1943): 196-198.

5378. Daro, Michael: "Report on Hungary: What Has Been Happening Behind the Censorship." Harper´s vol.184 #1111 (Feb., 1942): 308-312.

5379. Dijour, Ilja M.: "Refugee Problem." AJYB, vol.46 (1944/45): 302-311.

5380. "Documents." New Currents, vol.1 #2 (April, 1943): 28-29.

5381. "The First to Suffer: Editorial of the New York Times of December 2, 1942." CW, vol.9 #37 (Dec. 4, 1942): 15-16. * On the tragic fate of the Jews under Nazis.

5382. Fischer, Julius and Carol Klein: A Memorandum on the Situation of Hungarian Jewry [New York: WJC, 1944]

5383. Frank, Moses Z. R.: "The Most Tragic Year in Jewish History." JVP, vol.6 #7/8 (Oct./Nov., 1943): 11, 32.

5384. ___: "Review of the Year 5703: Eastern and Southern Europe." AJYB, vol.45 (1943/44): 298-331.

5385. Frank, Reuven: "5702: The Jewish Year in Review." HM, vol.23 #1 (Sept./Oct., 1942): 4-9.

5386. Fried, Hanna: "Movements for Better Understanding." AJYB, vol.43 (1941/42): 112-124.

5387. Gaster, Theodor H.: "Review of the Year: British Commonwealth." AJYB, vol.43 (1941/42): 125-146; vol.44 (1942/43): 166-178.

5388. ___ and M. Moskowitz: "Review of the Year 5700: Foreign Countries." AJYB, vol.42 (1940/41): 316-443.

5389. "German News Versus German Views: The Novy Kurier Warszawski." PFR, #35 (Jan. 1, 1942): 1-7.

5390. Glasgow, George: "Foreign Affairs." Cont Rev, vol.157 #894 (June, 1940): 731-742.

5391. Greenberg, Leonard A.: "Jews in the News." Lib Jud, vol.12 #5 (Sept., 1944): 54-60.

5392. Grossman, Meir: "Highlights of the Jewish Year." CW, vol.11 #27 (Sept. 15, 1944): 13-15.

5393. Herzberg, Arno: "The Blackout of Jewish News." CW, vol.9 #9 (Feb. 27, 1942): 8-9.

5394. Hevesi, Eugene: "Review of the Year." AJYB, vol.43 (1941/42): 216-229, 259-270; vol.44 (1942/43): 253-276; vol.46 (1944/45): 254-270. * Reviews Slovakia, Hungary, Rumania, and other Balkan countries, as well as events in Southern Europe.

5395. Himmelfarb, Milton: "Refugee Migration." AJYB, vol.45 (1943/44): 353-362.

5396. ___: Review of the Year 5704: Western Europe." AJYB, vol.46 (1944/45): 209-239.

5397. "Hitler Order to Exterminate Jews." CW, vol.9 #37 (Dec. 4, 1942): 5.

5398. Jelenko, Martha: "Review of the Year." AJYB, vol.43 (1941/42): 147-210; vol.44 (1942/43): 183-232; vol.45 (1943/44): 232-297. * Reviews events in Nazi Germany and Western Europe.

5399. "The Jewish Press on the Partition of Poland and its Consequences." CJR, #6 (Nov./Dec., 1939): 35-42.

5400. Lahtnehcie, Namreh: "Looking Backward: The Year 5700 in Review." JVP, vol.3 #9/10 (Sept./Oct., 1940): 6, 33, 38.

5401. Lestchinsky, Jacob: "Highlights of a Tragic Year." CW, vol.8 #31 (Sept. 19, 1941): 6-8.

5402. Lyons, Eugene: "Horror Unlimited." Am Mercury, vol.56 #230 (Feb., 1943): 199-203. * On the extermination of European Jewry.

5403. Margoshes, Samuel: "The Year 5704 - A Bloody Chapter in the Annals of Jewish Martyrdom." JVP, vol.7 #4 (Oct., 1944): 8-9, 32-34.

5404. "The Martyrdom of Polish Jewry." Am J Ch, vol.1 #1 (Nov. 15, 1939): 12-13; #2 (Dec. 1, 1939): 12-13; #3 (Dec. 15, 1939): 13-14; #4 (Jan. 1, 1940): 13.

5405. Moskowitz, Moses: "Review of the Year 5699." AJYB, vol.41 (1939/40): 233-374.

5406. "Nazis Determined to Complete Destruction of European Jewry, Declares President Roosevelt." Rescue, vol.1 #7/8 (July/Aug., 1944): 3, 14.

5407. "News from Poland." Am Heb, vol.153 #37 (July 14, 1944): 9; #40 (Aug. 4, 1944): 7, 14; vol.154 #11 (Jan. 19, 1945): 7.

5408. "Poland Under German Occupation According to the German Press." PFR, #5 (Sept. 16, 1940): 3-9.

5409. Posner, Elie: "Fugitive from Death Estimates 20,000 Warsaw Jews Alive." CJCh, vol.32 #19 (Sept. 22, 1944): 6, 15.

5410. "Public Opinion: The Fascist Press in America." CJR, vol.5 #3 (June, 1942): 291-298.

5411. "The Record of Nazi Atrocities as Submitted to President Roosevelt." CW, vol.9 #38 (Dec. 11, 1942): 4-7.

5412. "Report from Poland: The World Jewish Congress Gathers Some Eyewitness Accounts of Continued Massacres." Am Heb, vol.151 #43 (Feb. 26, 1943): 6, 11, 15.

5413. Rosmarin, A.: "The Year 5699 in Jewish Life." J Sp, vol.4 #11 (Sept., 1939): 10, 46-48.

5414. Schwarzbart, Isaac: "The Organized Slaughter of the Jews." PFR, #48 (July 15, 1942): 7-8.

5415. Segal, Simon: "Review of the Year." AJYB, vol.43 (1941/42): 210-216, 229-258, 314-323; vol.44 (1942/43): 232-253; vol.46 (1944/45): 240-253. * Reviews Eastern Europe.

5416. The Underground Reporter: "They Have a Rendezvous with Death." FW, vol.7 #1 (Jan. 1944): 49-50.

5417. Zygielbojm, Shmuel: "A Plan of Extermination of the Jews." PFR, #48 (July 15, 1942): 7.

Postwar Literature

5418. Abrahams, Olga: "The Catholic Press and Persecuted Jewry, 1939-1945." WLB, vol.18 #1 (Jan., 1964): 4, 9.

5419. Aronsfeld, C. C.: "The London Times and Hitler." Mid, vol.31 #4 (April, 1985): 39-41.

5420. Bauer, Yehuda: "When Did They Know?" Mid, vol.14 #4 (April, 1968): 51-58.

5421. Breitman, Richard and A. M. Kraut: "Who was the Mysterious Messenger." Com, vol.76 #4 (Oct., 1983): 44-47. * On Eduard Schulte.

5422. Brownstein, Ronald: "The New York Times on Nazism (1933-39)." Mid, vol.26 #4 (April, 1980): 14-18.

5423. Cohen, Augusta: "Reaction to Events Overseas." AJYB, vol.47 (1954/46): 291-303.

5424. Easterman, Alexander L.: "The British Press and the Nazis." WJ, vol.14 #3 (Sept., 1971): 14-15.

5425. Frankel, Henry: "Review of the Year 5706: Eastern Europe." AJYB, vol.48 (1946/47): 322-358.

5426. Gannon, F. R.: The British Press and Germany [Oxford: Clarendon Press, 1971]

5427. Goldbloom, M. J.: "Review of the Year 5706: Western Europe." AJYB, vol.48 (1946/47): 289-301.

5428. Green, G.: "New Year´s Cards from Vilna: The Cards Stopped Coming in 1939. We Knew Why." ADL Bul, vol.35 #2 (Feb., 1978): 7-8.

5429. Grobman, Alex: "The Warsaw Ghetto Uprising in the American Press." WLB, vol.29 #1 (1976): 53-61.

5430. ___: "What Did They Know? The American Jewish Press and the Holocaust 1 September 1939-17 December 1942." Am J His, vol.68 #3 (March, 1979): 327-352.

5431. Hevesi, E.: "Review of the Year: Southern Europe." AJYB, vol.47 (1945/46): 423/444; vol.48 (1946/47): 359-371.

5432. Kohanski, Alexander S.: "Review of the Year: Central and Western Europe." AJYB, vol.47 (1945/46): 375-390.

5433. Laqueur, Walter: "The First News of the Holocaust." LBML, #23 (1979).

5434. ___: "The Mysterious Messenger and the Final Solution." Com, vol.69 #3 (March, 1980): 54-64.

5435. Lipstadt, Deborah E.: Beyond Belief: The American Press and the Coming of the Holocaust [New York: The Free Press, 1986]

Study of the American press reaction to the Holocaust. Based on a broad review of North American daily newspapers. Can be considered definitive.

5436. Liskofsky, Sidney: "Review of the Year: International Events." AJYB, vol.48 (1946/47): 424-465.

5437. Nicholas, H. G. (ed.): Washington Despatches, 1941-1945: Weekly Political Reports from the British Embassy [Chicago: Univ. of Chicago Press, 1981]

5438. Norden, M. K.: "American Editorial Response to the Rise of Adolf Hitler: A Preliminary Consideration." AJHQ, vol.59 #3 (March, 1970): 290-301.

5439. Penkower, Monty N.: "Believe the Unbelievable." Mid, vol.27 #4 (April, 1981): 31-37.

5440. Pinchuk, Ben-Cion: "Soviet Media on the Fate of Jews in Nazi-Occupied Territory (1939-1941): YVS, vol.11 (1976): 221-233.

5441. Ross, Robert W.: "The Evidence Reveals: They Did Know." ADL Bul, vol.38 #5 (May, 1981): 1, 12-14.

5442. Shamir, Haim: "French Press Reaction in 1933 to Hitler's Anti-Jewish Policies." WLB, vol.25 #1/2 (Win./Spr., 1971): 23-32.

5443. Sharf, Andrew: "The British Press and the Holocaust." YVS, vol.5 (1961): 169-192.

5444. ___: Nazi Racialism and the British Press, 1933-1945 [London: World Jewish Congress, 1963]

5445. Singer, David G.: "The Prelude to Nazism: The German-American Press and the Jews 1919-1933." AJHQ, vol.66 #3 (March, 1977): 417-432.

5446. Twersky, D.: "Under the Axis: Jews in Eastern Europe from 1938-1942 as Reflected in the Pages of 'Jewish Frontier'." J Fr, vol.43 #4 (April, 1976): 24-34.

GENERAL STUDIES, 1933-1945

Overviews

5447. Ainsztein, Reuben: "Facing the Truth." JQ, vol.16 #1 (Spr., 1968): 35-39. * On the failure to rescue.

5448. ___: "The Failure of the West." JQ, vol.14 #4 (Win., 1966/67): 11-20.

5449. Bentwich, Norman: "A Grim and Humiliating Story." JQ, vol.16 #1 (Spr., 1968): 34-35.

5450. Druks, Herbert: The Failure to Rescue [New York: R. Speller and Son, 1977]

Historical survey of Allied reactions to the Holocaust. Short to the point of being facile, the book is still a useful introduction to the subject.

5451. Fox, John P.: "Japanese Reactions to Nazi Germany's Racial Legislation." WLB, vol.23 #2/3 (Spr./Sum., 1968): 46-50.

5452. Gutman, Yisrael and E. Zuroff (eds.): Rescue Attempts During the Holocaust [Jerusalem: Yad Vashem, 1977]

Papers from the Second Yad Vashem Historical Conference, held in Jerusalem on April 8-11, 1974. Covers a wide variety of sub-topics within the general topic of rescue.

5453. Lipstadt, Deborah E.: "Witness to the Persecution: The Allies and the Holocaust." MJ, vol.3 #3 (Oct., 1983): 319-338.

5454. Litvin, J.: "Partners in Guilt." J Sp, vol.28 #10 (Dec., 1963): 12-14.

5455. Macardle, Dorothy: Children of Europe [London: Victor Gollancz, 1949]

5456. Mashberg, Michael: "The West and the Holocaust: Prejudice that Meant Death." PoP, vol.12 #3 (May/June, 1978): 19-32.

5457. Penkower, Monty N.: The Jews Were Expendable: Free World Diplomacy and the Holocaust [Urbana: Univ. of Illinois Press, 1983]

Perhaps the best documented and most intensely researched study of the Free World's tardy reaction to the massacre of European Jewry. The work is set out in the form of independent but connected essays dealing with the Western Allies, neutral countries, and institutions, as well as free world Jewry.

5458. ___: "The Response of the Free World to the Holocaust." M&R, vol.9 #3 (Jan./Feb., 1983): 13, 14; #4 (March/ April, 1983): 10-11.

5459. Pilch, Judah: "The World Knew and Was Silent." Pilch: Catastrophe, pp.203-214.

5460. ___: "The World Was Silent." Chartock: Society, pp. 151-166.

5461. Shafir, Sh.: "Nazi Guilt and Western Indifference." Forum, #36 (Fall/Win., 1979): 99-107.

5462. Stillschweig, Kurt.: "International Protection of Human Rights and Fundamental Freedoms." HJ, vol.9 #1 (April, 1947): 35-56; vol.10 #1 (April, 1948): 43-60.

5463. Tartakower, Aryeh and Kurt R. Grossman: The Jewish Refugee [New York: Institue of Jewish Affairs, 1944]

5464. Tenenbaum, Joseph L.: "Religion and Rescue." YVB, #2 (Dec., 1957): 2-3.

5465. Wischnitzer, Marc: To Dwell in Safety: The Story of Jewish Migration Since 1800 [Philadelphia: J. P. S., 1948] * Chapters 6 and 7 deal with the Holocaust, Chapter 8 with the problems of DPs. Work includes important statistical appendices.

Canada and the Holocaust

5466. Abella, Irving and Harold Troper: "Jewish Refugees: Entry Denied." ADL Bul, vol.41 #1 (Jan., 1984): 6-8.

5467. ___: None is Too Many: Canada and the Jews of Europe, 1933-1948 [New York: Random House, 1982]

Important study of Canadian governmental policy towards Jewish refugees during the Nazi era. Especially important because of its broadening of the issue within the Anglo-American context.

5468. Belkin, S.: Through Narrow Gates [Montreal: Canadian Jewish Congress, 1966]

5469. Dirks, Gerald: Canada´s Refugee Policy: Indifference or Opportunism [Montreal: McGill-Queens Univ. Press, 1977]

Great Britain and the Holocaust

5470. Carsten, Francis L.: Britain and the Weimar Republic: The British Documents [New York: Schocken, 1984]

5471. Connell, John: The Office: A Study of British Foreign Policy and its Makers, 1919-1951 [New York: St. Martin´s Press, 1958]

5472. Hearst, Ernest A.: "The British and the Slaughter of the Jews." WLB, vol.21 #1 (Win., 1966/1967): 32-38; #2 (Spr., 1967): 30-40.

5473. Wasserstein, Bernard: Britain and the Jews of Europe 1939-1945 [Oxford: Clarendon Press for IJA, 1979]

Well documented examination of British policy toward the Jewish problem during World War II. Wasserstein places British policy in two contexts - refusal to see saving Jews as a war aim, and British fear that aid to Jews would mean assistance for Zionist goals in Palestine.

Switzerland and the Holocaust

5474. "Between Humanity and Expediency: Swiss Refugee Policy 1933-1945." WLB, vol.12 #1/2 (1958): 13, 16.

5475. Hasler, Alfred A.: The Lifeboat is Full: Switzerland and the Refugees 1933-1945 [New York: Funk & Wagnals, 1969]

5476. "Origins of the ´J´ Passport: A Controversy in Switzerland." WLB, vol.8 #3/4 (May/Aug., 1954): 20.

Russia, the Jews, and the Holocaust

5477. Delfinger, Henry: "Hitler´s Propaganda and Stalin´s Silence: Soviet and Nazi Antisemitism." PoP, vol.5 #4 (July/Aug., 1971): 1-9.

5478. Jabotinsky, Vladimir: "Zion and Communism." Hadar, vol.4 #1/2 (Feb./April, 1941): 31-33.

5479. Kohanski, A. S.: "Communist Propaganda for Jews: A New Line." CJR, vol.3 #5 (Sept./Oct., 1940): 470-483.

5480. Rosenberg, James N.: "Soviet Russia and the Jews." Menorah, vol.31 #3 (Oct./Dec., 1943): 296-299.

The United States and the Holocaust

5481. Adler, Selig: "The United States and the Holocaust." AJHQ, vol.64 #1 (Sept., 1974): 14-23.

5482. Divine, Robert A.: American Immigration Policy, 1924-1952 [New Haven, CT: Yale Univ. Press, 1957]

5483. Feingold, H.: "The Government Response." Friedlander: Ideology, pp.245-259.

5484. ___: The Politics of Rescue: The Roosevelt Administration and the Holocaust, 1938-1945 [New York: Holocaust Library, 1970]

Well balanced and scholarly account of the Roosevelt administration´s inactivity during the Holocaust. Still the best in a series of similar works rehashing the same subject.

5485. Felstiner, John: "The Popular Response." Friedlander: Ideology, pp.261-268.

5486. Fleming, D. and B. Bailyn (eds.): The Intellectual Migration: Europe and America, 1930-1960 [Cambridge, MA: The Beekmar Press of Harvard Univ., 1969]

5487. Genizi, Haim: American Apathy: The Plight of Christian Refugees from Nazism [Ramat-Gan, Isr.: Bar-Ilan Univ. Press, 1983]

5488. Hackett, Francis: What ´Mein Kampf´ Means to America [New York: Reynal & Hitchcock, 1941]

5489. Lippmann, W.: United States Foreign Policy: Shield of the Republic [Boston: Little, Brown & Co., 1943]

5490. Michael, Robert: "America and the Holocaust." Mid, vol.31 #2 (Feb., 1985): 13-16.

5491. Morse, Arthur D.: While Six Million Died: A Chronicle of American Apathy [New York: Hart Pub., 1967]

Journalistic account of America´s reactions to the Final Solution. Morse´s was the first full treatment of the subject. Full of moral fervor the work is largely a condemnation of United States policy vs. Jewish refugees from 1933-1945. Still a useful introduction, the work has largely been superceded by later scholarship.

5492. Saveth, Edward N.: "Franklin D. Roosevelt and the Jewish Crisis." AJYB, vol.47 (1945/46): 37-50.

5493. Schechtman, J. B.: "Roosevelt and the Jews." J World, vol.1 #5 (Feb., 1955): 7-10; #6/7 (March/April, 1955): 11-14.

5494. Simonhoff, Harry: "F. D. R. and the Jews." J Sp, vol. 24 #8 (Oct., 1959): 10-12.

5495. Strauss, H. A. (ed) (comp. by S. W. Siegel): Jewish Immigrants of the Nazi Period in the USA [Ridgewood, NJ: K. G. Saur, 1978]

5496. Yaffe, Richard: "U. S. Apathy While 6 Million Died." IH, vol.16 #4 (April, 1968): 14-18.

REFUGEES AND RESETTLEMENT, 1933-1939

The Refugee Crisis

5497. Adams, Walter: "Refugees in Europe." Annals, #203 (May, 1939): 37-44.

5498. Adelman, H.: "The Jewish Boat People in Historal Perspective." V CJQ, vol.10 #2 (Fall, 1979): 9-12.

5499. Barker, Ernest: "Scholars in Exile." Cont Rev, vol. 147 #831 (March, 1935): 305-312.

5500. Belth, Nathan: "The Refugee Problem." Korman: Hunter, pp.56-70.

5501. Bentwich, Norman: "The Problem of the Refugees in Europe." Cont Rev, vol.150 #847 (July, 1936): 35-42.

5502. ___: Shepherding the German Refugees." NJM, vol.48 #7 (April, 1934): 232-233, 253.

5503. Bernstein, John L.: "The Migration of Jews in Recent Years." AJYB, vol.38 (1936/37): 117-134.

5504. Bienstock, Victor M.: "On the Exile of Germany´s Jewish Intellectuals." J Digest, vol.29 #5 (Jan., 1984): 36-39.

5505. Bliven, Bruce: "Where Can the Refugees Go?" New Republic, vol.98 #1270 (April 5, 1939): 246-247.

5506. Burnstein, Alexander J.: "The Ethical Approach to the Refugee Problem." Recon, vol.5 #10 (June 30, 1939): 7-10.

5507. Cary, Mary G.: "People Without a Country." Survey Graphic, vol.25 #8 (Aug., 1936): 467-469.

5508. Dean, Vera M.: "European Power Politics and the Refugee Problem." Annals, #203 (May, 1939): 18-25.

5509. Feingold, Henry: "Rescue Through Mass Resettlement: Some New Documents, 1938-1943." in Lloyd P. Gartner, (ed.): Michael: On the History of the Jews in the Diaspora [Tel-Aviv: Diaspora Research Inst., 1975]: 302-335.

5510. George, Manfred: "Refugees in Prague, 1933-1938." Society: JoCz/II, pp.582-588.

5511. Huttenbach, Henry R.: "The Emigration of Jews from Worms (November 1938-October 1941): Hopes and Plans." Gutman: Rescue, pp.267-288.

5512. "Jews Out of Germany." New Republic, vol.82 #1054 (Feb. 13, 1935): 5-6.

5513. Jonas, H. J.: "People in Flight." CJR, vol.2 #5 (Sept./Oct., 1939): 30-42.

5514. Kornfeld, I.: "The Tragedy of People Without Nationality." CJR, vol.2 #3 (May/June, 1939): 42-48.

5515. Lightman, Jacob B.: "Relief Programs and Activities in Behalf of German Jewry." JSSQ, vol.10 32 (Dec., 1933): 170-172.

5516. Lowenstein, Solomon: "The German Jewish Children´s Aid." JSSQ, vol.11 #1 (Sept., 1934): 60-61.

5517. Margaliot, A.: "The Problem of the Rescue of German Jewry During the Years 1933-1939." Gutman: Rescue, pp.247-265.

5518. McDonald, J. G.: "Diplomacy Must Yield to Humanity." CJCh, vol.23 #33 (Jan. 3, 1936): 8, 12.

5519. Popper, David H.: "Mirage of Refugee Resettlement." Survey Graphic, vol.28 #1 (Jan., 1939): 23-25.

5520. Postal, Bernard: "German Refugees Circle the Globe." NJM, vol.50 #1 (Oct., 1935): 4-7; #2 (Nov., 1935): 50-51, 68-69; #3 (Dec., 1935): 84-85, 104.

5521. Roucek, Joseph S.: "Minorities - A Basis of the Refugee Problem." Annals, #203 (May, 1939): 1-17.

5522. Schwartz, Shulamith: "Immigration During the Terror." J Fr, vol.5 #12 (Dec., 1938): 26-27.

5523. Selver, Henry I.: "Problems in Placing Refugee Children." JSSQ, vol.16 #2 (Dec., 1939): 214-221.

5524. Simpson, John H.: "The Refugee Problem." Int Affairs, vol.17 #5 (Sept./Oct., 1938): 607-628.

5525. ___: The Refugee Problem: Report of a Survey [London: Oxford Univ. Press, 1939]

5526. Stankiewitz, Karl: "The Flight from the Nazis." J Digest, vol.26 #4 (Dec., 1980): 58-61.

5527. Thompson, Dorothy: "Escape in a Frozen World." Survey Graphic, vol.26 #2 (Feb., 1939): 93-96, 168-169.

5528. ___: "Refugees: A World Problem." F Affairs, vol.16 #3 (April, 1938): 375-387.

5529. Vorse, Mary H.: "Getting the Jews out of Germany." New Republic, vol.75 #972 (July 19, 1933): 255-258.

5530. Wischnitzer, Mark: "Jewish Emigration from Germany, 1933-1938." JSS, vol.2 31 (Jan., 1940): 23-44.

5531. Zarek, Otto: "The Children´s Migration." J Sp, vol.19 #3 (March, 1954): 18-20.

5532. Zukerman, Wm.: "Jewish Exodus from Germany. WJ, vol.2 #89 (Jan. 24, 1936): 10-11, 14.

The League of Nations and the Jews

5533. Bentwich, Norman: The League of Nations and Racial Persecution in Germany [London: Eastern Press, 1933]

5534. ___: "The League of Nations and Refugees." Cont Rev, vol.147 #824 (Aug., 1934): 151-157.

5535. ___: "Minorities and the League of Nations." Menorah, vol.24 #1 (Jan./March, 1936): 8-15; #2 (April/June, 1936): 169-176.

5536. ___: The Refugees Get Refuge." NJM, vol.52 #8 (April, 1938): 260, 275-276.

5537. "Bernheim Petition to the League of Nations." AJYB, vol.35 (1933/34): 74-101.

5538. Chamberlain, Joseph P.: "The High Commission for German Refugees." Survey Graphic, vol.23 #4 (April, 1934): 177-180.

5539. Genizi, Haim: "James G. McDonald: High Commissioner for Refugees, 1933-1935." WLB, vol.30 #2 (1976): 40-52.

5540. Goldstein, Sidney E.: The League of Nations and the Grounds for Action in Behalf of the Jews of Germany [New York: Correct Prtg Co., 1933]

5541. Holborne, Louise W.: "The League of Nations and the Refugee Problem." Annals, #203 (May, 1939): 168-176.

5542. "Minority and Refugee Questions Before the League of Nations." AJYB, vol.36 (1934/35): 89-119.

The Evian Conference

5543. Adler-Rudel, S.: "The Evian Conference." LBIYB, vol. 13 (1968): 235-273.

5544. Bentwich, Norman: "Evian: Basis for New Hope." NJM, vol.53 #1 (Aug./Sept., 1938): 6-7.

5545. ___: "The Evian Conference and After." Fortnightly, vol.150 #861 (Sept., 1938): 287-295.

5546. Estoric, Eric: "The Evian Conference and the Intergovernmental Committee." Annals, #203 (May, 1939): 136-145.

5547. Habe, Hans: "Evian: Secret Conference." ADL Bul, vol. 23 #6 (June, 1966): 7-8.

5548. "The Inter-Governmental Committee on Political Refugees." CJR, vol.2 #6 (Nov./Dec., 1939): 43-48.

5549. Katz, Shlomo Z.: "Public Opinion in Western Europe and the Evian Conference of July 1938." YVS, vol.9 (1973): 105-132.

5550. Lvovitch, David: "Negotiated Immigration and Colonization." Ort Eco Bul, vol.2 #3 (May/June, 1941): 1-2.

5551. "Resolution Adopted by the Evian Conference." CJR, vol.1 #1 (Sept., 1938): 21-23.

5552. Stein, Joshua B.: "Great Britain and the Evian Conference of 1938." WLB, vol.29 #1 (1976): 40-52.

5553. Taylor, M. C.: "The Evian Conference." CJR, vol.1 #1 (Sept., 1938): 17-21.

5554. Warburg, Gustav: "None to Comfort the Persecuted: The Failure of Refugee Conferences." WLB, vol.15 #3 (July, 1961): 43-44, 47.

5555. Wise, Jonah B.: "Impressions of Evian." CJR, vol.1 #1 (Sept., 1938): 40-42.

The Free World and the Refugees

China and the Refugees

5556. Jovishoff, Albert: "A City of Refugees: Shanghai." Menorah, vol.27 #2 (April/June, 1939): 209-216.

5557. Kranzler, David: "The Jewish Refugee Community of Shanghai 1938-1945." WLB, vol.26 #3/4 (Sum./Aut., 1972/73): 28-37.

5558. ___: "Restriction Against German-Jewish Refugee Immigration to Shanghai in 1939." JSS, vol.36 #1 (Jan., 1974): 40-60.

5559. Mars, Alvin: "A Note on the Jewish Refugees in Shanghai." JSS, vol.31 #4 (Oct., 1969): 286-291.

Great Britain and the Refugees

5560. Aronsfeld, C. C.: "The New Nazis and the Old: British Reactions to Hitler´s First Success in 1930." JOMER, vol.15 #48 (Dec. 2, 1966): 18-20.

5561. Baumel, Esther: The Jewish Refugee Children in Great Britain, 1938-1939 [Ramat-Gan, Isr.: Bar-Ilan Univ. Press, 1981]

5562. Benson, Arnold: "Germany, Britain, and the Jews." Am J Ch, vol.1 #3 (Dec. 15, 1939): 4-6.

5563. Bentwich, Norman: "Asylum for Birds of Passage." NJM, vol.54 #3 (Nov., 1939): 88-89.

5564. Fox, John: "Great Britain and the German Jews 1933." WLB, vol.26 #1/2 ((Win./Spr., 1972): 40-46.

5565. Gilbert, Martin: "British Government Policy Towards Jewish Refugees: November 1938-September 1939." YVS, vol.13 (1979): 127-167.

5566. Granzow, Brigitte: A Mirror of Nazism: British Opinion and the Emergence of Hitler, 1929-1933 [London: Victor Gollancz, 1964]

5567. Johnson, Geoffrey: "The Jewish Refugee in England." Ch J Forum, vol.16 #2 (Win., 1957/1958): 111-115.

5568. "Parliament and the Persecution of Jews in Germany." NJ, vol.9 #7 (April, 1933): 96-108.

5569. Scharf, Andrew: The British Press and Jews Under Nazi Rule [London: Oxford Univ. Press, 1964]

5570. Schimanski, Stefan K.: "Refugee Children in England." CJR, vol.2 #4 (July/Aug., 1939): 22-30.

5571. Sherman, A. J.: Island Refuge: Britain and Refugees from the Third Reich, 1933-1939 [London: Elek, 1973]

Charts the British refugee policy from the rise of the Nazis to the outbreak of World war II. The author notes that while Britain´s record on refugees, especially after the Anschluss, was inadequate it was, in light of the number of refugees, better than that of many other countries including the United States. Equal attention is given to both political and "racial" refugees thus obscuring the fact that relatively few Jewish refugees were admitted to English territory. The role of Palestine is downplayed as are British attempts to block the legal entry of Jews thereto.

5572. Wilson, Francesca M.: They Came as Strangers: The Story of Refugees to Great Britain [London: Hamilton, 1959]

5573. Wolfe, G.: "The London Conference for the Relief of German Jews." JSSQ, vol.10 #2 (Dec., 1933): 172-173.

<u>Other European Countries</u>

5574. Anderson, Evelyn: "Soviet Policies and the Rise of Hitler." <u>WLB</u>, vol.24 #4 (Aut., 1970): 29-35.

5575. Clark, Jane P.: ""Watchman: What of the Night? <u>Survey Graphic</u>, vol.27 #11 (Nov., 1938): 550-551.

5576. Grossman, Kurt R.: "Refugees to and from Czechoslovakia." Society: <u>JoCz/II</u>, pp.565-581.

5577. Lipsky, Shlomo: "Exiles on the Danube: A Visit to the Refugees from Austria Who Were Stranded on the Danube." <u>J Fr</u>, vol.5 #9 (Sept., 1938): 22-23.

5578. Ragatz, Lowell J.: <u>The German Refugees in France</u> [London: A. Thomas, 1934]

<u>Latin America and the Refugees</u>

5579. Henriques, C. Q. and A. Golovetz: "Ecuador: Prospects for Jewish Settlement." <u>WJ</u>, vol.2 #118 (Aug. 28, 1936): 3-4; #119 (Sept. 4, 1936): 3.

5580. Hirschberg, Alfred: "The Economic Adjustment of Jewish Refugees in Sao Paulo." <u>JSS</u>, vol.7 #1 (Jan., 1945): 31-40.

5581. Hochhauser, Jack: "The Forgotten Colony of Sosua: Dominican Republic." <u>J Digest</u>, vol.23 #4 (Dec., 1977): 52-54.

5582. Inman, Samuel: "South America Reacts to Hitlerism." PVP: <u>Nazism</u>, pp.284-305.

5583. Kilas, M.: "German Jews in Colombia." <u>Recon</u>, vol.19 #8 (May 29, 1953): 27-28.

5584. Savit, Julius A.: "British Guiana for Refugee Resettlement." <u>CJCh</u>, vol.26 #39 (Feb. 10, 1939): 5, 16.

5585. Schwartz, Barbara: "The General and His 300 Jews." <u>J Digest</u>, vol.6 #1 (Oct., 1960): 49-52.

5586. Weisbrod, R. G. and T. D. Morin: "The Caribbean Refuge." <u>CM</u>, vol.44 #2 (Feb., 1977): 13-16.

The United States and the Refugees

5587. Diamond, S. A.: "The Kristallnacht and the Reaction in America." YIVO Annual, vol.14 (1969): 196-208.

5588. Engels, Norbert: "Refugee Scholars Welcome in American Colleges." America, vol.65 #25 (Sept. 27, 1941): 677-678.

5589. Friedman, Saul S.: No Haven for the Oppressed: United States Policy Toward Jewish Refugees, 1933-1945 [Detroit, MI: Wayne State Univ. Press, 1973]

5590. Gellman, I. F.: "The St. Louis Tragedy." AJHQ, vol.61 #2 (Dec., 1971): 144-156.

5591. Gottlieb, Moshe: "The Berlin Riots of 1935 and Their Reprecussions in America." AJHQ, vol.59 #3 (March, 1970): 302-328.

5592. Kent, Donald P.: The Refugee Intellectual: The Americanization of the Immigrants of 1938-1941 [New York: Columbia Univ. Press, 1953]

5593. Kohler, Max J.: The United States and German Jewish Persecutions: Precedents for Popular and Governmental Action [New York: Jewish Academy of Arts & Sciences, 1933]

5594. Mann, Ruth Z.: "The Adjustment of Refugees in the USA in Relation to their Background." JSSQ, vol.16 #1 (Sept., 1939): 19-28.

5595. Mashberg, M.: "American Diplomacy and the Jewish Refugee 1938-1939." YIVO Annual, vol.15 (1974): 339-365.

5596. Moltmann, G.: "America´s Reaction to the Nov. 1938 Pogrom." WLB, vol.16 #4 (Oct., 1962): 70-71.

5597. Neumann, Franz L. et al (eds): The Cultural Migration [Philadelphia: Pennsylvania Univ. Press, 1953]

5598. Pickett, Clarence E.: "American Views on Admitting Refugee Children: 1939." Korman: Hunter, pp.71-85.

5599. Reynolds, Quentin: "American Views on Admitting Refugee Children: 1939." Korman: Hunter, pp.86-91.

5600. Rosenberg, Dan: "Resettling German Refugees Outside New York." JSSQ, vol.15 #2 (Dec., 1938): 254-257.

5601. Shafir, Shlomo: "American Diplomats in Berlin (1937-1939) and their Attitude to the Nazi Persecution of the Jews." YVS, vol.9 (1973): 71-104.

5602. Spear, Sheldon: "The U. S. and the Persecution of the Jews in Germany, 1933-1939." JSS, vol.30 #4 (Oct., 1968): 215-242.

5603. Sprafkin, B.: "Refugee Resettlement in the American Community." JJoS, vol.47 #1 (Fall, 1970): 54-61.

5604. "The S. S. St. Louis Tragedy." CJR, vol.2 #4 (July/Aug., 1939): 97-99.

5605. Szajkowski, Zosa: "Relief for German Jewry: Problems of American Involvement." AJHQ, vol.62 #2 (Dec., 1972): 111-145.

5606. Thomas, Gordon and Max M. Witts: Voyage of the Damned [New York: Stein and Day, 1974]

5607. Tuttle, Charles A.: "The American Reaction." PVP: Nazism, pp.250-256.

5608. Weil, Arthur T.: "Word from Washington: Exodus and a Quota." J Layman, vol.10 #6 (Feb., 1936): 6, 9.

5609. Wyman, David: Paper Walls: America and the Refugee Crisis 1938-1941 [Amherst, MA: Univ. of Massachusetts Press, 1968]

Well documented study of the failure of the United States to respond effectively to the Jewish refugee crisis from Kristallnacht to 1941. Gives several explanations, including American apathy and antisemitism. Focused almost exclusively on the United States government response.

WARTIME RESCUE AND RELIEF, 1939-1945

General Studies

5610. Arendt, Hannah: "The Stateless People." CJR, vol.8 #2 (April, 1945): 137-153.

5611. Belth, Nathan C.: "The Refugee Problem." AJYB, vol.41 (1939/40): 374-391; vol.42 (1940/41): 444-457.

5612. Bierman, John: Odyssey [New York: Simon and Schuster, 1984]

Journalistic account of the dramatic escape from Europe by the 500 refugees of the S.S. Pentcho. The journey which should have taken a month took four years and was fraught at every turn with danger and intrigue.

5613. Brutzkus, Julius: "The Jewish Children of Europe." J Fr, vol.12 #9 (Sept., 1945): 15-16.

5614. Chamberlain, Joseph P.: "Without a Country." Survey Graphic, vol.34 #3 (March, 1945): 85-88, 108-111.

5615. Chomsky, I.: "Among Refugees: Some Medical Observations." Am OSE Rev, vol.1 #3/4 (March/April, 1942): 12-14.

5616. Feldman, Maurice: "Persecution Stalks the Jews Across the Face of Europe." America, vol.67 #24 (Sept. 19, 1942): 654-655.

5617. Folkman, Adolf: "The Last Jew from Poland." J Sp, vol.5 #9 (July, 1944): 20-23.

5618. Fry, V.: "Operation Emergency Rescue." New Leader vol.48 #25 (Dec. 20, 1965): 11-14. * On the wartime rescue of artists.

5619. Gottschalk, Max: "The Jewish Emigrant - 1941." CJR, vol.4 #3 (June, 1941): 261-268.

5620. ___: "Prisoners of Hope." Ch J Forum, vol.1 #4 (Sum., 1943): 3-6.

5621. ___: "The Refugee Problem." AJYB, vol.43 (1941/42): 323-337.

5622. Grodzensky, Shlomo: "In Days of Darkness." Furrows, vol.2 #2 (Nov., 1943): 10-13.

5623. Grossmann, Kurt R.: "Refugees: Burden or Asset?" Nation, vol.155 #26 (Dec. 26, 1942): 708-710.

5624. ___: "Relief and Rehabilitation and the Jews." J Fr, vol.11 #1 (Jan., 1944): 24-29.

5625. Gumpert, M.: "Hitler´s Gift to America." Am Mercury, vol.57 #235 (July, 1943): 49-55.

5626. Hay, Malcolm: "The Nations Talked While Jews Died." J Digest, vol.23 #8 (April, 1978): 56-59.

5627. Hertz, R. C.: "Background of the Present German Refugee Problem." JSSQ, vol.17 #2 (Dec., 1940): 238-248.

5628. ___: "Interdenominational Refugee Aid." JSSQ, vol.17 #3 (March, 1941): 289-298.

5629. "The Jews of Europe: How to Help Them." New Republic, vol.109 #9 (Aug. 30, 1943): 299-315.

5630. Jordan, Charles H.: "Backgrounds of Some Refugees as Factors in Their Orientation." JSSQ, vol.18 #2 (Dec., 1941): 232-238.

5631. Kuh, Anton: "These Are the Refugees." J Fr, vol.7 #12 (Dec., 1940): 7-11.

5632. Kulisher, E. M.: Jewish Migrations: Past Experiences and Postwar Prospects [New York: Am. Jew. Com., 1943]

5633. Lande, Adolf: "Emigration of Jews As Related to Their Vocational Structure." JSSQ, vol.17 #3 (March, 1941): 299-308.

5634. Lewkovitz, Bert: "The Orthodox Refugee." Am J Ch, vol.1 #8 (March 1, 1940): 10-11.

5635. Loeb, Rene: "The Jewish Refugee from France." J Fo, vol.25 #1 (Jan., 1942): 6, 8, 12.

5636. Lundberg, Isabel: "Who Are These Refugees." Harper´s vol.182 #1088 (Jan., 1941): 164-172.

5637. McDonald, J. G.: "The Refugee Question: A Survey and a Program." Palestine, vol.1 #12 (Dec., 1944): 3-5.

5638. "Political Aspects of Relief." CW, vol.11 #38 (Dec. 29, 1944): 5-6.

5639. "Problems of Displaced Jews." CW, vol.11 #19 (May 19, 1944): 11-12.

5640. "Projects for Jewish Mass Colonization." IJA, vol.1 #4 (Nov., 1941): 1-15.

5641. Proudfoot, Malcolm J.: European Refugees, 1939-1952: A Study in Forced Population Movements [Evanston, IL: Northwestern Univ. Press, 1956]

5642. Rothkirchen, Livia: "Escape Routes and Contacts during the War." Y/V: Resistance, pp.408-414.

5643. Saenger, G.: "The Psychology of the Refugee." CJR, vol.3 #3 (May/June, 1940): 264-273.

5644. Schapiro, Michael: "German Refugees in France." CJR, vol.3 #2 (March/April, 1940): 134-140.

5645. Schechtman, Joseph B.: European Population Transfers, 1939-1945 [Ithaca, NY: Cornell Univ. Press, 1946]

5646. Scherer, Emanuel: "Motion to Rescue the Jews of Poland." GS, #20 (Feb. 1, 1944): 4-5.

5647. Schwarz, Maria: "The Tragedy of Europe´s Children." J Mirror, vol.1 #5 (Dec./Jan., 1942/1943): 36-40.

5648. Smolar, Boris: "The Plight of Refugees in War Time." J Fr, vol.7 #1 (Jan., 1940): 6-8.

5649. Steinberg, Milton: "A Bold Proposal." Recon, vol.7 #13 (Oct. 31, 1941): 14-17.

5650. Tartakower, Aryeh: "The Jewish Refugees: A Sociological Survey." JSS, vol.4 #4 (Oct., 1942): 317-348.

5651. Teller, Judson L.: "Refugees Take Root." J Fr, vol.10 #9 (Sept., 1943): 11-13.

5652. "The Tragedy of the Refugees." Cont Rev, vol.158 #896 (Aug., 1940): 170-176.

5653. Warburg, Gustav: "Rescuing Hungarian Jews." JM, vol.1 #7 (Oct., 1947): 26-37.

5654. Weis, P.: "Statelessness as a Legal Political Problem." WJC/BS Rep, #12 (July, 1944): 3-26.

5655. Wise, Stephen S.: "United Nations vs. Mass Murder." Opinion, vol.13 #3 (Jan., 1943): 5.

5656. W. J. C.: "Refugee Conditions in France." CW, vol.8 #8 (Feb. 21, 1941): 11-13.

5657. Zwergbaum, Aaron: "From Internment in Bratislava and Detention in Mauritius to Freedom." Society: JoCz/II, pp.599-654.

Jews in Allied Strategic Policy

5658. Adler-Rudel, S.: "A Chronicle of Rescue Efforts." LBIYB, vol.11 (1966): 214-241.

5659. Ainsztein, Reuben: "They Could Have Been Saved." J Sp, vol.32 #6 (June, 1967): 8-16.

5660. Amos, Paul: "Jews, the War, and After." Opinion, vol. 11 #7 (May, 1941): 6-8; #8 (June, 1941): 8-10; #9 (July, 1941): 18-21.

5661. Beveridge, William: "Rescue for the Doomed Jews." J Sp, vol.8 #10 (Aug., 1943): 9-10.

5662. Brand, Joel and Alex Weissberg (C. FitzGibbon and A. Foster-Melliar, transls.): Desperate Mission: Joel Brand´s Story [New York: Criterion Books, 1958]

One-sided but nonetheless important personal report on the efforts to save Hungarian Jewry from the Nazis. Fails to mention many details of the mission including the role of Bandy (Bernard) Grosz. This is, however, the only inside account of the Brand Mission and the Eichmann-Kastner negotiations available in English.

5663. Conway, John S.: "Between Apprehension and Indifference: Allied Attitudes to the Destruction of Hungarian Jewry." WLB, vol.27 #1/2 (Win./Spr., 1973/74): 37-48.

5664. Druks, H.: "The Rescue of Jews from Nazi Europe." M&R, vol.5 #2 (Nov./Dec., 1979): 7-8.

5665. Dunner, Joseph: "The Atlantic Charter and the Jews." NP, vol.33 #4 (Dec. 18, 1942): 6-9.

5666. Ettenberg, M.: "The Cry of the Refugee." Recon, vol.5 #20 (Feb. 2, 1940): 10-12.

5667. Feingold, Henry: "Failure to Rescue European Jewry: Wartime Britain and America." Annals, #450 (July, 1980): 113-121.

5668. ___: "The Importance of Wartime Priorities in the Failure to Rescue Jews." Grobman: Genocide, pp.300-307.

5669. Fischl, Viktor: "The Jews and the Conscience of the World." J Sp, vol.8 #7 (May, 1943): 20-21.

5670. Fuchs, Abraham: The Unheeded Cry [New York: Mesorah Pub., 1984]

Biographical history of Rabbi Michael Ber Weissmandel. Charts in particular his efforts to rescue Slovakian Jewry in 1944. Although the author is Israeli, his primary intent is to prove that Jewish leaders during the war did not do enough to save European Jewry by not following up on the Rabbi´s plan for ideological reasons.

5671. Gelb, Saadia: "Progress in Rescue." Furrows, vol.2 #4 (Feb., 1944): 9-11.

5672. Goldstein, J: "Hess for Grynszpan." Zionews, vol.4 #10 (June 1, 1942): 5-6.

5673. Goodman, H. A.: "Mission to Himmler." Ortho J Life, vol.20 #2 (Nov./Dec., 1952): 35-39.

5674. ___: "Now It Can Be Told." JM, vol.4 #9 (Dec., 1950): 578-582. * On Mussy´s negotiation with Himmler.

5675. "In the Diaspora: United Nations Declaration on Jewish Massacres." NJ, vol.19 #3 (Dec., 1942): 37-40.

5676. Johnson, Edwin C.: "Stop Mass Murder!" CW, vol.9 #40 (Dec. 25, 1942): 5-6. * Speech in U.S. Congress by Senator Johnson from Colorado.

5677. Kersten, Felix: "Himmler´s Last Deal With the Jews." J Digest, vol.6 #2 (Nov., 1960): 41-46.

5678. Laqueur, Walter: The Terrible Secret: Suppression of the Truth about Hitler's 'Final Solution' [Boston: Little, Brown and Co., 1980]

Extensive inquiry into the problem of the flow of information on the Final Solution. Laqueur argues cogently that understanding, will, and ability to act do not necessarily flow from knowledge.

5679. "The Lessons of Italy." CW, vol.16 #27 (Sept. 24, 1943): 14-15.

5680. "The Massacres in Europe: Historic Declaration by United Nations." J Standard, vol.3 #37 (Dec. 25, 1942): 1-2.

5681. Namier, L. B.: "Numbers and Exodus." NJ, vol.18 #5 (Feb., 1942): 61-63; #6 (March, 1942): 77-80.

5682. "Opportunity for Action." CW, vol.11 #12 (March 24, 1944): 12-14. * On Jewish status in Hungary.

5683. "The Relief Problem." CW, vol.10 #25 (July 16, 1943): 12-14.

5684. Schechtman, Joseph: "More Circumspection." Zionews, vol.4 #23/24 (Feb. 28, 1943): 16-18.

5685. Stone, I. F.: "For the Jews - Life or Death?" Nation, vol.158 #24 (June 10, 1944): 670-671.

5686. Syrkin, M.: "Eichmann's Last Offer: Goods for Blood." J Fr, vol.27 #7 (July, 1960): 7-13.

5687. Tenenbaum, Joseph: "They Might Have been Rescued." CW, vol.20 #5 (Feb. 2, 1953): 5-7.

5688. ___: "Rescue in the Framework of World War Strategy." YVB, #6/6 (June, 1960): 8-10.

5689. Trevor-Roper, Hugh R.: "The Strange Case of Himmler's Doctor: Felix Kersten and Count Bernadotte." Com, vol.23 #4 (April, 1957): 356-364.

5690. Vago, Bela: "The Horthy Offer: A Missed Opportunity for Rescuing Jews in 1944." Braham: Contemporary, pp. 23-45.

5691. Weizmann, Chaim: "Give Sanctuary to the Doomed!" J Mirror, vol.1 #6 (Feb./March, 1943): 17-18.

5692. Weybright, Victor: "Sympathy is not Enough." Survey Graphic, vol.29 #4 (April, 1940): 213-216, 265-269.

5693. "Where Rescue is Yet Possible." CW, vol.11 #13 (March 31, 1944): 5-6.

5694. Wiesenfeld, L.: "Heavy Clouds on the Jewish Horizon." JVP, vol.7 1/2 (Jan./Feb., 1944): 8-9, 21.

The Bermuda Conference

5695. "The Bermuda Affair." CW, vol.10 #19 (May 14, 1943): 11-13.

5696. Celler, Emanuel: "The Bermuda Conference: Diplomatic Mockery." FW, vol.6 #1 (July, 1943): 16-20.

5697. ___: "The Bermuda Conference: Just Another Gesture: What Now?" Am Heb, vol.152 #2 (May 14, 1943): 4, 9.

5698. Cohen, J. X.: "South of Bermuda." CW, vol.10 #19 (May 14, 1943): 6-8.

5699. "The Fringe of the Refugee Problem." J Comment, vol.1 #5 (June 4, 1943): 1-2.

5700. Goldstein, Israel: "Bermuda Failure." CW, vol.10 #18 (May 7, 1943): 5-6.

5701. "The Government and the Bermuda Conference." NJ, vol. 19 #8 (May, 1943): 120-126.

5702. "Memorandum to the Bermuda Conference." GS, #11 (May 1, 1943): 2-4.

5703. "A Note on Bermuda and After." WJC/BS Rep, #5 (July, 1943): 1-13.

5704. "Program for the Rescue of Jews from Nazi Occupied Europe Submitted April 14, 1943 to the Bermuda Refugee Conference by the Joint Emergency Committee for European Jewish Affairs." CW, vol.10 #17 (April 30, 1943): 11-18.

5705. Skidell, Kieve: "After Bermuda." Furrows, vol.1 #7 (May, 1943): 3-5.

5706. "Text of Final Communique of the Bermuda Conference on Refugees." CW, vol.10 #19 (May 14, 1943): 14.

5707. Zukermann, William: "The Bermuda Conference and the Jews." New Currents, vol.1 #2 (April, 1943): 22-23.

The Bombing of Auschwitz

5708. Brugioni, Dino A.: "Why World War Photography Interpreters Failed to Identify Auschwitz-Birkenau." M&R, vol.10 #1 (Sept./Oct., 1983): 5, 12.

5709. Druks, Herbert: "The Allies and Jewish Leadership on the Question of Bombing Auschwitz." Tradition, vol.19 #1 (Spr., 1981): 28-34.

5710. ___: "Why the Death Camps Were Not Bombed." M&R, vol. 3 #3 (March/April, 1977): 6, 10.

5711. Gilbert, Martin: Auschwitz and the Allies [New York: Holt, Rinehart and Winston, 1981]

Devastating account of Allied knowledge and inaction in face of the Nazi extermination of European Jewry. While primarily focussed upon the proposals to bomb Auschwitz-Birkenau, the work is in fact a chronicle of Free-World apathy toward Jewish suffering in World War II.

5712. Kulka, Erich: "Auschwitz Condoned - the Abortive Struggle Against the Final Solution." WLB, vol.23 #1 (Win., 1968/1969): 2-5.

5713. Tursky, L.: "Could the Death Camps Have Been Bombed?" J Fr, vol.31 #8 (Sept., 1964): 19-24.

5714. Williams, Roger M.: "An American Moral Tragedy: Why Wasn´t Auschwitz Bombed?" J Digest, vol.24 #8 (April, 1979): 7-14; #9 (May, 1979): 18-23.

The War Refugee Board and UNRRA

5715. Bolles, Blair: "Millions to Rescue." Survey Graphic, vol.33 #9 (Sept., 1944): 386-389.

5716. Dijour, Ilja M.: "The War Refugee Board." Rescue, vol.1 #3/4 (March/April, 1944): 5, 13.

5717. Evans, Jane: "UNRRA Goes to Work." J Fr, vol.11 #11 (Nov., 1944): 19-22.

5718. Hirschmann, Ira A.: "Assignment to Rescue." Rescue, vol.1 #11 (Nov., 1944): 3, 5.

5719. Landman, Isaac: "Chaos vs. a Better World." Lib Jud, vol.11 #1 (May, 1943): 4-7.

5720. Lehman, Herberet H.: "Relief for the Liberated." FW, vol.8 #2 (Aug., 1944): 107-110. Also in: Rescue, vol. 1 #9 (Sept., 1944): 3-4.

5721. ___: "UNRRA on the March." Survey Graphic, vol.33 #11 (Nov., 1944): 437-440, 470-471.

5722. Pehle, John W.: "Tackling Task of Rescue." Rescue, vol.1 #7/8 (July/Aug., 1944): 13-14.

5723. Perlzweig, Maurice: "UNRRA and the Jews of Europe." New Currents, vol.2 #10 (Dec., 1944): 3-5.

5724. Soloveytchik, G.: "After the Armies - UNRRA." Survey Graphic, vol.33 #7 (July, 1944): 311-312, 334-336.

5725. Tartakower, Aryeh: "UNRRA and the Jewish Case." J Fr, vol.10 #12 (Dec., 1943): 11-12.

5726. "U. S. War Refugee Board Confirms in Official Report Extermination of 1,765,000 Jews in Two Nazi Death Camps." Rescue, vol.1 #12 (Dec., 1944): 3-4, 10.

5727. United States War Refugee Board: Final Summary Report of the Executive Director of the War Refugee Board [Washington, DC: U. S. Gov. Printing Office, 1945]

5728. "The UNRRA Program and Jewish Needs." CW, vol.11 #27 (Sept. 15, 1944): 10-12.

5729. "The War Refugee Board." J Comment, vol.2 #3 (Feb. 4, 1944): 1-4.

5730. "The War Refugee Board and the Rescue of Polish Jewry." GS, #22 (March 1, 1944): 6-7.

5731. "War Refugee Board - Success or Failure." NJM, vol.59 #3 (Nov., 1944): 88-89.

The Free World and the Holocaust

The Far East

5732. Benz, David: "Refugee in Shanghai." CW, vol.8 #18 (May 9, 1941): 11-12.

5733. "Facts About Jews in Japan." J Sp, vol.7 #7 (May, 1942): 33-34.

5734. Gayn, Mark: "Refuge in Shanghai." J Fr, vol.7 #9 (Sept., 1940): 20-22.

5735. Grunberger, Felix: "The Jewish Refugees in Shanghai." JSS, vol.12 #4 (Oct., 1950): 329-348.

5736. "Jews in the Far East." IJA, vol.1 #6 (Jan., 1942): 1-7.

5737. Katz, L. G.: "Shanghai Story." CW, vol.16 #12 (March 21, 1949): 11-13.

5738. Krantzler, David: The Japanese, the Nazis, and the Jews [New York: Yeshiva Univ. Press/Sifria, 1976]

Pioneering study which takes the Holocaust out of the exclusively European environment. The book brings to light a previously unknown chapter of Jewish history.

5739. Margolis, Laura L.: "Race Against Time in Shanghai." Survey Graphic, vol.33 #3 (March, 1944): 168-171, 190-191.

5740. Tokayer, Marvin and Mary Swartz: The Fugu Plan: The Untold Story of the Japanese and the Jews during World War II [New York: Paddington Press, 1979]

Journalistic account of Japanese efforts to save millions of European Jews. Interspersed with the detailing of the plan are the adventures of Jewish refugees in Japan and Japanese held territory. The book seems to overplay the plan somewhat, although it is not possible to judge given the lack of direct citation of documents.

5741. Zuroff, Efraim: "Attempts to Obtain Shanghai Permits in 1941: A Case of Rescue Priority During the Holocaust." YVS, vol.13 (1979): 321-351.

The British Commonwealth

5742. Angell, Norman: "Britain and the Refugees." J Fr, vol.7 #9 (Sept., 1940): 7-10.

5743. Bentwich, Norman: "England and the Aliens." Political Quarterly, vol.12 #1 (Jan./March, 1941): 81-93.

5744. ___: "German-Jewish Refugees in England: 1933-1943." CJR, vol.7 #5 (Oct., 1944): 529-535.

5745. ___: "The Kitchner Refugee Camp." J Fo, vol.22 #8 (Dec., 1939): 173-174; vol.23 #1 (Jan., 1940): 6; #2 (Feb., 1940): 31-32.

5746. ___: "They helped a Continent." NJM, vol.66 #8 (April, 1952): 276-277, 295-296.

5747. ___: "Wartime Britain´s Alien Policy." CJR, vol.5 #1 (Feb., 1942): 41-50.

5748. Fox, John R.: "The Jewish Factor in British War Crimes Policy in 1942." EHR, vol.92 #1 (Jan., 1977): 82-106.

5749. Hirsch, Barnet: "Free Ports and the White Paper." J Fo, vol.27 #6 (June, 1944): 115-117, 118. * Analysis of Samuel Grafton´s plan.

5750. "The Massacre of the Jews: Plea for Urgent Action." NJ, vol.19 #6/7 (March/April, 1943): 96-105. * Appeal by the Archbishop of Cantenbury. Includes House of Lords debate on issue.

5751. Namier, Lewis B.: "The Core of the Jewish Question." Palestine, vol.1 #2 (Jan., 1944): 3-5.

5752. Rivlin, A. B.: "England and the Jews." CJCh, vol.32 #18 (Sept. 15, 1944): 25-26.

5753. Rosenthal, Eric: "Jewish Refugees in Rhodesia." J Sp, vol.7 #4 (Feb., 1942): 14-15, 21.

5754. Tocker, S.: "The Jewish Internees in Mauritius." Polish Jew, vol.4 #22 (April, 1944): 8-11.

5755. Vago, Bela: "The British Government and the Fate of Hungarian Jewry in 1944." Gutman: Rescue, pp.205-223.

5756. Van Passen, Pierre: "Britain´s Cause Supreme." CB, vol.7 #4 (Dec. 6, 1940): 7-8.

5757. Watt, D. C.: "Christian Essay in Appeasement: Lord Lothian and His Quaker Friends." WLB, vol.14 #2 (April, 1960): 30-31.

5758. Werner, Alfred: "German Refugees in England." CJR, vol.3 #4 (July/Aug., 1940): 381-387.

5759. ___: A Refugee Passover in England." Polish Jew, vol. 3 #16 (April, 1943): 4-5.

5760. Yarin, Mark: "A New Trend in Canada." CW, vol.10 #32 (Nov. 19, 1943): 9-11.

Latin America

5761. Baker, S.: "Dominican Haven for Refugees from Nazism." J Digest, vol.25 #9 (May, 1980): 63-66.

5762. "Dominican Refugee Settlement Agreement." CJR, vol.3 #2 (March/April, 1940): 195-199.

5763. Eck, Nathan: "The Rescue of Jews with the Aid of Passports and Citizenship Papers of Latin American States." YVS, vol.1 (1957): 125-152.

5764. Goldberg, Nathan: "Immigration Attitudes of Mexicans: An Insight." Rescue, vol.2 #7/8 (July/Aug., 1945): 3-4, 8.

5765. Hanson, Earl P.: "The Americas and the Refugees." Am Mercury, vol.52 #205 (Jan., 1941): 45-52.

5766. "Historic Document: The Agreement Between the Dominican Republic Settlement Association, Inc. of January 30, 1940." Ort Eco Bul, vol.1 #2 (March/April, 1940): 13-15.

5767. Kirchwey, Freda: "Caribbean Refuge." Nation, vol.150 #15 (April 13, 1940): 166-168. * On Sosua.

5768. Knudson, J. W.: "The Bolivian Immigration Bill 1942: A Case Study in Latin American Antisemitism." AJA, vol.22 #2 (Nov., 1970): 138-158.

5769. Locker, Berl: "Exit San Domingo." NJ, vol.19 #6/7 (March/April, 1943): 87-89.

5770. Neumann, Gerhardt: "German Jews in Colombia: A Study in Immigrant Adjustment." JSS, vol.3 #4 (Oct., 1941): 387-398.

5771. Oungre, Edouard: "Chile - a New Haven." Am Heb, vol. 152 #10 (July 9, 1943): 8-9.

5772. Price, A. G.: "Refugee Settlement in the Tropics." F Affairs, vol.18 #4 (July, 1940): 659-670.

5773. Schechtman, J. B.: "Failure of the Dominican Scheme." CW, vol.10 #3 (Jan. 15, 1943): 8-9.

5774. Schwarz, Ernst: "Trujillo Opens a Door." NJM, vol.54 #7 (March, 1940): 206-207.

5775. Stern, Heinrich: "The Jewish Immigration in Bolivia." Ort Eco Rev, vol.3 #2 (March/April, 1942): 7-12.

5776. Weston, J. A.: "The Jewish Refugee Problem in Costa Rica." J Fo, vol.22 #8 (Dec., 1939): 169-170, 172; vol.23 #1 (Jan., 1940): 13-14.

5777. Wischnitzer, Mark: "The Historical Background of the Settlement of Jewish Refugees in Santo Domingo." JSS, vol.4 #1 (Jan., 1942): 45-58.

5778. ___: "The Sosua Settlement." Ort Eco Bul, vol.2 #3 (May/June, 1941): 2-4.

The United States

5779. Adler, Selig: The Isolationist Impulse [New York: The Free Press, 1966]

5780. Allen, Jay: "Refugees and American Defense." Survey Graphic, vol.29 #10 (Oct., 1940): 486-488, 524-526.

5781. "Asylum in America. House and Senate Resolutions: The Voice of Labor." J Fr, vol.10 #11 (Nov., 1943): 9-17.
* Resolution of the American Federation of Labor.

5782. Baron, L.: "Haven from the Holocaust: Oswego, New York 1944-1946." NY History, vol.64 #1 (Jan., 1983): 5-34.

5783. Benedict, Libby: "Refugees and Red Tape: A Survey of Seven Years of Refugee Work." CW, vol.8 #5 (Jan. 31, 1941): 9-11.

5784. Blair, Leon B.: "Amateurs in Diplomacy: The American Vice Consuls in North Africa, 1941-1943." The Historian, vol.35 #4 (Aug., 1973): 607-620.

5785. Boraisha, M.: "Refugee Haven - Act One." CW, vol.11 #27 (Sept. 15, 1944): 6-8.

5786. Brand, Edward: "Oswego - a Study of Liberation." Am Heb, vol.155 #40 (Feb. 1, 1946): 14-15.

5787. Cohen, Felix S.: "Exclusionary Immigration Laws: Social and Economic Consequences." CJR, vol.3 #2 (March/April, 1940): 141-155.

5788. Cranston, Alan: "Congress and the Alien." CJR, vol.3 #3 (May/June, 1940): 245-252.

5789. Davie, Maurice R.: Refugees in America: Report of the Committee for the Study of Recent Immigration from Europe [New York: Harper & Brothers, 1947]

5790. Dingol, Solomon: "How Many Jewish Refugees from Nazi Persecution were Admitted to the U. S.?" Rescue, vol. 1, #2 (Feb., 1944): 1, 11-12.

5791. Druks, Herbert: "Congressional Responses to the Holocaust in 1943." M&R, vol.7 #4 (March/April, 1981): 4, 7; #5 (May/June, 1981): 4, 16.

5792. Feingold, Henry L.: "The Roosevelt Administration and the Effort to Save the Jews in Hungary." HJS, vol.2 (1969): 211-252.

5793. ___: "Roosevelt and the Holocaust: Reflections on New Deal Humanitarianism." Judaism, vol.18 #3 (Sum., 1969): 259-276.

5794. ___: "Roosevelt and the Resettlement Question." Gutman: Rescue, pp.123-181.

5795. Finkel, Herman: "Way-Station." Furrows, vol.3 #3 (Jan., 1945): 19-23. * On Oswego.

5796. Frank, Murray: "America and the Refugee Problem." Ch J Forum, vol.3 #1 (Fall, 1944): 35-41.

5797. ___: "Failure of the American Refuge." JM, vol.2 #7 (Oct., 1948): 429-440.

5798. Fry, Varian: "Our Consuls at Work." Nation, vol.154 #18 (May 2, 1942): 507-509.

5799. Graubart, B.: "Polish Jewish Refugees in America." Polish Jew, vol.2 #6/7 (March/April, 1942): 9-10.

5800. Gruber, Ruth: Haven: The Unknown Story of 1000 World War II Refugees [New York: Coward McCann, Geoghegan, 1983]

Journalistic account of the refuge granted to 1,000 Jews by the United States at Fort Oswego, New York. The book is an accurate picture of their life but is not sufficient as a historical record. Gruber has not paid enough attention to the overall context of the Roosevelt administration's apathy toward rescuing Jews. 1,000 refugees admitted in 1944 cannot offset the one million too few visas granted to political refugees (primarily Jews) before 1941.

5801. Haber, William: "The Refugees in America." Menorah, vol.28 #2 (April/June, 1940): 205-213.

5802. Johnson, Alvin: "Hitler and American Scholarship." J Fo, vol.24 #9 (Sept., 1941): 141-142.

5803. "Joint Protest on Jewish Wrongs." Am Heb, vol.151 #41 (Feb. 12, 1943): 5, 8, 12; #42 (Feb. 19, 1943): 9; #43 (Feb. 26, 1943): 12, 14.

5804. Karpf, R.: "Displaced Persons: A USA Closeup." Survey Graphic, vol.34 #6 (June, 1945): 282-284, 304.

5805. Kirchwey, Freda: "The State Department Versus Political Refugees." Nation, vol.151 #26 (Dec. 28, 1940): 648-649.

5806. Kish, Bruno: "The Jewish Refugee and America." J Fo, vol.25 #1 (Jan., 1942): 3-4; #2 (Feb., 1942): 27, 31.

5807. Lowenstein, Sharon: "A New Deal for Refugees: The Promise and Reality of Oswego." Am J His, vol.71 #3 (March, 1982): 325-341.

5808. Mashberg, Michael: "Documents Concerning the American State Department and the Stateless European Jews, 1942-1944." JSS, vol.39 #1/2 (Win./Spr., 1977): 163-182.

5809. "Mr. Breckinridge Long's Statement." CW, vol.10 #37 (Dec. 24, 1943): 14-17.

5810. Munro, Dana G. et al (ed.): Refugee Settlement in the Dominican Republic [Washington, DC: The Brookings Institution, 1942]

Study of the economic implications of mass Jewish resettlement in Sossua. Does not deal with the political or social aspects of the plan. The editors' decidedly negative finding was that only limited migration would be possible or desirable.

5811. "President Roosevelt's Statement of March 24, 1944 Against Nazi Crimes Against Jews." CW, vol.11 #14 (April 7, 1944): 14.

5812. "President Roosevelt to Act on Hitler Massacres." CW, vol.9 #38 (Dec.11, 1942): 2, 16.

5813. Sandrow, Edward T.: "The Thousand Who Were Saved." CW, vol.11 #26 (Aug. 11, 1944): 6-7.

5814. Shapiro, Edward S.: "The Approach of War: Congressional Isolationism and Antisemitism, 1939-1941." Am J His, vol.74 #1 (Sept., 1984): 66-72.

5815. "The State Department and the Jews." New Republic, vol.109 #25 (Dec. 20, 1943): 867-868.

5816. "Statement of the Hon. Breckinridge Long." J Comment, vol.1 #23 (Dec. 24, 1943): 1-4.

5817. Strum, Harvey: "Fort Ontario Refugee Shelter, 1944-1946." Am J His, vol.73 #4 (June, 1984): 422-444.

5818. Syrkin, Marie: "At Fort Ontario." J Fr, vol.11 #9 (Sept., 1944): 9-12.

5819. "U. S. Admits and Cares for 982 Refugees at Emergency Shelter in Oswego New York." Rescue, vol.1 #9 (Sept., 1944): 7-8.

5820. "U. S. Congress Condemns Nazi Outrages." CW, vol.10 #11 (March 12, 1943): 16.

5821. Van Passen, Pierre: "To the Conscience of America." J Sp, vol.8 #3 (Jan., 1941): 27.

5822. Wyman, David S.: The Abandonment of the Jews: America and the Holocaust, 1941-1945 [New York: Pantheon Books, 1984]

Important contribution to growing body of work on American government reactions to the Final Solution. Contains an especially important chapter on the bombing of Auschwitz.

5823. Zirin, Lester: "Roosevelt and American Jewry." New Currents, vol.2 #6 (June/July, 1944): 6-8, 30.

The Soviet Union

5824. Brainin, J.: "The Ehrlich-Alter Plot." New Currents, vol.1 #2 (April, 1943): 15-16.

5825. Carmel, Herman: Black Days, White Nights [New York: Hippocrene Books, 1985]

5826. Ehrenburg, Ilya: "I Cannot Remain Silent." New Currents, vol.1 #6 (Sept., 1943): 6-7.

5827. Ehrlich, H. and V. Alter: "A Letter to J. V. Stalin." GS, #13 (July 1, 1943): 2-4.

5828. Frank, F.: "On the Nazi-Soviet Border." J Fr, vol.7 #2 (Feb., 1940): 9-12.

5829. Hirszowicz, Lukasz (ed.): "The Soviet Union and the Jews during World War II: British Foreign Office Documents." SJA, vol.3 #1 (May, 1973): 103-109; #2 (Nov., 1973): 73-90; vol.4 #1 (May, 1974): 73-89.

5830. Husymans, Camille: "Memorial Meeting in London for the Executed Henryk Ehrlich and Victor Alter." GS, #12 (June 1, 1943):6-8.

5831. Jelenko, Edward W.: "Suppression of Antisemitism in Soviet Russia." Ch J Forum, vol.5 #1 (Fall, 1946): 10-14.

5832. Levin, Dov: "The Attitude of the Soviet Union to the Rescue of Jews." Gutman: Rescue, pp.225-236.

5833. Pinchuk, Ben-Cion: "Jewish Refugees in Soviet Poland, 1939-1941." JSS, vol.40 #2 (Spr., 1978): 141-158.

5834. Redlich, Shimon: "The Ehrlich-Alter Affair." SJA, vol.9 #2 (Oct., 1979): 24-45.

5835. ___: "The Jewish Anti-Fascist Committee in the Soviet Union." JSS, vol.31 #1 (Jan., 1969): 25-36.

5836. ___: "Jewish Refugees from Poland as a Factor in Relations Between the Polish and Soviet Governments During World War II." YVB, #14 (March, 1964): 32-35.

5837. Russia Set Them Free [New York: Jewish Council for Russian War Relief, 1943]

5838. "Statement by the American Representation of the General Jewish Workers Union of Poland on the Murder of Ehrlich and Alter." GS, #10 (April 1, 1943): 5-8.

5839. "Statement of Extraordinary State Committee on Crimes Committed by the German-Fascist Invaders During the Occupation." Lith Jew, vol.2 #5/6 (March, 1945): 2-4.

5840. "Statement on the Russian-Polish Controversy." GS, #21 (Feb. 5, 1944): 1-2.

Other Countries

5841. Druks, Herbert: "Rescue in Portugal and Spain." M&R, vol.5 #5 (May/June, 1979): 12, 15.

5842. Dzluznowsky, R.: "Across The Pyrenees Lies Spain." Am Heb, vol.154 #7 (Dec. 15, 1944): 16, 36-37, 40-43; #8 (Dec. 22, 1944): 9-10.

5843. Ezratty, H.: "The Consul Who Disobeyed: A Christian Who Sacraficed His Career to Save Jewish Lives." J Digest, vol.13 #12 (Sept., 1968): 54-56.

5844. ___: "The Potuguese Consul and the 10,000 Jews." Orhto J Life, vol.32 #1 (Sept./Oct., 1964): 17-20.

5845. Feldman, Maurice: "Where Sweden Stands." Nation, vol. 153 #15 (Oct. 11, 1941): 333-334. * On Refugees.

5846. "Follow Up the Scandinavian Example." J Comment, vol. 1 #15 (Oct. 29, 1943): 1-2.

5847. "He Saved 10,000 Jews." NJM, vol.75 #11 (July/Aug., 1961): 5-6. * On A. S. Mendes, Portugal´s consul in France.

5848. Hurwitz, H. A.: "An Oasis of Freedom." CW, vol.10 #13 (March 26, 1943): 7-9. * On Sweden.

5849. Landsberger, Herbert H.: "The Road to Freedom." CW, vol.10 #30 (Oct. 29, 1943): 10-11. * On Spain.

5850. Lestchinsky, Jacob: "Swiss Bravery." CW, vol.9 #39 (Dec. 18, 1942): 5-7.

5851. Pearson, Albert: "Jewish Relief Work in Sweden." Opinion, vol.10 #11 (Sept., 1940): 16-17.

5852. "Portugal on the Tightrope." WLB, vol.16 #2 (Spr., 1968): 27-28.

5853. Soderberg, Eugenie: "Sweden Against Antisemitism." J Fr, vol.10 #12 (Dec., 1943): 29-30.

5854. Valentin, Hugo: "Rescue and Relief Activities in Behalf of Jewish Victims of Nazism in Scandinavia." YIVO Annual, vol.8 (1953): 224-251.

5855. Yahil, Leni: "Scandinavian Countries to the Rescue of Concentration Camp Prisoners." YVS, vol.6 (1967): 181-220.

5856. Zukerman, William: "North Africa and the Jews." New Currents, vol.1 #1 (March, 1943): 27-28.

GOVERNMENTS-IN-EXILE AND THE JEWS

5857. Ainsztein, Reuben: "The Enemy Within: Antisemitism among Polish Soldiers in War-Time Britain." WLB, vol. 13 #5/6 (1959): 58-59.

5858. Aldridge, James: "Poles Abuse Jews." Lib Jud, vol.11 #12 (April, 1944): 50-52.

5859. Apenszlak, J.: "The Peculiar Reconstruction." Polish Jew, vol.2 #6/7 (March/April, 1942): 4-5.

5860. Avital, Zvi: "The Polish Government in Exile and the Jewish Question." WLB, vol.28 #1 (1975): 43-51.

5861. Davies, Rhys: "The Jews and the Polish Government." J Fr, vol.7 #4 (April, 1940): 22-24.

5862. Not Used.

5863. Goldberg, Abraham: "Polish Fascists Still Active." Polish Jew, vol.1 #2 (Nov., 1941): 1-2, 6.

5864. Iranek-Osmecki, Kazimierz et al: "The Polish Government in Exile and the Jewish Tragedy during World War Two." WLB, vol.29 #1 (1976): 62-67.

5865. "Is There a Polish Fascist Group at Work in this Country?" Polish Jew, vol.2 #5 (Feb., 1942): 8-9.

5866. Kacewicz, George V.: Great Britain, the Soviet Union, and the Polish Government in Exile (1939-1945) [The Hague: Martinus Nijhoff, 1979]

5867. Kusin, Vladimir V.: "T. G. Masaryk: The Conscience of His Nation." Bul S/EEJA, #5 (May, 1970): 52-55.

5868. "The Legal Position of the Jews in Poland." PFR, #27 (Sept. 1, 1941): Whole Issue.

5869. Lestchinsky, Jacob: "Attention, General Sikorsky!" CW, vol.8 #15 (April 11, 1941): 8-9.

5870. "A Letter to the Polish Premier." Menorah, vol.31 #2 (July/Sept., 1943): 174-175.

5871. Lewin, Isaac: "Attempts at Rescuing European Jews with the Help of Polish Diplomatic Missions During World War II." Polish Rev, vol.22 #4 (Dec., 1977): 3-23; vol.24 #1 (March, 1979): 46-61; vol.27 #1/2 (March/June, 1982); 99-111.

5872. Masaryk, Jan: "Free Czechoslovakia in a Free Europe." CEO, vol.17 #1 (Feb. 1, 1940): 4-5.

5873. "Memorandum to the Polish Delegation of the UNRRA in Atlantic City." GS, #20 (Feb. 1, 1944): 5-8.

5874. Pavlowitch, Stevan K.: "Out of Context - The Yugoslav Government in London, 1941-1945." JCH, vol.16 #1 (Jan., 1981): 89-118.

5875. "Poland's New Government." CJR, vol.2 #6 (Nov./Dec., 1939): 57-58.

5876. "The Polish Government in Exile." CJR, vol.3 #6 (Nov./Dec., 1940): 646-651.

5877. "Polish Government Protests." CW, vol.9 #37 (Dec. 4, 1942): 14-15. * On the Slaughter of Jews.

5878. Radwanski, Th.: "Poland and the Jews." New Currents, vol.2 #1 (Jan., 1944): 6-7.

5879. Roback, A. A.: "Polish-Jewish Relations." CJCh, vol. 27 #38 (Feb. 2, 1940): 6, 13.

5880. Rothkirchen, Livia: "The Czechoslovak Government in Exile: Jewish and Palestinian Aspects in the Light of the Documents." YVS, vol.9 (1973): 157-199.

5881. Schwartz, David: "The Press-in-Exile." CW, vol.8 #36 (Nov. 7, 1941): 9-11.

5882. Schwarzbart, Ignacy: "The Unification of the Polish Antisemites." Polish Jew, vol.2 #8/9 (May/June, 1942): 4-5.

5883. Sikorski, W.: "Poland: Once a Refuge." J Layman, vol. 17 #4 (Jan., 1943): 8-9.

5884. ___: "The Polish Government and the Polish Army Facing New Tasks." PFR, #2 (Aug. 1, 1940): 13-18.

5885. Slavik, Juraj: "Persecution of Jews in Slovakia and Aryanization of Jewish Property in Slovakia." CJRC/B, #11 (April, 1944): 3-4. * From a report by the Czech Government-in-Exile.

5886. Stanczyk, Jan: "Polish Jewish Problems." J Layman, vol.18 #8 (May, 1944): 14-15.

5887. Trepp, Leo: "Government in Exile." Recon, vol.9 #8 (May 28, 1943): 8-12.

5888. Wachsman, Zvi H.: The Governments-in-Exile and Their Attitudes Towards the Jews [New York: The Resistance, 1943]

5889. Wolf, Szymon: "Poland's New Leaders." Cont Rev, vol. 157 #890 (Feb., 1940): 185-189.

5890. Zukerman, William: "Antisemitism in Exile." Nation, vol.152 #20 (May 17, 1941): 579-581.

REACTION OF FREE WORLD JEWRY

Surveys

5891. Apenszlak, Jacob: "Program of the World Conference of Polish Jewry." Polish Jew, vol.5 #28 (April, 1945): 13-19.

5892. Avni, Haim: "Pattern of Jewish Leadership in Latin America during the Holocaust." Braham: Leadership, pp.87-130.

5893. Braham, Randolph L. (ed.): Jewish Leadership during the Nazi Era: Patterns of Behavior in the Free World [New York: Columbia Univ. Press for Holocaust Studies of the City Univ. of New York, 1985]

5894. Dawidowicz, Lucy S.: "Blaming the Jews: The Charge of Perfidy." Dawidowicz: Presence, pp.269-279.

5895. "Israel's Martyrdom." J Affairs, vol.3 #7 (Dec., 1943): 8 pp. * Special Day of Mourning issue.

5896. "Israel Mourns." J Affairs, vol.2 #7 (Dec., 1942): 12 pp. * Special issue detailing Nazi atrocities.

5897. "The Jewish People and the Present Hour." WJC/AS Bul, #1 (June, 1942): 1-2.

5898. Kircheway, Freda: "While the Jews Die." Nation, vol. 156 #11 (March 13, 1943): 366-367.

5899. Matz, E.: "Political Actions vs. Personal Relations." Mid, vol.27 #4 (April, 1981): 41-48.

5900. Riegner, Gerhart M.: "Switzerland and the Leadership of its Jewish Community During the Second World War." Braham: Leadership, pp.67-86.

5901. Sagi, Nana and Malcolm Lowe: "Research Report: Pre-War Reactions to Nazi Anti-Jewish Policies in the Jewish Press." YVS, vol.13 (1979): 387-408.

5902. Schwarz, Joseph J.: "Jewish Relief Picture in Central and Western Europe." JSSQ, vol.18 #1 (Sept., 1941): 55-59.

5903. Strauss, L.: "When the Nazis Tried to Blackmail World Jewry." J Digest, vol.12 #5 (Feb., 1967): 33-40.

5904. Wasserstein, Bernard: "The Myth of ´Jewish Silence´." Mid, vol.26 #7 (Aug./Sept., 1980): 10-16.

Anglo-Jewry

5905. Bentwich, Norman: "Anglo-Jewry in the War." Menorah, vol.29 #2 (April/June, 1941): 214-221.

5906. Hyamson, Albert M.: "British Jewry in Wartime." CJR, vol.6 #1 (Feb., 1943): 14-22.

5907. Leftwich, Joseph: "War Hits Anglo-Jewry." NJM, vol.54 #7 (March, 1940): 207, 214-215.

5908. Simpson, William W.: "Jewish-Christian Cooperation in Great Britain." CJR, vol.7 #6 (Dec., 1944): 641-645.

5909. Sompolinsky, Meier: "Anglo-Jewish Leadership and the British Government: Attempts at Rescue, 1944-1945." YVS, vol.13 (1979): 211-247.

5910. Wasserstein, B.: "Patterns of Jewish Leadership in Great Britain During the Nazi Era." Braham: Leadership, pp.29-43.

American Jewry

5911. Adler, Cyrus and Aaron M. Margalith: With Firmness in the Right [New York: Am. Jewish Committee, 1946]

5912. Baron, S. W.: "What War Has Meant to Communal Life." CJR, vol.5 #5 (Oct., 1942): 493-507.

5913. Bauer, Yehuda: "The Holocaust and American Jewry." Bauer: Perspective, pp.7-29.

5914. Beller, Jacob: "The Refugee in the American Jewish Community." JSSQ, vol.19 #4 (June, 1943): 315-321.

5915. Bernstein, Philip S.: "The Jews of Europe." Nation, vol.156 #1 (Jan. 2, 1943): 8-11; #2 (Jan. 9, 1943): 48-51; #5 (Jan. 30, 1943): 158-161; #6 (Feb. 6, 1943): 196-200.

5916. Bick, A.: "Justice and Mercy, Forgiveness and Revenge." Hamigdal, vol.4 #4 (April, 1944): 8-9.

5917. Bittleman, Alexander: Jewish Unity for Victory [New York: Workers Library Publishers, 1943]

5918. Braunstein, Baruch: "Jews and the War Chest." CW, vol.9 #27 (Sept. 11, 1942): 15-17.

5919. Brody, David: "American Jewry, the Refugees and Immigration Restriction (1932-1942)." PAJHS, vol.45, #4 (June, 1956): 219-247.

5920. Clark, Carnzu: "American Student Action for Refugee Students." Menorah, vol.27 #2 (April/June, 1939): 217-231.

5921. Cohen, Henry: "Crisis and Reaction: A Study in Jewish Group Attitudes (1929-1939)." AJA, vol.5 #2 (June, 1953): 71-113.

5922. Dawidowicz, Lucy S.: "Indicting American Jews." Com, vol.75 #6 (June, 1983): 36-44.

5923. Diamond, Jack: "Jewish Overseas Relief Organization: Report of a Survey." J Fr, vol.12 #8 (Aug., 1945): 14-21.

5924. Dinnerstein, L.: "Jews and the New Deal." Am J His, vol.72 #4 (June, 1983): 461-476.

5925. Eisenstein, Ira: "Jewish Ideology and the Present Crisis." JSSQ, vol.15 #3 (March, 1939): 291-298.

5926. Erlanger, S. B.: "The Volunteer in Refugee Work in New York City." JSSQ, vol.16 #1 (Sept., 1939): 40-45.

5927. Feingold, Henry L.: "Could American Jews Have Done More?" Grobman: Genocide, pp.308-312.

5928. ___: "Courage First and Intelligence Second: The American Jewish Secular Elite, Roosevelt and the Failure to Rescue." Am J His, vol.72 #4 (June, 1983): 424-460.

5929. ___: "Who Shall Bear Guilt for the Holocaust? The Human Dilemma." Am J His, vol.68 #3 (March, 1979): 261-282. Also in Porter: Genocide, pp.59-82.

5930. ___: "The Witness Role of American Jewry: A Second Look." Ryan: Responses, pp.81-91.

5931. Field, Allan G.: "And for the Sin of Callous Indifference." J Sp, vol.10 #11 (Sept., 1945): 16-17.

5932. ___: "The Man from Bergen-Belsen." J Sp, vol.11 #11 (Sept., 1946): 26-27. * Indicts American Jewry.

5933. Frommer, Samuel A.: "The Kingdom of Hate." NJM, vol. 48 #1 (Oct., 1933): 24-25, 38-39.

5934. Gelber, Lionel: "American Jewry, Bethink Ye!: A Plea for a Realistic Policy Abroad." Menorah, vol.31 #1 (Jan./March, 1943): 1-14.

5935. Gurock, Jeffrey: "The Response of American Jewry to Nazism and the Holocaust." Hirt: Issues, pp.96-107.

5936. Halpern, Ben: "We and the European Jews." J Fr, vol. 10 #8 (Aug., 1943): 15-18.

5937. Heller, Bernard: "War and the Spirit of Israel." CJR, vol.5 #4 (Aug., 1942): 347-356.

5938. Hellman, Ellen: "The Jewish American Scene." Furrows, vol.4 #1 (Nov., 1945): 14-17.

5939. "Hitler Must be Stopped: An Editorial." J Life, vol.2 #10 (Oct., 1938): 8-10.

5940. Horlings, A.: "Who Aids the Refugee?" New Republic, vol.104 #2 (Jan. 13, 1941): 43-45.

5941. Hyman, J. C.: "Coordination of Jewish Efforts Overseas." JSSQ, vol.14 #1 (Sept., 1937): 23-30.

5942. Igel, Amelia: "Case Work with Refugees." JSSQ, vol.16 #1 (Sept., 1939): 29-39.

5943. Lawrence, Samuel: "Design for Unity." Ch J Forum, vol.2 #1 (Fall, 1943): 41-48.

5944. Levin, Samuel M.: "Fascism and American Jewry." J Fo, vol.22 #2 (March, 1939): 23-24, 27; #3 (April, 1939): 41-43.

5945. Lookstein, Joseph H.: "Relief to Humanity, Inc." J Survey, vol.1 #10 (March, 1942): 9-11. * Appeal for aid to Russia.

5946. Minsky, Louis: "The Policy of Agression." Menorah, vol.23 #1 (April/June, 1935): 1-17.

5947. Monsky, Henry: "Vital Need for Unity." J Mirror, vol. 1 #5 (Dec./Jan., 1942/43): 26-27.

5948. "Nazi Atrocities in Poland Condemned at Huge Rally." NP, vol.29 #40 (Dec. 15, 1939) 1, 2.

5949. Neuringer, S. M.: American Jewry and United States Immigration Policy, 1881-1953 [New York: Arno Press, 1980]

5950. "The Role of American Jewry as Viewed from London." IP, #3 (Dec. 12, 1940): 3-4.

5951. Rothschild, Richard C.: "Are American Jews Falling into the Nazi Trap." CJR, vol.3 #1 (Jan./Feb., 1940): 9-17.

5952. Shafir, Shlomo: "American Jewish Leaders and the Emerging Nazi Threat, 1928-January 1933." AJA, vol.31 #2 (Nov., 1979): 150-183.

5953. Shelvin, B.: "American Jewry's Indifference." J Sp, vol.6 #11 (Nov., 1940): 21-22. * Events in Europe.

5954. Silver, Abba H.: "The American Jewish Community in War Time and After." JSSQ, vol.21 #1 (Dec., 1943): 16-27.

5955. ___: "Is Fascism a 'Domestic Affair'?" NJM, vol.53 #8 (April, 1939): 256-258.

5956. ___: "The World Crisis and Jewish Survival." CCAR/YB, vol.39 (1939): 309-330.

5957. Szajkowski, Zosa: "The Attitude of American Jews to Refugees from Germany in the 1930's." AJHQ, vol.61 #2 (Dec., 1971): 101-143.

5958. ___: "A Note on the American Jewish Struggle Against Nazism and Communism in the 1930's." AJHQ, vol.59 #3 (March, 1970): 272-289.

5959. Tenenbaum, J.: "The Contribution of American Jewry Towards Rescue in the Hitler Period." YVB, #1 (April, 1957): 2-4.

5960. Thompson, Dorothy and B. Stolberg: "Hitler and the American Jew." Scibner's, vol.94 #3 (Sept., 1933): 136-140. * American Jewry's response to the Nazis.

5961. Troper, M. C.: "On the European Relief Front." CJR, vol.3 #3 (May/June, 1940): 227-239.

5962. Unger, Menashe: "Can the Jews of Europe be Saved?" New Currents, vol.2 #2 (Feb., 1944): 9-11, 34.

5963. "Unity of Faith." CJR, vol.5 #2 (April, 1942): 200-202.

5964. Urofsky, M. I.: "American Jewry and the Holocaust." J Fr, vol.48 #8 (Oct., 1981): 8-12, 20.

5965. Waldman, Morris: "Problems Facing the Jews Throughout the World and Their Implications for American Jewry." JSSQ, vol.1 #1 (Sept., 1934): 54-56.

5966. "What Can We Do?" J Comment, vol.1 #22 (Dec. 17, 1943): 1-4. * American Jewry and the Holocaust.

5967. Wurm, Shalom: "When the Leaders Fail." Furrows, vol. 2 #3 (Jan., 1944): 14-17.

5968. Wyman, David S.: "The American Jewish Leadership and the Holocaust." Braham: Leadership, pp.1-27.

The Boycott

5969. A. T.: "A Blow at Oppression: The Jewish Anti-Nazi Boycott, 1933-1939." WLB, vol.14 #1 (Jan., 1960): 14-15.

5970. Gottlieb, Moshe R.: American Anti-Nazi Resistance, 1933-1941: An Historical Analysis [New York: Ktav, 1982]

Well documented and thorough history of the American Jewish anti-Nazi boycott. Argues that the boycott did have a negative impact on the German economy. While evidence for that seems a bit dubious, the author does realize that the boycott never accomplished its main goal - the downfall of the Nazi regime.

5971. ___: "The American Controversy Over the Olympic Games." AJHQ, vol.61 #3 (March, 1972): 181-213.

5972. ___: "The Anti-Nazi Boycott Movement in the United States: An Ideological and Sociological Appreciation." JSS, vol.35 #3/4 (July/Oct., 1973): 198-227.

5973. ___: "Boycott, Rescue, and Ransom: The Threefold Dilemma of American Jewry in 1938-1939." YIVO Annual, vol.15 (1974): 235-279.

5974. ___: "The First of April Boycott and the Reaction of the American Jewish Community." AJHQ, vol.57 #4 (June, 1968): 516-556.

5975. ___: "In the Shadow of War: The American Anti-Nazi Boycott Movement in 1939-1941." AJHQ, vol.62 #2 (Dec., 1972): 146-161.

5976. Krinkler, B.: "Boycotting Nazi Germany." WLB, vol.23 #4 (Aut., 1969): 26-32.

5977. Lipsky, L.: "Economic Blockade of Nazidom: A Cordon of Peace." CB, vol.1 #17 (May 17, 1935): 3-4.

5978. Rabinowitz, E.: "The Boycott Against Nazi Germany." CJCh, vol.21 #18 (Sept. 22, 1933): 7; #22 (Sept. 29, 1933): 16.

5979. Untermyer, Samuel: The Boycott is Our Only Weapon Against Nazi Germany [New York: Am. League for the Defense of Jewish Rights, 1933]

Organizations

The American Jewish Committee

5980. "Annual Report of the Executive Committee." AJYB, vol.34 (1932/33): 294-306; vol.35 (1933/34): 297-300; vol.36 (1934/35): 416-456; vol.37 (1935/36): 402-419; vol.38 (1936/37): 601-630; vol.39 (1937/38): 796-820; vol.40 (1938/39): 589-605; vol.41 (1939/40): 626-641; vol.42 (1940/41): 643-656; vol.43 (1941/42): 714-727; vol.44 (1942/43): 480-485; vol.45 (1943/44): 646-652; vol.46 (1944/45): 565-573; vol.47 (1945/46): 713-718.

5981. Cohen, Naomi W.: Not Free to Desist [Philadelphia: J. P. S., 1972]

5982. Jacobs, Naomi: "Lending a Hand." NJM, vol.54 #5 (Jan., 1940): 139-140.

5983. Lazin, F.: "The Response of the American Jewish Committee to the Crisis of German Jewry, 1933-1939." Am J His, vol.68 #3 (March, 1979): 283-304

5984. "We Cannot Remain Silent." Lib Jud, vol.12 #5 (Sept., 1944): 38-41. * Text of a rally in New York.

The American Jewish Conference

5985. Gelb, S.: "The Conference to the Rescue." Furrows, vol.2 #2 (Dec., 1943): 9-11.

5986. Graeber, I.: "The Birth and Death of the American Jewish Conference." J Life, vol.32 #1 (Sept./Oct., 1964): 26-40.

5987. Rappaport, D.: "American Jewish Conference, Limited." Furrows, vol.3 #3 (Jan., 1945): 9-11.

5988. Rittenberg, Louis: "American Jewish Conference." Lib Jud, vol.11 #5 (Sept., 1943): 4-7, 33-43.

5989. Steinbrink, Meyer: "The American Jewish Conference and its Possibilities." J Fo, vol.26 #11 (Dec., 1943): 211-212.

5990. Tenenbaum, Joseph: "The American Jewish Conference and Immediate Relief." J Fo, vol.26 #11 (Dec., 1943): 210, 224.

5991. Wise, Stephen S.: "The American Jewish Conference." Opinion, vol.13 #12 (Oct., 1943): 8-11.

The American Jewish Congress

5992. "The Day of Mourning and Protest." CW, vol.9 #39 (Dec. 18, 1942): 13, 16.

5993. "Declaration and Resolution." J Mirror, vol.1 #6 (Feb./March, 1943): 88-91.

5994. "The ´Stop Hitler Now´ Demonstration." CW, vol.10 #10 (March 5, 1943): Whole Issue. * Includes a full transcript of the rally at Madison Square Garden.

5995. Wise, Stephen S. et al: "Stop Hitler Now!" WJC/BS Rep, #3 (March, 1943): 3-10.

B´nai Brith

5996. "B´nai Brith in World War II." NJM, vol.60 #10 (June, 1946): 343-392 * Special issue.

5997. "B´nai Brith Shelters 3,500 Refugees." NJM, vol.50 #5 (Feb., 1936): 149, 164.

5998. Herbach, Joseph: "B´nai Brith and the Boycott." NJM, vol.48 #2 (Nov., 1933): 56, 61.

The Hebrew Committee for National Liberation

5999. Charles, Daniel: "Peter Bergson´s Irgun in America." Am Zionist, vol.65 #7 (March/April, 1975): 25-28.

6000. Grossman, Meir: "Self Appointed Liberators." CW, vol. 11 #20 (May 26, 1944): 4-7.

6001. Hecht, Ben: "Remember Us!" Am Mercury, vol.56 #230 (Feb., 1943): 194-199.

6002. ___ et al: "We Will Never Die: A Memorial in Three Episodes dedicated to the 2,000,000 Jewish Dead in Europe." Lib Jud, vol.11 #1 (May, 1943): 38-45; #2 (June, 1943): 55-63.

6003. Netanyahu, Benzion: "The Fiasco of the Hebrew Committee." Zionews, vol.5 #2 (July, 1944): 12-16. * Condemnation of Bergson's activities by the Rosh Nezivuth Betar in North America.

6004. Peck, Sarah E.: "The Campaign for an American Response to the Nazi Holocaust, 1943-1945." JCH, vol.15 #2 (April, 1980): 367-400.

6005. Penkower, Monty N.: "In Dramatic Dissent: The Bergson Boys." Am J His, vol.70 #3 (March, 1981): 281-309.

6006. "The Story of a 'Front' Organization." CW, vol.11 #1 (Jan. 7, 1944): 15-16. * On Bergson.

6007. Syrkin, Marie: "What American Jews Did During the Holocaust." Mid, vol.28 #8 (Oct., 1982): 6-12.

6008. ___: "Liberation by Double-Talk." CW, vol.11 #26 (Aug. 11, 1944): 7-9.

HIAS

6009. Bernstein, James: "Salvaging under Difficulties." Lib Jud, vol.11 #3 (July, 1943): 47-50.

The Joint Distribution Committee

6010. Agar, Herbert: The Saving Remnant: An Account of Jewish Survival [New York: Viking Press, 1960] * Focuses on the activities of the Joint. The book is well written but has been superseded. <see #6011/12>

6011. Bauer, Yehuda: American Jewry and the Holocaust: The American Jewish Joint Distribution Committee, 1939-1945 [Detroit: Wayne State Univ. Press, 1981]

Continuation of Bauer's history of the prewar Joint Distribution Committee covering the Committee's rescue and relief activities during the war. Primary focus is on attempts to rescue Jews by means of ransom and relocation. Special attention is given to the activities of Sally Mayer, the JDC representative in Geneva, Switzerland. JDC activities are not, however, taken out of context. The book is also a history of American Jewry's public response to the horrifying events transpiring in Europe.

6012. ___: My Brother's Keeper: A History of the American Jewish Joint Distribution Committee 1929-1939 [Philadelphia: J. P. S., 1974]

Organizational history of the Joint Distribution Committee for the years 1929-1939. Special focus is on aid given to German Jews, especially to the refugees in the years after the Nazi rise to power.

6013. Hyman, Joseph C.: "Twenty-Five Years of American Aid to Jews Overseas." AJYB, vol.41 (1939/40): 141-179.

6014. ___: "Whom Hitler Would Destroy." Ch J Forum, vol.2 #2 (Win., 1943/1944): 121-126.

6015. "J. D. C. Reports Vast Program." Lib Jud, vol.11 #9 (Jan., 1944): 27-31.

6016. Schwarz, Joseph J.: "The Joint Distribution Committee in War Time." JSSQ, vol.20 #2 (Dec., 1943): 93-102.

6017. "Statement Issued on Sept. 17, 1939 by the American Jewish Joint Distribution Committee on its Organization for War Emergency." CJR, vol.2 #5 (Sept./Oct., 1939): 63-64.

6018. Warburg, Edward M.: "How the JDC Does It." NJM, vol. 55 #6 (Feb., 1941): 176-177, 189.

6019. Zuroff, Ephraim: "Rescue Priority and Fund Raising as Issues during the Holocaust." Am J His, vol.68 #3 (March, 1979): 305-326.

Joint Emergency Committee for European Jewish Affairs

6020. "American Israel Speaks." Lib Jud, vol.11 #1 (May, 1943): 26-27.

6021. Pinsky, Edward: "American Jewish Unity During the Holocaust: The Joint Emergency Committee, 1943." Am J His, vol.72 #4 (June, 1983): 495-504.

6022. "Proposals to the Bermuda Conference." Am Heb, vol. 151 #51 (April 23, 1943): 2, 10. * Submitted by the Joint Emergency Committee.

ORT

6023. Akivisson, Vladimir: "ORT´s Work in the French Internment Camps." ORT Eco Rev, vol.2 #4/5 (July/Oct., 1941): 29-32.

6024. Brunschvig, J.: "The Swiss ORT at a Crucial Period." ORT Eco Rev, vol.5 #3/4 (March/June, 1946): 34-38.

6025. D. L.: "ORT´s Work During the Second World War." ORT Eco Rev, vol.2 #6 (Nov./Dec., 1941): 1-3.

United Jewish Appeal

6026. Gross, Joel: "New Horizons of Rescue." NJM, vol.57 #9 (May, 1943): 288-291.

6027. Heller, James G.: "The UJA Aids Jewish Survival." NJM, vol.58 #9 (May, 1944): 297-299.

6028. Wise, Jonah B.: "UJA Helps Fight the Axis." NJM, vol. 56 #9 (May, 1942): 293-295, 299.

The World Jewish Congress

6029. Eppler, Elizabeth E.: "The Rescue Work of the World Jewish Congress During the Nazi Period." Gutman: Rescue, pp.47-69.

6030. "The First World Jewish Congress." WJ, vol.2 #116 (Aug. 14, 1936): 5-7.

6031. Grossman, K. R.: "Rescue and Relief Work of the World Jewish Congress." JSSQ, vol.23 #1 (Sept., 1946): 22-24.

6032. Kubovy, A. Leon: "How did We Sit Solitary." YVB, #15 (Aug., 1964): 2-4.

6033. Kubowitzki (Kubovy), A. L.: "Snatching Jews from the Jaws of Death." J Sp, vol.10 #3 (Jan., 1945): 10-13.

6034. ___: Unity in Dispersion: A History of the World Jewish Congress [New York: WJC, 1948]

6035. Lestchinsky, Jacob: "Linking Scattered Israel." CW, vol.8 #34 (Oct. 24, 1941): 6-7.

6036. Mergler, Bernard: "Issues of War and Peace Face Jewish Congress." Today, vol.1 #1 (Nov., 1944): 8-10.

6037. Penkower, Monty N.: "Jewish Organizations and the Creation of the War Refugee Board." Annals, #450 (July, 1980): 122-139.

6038. ___: "The World Jewish Congress Confronts the Inter-National Red Cross during the Holocaust." JSS, vol.41 #3/4 (Sum./Fall, 1979): 229-256.

6039. "Relief and Rehabilitation of European Jewry: Memorandum submitted to the Council of the United Nations Relief and Rehabilitation Administration by the World Jewish Congress." CW, vol.10 #33 (Nov. 26, 1943): 14-20.

6040. Schwarzbart, Isaac I.: 25 Years in the Service of the Jewish People: A Chronicle of Activities of the World Jewish Congress [New York: WJC, 1957]

6041. World Jewish Congress: Outline of Activities, 1936-1946 [London: WJC/ British Section, 1948]

Zionist Organization of America

6042. Berman, Aaron: "American Zionism and the Rescue of European Jewry: An Ideological Perspective." Am J His, vol.70 #3 (March, 1981): 310-330.

6043. Biderman, D.: "Facts and Factors in Zionist Policy." Furrows, vol.1 #6 (April, 1943): 16-19.

6044. Cohen, Naomi W.: American Jews and the Zionist Idea [New York: Ktav, 1975]

6045. Fink, Reuben (ed.): America and Palestine [New York: American Zionist Emergency Council, 1944]

6046. Werner, Alfred: "Refugee Zionists in America." NP, vol.32 #13 (April 24, 1942): 11-12.

6047. Wurm, Shalom: "The Dangers of Anarchy." Furrows, vol. 1 #11 (Oct., 1943): 8-12.

PERSONALITIES

6048. Agar, Herbert: "The Incredible Sally Meyer: His Business was Snatching Jews from the Nazis." J Digest, vol.7 #4 (Jan., 1962): 53-56.

6049. Bauer, Yehuda: "The Negotiations Between Sally Meyer and the Representatives of the SS in 1944-1945." Gutman: Rescue, pp.5-45.

6050. Ganin, Zvi: "Activism Versus Moderation: The Conflict Between Abba Hillel Silver and Stephen S. Wise during the 1940s." SiZ, vol.5 #1 (Spr., 1984): 71-96.

6051. Lipsky, Louis: "Dr. Silver´s Historic Address." CBW, vol.30 #18 (Dec. 16, 1963): 16-19.

6052. Voss, Carl H.: "Let Stephen Wise Speak for Himself." Dimensions, vol.3 #1 (Fall, 1968): 35-39.

6053. Warburg, Gustav: "Rescuing Hungary´s Jews." JM, vol.1 #7 (Oct., 1947): 26-37. * On S. Meyer and R. Kastner.

THE GOLDBERG COMMITTEE REPORT

6054. Bauer, Yehuda: "The Goldberg Report." Mid, vol.31 #2 (Feb., 1985): 25-28. * Critical review of the report.

6055. Finger, Seymour M. (ed.): American Jewry During the Holocaust: A Report Sponsored by the American Jewish Commission on the Holocaust [New York: Holmes and Meier, 1985]

6056. Foxman, Abraham H.: "A Survivor Asks Why." ADL Bul, vol.41 #5 (May, 1984): 10-11.

6057. Goldstein, I.: "American Jewry During the Holocaust: A Review of the Blame and the Guilt." M&R, vol.10 #1 (Sept./Oct., 1983): 13; #2 (Nov./Dec., 1983): 11.

THE YISHUV DURING THE NAZI ERA

The New Exodus, 1933-1939

6058. Copeland, Royal S.: "A More Liberal Palestine Immigration Policy Wanted." P/P Herald, vol.3 #1/2 (Jan./Feb., 1934): 9-10.

6059. Frier, Recha: Let the Children Come: The Early History of Youth Aliyah [London: Weidenfeld, 1961]

6060. "The German Immigration." J Rev, #8 (March/June, 1934): 88-94.

6061. Gottgetreu, Erich: "The German Jews in Palestine." Menorah, vol.24 #1 (Jan./March, 1936): 55-67.

6062. Jabotinsky, Vladimir: "The Fata Morgana Land." Hadar, vol.2 #11 (Nov., 1939): 5-10, 14.

6063. Pinkus, Chasya: Come From the Four Winds: The Story of Youth Aliyah [New York: Herzl Press, 1970]

Surveys the role played by Youth Aliyah in rescuing children during the Nazi years. Their work in rebuilding Jewish youth, both physically and morally, is also described. Appropriately, the children, not the organization, are the center of the story.

6064. Rothenberg, Morris: "Palestine´s Part in Absorbing German Jewish Refugees." JSSQ, vol.11 #1 (Sept., 1934): 58-60.

6065. Russell, Ch. E.: "Help Open the Doors of Palestine." P/P Herald, vol.3 #1/2 (Jan./Feb., 1934): 1-2.

6066. "The Settlement of German Jews in Palestine." NJ, vol.10 #5 (Feb., 1934): 43-45.

6067. Szold, Henrietta: "The Problem of German-Jewish Youth." WJ, vol.1 #16 (Aug. 17, 1934): 367.

6068. Wormann, Curt: "German Jews in Israel: Their Cultural Situation Since 1933." LBIYB, vol.15 (1970): 73-103.

The Ha´avara

6069. Black, Edwin: The Transfer Agreement [New York: Macmillan, 1984]

Tendentious and ideologically motivated history of the Ha´avara Agreement. Does not put the crisis of Jewish immigration to Palestine into context and ignores Great Britain´s attempts to keep Jews out of the territory. Black further exaggerates the importance of the anti-Nazi boycott and the supposedly negative impact of the Ha´avara on its ability to oust the Nazis. Long on documentation but, ultimately, a polemic short on historical insight.

6070. Krojanker, Gustav: The Transfer: A Vital Question of the Zionist Movement [Tel-Aviv: Palestine Pub., 1936]

The Yishuv at War

6071. Bauer, Yehuda (A. M. Winters, transl.): From Diplomacy to Resistance: A History of Jewish Palestine, 1939-1945 [New York: Atheneum, 1973]

Meticulously researched history of the political developments in Palestine during World War II. Both internal and external developments are charted as are the frantic efforts to aid and rescue European Jewry.

6072. Beer, Israel: "The Yishuv as Ally." HM, vol.22 #3 (Dec./Jan., 1941/1942): 14-17.

6073. Ben-Ami, Yitshaq: "The Irgun and the Destruction of European Jewry." Braham: Perspectives, pp.71-91.

6074. Ben-Gurion, David: "Bevin Proposed a Jewish State." JOMER, vol.13 #12 (March 20, 1964): 20-22.

6075. ___: "The Only Solution." NJ, vol.21 #8 (May, 1945): 107-109.

6076. ___: "War and the Jewish People." NP, vol.29 #33 (Oct. 22, 1939): 5.

6077. Cohen, Israel: "Palestine and the Jewish Future." J Sp, vol.10 #2 ((Dec., 1944): 22-25.

6078. Duker, Abraham G.: "Palestine and Jewish Survival in a World of Democracy." Recon, vol.9 #2 (March 5, 1943): 15-18. * Address before Zionist convention of October 16, 1942.

6079. Eliash, Shulamit: "The ´Rescue´ Policy of the Chief Rabbinate of Palestine Before and During World War II." MJ, vol.3 #3 (Oct., 1983): 291-308.

6080. Epstein, Albert K.: Palestine at War [Washington, DC: The Zionist Organization of America, 1943]

6081. Executive of the Jewish Agency for Palestine: "To the Jews in all Countries." NJ, vol.9 #7 (April, 1933): 93-95. * Reaction of Yishuv to Nazi rise to power.

6082. "The Extermination of Jews: The Yishuv's Protest." NJ, vol.19 #5 (Feb., 1943): 67-68.

6083. Freedman, Joseph H.: "Palestine in Wartime." Opinion, vol.14 #9 (July, 1944): 6-8.

6084. Gelber, Yoav: "Zionist Policy and the Fate of European Jewry (1939-1942)." YVS, vol.13 (1979): 169-210.

6085. Hurewitz, J. C.: The Struggle for Palestine [New York: Norton and Co., 1950]

6086. Itzhaki, Solomon: "Tragic Aspects of Rescue Work." CW, vol.10 #35 (Dec. 10, 1943): 5-7.

6087. Jabotinsky, Vladimir: "The Fate of Jewry." CJCh, vol. 27 #51 (May 3, 1940): 7.

6088. Katzburg, N.: "European Jewry and the Palestine Question." YVS, (1979): 249-262.

6089. Locker, Berl: "Et Tu Brute!" NJ, vol.19 #9 (June, 1943): 131-134.

6090. McDonald, James G.: "Life or Death of a People." Palestine, vol.1 #1 (Dec., 1943): 9-10.

6091. Ofer, Dalia: "The Activities of the Jewish Agency Delegation in Istanbul in 1943." Gutman: Rescue, pp. 435-450.

6092. Popper, David H.: "A Homeland for Refugees." Annals, #203 (May, 1939): 168-176.

6093. Porat, Dina: "Al-Domi: Palestinian Intellectuals and the Holocaust 1943-1945." SiZ, vol.5 #1 (Spr., 1984): 97-124.

6094. Sachar, Howard M.: A History of Israel: From the Rise of Zionism to Our Time [New York: A. A. Knopf, 1976]

6095. Shertok, Moshe: "On the Battlefield, on the Farm and in the Factory - Jewish Palestine Contributes to the War Effort." IP, vol.2 #6 (Feb. 10, 1943): 1-2.

6096. Slutzki, Yehuda: "The Palestine Jewish Community and its Assistance to European Jewry in the Holocaust Years." Y/V: Resistance, pp.414-426.

6097. Tartakower, A.: "Efforts at Aid and Rescue During the Holocaust." Y/V: Resistance, pp.438-452.

6098. Vago, Bela: "Some Aspects of the Yishuv Leadership's Activities During the Holocaust." Braham: Leadership, pp.45-65.

6099. Vago, Raphael: "The Destruction of Hungarian Jewry as Reflected in the Palestine Press." HJS, vol.3 (1973): 291-324.

6100. Van Paassen, Pierre: The Forgotten Ally [New York: Dial Press, 1943]

Highly polemical but straightforward call for the establishment of a Jewish army in World War II, and for a fairer solution to the Palestine issue.

6101. Weizmann, Chaim: "The German-Jewish Tragedy and Palestine." NJ, vol.9 #89 (May/June, 1933): 135-157.

6102. ___: "Palestine's Role in the Solution of the Jewish Problem." F Affairs, vol.20 #2 (Jan., 1942): 324-338.

6103. Zel Lurie, Jesse: "Thorn in Hitler's Side." J Survey, vol.1 #9 (Feb., 1942): 16-17. * The Yishuv.

6104. The Zionist Executive: "To The Jewish People!" NJ, vol.16 #6/7 (March/April, 1940): 81. * Proclamation.

The International Context

6105. Abrahams, A.: Background of Unrest: Palestine Journey 1944 [London: Galil Pub., 1945]

6106. Aharoni, S.: "In Sheep's Clothing." Furrows, vol.1 #8 (June, 1943): 9-12.

6107. Alpert, Alice: "The White Paper: Relic of Munichism." New Currents, vol.2 #1 (Jan., 1944): 8-9.

6108. Celler, Emmanuel: "The Great Mockery." Zionews, vol.4 #27/28 (May, 1943): 14-16.

6109. Cohen, Michael J.: "Britain, Palestine and the Middle East, 1939-1945: Some Concepts and Misconceptions." P. Artzi (ed.): Bar-Ilan Studies in History [Ramat-Gan: Bar-Ilan Univ. Press, 1978]: 239-254.

6110. Donovan, William: "From the Vantage Point of O.S.S." Palestine, vol.2 #4 (April/May, 1946): 46-47.

6111. ___: "We Need An Open Door." Opinion, vol.16 #8 (June, 1946): 5-7.

6112. Frank, Gerold: The Deed [New York: Simon & Schuster, 1963]

Journalistic account of the 1944 assassination of the British Minister Resident in Cairo, Lord Moyne (Walter Edward Guiness), by members of LEHI (Lohame Herut Israel), known in English parlance as the "Stern Gang". Interesting for its perspective on the state of mind of the Yishuv in the shadow of the Holocaust, but otherwise of dubious veracity.

6113. Goldmann, Nahum: "Sovereignty and Human Rights." FW, vol.7 #1 (Jan., 1944): 63-66.

6114. Grose, P.: Israel in the Mind of America [New York: Schocken, 1984]

Survey of American interactions with Zionism and Jews for the last 200 years. Chapters five through seven deal with the Roosevelt years; pp. 122-133 cover the administration reaction to the Holocaust.

6115. Halperin, Samuel and Irwin Oder: "The United States in Search of a Policy: Franklin D. Roosevelt and Palestine." Rev of Politics, vol.24 #3 (July, 1962): 320-341.

6116. Hecht, Ben: Perfidy [New York: Julian Messner, 1961]

Oversensualized and ideologically motivated attack upon the Yishuv's efforts at rescue. Hecht based his contentions on the issues raised by the Kastner case but was, nonetheless, unable to prove his basic assertions.

6117. Hen-Tov, Jacob: "Contacts Between Soviet Ambassador Maisky and Zionist Leaders during World war II." SJA, vol.8 #1 (May, 1978): 46-56.

6118. Hyamson, H. M.: Palestine Under the Mandate [London: Methuen, 1950]

6119. Jabotinsky, Vladimir: "The Consequences of the White Paper." Hadar, vol.2 #8 (Aug., 1939): 4-6.

6120. Katzburg, Nathaniel: "British Policy on Immigration to Palestine During World War II." Gutman: Rescue, pp.183-203.

6121. Marlowe, John: The Seat of Pilate: An Account of the Palestine Mandate [London: Cresset, 1959]

6122. McDonald, J. G.: "The Time for Discussion is Past." NP, vol.33 #10 (March 19, 1943): 5-7.

6123. Rosenberg, Y.: "Meetings with Soviet Jewish Leaders, 1944-1945." SJA, vol.3 #1 (May, 1973): 65-70.

6124. Schechtman, Joseph B.: The United States and the Jewish State Movement: The Crucial Decade 1939-1949 [New York: Herzl Press, 1966]

6125. Sherfer, G.: "Political Considerations in British Policy-Making on Immigration to Palestine." SiZ, #4 (Aut., 1981): 237-294.

6126. Sykes, Christopher: Crossroads to Israel [London: Collins, 1965]

6127. Van Passen, P.: "World Destiny Pivots on Palestine." NP, vol.32 #6 (Dec. 12, 1941): 9-10.

6128. Ziff, William B.: The Rape of Palestine [New York: Longmans, Green and Co., 1938]

6129. Zweigbaum, Aaron: "Exile in Mauritius." YVS, vol.4 (1960): 191-260.

Immigration: Legal/Illegal

6130. Avriel, Ehud: Open the Gates! A Personal Story of ´Illegal´ Immigration to Israel [New York: Atheneum, 1975]

Memoir of the ´Mossad Le´aliyah Bet´ (illegal immigration department) and its activities from 1940 to 1947. An important primary source.

6131. Brada, Fini: "Emigration to Palestine." Society: JoCz/I, pp.589-598.

6132. Brodetsky, Selig: "Zionism Versus Evacuation." NP, vol.31 #24 (March 28, 1941): 12-13.

6133. Dekel, Ephraim: Shai: The Exploits of Haganah Intelligence [New York: Thomas Yoseloff, 1959]

6134. Frank, M. Z.: "Epic of Rescue." CBW, vol.26 #11 (June 15, 1959): 5-7.

6135. Gelbart, Bernhard: "Homeward Flight." HM, vol.22 #7 (May/June, 1942): 4-9.

6136. Habas, Bracha: "With the Children from Teheran." J Fr, vol.10 #7 (July, 1943): 13-16.

6137. Haestrup, Jorgen: Passage to Palestine: Young Jews in Denmark, 1932-1945 [Svendborg, Denmark: Odense Univ. Press, 1983]

6138. Hirschman, Ira S.: "Palestine - As a Refuge from Fascism." Survey Graphic, vol.34 #5 (May, 1945): 195-198, 265-269.

6139. Jabotinsky, Eri: "With the ´Outlaws´ to Palestine." Hadar, vol.4 #1/3 (Feb./April, 1941): 33-34.

6140. Kimche, Jon and David Kimche: The Secret Roads: The Illegal Migration of a People [Westport, CT: Hyperion Press, 1976]

6141. Kluger, Ruth and Peggy Mann: The Last Escape: The Launching of the Largest Secret Rescue Movement of all Time [Garden City, NY: Doubleday, 1973]

Memoir-history of the ´Mossad Le´aliyha Bet´. A moving and quite dramatic story, although not heavily documented. Contains nineteen appendices which explain some of the book´s less obvious sections.

6142. Ofer, D.: "The Rescue of European Jewry and Illegal Immigration to Palestine in 1940. Prospects and Reality: Berthold Storfar and the Mossad Le´aliyah Bet." MJ, vol.4 #2 (May, 1984): 159-182.

6143. Perl, William R.: The Four Front War: From the Holo-Caust to the Promised Land [New York: Crown Pubs., 1979] Also published as: Operation Action: Rescue from the Holocaust [New York: Frederick Ungar, 1979]

Memoir of one man's efforts to rescue Jews from the Nazis. Promised to be quite controversial but in fact much of the information is well known. The single most important contribution of the book is to show that rescuing Jews by sending them to Palestine would have been feasible had Great Britain been willing to cooperate.

6144. Sagi, Nana: "The Epic of Aliyah Bet (Illegal Immigration) to Palestine 1945-1948." Mid, vol.17 #3 (March, 1971): 29-56.

6145. Shepherd, Naomi: A Refuge from Darkness [New York: Pantheon Books, 1984]

Definitive biography of Wilfred Israel, an unsung hero of the Holocaust. Using his business connections, money, and personal charm, Israel attempted to find refuge for thousands of Jews threatened with extermination. In 1942 Israel became one of the earliest transmitters of news of the Final Solution. While he was on a flight to Lisbon, hoping to find refuge for a number of Jews in Portugal, his airplane was shot down, under unknown circumstances, by the Luftwaffe.

6146. Yahil, Leni: "Select British Documents on the Illegal Immigration to Palestine (1939-40)." YVS, vol.10 (1974): 241-276.

The Death Ships

6147. Eliav, Arie: The Voyage of the Ulua [New York: Funk and Wagnalls/Sabra Books, 1969]

6148. Goldberger, Hans: "On the Pentcho." Korman: Hunter, pp.149-155.

6149. Habas, Bracha: "Forty Days in a Fisherman's Skiff." Furrows, vol.1 #8 (June, 1943): 13-16.

6150. Helpern, Jeremiah: "Ships to the Rescue." Hadar, vol. 3 #4 (May/June, 1940): 58-60.

6151. Manning, Olivia: "The Story of the Struma." Mid, vol. 16 #6 (June/July, 1970): 48-57.

6152. "Palestine: Questions in Parliament." NJ, vol.17 #3 (Dec., 1940): 28-30. * On the Patria.

6153. Rosen, P.: "Death in the Bosporus: The Voyage of the Struma." Am Zionist, vol.70 #11/12 (Nov./Dec., 1979): 10-13.

6154. "Saga of the Refugee Ship Vitorul." IP, vol.2 #4 (Dec. 18, 1942): 2-3.

6155. Steiner, Erich G.: The Story of ´Patria´ [New York: Holocaust Library, 1982]

Semi-fictitious account of the sinking of the S.S. Patria in Haifa harbor on November 25, 1940. Based on real events - the Haganah sinking of an Aliyah-Bet ship which was to be returned to Europe by the British - the novelized dialogue makes the book of dubious value.

6156. "The ´Struma´ Protest." CJR, vol.5 #3 (June, 1942): 315-317.

PERSONAL RESPONSES

Prewar

6157. Archbishop of Canterbury: "Urging the Participation of Christians in the Special Services of Intercession on July 17th." CJR, vol.1 #1 (Sept., 1938): 25-26.

6158. Belth, Norton: "Can Nazism be Halted?" CJCh, vol.25 #40 (Feb. 25, 1938): 8, 13, 16.

6159. Boyd, Ernest: "As a Gentile Sees It." Scribner´s, vol.94 #4 (Oct., 1933): 242-243.

6160. Brandeis, Louis D.: "The Greatest Tragedy of the Twenty Centuries." WJ, vol.2 #32 (Dec. 7, 1934): 755.

6161. Dodd, William E.: "Germany Shocked Me." J Sp, vol.3 #11 (Sept., 1938): 13-15, 30.

6162. Durant, Will: "Brotherhood Will Return." CJCh, vol.24 #22 (Oct. 23, 1936): 5, 16.

6163. Dushaw, Amos I.: "The Menace of Hitler." P/P Herald, vol.3 #3/4 (March/April, 1934): 5-6.

6164. Farwell, G.: "Those Whom Hitler Seeks to Destroy." P/P Herald, vol.3 #3/4 (March/April, 1934): 25-28.

6165. Fox, Gresham G.: Democracy and Nazism [Chicago: Argus Book Shop, 1934]

6166. George, David L.: "A Remarkable Race - Why Are Jews Persecuted?" Am J Times, vol.2 #8 (April, 1937): 6, 32.

6167. Golding, Louis: A Letter to Adolf Hitler [London: L. & V. Woolf at the Hogarth Press, 1932]

6168. Holmes, John H.: "A Christian Speaks to Jews." J Sp, vol.4 #5 (March, 1939): 13-15.

6169. Hook, Sidney: "Promise Without Dogma: A Social Philosophy of Jews." Menorah, vol.25 #3 (Oct./Dec., 1937): 273-288.

6170. Jackson, Robert H.: "Challenge to America." NP, vol. 29 #3 (Jan. 20, 1939): 9.

6171. Janowski, Oscar: "Don´t Hush Attacks - Strike Back." CJCh, vol.22 #33 (Jan. 4, 1935): 5, 12.

6172. Lasker, Loula D.: "A Test for Civilization." Survey Graphic, vol.27 #12 (Dec., 1938): 601-603, 640.

6173. Lore, Ludwig: "Can Hitlerism Survive?" New Republic, vol.74 #954 (March 15, 1933): 120-123.

6174. McDonald, James G.: "I Cannot Remain Silent. Letter of Resignation Scores Germany´s Treatment of Jews." NJM, vol.50 #5 (Feb., 1936): 150-151, 162-164.

6175. Murray, G.: "In Defense of Civilization." Menorah, vol.27 #2 (April/June, 1939): 121-137.

6176. Niebuhr, R.: "Germany Must be Told." Ch Century, vol. 50 #32 (Aug. 9, 1933): 1014-1015.

6177. Noel-Baker, Philip J.: "A Speech on Persecutions in Germany." CJR, vol.2 #1 (Jan., 1939): 33-46

6178. Padover, Saul K.: "Who Are the Germans?" F Affairs, vol.13 #3 (April, 1935): 509-518.

6179. Parkes, James: "Judaism-Jews-Antisemites: Thoughts of a Non-Jew." J Rev, #8 (March/June, 1934): 26-34.

6180. Ravin, Selma: "A Plea for Common Humanity." J Sp, vol.4 #3 (Jan., 1939): 27-28.

6181. Russell, Charles E.: "To My Fellow Gentiles." P/P Herald, vol.3 #9/11 (Fall, 1934): 1-2.

6182. ___: "Wanted - An International Defense League." P/P Herald, vol.4 #1/3 (Jan./March, 1935): 1-2.

6183. Smith, Alfred E.: "The Challenge to America." PVP: Nazism, pp.306-310.

6184. Starr, S.: "A Dictator's War on Jehovah, His Prophets, and His People." J Fo, vol.22 #3 (April, 1939): 37-38, 47.

6185. Van Passen, Pierre: "A Plea to World Christendom." P/P Herald, vol.6 #6/11 (Fall, 1937): 17-18.

6186. Wagner, Robert F.: "Nazis Menace Civilization." NJM, vol.53 #5 (Jan., 1939): 162.

6187. Wells, H. G.: "Civilization on Trial." F Affairs, vol.13 #4 (July, 1935): 595-599.

6188. Wilson, Lloyd: "A Persecution Universally Condemned." Syn/LB, vol.6 #5 (Jan., 1939): 4-6.

6189. Zukerman, Wm: "Towards a New Solution of the Jewish Problem." WJ, vol.2 #74 (Oct. 4, 1935): 16-17, 20.

6190. ___: "Under the Whip of Fascism." Menorah, vol.25 #1 (Jan./March, 1937): 1-19.

6191. Zweig, Arnold: "Does the World Need Jews?" WJ, vol.2 #58 (June 14, 1935): 3-4.

Wartime

6192. Archbishop of Canterbury: "Help for Jews." J Fr, vol. 10 #8 (Aug., 1943): 24-26. * Address before the House of Lords.

6193. Arendt, Hannah: "We Refugees." Menorah, vol.31 #1 (Jan./March, 1943): 69-77.

6194. Arnot, R. Page: "Science Says: ´You´re a Mongrel, Brother, Be Proud of It´." Today, vol.1 #5 (March, 1945): 16-20. * Rebuts Nazi racial theory.

6195. Atkinson, Henry: "The Deadliest Challenge." Opinion, vol.11 #5 (March, 1941): 7-8.

6196. Barkley, Alben W.: "America Must Show the Way." CW, vol.10 #15 (April 9, 1943): 7-8. * Senator Barkley urges immediate rescue action.

6197. Baron, Salo W.: "The Effect of War on Jewish Community Life." JSSQ, vol.19 #1 (Sept., 1942): 10-72.

6198. Benes, Edouard: "What We Are Fighting For." FW, vol.1 #1 (Oct., 1941): 39-42.

6199. Biddle, Francis: "Immigration Stoppage Would be Unwise and Ungenerous." Rescue, vol.1 #3/4 (March/April, 1944): 1-2.

6200. Black, Norman F.: "A Christian Answers the Query: What About the Jews?" Today, vol.1 #2 (Dec., 1944): 1-3, 30-31.

6201. Ehrenburg, Ilya: "Crime and Punishment: Germany´s Responsibility." Am Heb, vol.153 #1 (Nov. 5, 1943): 8-9.

6202. ___: "The Dead Speak: Do Not Forget Us." Today, vol. 1 #3 (Jan., 1945): 21-22.

6203. ___: "It is Our Duty to Remember if We are to Save the World." Today, vol.1 #4 (Feb., 1945): 13-15.

6204. ___: "The Justification of Hate." J Sp, vol.9 #3 (Jan., 1944): 24-26.

6205. Frankenstein, Ernst: Justice for My People [New York: Dial Press, 1944]

6206. Goldin, Judah: "What is the Jewish Problem?" Recon, vol.8 #1 (Feb. 20, 1942): 11-16.

6207. Goldman, Nahum: "The Jewish Problem in the Light of World Events." J Sp, vol.5 #11 (Sept., 1940): 8-10.

6208. Green, William: "The Voice of American Labor." CW, vol.9 #26 (Aug. 14, 1942): 9-11.

6209. Holmes, John H.: "Through Gentile Eyes." Opinion, vol.11 #12 (Oct., 1941): 16-18.

6210. Hurley, Robert A.: "Justice for Jews - a War Aim." CW, vol.9 #27 (Sept. 11, 1942): 9-11.

6211. James, Stanley B.: A Catholic Angle on the Jewish Problem [London: Paternoster Pub., 1944]

6212. Not Used.

6213. Kravitz, Nathan: "To My Brother in Poland." Polish Jew, vol.4 #22 (April, 1944): 19-24.

6214. Langer, William R.: "Do Not Fail Them." Zionews, vol. 4 #25/26 (April, 1943): 12-15, 21-22.

6215. Littell, Norman: "Shadows of the Crooked Cross." New Currents, vol.2 #3 (March, 1944): 6-9.

6216. Lodge, Henry C.: "Warning to Hitler." CW, vol.9 #26 (Aug. 14, 1942): 5-6.

6217. Mann, Thomas: "Culture Against Barbarism." CJR, vol.3 #2 (March/April, 1940): 115-118.

6218. McConnell, Francis: "Our Christian Duty." J Mirror, vol.1 #6 (Feb./March, 1943): 5-8.

6219. Miller, Arthur: "Hitler´s Quarry: Despoiled, Driven Over the Seven Seas, Jews Seek Refuge." J Survey, vol.1 #1 (may, 1941): 8-9, 21.

6220. Montagu, M. F. A.: "Are Jews a ´Race´?" Ch J Forum, vol.2 #2 (Win., 1943/44): 77-86.

6221. Musatti, Raymondo: "We Who Have Seen Fascism." FW, vol.2 #2 (March, 1942): 157-160.

6222. Nussbaum, Max: "Is This a Religious War?" NJM, vol.56 #8 (April, 1942): 252, 270-271.

6223. "Prominent Americans On Antisemitism." J Sp, vol.5 #11 (Sept., 1940): 20-24, 46.

6224. Samuel, Maurice: "Antisemitism Is a Christian Problem." Am Mercury, vol.53 #211 (July, 1941): 56-63.

6225. Shirer, William L.: Berlin Diary: The Journal of a Foreign Correspondent, 1934-1941 [New York: Alfred A. Knopf, 1941]

6226. Silver, Abba H.: "The Mystery of Jewish Survival." JVP, vol.4 #9/10 (Oct., 1941): 8, 25.

6227. Smith, Rennie: "Concerning War Aims." CEO, vol.18 #4 (Feb. 17, 1941): 41-42.

6228. "Ten Years of Hitler." Opinion, vol.13 #4 (Feb., 1943): 7-20, 22, 24, 26, 28, 30, 32. * Statements by American public figures.

6229. Thompson, Dorothy: "Jews are a People." J Mirror, vol.2 #7 (April/May, 1943): 37-40.

6230. Tuwim, Julian: "We Polish Jews." FW, vol.8 #1 (July, 1944): 53-56. * Honoring martyred Jews of Poland.

6231. Wagner, Robert F.: "No Time for Red Tape." Am Heb, vol.153 #44 (Sept. 1, 1944): 10, 15.

6232. Weinstein, Jacob J.: "Amos in Times Square." Menorah, vol.30 #3 (Oct./Dec., 1942): 240-245.

6233. Weiss-Rosmarin, Trude: "Some Observations on Jewish Survival." J Sp, vol.6 #3 (Jan., 1941): 6-9.

6234. Wise, Stephen S.: "As I See It." Opinion, vol.11 #8 (June, 1941): 5-6.

6235. ___: "The Crime of Crimes." Opinion, vol.11 #5 (March, 1941): 9-10.

6236. ___: "Deliverance Will Come." Opinion, vol.12 #10 (Aug., 1942): 5-6.

6237. ___: "A New Year´s Message." Opinion, vol.10 #12 (Oct., 1940): 10-12; vol.12 #11 (Sept., 1942): 7-10.

6238. Zukerman, William: "The Jewish Spirit in Crisis." Menorah, vol.30 #2 (July/Sept., 1942): 105-115.

6239. ___: "Militarization of Antisemitism." J Fr, vol.9 #3 (March, 1942): 10-13. * Appeal to save Jewry.

6240. Zweig, Stefan: "Pointless Jewish Tragedy." CW, vol.10 #16 (April 18, 1943): 5-6.

6241. Zygielbojm, Szmul: "Speech at the International Protest Meeting Against German Atrocities in Poland and Czechoslovakia, Caxton Hall, London, Sept. 2, 1942." GS, #4 (Oct. 4, 1942): 3-4.

The Bystanders

Winston S. Churchill

6242. Krefetz, Gerald: "Churchill and the Jews." J Fr, vol. 25 #10 (Oct., 1958): 11-15.

6243. Rabinowicz, Oskar: "Churchill on Judaism and Jews." J Sp, vol.21 #7 (Sept., 1956): 9-13.

6244. ___: "Churchill's Place in Jewish History." Recon, vol.30 #16 (Dec. 11, 1964): 25-30.

6245. ___: Winston Churchill on Jewish Problems [London: Lincoln-Prager for World Jewish Congress, 1956]

Franklin D. Roosevelt

6246. Cohen, Jacob: "Roosevelt in Retrospect." Moment, vol. 5 #1 (Dec., 1979): 11-19.

6247. Dallek, Robert: Franklin D. Roosevelt and American Foreign Policy, 1932-1945 [New York: Oxford Univ. Press, 1980]

6248. Lehman, Herbert: "FDR Who was His Brother's Keeper." J Digest, vol.5 #4 (Jan., 1960): 33-37.

6249. Matzozky (Matz), Eliyahu: "An Episode: Roosevelt and the Mass Killing." Mid, vol.26 #7 (Aug./Sept., 1980): 17-19.

6250. Schwartz, D.: "Roosevelt's Place in Jewish History." CJCh, vol.32 #50 (April 27, 1945): 7.

Stephen S. Wise

6251. Martel, M.: "Stephen S. Wise: Remembering His Greatness." Recon, vol.40 #4 (May, 1974): 18-26.

6252. Urofsky, Melvin I.: "The Cause of Stephen Wise." J Fr, vol.47 #1 (Jan., 1980): 15-20.

6253. Weiler, Moses C.: "Stephen S. Wise." JRJ, vol.25 #3 (Sum., 1978): 23-41.

Szmul Zygelbojm

6254. Ainsztein, Reuben: "New Light on Szmuel Zygelbojm´s Suicide." YVB, #15 (Aug., 1964): 8-12.

6255. Kazin, Alfred: "In Every Voice, In Every Ban." New Republic, vol.110 #2 (Jan. 10, 1944): 44-46.

6256. Piorkowski, J.: "Homage to Szmul Zygelbojm." Poland, #5/153 (May, 1967): 2.

6257. Ravel, A.: Faithful Unto Death: The Story of Arthur Zygelbojm [Montreal: Arbeiter Ring, 1980]

6258. "Szmul Zygielbojm - The Death of a Fighter." GS, #12 (June, 1943): 1-3.

Other Bystanders

6259. Acheson, Dean: Morning and Noon [Boston: Houghton Mifflin, 1965]

6260. Berkman, Ted: "J. F. K., Fanny Holtzman, and the Refugees." J Digest, vol.22 #8 (April, 1977): 22-25.

6261. Blum, John M. (ed.): The Morgenthau Diaries 3 vols. [Boston: Houghton Mifflin, 1967]

6262. Finkelstein, Moses I.: "A Time for Decision on Sumner Welles." New Currents, vol.2 #8 (Sept., 1944): 10-12, 30.

6263. Francois-Poncet, Andre (J. Le Clerq, transl.): The Fateful Years: Memoirs of a French Ambassador in Berlin, 1931-1938 [New York: Harcourt, Brace & World, 1949]

6264. Genizi, H.: "James McDonald and the Roosevelt Administration." in Pinhas Artzi (ed.): Bar-Ilan Studies in History [Ramat-Gan, Israel: Bar-Ilan Univ. Press, 1978]: 285-306.

6265. Goldmann, Nahum (Helen Sebra, transl.): The Autobiography of Nahum Goldmann: Sixty Years of Jewish Life [New York: Holt, Rinehart & Winston, 1969]

6266. Hayes, Carlton J. H.: Wartime Mission in Spain, 1942-1945 [New York: Macmillan, 1945]

6267. Herman, Abraham: "Berl Katzenelson." Furrows, vol.4 #9 (Sept., 1946): 17-21.

6268. Hull, Cordell: The Memoirs of Cordell Hull [New York: Macmillan, 1948]

6269. Jedrzejewki, Waclaw (ed.): Diplomat in Berlin: Papers and Memoirs of Jozef Lipski, Ambassador of Poland [New York: Columbia Univ. Press, 1968]

6270. Lewis, Theodore N.: "Ambassador Dodd´s Diary." Recon, vol.7 #9 (June 13, 1941): 13-14.

6271. Melamet, Max: "The Labors of Henry Morgenthau." CW, vol.34 #4 (Feb. 20, 1967): 18-19.

6272. Millis, W. (ed.): The Forrestal Diaries [New York: Viking Press, 1951]

6273. Nadich, Judah: Eisenhower and the Jews [New York: Twayne Publishers, 1953]

6274. Rapoport, Louis: "Hillel Kook Alias Peter Bergson." PT, vol.10 #1 (Aut., 1982): 13-15.

6275. Ribalow, Harold U.: "Nahum Goldmann." J Sp, vol.19 #6 (June, 1954): 11-13.

6276. Rubin, Barry: "Ambassador Lawrence A. Steinhardt: The Perils of a Jewish Diplomat, 1940-1945." Am J His, vol.70 #3 (March, 1981): 311-346.

6277. Shafir, Shlomo: "George S. Messersmith: An Anti-Nazi Diplomat´s View of the German Jewish Crisis." JSS, vol.35 #1 (Jan., 1973): 32-41.

6278. Shirer, William L.: The Nightmare Years [Boston: Little, Brown and Co., 1984]

6279. Smith, Howard K.: Last Train From Berlin [New York: Alfred A. Knopf, 1942]

6280. Weizmann, Chaim: Trial and Error [New York: Harper & Row, 1949]

Memoir of perhaps the most famous Zionist leader of the twentieth century. Reviews the trials and tribulations of European and World Jewry during this most stormy period. His view is broad but at the same time highly personal.

6281. Wilson, John P.: "Carlton H. Hayes, Spain, and the Refugee Crisis, 1942-1945." AJHQ, vol.62 #2 (Dec., 1972): 99-110.

INSTITUTIONAL RESPONSES

The International Red Cross

6282. Dworzecki, Meir: "The International Red Cross and its Policy Vis-A-Vis the Jews in the Ghetto and Concentration Camps in Nazi-Occupied Europe." Gutman: Rescue, pp. 71-110.

6283. Grossmann, Kurt R.: "An Unfulfilled Testament." CW, vol.10 #31 (Nov. 14, 1943): 10-11.

6284. Kantor, S. Z.: "The International Red Cross Was Silent." J Fr, vol.12 #5 (May, 1945): 17-20.

6285. Tartakower, Aryeh: "Where the Red Cross Failed." CW, vol.13 #16 (May 3, 1946): 9-10.

6286. Tenenbaum, Joseph: "Red Cross to the Rescue." YVB, (Oct., 1959): 7-8.

Religious Groups

6287. Fishman, H.: American Protestanism and a Jewish State [Detroit: Wayne State Univ. Press, 1973]

6288. Genizi, Haim: "American Interfaith Cooperation on Behalf of Refugees from Nazism, 1933-1945." Am J His, vol.70 #3 (March, 1981): 347-361.

6289. Leslie, Kenneth: "Christianity Fights Antisemitism." J Sp, vol.9 #6 (April, 1944): 13-14.

6290. Levy, Henry W.: "Good Will to Men." NJM, vol.53 #4 (Dec., 1938): 128-130.

6291. Ludlow, P. W.: "The Refugee Problem in the 1930's: The Failures and Successes of Protestant Relief Programmes." EHR, vol.90 #356 (July, 1975): 564-603.

6292. Nawyn, William E.: American Protestantism's Response to Germany's Jews and Refugees, 1933-1941 [Ann Arbor, MI: UMI Research Press, 1981]

6293. Ross, Robert W.: "The Response of Institutionalized Religion to the Holocaust." Littell: Education, pp. 81-86.

6294. ___: So It Was True: The American Protestant Press and the Nazi Persecution of the Jews [Minneapolis: Univ. of Minnesota Press, 1980]

Study which attempts to debunk the "we didn't know" myth that has been used by apologists to explain the lack of pressure to rescue European Jewry. Ross has surveyed more than fifty American Protestant periodicals and found them informed about events in Europe. Few of their readers cared to translate knowledge of evil into action against it.

6295. Snoek, Johan M.: The Grey Book: A Collection of Protests Against Antisemitism and the Persecution of Jews [New York: Humanities Press, 1970]

6296. The Voice of Religion [New York: American Jewish Committee, 1933] * Short anthology by Christian religious leaders on the persecution of German Jewry.

Varia

6297. "Complete Text of American Labor's Memorandum to the State Department on Aid to Jews in Nazidom." V/Ung, vol.1 #6 (Nov., 1943): 6-7.

6298. Duggan, Stephen and B. Drury: The Rescue of Science and Learning: The Story of the Emergency Committee in Aid of Displaced Foreign Scholars [New York: Macmillan, 1948]

6299. Institute of Human Relations: American Democracy Against Totalitarianism [New York: National Conf. of Christians and Jews, 1938]

6300. The Rabbinical Assembly of America: "A Union of Democratic Nations." CJR, vol.5 #5 (Oct., 1942): 536-540.

6301. Wedlock, L.: The Reaction of Negro Publications and Organizations to German Antisemitism [Washington, DC: Graduate School, Howard Univ., 1942]

FASCISM/ANTISEMITISM IN THE UNITED NATIONS

Fascism in the British Commonwealth

6302. Barnes, James J.: "´Mein Kampf´ in Britain 1930-39." WLB, vol.27 #3 (Sum., 1974): 2-10.

6303. Brailsford, H.: "Fascism in England." New Republic, vol.80 #1029 (Aug. 22, 1934): 42-43.

6304. Cross, Colin: The Fascist in Britain [London: Barrie and Rockliff, 1961]

6305. Harap, L.: "Antisemitism in 1941 England." J Survey, vol.1 #2 (June, 1941): 3-5.

6306. Hoffman, G. H.: "Canadian Fascist Movements in the 1930´s." J Fr, vol.43 #1 (Jan., 1976): 26-29.

6307. Lebzelter, Gisela: "The ´Protocols´ in England." WLB, vol.31 #2 (1978): 111-117.

6308. Mandle, W. F.: Antisemitism and the British Union of Fascists [New York: Barnes & Noble, 1968]

6309. Orwell, George: "Antisemitism in Britain." CJR, vol.8 #2 (April, 1945): 163-171.

6310. Strachey, John: "Fascism in Great Britain." New Republic, vol.78 #1013 (May 2, 1934): 331-332.

6311. Wasner, Jonathan: Brothers Beyond the Sea: National Socialism in Canada [Waterloo, Ont.: Wilfrid Laurier Univ. Press, 1981]

6312. Zukerman, William: "Fascism Disrupts British Jewry." J Fr, vol.3 #11 (Dec., 1936): 22-24.

Fascism in Latin America

6313. Priestley, Gerard: "The Swastika in South America." CW, vol.8 #41 (Dec. 12, 1941): 7-8.

6314. Putnam, Samuel: "Antisemitism in Latin America." J Life, vol.2 #5 (May, 1938): 12-16.

6315. Simon, Carla: "Antisemitism in the Argentine." New Currents, vol.2 #1 (Jan., 1944): 3-5.

6316. Taubes, I. B.: "Why the Argentine Republic is Antisemitic." Am Heb, vol.153 #5 (Dec. 3, 1943): 7, 14.

Fascism in the United States

6317. Abrahams, Edward: "Fascism in the U.S.A." PoP, vol. 8 #2 (March/April, 1974): 23-26.

6318. Angoff, Ch.: "Nazi Jew Baiting in America." Nation, vol.140 #3643 (May 1, 1935): 501-503; #3644 (May 8, 1935): 531-535.

6319. Arnold, J.: "Fascism and the American Jews." J Life, vol.2 #1 (Jan., 1938): 8-15.

6320. Bell, Leland V.: "The Failure of Nazism in America: The German American Bund, 1936-1941." Pol Sci Q, vol. 85 #4 (Dec., 1970): 585-599.

6321. ___: In Hitler's Shadow: The Anatomy of American Nazism [Port Washington, NY: Kennikat Press, 1973]

6322. Bergel, L.: "How Nazism has Invaded U. S. Colleges." CB, vol.2 #17 (Feb. 2, 1936): 3-4.

6323. Carlson, John R.: "Our Fascist Enemies Within." Am Mercury, vol.54 #219 (March, 1942): 306-317.

6324. ___: Under Cover: My Four Years in the Nazi Underworld of America [New York: E. P. Dutton, 1943]

6325. Cohen, William: "Unholy Trinity of Fascism." CW, vol. 9 #2 (Jan. 2, 1942): 8-10.

6326. Compton, James: The Swastika and the Eagle [Boston: Houghton Mifflin, 1967]

6327. "Coughlin and the Christian Front." Opinion, vol.10 #4 (Feb., 1940): 3-4.

6328. Dennis, Lawrence: The Coming American Fascism [New York: AMS Press, 1972] Rep. 1936 Ed.

6329. ___: Fascism in America." Annals, #180 (July, 1935): 62-73.

6330. Diamond, Sander A.: The Nazi Movement in the U.S., 1924-1941 [Ithaca, NY: Cornell Univ. Press, 1974]

6331. ___: "The Years of Waiting: National Socialism in the United States, 1922-1933." AJHQ, vol.59 #3 (March, 1970): 256-271.

6332. Frye, Alton: Nazi Germany and the American Hemisphere 1933-1941 [New Haven, CT: Yale Univ. Press, 1967]

6333. Greenwald, L.: "Fascism in America: The Distaff Side." CJR, vol.4 #6 (Dec., 1941): 616-624.

6334. Hare, William: The Brown Network [New York: Knight, 1936]

6335. Higham, Charles: American Swastika [Garden City, NY: Doubleday, 1985]

Well documented review of nazism in the United States from the German American Bund of the thirties to the American Nazi party of the seventies. Also includes information on Nazi war criminals used by segments of the American government, and features the Klaus Barbie incident.

6336. Kahn, A. E.: "Offensive on the Fifth Column Front." New Currents, vol.1 #1 (March, 1943): 7-11.

6337. Katz, Isaac: "Fascism: American Style." Recon, vol.2 #6 (May 1, 1936): 13-16.

6338. Levine, Harold: Fifth Column in America [New York: Doubleday, 1940]

6339. Lewis, Walter K.: "Disciples of Disunity." CW, vol.9 #19 (May 1, 1942): 20-21.

6340. Libero, Mario: "Mussolini´s Puppets in America." CW, vol.8 #24 (June 20, 1941): 7-8.

6341. Littell, Norman M.: "Shadows of the Crooked Cross." CW, vol.11 #7 (Feb. 18, 1944): 10-14.

6342. Lore, Ludwig: "Nazi Unions in America." NJM, vol.56 #7 (March, 1942): 222-223.

6343. Richards, Bernard G.: "Crusade for Hitlerism." CW, vol.11 #24 (June 30, 1944): 6-8. * On Huey Long.

6344. Rorty, James: "American Fuehrer in Dress Rehearsal." Com, vol.1 #1 (Nov., 1945): 13-20.

6345. Shub, Boris: "White Russian Nazi Ring in U.S." CW, vol.8 #27 (July 25, 1941): 8-10.

6346. Spivak, John L.: Secret Armies: The New Technique of Nazi Warfare [New York: Modern Age/McLeod, 1939]

Journalistic expose of Nazi activities in America. Unafraid to name names, Spivak pays special attention to the secret world of nazism´s "antisemitic international".

6347. Straight, Michael: "Hitler´s Guerrillas Over Here." New Republic, vol.106 #15 (April 13, 1942): 481-483.

6348. Swing, Raymond G. (ed.): Forerunners of American Fascism [New York: Arno Press, 1969] Rep. 1935 Ed.

6349. Tozier, Roy B.: America´s Little Hitlers: Who´s Who and what´s up in U.S. Fascism [Girard, KS: Halderman Julius, 1940]

6350. von Hilderbrand, Dietrich: "Fascism and Catholicism." FW, vol.1 #2 (Nov., 1941): 197-199.

6351. Ward, Harry F.: "The Development of Fascism in the United States. Annals, #180 (July, 1935): 55-61.

American Industry and the Nazis

6352. Higham, Charles: Trading with the Enemy: An Expose of the Nazi-American Money Plot [New York: Delacorte Press, 1983]

Expose of the relations between major American corporations

and Nazi Germany before and during World War II. Many American corporations - through Swiss "subsidiaries" - chose to do business as usual rather than to break off relations with the Nazis. A well documented and chilling account of corporate irresponsibility.

6353. Tenenbaum, Joseph: American Investments and Business Interests in Germany [New York: Joint Boycott Council, 1939]

Antisemitism in the United States

6354. Arnold, John: "Antisemitism in the U.S.A." J Life, vol.2 #5 (May, 1938): 6-11.

6355. Belth, N.: "Problems of Antisemitism in the United States." CJR, vol.2 #3 (May/June, 1939): 6-19; #4 (July/Aug., 1939): 43-57.

6356. Berman, H.: "Political Antisemitism in Minnesota During the Great Depression." JSS, vol.38 #3/4 (Sum./Fall, 1970): 247-264.

6357. Boxerman, Burton: "Rise of Antisemitisn in St. Louis, 1933-1945." YIVO Annual, vol.14 (1969): 251-269.

6358. Fein, Helen: "Attitudes in the U.S.A. 1933-45: Toleration of Genocide." PoP, vol.7 #5 (Sept./Oct., 1973): 22-28.

6359. Frank, Reuven: "Isolationism and Antisemitism." CW, vol.8 #34 (Oct. 24, 1941): 7-9.

6360. Gunstadt, Richard E.: "How Strong is Jew-Hatred?" NJM, vol.56 #9 (May, 1942): 296-297, 307.

6361. Johnson, Alvin: "The Rising Tide of Antisemitism." Survey Graphic, vol.28 #2 (Feb., 1939): 113-116.

6362. Jonas, H. J.: "Antisemitica Americana." CJR, vol.4 #5 (Oct., 1941): 564-571.

6363. Lowenthal, Leo and N. Guterman: Prophets of Deceit: A Study of the Techniques of an American Agitator [Palo Alto, CA: Pacific Books, 1970]

6364. Martin, Louis E.: "Antisemites Like Detroit." New Currents, vol.1 #5 (Aug., 1943): 10-11.

6365. Nomad, Max: "Jewish Conspiracy." Am Heb, vol.154 #5 (Dec. 1, 1944): 7, 14-15.

6366. Riesman, D.: "The Politics of Persecution." Pub Op Q, vol.6 #1 (Spr., 1942): 41-56.

6367. Roe, W.: "Antisemitism in Congress." J Survey, vol.1 #6 (Nov., 1941): 4-6.

6368. Starr, Joshua: Antisemitic Activities and Propaganda in the United States [New York: AJC, 1940] * Survey

6369. Strong, Donald S.: Organized Antisemitism in America: The Rise of Group Prejudice During the Decade 1930-1940 [Washington, DC: Am. Council on Public Affairs, 1941]

6370. Teller, J. L.: "Assorted Hate-Mongers." CW, vol.11 #2 (Jan. 14, 1944): 7-8.

6371. Tumin, Melvin M.: An Inventory and Appraisal of Research on American Antisemitism [New York: Freedom Books, 1961]

6372. Wylie, P.: "Memorandum on Antisemitism." Am Mercury, vol.60 #253 (Jan., 1945): 66-73.

6373. Young, Stanley: "Antisemitism in Our Time." FW, vol.7 #3 (March, 1944): 198-199.

Father Coughlin

6374. Benson, Arnold: "The Catholic Church and the Jews." Am J Ch, vol.1 #7 (Feb. 15, 1940): 5-7.

6375. "Digest of Public Opinion: The Coughlin Broadcasts." CJR, vol.2 #1 (Jan., 1939): 51-53.

6376. Kolodny, Ralph L.: "Father Coughlin and the Jews: A Reminiscence for Younger Colleagues." JJoS, vol.53 #4 (Sum., 1977): 309-319. Also in CM, vol.44 #8 (Nov., 1977): 14-17. J Digest, vol.23 #7 (March, 1978): 66-72.

6377. Tull, Charles J.: Father Coughlin and the New Deal [Syracuse, NY: Syracuse Univ. Press, 1965]

Combatting American Antisemitism

6378. "Digest of Public Opinion: The Lindbergh Speech at Des Moines." CJR, vol.4 #6 (Dec., 1941): 637-648.

6379. Engel, Joseph: "Jewish Youth and the Defeatists." New Currents, vol.1 #4 (July, 1943): 22-23.

6380. Minsky, Louis: "Jewry and Democracy." Recon, vol.4 #3 (March 25, 1938): 5-10.

6381. Murphy, Frank: "Race Hatred: The Enemy Bullets Can't Stop." Am Heb, vol.154 #14 (Feb. 16, 1945): 6-7, 15.

6382. Pearlman, Nathan D.: "Combatting Enemy Propaganda." CW, vol.10 #33 (Nov. 26, 1943): 5-6.

6383. Wise, Stephen S.: "Antisemitism is Anti-American." CW, vol.11 #7 (Feb. 18, 1944): 6-9.

6384. Zirin, L.: "The Community Fights Back." New Currents, vol.2 #2 (Feb., 1944): 5-7.

WARTIME PLANNING FOR RECOVERY

Europe

6385. Belkin, Samuel: "World At the Cross Roads: Concept of Universal Justice Must be Blue Print of New Social Order." Am Heb, vol.153 #9 (Dec. 31, 1943): 9, 13.

6386. Benedict, Libby: "After Germany is Liberated." CW, vol.8 #37 (Nov. 14, 1941): 8-10.

6387. Bickel, Alexander M.: "Fundamentals of a European Order." CW, vol.10 #14 (April 2, 1943): 5-6.

6388. Carr, Edward H.: Conditions of Peace [New York: Macmillan, 1942]

6389. Condlife, J. B.: Agenda for a Post-War World [New York: W. W. Norton, 1942]

6390. "The Declaration of Human Rights." CJR, vol.8 #2 (April, 1945): 207-209.

6391. Duncan, Ivor: "Occupation Armies in Germany." CEO, vol.19 #17 (Aug. 21, 1942): 262-263.

6392. Eichelberger, C. M.: "When Peace Comes: A Challenge to America." CJR, vol.5 #2 (April, 1942): 123-130.

6393. Emerson, Sir Herbert: "Postwar Problems of Refugees." F Affairs, vol.21 #2 (Jan., 1943): 211-220.

6394. Friedrich Carl J.: "Military Government as a Step Toward Self-Rule." Pub Op Q, vol.7 #4 (Win., 1943): 527-541.

6395. Hafftka, Alexander Z.: "The National Minorities in Post-War Poland." Polish Jew, vol.1 #3 (Dec., 1941): 3-5.

6396. Halecki, Oscar: "Post-War Poland." Am Slavic/EER, vol.3 (1944): 28-40.

6397. King, Frank: "Allied Negotiations and the Dismemberment of Germany." JCH, vol.16 #3 (July, 1981): 585-596.

6398. Kohn, H.: "Russia and Germany in the Post-War World." Ort Eco Rev, vol.4 #2 (Nov., 1944): 39-47.

6399. Kulisher, E. M.: The Displacement of Population in Europe [Montreal: International Labour Office, 1943]

6400. Lasker, Bruno: "A Cornerstone for World Reconstruction." Survey Graphic, vol.30 #10 (Oct., 1941): 522-526, 536.

6401. Marburg, Fr.: "Poland´s Future Regime and National Minorities." Polish Jew, vol.2 #6/7 (March/April, 1942): 7-8.

6402. "Minorities After this War." IJA, vol.1 #9/10 (April/May, 1942): 1-23.

6403. Minsky, Louis: "Religious Groups and the Postwar World." CJR, vol.5 #4 (Aug., 1942): 357-372.

6404. Noskin, Bernard: "Blueprint for a Post-War World." J Fr, vol.6 #11 (Nov., 1939): 13-16.

6405. Pickett, Clarence: "Handling Displaced Populations." Pub Op Q, vol.7 #4 (Win., 1943): 592-605.

6406. Soffner, H.: "Winning the Peace with Germany." Survey Graphic, vol.32 #7 (July, 1943): 296-298, 302-303.

6407. Vansittart, Robert: The Black Record [Toronto: Musson Book Co., 1941]

6408. Wright, Quincy: "Dilemmas for a Post-War World." FW, vol.1 #1 (Oct., 1941): 14-16.

On Justice for the Perpetrators

6409. "America and the Postwar World: What Shall We Do With Germany?" New Republic, vol.109 #22 (Nov. 29, 1943): 768-772.

6410. Benes, V.: "The Question of the Definition of War Crimes." CEO, vol.20 #19 (Sept. 17, 1943): 282-283.

6411. Edelman, Maurice: "Will the War Criminals Escape?" New Republic, vol.112 #8 (Feb. 19, 1945): 259-260.

6412. Farrin, A.: "The Responsibility for Nazi Crimes." CEO, vol.20 #18 (Sept. 17, 1943): 281-282.

6413. Not Used.

6414. Glueck, Sheldon: "Punish Axis War Criminals." CW, vol.12 #5 (Feb. 2, 1945): 11-13.

6415. ___: "Punishing the War Criminals." New Republic, vol.109 #21 (Nov. 22, 1943): 706-709.

6416. ___: "Trial and Punishment of the Axis War Criminals." FW, vol.4 #2 (Nov., 1942): 138-146.

6417. Grossman, Meir: "By Whom Will They be Tried?" CW, vol.10 #31 (Nov. 12, 1943): 6-8.

6418. Kaufman, Theodore: Germany Must Perish [Newark, NJ: Argyle Press, 1941]

6419. Lelewer, Georg: "Punishment of War Criminals." CEO, vol.20 #19 (Sept. 17, 1943): 283-284.

6420. Lewin, Kurt: "The Special Case of Germany." Pub Op Q, vol.7 #4 (Win., 1943): 555-566.

6421. Marx, Hugo: "The Problem of Germany." Menorah, vol.30 #3 (Oct./Dec., 1942): 300-306.

6422. Minshall, T.: "The Problem of Germany." Int Affairs, vol.20 #1 (Jan., 1944): 3-18.

6423. Nizer, Louis: What To Do With Germany [Chicago: Ziff-Davis Pub., 1944]

Wartime proposal for the denazification of Germany after the eventual Allied victory. Interesting in light of what the Western Allies failed to do after the war. Focuses on the neutralization of German nationalism and the reeducation of the German people.

6424. Pepper, Claude D.: "Punishment of War Criminals: A Major War Aim." FW, vol.8 #1 (July, 1944): 72-74.

6425. Pinson, Koppel S.: "On the Future of Germany: A Survey of Opinions and Proposals." Menorah, vol.32 #2 (Oct./Dec., 1944): 125-160.

6426. Pol, Heinz: The Hidden Enemy: The German Threat to Post-War Peace [New York: Julian Messner, 1943]

6427. "Punishment of War Criminals." J Comment, vol.2 #19 (July 28, 1944): 1-4.

6428. "Punishment of War Criminals." CW, vol.11 #28 (Oct. 6, 1944): 8-10. * Statement of policy adopted by the Executive Committee of the WJC.

6429. Ribalow, Harold U.: "Must Germany Perish?" CW, vol.10 #11 (March 12, 1943): 7-9.

6430. Rosengarten, Issac: "Punishment of Germany and World Peace." J Fo, vol.27 #1 (Jan., 1944): 5-6, 19.

6431. Shotwell, James T.: "What Shall We do About Germany?" Survey Graphic, vol.34 #3 (March, 1945): 99-100.

6432. Sinclair, Upton: "What Shall be Done with Hitler?" FW, vol.7 #2 (Feb., 1944): 121-124.

6433. Unsdet, Sigrid: "The War Criminals and the Future." FW, vol.6 #6 (Dec., 1943): 490-491.

6434. "Will War Criminals Find Asylum? J Comment, vol.1 #24 (Dec. 31, 1943): 1-3.

6435. Ziemer, Gregor: "Rehabilitating Fascist Youth." Pub Op Q, vol.7 #4 (Win., 1943): 583-591.

On the Jewish Question

6436. Abrahams, I.: "Jewish Aspects of the Peace." J Sp, vol.10 #7 (May, 1945): 19-21.

6437. Apenszlak, Jacob: "Polish Jewry - Nucleus of Jewish National Resurrection." Polish Jew, vol.4 #25 (Sept./Oct., 1944): 7-8, 33-34.

6438. ___: "The Reconstruction of Polish Jewry." J Fo, vol. 27 #8 (Aug., 1944): 159, 162.

6439. Aufricht, Hans: "Some Prerequisites of Jewish Post-War Adjustment." J Fo, vol.26 #3 (April, 1943): 43-44, 62-63.

6440. Baird, Alexander: "The Future of the Jews in Eastern Europe." CJR, vol.8 #1 (Feb., 1945): 3-14.

6441. Baron, Salo W.: "Reflections on the Future Conditions of European Jewry." JSSQ, vol.17 #1 (Sept., 1940): 5-19.

6442. ___: "Reflections on the Future of the Jews of Europe." CJR, vol.3 #4 (July/Aug., 1940): 355-369.

6443. Bernstein, E.: "Jewry After the War: The Problem of Relief, Reparations and Future Security." J Affairs, vol.1 #9 (Feb., 1942): 3-4.

6444. Bernstein, Henri: "A Fighting Program for Jews." CW, vol.8 #43 (Dec. 26, 1941): 9-10.

6445. Brodetsky, Selig: "Jews in the Post-War Settlement." J Affairs, vol.2 #2 (July, 1942): 3-4.

6446. Brutzkus, J.: "On the Morrow After the War." Am OSE Rev, vol.1 #3/4 (March/April, 1942): 10-12.

6447. Chapman, Abraham: "Teheran Concord and the Jews." New Currents, vol.2 #5 (May, 1944): 12-13, 31.

6448. Cohen, Morris: "Jewish Studies of Peace and Post-War Problems." CJR, vol.4 #2 (April, 1941): 110-126.

6449. Dijour, Ilja M.: "Jewish Migration - Past and Post-War." JSSQ, vol.20 #1 (Sept., 1943): 3-10.

6450. Duker, Abraham G.: "Political and Cultural Aspects of Jewish Post-War Problems." JSSQ, vol.19 #1 (Sept., 1942): 56-66.

6451. Dunner, Joseph: "Jews in the Post-War World." NJM, vol.57 #4 (Dec., 1942): 119-120.

6452. Emerson, Herbert: "Repatriation Alone will not Solve Problems of Europe´s Displaced Persons." Rescue, vol. 2 #3/4 (March/April, 1945): 1-2.

6453. Fischbein, Bernard B.: "German Jews Must Not Return." CW, vol.11 #38 (Dec. 29, 1944): 6-8.

6454. Goldmann, Nahum: "Europe´s Jews and the Future." Opinion, vol.12 #10 (Aug., 1942): 7-10.

6455. ___: "Post-War Problems." CW, vol.8 #39 (Nov. 28, 1941): 5-7.

6456. Gottschalk, Max: "Jewry´s Post-War Problems: The Need for a Scientific Approach." J Affairs, vol.2 #10 (March, 1943): 4-5.

6457. ___ and Abraham G. Duker: Jews in the Post-War World [New York: American Jewish Committee, 1945]

Textbook written for the American Jewish Committee as part of the "Study Course on Jewish Post-War Problems." Reviews the Jewish situation in Europe from 1919 to 1945 and possible solutions for Jewish homelessness and powerlessness.

6458. Graeber, Isaque: "Europe´s Jews After the War." NJM, vol.59 #5 (Jan., 1945): 152, 159.

6459. Greenberg, Hayim: "Migration in the Post-War World." J Fr, vol.10 #9 (Sept., 1943): 14-18.

6460. ___: "Proposed Homes for Jews." J Fr, vol.9 #4 (April, 1942): 14-17.

6461. Halpern, Ben: "In the Light of History." J Fr, vol.11 #6 (June, 1944): 20-25.

6462. Hirschberg, A.: "Human Rights ´or´ Minority Rights." CJR, vol.8 #1 (Feb., 1945): 43-47.

6463. Horowitz, P.: The Jews, the War, and After [London: Loyd Cole, 1943]

6464. Hyman, Joseph C.: "Observations on Problems of Jewish Readjustment Overseas." JSSQ, vol.17 #1 (Sept., 1940): 20-30.

6465. The Jews in Europe, their Martyrology, and their Future [London: Board of Deputies of British Jews, 1945]

6466. Janowsky, Oscar I.: "Jewish Rights in the Post-War World." Survey Graphic, vol.32 #9 (Sept., 1943): 348-350, 365.

6467. "Judaism and a Just and Enduring Peace." CCAR/YB, vol.43 (1943): 278-290.

6468. Kaplan, Mordecai M.: "What The American Jewish Conference Should Ask For." Recon, vol.9 #10 (June 25, 1943): 7-13.

6469. Karbach, Oscar: "The Problem of ´Living Corpses´." CW, vol.11 #25 (July 14, 1944): 18-20.

6470. Kargman, M. R.: "The Jew in the Post-War World." Ch J Forum, vol.1 #1 (Fall, 1942): 58-61.

6471. Kulisher, E. M.: Jewish Migrations: Past Experiences and Post-War Prospects [New York: Am. Jewish Com., 1943]

6472. Lamm, Hans: "The Challenge of Post-War Antisemitism." J Fo, vol.26 #3 (April, 1943): 55-56, 61, 69.

6473. Laserson, Max M.: "The Legal Rehabilitation of European Jews." Recon, vol.10 #4 (March 31, 1944): 10-15.

6474. Lestchinsky, Jacob: "The Post-War Outlook for Jewry in Europe." Menorah, vol.30 #1 (Jan./March, 1942): 13-37.

6475. ___: "Toward an ORT Post-War Program." Ort Eco Rev, vol.4 #1 (Aug., 1944): 29-52; #2 (Nov., 1944): 19-29.

6476. Lewisohn, Ludwig: "Looking Before and After: After the War There is no Future for the Jews in Europe." NP, vol.32 #17 (Sept. 11, 1942): 6-8.

6477. Liebenstein, Elazar: "The Jewish Future." HM, vol.22 #1 (Sept./Oct., 1941): 8-11.

6478. Lvovitch, David: "The Jews in the Post-War Economy." Ort Eco Rev, vol.2 #4/5 (July/Oct., 1941): 1-3.

6479. Mahler, Raphael: "The Future of the Jews in Poland." CJR, vol.7 #3 (June, 1944): 269-278.

6480. Mattuck, I. I.: "The Position of Jews in the Post-War World." Am Heb, vol.152 #23 (Oct. 8, 1943): 9-10.

6481. Meyerowitz, Arthur: "Jewish Migration and the Coming Peace." J Fo, vol.25 #7 (July, 1942): 107-109.

6482. Netanyahu, B.: "Our Post-War Problems." CW, vol.8 #11 (March 14, 1941): 7-9.

6483. Niebuhr, Reinhold: "Jews After the War." Nation, vol. 154 #8 (Feb. 21, 1942): 214-216; #9 (Feb. 28, 1942): 253-255.

6484. Parkes, James: "The Jews in the Post-War World." J Sp, vol.7 #12 (Oct., 1942): 19-20.

6485. Pickel, Clarence E.: "Post-War Relief and Rehabilitation." JSSQ, vol.19 #1 (Sept., 1942): 51-55.

6486. Revusky, Abraham: "The First Post-War Task." NP, vol. 33 #9 (March 5, 1943): 9-11.

6487. Rittenberg, Louis: "Masaryk Charts Jewish Future." Lib Jud, vol.11 #9 (Jan., 1944): 5-9, 50-51.

6488. Robinson, Jacob: "Equity - Not Equality: An Analysis of the Problem of European Jewry." J Affairs, vol.2 #12 (May, 1943): 4-5.

6489. ___: "Minorities in a Free World." FW, vol.5 #5 (May, 1943): 450-454.

6490. ___: "Preparing for Peace." CW, vol.8 #8 (Feb. 21, 1941): 5-6.

6491. ___: Realities of Jewish Life." CW, vol.10 #5 (Jan. 29, 1943): 6-8.

6492. Roth, Cecil: "The Jewish Problem Today and Tomorrow." Am Heb, vol.152 #20 (Sept. 17, 1943): 20, 24-25.

6493. ___: "The Restoration of Jewish Libraries, Archives and Museums." CJR, vol.7 #3 (June, 1944): 253-257.

6494. Schechtman, Joseph B.: "Realistic Auguries of a Post-War Europe." Zionews, vol.4 #29/30 (July/Aug., 1943): 28-29, 32.

6495. Schlossberg, Joseph: "The Jews After the War." CW, vol.9 #2 (Jan. 9, 1942): 5-7.

6496. Shapiro, William: "Post-War Migrations and European Jewry." J Horizon, vol.7 #4 (Sept., 1944): 7-8.

6497. Stanczyk, Jan: "Jews in Post-War Poland." Polish Jew, vol.2 #10 (Sept., 1942): 5-6.

6498. Stefansky, George: Does the Refugee Have a Future? An Analysis of the Position of Homeless Jews in the Postwar World [New York: United Palestine Appeal, 1945]

6499. Stein, Kalman: "The Future of Polish Jewry." Polish Jew, vol.2 #4 (Jan., 1942): 2-3.

6500. ___: "Jews in Europe of Tomorrow." CW, vol.12 #15 (April 27, 1945): 6-8.

6501. ___: "Reconstruction in Poland." CW, vol.9 #19 (May 15, 1942): 10-11.

6502. Stone, Edith: "Training Programs for the Post-War World." Ort Eco Rev, vol.4 #1 (Aug., 1944): 65-67.

6503. A Survey of Facts and Opinions on Problems of Postwar Jewry in Europe and Palestine [New York: Am. Jewish Conference, 1943]

6504. Wachsman, Zvi H. (ed.): Jews in Post-War Europe [New York: H. H. Glanz, 1944]

6505. Wechsler, Israel: "Jewish Youth in Post-War Europe." CW, vol.10 #33 (Nov. 26, 1943): 6-8.

6506. Weinryb, Bernard W.: "Jewish Economic Reconstruction Problem." J Fo, vol.26 #3 (April, 1943): 51-52, 59.

6507. Weiss-Rosmarin, Trude: "Jewish Post-War Problems." J Sp, vol.10 #1 (Nov., 1944): 7-11.

6508. Weizmann, Chaim: "Jews in the Post-War World." J Sp, vol.7 #8 (June, 1942): 6-7, 19.

6509. Werner, Alfred: "Defeat by Antisemitism." CW, vol.10 #28 (Oct. 8, 1943): 6-8.

6510. Wischnitzer, Mark: "We Must Prepare Today for the Emigration Problems of Tomorrow." Rescue, vol.1 #5 (May, 1944): 5, 12.

6511. Wise, Stephen S. and Nahum Goldmann: "Memorandum on the Post-War Relief and Rehabilitation of European Jewry Submitted to the Council of the United Nations Relief and Rehabilitation Administration." WJC/BS Rep, #10 (Dec., 1943): 3-17.

6512. Wulman, L.: "Health Problems Among Jews in Europe After the War." Am OSE Rev, vol.3 #1 (Spr., 1944): 3-7.

6513. Zukerman, William: "Towards Regeneration in Europe: Against the Folly of ´Evacuation´." Menorah, vol.31 #3 (Oct./Dec., 1943): 215-226.

LIBERATION

The Liberation of North African Jewry

6514. "Giraud Action Termed Unconstitutional." Lib Jud, vol.11 #2 (June, 1943); 73-76. * Protest against abrogation of the Cremieux Laws.

6515. Herbert, Edward: "Gen. Giraud and the Jews of North Africa." Am Heb, vol.151 #49 (April, 1943): 6, 15.

6516. McKay, Claude: "North African Triangle." Nation, vol. 156 #15 (May 8, 1943): 663-665.

6517. Rabinowitz, Louis: "Liberation in North Africa: With an Account of German and Italian Behavior." Menorah, vol.33 #1 (April/June, 1945): 115-130.

6518. Spectator: "In the Light of Casablanca." Hamigdal, vol.3 #3 (Feb., 1943): 9-10.

6519. "The Stages of Rehabilitation in Algeria." J Comment, vol.1 #16 (Nov. 5, 1943): 1-4.

6520. Stone, I. F.: "Moral Issues for Mr. Hull." Nation, vol.156 #5 (Jan. 30, 1943): 151-152. * On the legal status of North African Jews.

6521. "Tripoli Jews Observe Happiest Sabbath." IP, vol.2 #8 (March 12, 1943): 2-3.

The Liberators

6522. Abzug, Robert H.: Inside the Vicious Heart: Americans and the Liberation of Nazi Concentration Camps [New York: Oxford Univ. Press, 1985]

Study of the reactions of U. S. troops to the liberation of Hitler´s concentration camps. In words and photos Abzug describes the horror that American troops found and their reactions. Includes information on the attitude of U. S. military governors to Jewish displaced persons.

6523. Dobkin, Eliahu: "Face to Face with the Survivors." Palestine, vol.2 #8 (Oct., 1945): 6-8.

6524. Eliach, Yaffa and Brama Gurewitsch: The Liberators [Brooklyn, NY: Center for Holocaust Studies, 1981]

6525. Fellenz, Walter J.: "I Liberated Dachau..." ADL Bul, vol.35 #6 (June, 1978): 4. Also in J Digest, vol.24 #1 (Sept., 1978): 3-5.

6526. Grobman, Alex: "Jewish GI´s and Holocaust Survivors." J Sp, vol.43 #1 (Spr., 1978): 49-52.

6527. Gun, Nerin E.: The Day of the Americans [New York: Fleet Publishing, 1966]

6528. Guttman, Nahum: "A GI Views Marseilles Jews." CW, vol.12 #5 (Feb. 2, 1945): 10-11.

6529. Hay, Malcolm: "Five Scottish Soldiers Bear Witness." Mid, vol.2 #3 (Sum., 1956): 104-106.

6530. Klein, Isaac: The Anguish and the Ecstasy of a Jewish Chaplain [New York: Vantage Press, 1974]

Documentary memoir by one of the first Jewish chaplain´s in newly liberated Europe. Basically a series of anecdotes, the book offers an interesting perspective on the liberation and rebuilding of European Jewry.

6531. ___: "The French that Became Yiddish: How I Met the First Survivors in Nazi Occupied Territory. J Digest, vol.9 #6 (March, 1964): 46-48.

6532. ___: "Meeting the First Jewish Survivor." J Digest, vol.20 #2 (Nov., 1974): 17-21.

6533. Levin, Meyer: "I Witnessed the Liberation." CW, vol. 22 #15 (April 18, 1955): 3-4.

6534. "The Liberators as Witnesses." Shoa, vol.2 #3 (Fall/Win., 1981/82): 14-16.

6535. Marcus, Robert S.: " A Chaplain in Germany." CW, vol. 12 #14 (April 20, 1945): 8-10.

6536. Margolin, J.: "When the Red Army Liberated Pinsk." Com, vol.14 #6 (Dec., 1952): 517-528.

6537. Massinson, M.: "Dachau." J Horizon, vol.9 #4 (Jan., 1946): 15-16.

6538. Not Used.

6539. "Nauseated by the Sights and Odors." AJA, vol.31 #1 (April, 1979): 51-61.

6540. Orleck, Annelise: "International Liberators Conference: When the Political and Historical Merge." Shoa, vol.2 #3 (Fall/Win., 1981/82): 12-13, 22.

6541. Salzberg, Marc: "Jewish GI´s in Germany." J Digest, vol.19 #4 (Jan., 1974): 11-14.

6542. Seltzer, Michael: Deliverance Day: The Last Hours at Dachau [Philadelphia: J. B. Lippincott, 1978]

Fictionalized account of the liberation of Dachau. Based on interviews with witnesses. The dialogue is, however, mostly fictional. Does contain some useful insights, but is not a classic account.

6543. Strong, Anna: "With the Red Army in Minsk." Nation, vol.159 #5 (July 29, 1944): 121-122.

Liberated Communities

6544. Arnothy, Christine: "The Yellow Badge of Courage." J Digest, vol.2 #1 (Oct., 1956): 23-24. * On the liberation of Hungary.

6545. Benoschofsky, Ilona: "The Position of Hungarian Jewry after the Liberation." HJS, vol.1 (1966): 237-260.

6546. Blondheim, S. Hillel: "New Year in France, 5705. Oct. 1, 1944." Menorah, vol.32 #2 (Oct./Dec., 1944): 216-220. * Jewish life in liberated Paris.

6547. Brutzkus, J.: "Medical Aid in Liberated Regions." Am OSE Rev, vol.3 #1 (Spr., 1944): 8-11.

6548. Gekham, Efim: "The ´Bunker´ Folk in Warsaw." Rescue, vol.2 #3/4 (March/April, 1944): 5-6.

6549. Kleinlerer, Edward D.: "Roman Jewry Comes Back." Am Heb, vol.153 #34 (June 23, 1944): 6, 16.

6550. Meystal, Sidney: "Diary Without Dates." Furrows, vol. 2 #10 (Aug., 1944): 15-19 * Liberated Roman Jews.

6551. Schwarz, Leo W.: "When Liberation Came." CW, vol.32 #10 (May 24, 1965): 5-6.

6552. Stern, Alfred: "Rebirth of French Jewry." Lib Jud, vol.12 #8 (Dec., 1944): 37-44, 56.

6553. Werner, Alfred: "Belgium Back On Her Old Road." Am Heb, vol.153 #47 (Sept. 22, 1944): 7, 14-15.

PART IV

Aftermath

Introduction

REPATRIATION

With the war´s end the tragedy that befell the Jewish people was revealed to the world in all its terrifying detail. Yet, even in 1945 the Jewish crisis was far from over. Although the Jews made up only a small percentage of the displaced persons, their very existence created a new refugee crisis. Most of the other newly liberated nationals sought repatriation and were soon on their way home. Others with useful professions, as well as many Nazis posing as refugees, sought and obtained immigration visas for countries in the Americas and were soon on their way to a new life. To be sure, Jews also sought these avenues of return to normality. But the Jews´ former neighbors wanted no more of them in 1945 than they had in 1939. In Poland, Czechoslovakia, and other East European countries, there were renewed pogroms and blood libels. Survivors who had managed to return "home" were greeted with mob violence. Gentiles greeted their returning Jewish neighbors with shock and disbelief; they thought that the Jewish Problem had been completely solved and that the former Jewish properties that they now occupied would be their´s to keep.

Similarly, mass migration of Jews out of Europe, primarily to the United States, was still not an option. Renewed anti-Jewish violence in Eastern Europe led to a mass exodus of Jews to the United States Zone of Occupation in Germany. This influx of Jewish refugees created, in turn, new political and social problems.

THE YISHUV

The problem of the Jewish remnant on the blood-soaked soil of Europe accelerated the fight for the Jewish National Home. Long presented as the only serious option for the rescue of Europe's Jews, the Yishuv was no longer willing to be reduced, via the 1939 White Paper, to a minority in the Jewish National Home. A three-year political and military struggle culminated in the rebirth of the State of Israel (May 14, 1948) and the ingathering of exiles from the four corners of the earth. Not only Jews from Europe, but also Jews from Arab countries threatened with a rising tide of genocidal antisemtism, and Jews from "safe" diasporas, finally came home.

THE NUREMBERG TRIALS

For the victorious Allies, the first order of business was to expunge the Nazi cancer once and for all. The Western governments placed a great deal of emphasis upon a program of denazification, hoping to re-educate the Germans and wean them away from fascism. Unfortunately, cold war politics prevented the program from being fully carried out. Even as the denazification program was moving into full gear, it was wound down and eventually discarded entirely.

The Allies also began a series of war-crimes trials, appropriately held at the sight of previous Nazi victories, Nuremberg. The Allied powers established an International Military Tribunal to punish Nazi war criminals. Twenty-three top Nazis were included in the first trial presided over by a court composed of justices from the United States, Britain, France, and the Soviet Union. Among the twenty-three were Hermann Goering, Julius Streicher, Alfred Rosenberg, Hans Frank, Joachim von Ribbentrop, Ernst Kaltenbrunner, and most of the German general staff. All the defendants pleaded innocent to all the charges. Julius Streicher stated his case quite succinctly: The Final Solution was not a crime because it was what Martin Luther had bidden every good Christian to do.

After these initial trials another series of trials was begun on a smaller scale. At these trials members of the German bureaucracy were held responsible for their individual and collective parts in Nazi crimes. Unfortunately, postwar realignments in the balance of power and the confrontation between the United States and the Soviet Union weakened Western resolve to bring Nazi war criminals to justice. Although hundreds of Nazis were tried, with sentences meted out ranging from death to a few months imprisonment, thousands and even tens of thousands of Nazi and Fascist criminals were left untouched - overlooked and left to roam free, to become once more a part of respected society. Many high-ranking Nazis were set free, among them some of the commanders of the dreaded Einsatzgruppen (the killer task forces) and Higher SS Police Leaders (HSSPF). Some of these criminals and thousands of lesser Nazis even received pensions from the reconstituted German government.

Still, these trials set a major precedent in international law. The International Military Tribunal sitting in judgment at Nuremberg concluded that every member of a government is responsible both legally and morally for actions that break the bounds of humanity and common decency.

ESCAPED WAR CRIMINALS

Certain war criminals - Joseph Mengele, Martin Bormann, and Adolf Eichmann among them - managed to escape altogether. Yet, their escape has not gone unnoticed. Their victims, in concert with men and women of conscience from all over the world, have given chase. Simon Wiesenthal, Tuvia Friedman, Serge and Beate Klarsfeld, among others, have dedicated their lives to bringing Nazi criminals to justice.

On May 23, 1960, the Israeli government made a dramatic announcement: SS Lieutenant Colonel Adolf Eichmann, head of the Jewish office of the Gestapo, had been tracked down and captured in Argentina and would soon be standing trial before a Jewish court for crimes against the Jewish people. The trial, which was televised throughout the world, and Eichmann's subsequent execution aroused a swirl of controversy about legal issues raised by the kidnapping and trial of this Nazi war criminal. The televising of the proceedings and the issues raised by witness after witness brought the magnitude of the Final Solution into millions of homes for the first time and led to a renewed interest in the history of the Holocaust. The Eichmann trial was the catalyst for a good deal of the research carried out in the late 1960s and early 1970s.

The Eichmann case and other more recent ones have shown clearly that Latin American, Arab, and many other Third World countries, as well as the United States and Canada, have become fertile soil for countless Nazi criminals evading justice. As a result of the extradition of Klaus Barbie, the notorious "butcher of Lyon", and revelations about U.S. military intelligence aid in his escape, the fact that the

Allies actually punished only a few of the Nazi war criminals has come under close scrutiny. Similar questions were raised in 1985 after the discovery of what appear to be the remains of Joseph Mengele, the "angel of death" of Auschwitz. Continuing investigations and periodic trials have also brought to light dozens and perhaps hundreds of Nazi criminals at large in the United States and Canada. All entered illegally, some with the tacit approval of the governments involved, posing as legitimate refugees. The exigencies of postwar politics were the primary cause of the premeditated obstruction of justice.

THE SURVIVORS

The establishment of Israel and the continuing search for justice have been only part of the saga of post-Holocaust Jewry. On both the individual and communal levels, survivors have been beset by the problem of rebuilding. Whereas in Eastern Europe the attempts to reestablish Jewish communal life have largely failed, the same has not held true in Western countries, especially in the United States. Physical problems, ranging from making a living to poor health as a result of Nazi mistreatment, have plagued the survivors as individuals. A nexus between the interests of individual survivors, the survivors as a group, and the State of Israel became an issue when the government of the Federal Republic of Germany offered reparations. Their term was the controversial Wiedergutmachung (reparation), to all individual survivors and to Israel as the collective representative of those who perished. Many Jews refused the offer to make amends; others accepted the "blood money" only reluctantly. Israel, then in the midst of an economic and political crisis, had little choice but to accept. The issues raised have been part of the legacy that the survivors must impart to future generations.

IMPARTING THE LESSONS

Over the last forty years the lessons of World War II in general and the Holocaust in particular have been expressed in a variety of ways. Every possible discipline has been used to try to understand the Holocaust and its implications: history, political science, sociology, psychology, and theology, among others.

Education. Teachers sensitive to the problems of transmitting the events of the Holocaust to their students have had to grapple with the enormity of the subject at hand in order to answer the questions involved: How can the Holocaust be taught? How can the events be transmitted from generation to generation? Do we dare to teach impressionable youngsters about these horrifying events? How and at what age should that education begin? In recent years, as Holocaust studies programs have grown in number and scope, these more general concerns have been supplemented by more practical ones, including the formulation of syllabi, lesson plans, and course outlines to aid in the translation of historical events into the classroom.

By and large teachers try to cover a variety of topics. The background - Jewish life before the Holocaust, anti-semitism, and German history - as well as topics directly relating to the extermination of European Jewry, are covered in almost every course on the Holocaust. Clearly, lesson plans must place emphasis on different aspects of the history of the Holocaust in order to tailor the lessons to the level of the students in elementary schools, high schools, and colleges. Original documents and audiovisual materials must also be integrated, although again care must be taken to tailor the use of these materials to the level of the students.

Art: Literature and Film. The effort to translate the experiences of the Holocaust into literature and onto the screen has been greeted with both censure and acclaim. Given the nature of the subject, there are many who deplore its commercial exploitation and who categorically reject the advent of the Holocaust as entertainment. For many survivors, the enormity of the experience of the Holocaust remains ineffable, beyond human imagination, virtually supraverbal. Fictionalized or semifictionalized accounts, either literary or cinematic, are judged to be diluted or narrow, even when produced with the best of intentions. Misleading stereotypes have emerged, such as the guilt-ridden survivor, the evil Judenraete, and the overprotective parent. Especially in film, owing to the limitations of time and of the genre itself, the complex range of reactions before, during, and after the war is not presented. For some the knowledge that artistic license has been used to simulate, even if only partially, the horrors of a concentration camp is jarring. For others, the memory is far too raw to be fictionalized at all. Those who censure all commercial exploitation of the Holocaust justifiably fear that the unknowing spectator, confused by the mixture of fact and fantasy, may reject what is seen or written as untrue. Without a thorough education in the facts of the Holocaust, the spectator or reader is not in a position to distinguish between truth and fiction when they are blended in a single work.

Other survivors and educators hail the release of films and television docudramas. Recognizing the emotional impact of film on the spectator, and in view of the current paucity of educational programs on the Holocaust in high schools and universities, they welcome the aforementioned attempts as the best educational vehicle to reach the masses. Faced with the alternatives of utter ignorance and partial knowledge, the latter is seen as the lesser of the two evils.

Literary attempts by survivors are met with less ambivalence. The few successful novelists of the Holocaust are, in fact, survivors, and they place artistic expression at the service of their own personal truth. One might also argue that the novel or poem, unlike film, are genres that force the human imagination to provide the color and texture of a scene; the author or poet may describe and intimate, but the reader must visualize the scene on his own. The simulation is not partial or external, but subjective.

The plastic arts, painting and sculpture, have proved the least controversial of the artistic media concretizing the Holocaust. The conflict between fact and fantasy in so sensitive a subject is eliminated because the plastic arts are, by their very nature, symbolic. Moreover, many of the sculptures and monuments have been commissioned by survivors themselves so as to honor the memory of the six million victims in a lasting, rather than an ephemeral, medium.

THE YIZKOR BUCH

The awesome dimensions of the Holocaust have created a field of study unparalleled in modern history. Simultaneously the Holocaust has produced a distinct and unique literary form - the Yizkor Buch, or memorial volume.

Before World War II many vibrant Jewish communities existed throughout Europe. Most of them were destroyed, along with the masses of their Jews, and the few survivors scattered to the four corners of the globe. Yet, no matter where one went, one had always come from the old country. Despite the travails, the survivors carried the legacy of their towns, villages, and cities with them at all times. They carried bits and pieces, trivia, history, and legend. They also carried the need to put their recollections on paper, to set the record straight and to close the circle. In a word, to publish a volume that would not only provide a source of nostalgia for those who had actually lived in the community, but also provide a link to the past for the next generation so that the memory of what once was would never be erased.

All Yizkor books follow this general ideal, some more successfully than others. Generally, a committee of the Landsmanschaft (society) of the locality would be formed. In some instances, a historian - either himself a member of the Landsleit or hired by them - would do the actual research and record the communal history. Obviously, not all towns were large enough to warrant an individual volume. Thus, some groups of neighboring villages - or rather their Landsmanschaften - would collaborate on a single composite volume on a county-wide scale.

The numerous volumes almost inevitably have the same contents: a sketch of communal history from foundation until the Nazi invasion; a list of the most important citizens who made a name for themselves inside and outside their respective community; anecdotes of daily life in the community; world and local situation just prior the Nazi invasion; and finally, the struggle and destruction of the community during the Nazi occupation. Most of the memorial volumes also include photographs of people and places of importance and a map of the town and its environs.

POLITICIZATION OF THE HOLOCAUST

Since 1945 the Holocaust has been appropriated by those who distort, mystify, and use it for political purposes. Signaling the rise of neo-antisemitism, this conscious distortion of history represents a threat to world Jewry´s physical security.

A major source of this type of propaganda has been the Soviet Union and its allies. The Soviets have never willingly accepted the existence of Jewish victims of nazism, subsuming Jews under more general rubrics. They have not even been willing to accept the idea of a specifically Jewish aspect to Nazi crimes, opting for a class perspective rather than a racial one. In recent years the Soviets have taken this even one step further: Because there were no Jewish victims and because Zionism (which equates with Judaism) is a form of fascism, then it follows that the Zionists must have collaborated with the Nazis.

A second trend is the assault from the right. Neo-Nazi groups, in collusion with "revisionist" historians, have begun to deny that the Holocaust ever happened. We are thus told that Jews created the Holocaust story for their own purposes: to further the aims of Jewish world domination. We are asked to believe that nine million Jews entered the United States illegally after World War II. They claim that no Jews were ever murdered; that gas chambers, crematoria, mobile murder vans, and shooting pits never existed; that only a few thousand Jews were judicially dealt with, in connection with their underhanded wartime black-market activities; that, in plain English, the atrocity stories are a fake - a conspiracy foisted upon the unsuspecting gentile world to gain sympathy for the Jews.

Even more invidious are the activities of certain "friends" of the Jews. Some historians, theologians, novelists, and others who do not deny the Holocaust feel the need to obfuscate it with the argument that "others also suffered" under the oppressive heel of nazism. We are told that Poles, gypsies, homosexuals, the insane, and even Jehovah's Witnesses were all targets for the Holocaust. The Jewish aspect is watered down until, when one considers the Armenian massacres, the slaughter of Biafrans, American Indians, Cambodians, and the mass genocide of the Chinese Cultural Revolution, the Holocaust becomes almost irrelevant.

What can our answer be to such assertions? To be sure, as befits the greatest gangster state in history, the Nazis acted brutally toward almost everyone. In their apocalyptic zeal they persecuted all of the above groups. And, in fact, genocide is not an unknown phenomenon in human history. Yet, the Holocaust was unique. Others might be enslaved by the Nazis, they were brutalized and many perished, but only the Jews were marked for total extermination. Every group had a place in Nazi society. The Poles, for instance, might have been considered "two legged-cattle" in Reinhard Heydrich's terminology, but at least they could live. Almost any gentile in Nazi-occupied Europe who obeyed the laws of the New Order would be left to himself. Some gypsies were murdered, others allowed to volunteer for the Waffen-SS. Homosexuals were persecuted, yet many high Nazi party officials were themselves homosexual. Jehovah's Witnesses had merely to swear an oath in Hitler's name and they too were free.

On the other hand, Jews - all Jews - were to be specially dealt with, sonderbehandelt. Irrespective of political ideology, age, sex, sexual orientation, and economic status, all Jews were destined for murder. There can be no denial that Poles and Czechs suffered much because of the Nazi racial formula in which they were considered to be a part of the inferior Eastern European (Slav) race, Ostmenschen, created to serve and obey their masters. No Jew in any part - east or west - of Nazi-occupied Europe had the honor of even belonging to this lowest Nazi-designated category. Under the National Socialist racial formula, the Jew was less than subhuman, an untermensch. To insure the apocalypse, the Nazis had to hunt them down and destroy them utterly. _Endloesung_ had to be carried out - a final and complete solution. Never before had a people been marked for total extermination solely for the sin of existing.

CONCLUSION

It would be rather presumptuous to attempt to offer a definitive conclusion on the Holocaust. Even as these words are being written, the few remaining links with the Holocaust - the survivors and witnesses - are passing on. So, too, are many of the Nazi war criminals who evaded justice. Some of the source material listed in this bibliography is in danger of being lost to future historians as the material yellows and crumbles with age.

At the same time the Jewish people have not yet fully recovered from the catastrophe. The demographic impact of the destruction of European Jewry has not yet fully been counted. Jews are still a small minority in an apathetic and, at times, hostile world. The Jews are still as beleaguered as they ever were; beset by enemies on all sides.

Holocaust research is far from complete. New questions are being asked and old ones are amplified on an almost daily basis. New issues, many still in an embryonic stage, have been raised in recent years by scholars and authors. New sources are becoming available as archival collections are opened in many countries.

Nevertheless, if our study offers any clear conclusion, it is that mankind must be eternally vigilant. The bonds of humanity proved to be frail indeed, yet these are the very bonds that insure our survival.

14

From Holocaust to Rebirth

THE SHEARIT HA´PLETA: THE REMNANT

The Displaced Persons

6554. Alderstein, F. R.: "How Europe´s Lost Are Found." Am Mercury, vol.61 #262 (Oct., 1945): 485-491.

6555. Alpin, E. M.: "I Saw Belsen... My Conscience Cannot Wait." Today, vol.2 #5 (April, 1946): 18-19, 38.

6556. Appelfeld, A.: "Witness." Jer Q, #16 (Sum., 1980): 91-96. * Survivors in Italy.

6557. Bar-Adon, Dorothy: "Escape to Life." HM, vol.25 #6 (Oct., 1945): 5-9.

6558. Barav, Shmuel: "European Expectations." J Outlook, vol.13 #6 (June, 1949): 6-7.

6559. Baruch, N. with Y. Feitman: "30 Years Ago: Problems of Post-Liberation." J Observer, vol.11 #1 (Sum., 1975): 12-13.

6560. Ben-Horin, Meir: "The Years That Followed." Pilch: Catastrophe, pp.215-226.

6561. Berl, Fred: "Adjustment of Displaced Persons." JSSQ, vol.25 #2 (Dec., 1948): 254-263.

6562. Bernard, Wm. S.: "Homeless, Tempest Tossed." Survey Graphic, vol.37 #4 (April, 1948): 189-192.

6563. ___: "Not Sympathy but Action." Survey Graphic, vol. 36 #2 (Feb., 1947): 132-137, 170.

6564. Bernstein, D.: "Europe´s Jews: Summer, 1947. A First-hand Report by an American Observer." Com, vol.4 #2 (Aug., 1947): 101-109.

6565. Bernstein, Joseph M.: "Immigration and Refugee Aid." AJYB, vol.47 (1945/46): 316-324.

6566. Bernstein, Philip S.: "Displaced Persons." AJYB, vol. 49 (1947/48): 520-533.

6567. ___: "Jewish Displaced Persons." PYB, #3 (1946/47): 67-76.

6568. Betari, Josef: "I Found the Answer." Schwarz: Root, pp.136-141.

6569. Brown, S.: "A Jewish Chaplain in Post-War Europe." JM, vol.4 #7 (Oct., 1950): 448-454.

6570. Carlebach, Alexander: "The Future of German Jewry." JM, vol.2 #5 (Aug., 1948): 288-297.

6571. Cohen, Henry: "The Jewish Displaced Persons." J Fr, vol.14 #3 (March, 1947): 26-29.

6572. ___: "Life in a DP Camp." CW, vol.14 #1 (Jan. 3, 1947): 14-15.

6573. de Vahl Davis, G.: "An End and a Beginning." WJC/ASB, #6 (July, 1945): 1-10.

6574. Dijour, Ilja: "How to Alleviate Plight of Displaced Persons." Rescue, vol.2 #12 (Dec., 1945): 1-2, 11-12.

6575. ___: "Jewish Migration in Post-War Period." JJoS, vol.4 #1 (June, 1962): 72-81.

6576. "The Displaced and Destitute." J Fr, vol.13 #1 (Jan., 1946): 24-25.

6577. Displaced Persons [Frankfort-am-Main, Germany: Office of the Chief Historian, European Command, 1947]

6578. Ebon, Martin: "The Homeless Return." FW, vol.10 #1 (July, 1945): 59-62.

6579. Eigen, M.: "Current Problems of Jewish Migration." JSSQ, vol.25 #1 (Sept., 1948): 42-48.

6580. Fantlowa, Zdenka.: "Long Live Fife." Schwarz: Root, pp.201-227.

6581. Frank, G.: "The Tragedy of the DP´s." New Republic, vol.114 #13 (April 1, 1946): 436-438.

6582. Gertz, Elmer: "The DP Story." Ch J Forum, vol.11 #3 (Spr., 1953): 180-184.

6583. Goldfeder, Pinchas: "A Practical Scheme to Settle the DP´s: With Malice to None, with Profit to All." Com, vol.6 #2 (Aug., 1948): 108-113.

6584. Goldman, Solomon: "The Survivors." Mid, vol.31 #4 (April, 1985): 26-29.

6585. Gottschalk, Max: "Jewish Problems of Today." Rescue, vol.2 #9 (Sept., 1945): 1-2.

6586. Gringauz, Samuel: "Jewish Destiny As the DP´s See It: The Ideology of the Surviving Remnant." Com, vol.4 #6 (Dec., 1947): 501-509.

6587. ___: "Our New German Policy and the DP´s." Com, vol.5 #6 (June, 1948): 508-514.

6588. Grossman, Vladimir: "First Aid and Personal Rehabilitation for Displaced Persons." Ort Eco Rev, vol.5 #2 (Dec., 1945): 38-44.

6589. Grossmann, Kurt R.: "Can They Live Again?" J Sp, vol. 21 #7 (Sept., 1956): 14-18.

6590. ___: "Forgotten People." CW, vol.15 #8 (Feb. 27, 1948): 13-15.

6591. ___: The Jewish DP Problem: Its Origins, Scope, and Liquidation [New York: IJA, 1951]

6592. ___: "Jewish Migration Today." J Sp, vol.14 #12 (Nov. 1949): 22-26.

6593. ___: "Report on the Displaced Persons." CW, vol.15 #6 (Feb. 13, 1948): 5-7.

6594. Gruber, Ruth: "The First Witnesses." ADL Bul, vol.41 #4 (April, 1984): 5-8.

6595. Gruss, Emanuel: "In a Camp of Displaced Jews." CW, vol.12 #23 (June 29, 1945): 12-13.

6596. Handler, Arieh: "Report on Europe." J Horizon, vol.9 #8 (Sept., 1946): 8-10.

6597. Hardman, Leslie H.: The Survivors: The Story of the Belsen Remnant [London: Valentine, Mitchell, 1958] * Memoir-history by a Jewish Royal Army Chaplain who served at the newly liberated Belsen concentration camp.

6598. Harrison, Earl G.: "Report from Central Europe." NJM, vol.60 #3 (Nov., 1945): 85-86, 198-199. * On report to President Truman on conditions in the DP camps.

6599. ___: "Report to the President on Plight of Jews in Concentration Camps of Occupied Germany." Rescue, vol.2 #10 (Oct., 1945): 1-2, 9-12.

6600. Heymont, Irving: Among the Survivors of the Holocaust 1945: The Landsberg DP Camp Letters of Major Irving Heymont, United States Army [Cincinnati, OH: American Jewish Archives, 1982]

6601. Horowitz, Isac: "Jewish Refugees." J Sp, vol.14 #8 (June, 1949): 18-20.

6602. "How Do Jews Live in DP Camps? An Eywitness Report." J Life, vol.1 #2 (Dec., 1946): 1, 26-28.

6603. Hurwitz, M.: "The Jewish DP Papers in Germany." CW, vol.13 #6 (Feb. 8, 1946): 7-8.

6604. Hyman, Abraham S.: "Displaced Persons." AJYB, vol.50 (1948/49): 455-473.

6605. Indig, Joseph: "Five Years of Wandering." HM, vol.26 #6 (Oct., 1946): 12-15.

6606. Jacobs, Theodore: "Antisemitism on DP Transports." J Life, vol.6 #10 (Aug., 1952): 7-8.

6607. Jacoby, Gerhard: "The Story of the Jewish DP." IJA, vol.2 #6 (Nov. 15, 1948): 1-30.

6608. Jordan, Charles H.: "Current European Emigration Problems." JSSQ, vol.26 #3 (March, 1950): 354-361.

6609. Katz, Sh.: "The Jewish Displaced Persons. A Survey." J Fr, vol.13 #7 (July, 1946): 6-8.

6610. Kenneth, G.: "Life at Bergen Belsen Today." Rescue, vol.2 #12 (Dec., 1945): 4.

6611. Klausner, Abraham J. (ed.): Sharit ha-Platah [Munich: Central Committee of Liberated Jews in Bavaria, 1945]
* List of survivors in the American and British zones of occupation in Germany and Austria.

6612. Klein, Isaac: "Jewish Communities in Germany." Con Jud, vol.6 #1 (Oct., 1949): 74-82.

6613. Klerr (Kleinlerer), Edward D.: "What Next for DP´s in Italy?" NJM, vol.62 #1 (Sept., 1947): 26, 54.

6614. Korman, Max O.: "On Being a Refugee." Korman: Hunter, pp.47-55.

6615. Kubowitzki, Leon: "In the Wake of Ruin." Furrows, vol.3 #8 (June, 1945): 10-12.

6616. Laderman, Manuel: "Exit DP´s." J Horizon, vol.12 #2 (Oct., 1949): 8-10.

6617. Lang, Leon S.: "Notes on a Tour Through Germany." Con Jud, vol.6 #1 (Oct., 1949): 68-73.

6618. Lehman, Herbert H.: "It Is Within Our Power." NJM, vol.60 #8 (April, 1946): 269, 299.

6619. Lehrman, Hal: "Austria: Way-Station of Exodus. Pages from a Correspondents Notebook." Com, vol.2 #6 (Dec., 1946): 565-572.

6620. Leivick, H.: "Vignettes from the DP Camps." CW, vol. 13 #25 (Oct. 25, 1946): 8-10.

6621. ___ and Israel Efros: "They Must be Rescued." CW, vol.13 #21 (July 19, 1946): 6-8.

6622. Lestschinsky, Jacob: "The Jew in Ruined Europe." Ch J Forum, vol.4 #1 (Fall, 1945): 10-16.

6623. ___: "Jews in 1945." PYB, vol.1 (1945): 23-42.

6624. ___: "A Year of Disillusionment and Despair." PYB, vol.2 (1945/46): 53-68.

6625. Levin, Moshe: "Amidst the Ruins." Furrows, vol.4 #3 (Jan./Feb., 1946): 26-28.

6626. Liepman, Heinz: "The Survivors." Menorah, vol.35 #3 (Oct./Dec., 1947): 300-313.

6627. Liskofsky, Sidney: "Jewish Migration." AJYB, vol.50 (1948/49): 725-766.

6628. Lorge, Ernst M.: "A Tragic Object-Lesson." J Fr, vol. 12 #8 (Aug., 1945): 11-14.

6629. Mann, Seymour: "Portrait of a DP." CW, vol.13 #24 (Oct. 4, 1946): 12-13.

6630. Marcus, Robert S.: "A Conference of Survivors." CW, vol.12 #25 (Aug. 17, 1945): 6-8.

6631. ___: "The Thousands Who Were Saved. Report from a German Concentration Camp." CW, vol.12 #17 (May 11, 1945): 11, 16.

6632. Marston, Horace: "Vignettes of the Displaced." NJM, vol.60 #9 (May, 1946): 314-315, 334-335.

6633. Martin, David: "Jews, Christians and Collaborators." America, vol.80 #13 (Jan. 1, 1949): 344-345. * On the necessity to screen DP´s.

6634. Mayne, Richard: "The Uprooted." Chertock: Society, pp.205-206.

6635. McNarney, Joseph T.: "The Only Solution." CW, vol.15 #16 (April 23, 1948): 11-12.

6636. Meystal, Sidney: "Rebirth in Rome." Furrows, vol.3 #5 (March, 1945): 15-18.

6637. Mintzer, Oscar A.: "Munich in 1945." J Sp, vol.25 #6 (June, 1960): 11-12.

6638. Novick, Paul: "Jews Are not Expendable." J Life, vol. 1 #7 (May, 1947): 19-22.

6639. Pauley, Edwin W.: "Memorandum for the President, Re: Jewish People in Europe." PYB, #2 (1945/46): 45-52.

6640. Petrov, N.: "The Jews Who Survived the Storm." CEO, vol.23 #10 (May 10, 1946): 156.

6641. Prager, Moshe: "Sketches of a Heroic Era." J Fr, vol. 15 #12 (Dec., 1948): 24-29.

6642. Richman, Milton H.: "Truth About the Displaced." Am Heb, vol.156 #49 (April 4, 1947): 44-46.

6643. Rifkind, Simon H.: "I Lived with the Jewish DP´s." CW, vol.13 #15 (April 12, 1946): 9-12.

6644. ___: "They are not Expendable." Survey Graphic, vol. 35 #6 (June, 1946): 205-207, 234-236.

6645. Rothberg, Babette: "Jewish Children in Europe." J Fo, vol.29 #2 (Feb., 1946): 35-36.

6646. Schwarz, Leo W.: "Close of the DP Epic." J Fr, vol.17 #8 (Aug., 1950): 9-11.

6647. Schwarzbart, Isaac: "Our People´s Rebirth." CW, vol. 11 #32 (Nov. 10, 1944): 10-11.

6648. Shafter, Toby: "How DP Children Play." CW, vol.15 #12 (March 26, 1948): 8-11.

6649. Shneiderman, S. L.: "DP´s Are at the Breaking Point." NJM, vol.61 #5 (Jan., 1947): 158-159, 180-181.

6650. Skidell, Kieve: "Kibbutz Buchenwald." Furrows, vol.3 #10 (Aug./Sept., 1945): 19-22.

6651. Stein, Reta L.: "Problems of Jewish Migration." JSSQ, vol.25 #1 (Sept., 1948): 49-53.

6652. Syrkin, Marie: "The DP School." J Fr, vol.15 #3 (March, 1948): 14-19.

6653. ___: "My DP Students." J Fr, vol.32 #5 (June, 1965): 7-12.

6654. Toland, John: "Salzwedel: Death to the Jews." Korman: Hunter, pp.296-300.

6655. Varchaver, Catherine: "The Letters of European Jewish Children." JSSQ, vol.23 #2 (Dec., 1946): 119-124.

6656. Vida, George: From Doom to Dawn: A Jewish Chaplain´s Story of Displaced Persons [New York: J. David, 1967]

6657. Warhaftig, Zorach: "Five Months in Europe." Hamigdal, vol.6 #3 (Feb., 1946): 13-14.

6658. Werner, Alfred: "The New Refugees." J Fr, vol.13 #7 (July, 1946): 21-23.

6659. World Jewish Congress: "Jewish Migration: Where They Have Gone." JOMER, vol.1 #26 (Aug. 1, 1952): 12-13.

6660. Zimmerman, Charles S.: "What I Saw in Europe." V/Ung, vol.4 #1/2 (Jan./Feb., 1946): 2, 10-11.

6661. Zukerman, William: "The Jewish Exodus from Europe." J Newsletter, vol.2 #7 (Feb. 18, 1949): 1-2.

Organizational Assistance

6662. Abramowitz, Mayer: "DPs, GIs and COs: Working Undercover in Post-War Europe." Moment, vol.7 #4 (April, 1982): 44-48.

6663. Alexander, Lester: "From War to Peace." Lib Jud, vol. 14 #3 (July, 1946): 48-50. * On the JWB.

6664. American Jewish Committee: "The IRO." AJYB, vol.49 (1947/48): 533-540.

6665. Bauer, Y.: "The Initial Organization of the Holocaust Survivors in Bavaria." YVS, vol.8 (1970): 127-158.

6666. Bentwich, N.: "The Jewish Relief Units in Germany." JM, vol.1 #11 (Feb., 1948): 30-36.

6667. Boudin, Anna P.: "ORT Work in the Post-War World." Ort Eco Rev, vol.5 #3/4 (March/June, 1946): 39-43.

6668. Cohen, H.: "The International Refugee Organization." J Fr, vol.14 #5 (May, 1947): 21-23.

6669. Cohen, Leonard: "Jewish Relief and Rehabilitation." JM, vol.2 #9 (Dec., 1948): 609-611.

6670. Crystal, David: <u>The Displaced Person and the Social Agency</u> [New York: United HIAS Service, 1958]

6671. Davie, Maurice R.: "Refugee Aid." <u>AJYB</u>, vol.49 (1947/48): 212-222.

6672. Donovan, William: "The U. J. A.: Answer to Hitler." <u>NJM</u>, vol.60 #9 (May, 1946): 312-313, 333.

6673. Dushkin, Alexander M.: "The Educational Activities of the J. D. C. in European Countries." <u>JSSQ</u>, vol.25 #4 (June, 1949): 444-451.

6674. Forster, W. Arnold: "UNRRA´s Work for Displaced Persons in Germany." <u>Int Affairs</u>, vol.22 #1 (Jan., 1946): 1-13.

6675. Frank, Murray: "UNRRA - and Jewish Reconstruction." <u>Ch J Forum</u>, vol.3 #3 (Spr., 1945): 168-173.

6676. Glassberg, Benjamin: "The Organization of Services for Overseas Jewry: The Work of UNRRA and IGC." <u>JSSQ</u>, vol.23 #1 (Sept., 1946): 13-20.

6677. Gray, H. A.: "JVS Services for Europe and Palestine." <u>JSSQ</u>, vol.25 #1 (Sept., 1948): 86-87.

6678. Greenleich, Arthur: "The Overseas Program and Its Relation in National Planning." <u>JSSQ</u>, vol.27 #1 (Sept., 1950): 80-85.

6679. Grinberg, Zalman: "ORT´s Great Task in the DP Camps." <u>ORT Eco Rev</u>, vol.5 #3/4 (March/June, 1946): 17-23.

6680. Hermann, Leo: "U.N.R.R.A.´s Special Jewish Problems." <u>Rescue</u>, vol.2 #9 (Sept., 1945): 3-4.

6681. Joffe, B.: "Vocational Training of Jews in Europe." <u>JSSQ</u>, vol.25 #1 (Sept., 1948): 76-85.

6682. Lehrman, Hal: "The ´Joint´ Takes a Human Inventory: The End of the DP Problem is in Sight." <u>Com</u>, vol.7 #1 (Jan., 1949): 19-27.

6683. Levinger, Lee J.: "Chaplains to the Rescue: The Saga of the Prisoners in DP Camps and the Rabbis in Uniform." <u>J Digest</u>, vol.7 #7 (April, 1962): 73-88.

6684. Lvovitch, David: "ORT and the Rehabilitation of Jewish Life in Europe." ORT Eco Rev, vol.5 #3/4 (March/June, 1946): 24-33.

6685. Newman, Jean: "ORT and the Jewish DP´s in Germany." ORT Eco Rev, vol.5 #3/4 (March/June, 1946): 7-12.

6686. Reich, Norman: "Overseas Aid." AJYB, vol.49 (1947/48): 223-244.

6687. Rice, James P.: "Some Aspects of Jewish Social Work in Europe." JSSQ, vol.23 #2 (Dec., 1946): 113-118.

6688. Schotland, Charles I.: "The Organization of Services for Overseas Jewry: Role of the Armed Services." JSSQ, vol.23 #1 (Sept., 1946): 4-12.

6689. Schwartz, Abba P.: "International Refugee Organization." AJYB, vol.50 (1948/49): 473-483.

6690. Schwarz, Leo W.: "Summary Analysis of AJDC Program in the U. S. Zone of Occupation, Germany." Menorah, vol. 35 #2 (April/June, 1947): 217-239.

6691. ___: "Toward the Rehabilitation of European Jewry." JSSQ, vol.24 #1 (Sept., 1947): 179-184.

6692. Warhaftig, Zorach: Uprooted: Jewish Refugees and Displaced Persons After Liberation [New York: WJC, 1946]

6693. Zimmerman, Charles: "ORT Must Do and Ask for More." ORT Eco Rev, vol.5 #3/4 (March/June, 1946): 13-16.

Solution for the DP Problem

6694. George, Manfred: "German Jews Oppose Return." CW, vol.12 #24 (July 20, 1945): 12.

6695. Gerson, A.: "Poland´s Jews Cry Out." CW, vol.12 #35 (Nov. 30, 1945): 7-8.

6696. Goldberg, Celia: "Displaced Jews in Germany Want New Homes." Today, vol.2 #9 (Sept., 1946): 7-8.

6697. Itzhaki, Solomon: "Whither Surviving Jews?" CW, vol. 12 #19 (May 25, 1945): 9-10.

6698. Katz, Shlomo: "No Hope Except Exodus. Does History Spell the Doom of Western Jewry." Com, vol.1 #6 (April, 1946): 12-19.

6699. Kubowitzki, A. Leon: "Jews in Western Europe." CW, vol.12 #26 (June 8, 1945): 8-10.

6700. Rosenstock, Werner: "Jewry in Germany and Britain." JM, vol.3 #3 (Jan., 1949): 149-157.

6701. Shuster, Zacharia: "Between the Millstones in Poland: The Story Behind the Mass Flight of Polish Jews." Com, vol.2 #2 (Aug., 1946): 107-115.

6702. Solomon, Michel: "In the Lands of the Benelux." J Fr, vol.17 #2 (Feb., 1950): 9-11.

6703. Tenenbaum, Joseph L.: Peace for the Jews [New York: American Federation of Polish Jews, 1945]

America and the DP´s

6704. Bernstein, Philip S.: "The DP´s and America." CW, vol.15 #16 (April 23, 1948): 12-13.

6705. Clark, Tom C.: "Let´s Admit Our Share of DP´s." NJM, vol.61 #10 (June, 1947): 350-351.

6706. Dicker, Herman: "The U. S. Army and Jewish Displaced Persons." Ch J Forum, vol.19 #4 (Sum, 1961): 290-298.

6707. Dinnerstein, Leonard: America and the Survivors of the Holocaust [New York: Columbia Univ. Press, 1982]

Well documented analysis of American attitudes to Jewish DP´s from 1945 to 1950. Notes that only after the State of Israel was established did the U. S. remove blatantly anti-semitic elements from immigrant quotas.

6708. ___: "The U. S. Army and the Jews: Policies Toward the Displaced Persons after World War II." Am J His, vol.68 #3 (March, 1979): 353-356.

6709. Dobkowski, Michael N.(ed.): The Politics of Indifference: A Documentary History of Holocaust Victims in America [Washington, D. C.: Univ. Press of America, 1983]

6710. Drutman, D.: "Displaced Jewry in the American Zone of Germany." JJoS, vol.3 #2 (Dec., 1961): 261-263.

6711. Duker, Abraham G.: "Admitting Pogromists and Excluding Their Victims." Recon, vol.14 #11 (Oct. 1, 1948): 21-27.

6712. Goldstein, L.: "Vital Statistics on the Jewish Displaced Persons in the U.S. Zone of Germany." Am OSE Rev, vol.6 #1 (Spr., 1949): 29-34.

6713. Herman, Joseph: "Shall We Keep our Doors Shut to the Refugees?" Today, vol.2 #6 9May, 1946): 4-5, 33.

6714. Korman, Gerd: "Survivors´ Talmud and the U. S. Army." Am J His, vol.73 #3 (March, 1984): 286-306.

6715. Liskofsky, Sidney: "Immigration Prospects." AJYB, vol.49 (1947/48): 541-562.

6716. Newman, Edwin S.: "Our Post-War Immigration Policy." J Fr, vol.13 #9 (Sept., 1946): 12-14.

6717. Sachar, Abram L.: The Redemption of the Unwanted: From the Liberation of the Death Camps to the Founding of Israel [New York: St. Martin´s Press, 1983]

Expose of Western policy on Jewish refugees from 1945 to 1948. Argues that the U.S. consciously tried to retain its prewar immigration policy, thereby keeping out Jews, until the establishment of Israel ended the perceived threat of a massive influx of poor Jews.

6718. Sprafkin, Benjamin R.: "Displaced Persons and Public Assistance." JSSQ, vol.26 #3 (March, 1950): 400-403.

6719. Steinberg, Milton: "They Shall Live Again: 1,500,000 Survivors of Nazism Look to USA to Help Them Rebuild their Broken Lives." NJM, vol.60 #7 (March, 1946): 224-227.

6720. Tennenbaum, Samuel: "America and Displaced Persons." NJM, vol.63 #5 (Jan., 1949): 150-151.

THE HOLOCAUST AND THE STATE OF ISRAEL

Contemporary Literature

6721. Aharoni, S.: "The 'Enzo Sereni' Arrives." Furrows, vol.4 #4 (March, 1946): 24-25.

6722. Ben-Gurion, David: "The Only Solution to the Jewish Problem." PYB, vol.1 (1945/46): 11-20.

6723. Crum, Bartley: Behind the Silken Curtain: A Personal Account of Anglo-American Diplomacy in Palestine and the Middle East [New York: Simon and Schuster, 1947]

6724. ___: "I Served on the Palestine Inquiry." J Sp, vol. 11 #10 (Aug., 1946): 9-12.

6725. de Sola Pool, Tamar: "The Exile in Cyprus." Survey Graphic, vol.36 #6 (June, 1947): 335-338, 364-365.

6726. Duker, Abraham G.: "This, Our Last Stand: A Reply to Rabbis Eisenstein and Agus." Recon, vol.12 #17 (Dec. 27, 1946): 17-23. <see #6728>

6727. ___: "The War to Annihilate the Jews - the Second Phase: A Memorandum to Jewish Leaders." Recon, vol.12 #13 (Nov. 1, 1946): 10-16.

6728. Eisenstein, Ira: "The British Are Not Nazis - A Reply to Mr. Duker." Recon, vol.12 #14 (Nov. 15, 1946): 13-15. <see #6726>

6729. Frank, M. Z.: "The Palestine Homeland." FW, vol.12 #2 (Sept., 1946): 61-64.

6730. Garcia-Granados, Jorge: The Birth of Israel [New York: A. A. Knopf, 1948]

Eyewitness account of the rebirth of Israel as told by the President of the U.N. General Assembly. Includes some information on the Holocaust and antisemitism.

6731. ___: "Why the Jews Must Have a State." J Outlook, vol.12 #4 (Jan., 1948): 4-5.

6732. Goldman, Nahum: "The Jewish Problem Must be Solved Now." FW, vol.10 #5 (Nov., 1945): 41-43.

6733. Gruber, Ruth: "Destination Cyprus." New Republic, vol.118 #7 (Feb. 16, 1948): 16-20. * On Exodus.

6734. ___: "Destination Germany." New Republic, vol.118 #8 (Feb. 23, 1948): 15-19. * On Exodus.

6735. ___: "Destination Palestine." New Republic, vol.118 #6 (Feb. 9, 1948): 14-18.

6736. ___: Destination Palestine: The Story of the Haganah Ship Exodus 1947 [New York: Current Books, 1948]

Journalistic account of the Haganah ship Exodus 1947. Places the dramatic events against a colorfully painted background. Also discusses the imprisonment of "illegal" immigrants on the Island of Cyprus.

6737. "The Illegals: Picture Story Based Upon a Historic Film." Ortho J Life, vol.16 #1 (Oct., 1948): 48-55.

6738. Journal/Kibbutz Buchenwald: "Homecoming in Israel." Schwarz: Root, pp.309-345.

6739. Kohlberg, Laurence: "Beds for Bananas: A First-Hand Story of the S. S. Redemption." Menorah, vol.36 #4 (Aut., 1948): 385-394. * Aliya Bet - doomed ships.

6740. Kovner, Abba: "Israel, Unite!" HM, vol.26 #6 (Oct., 1946): 4-6.

6741. Lader, L.: "The Road from Buchenwald." New Repulic, vol.119 #12 (Sept. 20, 1948): 16-19.

6742. Levin, Meyer: "Journal Kibbutz Buchenwald: From Concentration Camp to Palestine." Com, vol.1 #8 (June, 1946): 31-39; vol.2 #2 (Aug., 1946): 150-160.

6743. Levine, H.: "Immigration, Settlement, Self-Defense." Furrows, vol.4 #2 (Dec., 1945): 9-13.

6744. Levy, Henry: "Anglo-American Committee of Inquiry." AJYB, vol.48 (1946/47): 395-423.

6745. Lipser, Abraham: "Escape." Schwarz: Root, pp.304-307.

6746. Marcus, Robert S.: "From Buchenwald to Palestine." CW, vol.12 #27 (Oct. 6, 1945): 5-6.

6747. ___: "Voice of the Survivors." CW, vol.13 #7 (Feb. 15, 1946): 6-8.

6748. Neikind, C.: "I Tried to Run the British Blockade." HM, vol.27 #3 (May, 1947): 8-13.

6749. ___: "The Royal Navy Battles the DPs." Palestine, vol.3 #9 (Nov./Dec., 1946): 127-131.

6750. Report of the Anglo-American Committee of Inquiry: Report to the United States Government and His Majesty´s Government in the United Kingdom [Washington, DC: U. S. Department of State, 1946]

6751. "Send Them to Palestine." New Republic, vol.114 #1 (Jan. 7, 1946): 7-8.

6752. Silver, Abba Hillel: "We Need the Jewish State Now." J Sp, vol.10 #7 (May, 1945): 15-18.

6753. Steinberg, Milton: "Centers for Large Colonization of Jews Must be Designated by United Nations." Rescue, vol.2 #11 (Nov., 1945): 3-4, 11.

6754. Weizmann, Chaim: "I Appeal to the Conscience of the World." J Sp, vol.10 #11 (Oct., 1945): 13-15.

Historical Works

6755. Bauer, Yehuda: Flight and Rescue: Brichah [New York: Random House, 1970]

The first fully documented history of the organized mass flight of Jewish survivors from Eastern Europe to displaced persons camps in the west and thence to Palestine/Israel.

6756. ___: "The Holocaust and the Struggle of the Yishuv as Factors in the Establishment of the State of Israel." Gutman: Catastrophe, pp.611-632; Y/V: Hol/Reb, pp. 105-140.

6757. ___: The Jewish Emergence from Powerlessness [Toronto: Univ. of Toronto Press, 1979]

Seminal work evaluating Jewish capabilities and position of world Jewry during the Holocaust. Bauer´s conclusions, that during World War II Jews were powerless to affect their fate, is beyond question. As Bauer correctly points out, however, the Jewish world was able to recover immediately after the war and emerge from powerlessness with the rise of the State of Israel.

6758. Ben-Gurion, David: "First Conflict with Labour Government." JOMER, vol.13 #29 (July 17, 1964): 15-17.

6759. ___ (Mordechai Nurock, ed. and transl.): Rebirth and Destiny [New York: Philosophical Library, 1954]

6760. Birnbaum, Ervin: "On the Exodus 1947." J Fr, vol.24 #5 (May, 1957): 13-18; #8 (Aug., 1957): 16-20.

6761. Cohen, Michael J.: "Truman, the Holocaust and the Establishment of the State of Israel." Jer Q, #23 (Spr., 1982): 79-94.

6762. Dekel, Ephraim: B´richa: Flight to the Homeland [New York: Herzl Press, 1972]

6763. Eban, Abba: My Country: The Story of Modern Israel [New York: Random House, 1972]

6764. Ettinger, Shmuel: "The Holocaust as a Factor in the National Awakening of Soviet Jewry." Y/V: Hol/Reb, pp.159-189.

6765. Gilbert, Martin: Exile and Return: The Struggle for a Jewish Homeland [Philadelphia: Lippincott, 1978]

6766. Goldmann, Nahum: "The Influence of the Holocaust on the Change in the Attitude of World Jewry to Zionism and the State of Israel." Y/V: Hol/Reb, pp.77-103.

6767. Grobman, Alex: "From the Holocaust to the Establishment of the State of Israel." Grobman: Genocide, pp. 315-337.

6768. Habas, Bracha (D. Segal, transl): The Gate Breakers [New York: Thomas Yoseloff, 1963]

6769. Halpern, B.: The Idea of the Jewish State [Cambridge, MA: Harvard Univ. Press, 1961]

6770. Haron, M. J.: "Note: United States - British Collaboration on Illegal Immigration to Palestine, 1945 - 1947." JSS, vol.42 #2 (Spr., 1980): 177-182.

6771. Holly, David C.: Exodus 1947 [Boston: Little, Brown & Company, 1969]

6772. Horowitz, David: "The Holocaust as Background for the Decision of the United Nations to Establish a Jewish State." Y/V: Hol/Reb, pp.141-158.

6773. Hurewitz, J. C.: The Struggle for Palestine [New York: W. W. Norton, 1950]

6774. Klausner, Carla and Joseph P. Schultz (eds): From Destruction to Rebirth: The Holocaust and the State of Israel [Washington, DC: Univ. Press of America, 1978]

Anthology of historical documents on the Holocaust and the State of Israel. The book is geared to High School and College courses; most of the documents were previously published in English.

6775. Laqueur, Walter Z.: A History of Zionism [New York: Holt, Rinehart & Winston, 1972]

6776. Lasher, Ari: "Zero Hour." Furrows, vol.4 #2 (Dec., 1945): 5-8.

6777. Laub, Morris: Last Barrier to Freedom: Internment of Jewish Holocaust Survivors on Cyprus, 1946-1949 [Berkeley, CA: Judah Magnes Museum, 1985]

6778. Lestchinsky, Jacob (N. Shapiro, transl.): "Migration and Aliyah." Ortho J Life, vol.19 #4 (March/April, 1952): 43-48.

6779. ___(S. Rabinowitz, transl.): "Up from Despair." Ortho J Life, vol.20 #4 (March/April, 1953): 49-57.

6780. Pomeranz, F.: "The State of Israel." His/WWII, #118 (1974): 3295-3299.

6781. Prager, Moshe: "Men of the Jewish Underground." Zion, vol.1 #2 (Oct., 1949): 29-35.

6782. ___: "The Silent Heroes: Tales of the Ma´apilim." Zion, vol.1 #3 (Nov., 1949): 19-28.

6783. Schwartz, Leo W.: The Redeemers: A Saga of the Years 1945-1952 [New York: Farrar, Straus and Young, 1953]

A personalized history of the Jewish rebirth at the end of World War II. Deals with the most famous actors in the drama as well as with the unknown. An important and useful book.

6784. ___: "The Survivors and Israel." J Fr, vol.33 #8 (Oct., 1966): 8-12.

6785. ___: "With the Ma´apilim of the Exodus." Dispersion, #5/6 (Spr., 1966): 184-209.

6786. Stone, Isidore F.: Underground to Palestine [New York: Boni & Gaer, 1946]

Personal account by an American journalist of the "illegal" immigration of Holocaust survivors to pre-state Israel. Covers almost every aspect of the Bricha (flight) from Europe.

6787. Weingrod, Avraham: "Reminiscinces of Aliyah Bet." J Fr, vol.28 #3 (March, 1961): 45-49.

6788. Yad Vashem (E. Zuroff, transl.): Holocaust and Rebirth: A Symposium [Jerusalem: Yad Vashem, 1974]

Lectures at a symposium marking Israel´s 25th aniversary, held in Jerusalem, April, 1973.

6789. Zaar, Isaac: Rescue and Liberation: America´s Part in the Birth of Israel [New York: Bloch Pub., 1954]

6790. Zigler, Moshe: "From the Lands of the Holocaust to the War of Liberation in Israel." YVB, #13 (Oct., 1963): 45-47.

REBUILDING EUROPEAN JEWRY

Surveys

6791. Baron, Salo W.: "The Spiritual Reconstruction of European Jewry." Com, vol.1 #1 (Nov., 1945): 4-12.

6792. Bisgyer, Maurice: "Program for Overseas." NJM, vol.61 #1 (Sept., 1946): 12-13, 28-29.

6793. Cohen, Israel: "How Many Jews?" J Sp, vol.15 #5 (April, 1950): 9, 11, 13,

6794. Elazar, Daniel J.: "The Reconstruction of Jewish Communities in the Post-War Period." JJoS, vol.11 #2 (Dec., 1969): 187-226.

6795. Fishman, Joel S.: "The European Jewish Communities After the Holocaust." Grobman: Genocide, pp.338-347.

6796. Gerber, J.: "The Impact of the Holocaust on Sephardic and Oriental Jews." Grobman: Genocide, pp.348-351.

6797. Grossman, Meir: "Viewing the Brighter Side." CW, vol. 12 #3 (Jan. 19, 1945): 6-8.

6798. Hersch, L.: "The Downward Trend of Jewish Population: An Examination of Some Vital Statistics." Com, vol.7 #2 (Feb., 1949): 185-191.

6799. Institute of Jewish Affairs: European Jewry Ten Years After the War [New York: WJC, 1956] * Development and status of the decimated communities.

6800. Laderman, Manuel: "Judaism in Europe Today." J Sp, vol.15 #7 (June, 1950): 11-14.

6801. Landes, Daniel: "Renewal of Religious Life After the Holocaust." Grobman: Genocide, pp.352-370.

6802. Lestchinsky, J.: "The Biological Growth of the Jewish People." PYB, vol.4 (1948/49): 45-58.

6803. ___: "How Many Jews are There Really?" J Sp, vol.15 #8 (July/Aug., 1950): 12-14.

6804. ___: "New Conditions of Jewish Survival." J Fr, vol. 14 #4 (April, 1947): 40-48.

6805. Newman, Edwin S.: "Europe's Jewry: Resettlement and Rehabilitation." Recon, vol.12 #15 (Nov. 29, 1946): 10-13.

6806. Shapiro, Leon and Boris Sapir: "Jewish Population of the World." AJYB, vol.50 (1948/49): 691-724.

6807. Stein, Herman D.: "Welfare and Child Care Needs of European Jewry." JSSQ, vol.25 #3 (March, 1949): 297-307.

6808. Syngalowski, A.: "The Rehabilitation of Work." Ort Eco Rev, vol.5 #3/4 (March/June, 1946): 3-6.

6809. Syrkin, Marie: "Mass Graves and Mass Synagogues." J Fr, vol.14 #11 (Nov., 1947): 11-14.

6810. Szyfman, Leib and W. M. Schmidt." "Jewish Health and Medical Work in Europe." JSSQ, vol.25 #4 (June, 1949): 423-443.

6811. Tartakower, Aryeh: "The Dying Communities." J Fr, vol.14 #9 (Sept., 1947): 13-19.

6812. ___: "Jews in ´New-Europe´." J Fr, vol.12 #7 (July, 1945): 13-14.

6813. Werner, Alfred: "For the Jews in Europe." CW, vol.14 #14 (April 18, 1947): 12-13.

Central Europe

6814. Bentwich, Norman: "The Jewish Remnant in Germany." Cont Rev, vol.183 #1046 (Feb., 1953): 73-76.

6815. ___: "The Jews in Germany, 1945-1956." Cont Rev, vol. 190 #1091 (Nov., 1956): 268-272.

6816. Bergner, Alois: "Return to a Sudeten German Town." CEO, vol.22 #1 (June 15, 1945): 180-181.

6817. Carlebach, Alexander: "The Future of German Jewry." JM, vol.2 #5 (Aug., 1948): 288-297.

6818. Katcher, Leo: "The Vanishing Jews of East Germany." J Digest, vol.15 #3 (Dec., 1969): 59-65.

6819. Kramer, Simon G.: "German Jewry: The Shadow that Remains." Ortho J Life, vol.16 #5 (June, 1949):38-48.

6820. Levinson, N. Peter: "Jews in Post-War Germany." J Sp, vol.19 #3 (March, 1954): 25-27.

6821. Marcus, Robert S.: "Austria: Danger Zone." CW, vol.16 #23 (Aug., 1949): 8-10.

6822. Muehlen, Norbert: The Survivors: A Report on the Jews in Germany Today [New York: Crowell, 1962]

6823. Pinson, Koppel: "Jewish Life in Liberated Germany." JSS, vol.9 #2 (Dec., 1947): 101-126.

6824. Salit, Norman: "Amidst the Ruins." J Horizon, vol.16 #6 (Feb., 1954): 3-5.

6825. Salomon, Michel: "Jews in East Germany." J Fr, vol.19 #6 (June, 1952): 13-15.

6826. ___: "Report from Austria." J Fr, vol.19 #7 (July, 1952): 15-18.

6827. Sapir, Boris: "Germany and Austria." AJYB, vol.49 (1947/48): 362-380; vol.50 (1948/49): 375-387; vol.51 (1950): 325-335; vol.52 (1951): 313-325.

6828. Schecter, Edmund: "Vienna´s Jews Today." CW, vol.12 #26 (Oct. 12, 1945): 6-8.

6829. Schmidt, Samuel M.: "What I saw in Germany." J Sp, vol.11 #1 (Nov., 1945): 23-24.

6830. Srole, Leo: "Landsberg, A Vibrant Community Emerges from Rubble." HM, vol.26 #8 (Dec., 1946): 14-15.

6831. Steinberg, K.: "German Jewry Today." J Affairs, vol. 6 #4 (April, 1951): 23-25.

6832. Weinryb, Bernard D.: "Jews in Central Europe." JCEA, vol.6 #1 (April, 1946): 43-77.

6833. Weiss-Rosmarin, Trude: "German-Jewry: A Post-Mortem." J Sp, vol.10 #9 (July, 1945): 28-31.

6834. Werner, Alfred: "Postwar Austria and the Jews." CW, vol.12 #2 (Jan. 12, 1945):7-10.

6835. ___: "Vienna Paradise Lost." Ch J Forum, vol.7 #4 (Sum., 1949): 230-235.

6836. Yahil, Ch.: "All Jews Must Leave Germany." J Fr, vol. 18 #5 (May, 1951): 18-21.

Eastern Europe

6837. Apenslak, Jacob: "Polish Jewry Today." CW, vol.22 #28 (Nov. 15, 1946): 11-13.

6838. Cang, Joel: "Poland´s Millenium and Polish Jews." JQ, vol.14 #1 (Spr., 1966): 31-34.

6839. Chanin, Nathan: "Can East Europe´s Jews Survive?" New Leader, vol.34 #19 (May 7, 1951): 9-10.

6840. Checinski, M.: "The Kielce Pogrom: Some Unanswered Questions." SJA, vol.5 #1 (May, 1975): 57-72.

6841. ___: Poland: Communism, Nationalism, Antisemitism [New York: Karz-Cohl Pub., 1982]

6842. Cohen, I.: "Dissolving Jewries: The Jews of Czecho-slovakia." CW, vol.18 #17 (May 14, 1951): 11-13.

6843. Dobroszycki, Lucjan: "Restoring Jewish Life in Post-War Poland." SJA, vol.3 #2 (1973): 58-72

6844. Furst, Peter: "The Jews of Eastern Europe." J Life, vol.5 #8 (June, 1951): 9-11.

6845. Gliksman, George J.: "Soviet Union." AJYB, vol.49 (1947/48): 393-409.

6846. Grossman, A.: "Jews in Poland Today and Yesterday." J Fo, vol.33 #8 (Aug., 1950): 134-136.

6847. Gutman, I.: "The Jews of Poland after World War II." Dispersion, #1 (Jan., 1962): 81-92.

6848. Jelinek, Yeshayahu: "The Jews of Slovakia, 1945 - 1949." SJA, vol.8 #2 (Oct., 1978): 45-56.

6849. "The Kielce Massacre." J Fr, vol.13 #8 (Aug., 1946): 6-7. * On the attitude of Cardinal Hlond.

6850. Korey, William: "The Oigins and Development of Soviet Antisemitism: An Analysis." Slavic Review, vol.31 #1 (March, 1972): 111-135.

6851. Lestchinsky, Jacob: "Anti-Zionism in Poland." J Fr, vol.16 #3 (March, 1949): 6-9.

6852. ___: "In Poland Today." CW, vol.15 #7 (Feb. 20, 1948): 11-12.

6853. Levin, Nora: "The Holocaust and the Rise of Soviet Jewish National Consciousness." Forum, #51/52 (1984): 41-52.

6854. Niemira, P.: "The Situation of the Jews in Poland." JCEA, vol.11 #2 (July, 1951): 172-183.

6855. Novick, Paul: "Polish Diary." J Life, vol.1 #3 (Jan., 1947): 20-23.

6856. Ott, Jacob M.: "The Polish Pogroms and Press Suppression." J Fo, vol.29 #1 (Jan., 1946): 3-4.

6857. Patron, Rachel: "Again Poland - 1948." HM, vol.63 #7 (March, 1982): 24-25, 53-54.

6858. Polonsky, Antony (ed.): "Jews in Eastern Europe after World War II: Documents from the British Foreign Office." SJA, vol.10 #1 (Feb., 1980): 52-70.

6859. Reiss, Anselm: "The Situation in Poland." CW, vol.14 #10 (March 7, 1947): 12-13.

6860. Seidman, Hillel: "To the Rescue of Jews in Poland." J Fo, vol.29 #8 (Aug., 1946): 166-167.

6861. Sharf, M.: "Exodus from Poland." J Fr, vol.16 #12 (Dec., 1949): 8-10.

6862. Shneiderman, S. L. (N. Guterman, transl.): Between Fear and Hope [New York: Arco, 1947]

A firsthand report on the hardship and new/old antisemitism encountered by the few returning survivors in post-Nazi Poland. Includes a brief survey of Nazi atrocities during the occupation.

6863. ___: "I Saw Kielce: The Worst Pogrom." NJM, vol.61 #4 (Dec., 1946): 126-127, 134-135.

6864. ___: "Polish Repatriates from Russia." NJM, vol.61 #6 (Feb., 1947): 196-197.

6865. Suhl, Yuri: "Out of the Ashes." J Life, vol.3 #6 (April, 1949): 12-14.

6866. Tartakower, Aryeh: "Jewish Fate and Future in Eastern Europe." Zion, vol.2 #5 (Aug., 1951): 74-80.

6867. Tenenbaum, Joseph L.: In Search of a Lost People: The Old and the New Poland [New York: Beechhurst Press, 1948] * The author chronicles the destruction of Polish Jewry and the attempt by a few broken survivors to make a new start.

6868. Yaffe, Richard: "A Report on Poland." CW, vol.16 #24 (Sept. 19, 1949): 5-6.

6869. Zukerman, W.: "The Future of Polish Jewry." Today, vol.1 #9 (Sept., 1945): 8-9.

Southern Europe

6270. Alcalay, Ora: "Bulgaria." Eur Jud, vol.3 #2 (Win, 1968/69): 26-33.

6871. Bashby, A.: "The Anti-Zionist Campaign in Rumania." J Fr, vol.16 #2 (Feb., 1949): 15-18.

6872. Cohen, Israel: "The Jews of Bulgaria." CW, vol.18 #10 (March 12, 1951): 9-11.

6873. ___: "The Jews of Greece." CW, vol.18 #21 (June 25, 1951): 11-12.

6874. ___: "The Jews of Yugoslavia." CW, vol.18 #13 (April 2, 1951): 9-11.

6875. Du Broff, Sidney: "Bulgarian Jewry Today." J Digest, vol.14 #7 (April, 1969): 25-30.

6876. Elazar, Daniel J.: "The Sunset of Balkan Jewry." Forum, #27 (1977): 135-141.

6877. Fabian, Bela: "Hungary´s Jewry Faces Liquidation: Again the Concentration Camps." Com, vol.12 #4 (Oct., 1951): 330-335.

6878. Hevesi, Frances: "Spiritual Survival in Budapest." Lib Jud, vol.14 #11 (March, 1947): 31-38.

6879. Lehrman, Hal: "Greece: ´Unused Cakes of Soap.´" Com, vol.1 #7 (May, 1946): 48-52

6880. ___: "Rumania: Equality with Reservations." Com, vol. 1 #5 (March, 1946): 25-29.

6881. Major, Robert: "Jews in Post-War Hungary." JM, vol.4 #8 (Nov., 1950): 517-525.

6882. Pearlman, Maurice: "Jews in Postwar Yugoslavia." JVP, vol.10 #34 (Sept./Oct., 1947): 24-25, 37.

6883. Roth, Cecil: "Greece: Can Its Jews Survive?" NJM, vol.61 #9 (May, 1947): 312-313.

Western Europe

6884. Abrahamson, Samuel: "The Saga of Norway's Jews." CW, vol.18 #25 (Oct. 8, 1951): 8-10.

6885. Bulawko, Henri: "Erasing the Record of Nazi Crimes." IH, vol.1 #4 (Feb., 1953): 27-28.

6886. Fischer, Alfred J.: "Rehabilitation in Norway." J Fr, vol.17 #10 (Oct., 1950): 20-33.

6887. Fishman, Joel S.: "The Jewish Community in Post-War Netherlands, 1944-1975." Mid, vol.22 #1 (Jan., 1976): 42-54.

6888. Fleg, Edmond: "Revival in France." Menorah, vol.33 #2 (Oct./Dec., 1945): 214-218.

6889. Level, Hildegard: "Return to Holland." CW, vol.17 #1 (Jan. 2, 1950): 9-11.

6890. Lyon, Mabel: "Judaism Revived in Italy." Lib Jud, vol.12 #3 (July, 1944): 33-42.

6891. Rivkin, Malcolm D.: "The Return of Amsterdam Jewry." J Fr, vol.23 #2 (Feb., 1956): 20-24.

6892. Rossi, Mario: "Italy: 'Viva la Palestina Ebraica'." Com, vol.4 #1 (July, 1947): 23-27.

6893. Ruhstrat, Paul: "Antismitism in Postwar France." CW, vol.15 #22 (July 16, 1948): 12-13.

6894. Szenberg-Hatalgi, Theodore: "Report From Italy." CW, vol.14 #6 (Feb. 7, 1947): 6-7.

The Recovery of Cultural Treasures

6895. Aharoni, A. and J. H. Bachman: "Europe´s Jewish Cultural Material." NJM, vol.61 #9 (May, 1947): 309-311.

6896. Arendt, Hannah: "New Homes for Jewish Books." Am Heb, vol.159 #30 (Nov. 18, 1949): 2, 14.

6897. Blatberg, Wolf: "Recovering Cultural Treasures." CW, vol.17 #27 (Oct. 30, 1950): 5-6.

6898. Cats, Elizabeth: "Danzig, 1939: Treasures of a Destroyed Community." Moment, vol.5 #3 (March, 1980): 42-48. * Based on the ´Danzig Exhibit.´

6899. Goldreich, Gloria: "The Case(s) of the Missing Jewish Books." J Digest, vol.9 #8 (May, 1964): 53-57.

6900. Heller, Bernard: "Operation Salvage." J Horizon, vol. 12 #6 (Feb., 1950): 12-14.

6901. ___: "Our Orphaned Books." J Horizon, vol.17 #1 (Sept., 1954): 9-11, 17.

6902. ___: "Recovery of Looted Sacred Objects." Lib Jud, vol.17 #4 (March, 1950): 9-12.

6903. Hyams, Barry: "How YIVO Came out of the Abyss." J Digest, vol.26 #8 (April, 1981): 55-60.

6904. Iltis, Rudolf: "Jewish Treasures in Czechoslovakia." J Sp, vol.28 #5 (May, 1963): 21-23.

6905. Ya´ari, Avraham: "The Power of Faith: How a Manuscript of Benzion Rapaport was Saved." YVB, #2 (Dec., 1957): 7-9.

SURVIVORS AND THEIR PROBLEMS

General Studies

6906. Boder, David: I Did Not Interview the Dead [Urbana: Univ. of Illinois Press, 1949]

6907. Dimsdale, Joel E. (ed.): Survivors, Victims, and Perpetrators: Essays on the Nazi Holocaust [New York: Hemisphere Pub., 1980]

6908. Friedman, Saul S.: Amcha: An Oral Testament of the Holocaust [Washington, DC: University Publishers of America, 1979]

6909. Halperin, I.: "On Stepping Into the 'Fiery Gates'." Judaism, vol.21 #4 (Fall, 1972): 405-408.

6910. Peck, A. J.: "The Lost Legacy of Holocaust Survivors." Shoa, vol.3 #2/3 (Fall/Win., 1982/83): 33-37.

6911. Rabinowitz, Dorothy: New Lives: Survivors of the Holocaust Living in America [New York: Knopf, 1976]

6912. Ribalow, Harold U.: "Those Jews Who Survived." CW, vol.13 #23 (Sept. 20, 1946): 10-12.

6913. Schwimmer, Sydney: "'Holocaust Survivor': An Interpretation to Account for Varied Forms of Survival." M&R, vol.10 #4 (March/April, 1984): 5, 14.

Psychological Studies

6914. Baron, L.: "Surviving the Holocaust." JP/J, vol.1 #2 (Spr., 1977): 25-37.

6915. Benner, Patricia et al: "Stress and Coping under Extreme Conditions." Dimsdale: Survivors, pp.219-258.

6916. Berger, Leslie: "A Psychological Perspective of the Holocaust: Is Mass Murder Part of Human Behavior?" Braham: Perspectives, pp.19-32.

6917. Bettelheim, Bruno: The Informed Heart: Autonomy in a Mass Age [New York: Avon Books, 1971]

Ostensibly a study on the psychology of Holocaust survivors, the book is actually a diatribe against the victims of nazism. Bettelheim argues that by not resisting, Jews caused their own deaths. Based mainly on Bettelheim's brief experience in a concentration camp in 1938.

6918. Bloch, Herbert A.: "The Personality of Inmates of Concentration Camps." Am Jnl Soc, vol.52 #4 (Jan., 1947): 335-341.

6919. Bulka, Reuven P. (ed.): "Holocaust Aftermath: The Continuing Impact on the Generations." JP/J, (1981): Special Issue.

6920. Carmelly, Felicia: "Guilt Feelings in Concentration Camp Survivors: Comments of a Survivor." JJCS, vol.52 #2 (Win., 1975): 139-144.

6921. Chodoff, Paul: "Psychotherapy of the Survivor." Dimsdale: Survivor, 205-218.

6922. Conrad, G.: "Casework with Survivors of Nazi Persecutions Twenty Years After Liberation." JJCS, vol.46 #2 (Win., 1969): 170-175.

6923. Crystal, David: "The Relation Between Agency Service and Subsequent Social Adjustment of Refugees." JJCS, vol.43 #3 (Spr., 1967): 221-227.

6924. Des Pres, Terrence: "The Edge of Decency." Moment, vol.1 #7 (Feb., 1976): 43-51.

6925. Dimsdale, Joel E.: "The Coping Behavior of Nazi Concentration Camp Survivors." Dimsdale: Survivors, pp. 163-174.

6926. Dvorjetski, Marc: "Adjustment of Detainees to Camp and Ghetto Life and their Subsequent Readjustment to Normal Life." YVS, vol.5 (1961): 193-220.

6927. Eitinger, Leo: Concentration Camp Survivors in Norway and Israel [London: Allen & Unwin, 1964]

6928. ___: "The Concentration Camp Syndrome and Its Late Sequelae." Dimsdale: Survivors, pp.127-162.

6929. Feuerstein, Chester W.: "Working with the Holocaust Victims Psychologically: Some Vital Cautions." JCP, vol.11 #1 (Spr./Sum., 1980): 70-77.

6930. Frankl, Victor E.: From Death-Camp to Existentialism: A Psychiatrist´s Path to a New Therapy [Boston: Beacon Press, 1959]

6931. ___: Man´s Search for Meaning [Boston: Beacon Press, 1963]

Psychiatric reaction to the Holocaust. As a result of his experiences in Nazi concentration camps Frankl developed the theory of logotherapy, which focuses on man as a whole and on man´s search for a higher meaning to life.

6932. Friedman, Paul: "The Road Back for the DP´s: Healing the Psychological Scars of Nazism." Com, vol.6 #6 (Dec., 1948): 502-510.

6933. Goldberger, A.: "Religious Experiences in the Concentration Camps." Recon, vol.34 #5 (April 19, 1968): 12-16, 18.

6934. Goldstein, J. et al: "A Case History of a Concentration Camp Survivor." Am OSE Rev, vol.8 #1 (Fall, 1951): 11-28.

6935. Groliman, Earl A.: "The Logotherapy of Victor E. Frankl. A Search for the Authentic Self." Judaism, vol.13 #1 (Win., 1975): 23-38.

6936. Hogman, Flora: "Adoptive Mechanisms of Displaced Jewish Children During World War II and their Later Adult Adjustment." Shoa, vol.1 #3 (Win, 1979): 10-13.

6937. Holocaust Survivors: Psychological and Social Sequelae [New York: Human Sciences Press, 1980] * First New York Holocaust Memorial Symposium.

6938. Hoppe, K. D.: "Severed Ties." Luel: Psycho, pp.95-111.

6939. Jaffe, Ruth: "Sense of Guilt Within Holocaust Survivors." JSS, vol.32 #4 (Oct., 1970): 307-314.

6940. Kanter, Isaac: "Social Psychiatry and the Holocaust." JP/J, vol.1 #1 (Fall, 1976): 55-56.

6941. Krell, Robert: "Aspects of Psychological Trauma in Holocaust Survivors and their Children." Grobman: Genocide, pp.371-380.

6942. Krystal, Henry: "Integration and Self-Healing in Posttraumatic States." Luel: Psycho, pp.113-133.

6943. Laub, D.: "Holocaust Survivors Adaptation to Trauma." PoP, vol.13 #1 (Jan./Feb., 1979): 17-25.

6944. ___ and N. C. Auerhahn: "Reverberations of Genocide: Its Expression in the Concious and Unconcious of Post-Holocaust Generations." Luel: Psycho, pp.151-167

6945. Lifton, Robert Jay: "The Concept of the Survivor." Dimsdale: Survivors, pp.113-126.

6946. Lore, Shelly: Jewish Holocaust Survivor's Attitudes Toward Contemporary Beliefs About Themselves [Ann Arbor, MI: UMI Publications, 1984]

6947. Luel, Steven L.: "Living with the Holocaust: Thoughts on Revitalization." Luel: Psycho, pp.169-177.

6948. ___ and P. Marcus (eds.): Psychoanalytic Reflections on the Holocaust: Selected Essays [New York: Ktav for Holocaust Awareness Institute, Univ. of Denver, 1984]

6949. Marcus, Paul: "Jewish Consciousness After the Holocaust." Luel: Psycho, pp.179-195.

6950. Minkowski, E.: "Observations on the Psychological and Psychopathological Consequences of War and Nazism." Am OSE Rev, vol.6 #1 (Spr., 1949): 3-10.

6951. ___: "The Psychology of the Deportees." Am OSE Rev, vol.4 #2/3 (Sum./Fall, 1947): 17-22.

6952. Moses, Rafael: "An Israeli Psychoanalyst Looks Back in 1983." Luel: Psycho, pp.53-69.

6953. Niederland, W. G.: "Clinical, Social and Rehabilitation Problems in Concentration Camp Survivors." JJCS, vol.42 #2 (Win., 1965): 186-191.

6954. Novins, S.: "The Holocaust and the Age of Absurdity." Recon, vol.44 #4 (May, 1978): 11-13.

6955. Noyce, Wilfrid: They Survived: A Study of the Will to Live [London: Heinemann, 1962]

6956. Pattison, E. Mansell: "The Holocaust as Sin: Requirements in Psychoanalytic Theory for Human Evil and Mature Morality." Luel: Psycho, pp.71-91.

6957. Porter, J. N.: "Is There a Survivor's Syndrome? Psychological and Socio-Political Implications." Porter: Confronting, pp.83-105.

6958. ___: "On Therapy, Research, and Other Dangerous Phenomena." Shoa, vol.1 #3 (Win., 1979): 14-15. Also in Porter: Confronting, pp.79-82.

6959. ___: "Social-Psychological Aspects of the Holocaust." Sherwin: Encountering, pp.189-222.

6960. Prince, Robert: "A Case Study of a Psychohistorical Figure: The Influence of the Holocaust on Identity." JCP, vol.11 #1 (Spr./Sum., 1980): 44-60.

6961. "Psychoanalysis and the Holocaust: A Roundtable." Luel: Psycho, pp.209-229.

6962. Rakoff, Vivian: "Long Term Effects of the Concentration Camp Experience." V CJQ, vol.1 #2 (March, 1966): 17-21.

6963. Russell, Axel: "Late Effects-Influence on the Children of the Concentration Camp Survivor." Dimsdale: Survivors, pp.175-204.

6964. Rustin, Stanley L.: "The Legacy is Loss." JCP, vol.11 #1 (Spr./Sum., 1980): 32-43.

6965. ___: "The Post-Holocaust Generations: A Psychological Perspective." Braham: Perspectives, pp.33-40.

6966. Schachter, Stanley J.: "Bettelheim and Frankl: Contrasting Views of the Holocaust." Recon, vol.26 #20 (Feb. 10, 1961): 6-11.

6967. Schneider, G.: "Survival and Guilt Feelings of Jewish Concentration Camp Victims." JSS, vol.37 #11 (Jan., 1975): 74-83. Reply with Rejoinder: Jack Nusan Porter vol.38 #1 (Win., 1976): 91-94.

6968. Segalman, Ralph: "The Psychology of Jewish Displaced Persons." JSSQ, vol.23 #4 (June, 1947): 361-369.

6969. Siegel, Lloyd M.: "Holocaust Survivors in Hasidic and Ultra-Orthodox Jewish Populations." JCP, vol.11 #1 (Spr./Sum., 1980): 15-31.

6970. Terry, Jack: "The Damaging Effects of the ´Survivor Syndrome´." Luel: Psycho, pp.135-148.

6971. Wangh, M.: "On Obstacles to the Working-Through of the Nazi Holocaust Experience and on the Consequences of Failing to Do So." Luel: Psycho, pp.197-205.

Children Who Survived

6972. Baumgold, Z.: "The Lost Children of Israel." J Fr, vol.20 #1 (Jan., 1953): 12-13.

6973. Bergman, Martin S. and Milton Jucovy: Generations of the Holocaust [New York: Basic Books, 1982]

Intensive psychological study of the longterm impact of the Holocaust. Studies children of both the survivors and the persecutors. As a first study it makes some interesting observations.

6974. Brutzkus, Julius: "The Jewish Children in Europe." J Fr, vol.12 #9 (Sept., 1945): 15-16.

6975. Danan, Alexis: "The Incredible Finaly Case." J Fr, vol.20 #6 (June, 1953): 7-12.

6976. Fishman, Joel S.: "Jewish War Orphans in the Netherlands: The Guardianship Issue 1945-1950." WLB, vol.27 #1/2 (Win./Spr., 1973/74): 31-36.

6977. Flannery, Edward H.: "The Finaly Case." Bridge, vol.1 (1955): 292-313.

6978. Goldstein, Goldie: "Discussion on Adolescent Refugees." JSSQ, vol.24 #1 (Sept., 1947): 150-152.

6979. Grossman, Frances G.: "A Psychological Study of Children´s Concentration Camp Art." IH, vol.21 #7/8 (July/Aug., 1973): 9-17.

6980. Grunfeld, I.: "The Jewish War Orphans in Europe." Ortho J Life, vol.17 #5 (Sum., 1950): 5-12.

6981. Hirsh, Elizabeth: "OSE Child care Activities in France, Hungary and Rumania." JSSQ, vol.24 #4 (June, 1948): 418-421.

6982. Hochberg-Marianska, M.: "Working with Rescued Children." YVB, #1 (April, 1957): 15-16.

6983. Keller, M.: "The case of the Finaly Orphans." CW, vol.20 #12 (March 23, 1953): 7-11.

6984. Kovarsky, Marcel: "Case Work with Refugee Children." JSSQ, vol.24 #4 (June, 1948): 402-407.

6985. Lappin, Ben: The Redeemed Children: The Story of the Rescue of War Orphans by the Jewish Community of Canada [Toronto: Univ. of Toronto Press, 1963]

6986. Lebeson, Anita L.: "Death-Cry in Holland." CW, vol.21 #22 (June 14, 1954): 11-13.

6987. ___: Of the Generation of Anne Frank." CW, vol.21 #9 (March 1, 1954): 8-10.

6988. Lowrie, Donald R.: The Hunted Children [New York: W. W. Norton, 1963]

6989. Moskovitz, Sarah: Love Despite Hate: Child Survivors of the Holocaust and their Adult Lives [New York: Schocken, 1983]

Psychological study of the make-up of child survivors. Based on interviews with twenty-four survivors now living in the United States and Israel.

6990. Paneth, Marie: "Rebuild Those Lives." FW, vol.11 #4 (April, 1946): 53-55.

6991. Papanek, Ernst: "Social Services for European Jewish Children." JSSQ, vol.24 #4 (June, 1948): 412-417.

6992. Perlzweig, Maurice: "The Finaly Affair." Ch Century, vol.70 #22 (June 3, 1953): 660-661.

6993. Portnoy, Deborah: "The Adolescent Immigrant." JSSQ, vol.25 #2 (Dec., 1948): 268-273.

6994. Puner, Morton: "Where Are the Finaly Children?" ADL Bul, vol.10 #4 (April, 1953): 6, 8.

6995. Varchaver, Catherine: "Rehabilitation of European Jewish Children Through Personal Contact." JSSQ, vol. 24 #4 (June, 1948): 408-411.

6996. Vegh, Claudine: I Didn´t Say Goodby: Interviews with Children of the Holocaust [New York: Dutton, 1985]

Interviews with French Jews who were child survivors of the Holocaust. Focused on psychological issues related to child survivors.

6997. Wulman, Leon: "European Jewish Children in the Post-War Period." Am OSE Rev, vol.5 #1/2 (Win./Spr., 1948): 4-11.

The Second Generation

6998. Abelson, Norman: "Marrying into Memory." Moment, vol. 8 #5 (May, 1983): 62-63.

6999. Alexanderowicz, D. R.: Children of Concentration Camp Survivors [Tel-Aviv: Univ. Medical School, 1970]

7000. Barocas, Harvey A. and Carol B. Barocas: "Separation-Individuation Conflicts in Children of Holocaust Survivors." JCP, vol.11 #1 (Spr./Sum., 1980): 6-14.

7001. Blitzer, Wolf: "In Congress, the Memory Lives." HM, vol.65 #8 (April, 1984): 13, 40-42.

7002. Epstein, Helen: Children of the Holocaust [New York: G. P. Putnam's Sons, 1979]

7003. Frankle, Helen: "The Survivor as Parent." JJCS, vol. 54 #3 (Spr., 1978): 241-246.

7004. Greenblatt, Steven: "The Influence of Survival Guilt on Chronic Family Crises." JP/J, vol.2 #2 (Spr., 1978): 19-28.

7005. Katz, Cipera and F. A. Keleman: "The Children of Holocaust Survivors: Issues of Separation." JJCS, vol.58 #3 (Spr., 1981): 257-263.

7006. Ludzki, Marilyn: "Children of Survivors." J Sp, vol. 42 #3 (Fall, 1977): 41-43.

7007. Mostysser, Toby: "Children of Survivors Growing Up in America with a Holocaust Heritage." M&R, vol.1 #6 (July/Aug., 1975): 4-5.

7008. ___: The Weight of the Past: Reminiscences of a Survivors' Child." Response, vol.9 #1 (Spr., 1975): 3-32.

7009. Podietz, Lenore: "The Holocaust Revisited in the Next Generation." J Digest, vol.21 #7 (April, 1976): 40-47.

7010. Rosensaft, Menachem Z.: "Reflections of a Child of Holocaust Survivors." Mid, vol.27 #9 (Nov., 1981): 31-33.

7011. Seligman, Ruth: "Children of Survivors: The Israeli Difference." HM, vol.64 #8 (April, 1983): 33-34, 36.

7012. Steinitz, Lucy Y.: "Their Legacy, Our Duty." J Fr, vol.46 #4 (April, 1979): 22-24.

7013. Trachtenberg, Martin and M. Davis: "Breaking Silence: Serving Children of Holocaust Survivors." JJCS, vol. 54 #4 (Sum., 1978): 294-302.

7014. Weiner, S. A. and B. Spilka: "Holocaust Survivors' Children as Jews." Sh'ma, vol.10 #192 (April 18, 1980): 89-90.

THE REPARATIONS ISSUE

7015. Adler-Rudel, S.: "Reparations from Germany." Zion, vol.2 #5 (Aug., 1951): 84-90.

7016. Balabkins, Nicholas: "The Birth of Restitution: The Making of the Shilumim Agreement." WLB, vol.21 #1 (Aut., 1967): 8-16.

7017. __: West German Reparations to Israel [New Brunswick: Rutgers Univ. Press, 1971]

7018. Barou, N.: "Origin of the German Agreement." CW, vol. 19 #24 (Oct. 13, 1952): 6-8.

7019. Ben-Horin, Eliahu: "Muddled Thinking in Jerusalem." CW, vol.19 #3 (Jan. 21, 1952): 7-9. * Debate.

7020. Bentwich, Norman: "Compensation for Nazi Victims." Cont Rev, vol.188 #1076 (Aug., 1955): 88-92.

7021. ___: "German 'Atonement' for Nazi Crimes." JQ, vol.5 #3 (Win., 1958): 19-22.

7022. ___: "German Restitution and Reparation." Fortnightly, #1021 (Jan., 1952): 31-36.

7023. ___: The United Restitution Organization [London: Valentine Mitchell, 1969]

7024. Courtney, David: "The German Reparations Agreement." J Fr, vol.19 #11 (Nov., 1952): 5-9.

7025. Dawidowicz, Lucy S.: "The Conference on Jewish Material Claims Against Germany: 1953-58." AJYB, vol.61 (1960): 110-127.

7026. ___: "German Collective Indemnity to Israel and the Conference on Jewish Material Claims Against Germany." AJYB, vol.54 (1953): 471-485.

7027. Deutschkorn, Inge: Bonn and Jerusalem: The Strange: Coalition [Philadelphia: Chilton Book Co., 1970]

Authoritative journalistic account of the relations between Israel and West Germany. Includes military, political, and economic relations as well as the context of German-Arab and German-Allied relations.

7028. Dunner, Joseph: "Jews and Germans: Contrasting Views, Appeal to Reason." CW, vol.19 #4 (Jan. 28, 1952): 5-7.

7029. Easterman, Alexander L.: "Jewish Claims on Germany." CW, vol.17 #22 (Aug. 21, 1950): 5-7.

7030. Frank, Murray: "What Can Nazi Victims Expect?" NJM, vol.64 #5 (Jan., 1950): 150-151, 169-170.

7031. Goldman, Frank: "The Significance of German Claims Agreement." NJM, vol.67 #2 (Oct., 1952): 58, 73-75.

7032. Goldman, Nahum: "Direct Israel-German Negotiations? Yes." Zionist Q, vol.1 #3 (Win., 1952): 9-13.

7033. Goldschmidt, Siegried: Legal Claims Against Germany: Compensation and Losses Resulting from Anti-Racial Measures [New York: American Jewish Committee, 1945]

7034. Gringauz, Samuel: "Indemnification from Germany." J Fr, vol.18 #5 (May, 1951): 11-15.

7035. Grossmann, Kurt R.: "The German Indemnification Program." J Sp, vol.23 #6 (June, 1958): 15-19.

7036. ___: "The German-Israeli Agreement." Ch J Forum, vol. 12 #2 (Win., 1953/1954): 73-79.

7037. ___: Germany's Moral Debt [Washington, DC: Public Affairs Press, 1954]

7038. Grusd, Edward E.: "The Claims Against Germany." NJM, vol.66 #9 (May, 1952): 306-307.

7039. Heller, Bernard: "To the Victims Belong the Spoils." Lib Jud, vol.18 31 (June, 1950): 21-24.

7040. Hyman, Abraham S.: "The Heirless Property Paradox." CW, vol.20 #20 (June 1, 1953): 5-6.

7041. Ivry, Itzhak: "Reparations but Not Reconciliation." CW, vol.19 #7 (Feb. 18, 1952): 5-7.

7042. Kapralik, Charles I.: Reclaiming the Nazi Loot: The History of the Jewish Trust Corporation for Germany. A Report [London: Jewish Trust Corp., 1962]

7043. Landauer, Georg: "Restitution of Jewish Property in Germany." Zion, vol.2 #1 (Dec., 1953): 18-22.

7044. ___: "Urgency of Jewish Restitution." Zion, vol.2 #3 (March/April, 1951): 11-14.

7045. Lehrman, Hal: "Austria and Jewish Indemnity Claims." New Leader, vol.36 #48 (Nov. 30, 1953): 11-12.

7046. ___: "Austria and the Jews: Struggle for Restitution." Com, vol.18 #4 (Oct., 1954): 308-318.

7047. Leivick, H.: "No Blood-Money from Germany." J Fr, vol.17 #5 (May, 1950): 14-15.

7048. Levin, I. Halevi: "Reparations from Germany." Ortho J Life, vol.19 #4 (March/April, 1952): 29-35.

7049. Marx, Hugo: "The Indemnification of Victims of Nazi Persecution." JSS, vol.7 #3 (July, 1945): 265-274.

7050. Nassauer, Rudolf: Reparations [London: Cape, 1981]

7051. Nurock, M.: "To Negotiate Is to Condone." J Horizon, vol.14 #5 (Jan., 1952): 4-5.

7052. Robinson, Nehemiah: "Germany´s Debts." CW, vol.18 #33 (Dec. 17, 1951): 3-7.

7053. ___: Indemnification and Reparations [New York: Inst. of Jewish Affairs, 1944]

7054. ___: Ten Years of German Indemnification [New York: Conference on Jewish Material Claims Against Germany, 1964]

7055. Roth, S. J.: "West German Recompense for Nazi Wrongs: 30 Years of the Luxembourg Agreement." IJA Res Rep, #16/17 (Nov., 1982): 1-32.

7056. Rubinstein, A.: "German Reparations in Retrospect." Mid, vol.8 #1 (Win., 1962): 29-42.

7057. ___: "Ten Years of German Reparations to Israel: Impact and Implications of an Historic Decision." J Digest, vol.8 #2 (Nov., 1962): 41-53.

7058. Saphire, William B.: "Jewish Claims Against Germany." J Affairs, vol.6 #11 (Nov., 1951): 11-14.

7059. Schechtman, Joseph B.: "Direct Israel-German Negotiations? No." Zionist Q, vol.1 #3 (Win., 1952): 10-20.

7060. Sebba, Leslie: "The Reparations Agreements: A New Perspective." Annals, #450 (July, 1980): 202-212.

7061. Silvers, Dean: "The Future of International Law as seen Through the Material Claims Conference Against Germany." JSS, vol.42 #3/4 (Sum./Fall, 1980): 215-228.

7062. Werner, Alfred: "Austria´s Moral Debt." J Fr, vol.22 #4 (April, 1955): 19-22.

QUESTIONABLE BEHAVIOR BY JEWS

7063. Bauer, Yehuda: "The Mission of Joel Brand." Bauer: Perspective, pp.94-155.

7064. Cale, Ruth: "The Kastner Case Closed." CW, vol.25 #5 (March 3, 1958): 5-7.

7065. Dean, Gideon: "The Kastner Affair." Recon, vol.21 #19 (Jan. 27, 1956): 9-15; #20 (Feb. 10, 1956): 13-19.

7066. Levin, Meyer: "Eichmann´s Last Victim." Coronet, vol. 50 #3 (July, 1961): 98-107. * On Rudolf Kastner.

7067. Levine, Herbert S.: "A Jewish Collaborator in Nazi Germany: The Strange Career of Georg Kareski." CEH, vol.8 #3 (Sept., 1975): 251-281.

7068. Major, Robert: "The Holocaust in Hungary. About the ´Rescue´ of Hungarian Jewry in World War II." J Currents, vol.19 #11 (Dec., 1965): 6-13. * On Kastner.

7069. Sehlag, Maurice: "Jews Who Helped Hitler." JVP, vol.4 #9/10 (Oct., 1941): 16, 27-28.

7070. Shtrigler, Mordecai: "The Kastner Case." J Fr, vol.22 #8 (Aug., 1955): 10-16.

7071. Sloan, Jacob: "From the Trial of Rudolf Kastner." Recon, vol.24 #17 (Dec. 26, 1958): 29-31.

7072. Wainwright, Landon S.: "You Are the Man Who Killed My Brother." Life, vol.26 #24 (Dec. 11, 1950): 132-150. * Proceedings of the Beth-Din trial of the Krieger-Mittelman case held at the offices of the American Jewish Congress in New York City.

7073. Werner, Alfred: "Jewish Renegades with Hitler." J Fo, vol.24 #12 (Dec., 1941): 203-204, 214; vol.25 #1 (Jan., 1942): 13-14; #3 (March, 1942): 48.

15

Reflection on the Holocaust

THEOLOGICAL REFLECTIONS

General Studies

7074. Brown, R. M.: "The Holocaust: The Crisis of Indifference." Con Jud, vol.31 #1 (Fall/Win., 1976/1977): 16-20.

7075. Eckardt, Alice L.: "The Holocaust: Christian-Jewish Responses." CM, vol.42 #4 (April, 1975): 10-14; #5 (May, 1975): 10-14.

7076. ___ and A. Roy Eckardt: "The Holocaust and the Enigma of Uniqueness: A Philosophical Effort at Practical Clarification." Annals, #450 (July, 1980): 165-178.

7077. Fleischner, Eva (ed.): Auschwitz: Beginning of a New Era? Reflections on the Holocaust [New York: Ktav, 1974] * Collection of reflective works on the Holocaust based upon a June 1973 symposium held in New York City.

7078. Friedlander, A. H.: "Bonhoeffer and Baeck: Theology After Auschwitz." Eur Jud, vol.14 #1 (Sum., 1980): 26-32.

7079. Greenberg, Irving: "The State of Israel and the Challenge of Power to Jewish and Christian Theology." Shoa, vol.1 #2 (Fall, 1978): 21-23.

7080. Jonas, Hans: "The Concept of God After Auschwitz." Friedlander: Whirlwind, pp.465-476.

7081. Knopp, Josephine (ed.): International Theological Symposium On the Holocaust [Philadelphia: National Institute of the Holocaust, 1978] * Papers of Symposium held October 15-17, 1978.

7082. Magurshak, Dan: "The Incomprehensibility of the Holocaust: Tightening Up Some Loose Usage." Judaism, vol. 29 #2 (Spr., 1980): 233-242.

7083. Niger, Shin: "Freedom from Fear." Lib Jud, vol.14 #5 (Sept., 1946): 7-12, 25.

7084. Peck, Abraham J. (ed.): Jews and Christians After the Holocaust [Philadelphia: Fortress Press, 1982]

7085. Rosenberg, Alan: "The Philosophical Implications of the Holocaust." Braham: Perspectives, pp.1-18.

7086. Roth, John K.: "The Holocaust and Freedom to Choose." Shoa, vol.2 #1 (Spr./Sum., 1980): 19-22.

7087. Rubinoff, Lionel: "Auschwitz and the Pathology of Jew-Hatred." Fleischner: Auschwitz, pp.347-371.

7088. Ryan, Michael D. (ed.): Human Response to the Holocaust [New York: Mellon Edition, 1981]

7089. Seeskin, Kenneth R.: "The Reality of Radical Evil." Judaism, vol.29 #4 (Fall, 1980): 440-453.

7090. Sherwin, B. L.: "Jewish and Christian Theology Encounters the Holocaust." Sherwin: Encountering, pp. 407-442.

7091. ___: "Philosophical Reactions to and Moral Implications of the Holocaust." Sherwin: Encountering, pp. 443-472.

7092. Simon, Ulrich: A Theology of Auschwitz [Atlanta, GA: Knox Press, 1979]

7093. Tiefel, Hans O.: "Holocaust Interpretations and Religious Assumptions." Judaism, vol.25 #2 (Spr., 1976): 135-149.

7094. Weiler, M. C.: "Has God Hidden Himself from Man?" Recon, vol.22 #4 (April 6, 1956): 23-28.

7095. Winograd, L.: "Genocide and Religion." J Sp, vol.29 #2 (Feb., 1964): 19-21.

Jewish Theology

7096. Agus, Jacob B.: "The Future of Jewish Messianism." Ryan: Responses, pp.225-237.

7097. ___: "God and the Catastrophe." Con Jud, vol.18 #4 (Sum., 1964): 13-21.

7098. Berenbaum, M.: "Our Ancient Covenant has been Shattered." Sh´ma, vol.14 #272 (April 13, 1984): 91-93.

7099. Berkovits, Eliezer: "Approaching the Holocaust." Judaism, vol.23 #1 (Win., 1973): 18-20.

7100. ___: "Crisis and Faith." Tradition, vol.14 #4 (Fall, 1974): 5-19.

7101. ___: Faith After the Holocaust [New York: Ktav, 1973]

Attempts to integrate the Holocaust into the thought patterns of contemporary orthodox Judaism. Berkovits presumes the affirmation of the "God of History" and seeks evidence for this in both the destruction of European Jewry and the rebirth of Israel.

7102. ___: God, Man, and History: A Jewish Interpretation [New York: Jonathan David Pub., 1959]

7103. ___: "The Hiding God of History." Gutman: Catastrophe, pp.684-704.

7104. ___: With God in Hell [New York: Sanhedrin Press, 1979]

7105. Besdin, A. R.: "Reflections on the Agony and the Ecstasy." Tradition, vol.11 #4 (Spr., 1971): 64-70.

7106. Blumenthal, David R.: "The Popular Jewish Response to the Holocaust: An Initial Reflection." Shoa, vol.2 #1 (Spr./Sum., 1980): 3-5.

7107. Borowitz, E. B.: "The 614th Commandment." J Digest, Vol.16 #4 (Jan., 1971): 23-31.

7108. Brenner, Reeve R.: "Belief and Unbelief After the Holocaust." J Sp, vol.46 #1 (Spr., 1981): 31-35.

7109. ___: The Faith and Doubt of Holocaust Survivors [New York: Free Press, 1980]

7110. Cain, Seymour: "Jewish Faith After Nazism: The Question and the Answers After Auschwitz." Judaism, vol. 20 #3 (Sum., 1971): 263-278.

7111. Carr, Maurice: "The Revelation and the Lessons of Auschwitz." JQ, vol.12 #3 (Aut., 1964): 3-5.

7112. Cohen, Arthur A.: Arguments and Doctrines: A Reader of Jewish Thinking in the Aftermath of the Holocaust [New York: Harper & Row, 1970]

7113. ___: The Natural and Supernatural Jew: An Historical and Theological Introduction [New York: Pantheon Books, 1962]

7114. ___: "Thinking the Tremendum: Some Theological Implications of the Death-Camps." LBML #18 (1974). Also in Forum, #30/31 (1978): 121-134.

7115. ___: The Tremendum: A Theological Interpretation of the Holocaust [New York: Crossroad Press, 1981]

Theological reflection on the centrality of the Holocaust to the understanding of the role that Judaism and Christianity play in the modern world.

7116. Cohn, R. L.: "Being Human After Auschwitz." JRJ, vol. 26 #4 (Aut., 1979): 51-56.

7117. Dorff, E. N.: "God and The Holocaust." Judaism, vol. 26 #1 (Win., 1977): 27-34.

7118. Eckstein, J.: "The Holocaust and Jewish Theology." Mid, vol.23 #4 (April, 1977): 36-45.

7119. Elias, J.: "Dealing with Churban Europa." J Observer, vol.12 #8 (Oct., 1977): 10-18.

7120. Fackenheim, Emil: God's Presence in History: Jewish Affirmation and Philosophic Reflections [New York: Harper & Row, 1972]

7121. ___: "The Human Condition After Auschwitz." CBW, vol. 39 #7 (April 28, 1972): 6-10; #8 (May 19, 1972): 5-8.

7122. ___: "Jewish Faith and the Holocaust: A Fragment." Com, vol.46 #2 (Aug., 1968): 30-36.

7123. ___: The Jewish Return Into History: Reflections in the Age of Auschwitz and a New Jerusalem [New York: Schocken, 1978]

Collection of Fackenheim's essays on three basic themes: Man's place in the world; the place of the Holocaust in Jewish theology; and the central role played by Israel in contemporary Jewish life. These essays are a serious attempt at a new philosophy of Jewish history.

7124. ___: "Jewish Values in the Post-Holocaust Future." Judaism, vol.16 #3 (Sum., 1967): 269-273.

7125. ___: "On Faith in the Secular World." Friedlander: Whirlwind, pp.493-514.

7126. ___: "Why Jews Can Only Survive as Jews." J Digest, vol.19 #7 (April, 1974): 5-13; #8 (May, 1974): 49-59.

7127. Fischer, J.: "God After the Holocaust: An Attempted Reconciliation." Judaism, vol.32 #3 (Sum., 1983): 309-320.

7128. Friedlander, Albert H.: "A Final Conversation with Paul Tillich." Friedlander: Whirlwind, pp.515-521.

7129. Gelber, Shlome M.: "Wherein is this Night Different? A Report from Bergen Belsen, Germany." Menorah, vol. 35 #1 (Jan./March, 1947): 21-30.

7130. Gilbert, Arthur: "The Meaning and Purpose of Jewish Survival." Recon, vol.34 #13 (Nov. 8, 1968): 11-17.

7131. Glatzer, Nahum N.: The Passover Haggadah: Including Readings on the Holocaust [New York: Schocken, 1982]

7132. Goldberg, Hillel: "Holocaust Theology: The Survivors´ Statement." Tradition, vol.20 #2 (Sum., 1982): 141-154; #4 (Win., 1982): 341-357.

7133. Gordis, R.: "A Cruel God or None: Is There No Other Choice?" Judaism, vol.21 #4 (Fall, 1972): 277-284.

7134. Gottschalk, Alfred: "Religion in a Post-Holocaust World." Peck: Jews/Chr, pp.1-9.

7135. Greenberg, Irving: "Cloud of Smoke, Pillar of Fire: Judaism, Christianity, and Modernity after the Holocaust." Fleischner: Auschwitz, pp.7-55.

7136. ___: "Religious Values After the Holocaust: A Jewish View." Peck: Jew/Chr, pp.63-86.

7137. Gruenwald, Max: "The Remnant of Israel." Con Jud, vol.18 #4 (Sum., 1964): 10-12.

7138. Hammer, R. A.: "The God of Suffering." Con Jud, vol. 31 #1 (Fall/Win., 1976/1977): 34-41.

7139. Hartman, David: "Auschwitz or Sinai." Shofar, vol.2 #2 (Win., 1984): 40-43.

7140. Helfand, J. I.: "Halakhah and the Holocaust: Historical Perspectives." Braham: Perspectives, pp.93-103.

7141. Heschel, Abraham Joshua: "The Meaning of this Hour." Friedlander: Whirlwind, pp.488-492.

7142. Hutner, Yitzchak: "Holocaust." J Observer, vol.12 #8 (Oct., 1977): 3-9.

7143. Kaplan, L.: "Rabbi Isaac Hutner´s ´Daat Torah´ Perspective on the Holocaust: A Critical Analysis." Tadition, vol.18 #3 (Fall, 1980): 235-248.

7144. Katz, Steven T.: Post-Holocaust Dialogues: Critical Studies in Modern Jewish Thought [New York: New York Univ. Press, 1983]

Collection of essays by Katz on Jewish philosophy. Focuses on how recent Jewish philosophers have dealt with the Holocaust. Also includes some of the author´s musing on the philosophical implications of the Holocaust. A useful review book and guide.

7145. Kirschner, Robert (ed. and transl): Rabbinic Responsa of the Holocaust Era [New York: Schocken, 1985]

7146. Klagsburn, Francine: "The Value of Life: Jewish Ethics and the Holocaust." Braham: Contemporay, pp.3-19.

7147. Klausner, Carla L. and J. P. Schultz: "The Holocaust, Israel and Jewish Chosenness." Forum, #32/33 (1978): 71-77.

7148. Korn, Bertram W.: "How to Understand the Meaning of Churban." J Digest, vol.12 #11 (Aug., 1967): 32-36.

7149. Kraut, Benny: "Faith and the Holocaust." Judaism, vol.31 #2 (Spr., 1982): 185-201.

7150. Landes, Daniel: "A Jewish Reflection on Christian Responses." Grobman: Genocide, pp.419-421.

7151. ___: "The Threefold Covenant: Jewish Belief After the Holocaust." Grobman: Genocide, pp.402-409.

7152. Lipstadt, Deborah E.: "We Are Not Job's Children." Shoa, vol.1 #4 (1979): 12-16.

7153. Maybaum, Ignaz: The Face of God After Auschwitz [New York: Dell, 1976]

7154. Montefiore, A.: "The Moral Philosopher's View on the Holocaust." Eur Jud, vol.11 #2 (Sum., 1977): 13-22.

7155. Neusner, Jacob: "Beyond Catastrophe, Before Redemption." Recon, vol.46 #2 (April, 1980): 7-12.

7156. Orbach, William W.: "Post-Holocaust Jewish Theology: The State of the Art." Recon, vol.43 #10 (Jan., 1978): 7-15.

7157. Oshry, Ephraim: Responsa from the Holocaust [New York: Judaica Press, 1984]

7158. Patai, Raphael: "The Impotence of God: From Adam to Auschwitz." Mid, vol.28 #7 (Aug./Sept.,1982): 34-38.

7159. Peli, Pinhas H.: "In Search of Religious Language for the Holocaust." Con Jud, vol.33 #2 (Win., 1979): 3-24.

7160. Plaut, Gunther: "A Voice From the Grave." J Digest, vol.5 #2 (Nov., 1959): 21-26.

7161. Rose, Herbert H.: "Auschwitz and God." J Sp, vol.32 #2 (Feb., 1967): 8-9.

7162. Rosenbaum, Irving J.: The Holocaust and Halakhah [New York: Ktav, 1976]

Surveys the reaction of Halachic scholars to the Holocaust. Quotes extensively from contemporary and postwar responsa literature on a wide variety of topics.

7163. Rosensaft, Menachem Z.: "Jewish Values in the Post-Holocaust Future." Judaism, vol.16 #3 (Sum., 1967): 294-295.

7164. Rothschild, F.: "Jewish Values in the Post-Holocaust Future: Comments." Judaism, vol.16 #3 (Sum., 1967): 291-292. <see #7163>

7165. Rubenstein, Richard L.: After Auschwitz: Radical Theology and Contemporary Judaism [Indianapolis, IN: Bobbs-Merrill Co., 1966]

Interesting although not completely convincing effort at a philosophical response to the Holocaust. Propounds the "God is dead" hypothesis.

7166. ___: The Cunning of History: The Holocaust and the American Future [New York: Harper & Row, 1975]

7167. ___: "Religious Origins of the Death Camps." Recon, vol.27 #6 (May 5, 1961): 10-14; #7 (May 19, 1961): 20-27.

7168. ___ and A. A. Cohen: "Theology After the Holocaust." JRJ, vol.31 #2 (Spr., 1984): 43-65.

7169. Samuels, Marc E.: "Can I Still Believe in God?" J Sp, vol.27 #2 (Feb., 1962): 18-19.

7170. ___: "Why This Great Evil?" J Sp, vol.30 #3/4 (March/April, 1965): 40-41.

7171. Schindler, Pesach: "The Holocaust and Kiddush Hashem in Hasidic Thought." Tradition, vol.13 #4/vol.14 #1 (Spr./Sum., 1973): 88-104.

7172. Schulweis, H. M.: "The Prophet in a Post-Holocaust Age." Recon, vol.45 #2 (April, 1979): 7-10.

7173. Schwarzschild, Steven S.: "Jewish Values in the Post-Holocaust Future." Judaism, vol.16 #3 (Sum., 1967): 266-269. <see #7163>

7174. Seeskin, Kenneth R.: "The Perfection of God and the Presence of Evil." Judaism, vol.31 #2 (Spr., 1982): 202-210.

7175. Sherwin, Byron L.: "The Impotence of Explanation and the European Holocaust." Tradition, vol.12 #3/4 (Win./Spr., 1972): 99-106.

7176. Siegel, Seymour: "Theological Reflections on the Destruction of European Jewry." Con Jud, vol.18 #4 (Sum., 1964): 2-9.

7177. Steckel, Charles: "God and the Holocaust." Judaism, vol.20 #3 (Sum., 1971): 279-285.

7178. Steiner, George: "Jewish Values in the Post-Holocaust Future." Judaism, vol.16 #3 (Sum., 1967): 276-281.

7179. Swirsky, M.: Readings for Tish´ah B´av [Jerusalem: W. Z. O. Youth Dept., 1971]

7180. Weinberg, Yaacov: "A Churban of Singular Dimensions." J Observer, vol.11 #8 (June, 1976): 4-6.

7181. Weiss, David W.: "After Auschwitz, After Eden." J Sp, vol.39 #2 (Sum., 1974): 18-22.

7182. ___: "After the Holocaust, Another Covenant?" Sh´ma, vol.14 #272 (April 13, 1984): 89-91.

7183. Wurzburger, Walter S.: "The Holocaust - Meaning or Impact?" Shoa, vol.2 #1 (Spr./Sum., 1980): 14-16.

7184. ___: "Theological and Philosophiocal Responses to the Holocaust." Hirt: Issues, pp.27-32.

7185. Wyschogrod, Michael: "Auschwitz: The Beginning of a New Era? Reflections on the Holocaust." Tradition, vol.17 #1 (Fall, 1977): 63-78.

7186. ___: "Some Theological Reflections of the Holocaust." Response, vol.9 #1 (Spr., 1975): 65-68.

7187. Zimmels, Hirsch J.: The Echo of the Nazi Holocaust in Rabbinic Literature [New York: Ktav, 1977]

Christian Theology

7188. Anderson, Terence: "An Ethical Critique: Antisemitism and the Shape of Christian Repentance." Davies: Foundations, pp.208-229.

7189. Baum, Gregory: "Catholic Dogma after Auschwitz." Davies: Foundations, pp.137-150.

7190. ___: Christian Theology After Auschwitz [London: Council of Christians and Jews, 1976]

7191. Boyens, Armin F. C.: "The Ecumenical Community and the Holocaust." Annals, #450 (July, 1980): 140-152.

7192. Brockway, Allan R.: "Religious Values after the Holocaust: A Protestant View." Peck: Jews/Chr, pp.53-62.

7193. Brown, Robert M.: "The Coming of the Messiah: From Divergence to Convergence?" Ryan: Responses, pp.205-223.

7194. Cargas, Harry J.: "Headlines and Footnotes: Christians Face the Holocaust." NJM, vol.94 #9 (May, 1980): 48-50.

7195. Christians Confront the Holocaust: A Collection of Sermons [New York: Nat´l Conference of Christians And Jews, 1980]

7196. Davies, Alan: "On Religious Myths and their Secular Translation: Some Historical Reflections." Davies: Foundations, pp.188-207.

7197. Drinan, Robert F.: "The Christian Response to the Holocaust." Annals, #450 (July, 1980): 179-189.

7198. Eckardt, Alice L.: "Christian Responses to the Holocaust." Hirt: Issues, pp.69-95.

7199. ___ and A. Roy Eckardt: "How German Thinkers View the Holocaust." Ch Century, vol.93 #9 (March 17, 1976): 249-252.

7200. Eckardt, A. Roy: "Contemporary Christian Theology and a Protestant Witness for the Shoah." Shoa, vol.2 #1 (Spr./Sum.,1980): 10-13.

7201. ___ and A. L. Eckardt: Long Night´s Journey into Day: Life and Faith After the Holocaust [Detroit: Wayne State Univ. Press, 1981]

7202. Fisher, E. J.: "Holocaust and Christian Responsibility." America, vol.144 #6 (Feb. 14, 1981): 118-121.

7203. Haverwas, S.: The Holocaust and the Duty to Forgive." Sh´ma, vol.10 #198 (Oct. 3, 1980): 137-139.

7204. Kremers, Heinz: "The First German Church Faces the Challenge of the Holocaust." Annals, #450 (July, 1980): 190-201.

7205. Littell, Franklin H.: "Christendom, Holocaust and Israel: The Importance for Christians of Recent Major Events in Jewish History." Jnl/Ec Studies, vol.10 #3 (Sum., 1973): 496-497.

7206. ___: Christian Involvement During the Holocaust." M&R, vol.6 #5 (May/June, 1980): 6, 15.

7207. ___: "Christians and Jews in the Historical Process." Judaism, vol.22 #3 (Sum., 1973): 263-277.

7208. ___: The Crucifiction of the Jews [New York: Harper & Row, 1975]

Effort to come to grips with the modern Jewish experience as seen through the eyes of Christian theology. Surveys the role that antisemitism has played in Christian thought and suggests alternative models to demythologize Judaism. Includes an interesting Yom Ha´shoa liturgy for Christians.

7209. Michael, Robert: "Christian Theology and the Holocaust." Mid, vol.30 #4 (April, 1984): 6-9.

7210. Oestrreicher, J. M.: "Challenge of the Holocaust." America, vol.136 #23 (June 11, 1977): 525-527.

7211. Pawlikowski, John: The Challenge of the Holocaust for Christian Theology [New York: ADL, 1978]

7212. ___: "Christian Perspectives and Moral Implications." Friedlander: Ideology, pp.295-308.

7213. ___: "The Holocaust and Catholic Theology: Some Reflections." Shoa, vol.2 #1 ((Spr./Sum., 1980): 6-9.

7214. ___: Implications of the Holocaust for the Christian Churches." Grobman: Genocide, pp.410-418.

7215. Rausch, David A.: Legacy of Hatred: Christians Must Not Forget the Holocaust [Chicago: Moody Press, 1984]

7216. Ruether, Rosemary: "Antisemitism and Christian Theology." Fleischner: Auschwitz, pp.79-92.

7217. ___: "Christianity and Jewish-Christian Relations." Peck: Jews/Chr, pp.25-38.

7218. St. John, Robert: "Time for Christianity to Shed Prejudice." M&R, vol.5 #2 (Nov./Dec., 1979):3.

7219. Schlink, K. (A. and T. Wiener, transls): Israel, My Chosen People: A German Confession Before God and the Jews [London: Canterburry Press, 1963]

7220. Siirala, Aarne: "Reflections from a Luthern Perspective." Fleischner: Auschwitz, pp.135-148.

7221. Tracy, David: "Religious Values After the Holocaust: A Catholic View." Peck: Jews/Chr, pp.87-107.

7222. Van Buren, Paul M.: "Changes in Christian Theology." Friedlander: Ideology, pp.285-293.

MEMORIALIZATION AND COMMEMORATION

Yom Ha´shoa Commemoration

7223. Berenbaum, Michael: "On the Politics of Public Commemoration of the Holocaust." Shoa, vol.2 #3 (Fall/Win., 1981/82): 6-9, 37.

7224. Cain, Seymour: "Commemorating the Holocaust." Mid, vol.26 #4 (April, 1980): 23-25.

7225. Eckardt, Alice L.: "In Consideration of Christian Yom Hashoa Liturgies." Shoa, vol.1 #4 (Aug./Sept., 1979): 1-4.

7226. ___: "Yom Ha´Shoah Commandments: A Christian Declaration." Mid, vol.27 #4 (April, 1981): 37-41.

7227. Feinberg, Abraham L.: "Why We Must Never Forget...the 6,000,000." NJM, vol.73 #4 (Jan., 1959): 10-11.

7228. Grossman, Chaya: "Why We Must Not Forget." IH, vol.6 #10 (Dec., 1958): 11-13.

7229. Hammer, Robert A.: "Not to Mourn is Impossible." Con Jud, vol.25 #4 (Sum., 1971): 46-50.

7230. "Holocaust Remembrance in Local Communities." Shoa, vol.2 #3 (Fall/Win., 1981/1982): 17-22.

7231. "The Image of Remembrance." YVN, #2 (June, 1969/June, 1970): 4-7.

7232. Knox, I.: "The Holocaust: For Remembrance and for Kaddish." CM, vol.43 #4 (April, 1976): 12-14.

7233. Korman, Gerd: "Hunter and Hunted: The Holocaust Remembered." JH, vol.14 #1 (Spr., 1972): 6-8.

7234. Kubovy, Aryeh L.: "The Day of Remembrance Law." YVB, #4/5 (Oct., 1959): 2.

7235. Learsi, Rufus: "Lest We Forget: A Ritual of Remembrance." CW, vol.19 #7 (Feb. 18, 1952): 8-10.

7236. ___: "We Must Will to Remember." CW, vol.25 #7 (March 31, 1958): 8-9. * On remebering the Holocaust at the Seder table.

7237. Levin, Nora: "20th Anniversary of the Liberation." HM, vol.46 #8 (April, 1965): 7, 27, 29-30.

7238. Michel, Ernest W.: "We Must Remind the World." Shoa, vol.2 #3 (Fall/Win., 1981/82): 10-11.

7239. Schary, Dore: "The Pain Stays... Six Million Humans Died." ADL Bul, vol.29 #5 (May, 1972): 3-4.

7240. Shapiro, Morris: "For Yom Ha´shoah." Con Jud, vol.28 #3 (Spr., 1974): 57-59.

7241. Shashar, Michael: "Yom Hashoa: Heroism and the Holocaust." Recon, vol.39 #3 (April, 1973): 7-12.

7242. Shmulewitz, I. (H. Berliner-Fischthal, transl.): "Our Obligation to Remember." Yiddish, vol.1 #3 (Win., 1973/1974): 49-54.

7243. Smolar, Leivy: Lest We Forget: The Murder of the Six Million Jews of Europe [Washington, DC: Bnai Brith Youth Organization, 1973]

7244. Thornburgh, Dick: "Renewing Our Commitment." Littell: Education, pp.1-3.

7245. Weinroth, Aryeh: "To Remember, and Not to Forget..." IH, vol.2 #4 (April, 1954): 10-12.

7246. Wiesel, Elie: "Let Us Remember." J Digest, vol.25 #8 (April, 1980): 77-80.

7247. Zborowski, Eli: "Reflections on Yom Hashoa: Holocaust and Resistance Day." M&R, vol.2 #3 (April/May. 1976): 1, 3.

7248. ___: "Reflections on Yom Hashoa: Life in a World of Ironies." M&R, vol.3 #3 (March/April, 1977): 1, 12.

7249. ___: "Yom Hashoa: Renewal of Commitment." M&R, vol.4 #3 (March/April, 1978): 1, 10.

7250. ___: "Yom Hashoa: The Task That Lies Ahead." M&R, vol.5 #4 (March/April, 1979): 1, 10.

Speeches and Addresses

7251. Eisner, Jack P.: "The Genocide Bomb: The Holocaust Through the Eyes of a Survivor." Braham: Perspectives pp.149-163.

7252. Goldmann, Nahum: "The Lesson of Belsen." CW, vol.19 #33 (Dec. 15, 1952): 13-15.

7253. Katsh, Abraham I.: "Remember Not to Forget." J Sp, vol.32 #4 (April, 1967): 7-8.

7254. Kazin, Alfred: "Living with the Holocaust." Mid, vol. 16 #6 (June/July, 1970): 3-7.

7255. Kovner, Abba (R. Rass, transl.): "Once There Was a Shtetl." J Sp, vol.44 #4 (Win., 1979): 13-17.

7256. Michel, Ernst: "We Have Survived." J Digest, vol.27 #1 (Sept., 1981): 17-19.

7257. Reagan, Ronald: "The President´s Remarks for Yom Ha´ shoa." M&R, vol.7 #5 (May/June, 1981): 9.

7258. Rosensaft, Menachem Z.: "My Grandfather, a Presence." Mid, vol.22 #1 (Jan., 1976): 62-64.

7259. Saragat, Giuseppe: "The Duty to Remember." Poland, #3/139 (March, 1966): 17. * Memorial address by the President of Italy delivered in Auschwitz on October 16, 1965.

7260. Schappes, Morris U.: "Holocaust and Resistance." JCP, vol.11 #1 (Spr./Sum., 1980): 61-69.

7261. Schmidt, Helmut: "Kristallnacht: Recall of Crimes of the Past." M&R, vol.9 #1 (Sept./Oct., 1982): 12, 16. * Memorial address by the West German Chancellor.

7262. Sultanik, Kalman: "36 Years after Liberation." Mid, vol.27 #5 (May, 1981): 27-28.

7263. Wiesel, Elie: "Address of the Chairman of the Holocaust Commission." M&R, vol.7 #5 (May/June, 1981): 9.

7264. ___: Address of the Chairman of U.S. Holocaust Council." M&R, vol.8 #4/5 (May/June, 1982): 9, 13.

7265. ___: "Eichmann´s Victims and the Unheard Testimony." Com, vol.32 #6 (Dec., 1961): 510-516.

7266. ___: "For Some Measure of Humility." Sh´ma, vol.5 #100 (Oct. 31, 1975): 314-316.

7267. ___: "Holocaust Twenty-Five Years Later." HM, vol.52 #1 (Sept., 1970): 8-9, 42-43.

7268. ___: "A Plea for the Dead." HM, vol.50 #1 (Sept., 1968): 8-11.

7269. ___: "Statement to the President." Mid, vol.26 #1 (Jan., 1980): 27-28.

7270. ___: "To Remain Human in the Face of Inhumanity." J Digest, vol.17 #12 (Sept., 1972): 37-42.

7271. ___: "Words from a Witness." Con Jud, vol.21 #3 (Spr., 1967): 40-48.

7272. ___: "Words from a Witness who Survived." J Digest, vol.13 #8 (May, 1968): 27-30.

7273. Wolf, Kurt H.: "Exercise in Commemoration." JQ, vol.8 #2 (Spr., 1961): 14-17.

RETURN TO THE PLACES OF HORROR

Eastern Europe

7274. Benkler, Rafi: "Auschwitz Revisited." IH, vol.15 #5 (May/June, 1967): 12-16.

7275. Bikales, Gerda: "The Last Jew of Skierniewice." CM, vol.45 #8 (Dec., 1978): 6-9.

7276. Einhorn, Moses: "A Journey to Poland: Birkenau - The Land of Human Ashes." J Fo, vol.40 #2 (Feb., 1957): 25-27; #3 (March, 1957): 42-44.

7277. Fenster, Myron M.: "Return to Streslik." HM, vol.57 #5 (Jan., 1976): 14-17.

7278. Fuerst, Dorothy: "Summer in Auschwitz." M&R, vol.11 #2 (Nov./Dec., 1984): 7, 11.

7279. Grade, Hayim: "Revisiting the Ghetto." J Sp, vol.17 #2 (Feb., 1952): 16-21.

7280. Hart, Kitty: Return to Auschwitz [New York: Atheneum, 1983]

7281. Helmreich, William: "A Visit to Auschwitz." Chartock: Society, pp.226-227.

7282. Leff, Sylvia: "Encounter at Babi Yar." Moment, vol.8 #7 (July/Aug., 1983): 46-48.

7283. Levenberg, S.: "Anguish on the Sands of Babi Yar." J Observer, vol.25 #40 (Oct. 1, 1976): 14-15.

7284. Lewis, Philippa: "The Road to Babi Yar." J Digest, vol.15 #5 (Feb., 1970): 60-62.

7285. Lewis, Theodore N.: "Auschwitz Revisited." J Sp, vol.25 #2 (Feb., 1960): 19-22.

7286. Rosenthal, A. M.: "There is no News from Auschwitz." J Digest, vol.4 #7 (April, 1959): 30-32.

7287. Parker, Frank S.: "A Visit to Majdanek." Judaism, vol.25 #2 (Spr., 1976): 158-166.

7288. Schechtman, Joseph B.: " "A Visit to Babi Yar." Mid, vol.5 #4 (Aut., 1959): 49-57.

7289. Schenker, Jonathan: "Babi Yar Still Boils." J Digest, vol.24 #5 (Jan, 1979): 12-13.

7290. Wiesel, Elie: "40 Years After: Remembering Babi Yar." HM, vol.63 #1 (Aug./Sept., 1981): 14-15.

7291. Zvielli, Alexander: "Israelis Return to Auschwitz." HM, vol.59 #10 (June/July, 1978): 19, 32-33.

Western Europe

7292. Bearfield, Lev: "What Do You Say at Dachau?" HM, vol. 64 #8 (April, 1983): 14-15, 38-39.

7293. Bettelheim, Bruno: "Returning to Dachau: The Living and the Dead." Com, vol.21 #2 (Feb., 1956): 144-151.

7294. Dawidowicz, Lucy S.: "Belsen Remembered." Com, vol.41 #3 (March, 1966): 82-85. Also in Dawidowicz: Presence pp.289-297.

7295. Elkin, L.: "The Flowers that Bloom in Dachau." CBW, vol.36 #13 (Nov. 21, 1969): 8-10.

7296. Gersh, Gabriel: "Zone of Silence." CW, vol.23 #6 (Feb. 6, 1956): 6-7. * On Stutthof.

7297. Gilor, Dov: "Impressions from Dachau." M&R, vol.11 #3 (Jan./Feb., 1985): 6, 15.

7298. Halperin, I.: "Dachau: 1964." J Fr, vol.32 #1 (Jan., 1965): 25-27.

7299. Horwitz, Julius: "Dachau: 1955." Mid, vol.1 #1 (Aut., 1955): 2-4.

7300. Levenberg, S.: "My Visit to Belsen." JOMER, vol.24 #16 (April 18, 1975): 10-11.

7301. Levine, Herbert S.: "Munich Thirty Years Later." PT, vol.2 #3 (April, 1975): 31-35.

7302. Mork, Gordon: "Confronting the Past: A Visit to the Struthof-Natzwiller Concentration camp." Shofar, vol. 2 #2 (Win., 1984): 31-32.

7303. Prittie, Terence: "Dachau Revisited." CW, vol.22 #10 (March 7, 1955): 12-13.

7304. Robinson, Jacob: "Not Far from Munich." CBW, vol.38 #12 (Nov. 26, 1971): 9-11.

7305. Rosensaft, M. Z.: "The Mass Graves of Bergen-Belsen: Focus for Confrontation." JSS, vol.41 #2 (Spr., 1979): 155-186.

7306. Rosenthal, D.: "Thirty Years After the Liberation and Bergen-Belsen." J Fr, vol.42 #3 (March, 1975): 4-10.

7307. Spigelglass, L.: "An American Tourist Visits Dachau." CW, vol.30 #7 (April 1, 1963): 21-22.

7308. Wakin, E.: "Visit to a Munich Suburb." America, vol. 111 #10 (Sept. 5, 1964): 235-236.

7309. Werner, A.: "Return to Dachau: ´Not All the Perfumes of Arabia´." Com, vol.12 #6 (Dec., 1951): 542-545.

7310. Wiesel, Elie: "Remembrance at Bergen-Belsen." HM, vol.47 #1 (Sept., 1965): 9, 16.

7311. Wurtman, Richard J.: "Go to Dachau." J Digest, vol.2 #6 (March, 1957): 1-4.

7312. Zyd, Marian: "A Visit to Buchenwald." J Sp, vol.11 #1 (Nov., 1945): 21-23.

MONUMENTS

7313. Ainsztein, Reuben: "22 Years to Erect a Monument: The Meaning of Babi Yar." JOMER, vol.14 #40 (Oct. 1, 1965): 14-16.

7314. "Babi Yar Memorial: No Mention of Jews." JIEE, vol.3 #6 (May, 1967): 32-34.

7315. Cang, Joel: "An Appeal for the Dead: The Need to Preserve Monuments to the Jewish Past." J Digest, vol.12 #11 (Aug., 1967): 53-55.

7316. "For a Permanent British Memorial to the Victims of Nazism." JQ, vol.9 #2 (Spr., 1962): 15-17.

7317. Goldsmith, Samuel J.: "Laments in Stone: Monuments to the Catastrophe." J Digest, vol.6 #4 (Jan., 1961): 23-27.

7318. Iltis, Rudolf: "Unique Memorial to the Nazi Victims in Czechoslovakia." JQ, vol.8 #3 (Sum., 1961): 16.

7319. Klerr (Kleinlerer), E. D.: "A Monument of the (8,000) Martyrs (in Milan, Italy)." NJM, vol.62 #4 (Dec., 1947): 130, 158.

7320. Korey, William: "Babi Yar." Ch J Forum, vol.25 #3 (Spr., 1967): 187-190.

7321. ___: "A Monument for Babi Yar." ADL Bul, vol.23 #8 (Oct., 1966): 7-8.

7322. ___: "A Monument to Jewish Martyrdom: The Story of Babi Yar." J Digest, vol.13 #2 ((Nov., 1967): 9-13.

7323. Lapid, Mordecai (M. Z. Frank, transl.): "The Memorial at Rumbuli: A First-Hand Account from Soviet Russia." J Fr, vol.38 #6 (June, 1971): 10-19.

7324. "Monument to the Holocaust." ADL Bul, vol.39 #6 (June, 1982): 8-9. * On monument in New York City.

7325. Novitch, M.: "Memorial Monuments in the Concentration and Extermination Camps of Poland and Germany." YVB, #13 (Oct., 1963): 72-74.

7326. Rieth, A.: Momuments to the Vicitms of Tyranny [New York: F. A. Praeger, 1969]

7327. Shneiderman, S. L.: "The Monument Controversy." CBW, vol.32 #5 (March 1, 1965): 5-6.

7328. ___: "Remembering the Six Million, A Monument in Philadelphia." CBW, vol.31 #7 (April 13, 1964): 13-15,

7329. "Treblinka Memorial." JIEE, vol.3 #1 (Nov. 1964): 101-102.

7330. Zachwatowicz, Jan: "The International Memorial at Auschwitz. " Poland, #1/125 (Jan., 1965): 10-11, 20.

INSTITUTIONS

Anne Frank House

7331. Goldfarb, Jack: "Echoes from a Shrine: The Anne Frank House in Amsterdam." NJM, vol.75 #11 (June, 1961): 7-8.

7332. Koestler, F. A.: "The House of the Prince Canal." NJM, vol.83 #6 (Feb., 1969): 20, 22-23

The Arlosen Archives

7333. Arnsberg, Paul: "Where Numbers are Turned into Men." JOMER, vol.13 #41 (Oct. 9, 1964): 15-17.

7334. Baum, K.: "A Neglected Area." CW, vol.24 #21 (July 22, 1957): 5-6.

Amsterdam Jewish Museum

7335. Heidenfeld, W.: "Storehouse of Jewish Culture." J Affairs, vol.11 #6 (June 1956): 32-34.

Auschwitz Museum

7336. "Reserved and Subdued." Poland, #5/153 (May 1967): 3-5.

The Bergen-Belsen Memorial (Jerusalem)

7337. Ben Zvi, Moshe: "The Chamber of Horrors." J Horizon, vol.15 #9 (May, 1953): 11.

The Jewish Museum of Prague

7338. Iltis, Rudolf: "The Jewish Museum in Prague." J Sp, vol.28 #1 (Jan., 1963): 26-27.

7339. Shneiderman, S. L.: "Museum of a Lost Jewish World: Remnants of Prague." J Digest, vol.11 #11 (Aug., 1966): 61-65.

7340. Silbert, Harry A.: "The Prague Museum." J Layman, vol.21 #2 (Nov., 1946): 3-4.

Kibbutz Lohame Ha´getaot

7341. Freeden, Herbert: "The Village of Ghetto Fighters." J Affairs, vol.16 #6 (June, 1961): 23-25.

7342. Friedler, Yaacov: "Breaking Down Ghetto Walls." HM, vol.41 #1 (Sept., 1960): 10, 21.

The President´s Holocaust Commission (U.S.A.)

7343. Edelman, Lily: "In search of Memory: Journey with the President´s Commission on the Holocaust." ADL Bul, vol.36 #8 (Oct.,. 1979): 13-15.

7344. Foxman, Abraham H.: "A Mandate to Remember." ADL Bul, vol.36 #2/3 (March/April, 1979): 15.

7345. Zborowski, Eli: "President´s Commission: Establishing A Memorial Reflecting the Holocaust." M&R, vol.6 #1 (Sept./Oct., 1979): 7.

The Wiener Library

7346. J. L.: "In Re the Wiener Library." Menorah, vol.40 #1 (Spr., 1952): 117-121.

7347. Rabinowicz, Harry M.: "Archives of Nazi Crimes." J Digest, vol.15 #10 (July, 1970): 41-48.

7348. ___: "The Wiener Library, London." Ch J Forum, vol. 25 #2 (Win., 1966/1967): 129-135.

The World Gathering

7349. Gerson, A.: "The World Gathering of Jewish Holocaust Survivors: Notes of a Survivor´s Son." Mid, vol.28 #4 (April, 1982): 28-31.

7350. Holocaust: The Obligation to Remember [Washington, D.C.: The Washington Post, 1983]

7351. Lerner, Israel: "Lessons From World Gathering of Holcaust Survivors." J Ed, vol.49 #3 (Fall, 1981): 12-16.

7352. Mozes, Samuel R.: "The World Gathering of Jewish Holocaust Survivors." IH, vol.29 #1 (Jan./Feb., 1981): 12-15.

7353. Passow, Emilie S.: "Reflections on a Gathering." Mid, vol.31 #4 (April, 1985): 41-43.

Yad Vashem

7354. Dinur, Benzion: "Problems Confronting ´Yad Vashem´ in its Work of Research." YVS, vol.1 (1957): 7-30.

7355. Feinstein, Sara: "Yad Vashem: Lest We Forget." Recon, vol.28 #6 (May 4, 1962): 15-19

7356. Friedland, E.: " Remebrance and Redemption: The Story of Yad Vashem." Ch J Forum, vol.21 #4 (Sum., 1963): 286-290.

7357. "The Hall of Names." YVN, #1 (1969): 11-12.

7358. "Hans Habe on Yad Vashem." YVN, #3 (June, 1970/June, 1971):27-29.

7359. Heiman, Leo: "Yad Vashem: Tabernacle of Tears and Suffering." JH, vol.4 #1 (Sum., 1961): 12-15.

7360. Korinsky, Leibl: "The Ashes of the Jewish Fighters." Kowalski: Anthology, pp.628-630.

7361. Mann, Peggy: "The File of Mass Murder: A Visit to Yad Vashem." J Digest, vol.6 #10 (July, 1961): 37-40.

7362. "Memorial to the Unkown Jewish Martyr." J Affairs, vol.14 #4 (April, 1959): 33-34.

7363. Nadler, Eugenia: "So that it is not Forgotten: Reflection of Yad Vashem." M&R, vol.10 #5 (May/June, 1984): 6, 14.

7364. "New Museum Inaugurated at Yad Vashem." YVN, #4 (1973): 2-3.

7365. "Remembrance Day Assembly at Yad Vashem." YVN, #3 (June, 1970/June, 1971): 8-10.

7366. "Research At Yad Vashem." YVN, #3 (June, 1970/June, 1971): 17-18.

7367. "The Scientific Advisory Council of Yad Vashem." YVN, #1 (1969): 8, 10.

7368. Shenhabi, Mordehai: "Memorial to the 6 Million." IH, vol.2 #7 (Sept, 1954): 28-29.

7369. "Yad Vashem and the Diaspora." YVN, #2 (June, 1969/ June, 1970): 3, 15.

7370. "Yad Vashem Archives." YVN, #1 (1969): 10; #4 (1973): 13-15; #3 (June 1970/June 1971): 11-16.

7371. "The Yad Vashem Council." YVN, #1 (1969): 2-3.

7372. "Yad Vashem´s Research Activity." YVN, #1 (1969): 6-7.

7373. Zerubavel, J.: "The Controversy Around Yad Vashem." JQ, vol.6 #2 (Win., 1958/1959): 8-10.

7374. Zuroff, E.: "Travails of a Holocaust Professional." J Digest, vol. 24 #6 (Feb., 1979): 58-63.

7375. ___: "Yad Vashem: More than a Memorial, More than a Name." Shoa, vol.1 #3 (Win., 1979): 4-9.

YIVO

7376. Flakser, David: "YIVO: The Archives of a People." IH, vol.11 #2 (Feb., 1963): 20-22.

7377. Gilson, Estelle: "YIVO - Where Yiddish Scholarship Lives." PT, vol.4 #1 (Aut., 1976): 57-65.

Zydowski Institut Historyczny (Poland)

7378. Teitelbaum, Dora: "Visit to Warsaw Jewish Institute." J Life, vol. 7 #1 (Nov., 1952): 14-15.

7379. Wein, Abraham: "The Jewish Historical Institute in Warsaw." YVS, vol.8 (1970): 203-214.

TEACHING THE HOLOCAUST

7380. Arian, Philip: "Teaching the Holocaust." J Ed, vol. vol. 41 #4 (Fall, 1972): 41-66.

7381. ___: Zakhor [Chicago: Board of Jewish Educaton, 1972]

7382. "Attitudes of Youth to the Holocaust." YVN, #4 (1973): 19-22.

7383. Barnes, I. S.: "Stamps - A New Way of Studying the Holocaust." Mid, vol. 31 #4 (April, 1985): 44-45.

7384. Baron, Lawrence: "Teaching the Holocaust to Non-Jews." Shoa, vol.2 #2 (Spr., 1981): 14-15. Also in J Digest, vol. 26 #11 (July, 1981): 35-39.

7385. Bauminger, Aryeh: "Israel Youth and the European Catastrophe." YVB, #2 (Dec., 1962): 76-79.

7386. Bayfield, Tony: Churban, the Murder of the Jews of Europe [London: Michael Goulston, 1981]

7387. Bayme, Steven and J. Roberts: "Yeshiva University´s Summer Institute on Teaching the Holocaust." Shoa, vol.1 #3 (Win., 1979): 16-17.

7388. Ben-Horin, M.: "Teaching about the Holocaust." Recon, vol.27 #6 (May 5, 1961): 5-9.

7389. Bennett, Alan D.: "Toward a Holocaust Curriculum." J Ed, vol.43 #2 (Spr., 1974): 22-26.

7390. Berger, A. L.: "Academia and the Holocaust." Judaism, vol.31 #2 (Spr., 1982): 166-176.

7391. ___: "Reflections on Teaching the Holocaust: The American Setting." Shofar, vol.2 #2 (Win., 1984): 21-26.

7392. Blumberg, Herman J.: "Some Problems of Teaching the Holocaust." Recon, vol.34 #16 (Dec. 20, 1968): 13-20.

7393. Blumenthal, David R.: "On Teaching the Holocaust." Recon, vol.64 #2 (April, 1980): 12-18.

7394. Boyle, Kaye: Breaking the Silence [New York: Am. Jew. Committee, 1962]

7395. Brayer, M.: "Jewish and Psychological Factors in the Teaching of the Holocaust." Hirt: Issues, pp.19-26.

7396. Bronznick, Norman M.: "A Theological View of the Holocaust: A Traditional Approach for Traditional Jewish Education." J Ed, vol.42 #4 (Sum., 1973): 13-28.

7397. Carmon, Arye: "The Holocaust as an Educational Dilemma: To Humanize or to Dehumanize?" Forum, #41 (1981): 53-62.

7398. ___: "Holocaust Teaching in Israel." Shoa, vol.3 #2/3 (Fall/Win., 1982/1983): 22-25.

7399. ___: "Problems in Coping with the Holocaust: Experiences with Students in a Multi-National Program." Annals, #450 (July, 1980): 227-236.

7400. ___: "Teaching the Holocaust." J Fr, vol.47 #4 (April, 1980): 11-13.

7401. Chanover, Hyman (ed.): "Teaching and Commemorating the Holocaust." P/Rep, vol.25 #2 (Win., 1974): 1-20.

7402. Charny, Isaac W.: "Teaching the Violence of the Holocaust." J Ed, vol.38 #2 (March, 1968): 15-24.

7403. Cohen, M.: "Teaching the Holocaust in San Antonio." Shoa, vol.3 #2/3 (Fall/Win., 1982/1983): 16-17.

7404. Dachslager, Earl L.: "The Holocaust as a Subject." Sh´ma, vol.8 #141 (Nov. 11, 1977): 181-184.

7405. Davis, P.: "Lessons for Humanity: Teaching the Holocaust in New York City´s Public Schools." Moment, vol.3 #3 (Jan./Feb., 1978): 13-16.

7406. ___: "The New York City Holocaust Curriculum." Shoa, vol.1 #2 (Fall, 1978): 4-7.

7407. Dawidowicz, Lucy S.: "Some Counsels and Cautions in Teaching the Holocaust." Hirt: Issues, pp.33-35.

7408. Douglas, Donald M.: "Teaching the Holocaust - the Kansas Experience." Shoa, vol.1 #4 (1979): 17-18.

7409. Eckardt, Alice L.: "The ´Kingdom of Night´ in the Classroom." Shofar, vol.2 #2 (Win., 1984): 6-12.

7410. ___: "Syllabus - The Holocaust: Its History and Meaning." Shofar, vol.2 #2 (Win., 1984): 13-20.

7411. ___ and Roy Eckardt: "Studying the Holocaust Impact Today: Some Dilemmas of Language and Method." Judaism, vol.27 #2 (Spr., 1978): 222-232.

7412. Eliach, Yaffa: "Despair is Search of a Method." J Sp, vol. 42 #1 (Spr., 1977): 18-20.

7413. Feinstein, S.: "Journey Into the Holocaust." HM, vol. 54 #8 (April, 1973): 11, 38-40.

7414. Fleming, Gerald: "Germany 1933-1945." Eur Jud, vol.11 #1 (Win., 1976/1977): 9-12. * Teaching about nazism.

7415. French, Isaac: "Teaching the Tragic Events of Jewish History." J Ed, vol.34 #3 (Spr., 1964): 173-180.

7416. Friedenreich, F. and L. Rubin: Holocaust Education in Informal Settings: Program Resource Manual [New York: JWB and the Am. Assoc. for Jewish Education, 1981]

7417. Friedlander, Henry: On the Holocaust: A Critique of the Treatment of the Holocaust in History Textbooks [New York: Anti-Defamation League, 1972]

7418. ___: "Postscript: Toward a Methodology of Teaching About the Holocaust." Friedlander: Ideology, pp. 323-345.

7419. Friedman, Saul S.: "Teaching the Holocaust." J Fr, vol.39 #7 (July/Aug., 1972): 8-15.

7420. Friedman, Theodore: "Teaching About the Holocaust." ADL Bul, vol.37 #3 (March, 1980): 7-10.

7421. Furman, Harry: "Heir of the Holocaust." ADL Bul, vol. 41 #2 (Feb., 1984): 8-9, 11.

7422. Glicksman, Wm.: "Reactions of Jewish Youth in America to the Destruction of European Jewry." YVB, #14 (March, 1964); 53-58.

7423. ___: "Teaching the Shoa in Jewish Schools." J Ed, vol. 36 #3/4 (Spr./Sum., 1966): 174-178.

7424. Glynn, Mary T. and G. Bock: "American Youth and the Holocaust." Shoa, vol.3 #2-3 (Fall/Win., 1982/1983): 8-11.

7425. Goldhagen, Erich: "Propaganda in Education." Shoa, vol.3 #2/3 (Fall/Win., 1982/1983): 31-32.

7426. Greenberg, Martin and Marie Grieco: The Third Reich in Perspective [New York: ADL, 1973]

7427. Guri, Sara and Naama Sabar: "The Effect of Teaching a Special Holocaust Curriculum: An Assessment of Cognitive and Affective Changes." J Ed, vol.48 #3 (Fall, 1980): 27-39.

7428. Gutman, Y.: "Teaching the Catastrophe." Dispersion, #3 (Win., 1964): 132-138.

7429. ___: "Teaching the Holocaust." IH, vol.14 #4 (April, 1966): 12-19.

7430. Haberer, Rose: "Teaching About the Holocaust in the Community." Shofar, vol.2 #2 (Win., 1984): 33-34.

7431. Halperin, Irving: "Reflections on Teaching the Holocaust." Judaism, vol.24 #3 (Sum., 1975): 339-347.

7432. Hausdorff, Henry and I. Kuperstein: "The Holocaust in Holocaust Education." Shoa, vol.3 #2/3 (Fall/Win., 1982/1983): 12-15, 21.

7433. Helmreich, William B.: "How Jewish Students View the Holocaust: A Preliminary Appraisal." Response, vol.9 #1 (Spr., 1975): 101-114.

7434. ___: "Making the Awful Meaningful." Society, vol.19 #6 (Sept/Oct., 1982): 62-66.

7435. Hirt, Robert S. and Thomas Kessner (eds.): Issues In Teaching the Holocaust: A Guide [New York: Yeshiva Univ. Press, 1981]

Anthology of papers from Yeshiva University's Summer Institute for Teaching the Holocaust held in 1978 and 1980. Aimed at bringing the Holocaust out of history and into the classroom.

7436. Holocaust Curriculum for Jewish Schools [New York: The Jewish Education Service of North America, 1981]

7437. Jacob, Walter: "On Teaching the Holocaust." JRJ, vol.31 #1 (Win., 1984): 81-85.

7438. Kalfus, Richard: "Culture During the Nazi Era: An Interdisciplinary Course in the College." Shoa, vol.2 #2 (Spr., 1981): 16-18.

7439. Kane, Leslie and J. Friedman (comps.): Resistance: Jewish Ghetto Fighters and Partisans in Central Eastern Europe. Teachers Manual [New York: Board of Jewish Education and YIVO, 1976]

7440. Kaufner, Neal: "An Inquiry Model as a Focus for Teaching the Holocaust." J Ed, vol.44 #3/4 (Spr./Sum., 1976): 31-34.

7441. Korman, Gerd: "Silence in the American Textbooks." YVS, vol.8 (1970): 183-202.

7442. Krefetz, Gerald: "Nazism: The Textbook Treatment." CBW, vol.28 #16 (Nov. 13, 1961): 5-7.

7443. Lamm, Norman: "Teaching the Holocaust." Forum, #24 (1976): 51-60. Also in Hirt: Issues, pp.5-18.

7444. Lampert, Suzy: "How Students Perceive the Holocaust." Mid, vol.30 #4 (April, 1984): 29-31.

7445. Levine, J. H.: "Teaching the Holocaust Ecumenically." Sh'ma, vol.8 #159 (Sept. 29, 1978): 179-180.

7446. Lewis, Judith S.: "A Graded Curriculum for the Holocaust." M&R, vol.10 #4 (Jan./Feb., 1984): 12, vol.10 #5 (March/April, 1984): 4, 15.

7447. Libowitz, Richard: "On Teaching the Holocaust to Non-Jews." Recon, vol.41 #5 (June, 1975): 20-23.

7448. Littell, Marcia S. (ed.): Holocaust Education: A Resource Book for Teachers and Professional Leaders [New York: Edwin Mellen Press, 1985]

7449. Littell, F. H.: "Fundamentals in Holocaust Studies." Annals, #450 (July, 1980): 213-217.

7450. ___: "The Future of Holocaust Education." Littell: Education, pp.5-12.

7451. Maller, Allen S.: "The Shoa and Its Teaching." CCARJ, vol.16 #3 (June, 1969): 61-66.

7452. Marianska, Miriam: "How Today´s Youth Regard the History of the European Catastrophe." YVB, #12 (Dec., 1962): 72-76.

7453. Matteoni, Louis: "Why Teach the Holocaust." J Ed, vol.49 #2 (Sum., 1981): 4-7. Also in J Digest, vol.27 #6 (Feb., 1972): 71-75.

7454. Meisel, E.: "The Use of Literature in the Teaching of the Holocaust: Suggestions for the Secondary School Classroom." Shoa, vol.2 #1 (Spr./Sum., 1980): 26-30.

7455. Muffs, Judith H.: "Teaching about the Holocaust." ADL Bul, vol.33 #9 (Sept., 1976): 1, 8. Also in J Digest, vol.22 #7 (March, 1977): 38-40.

7456. ___: "U.S. Teaching on the Holocaust." PoP, vol.11 #3 (May/June, 1977): 28-29.

7457. Nadel, Max and S. Frost: "Teaching the Holocaust in the Jewish School." J Ed, vol.49 #1 (Sept., 1981): 30-33.

7458. Netzer, Shlomo: "Educating Israeli Youth Towards a Consciousness of Holocaust Experience." M&R, vol.6 #5 (May/June, 1980): 13-14.

7459. Pate, G. S.: The Treatment of the Holocaust in United States History Textbooks [New York: ADL, 1980]

7460. Pawlikowski, John T.: "The Holocaust and Catholic Education." Shoa, vol.3 #2/3 (Fall/Win., 1982/1983): 18-20.

7461. Pilch, J. et al: "Symposium: The Shoah and the Jewish School." *J Ed*, vol.34 #3 (Spr., 1964): 162-172.

7462. Post, Albert: *The Holocaust: A Case Study of Genocide* [New York: Experimental Edition for the New York City Public Schools, 1973]

7463. ___: "Teaching the Holocaust - A Mini-Guide." *The Principal*, vol.24 #7 (March, 1979): 7-23.

7464. Quenzer, W.: "Young Germans´ View of Auschwitz." *PoP*, vol.14 #4 (Oct., 1980): 10-17.

7465. Rabinsky, Leatrice and Gertrude Mann: *Journey of Conscience: Young People Respond to the Holocaust* [New York: William Collins, 1979]

7466. Raphael, Marc L.: "Yom Ha´shoah and Holocaust Education in an Israeli High School." *Shoa*, vol.2 #2 (Spr., 1981): 12-13.

7467. *The Record: The Holocaust in History, 1933-1945* [New York: Anti-Defamation League, 1978]

7468. Redlich, Simon: "Israeli Pupils on the Lesson of the Eichmann Trial." *YVB*, #12 (Dec., 1962): 68-69.

7469. Rosenberg, Alan with A. Bardosh: "The Problematic Character of Teaching the Holocaust." *Shoa*, vol.3 #2/3 (Fall/Win., 1982/1983): 3-7, 20.

7470. Rosenfeld, Max: "Parents´ Corner: Presenting the Holocaust to Teenagers." *J Currents*, vol.20 #4 (April, 1966): 27-29.

7471. Roskies, David and Diane K. Roskies: *Teaching the Holocaust to Children* [New York: Ktav, 1975]

7472. Ross, Robert W.: "The Nazi Persecution of the Jews and the Holocaust." *Shofar*, vol.2 #2 (Win., 1984): 27-31.

7473. Roth, John K.: "Difficulties Everywhere: Sober Reflections on Teaching About the Holocaust." *Shoa*, vol.1 #2 (Fall, 1978): 1-3.

7474. Salz, Bob: "Towards a Framework for Teaching the Holocaust." *Response*, vol.9 #1 (Spr., 1975): 75-82.

7475. Schatzker, Ch.: "Formation vs. Information: Trends in Holocaust Education in Israel." Forum, #30/31 (Spr./Sum., 1978): 135-141.

7476. ___: "The Teaching of the Holocaust: Dilemmas and Considerations." Annals, #450 (July, 1980): 218-226.

7477. Schechter, Jay and Al Zachter (Comps): The Holocaust: A Study of Genocide [New York: Board of Education, Division of Curriculum and Instruction, 1977]

Comprehensive curriculum guide to the Holocaust written for use in New York City public schools. Part One contains a series of lesson plans for the course; Part Two, an anthology of sources for classroom use. Includes extensive bibliography.

7478. "Schools Perpetuate the Memory of Jewish Communities." YVN, #3 (June, 1970/June, 1971): 21-22.

7479. Shilav, Yaakov: "A Turning Point in the Teaching of the Heroism and the Holocaust: A Survey." YVB, #12 (Dec., 1962): 57-62.

7480. Siegel, Danny: "Showing Holocaust Slides: Questions and Answers and Doubts." NJM, vol.95 #5 (Jan., 1981): 10-14.

7481. Silverberg, D.: "Studying and Teaching the Holocaust." PT, vol.6 #3 (Spr., 1979): 43-47.

7482. Spicehandler, Arnold: "Teaching the Holocaust." Mid, vol.26 #4 (April, 1980): 37-39.

7483. Syrkin, Marie: "The Teaching of the Holocaust." Mid, vol.31 #2 (Feb., 1985): 47-49.

7484. Toubin, Isaac: "How to Teach the Shoah." Con Jud, vol.18 #4 (Sum., 1964): 22-26.

7485. Ury, Zalman and Irwin Sorff: An Outline for Teaching the Shoa [Los Angeles: Board of Jewish Ed., 1966]

7486. ___: Teaching the Shoah: The Destruction of European Jewry [Los Angeles: Bureau of Jewish Education, 1963]
* Papers from the Summer Institute for Teachers and Principals held in Los Angeles, August, 1963.

7487. What the High School Students Say: A Survey of Attitudes and Knowledge About Jews and Nazism [New York: Anti-Defamation League, 1961]

7488. Yerushalmi, E.: "A Model Lesson on the Catastrophe." YVB, #12 (Dec., 1962): 62-67.

7489. Zamichow, A.: "Holocaust Curriculum in a Yeshiva." M&R, vol.9 #3 (Jan./Feb., 1983): 11, 12.

7490. Zornberg, I.: Classroom Strategies for Teaching About the Holocaust: Ten Lessons for Classroom Use [New York: Anti-Defamation League, 1982]

REFLECTIONS ON PAST AND FUTURE

Historical Reflections

7491. Aronsfeld, C. C.: "The November Pogrom, 1938 - Half Way to the Final Solution." JOMER, vol.17 #45 (Nov. 8, 1968): 14-15.

7492. Bauer, Yehuda: "The Holocaust Redefined." IH, vol.28 #5/6 (May/June, 1980): 44-45.

7493. ___ et al: "Was the Holocaust Unique? Responses to Pierre Papazin." Mid, vol.30 #4 (April, 1984): 19-25. <see #7511>

7494. Ben-Horin, Meir: "Annihilism: Reflections on the Nazi Holocaust." J Sp, vol.33 #10 (Dec., 1968): 12-15.

7495. Eban, Abba: The Final Solution: Reflection on the Tragedy of European Jewry [London: The Council of Christians and Jews, 1961] * Robert Whaley Cohen Memorial Lecture, 1961.

7496. Eck, Nathan: "Jewish Heroism in Israel and in Countries of the Holocaust." YVB, #22 (May. 1968): 3-8.

7497. Feingold, Henry L.: "German Jewry and the American Jewish Condition: A View from Weimar." Judaism, vol. 20 #1 (Win., 1971): 108-119. Also in J Digest, vol. 17 #4 (Jan., 1972): 1-10.

7498. ___: "How Unique Is the Holocaust?" Grobman: Genocide pp.397-401.

7499. Grobman, Alex: "Approaching Genocide and the Holocaust." Grobman: *Genocide*, pp.3-5.

7500. Hahn-Cohn, Miriam: "Thoughts on ´Kristallnacht´." *Sh´ma*, vol.15 #291 (April 5, 1985): 84-85.

7501. Hilberg, Raul: "The Occurrence Is Past: The Phenomenon Remains." Chartock: *Society*, pp.282-284.

7502. __: "The Significance of the Holocaust." Friedlander: *Ideology*, pp.95-102.

7503. Kahn, Lothar: "The Holocaust: Missed Opportunities." *J Sp*, vol.48 #1 (Spr., 1983): 13-15.

7504. Katz, Steven T.: "The Unique Intentionality of the Holocaust." *MJ*, vol.1 #2 (Sept., 1981): 161-183.

7505. Kirschenbaum, Mira: "Levels of the Holocaust." *M&R*, vol.11 #3 (Jan./Feb., 1985): 7, 8.

7506. Korey, William: "Babi Yar Remembered." *Mid*, vol.15 #3 (March, 1969): 24-39.

7507. ___: "The Silent Screams of Babi Yar." *HM*, vol.58 #5 (Jan., 1977): 12-13, 36-39.

7508. Kren, George M.: *The Holocaust and the Crisis of Human Behavior* [New York: Holmes & Meier, 1980]

7509. Landes, Daniel: "The Holocaust and Israel." Grobman: *Genocide*, pp.422-431.

7510. Laqueur, Walter Z.: "The View from the Reichstag: 50 Years Ago Adolf Hitler Glided Into Power." *New Republic*, vol.188 #6 (Feb. 14, 1983): 13-14, 16-18.

7511. Papazian, Pierre: "A ´Unique Uniqueness´?" *Mid*, vol. 30 #4 (April, 1984): 14-18. <see #7493>

7512. Robinson, Nehemiah: "Hitler - 25 Years After." *CW*, vol.25 #3 (Feb. 3, 1958): 7-8.

7513. ___: "Twenty Years Ago." *CBW*, vol.26 #14 (Sept. 21, 1959): 7-8.

7514. Rosenberg, Alan: "The Genocidal Universe: A Framework for Understanding the Holocaust." Eur Jud, vol.13 #1 (Aut., 1979): 29-34. Also in Porter: Genocide, pp.46-58.

7515. Russell, Edward F. L.: "Germany: Yesterday, Today and Tomorrow." Mid, vol.3 #4 (Aut., 1957): 5-14.

7516. Schorsch, Ismar: "Historical Reflections on the Holocaust." Con Jud, vol.31 #1 (Fall/Win., 1976/1977): 26-33.

7517. Talmon, Ya´acov L.: "Prophetism and Ideology: The Jewish Presence in History." Jer Q, #3 (Spr., 1977): 3-16.

7518. Werner, Alfred: "Twenty Years After." J Sp, vol.18 #2 (Feb., 1953): 21-24.

7519. Zohn, H.: "Twenty-Five Years After the Book Burning." J Fo, vol.41 #9 (Sept., 1958): 140-143.

Implications and Lessons

7520. Askenasy, Hans: Are We All Nazis? [Secaucus, NJ: Lyle Stuart, 1978]

7521. Ball-Kaduri, Kurt J.: "What is Not Preserved in the Archives." YVB, #1 (April. 1957): 26-27.

7522. Bemporad, Jack: "The Concept of Man After Auschwitz." Friedlander: Whirlwind, 477-487.

7523. Benavie, Barbara S.: "The Holocaust: Something for Everybody." Forum, #40 (1980/1981): 89-92.

7524. Berenbaum, Michael: "The Holocaust as Commandment." Sh´ma, vol.9 #180 (Nov. 2, 1979): 165-166.

7525. ___: "Lessons of the Holocaust are All-Important." NJM, vol.95 #2 (Oct., 1980): 9-13.

7526. Berkovits, Eliezer: "A Strategy for the Galut." J Sp, vol.12 #6 (April, 1947): 11-13.

7527. Berman, Aaron et al: Thinking About the Unthinkable: An Encounter with the Holocaust [Amherst, MA: Social Science Division, Hampshire College, 1972]

7528. Blumenthal, D. R.: "In the Shadow of the Holocaust." *J Sp*, vol.46 #4 (Win., 1981): 11-14.

7529. Boyd, Malcolm: "Will There be Another Holocaust?" *J Digest*, vol.20 #5 (Feb., 1975): 3-6.

7530. Crawford, Fred R.: "The Holocaust: A Never-Ending Agony." *Annals*, #450 (July, 1980): 250-255.

7531. Dawidowicz, Lucy S.: *The Jewish Presence* [New York: Holt, Rinehart and Winston, 1977]

7532. Ebel, Julia: "The Holocaust, a Time for Silence." *Sh´ma*, vol.3 #56 (Sept. 7, 1973): 123-124.

7533. Eckardt, Alice L.: "Bystanders? Resisters? Killers? Which Category is Ours? Biomedical Issues After the Holocaust." Ryan: *Responses*, pp.239-259.

7534. Efroymson, Sharon: "Do Israeli and Diaspora Responses to Holocaust Differ?" *J Digest*, vol.27 #1 (Sept., 1981): 20-24.

7535. Eliach, Yaffa: "The Holocaust as Obligation and Excuse." *Sh´ma*, vol.9 #181 (Nov. 16, 1979): 1-3.

7536. Eller, Lisa A.: "Facing the Holocaust, Finding Ourselves." *Sh´ma*, vol.7 #133 (April 29, 1977): 105-107.

7537. Fackenheim, Emil L.: "The Holocaust and the State of Israel: Their Relation." Fleischner: *Auschwitz*, pp. 205-215. * Responses by: Seymour Siegel, pp.217-223; Eva Fleischner, pp.225-235.

7538. Fein, Leonard (ed.): "The Valley of Death, the Armies of Life." *Moment*, vol.6 #9 (Oct., 1981): 13-24.

7539. Fever, M.: "From Generation to Generation." Littell: *Education*, pp.103-105.

7540. Fiorenza, E. S. and D. Tracy (eds.): *Holocaust as Event of Interruption* [Philadelphia: Concilium Books/ Fortress Press, 1985]

7541. Flescher, Joachim: *Nazi Holocaust and Mankind´s Final Solution* [New York: D. T. R. B. Editions, 1971] * On the necessity to learn the lessons of the Holocaust.

7542. Fromm, Erich: The Heart of Man: The Genius of Good and Evil [New York: Harper & Row, 1964]

7543. Goldsmith, S. J.: "After Belsen and Dachau." Mid, vol.31 #4 (April, 1985): 37-39.

7544. Grossman, Frances G.: "The Holocaust: Beyond Understanding and Yet Must be Understood." IH, vol.27 #8 (Sept., 1979): 14-15.

7545. Grossmann, Kurt R.: "The Problem of Remembering." CBW, vol.26 #5 (March 2, 1959): 9-11.

7546. Halperin, Irving: "Israel, the Holocaust and the Survivors." Recon, vol.32 #5 (April 15, 1966): 17-24.

7547. Hausner, Gideon: "Can It Happen Again." NJM, vol.76 #10 (June, 1962): 10, 34.

7548. Katzew, Henry: "How Could It Have Happened." J Sp, vol.15 #11 (Nov., 1950): 15-17.

7549. Kazin, A.: "Living with the Holocaust." J Digest, vol.18 #9 (June, 1973): 64-70.

7550. Kirschner, R.: "The Yoke of Auschwitz." J Sp, vol.41 #3 (Fall, 1976): 51-53.

7551. Legters, Lyman H. (ed.): Western Society After the Holocaust [Boulder, CO: Westview Press, 1983]

7552. Levin, N.: "Life Over Death." CBW, vol.40 #8 (May 18, 1973): 22-23.

7553. Levine, Hillel (ed.): "The Meaning and Demeaning of the Holocaust." Moment, vol.6 #3/4 (March/April, 1981): 29-35.

7554. Lifton, Robert J.: "Witnessing Survival." Society, vol.15 #3 (March/April, 1978): 40-44.

7555. Lipstadt, Deborah: "The Holocaust: Symbol and Myth in American Jewish Life." Forum, #40 (1980/1981): 73-86.

7556. Littell, F. H.: "The Credibility Crisis of the Modern University." Friedlander: Ideology, pp.271-283.

7557. Manowitz, Rosalyn: Reflections on the Holocaust [New York: Hebrew Tabernacle Congregation of Washington Heights, 1978]

7558. Merti, Betty: Understanding the Holocaust [Portland, ME: J. Weston Walch, 1982]

7559. Nachman, Larry D.: "Reflections on the Holocaust." Recon, vol.41 #10 (Jan., 1976): 13-18.

7560. Neher, Andre (D. Maisel, transl.): Exile of the Word: From the Silence of the Bible to the Silence of Auschwitz [Philadelphia: J. P. S., 1980]

7561. Neusner, Jacob: "Holocaust Primer." National Review, vol.31 #31 (Aug. 3, 1979): 975-979.

7562. ___: The Jewish War Against the Jews: Reflections on Golah, Shoa, and Torah [New York: Ktav, 1984]

7563. ___: Stranger at Home: The Holocaust, Zionism and American Judaism [Chicago: Univ. of Chicago Press, 1981]

7564. ___: "Wanted: A New Myth." Moment, vol.5 #3 (March, 1980): 34-36, 61. * On Holocaust and State of Israel.

7565. Norich, Samuel: "The Legacy of Rebirth." J Fr, vol.49 #1 (Jan., 1982): 9-11.

7566. Ozick, Cynthia: "A Liberal's Auschwitz." J Digest, vol.21 #2 (Nov., 1975): 18-21.

7567. Petuchowski, Jacob J.: "Dissenting Thoughts About the Holocaust." JRJ, vol.28 #4 (Fall, 1981): 1-9. Also in J Digest, vol.27 #7 (March, 1982): 18-25.

7568. Ranz, John: "The Relevance of the Holocaust: Misconceptions and Truths." IH, vol.25 #10 (Fall/Win., 1977): 23-26.

7569. Not Used.

7570. Rosensaft, Menahem: "The Holocaust: History as Aberration." Mid, vol.23 #5 (May, 1977): 53-55.

7571. Rosenthal, A. M.: "Forgive Them Not, For They Knew What They Did." Friedlander: Whirlwind, pp.451-457.

7572. Rotenstreich, Nathan: "The Individual and Personal Responsibility." YVS, vol.5 (1963): 17-34.

7573. Rubenstein, R. L.: "Anticipations of the Holocaust in the Political Sociology of Max Weber." Legters: Western, pp.165-183. Comments: G. Zahn, pp.184-187; E. Roth, pp.187-190. Rejoinder: pp.190-196.

7574. Sandler, Robert: "Could A Holocaust Happen Again?" J Sp, vol.47 #2 (Sum., 1982): 34-37.

7575. Schorsch, Ismar: "The Holocaust and Jewish Survival." Mid, vol.27 #1 (Jan., 1981): 38-42. Also in J Digest, vol.26 #8 (April, 1981): 37-46.

7576. Schulweis, Harold: "The Bias Against Man." J Ed, vol. 34 #1 (Fall, 1963): 6-14.

7577. ___: "The Holocaust Dybbuk." Moment, vol.1 #7 (Feb., 1976): 36-41.

7578. Schwarzbart, Isaac: Remembering and Rebuilding [New York: World Jewish Congress, 1955]

7579. Seeliger, R.: "Witness to a Recent Past?" J Affairs, vol.16 #9 (Sept., 1961): 35-36.

7580. Shelhav, Yaacov: "The Holocaust in the Consciousness of Our Generation." YVB, #3 (April, 1958): 2-4, 14.

7581. Silverman, David W.: "The Holocaust: A Living Force." Con Jud, vol.31 #1 (Fall/Win., 1976/1977): 26-33.

7582. Steinitz, Lucy and David Szonyi: Living After the Holocaust: Reflections by the Post-War Generation in America [New York: Bloch Pub. House, 1976]

7583. Strom, M. S. and Wm. S. Parsons: Facing History and Ourselves: Holocaust and Human Behavior [Watertown, MA: Intentional Educations, 1982]

7584. Syrkin, Marie: The State of the Jews: An Evolving Account of the Jewish Experience Since the Holocaust [New York: Herzl Press, 1980]

7585. Tubin, Yehuda: "The Lessons of the Nazi Catastrophe." IH, vol.13 #8 (Oct., 1965): 10-14.

7586. Weinberg, Berthold: "The Meaning of Jewish Existence: In Memory of the Martyred of our People." Recon, vol. 26 #4 (April 1, 1960): 8-11.

7587. Whitfield, Stephen J.: "The Holocaust and the American Jewish Intellectual." Judaism, vol.28 #4 (Fall, 1979): 391-401. Also in J Digest, vol.27 #3 (Nov., 1981): 22-31.

7588. Wiesel, Elie (L. Edelman, transl.): One Generation After [New York: Random House, 1970]

7589. ___ et al: Dimensions of the Holocaust [Evanston, IL: Northwestern Univ. Press, 1977]

7590. Wolf, Arnold J.: "The Centrality of the Holocaust is a Mistake." NJM, vol.95 #2 (Oct., 1980): 9, 14-17.

7591. ___: "The Holocaust as Temptation." Sh´ma, vol.9 #180 (Nov. 2, 1979): 162-165.

7592. Yaffe, Richard: "Coming to Grips with the Holocaust." IH, vol.23 #3/4 (March/April, 1975): 5-10.

7593. ___: "The Nazi was Wrong: the Ghetto Lives." IH, vol. 21 #4/5 (May/June, 1973): 12-15.

Survivors´Reflections

7594. Amery, Jean (Sidney and S. P. Rosenfeld, transls.): At the Mind´s Limits: Contemplations by a Survivor on Auschwitz and its Realities [Bloomington, IN: Indiana Univ. Press, 1980]

7595. Donat, Alexander: "A Letter to My Grandson." Mid, vol.16 #6 (June/July, 1970): 41-45.

7596. Dworzecki, Mark: "Confession of a Survivor." J Fr, vol.12 #10 (Oct., 1945): 7-10.

7597. Not Used.

7598. Hertzberg, Arthur: "A Generation Later." Mid, vol.16 #6 (June/July, 1970): 8-13.

7599. Kline, Dana L.: The Holocaust: Survivors Remember [Storrs, CT: Univ. of Connecticut - Center for Judaic Studies, 1983]

7600. Kovner, Abba: "The Mission of the Survivors." Gutman: Catastrophe, pp.671-683.

7601. Kuznestov, Anatoly: "Dina Mironovna Pronichev Remembers Babi Yar." NY Times Mag, (Dec. 11, 1966): 45, 164-176.

7602. Levi, Primo: "After Thirty Years." JQ, vol.24 #1/2 (Spr./Sum., 1976): 39-40.

7603. Lunati-Marmor, Elizabeth (A. Sinai, transl): "To a Mother Who is No More: A Mother´s Day Letter." J Digest, vol.11 #8 (May, 1966): 14-16.

7604. Rosensaft, M. Z.: "After Three Decades: More Reflections on the Holocaust." JQ, vol.20 #1 (Spr., 1972): 18-19.

7605. Scharf, Rafael: "After Thirty Years: Reflections on the ´Age of Auschwitz´." JQ, vol.23 #3 (Aut., 1975): 31-34.

7606. Soifer, Paul E.: "Remembrance and the Victim´s Covenant." Recon, vol.46 #2 (April, 1980): 19-22.

7607. Weinberg, Werner: "On Being a Survivor." Ch Century, vol.98 #12 (April 8, 1981): 378-383.

7608. Wells, Leon W.: "I Do Not Say Kaddish." Con Jud, vol. 31 #4 (Sum., 1977): 3-6.

7609. Werner, A.: "From Boxheimer to Majdanek: A Warning from the Past." Today, vol.1 #7 (May/June, 1945): 14-16, 28.

7610. Wiesel, Elie: "An Appointment with Hate." Com, vol.34 #6 (Dec., 1962): 470-476. Also in J Digest, vol.8 #8 (May, 1963): 41-49.

7611. ___: "A House of Strangers." PT, vol.5 #4 (Sum., 1978): 25-26.

7612. ___: "Rethinking Swallowed-Up Worlds." Ch Century, vol.98 #19 (May 27, 1980): 609-612.

16

Europe After World War II

WAR CRIME TRIALS

The Pursuit of Justice

7613. Ainsztein, Reuben: "Is This Justice?" JOMER, vol.14 #15 (April 9, 1965): 16, 18.

7614. Baker, Jack: "Amnesty for Nazis." ADL Bul, vol.22 #1 (Jan., 1965): 3, 8. * On statute of limitation.

7615. Baum, Phil: "Time and War Crimes." CW, vol.35 #13 (Nov. 25, 1968): 4-5.

7616. Brand, E.: "Material from Trials of War Criminals in West Germany Sent to Yad Vashem." YVB, #14 (March, 1964): 58-62.

7617. ___: "Nazi Criminals on Trial in the Soviet Union (1961-1965)." YVB, #19 (Oct., 1966): 36-44.

7618. ___: "Prosecution of Nazi Criminals in West Germany, Austria and East Germany 1965-1966." YVB, #20 (April, 1967): 14-28.

7619. Brook-Shepherd, G.: "The Pursuit of Guilt: Germany's Final Roundup of War Criminals." Atlantic, vol.214 #3 (Sept., 1964): 76-80.

7620. Cherner, L.: "Why Punish War Criminals?" Ort Eco Rev, vol.4 #4 (June, 1945): 16-23.

7621. "A German Government Report on the Prosecution of Nazi War Criminals, 1945-1969." PoP, vol.5 #2 (March/April, 1971): 15-18.

7622. Glueck, Sheldon: "Justice for War Criminals (Through the United Nations). Against Leaving the Punishment to the Germans Themselves." Am Mercury, vol.60 #255 (March, 1945): 274-280.

7623. Goldstein, Anatole: "Forgotten Pledge." CW, vol.15 #24 (Sept. 17, 1948): 11-12.

7624. Grossmann, Kurt R.: "Germany´s Moral Crossroads." CW, vol.32 #4 (Feb. 15, 1965): 5-7.

7625. Gruber-Michaels, Ruth: "Germany: War-Crime Trials Continue." HM, vol.48 #6 (Feb., 1967): 4-5.

7626. Hellendall, F.: "Nazi Crimes Before German Courts - The Immediate Post-War Era." WLB, vol.24 #3 (Sum., 1970): 14-20.

7627. Hudes, Ted: "Crime Without Punishment - Nazi Killers and Kindly Courts." Am Zionist, vol.56 #6 (Feb., 1966): 21-23.

7628. Jackson, Robert H.: "The Jewish Case Against the Nazis." J Sp, vol.11 #5 (March, 1946): 7-10.

7629. Jaworski, Leon: After Fifteen Years [Houston, TX: Gulf Publishing Company, 1961]

7630. Kempner, Robert M.: "Cross-Examining War Criminals." YVS, vol.5 (1963): 43-68.

7631. Kent, G.: "200,000 Persecutions Prevented." Reader´s Digest, vol.82 #491 (March, 1963): 169-175.

7632. Kilgore, H. M.: "Punishing the War Criminals: What is the Problem?" Today, vol.1 #6 (April, 1945): 3-5.

7633. Langbein, H.: "Trials Without Echo." YVB, #19 (Oct., 1966): 52-57.

7634. Levai, Eugene (Jeno): "The War Crimes Trials Relating to Hungary." HJS, vol.2 (1969): 252-296.

7635. ___: "The War Crimes Trials Relating to Hungary: A Follow-Up." HJS, vol.3 (1973): 251-290.

7636. Litvin, J.: "The Guilty Men: Call for an International Tribunal." JQ, vol.12 #2 (Sum., 1964): 9-13.

7637. Marcus, Robert S.: "Nazi Crimes to Be Remembered." CW, vol.15 #29 (Nov. 22, 1948): 10-13.

7638. ___: "Why Nazis Go Free." CW, vol.15 #27 (Nov. 8, 1948): 5-7.

7639. Martin, James S.: All Honorable Men [Boston: Little, Brown, 1950]

7640. May, Michael: "Nazi War Criminals: The Search and the Legal Process Continue." IJA Res Rep, #4 (March, 1983): 1-14.

7641. ___: "Trials of Nazi War Criminals: Has Justice Been Done?" IJA Res Rep, #12 (Aug., 1981): 1-11.

7642. Mushkat, Marion: "The Concept ´Crime Against the Jewish People´ in the Light of International Law." YVS, vol.5 (1961): 237-254.

7643. Ormond, Henry: "Nazi Crime and German Law." WLB, vol. 21 #1 (Win., 1966/1967): 16-21.

7644. Perlzweig, Maurice L.: "The Guilty Must Not Escape!" Today, vol.1 #6 (April, 1945): 6-8.

7645. ___: "Is Murder a Crime?" WJC/ASB, #7 (Oct., 1945): 2-5.

7646. Pilichowski, C.: No Time-Limit for These Crimes [Warsaw: Interpress Publishers, 1980]

7647. Reitlinger, Gerald: "Postscript to the War Trials." JQ, vol.1 #3 (Win., 1954): 9-17.

7648. Rosenthal, D.: "The Statute of Limitations and the War Crimes in Germany." J Fr, vol.46 #3 (March, 1979): 18-20.

7649. Rueckerl, Adalbert (D. Rutter, transl.): The Investigation on Nazi Crimes, 1945-1978: A Documentation [Hamden, CT: Archon Books, 1980]

7650. Ryan, Allan A. Jr.: "Attitudes Toward the Prosecution of Nazi War Criminals in the United States." Braham: Contemporary, pp.201-226.

7651. Spiegler, S.: "Difficulties in Prosecuting Nazi War Criminals." JJCS, vol.56 #1 (Fall, 1979): 110-111.

7652. Werner, Alfred: "Hitler's Apostles: Let Their Crimes be Remembered!" Today, vol.1 #8 (July/Aug., 1945): 20-22, 29.

The Nuremberg Trials

7653. Alexander, Ch. and A. Keeshan: Justice At Nuremberg: A Pictorial Record of the Trial of Nazi War Criminals by the International Tribunal at Nuremberg, Germany, 1945-1946 [New York: Marvel Press, 1946]

7654. Andrus, B. C. and Zwar Desmond: I Was the Nuremberg Jailer [New York: Coward McCann, 1969]

7655. Benton, Wilbourn and Georg Grimm (eds.): Nuremberg: German Views of the War Trials [Dallas, TX: Southern Methodist Univ. Press, 1955]

7656. Bernays, Murray C.: "Legal Basis of the Nuremberg Trials." Survey Graphic, vol.35 #1 (Jan., 1946): 5-9.

7657. ___: "Nuremberg." Survey Graphic, vol.35 #11 (Nov., 1946): 390-391.

7658. Bernstein, Victor H.: Final Judgment: The Story of Nuremberg [New York: Boni & Gaer, 1947]

Eyewitness account, originaly published in 1947, of the Nuremberg trials. Details Nazi crimes and the punishment meted out by the International Military Tribunal. Reprinted as The Holocaust: Final Judgment [Indianapolis, IN: Bobbs-Merrill, 1980]

7659. Biddis, Michael: "The Nuremberg Trial: Two Exercises in Judgment." JCH, vol.16 #3 (July, 1981): 597-615.

7660. Bosch, Wm. J.: Judgment at Nuremberg [Chapel Hill: Univ. of North Carolina Press, 1970]

7661. Conot, Robert E.: Justice at Nuremberg [New York: Harper & Row, 1983]

Comprehensive account of the International Military Tribunals held in Nuremberg. The book is also an investigation, using the evidence from the trials, into the inner life of the Third Reich.

7662. Cooper, R. W.: The Nuremberg Trial [London: Penguin Books, 1947]

7663. Davidson, E.: The Trial of the Germans: An Account of 22 Defendants before the International Military Tribunal at Nuremberg [New York: Macmillan, 1967]

7664. Doman, N.: "Political Consequences of the Nuremberg Trial." Annals, #246 (July, 1946): 81-90.

7665. Ecer, B.: "Lessons of the Nuremberg Trial." CEO, vol. 24 #5 (March 21, 1947): 70-71; #7 (April 18, 1947): 103-105.

7666. Ehrenburg, Ilya: "Evil at Nuremberg." Am Heb, vol.155 #35 (Dec. 28, 1945): 2, 10, 14-15.

7667. Fandlik, V.: "The Verdict of the Nuremberg Tribunal." CEO, vol.30 #21 (Oct. 11, 1946): 325-326.

7668. Fishman, Jack: The Seven Men of Spandau [New York: Reinhart, 1954]

7669. Friedlander, Henry: "Nuremberg and Other Trials." Grobman: Genocide, pp.381-383.

7670. Galagher, Richard: Nuremberg: The Third Reich on Trial [New York: Avon Books, 1961]

7671. Gide, Marjan: "Nuremberg Story." Furrows, vol.1 #6 (May, 1946): 18-21.

7672. Gilbert, G. M.: Nuremberg Diary [New York: New American Library, 1961]

7673. Goldbloom, Maurice J.: "War Crimes." AJYB, vol.49 (1947/1948): 580-590.

7674. ___: "War Crimes Trials." AJYB, vol.50 (1948/1949): 494-500.

7675. Goldsmith, S. J.: "Thirty Years after Nuremberg." JQ, vol.24 #3 (Aut., 1976): 42-43.

7676. Goldstein, Anatole: "Nuremberg: A Fair Trial." CW, vol.13 #26 (Nov. 1, 1946): 5-7.

7677. ___: "Nuremberg Will Serve Justice." CW, vol.13 #12 (March 22, 1946): 7-9.

7678. Gringauz, Samuel: "Ten Years After Nuremberg." J Sp, vol.21 #6 (June, 1956): 15-18.

7679. Halpern, Ben: "The Nuremberg Trial." J Fr, vol.13 #1 (Jan., 1946): 30-32.

7680. Harris, Whitney R.: Tyranny on Trial: The Evidence of Nuremberg [Dallas: Southern Methodist Univ. Press, 1954]

7681. Heydecker, G. A. and J. Leeb (E. A. Downie, transl.): The Nuremberg Trial [Cleveland: World Pub., 1962]

Extensive history of Nazi Germany based on the evidence collected at the Nuremberg trials. Deals also with the trials themselves and with the issue of Nazi and Soviet war crimes. The extermination of the Jews is covered on pp. 327-358.

7682. Hilu, Nathan: "My Memoirs as a G.I. Guard in the Nuremberg Prison: Observations of a Jewish Soldier." J Currents, vol.24 #4 (April, 1970): 5-11, 30-32; #5 (May, 1970): 14-23.

7683. International Military Tribunal: The Trial of German Major Criminals by the International Military Tribunal Sitting in Nuremberg: Opening Speeches of the Chief Prosecutors [London: HMSO, 1946/1951]

7684. ___: The Trial of the German Major War Criminals: Proceedings of the International Military Tribunal Sitting at Nuremberg, Germany [London: HMSO, 1946/1951] * Red Series, 23 vols.

7685. ___: Trial of the Major War Criminals before the International Military Tribunal: The Official Text [Nuremberg: International Military Tribunal, 1947/1949] * Blue Series, 42 vols.

7686. Jackson, R. H.: The Case Against the Nazi Criminals [New York: A. A. Knopf, 1946]

7687. ___: The Nuremberg Case and Other Documents [New York: A. A. Knopf, 1947]

7688. Jacoby, Gerhard: "The Verdict of Nuremberg." J Fr, vol.13 #11 (Nov., 1946): 32-35.

7689. Jones, Elwyn: "Judgement on Nuremberg." WJ, vol.15 #1 (Feb., 1972): 10-13. Also in J Digest, vol.7 #9 (June, 1972): 6-10.

7690. Kahn, Leo: "The Nuremberg Trials." Chartock: Society, pp.212-220.

7691. Keegan, John: "The Men in the Dock." Hist/WWII, #117 (1974): 3263-3270.

7692. Konvitz, Milton R.: "Will Nuremberg Serve Justice?" Com, vol.1 #3 (Jan., 1946): 9-15.

7693. Lasby, C. G.: Project Paperclip [New York: Atheneum, 1971]

7694. Lunau, Heinz: The Germans on Trial [New York: Storm Publishers, 1948]

7695. Manvell, R. and H. Fraenkel: "The Nuremberg Trial." Hist/WWII, #117 (1974): 3249-3251, 3254-3262.

7696. Martin, George S.: "Epilogue at Nuremberg." FW, vol. 12 #3 (Oct., 1946): 23-25.

7697. Maser, Werner: Nuremberg: A Nation on Trial [London: Allen Lane, 1979]

7698. Mushkat, M.: "Twenty Years After Nuremberg." YVB, #21 (Nov., 1967): 3-10.

7699. Musmanno, M. A.: "War-Criminal Trials." Ch J Forum, vol.18 #1 (Fall, 1959): 10-13.

7700. Nash, Arnold: "The Nuremberg Trials." Ch Century, vol.63 #46 (Sept. 25, 1946): 1148-1150.

7701. Nazi Conspiracy and Aggression [Washington, DC: U.S. Government Printing Office, 1946/1947] * 10 vols.

7702. Neave, Airey: On Trial at Nuremberg [Boston: Little, Brown, and Company, 1978]

7703. Oasksey (Justice), Lawrence: "The Nuremberg Trial." Int Affairs, vol.23 #2 (April, 1947): 151-159.

7704. Orren, Isaac: "The Nuremberg Trial." YVS, vol.5 (1961): 387-404.

7705. Perlzweig, Maurice L.: "The Trial of War Criminals: A Comment on Justice Jackson´s Report." J Affairs, vol. 5 #4 (Sept., 1945): 3-4.

7706. Pheleger, H.: "Nuremberg: A Fair Trial?" Atlantic, vol.177 #4 (April, 1946): 232-233.

7707. Poltorak, A. (D. Skvirsky, transl.): The Nuremberg Epilogue [Moscow: Progress Publishers, 1971]

7708. Radin, Max: "Justice at Nuremberg." F Affairs, vol.24 #3 (April, 1946): 369-384.

7709. Robinson, Jacob: "The Jewish Tragedy in Nuremberg." HM, vol.26 #8 (Dec., 1946): 9-11, 30.

7710. ___: "The Nuremberg Judgment." CW, vol.13 #25 (Oct. 25, 1946): 6-8.

7711. Sawicki, Jerzy: "Twenty Years After the Nuremberg Verdict." Poland, #4/152 (April, 1967): 4, 36.

7712. Settel, Arthur: "Seven Nazis Were Hanged: The Diary of a Witness." Com, vol.29 #5 (May, 1960): 369-379.

7713. Smith, Bradley F.: Reaching Judgment at Nuremberg [New York: Basic Books, 1977]

7714. ___: The Road to Nuremberg [New York: Basic Books, 1980]

7715. Stein, Leo: "The Meaning of Nuremberg." NJM, vol.60 #4 (Dec., 1945): 126-127.

7716. Stimson, Henry L.: "The Nuremberg Trial, Landmark in Law." F Affairs, vol.15 #2 (Jan., 1947): 179-189.

7717. Strahan, Charles: "Finale in Nuremberg." CEO, vol.23 #19 (Sept. 13, 1946): 297-298.

7718. Taylor, Telford: "The Legality of the Trials." Hist/WWII, #117 (1974): 3273-3276.

7719-7733. Trials of War Criminals before the Nuremberg Military Tribunals under Control Council Law # 10 15 vols. [Washington, DC: United States Gov't Printing Office, 1949/1952]

1. The Medical Case
2. The Medical Case (cont.) The Milch Case
3. The Justice Case
4. The Einsatzgruppen Case; The RUSHA Case
5. The RUSHA Case (cont.) The Pohl Case
6. The Flick Case
7-8. The I. G. Farben Case
9. The Krupp Case
10. The High Command Case
11. The High Command Case (cont.) The Hostage Case
12-14. The Ministries Case
15. Procedure, Practice and Administration

7734. Tusa, Ann and John Tusa: The Nuremberg Trial [New York: Atheneum, 1984]

7735. "Twenty Five Years After the Nuremberg Trials." YVN, #3 (June 1970/June 1971): 5-7.

7736. United Nations War Crimes Commission: Law Reports of Trials of War Criminals [London: HMSO, 1947/1949]

7737. von Knierim, August: The Nuremberg Trials [Chicago: H. Regnery, 1959]

7738. Walm, Nora: "Crime and Punishment." Atlantic, vol.177 #1 (Jan., 1946): 43-47.

7739. Walsh, William F.: "The Evidence at Nuremberg." CW, vol.13 #9 (March 1, 1946): 13-14.

7740. Werner, Alfred: "The Murderers' Defense." CW, vol.12 #34 (Nov. 23, 1945): 7-9.

7741. Wolfe, Robert: "Putative Threat to National Security as a Nuremberg Defense for Genocide." Annals, #450 (July, 1980): 46-67.

7742. Wright, Quincy: "The Nuremberg Trial." Annals, #246 (July, 1946): 72-80.

7743. Woetzel, Robert K.: The Nuremberg Trials in International Law [New York: F. A. Praeger, 1962]

7744. Wyzanski, Charles E., Jr.: "Nuremberg in Retrospect." Atlantic, vol.178 #6 (Dec., 1946): 56-59.

The Camp Trials

Auschwitz

7745. Arnsberg, Paul: "Deceptive Calm at Frankfurt Trial." JOMER, vol.13 #1 (Jan. 3, 1964): 22-23.

7746. Beigel, Greta: "The Auschwitz Trial in the World Press." IH, vol.14 32 (Feb., 1966): 24-28.

7747. Brand, Emanuel: "The Auschwitz Trial: An Evaluation." Dispersion, #5/6 (Spr., 1966): 161-171.

7748. ___: "Trials of Auschwitz Hangmen Held from the End of the War Until Now." YVB, #15 (Aug., 1964): 43-47.

7749. Elovitz, Mark H.: "Reflections on Auschwitz." J Sp, vol.32 #4 (April, 1967): 18-21. * The Trial of Auschwitz guards.

7750. Gordy, Michel: "Echoes from Auschwitz." New Republic, vol.117 #25 (Dec. 22, 1947): 14-15.

7751. Kulka, E.: "Photography as Evidence in the Frankfurt Court." YVB, #17 (Dec., 1965): 56-58.

7752. Lindquist, Irmela and J. J. Shapiro: "The Auschwitz Trial and the Absence of Nemesis." Recon, vol.30 #10 (June 6, 1964): 7-14.

7753. Naumann, Bernard (J. Steinberg, transl): Auschwitz: A Report on the Proceedings Against R. K. L. Mulka and Others Before the Court at Frankfurt [New York: F. A. Praeger, 1966]

7754. Shneiderman, S. L.: "Auschwitz Trial in Frankfurt." CBW, vol.31 #1 (Jan. 13, 1964): 8, 13.

7755. Weiss-Rosmarin, Trude: "Auschwitz Mass Murderers." J Sp, vol.29 #2 (Feb., 1964): 3.

7756. Wilchek, S.: "A Little Trial in Frankfurt." PT, vol.7 #3 (Spr., 1980): 46-50.

Majdanek

7757. Bemier, L.: "The Majdanek Trial: A Witness Who Would Not be Cowed." HM, vol.61 #4 (Dec., 1979): 18-19.

7758. Friedler, Y.: "Light Sentences for Nazi Camp Guards." J Digest, vol.27 #1 (Sept., 1981): 33-35.

7759. Reiss, Frank: "The Majdanek Trial: A Personal Assessment." ADL Bul, vol.27 #1 (Sept., 1981): 3-4. Also in J Digest, vol.27 #1 (Sept., 1981): 30-32.

Other Places of Horror

7760. Brand, E.: "The Lesson of the Treblinka Trial." YVB, #17 (Dec., 1965): 49-53.

7761. Kintner, Earl W.: The Hadamar Trial: Trial of Alfons Klein (and Others) [London: Hodge, 1949]

7762. Land, Thomas: "Exterminator of Treblinka: The Trial of a Dutiful Man." Nation, vol.211 #11 (Oct. 12, 1970): 339-340. * On camp commandant Franz Stangl.

7763. Pechersky, Alex.: "West Germany Tries Sobibor Nazis: Revolt Leader's Impassioned Appeal." JOMER, vol.15 #79 (July 22, 1966): 13-14.

7764. Phillips, Raymond (ed.): The Belsen Trial: Trial of Joseph Kramer and Forty-Four Others [London: Hodge, 1949]

7765. Rodney, C. M.: "The Trial of Sachsenhausen." CEO, vol. 24 #21 (Nov. 14, 1947): 329-330.

7766. Webb, A. M.: The Natzweiler Trial [London: Hodge, 1949]

Institutional Cases

7767. Dubois, Josiah E.: Generals in Grey Suits: The Directors of the I. G. Farben Cartel. Their Conspiracy and Trial at Nuremberg [London: The Bodley Head, 1953]

7768. "The End of I. G. Farben." CEO, vol.22 #21 (Nov. 16, 1945): 339-340.

7769. Goldstein, Anatole: "From Madagascar to Auschwitz." CW, vol.15 #19 (May 21, 1948): 5-7. * The Ministries case.

7770. Grossmann, K. R.: "Killing the Hydra-Headed Serpent." CW, vol.17 #25 (Oct. 16, 1950): 9-11. * The I. G. Farben case.

7771. Marcus, Robert S.: "The Greatest Murder Trial in History." CW, vol.15 #18 (May 14, 1948): 5-7. * The Einsatzgruppen case.

7772. ___: "Murder by Diplomacy." CW, vol.16 #19 (May 23, 1949): 5-9. * The Ministries case.

Individual Cases

7773. Ainsztein, Reuben: "The Bandera-Oberlander Case." Mid, vol.6 #2 (Spr., 1960): 17-25.

7774. "The Butcher Listens." Life, vol.36 #10 (March 8, 1954): 41-42. * On SS General Karl Oberg.

7775. "Casebook on Oberlander." JOMER, vol.9 #8 (Feb. 19, 1960): 15-17.

7776. Gersh, Gabriel: "Trial of a Nazi." J Digest, vol.4 #6 (March, 1959): 9-10. * On Wolfgang Heller.

7777. Goldstein, Anatole: "The Germans Learn Fast." CW, vol. 19 #13 (March 31, 1952): 8-9. * On Franz Rademacher.

7778. Grossmann, Kurt R.: "The Case Against Dr. Clauberg." CW, vol.23 #1 (Jan. 2, 1956): 8-9.

7779. ___: "The Trial of Ilse Koch." CW, vol.17 #34 (Dec. 18, 1950): 7-9.

7780. Gruber-Michaelis, Ruth: "Austrian Justice - After a Fashion." CW, vol.33 #17 (Dec. 19, 1966): 14-16. * On the Maurer brothers case.

7781. Kwaterko, A.: "Trial of the Ghetto´s Executioner." J Life, vol.5 #12 (Oct., 1951): 22-24. * On Juergen Stroop.

7782. Mayer, R.: "Last Words of Colonel Walter Gierecke." Ch J Forum, vol.8 #1 (Fall, 1949): 44-49.

7783. Reitlinger, Gerald: "Last of the War Criminals: The Mystery of Erich Koch." Com, vol.27 #1 (Jan., 1959): 30-42.

7784. Thompson, H. K. Jr. and Henry Strutz (eds.): Doenitz At Nuremberg: A Re-Appraisal [New York: Amber Pub., 1976]

DENAZIFICATION

Allied Occupation and Denazification

7785. Bach, Julian: America's Germany: An Account of the Occupation [New York: Random House, 1946]

7786. Botting, D.: From the Ruins of the Reich: Germany, 1945-1949 [New York: Crown Pub., 1985]

Study of the immediate impact of the collapse of the Nazi regime. The author surveys the occupation of Germany from the end of the war until 1949. Apologetic from the viewpoint of the Germans. Overuses the term genocide in categorizing the supposed harshness of the Allied occupation.

7787. Bower, Tom: The Pledge Betrayed: America and Britain and the Denazification of Postwar Germany [Garden City, NY: Doubleday, 1982] Also published as: Blind Eye to Murder: America & the Purging of Nazi Germany. A Pledge Betrayed [London: Andre Deutsch, 1981]

Chronicles the failures of the Allied policy of denazification. American and British administrators employed former Nazis to carry out the denazification programs, thereby undercutting and making a shambles of the entire program. An unsettling and well documented book.

7788. FitzGibbon, Constantine: Denazification [London: M. Joseph, 1969]

7789. Gedye, G. E. R.: "Austria: Rebuilding of a Volcano. Progress Report, with Reservations." Com, vol.7 #2 (Feb., 1949): 140-145.

7790. Greenstein, Harry: "A Prophet with Honor in His Own Country." J Digest, vol.12 #7 (April, 1967): 29-34.

7791. Joesten, Joachim: Germany: What Now? [Chicago: Ziff-Davis Pub., 1948]

Analysis of the social, political, and economic conditions in postwar Germany. Also includes considerable background material on Nazi Germany. Sees a reconstituted Germany as a potential obstacle to world peace.

7792. Kimbal, W. F.: Swords or Plowshears: The Morgenthau Plan for Defeated Germany, 1943-1946 [Philadelphia: Lippincott, 1976]

7793. Liddell, Helen: "Education in Occupied Germany." Int Affairs, vol.24 #1 (Jan., 1948): 30-62.

7794. Not Used.

7795. Marshal, Barbara: "German Attitudes to British Military Government, 1945-1947." JCH, vol.15 #4 (Oct., 1980): 655-684.

7796. Merritt, Anna J. and R. L. Merritt (eds.): Public Opinion in Occupied Germany: The OMGUS Surveys, 1945-1949 [Urbana: Univ. of Illinois Press, 1970]

7797. Morgenthau, H. Jr.: "Postwar Treatment of Germany." Annals, #246 (July, 1946): 125-129.

7798. Neumann, Franz L.: "Re-Educating the Germans." Com, vol.3 #6 (June, 1957): 508-516.

7799. Schmidt, Hans (ed.): U.S. Occupation in Europe After World War II [Lawrence, KS: Regents Press, 1978]

7800. Tent, James F.: Mission on the Rhine: Reeducation and Denazification in American Occupied Germany [Chicago: Univ. of Chicago Press, 1982]

7801. Viner, Jacob: "The Treatment of Germany." FW, vol.23 #4 (July, 1945): 567-581.

7802. Ziemke, Earl F.: The U.S. Army in the Occupation of Germany 1944-1946 [Washington, DC: USGPO, 1975]

7803. Zink, Harold: "The American Denazification Program in Germany." JCEA, vol.6 #3 (Oct., 1946): 227-240.

7804. ___: American Military Government in Germany [New York: Macmillan, 1947]

Evaluating the Denazification

7805. Allemann, F. R.: "Will History Repeat Itself in Germany?" Com, vol.19 #3 (March, 1955): 217-224.

7806. Arendt, Hannah: "The Aftermath of Nazi Rule: Report from Germany." Com, vol.10 #4 (Oct., 1950): 342-353.

7807. Clarion, Nicolas: "Does Democracy Need Nazi Partners? The Dangerous Course of Our German Reconstruction." Com, vol.7 #4 (April, 1949): 309-318.

7808. Dulles, Allen: "Alternatives for Germany." F Affairs, vol.25 #3 (April, 1947): 421-432.

7809. Edinger, D.: "A Glimpse Into the German Mind." Recon, vol.15 #10 (June 24, 1949): 23-29.

7810. Goldman, Frank: "The Failure of Denazification." NJM, vol.64 #11 (July/Aug., 1950): 394-397.

7811. Lendvai, P.: "The New Austria and the Old Nazis." Com, vol.44 #3 (Sept., 1967): 81-88.

7812. Mason, Edward S.: "Has Our Policy in Germany Failed?" F Affairs, vol.24 #4 (July, 1946): 579-590.

7813. Mushkat, Marion: "New Trends in ´Rehabilitating´ Nazi War Criminals." YVB, #16 (Feb., 1965): 26-33.

7814. Prittie, Terence: "How New is the New Germany." Com, vol.19 #6 (June, 1955): 513-521.

7815. Schoenbaum, D.: "Nazi Murders and German Politics." Com, vol.39 #6 (June, 1965): 72-77.

7816. Warburg, Gustav: "Know Your Germans." JM, vol.5 #6 (Sept., 1951): 334-338.

Establishing German War Guilt

7817. Goldstein, Anatole: "German Guilt." CW, vol.15 #8 (Feb. 27, 1948): 6-9.

7818. Jaspers, Karl (E. B. Ashton, transl.): The Question of German Guilt [New York: Dial Press, 1947]

7819. Massing, Paul W.: "Is Every German Guilty?" Com, vol. 3 #5 (May, 1947): 442-446.

7820. Themel, Uri: "The Sins of the Fathers." Dimensions, vol.1 #1 (Spr., 1967): 33-34.

NEO-NAZISM/NEO-ANTISEMITISM

The Emergence of Neo-Nazism

7821. Anglo-Jewish Association (eds.): Germany´s New Nazis [London: Jewish Chronicle Publications, 1951]

7822. Eisenberg, Dennis: The Re-emergence of Fascism [New York: A. S. Barnes, 1967]

7823. Ellerin, Milton and Samuel Rabinove: "Does Neo-Nazism Have a Future?" Mid, vol.29 #8 (Oct., 1983): 7-12.

7824. Hirschmann, Ira A.: The Embers Still Burn [New York: Simon and Schuster, 1949] * Eyewitness view.

7825. Jaeger, H.: Reappearence of the Swastika: Neo-Nazism and Fascist International [London: Gamma Pub., 1960]

7826. Mandellaub, Max: "Fascists at Work in Liberated Europe." FW, vol.10 #4 (Oct., 1945): 47-50.

7827. Oesterreicher, John M.: "The Swastika Reappears." Bridge, vol.4 (1962): 344-352.

7828. Purcell, J. Q.: "The New Right Promotes Neo-Nazi Ideology." J Digest, vol.16 #9 (June, 1971): 12-16.

7829. Riedelsperger, Max E.: The Lingering Shadow of Nazism [New York: Columbia Univ. Press, 1978]

7830. Tilton, T. A.: Nazism, Neo-Nazism and the Peasantry [Bloomington: Indiana Univ. Press, 1975]

7831. Werner, Alfred: "Hitler Isn´t Dead." J Sp, vol.17 #1 (Jan., 1952): 13-15.

7832. Wilkinson, Paul: The New Fascists [London: PAN, 1983]

Reviews the rise of neo-nazism in Western Europe and the United States. Includes useful information on a variety of movements and personalities. Also discusses distortion and denial of the Holocaust by neo-Nazi groups. More controversial is his discussion of "Israeli fascism", especially his comments about Rabbi Meyer Kahane.

Neo-Nazism in Germany/Austria

7833. Aronsfeld, C. C.: "Right Wing Over Germany." J Fr, vol.35 #4 (April, 1968): 18-19.

7834. Baum, Phil and C. Weisbrod: "Austria´s Lingering Shadows." CBW, vol.33 #12 (Sept. 12, 1966): Special Issue.

7835. Bernstein, Philip S.: "Is Germany Going Nazi Again?" Recon, vol.16 #3 (March 24, 1950): 10-18.

7836. Bernstein, Victor H.: "Unser Kameraden." IH, vol.3 #1 (Nov./Dec., 1954): 4-5, 27.

7837. Broch, Nathan: "The Plague of Swastikas." J Digest, vol.5 #5 (Feb., 1960): 73-76.

7838. Clark, Delbert: Again the Goose Step: The Lost Fruit of Victory [Indianapolis, IN: Bobbs-Merrill, 1949]

7839. Emmet, Christopher and Norbert Muhlen: The Vanishing Swastika: Facts and Figures on Nazism in West Germany [Chicago: H. Regnery Company, 1961]

7840. Grossman, Kurt R.: "Return of Hitler´s ´Wolves´." CW, vol.24 #18 (May 20, 1957): 4-7.

7841. Hindels, Josef: "Unmasking the NPD." J Digest, vol.14 #11 (Aug., 1969): 51-52.

7842. Knutter, H. H.: "Nation Europa - A Mouthpiece of the Fascist International." WLB, vol.17 #1 (Jan., 1963): 8-9.

7843. Long, W.: The New Nazis of Germany [Philadelphia: Chilton Books, 1968]

7844. Marcus, Robert S.: "Neo-Nazism in Austria." CW, vol. 17 #12 (March 20, 1950): 5-7.

7845. Montagu, Ivor: Germany´s New Nazis [London: Panther Books, 1967]

7846. Roth, S. J.: "How Popular is Neo-Nazism in West Germany?" IJA Res Rep, #6 (May, 1981): 1-12.

7847. Russell, Edward F. L.: Return of the Swastika: The Rising Threat of Resurgent Nazism in Germany [New York: David Mckay, 1969]

Beginning with 1945 the author reviews the ominous signs of a Nazi resurgence in Germany. Writing in the mid-sixties the author could not possibly have predicted the revival of Nazi, Fascist, and quasi-Fascist parties in recent years. His analysis still bears study, especially in light of its appreciation of the threat.

7848. Seidman, Hillel: "Der Fuehrer Trained Them, Der Alte Retains Them." J Fo, vol.45 #2 (Feb., 1962): 8-11.

7849. Snyder, Louis: "Nazism Resurgent: What Should Be Done About It?" Menorah, vol.40 #1 (Spr., 1952): 37-54.

7850. Straus, Nathan: "The Nazis Have Already Returned to Bonn." J Currents, vol.13 #7 (July/Aug., 1959): 7-10.

7851. Tetens, T. H.: The New Germany and the Old Nazis [New York: Random House, 1961]

7852. von Salomon, E. (C. FitzGibbon, transl.): The Answers to the 131 Questions in the Allied Military Government Fragebogen [New York: G. P. Putnam´s Sons, 1954]

7853. ___: Fragebogen, the Questionnaire [Garden City, NY: Doubleday, 1954]

7854. Werner, Alfred: "Postwar Nazism." CW, vol.15 #20 (May 28, 1948): 9-11.

7855. ___: "A Shocking Tale." CW, vol.22 #2 (Jan. 10, 1955): 5-8. * Essay on the Fragebogen.

Neo-Nazism in France

7856. Field, F.: "Peguy on the Jews." WLB, vol.23 #2/3 (Spr./Sum., 1968): 71-77.

7857. Hanan, Ben: "Poujade: Danger to France and Israel." IH, vol.4 #3 (Feb., 1956): 25-27.

7858. Kamai, Z.: "Poujade - The Enigma of Europe." J Fr, vol.23 #2 (Feb., 1956): 8-10.

7859. Lambert, David: "The Poujade Menace in France." CW, vol.23 #9 (Feb. 27, 1956): 6-8.

7860. ___: "The Truth About Poujade." J Digest, vol.1 #10 (July, 1956): 1-5.

7861. Puner, Morton: "What About Poujade?" ADL Bul, vol.13 #2 (Feb., 1956): 1-4.

Neo-Nazism in the United States

7862. Ellerin, Milton: The American Nazis [New York: Am. Jewish Congress, 1974]

7863. ___: "American Nazis: Myth or Menace?" J Digest, vol. 23 #11 (July/Aug., 1978): 83-92.

7864. Hamlin, David: The Nazi/Skokie Conflict: A Civil Liberties Battle [Boston: Beacon Press, 1980]

7865. Mann, T. R.: "The Nazis and the First Amendment." CM, vol.45 #2 (Feb., 1978): 6-9.

7866. Porter, Jack N.: "What Happens when Nazis are Elected to U. S. Office?" Porter: Confronting, pp.119-121.

Neo-Nazism and National Bolshevism

7867. Agursky, Mikhail: "Russian Neo-Nazism - A Growing Threat." Mid, vol.22 #2 (Feb., 1976): 35-42.

7868. Du Broff, S.: "The Nazi Role of East Germany." Am Zionist, vol.65 #4 (Dec., 1974): 25-27.

7869. Fabian, Bela: "Hungary´s and Rumania´s Nazis-in-Red." Com, vol.11 #5 (May, 1951): 470-474.

7870. Fried, J.: "The Truth About Communist Antisemitism." Ortho J Life, vol.23 #3 (Jan./Feb., 1956): 13-21.

7871. Korey, Wm: The Soviet Cage: Antisemitism in Russia [New York: Viking Press, 1973]

7872. Kovacs, Janos: "Neo-Antisemitism in Hungary." JSS, vol.8 #3 (July, 1946): 147-160.

7873. Meyer, Peter: "Soviet Antisemitism in High Gear." Com, vol.15 #2 (Feb., 1953): 115-120.

7874. Muhlen, N.: "The New Nazis of Germany: The Totalitarians of the Eastern Zone." Com, vol.11 #1 (Jan., 1951): 1-10.

7875. Schapiro, Leonard B.: "Antisemitism in the Communist World." SJA, vol.9 #1 (May, 1979): 42-52.

7876. Schwarz, Solomon M.: "The New Antisemitism of the Soviet Union: Its Background and Its Meaning." Com, vol.7 #6 (June, 1949): 535-545.

7877. Wiesenthal, Simon: Anti-Jewish Agitation in Poland: A Documentary Report [Bonn, Germany: R. Vogel, 1969]

Antisemitism After the Holocaust

7878. Arad, Yitzhak: "New Aspects of Antisemitism." YVN, #4 (1973): 16-18.

7879. Fischer, Eugene: "Antisemitism: A Contemporary Christian Perspective." Judaism, vol.30 #3 (Sum., 1981): 276-282.

7880. Flannery, Edward H.: "Underlying Christian Indifference to Holocaust and Unfriendly Reaction to Israel." J Digest, vol.15 #4 (Jan., 1970): 21-28.

7881. Grunfeld, I.: "The Challenge of Antisemitism." Ortho J Life, vol.27 #4 (April, 1960): 51-56.

7882. Heller, Bernard: Dawn or Dusk? [New York: Bookman's Press, 1961]

Investigation into the roots of nazism and antisemitism. Suggests possible alternatives to reshaping German national character through education. Also calls for a thorough reform of Christian attitudes towards Jews and Judaism as a step in reducing antisemitism.

7883. Kahn, Lothar: "Germans and Jews: New Perspectives." J Digest, vol.26 #4 (Dec., 1980): 52-57.

7884. Lever, H.: "The Defacement of a Ghetto Exhibition." JJoS, vol.6 #2 (Dec., 1964): 213-219.

7885. Lewin, Isaac: "The United Nations Survey on Antisemitism: Prologue or Epilogue." Ortho J Life, vol.28 #4 (April, 1961): 31-37.

7886. Lipset, S. M.: "Antisemitism of the Old Left and the New Left." J Digest, vol.15 #10 (July, 1970): 1-11; #11 (Aug., 1970): 41-48.

7887. May, Michael: "Antisemitism and the Law." IJA Res Rep #20/21 (Dec., 1982): 1-28

7888. Mintzer, George: Antisemitism: The World Scene [New York: Am. Jewish Committee, 1948]

7889. Moskowitz, Moses: "The Germans and the Jews. Postwar Report: The Enigma of German Irresponsibility." Com, vol.2 #1 (July, 1946): 7-14.

7890. Muhlen, Norbert: "In the Backwash of the Great Crime: Today's Barriers Between Jew and German." Com, vol.13 #2 (Feb., 1952): 107-114.

7891. Pinson, K. S.: "Antisemitism in the Post-War World." JSS, vol.7 #2 (April, 1945): 99-118.

7892. Poliakov, Leon: "European Antisemitism East and West: The Jewish Stake in Democracy." Com, vol.23 #6 (June, 1957): 553-560.

7893. "The Post-War Career of the 'Protocols of Zion'." IJA Res Rep, #15 (Dec., 1981): 1-11.

7894. Prinz, Joachim: "Beginning a Dialogue Between Germans and Jews." J Digest, vol.11 #12 (Sept., 1960): 27-32.

7895. Rubinstein, W. D.: The Left, the Right and the Jews [New York: Universe Books, 1982]

7896. Van Bergh, Hendrik: "The Swastika Neurosis." J Digest vol.11 #1 (Oct., 1965): 1-5.

7897. Vishniak, Mark: An International Convention Against Antisemitism [New York: Research Inst. of the Jewish Labor Committee, 1946]

7898. Wagner, Geoffrey: "The Classical Revival: A Dossier of Antisemitism." Ch J Forum, vol.12 #4 (Sum., 1954): 207-212.

7899. Wiesel, E.: "Ominous Signs and Unspeakable Thoughts." Chartock: Society, pp.284-286.

THE HUNT FOR NAZI WAR CRIMINALS

The Hunters

7900. Bar-Zohar, Michael: The Avengers [New York: Hawthorn Books, 1967]

7901. Benami, Shaddai: "Dead Nazis Who Are Still Alive." J Digest, vol.8 #3 (Dec., 1962): 78-80. * On Abner Less, of the Israel Police.

7902. Berkowitz, P.: "Simon Wiesenthal: The Lonely Hunter." J Digest, vol.20 #2 (Nov., 1974): 39-41.

7903. Blank, J.: "Man Who Will Not Forget." Readers Digest, vol.102 #610 (Feb., 1973): 154-164.

7904. Bligh, Ben-Mordechay: "Jewish ´Carabinieri´ Pursue Nazi-Collaborators." J Affairs, vol.11 #10 (Oct., 1956): 26-29. * On Compagnia Ebraica, Italy.

7905. Brandt, E.: "Jewish Agency Activities Against Nazi Criminals During World War II." Dispersion, #4 (Win., 1964/1965): 169-172.

7906. Clarke, Bernard: "I Helped Capture Rudolph Hoess: How a Jewish Officer Found the Commandant of Auschwitz." J Digest, vol.7 #6 (March, 1962): 48-50.

7907. Cooper, Abraham: "Simon Wiesenthal: The Man, the Mission, His Message." Grobman: Genocide, pp.384-388.

7908. Faerber, R.: "The German Who Hunts Nazi Criminals." J Digest, vol.21 #1 (Oct., 1975): 46-49. * On German Prosecutor Adalbert Rueckerl.

7909. Farnsworth, Clyde A.: "Sleuth with 6,000,000 Clients: Simon Wiesenthal who Devoted His Life to Bringing Nazis to Justice." J Digest, vol.10 #8 (May, 1965): 5-10.

7910. Friedman, Tuviah (D. G. Gross, ed. and transl.): The Hunter [Garden City, NY: Doubleday, 1961] Excerpted in Friedlander: Whirlwind pp.434-450.

Memoir of one of the most famous and active Nazi hunters. Friedman, a survivor who works out of Haifa, was directly involved in the hunt for and capture of Adolf Eichmann.

7911. Heiman, Leo: "He Hunts Nazis." J Digest, vol.3 #6 (March, 1958): 30-40.

7912. Kachleff, Owen: "Two German Women and the Nazi Spectre." J Digest, vol.20 #8 (May, 1975): 24-31. * On Beate Klarsfeld and Leni Riefenstahl.

7913. Klaidman, S.: "The Nazi Hunters." PT, vol.4 #2 (Win., 1977): 21-26.

7914. Klarsfeld, B. (M. Stearns and N. Gerardi, transls.): Wherever They May Be [New York: Vanguard Press, 1975]

7915. Lyttle, Richard B.: Nazi Hunting [New York: F. Watts, 1982]

7916. McGovern, George: "Simon Wiesenthal: Champion of Justice." IH, vol.27 #10 (Dec., 1979): 23-25.

7917. Mendelsohn, Janet: "The Klarsfeld´s Mission." CM, vol.46 #8 (Dec., 1979): 14-15.

7918. Noble, Iris: Nazi Hunter, Simon Wiesenthal [New York: Messner, 1979]

7919. Olshaker, E.: "The German Lady Who Hunts Nazis." J Digest, vol.23 #8 (April, 1978): 63-69. * On Beate Klarsfeld.

7920. Pruden, Wesley Jr.: "The Housewife Who Hunts Nazis." J Digest, vol.21 #4 (Jan., 1976): 40-43. * On Beate Klarsfeld.

7921. Ryan, A. A.: "The Clock is Still Against Us." ADL Bul vol.40 #7 (Sept., 1983): 10-12.

7922. Wiesenthal, Simon: The Murderers Among Us [New York: McGraw-Hill, 1976]

Memoir of one of the world´s best known Nazi hunters. Details Wiesenthal´s efforts on five continents to locate, track, and bring to justice Nazi war criminals still at large.

7923. Zimmerman, Golda: "Private Vengeance or Public Duty." JOMER, vol.13 #33 (Aug. 14, 1964): 14-15. * On Simon Wiesenthal.

The Hunted

7924. "Absentees from Nuremberg." Hist/WWII, #117 (1974): 3271-3272.

7925. Beigel, Greta: "War Criminals in Austria." IH, vol.14 #6 (June/July, 1966): 18-21.

7926. "Bonn´s Diplomats: 58 Nazi Associates Listed." JOMER, vol.11 #5 (Feb. 2, 1962): 2-5.

7927. Dornberg, John: "Can Nazi War Criminals Escape Justice." J Digest, vol.24 #5 (Jan., 1979): 14-16.

7928. Erdstein, Erich and Barbara Eden: Inside the Fourth Reich [New York: St. Martin´s Press, 1977]

7929. Garcia, Joaquin: "Nazi Haven in Spain." New Republic, vol.113 #26 (Dec. 24, 1945): 859-861.

7930. Grossmann, Kurt R.: "The Nazis and the Right of Asylum." Ch J Forum, vol.3 #2 (Win., 1944/45): 85-91.

7931. Heiman, Leo: "A Who´s Who of the World´s Top Nazis: Where They Are Now and What They Are Doing." J Digest, vol.12 #5 (Feb., 1967): 75-80.

7932. Knoop, H. (R. M. Rudnick, transl.): The Menten Affair [New York: Macmillan, 1978]

7933. Lahav, Ephraim: "Exposing Ulbrich´s Nazis." J Digest, vol.15 #6 (March, 1969): 30-32.

7934. MacPherson, Malcolm C: The Blood of His Servants [New York: Times Books, 1984] * On the Menten Affairs.

7935. Major, Robert: "Hungarian Hate Groups." CBW, vol.27 #4 (Feb. 22, 1960): 5-8.

7936. Robinson, Nehemiah: "The Fate of Hitler´s Confederates: The Lesser Nazis and What Happened to Them." J Digest, vol.8 #7 (April, 1963): 21-24.

7937. Samuels, G.: "Wanted: 1,000 Nazis Still at Large." NY Times Mag, (Feb. 28, 1965): 26-27, 96-98, 110.

7938. Varon, Benno W.: "The Nazis´ Friends in Rome." Mid, vol.30 #4 (April, 1984): 10-13.

Nazis in Arab Lands

7939. Aronsfeld, C. C.: "Ex-Nazis in Egypt." J Digest, vol. 2 #8 (May, 1957): 37-40.

7940. Dorn, Phillip: "Germany on the Nile." New Leader, vol. 48 #18 (Sept. 13, 1965): 3-5.

7941. Eytan, Steve (pseud.): "Shalom Herr Major." J Digest, vol.16 #5 (Feb., 1971): 15-20.

7942. Lust, Peter: "Nasser´s Nazis: Egypt a Home for Wanted Hitlerites." J Digest, vol.13 #6 (March, 1968): 63-66

7943. "Nazis in Cairo." PoP, vol.1 #3 (May/June, 1967): 6-8. * Biographical list.

7944. Raymist, Malkah: "Egypt´s Nazi Propagandist" CW, vol. 23 #30 (Nov. 19, 1956): 5-6.

7945. Wiesenthal, Simon: "Nazi Criminals in Arab States." IH, vol.15 #7 (Sept., 1967): 10-12.

Nazi War Criminals in the Americas

7946. Allen, Charles R.: "Heusinger and the Einsatzgruppen: State Department Refuted - Heusinger Shares Responsibility for Executions." J Currents, vol.15 #9 (Oct., 1961): 7-11, 36. * Documentation.

7947. ___: "Heusinger's Nazi Record: The War Crimes of the Chairman of the NATO General Staff." J Currents, vol. 15 #4 (April, 1961): 7-10.

7948. ___: "Nazi War Criminals Living Among Us." J Currents, vol.17 #1 (Jan., 1963): 3-12; #2 (Feb., 1963): 3-16; #3 (March, 1963): 3-16.

7949. Aronsfeld, C. C.: "Nazis in South America." J Fr, vol.17 #5 (May, 1950): 12-14.

7950. Blum, Howard: Wanted! The Search for Nazis in America [New York: Quadrangle Books, 1977]

7951. Druks, Herbert: "The Belated Hunt for Nazi Criminals in America." Am Zionist, vol.67 #6 (Feb., 1977): 9-12.

7952. Holtzman, Elizabeth: "Nazi War Criminals in America." IH, vol.27 #3 (March, 1979): 6-9.

7953. Lichten, Joseph L.: "Who Let Them In?" ADL Bul, vol. 10 #6 (Sept., 1953): 1, 7-8; #7 (Oct., 1953): 4-5; #8 (Nov., 1953): 6-7.

7954. Loftus, John: The Belarus Secret [New York: Alfred A. Knopf, 1982]

Revealing account of the use made by American intelligence organizations of Nazi war criminals, the help given murderers to escape justice, and the continuing protection given them by agencies of the U. S. government. Written by a former attorney for the United States Justice Department's Office of Special Investigations.

7955. Mann, P.: "The Dentist and the Bishop." PT, vol.1 #4 (Sum., 1974): 29-35.

7956. Mendelsohn, Martin: "World War II Nazis in the United States." Grobman: Genocide, pp.389-393.

7957. Rachleff, Owen: "Bishop Trifa and the Iron Guard." ADL Bul, vol.31 #3 (March, 1974): 3-4.

7958. Rinaldi, Matthew: "The Disturbing Case of Feodor Fedorenko." Judaism, vol.28 #3 (Sum., 1979): 293-303.

7959. Rosen, Philip: "America's Prosecution of Nazis in Danger." J Digest, vol.24 #3 (Nov., 1978): 62-64.

7960. Rosenthal, Morton and E. Welles: "Latin America: Safe Haven for Nazis." ADL Bul, vol.40 #5 (May, 1983): 1, 10, 12-14.

7961. Ryan, Allan A. Jr.: Quiet Neighbors: Prosecuting Nazi War Criminals in America [San Diego, CA: Harcourt, Brace Jovanovich, 1984]

Authoritative account by the former director of the Justice Department's Office for Special Investigation of his search for Nazi war criminals at large in the United States.

7962. Saidel, Rochelle G.: The Outraged Conscience: Seekers of Justice for Nazi War Criminals in America [Albany, NY: SUNY Press, 1984]

Journalistic account of the hunt for Nazi war criminals in the U.S.. Main focus is on the role of the American Jewish community and its organs. The book is more of an interim summary, rather than a definitive history.

7963. Schwartz, Martin: "The Search for Nazis in America." J Digest, vol.22 #9 (May, 1977): 3-6.

7964. Silverstock, M. J.: "War Criminals in Canada." V CJQ, vol.10 #2 (Fall, 1979): 26-34.

7965. Wiesenthal, Simon: "Latvian War Criminals in USA." J Currents, vol.20 #7 (July/Aug., 1966): 4-8; #10 (Nov., 1966): 24.

7966. ___: "There are Still Murderers Among Us." NJM, vol. 82 #2 (Oct., 1967): 8-9.

The Criminals

Klaus Barbie

7967. Ascherson, Neal et al: The Nazi Legacy: Klaus Barbie and the International Fascist Connection [New York: Holt, Rinehart and Winston, 1984]

7968. Dabringhaus, Erhard: Klaus Barbie: The Shocking Story of How the U.S. Used this Nazi War Criminal as an Intelligence Agent [Washington, DC: Acropolis, 1984]

7969. Ryan, Alan J. Jr. (ed.): Klaus Barbie and the United States Government [Frederick, MD: University Publications of America, 1984]

Documentary study, written as a report to the U. S. Justice Department, on the relations between the U.S. intelligence service and Nazi war criminal Klaus Barbie. Concludes that, although the Americans had not acted maliciously, this connection was unlawful and immoral. The book is disappointing because it offers no specific recommendations on how to deal with the issue of illicit American governmental protection of Nazi war criminals.

Martin Bormann

7970. Baker, Jack: "Is the Deputy Fuehrer Alive?" ADL Bul, vol.21 #5 (May, 1964): 3, 7.

7971. Clark, Eric: "The Case of Martin Bormann: Alive and Running." Atlas, vol.14 #4 (Oct., 1967): 40-41.

7972. Farago, Ladislas: Aftermath: Martin Bormann and the Fourth Reich [New York: Simon and Schuster, 1974]

7973. Manning, P.: Martin Bormann: Nazi in Exile [Secaucus, NJ: Lyle Stuart, 1981]

Journalistic account of the hunt for Martin Bormann. The author concludes from his research that Bormann is still alive.

7974. Stevenson, Wm: The Bormann Brotherhood [New York: Harcourt, Brace, Jovanovich, 1973]

7975. Terry, Antony: "The Case of Martin Bormann: The Impregnable Hideout." Atlas, vol.15 #3 (March, 1968): 52-54.

Joseph Mengele

7976. Baker, Jack: "The Case of the Nazi Doctor." ADL Bul, vol.21 #9 (Nov., 1964): 7-8.

7977. Emanuel, Myron: "Back-Page Story." New Republic, vol. 116 #7 (Feb. 17, 1947): 12-15.

7978. Varon, Benno W.: "The Diplomat and Dr. Mengele." J Digest, vol.25 #5 (Jan., 1980): 19-26.

7979. ___: "The Hunt for Mengele." PT, vol.10 #4 (Sum., 1983): 12-16.

7980. ___: "Living with Mengele." Mid, vol.29 #10 (Dec., 1983): 24-29.

JUSTICE BEFORE A JEWISH COURT OF LAW

The Capture and Interrogation of Eichmann

7981. "Behind the Eichmann Headlines: Secret Service Details Made Public." JOMER, vol.9 #23 (June 3, 1960): 11-13.

7982. Friedman, Tuvia: "I Tracked Down Eichmann: The Fifteen Year Hunt that Led to the Capture of the Mass Murderer." J Digest, vol.6 #7 (April, 1961): 7-16.

7983. ___: "My Search for Vengeance." Life, vol.50 #8 (Feb. 24, 1961): 90-100.

7984. Harel, Isser: The House on Garibaldi Street [New York: Viking Press, 1975] * The inside story of the capture of Adolf Eichmann by members of the Israeli secret service, written by the organization's former chief.

7985. Heiman, Leo: "Eichmann's Capture." NJM, vol.74 #10 (July, 1960): 10, 28.

7986. ___: "The Hunt for Eichmann." NJM, vol.74 #4 (Jan., 1960): 7, 23-24.

7987. ___: "Operation Eichmann." J Sp, vol.25 #9 (Nov., 1960): 15-17.

7988. Less, Avner W.: "Interrogating Eichmann." Com, vol.75 #5 (May, 1983): 45-51.

7989. Pearlman, M.: The Capture and Trial of Adolf Eichmann [New York: Simon and Schuster, 1963]

Definitive work on the Eichmann case written by an Israeli military and political historian. Although the chapters on the capture have been superseded by more recent literature, the book is still the best overall coverage of all the issues involved.

7990. Safire, Wm: "How they Captured Eichmann." J Digest, vol.21 #1 (Oct., 1975): 42-45.

7991. von Block, Bela W.: "The Chase and Capture of Adolf Eichmann." Reader´s Digest, vol.77 #462 (Oct., 1960): 60-65.

7992. von Lang, Jochen with Claus Sibyll (eds) (R. Manheim, transl.): Eichmann Interrogated: Transcripts from the Archives of the Israeli Police [New York: Farrar, Straus & Giroux, 1983]

Transcripts of the Israeli police interrogation of Adolf Eichmann. Useful as a microscope under which the Nazi personality may be examined in careful detail. Includes an introduction by Avner W. Less, the Israeli police captain who conducted the interrogation.

Legal Aspects

7993. Bergman, Shmuel H.: "Can Transgression Have an Agent? On the Moral-Judicial Problem of the Eichmann Trial." YVS, vol.5 (1961): 7-16.

7994. Draper, G. I. A. D.: "The Eichmann Trial: A Judicial Precedent." Int Affairs, vol.38 #4 (Oct., 1962): 485-500.

7995. "The Eichmann Case." J Newsletter, vol.16 #13 (June 27, 1960): 5-6.

7996. Gollancz, Victor: The Case of Adolf Eichmann [London: Victor Gollancz, 1961]

7997. Goodman, Arnold: "Capital Punishment and Eichmann." CBW, vol.29 #7 (April 2, 1962): 8, 32-33.

7998. Hanan, Ben: "Israel´s Right to Try Eichmann." IH, vol.9 #1 (Jan./Feb., 1961): 24-27.

7999. Hausner, Gideon: "Eichmann and His Trial." SEP, vol. 235 #39 (Nov. 3, 1962): 19-25; #40 (Nov. 10, 1962): 58-61; #41 (Nov. 17, 1962): 85-90.

8000. ___: "The Indictment." Mid, vol.7 #3 (Sum., 1961): 3-13.

8001. ___: Text of the Indictment Against Eichmann." AJYB, vol.63 (1962): 120-131.

8002. Levy, Robert: "Some International Conclusions of the Eichmann Trial." YVB, #11 (April/May, 1962): 26-29.

8003. Liskofsky, S.: "The Judgment." AJYB, vol.63 (1962): 104-119.

8004. Muszkat, Marion: "The Eichmann Trial - International Aspects." YVB, #11 (April/May, 1962): 19-26.

8005. ___: "The Problems of the Eichmann Trial." YVB, #10 (April, 1961): 6-8.

8006. Parsons, George R.: "Israel´s Right to Try Eichmann." New Republic, vol.144 #12 (March 20, 1961): 13-15.

8007. Playfair, G.: "Eichmann and the Problem of Justice." New Republic, vol.143 #22 (Nov. 21, 1960): 15-17.

8008. Robinson, Jacob: "Eichmann and the Question of Jurisdiction." Com, vol.30 #1 (July, 1960): 1-5.

8009. Rogat, Yosal: The Eichmann Trial and the Rule of Law [Santa Barbara, CA: Center for the Study of Democratic Institutions, 1961]

8010. Taylor, Telford: "Large Questions in the Eichmann Case." NY Times Mag, (Jan. 22, 1961): 11, 22-25.

8011. Weintraub, R. J.: "Does Israel Have Jurisdiction Over Eichmann?" NJM, vol.75 #8 (April, 1961): 5, 32-33.

The Trial

8012. Allon, Dafna: "The Eichmann Trial." J Fr, vol.28 #9 (Sept., 1961): 16-20.

8013. Auerbach, Rachel: "Witnesses and Testimony in the Eichmann Trial." YVB, #11 (April/May, 1962): 45-54.

8014. Bar-Nathan, M.: "Background to the Eichmann Trial." J Fr, vol.28 #5 (May, 1961): 4-7.

8015. ___: "The Eichmann Verdict." J Fr, vol.29 #1 (Jan., 1962): 3-5.

8016. Braham, Randolph L.: The Eichmann Case: A Source Book [New York: World Federation of Hungarian Jews, 1969]

8017. Caplan, Samuel: "At the Eichmann Trial: Six Million Prosecutors." CBW, vol.28 #9 (May 1, 1961): 5-7.

8018. "Digest of Testimony at the Trial." YVB, #11 (April/ May, 1962): 60-76.

8019. "The Eichmann Indictment." JOMER, vol.10 #9 (March 3, 1961): 17-21.

8020. "Eichmann - the Final Pleas." JOMER, vol.10 #33 (Aug. 18, 1961): 14-16.

8021. "Eichmann´s Own Story: ´I Transported them... to the Butcher.´" Life, vol.49 #22 (Nov. 28, 1960): 19-25, 101-112. * Edited by Life Magazine.

8022. "Eichmann´s Own Story: ´To Sum it all up, I Regret Nothing´." Life, vol.49 #23 (Dec. 5, 1960): 146-161.

8023. Forster, Arnold: "The Eichmann Case." ADL Bul, vol.18 #3 (March, 1961): 1-3.

8024. Freeden, Herbert: "At the Eichmann Trial: The Slain and the Slayer." CBW, vol.28 #10 (May 15, 1961): 6-7.

8025. "From Israel: The Charges Against Eichmann." ADL Bul, vol.18 #3 (March, 1961): 6-7.

8026. Gouri, H.: The Glass Cage: A Journal of the Eichmann Trial [New York: Orion Press, 1964]

8027. Halevi-Levi, I.: "Israeli Aspects of the Eichmann Case." Ortho J Life, vol.27 #6 (Aug., 1960): 6-11.

8028. Hausner, Gideon: Justice in Jerusalem [New York: Holocaust Library, 1968]

Prosecution brief of the Eichmann trial, written by the former Attorney General of Israel. Primarily focussed on legal issues the work is an answer to Hannah Arendt´s controversial Eichmann in Jerusalem <see #8069>.

8029. Heiman, Leo: "The Eichmann Trial: In and Around the Courtroom." J Fr, vol.28 #6 (June, 1961): 6-9.

8030. ___: "The Eichmann Trial: Witnesses for the Prosecution." J Fr, vol.28 #4 (April, 1961): 10-13.

8031. ___: "Eichmann's Trial to Show World's Indifference to Fate of Jews." J Digest, vol.6 #5 (Feb., 1961): 11-16.

8032. ___: "Preparing for the Eichmann Trial." CBW, vol.27 #14 (Oct. 10, 1960): 8-10.

8033. ___: "A Visit to Eichmann's Jail." CBW, vol.27 #11 (July 25, 1960): 4-6.

8034. "How Israel Will Try Eichmann." J Digest, vol.5 #11 (Aug., 1960): 18-22.

8035. Katz, Shlomo: "Notes on the Eichmann Case." Mid, vol. 6 #3 (Sum., 1960): 83-87.

8036. Liskofsky, Sidney: "The Eichmann Case." AJYB, vol.62 (1961): 199-208.

8037. Miron, S.: The Dread Symbol: A Portrait of the Eichmann Trial [Jerusalem: Yad Vashem, 1972]

8038. Papadatos, Peter: The Eichmann Trial [New York: F. A. Praeger, 1964]

8039. Poliakov, L.: "The Proceedings." AJYB, vol.63 (1962): 54-84.

8040. Rabkin, Sol: "Seven Key Legal Points." ADL Bul, vol. 18 #3 (March, 1961): 3-5.

8041. Rosenberg, Harold: "The Trial and Eichmann." Com, vol.32 #5 (Nov., 1961): 369-381.

8042. Russell, Edward F. L.: The Record: The Trial of Adolf Eichmann for His Crimes Against the Jewish People and Against Humanity [New York: A. A. Knopf, 1963]

Account of the Eichmann trial based on the official court records. Attempts to assess Eichmann's role in the Final Solution. Also deals with the legal aspects of the trial and the "superiors orders" defense.

8043. Schechtman, Joseph B.: "The Eichmann Story." CBW, vol.27 #10 (June 20, 1960): 5-8.

8044. "This Is My Life: Self Portrait of a Mass Murderer." JOMER, vol.9 #49 (Dec. 2, 1960): 4-7.

8045. Zeiger, Henry A.: The Case Against Adolf Eichmann [New York: New American Library, 1960]

Reactions

8046. Bauminger, Aryeh: "The Effect of the Eichmann Trial on Israel Youth." YVB, #11 (April/May, 1962): 9-12.

8047. Ben-Asher, Naomi: "Israelis Look at Eichmann Trial." CBW, vol.28 #13 (Sept. 4, 1961): 12-15.

8048. Ben-Dor, Ephraim: "As Seen in Israel." CBW, vol.27 #10 (June 20, 1960): 8-9.

8049. Ben-Nathan, Moshe: "Israel Relives the Holocaust." J Fr, vol.28 #6 (June, 1961): 4-6.

8050. Carmichael, Joel: "Reactions in Germany." Mid, vol.7 #3 (Sum., 1961): 13-27.

8051. Crespi, Irving: "Public Reaction to the Eichmann Trial." Pub Op Q, vol.28 #1 (Spr., 1964): 91-103.

8052. Deutsch, Akiva W.: The Eichmann Trial in the Eyes of Israeli Youngsters [Ramat-Gan, Israel: Bar-Ilan Univ. Press, 1974]

8053. The Eichmann Case in the American Press [New York: American Jewish Committee, 1963]

8054. "The Eichmann Trial: How the World´s Press Reacted." ADL Bul, vol.18 #7 (Sept., 1961): 6-7.

8055. Engel, Gerald: "Campus Reactions to Eichmann." CBW, vol.28 #11 (May 29, 1961): 7-8, 13.

8056. "From the Nations Press: Approval and Dissent." ADL Bul, vol.18 #3 (March, 1961): 7-8.

8057. Gellhorn, M: "Eichmann and the Private Conscience." Atlantic, vol.209 #2 (Feb., 1962): 52-59.

8058. Glock, Charles, Gertrude Selznik and Joe Spaeth: The Apathetic Majority: A Study Based on Public Response to the Eichmann Trial [New York: Harper & Row, 1966]

8059. Groner, Oscar: "How Students Reacted to the Eichmann Trial." NJM, vol.76 #5 (Jan., 1962): 27-28.

8060. "How Americans Reacted to the Eichmann Trial." J Digest, vol.12 #7 (April, 1967): 25-28.

8061. Jacobs, Paul: "Eichmann and Jewish Identity." Mid, vol.7 #3 (Sum., 1961): 33-38.

8062. Muszkat, Marion: "Eichmann in New York." YVB #14 (March, 1964): 3-12.

8063. ___: "Reactions to the Eichmann Trial." YVB, #13 (Oct., 1963): 48-53.

8064. Nissenson, H.: "Israel During the Trial: A Journal." Com, vol.32 #1 (July, 1961): 12-18.

8065. Pendorf, Robert: "Eichmann: A German Summing Up." Atlas, vol.2 #2 (Aug., 1961): 123-125.

8066. Prittie, Terence: "Eichmann and the Germans." New Republic, vol.144 #17 (April 24, 1961): 5-6.

8067. Rockman, A.: "World Opinion on the Eichmann Trial." YVB, #11 (April/May, 1962): 77-96.

8068. Salomon, George: "America´s Response." AJYB, vol.63 (1962): 85-103; vol.64 (1963): 247-259.

Implications

8069. Arendt, Hannah: Eichmann in Jerusalem: A Report on the Banality of Evil [New York: Viking Press, 1964]

Journalistic investigation of the Eichmann trial. Controversial on three points - the author rejected the right of Israel to try Eichmann, saw the trial as attempting to try Eichmann for crime with which he was not involved, and placed special emphasis on the role Jews, especially the Judenraete (Jewish Councils), played in the murder process. Arendt´s special point, however, is her effort at portraying the Nazi crimes in light of the "banality of evil", a philosophical concept that is not wholly irrelevant.

8070. Astor, David: The Meaning of Eichmann [Royoston, England: Hertz/Parkes Library Pamphlet #5, 1961]

8071. Bettelheim, B.: "Eichmann: The System: The Victims." New Republic, vol.148 #24 (June 15, 1963): 23-33.

8072. Blumenthal, Nachman: "Eichmann Trial Throws New Light on History." YVB, #11 (April/May, 1962): 2-9.

8073. Carmel, Israel: "Hans Frank´s Diary in the Eichmann Trial." YVB, #11 (April/May, 1962): 35-36.

8074. De Sola Pool, David and Tamar De Sola Pool: "The Impact of the Eichmann Trial." J Fo, vol.44 #5 (Nov., 1961): 17-18.

8075. Eban, Abba: "Lessons of the Eichmann Trial." J Sp, vol.27 #6 (June, 1962): 7-10; #7 (Sept., 1962): 7-9.

8076. Fleishman, A.: "Antisemitism and the Eichmann Trial." J Digest, vol.10 #3 (Dec., 1964): 9-12.

8077. Gilbert, Arthur and W. M. Abbott: "Christians Failed Jewish Hopes." America, vol.106 #24 (March 24, 1962): 825-828.

8078. Halpern, Ben: "Reflections on the Eichmann Trial." J Fr, vol.28 #3 (March, 1961): 30-35.

8079. Herman, Simon N.: "In the Shadow of the Holocaust." Jer Q, #3 (Spr., 1977): 85-97.

8080. Kelen, Emery: "Bureaucrat or Beelzebub?" Atlas, vol.2 #2 (Aug., 1961): 125-127. * The Eichmann personality.

8081. Kermish, Josef: "Yad Vashem Archives´ Contribution to Preparation of the Eichmann Trial." YVB, #11 (April/May, 1962): 37-45.

8082. Levin, M.: "Eichmann: The Lesson Yet to be Learned." CBW, vol.29 #1 (Jan. 8, 1962): 5-7.

8083. Melchior, D.: "Documents from the German Foreign Ministry in the Eichmann Trial." YVB, #11 (April/May, 1962): 54-55.

8084. O´Donovan, P.: "Reflections on the Eichmann Trial." New Republic, vol.144 #20 (May 15, 1961): 6-8.

8085. Schappes, Morris: "The Eichmann Trial." J Currents, vol.14 #8 (Sept., 1960): 3-6.

8086. ___: "6,000,000 Prosecutors." J Currents, vol.15 #5 (May, 1961): 3-4.

8087. Segall, Arie: "Books Around the Eichmann Trial." YVB, #11 (April/May, 1962): 29-35.

8088. "The Soviet Version." Mid, vol.7 #3 (Sum., 1961): 28-33.

8089. Sulzberger, C. L.: "The True Meaning of the Eichmann Trial." Comm Rep, vol.18 #2 (May, 1961): 18-19.

8090. Whartman, Eliezer: "Thoughts on the Eichmann Trial." Recon, vol.27 #9 (June 16, 1961): 5-8.

8091. Zukerman, William: "Lessons of the Eichmann Trial." J Newsletter, vol.17 #14 (Aug. 7, 1961): 1-2.

ESTABLISHING THE RULE OF LAW

8092. Aronson, R.: "Defining and Preventing Genocide." J Currents, vol.37 #4 (April, 1983): 5-7, 36.

8093. Auerbach, J. S.: "Human Rights at San Francisco." AJA, vol.16 #1 (April, 1964): 51-70.

8094. Bassiouni, M. Cherif: "International Law and the Holocaust." Sherwin: Encountering, pp.146-188.

8095. Bauer, Yehuda: "Lessons of the Holocaust: Signs of Oppression." Littell: Education, pp.13-21.

8096. Berenbaum, M.: "The Holocaust, Human Rights, and the Jewish Condition." Recon, vol.47 #2 (April, 1981): 7-16.

8097. Fried, Jacob: "The Genocide Convention." Ch J Forum, vol.9 #1 (Fall, 1950): 43-49.

8098. Goldstein, Anatole: "New Concepts of Justice." CW, vol.12 #31 (Nov. 2, 1945): 7-8.

8099. Grossmann, Kurt R.: "Shielding Victims of War." CW, vol.16 #17 (May 9, 1949): 5-6.

8100. Harf, B.: Genocide and Human Rights: International Legal and Political Issues [Denver: Univ. of Colorado Press, 1984]

8101. Horowitz, Irving L.: "Many Genocides, One Holocaust?: The Limits of the Rights of States and the Obligations of Individuals." MJ, vol.1 #1 (May, 1981): 74-89.

8102. "International Legal Theories Evolved at Nuremberg." Int Affairs, vol.23 #3 (July, 1947): 317-325.

8103. Jackson, William E.: "Putting the Nuremberg Law to Work." F Affairs, vol.25 #4 (July, 1947): 550-565.

8104. Kubowitzki, A. L.: "The Declaration of Human Rights." J Fr, vol.16 #3 (March, 1949): 12-15.

8105. Lemkin, Raphael: "Is it Genocide?" ADL Bul, vol.10 #1 (Jan., 1953): 3, 8.

8106. Liskofsky, S.: "Human Rights." AJYB, vol.49 (1947/1948): 572-579.

8107. Mates, Leo: "The Holocaust and International Relations." Legters: Western, pp.131-147. Comments and rejoinder: H. R. Huttenbach, pp.148-158; D. S. Lev, pp.158-160; L. Mates, pp.160-163.

8108. Proskauer, Joseph M.: "Restoration of Jewish Rights Throughout the World." AJYB, vol.46 (1944/1945): 559-565.

8109. Robinson, Nehemiah: "Establishing the Rule of Law." CW, vol.24 #28 (Nov. 11, 1957): 5-7.

8110. ___: "Genocide and the U. N." CW, vol.15 #4 (Jan. 30, 1948): 7-9.

8111. ___: The Genocide Convention [New York: IJA, 1949]

8112. Not Used.

8113. Stanciu, V. V.: "Reflections on the Congress for the Prevention of Genocide." YVS, vol.7 (1968): 185-188.

17

The Holocaust and the Literary Imagination

ART AND ART REVIEWS

8114. Adler, D.: "Sketches from Dachau: 1971." Ortho J Life, vol.39 #1 (Jan., 1972): 63-64.

8115. "Affirmations: Artists in the Holocaust." Moment, vol. 5 #1 (Dec., 1979): 53-62.

8116. Ansbacher, M.: "Art in the Period of the European Jewish Disaster: The Art Section of Thereisenstadt." YVB, #6/7 (June, 1960): 15-17.

8117. Aptecker, George: Beyond Despair [Morristown, NJ: Kahn and Kahn, 1980] * Includes an essay by Elie Wiesel.

8118. Belfer, Itzak: The Holocaust [Tel Aviv: United Artist Ltd., 1971]

8119. Berliner, Gert: "Living with the Knowledge of the Holocaust: A Photographic essay." Mid, vol.16 #6 (June/ July, 1970): 33-40.

8120. Bernbaum, Israel: My Brother´s Keeper: The Holocaust Through the Eyes of an Artist [New York: G.P. Putnam´s Sons, 1985] * For young people.

8121. Blatter, Janet and Sybil Milton (eds): Art of the Holocaust [New York: Rutledge Press, 1981]

A collection of artistic interpretations of the Holocaust. Contains over 350 works of art by Jewish victims of Nazi ghettos, concentration, and death camps as well as by some of the early liberators. Includes a preface by Irving Howe and a useful historical introduction by the editors.

8122. "Children's Drawings and Poems: Terezin, 1942-1944." J Currents, vol.15 #4 (April, 1961): 11-15.

8123. Dawidowicz, Lucy S. et al: Spiritual Resistance: Art from the Concentration Camps, 1940-1945 [Philadelphia: J. P. S., 1981]

8124. Dorfman, Lois: "Personal Reflections by the Artist: Making a Holocaust Memorial." Shoa, vol.2 #3 (Fall/ Win., 1981/1982): 25-26, 38.

8125. Frackiewicz, J.: Auschwitz in Artistic Photography [Oswiecim: Wydawnictwo Panstwowego, 1962]

8126. Friedman, Tuviah: We Shall Never Forget: An Album of Photographs, Articles and Documents [New York: Saphrograph, 1968]

8127. Green, Gerald (ed.): The Artist of Terezin [New York: Hawthorn Books, 1969]

8128. Hellman, Peter (text): The Auschwitz Album [New York: Random House, 1981]

Photo collection made by a Nazi camp guard and found by Lili Jacob Meier, a survivor of the camp. Provides a chilling testimonial to the Holocaust and clear evidence against those who deny its events.

8129. Jankowski, Stanislaw: Amidst a Nightmare of Crime [Oswiecim: Panstwowe Muzeum, 1973]

8130. Kaliszan, Jozef (C. Z. Banasiewicz, ed.): The Warsaw Ghetto [New York: Thomas Yoseloff, 1968]

8131. Kantor, Alfred: The Book of Alfred Kantor [New York: McGraw-Hill, 1971]

Artistic rendition of the Holocaust by a Czech Jew who survived the Terezin, Auschwitz, and Schwarzheide concentration camps. Gives a graphic day by day picture of inmate life in the camps, along with explanatory notes. Appended is a short preface by John Wykert.

8132. Langer, Lawrence L.: "The Art of the Concentration Camps." Sh´ma, vol.8 #159 (Sept. 29, 1978): 177-179.

8133. Lishinsky, Saul: "Art Out of Terezin." J Currents, vol.24 #4 (April, 1970): 16-19.

8134. Lurie, Esther: A Living Witness: Kovno Ghetto. Portfolio [Jerusalem: Dvir, 1958] * English captions.

8135. ___: Sketches from a Women´s Labour Camp [Tel Aviv: J. L. Peretz Pub., 1962] Heb./Yid./Eng.

8136. Milton, Sybil: "Concentration Camp Art and Artists." Shoa, vol.1 #2 (Fall, 1978): 10-15.

8137. Olevski, R. et al (eds): Our Destruction in Pictures [Bergen-Belsen: Central Com. for the Liberated Jews in the British Zone, 1946]

8138. Poznanski, Stanislaw: Struggle, Death, Memory, 1939-1945: On the 25th Anniversary of the Rising of the Warsaw Ghetto 1943-1963 [Warsaw: Council for the Preservation of the Monuments of Struggle and Martyrdom, 1963]

8139. Reiss, Lionel S.: "Nazi Warfare: Eight Water Colors." Menorah, vol.32 #2 (Oct./Dec., 1944): 202-203x. * In memoriam to the victims of Nazism.

8140. Rothkirchen, Livia: "Creative Life in the Shadow of Death." YVB, #18 (April, 1966): 57-59. * Terezin.

8141. Smolen, K.: In Memory of a Human Tragedy [Warsaw: Wydawnictwo Katalogow-Cennikow, 1976]

8142. "Spiritual Resistance: Art from the Concentration Camps." PT, vol.5 #2 (Win., 1978): 25-32.

8143. Szonyi, David M.: "Art from the Holocaust at the Jewish Museum." Shoa, vol.1 #2 (Fall, 1978): 24-25.

8144. Toll, N.: "Without Surrender: A Survivor´s Art." Response, vol.11 #4 (Win., 1978/1979): 52-59.

8145. Walkowitz, Abraham: Faces from the Ghetto [New York: Machmadim Art Editions, 1946]

8146. Werner, Alfred: "Art of the Holocaust." Dimensions, vol.4 #1 (Fall, 1969): 44-47.

8147. Zuroff, Efraim (ed.): Yad Vashem Album [Jerusalem: Yad Vashem, 1976]

DRAMA AND FILMS, REVIEWS

Drama

8148. Alexander, Edgar: "Rolf Hochhuth: Equivocal Deputy." America, vol.109 #15 (Oct. 12, 1963): 416-418, 423.

8149. Baal-Teshuva, Jacob: "Awaiting the ´Deputy´." New Leader, vol.47 #4 (Feb. 17, 1964): 14-17.

8150. Ben-Horin, Eliahu: "A Jerusalem Manifesto." Recon, vol.29 #17 (Dec. 27, 1963): 18-20.

8151. Bentley, E. (ed.): The Storm Over the Deputy: Essays and Articles about Hochhuth´s Explosive Drama [New York: Grove Press, 1964]

8152. Bloomgarden, Kermit: "Meyer Levin and Anne Frank´s Diary." CW, vol.24 #20 (June 17, 1957): 5-7.

8153. "The Deputy: The Dimensions of Controversy." ADL Bul, vol.21 #2 (Feb., 1964): 1-2, 8.

8154. Dworkin, Martin: "The Vanishing Diary of Anne Frank." J Affairs, vol.14 #9 (Sept., 1959): 32-36, 43. Also in J Fr, vol.27 #4 (April, 1960): 7-10.

8155. Ehrlich, Hedy: "´The Investigation´: A Review." J Fr, vol.33 #10 (Dec., 1966): 20-26.

8156. Eliach, Yaffa: " The Holocaust in Hebrew Drama." JBA, vol.36 (1978/1979): 37-49.

8157. ___: "Holocaust Literature III: Poetry and Drama." Sherwin: Encountering, pp.316-350.

8158. Fisher, Desmond: Pope Pius XII and the Jews: An Answer to Hochhuth´s Play, ´Der Stelvertreter´ [Glen Rock, NJ: Paulist Press, 1963]

8159. Friedlander, Albert H.: "´The Deputy´ on the College Campus." CCARJ, vol.12 #2 (June, 1964): 44-46.

8160. Hyams, Barry: "An ´Investigation´." Recon, vol.32 #17 (Jan. 6, 1967): 20-26.

8161. ___: "´The Deputy´: An Advance Report." Recon, vol.30 #1 (Feb. 21, 1964): 24-28.

8162. ___: "´The Deputy´ - An Evaluation." Recon, vol.30 #3 (March 20, 1964): 20-24.

8163. Isaac, Dan: "A Jewish Horror Show." Dimensions, vol.3 #3 (Spr., 1969): 41-43. * Review of ´The Man in the Glass Booth´.

8164. Klausner, A. J.: "Meyer Levin´s Obsession." CCARJ, vol.21 #4 (Aut., 1974): 57-61.

8165. Kubovy, Aryeh L.: "The Holocaust´s Accounts Remain Unsettled." IH, vol.13 #4 (April, 1965): 9-13. * On ´The Deputy´.

8166. Lampell, Millard: "Bringing ´The Wall´ to the Stage." Mid, vol.6 #4 (Aut., 1960): 14-19.

8167. Lewin, Marlin: "´The Deputy´: Where Lies the Guilt? An Analysis of a Controversial Play." HM, vol.45 #6 (Feb., 1964): 20-22.

8168. Oestreicher, John M.: "As We Await ´The Deputy´." America, vol.109 #19 (Nov. 9, 1963): 570-573, 576-582.

8169. Schappes, M. U.: "Peter Weiss´s ´The Investigation´." J Currents, vol.20 #11 (Dec., 1966): 4-6.

8170. Shulman, Charles E.: "The Deputy." CCARJ, vol.12 #2 (June, 1964): 39-43.

8171. Spelman, Franz: "The Pope, the Fuehrer, and the Jews: A Play Rocks West Germany." J Digest, vol.9 #1 (Oct., 1963): 1-7.

8172. Varon, Benno W.: "Anne Frank´s Voice, Uncensored." PT, vol.10 #3 (Spr., 1983): 5-6.

8173. Vogel, A.: "Pius XII's Crown of Silence." J Currents, vol.18 #5 (May, 1964): 26-29. * On Hochhuth's Play.

8174. von Kessel, Albrech: "A Play Rocks West Germany: The Pope and the Jews." Atlas, vol.5 #6 (June, 1963): 345-348.

8175. Weinstein, Jacob: "Anne Frank: Has Justice been Done to Her Diary?" J Affairs, vol.12 #7 (July, 1957): 34-36.

8176. ___: "Betrayal of Anne Frank." CW, vol.24 #17 (May 13, 1957): 5-7.

8177. Zohn, Harry: "An Angry Young German's 'J'Accuse'." JQ, vol.11 #3 (Aut., 1963): 9-12. Also in J Currents, vol.18 #2 (Feb., 1964): 4-8.

Film

8178. Bird, Keith: "Germany Awakes: The 'Holocaust' - Background and Aftermath." Shoa, vol.1 #4 (1979): 5-9.

8179. Dawidowicz, L. S.: "Boy Meets Girl in Warsaw Ghetto." Mid, vol.6 #3 (Sum., 1960): 109-112.

8180. ___: "Visualizing the Warsaw Ghetto: Nazi Images of the Jews Refiltered by the BBC. A Critical Review of the BBC Film 'The Warsaw Ghetto'." Shoa, vol.1 #1 (1979): 5-6, 17-18.

8181. Doneson, Judith E.: "The Jew as a Female Figure in Holocaust Film." Shoa, vol.1 #1 (1979): 11-13, 18.

8182. Dworkin, Martin: "White-Washing the German Soldier: Disturbing Trend in New War Films." J Affairs, vol.16 #7 (July, 1961): 7-12.

8183. Eglington, Charles: "The Man and the Nation: A Plea and a Warning." J Affairs, vol.16 #12 (Dec., 1961): 31-32. * Documentary on Hitler.

8184. Eskin, Stanley G.: "Narrating 'The Holocaust'." Mid, vol.19 #10 (Dec., 1973): 84-88.

8185. Feingold, H. L.: "'Finzi-Continis': Afterthoughts." CBW, vol.39 #9 (June 30, 1972): 13, 20-21.

8186. ___: "Four Days in April: A Review of NBC´s Dramatization of ´The Holocaust´." Shoa, vol.1 #1 (1979): 15-17.

8187. ___: "NBC´s ´Holocaust´ - an Assessment." CM, vol.45 #4 (May, 1978): 14-16.

8188. Friedman, Saul S.: "In Defense of ´Holocaust´." J Fr, vol.45 #7 (Aug./Sept., 1978): 7-9.

8189. Hier, Marvin: "Postscript: The Making of the Film ´Genocide´." Grobman: Genocide, pp.432-436.

8190. Kellen, Konrad: "Exploiting the Holocaust." Mid, vol. 24 #6 (June/July, 1978): 56-59. <see #8204 and #8206>

8191. ___: "Seven Beauties: Auschwitz - the Ultimate Joke?" Mid, vol.22 #8 (Oct., 1976): 59-66.

8192. Kolinsky, E.: "Germans Struggle with the Past after the ´Holocaust´ Film." PoP, vol.13 #2 (March/June, 1979): 13-18.

8193. Lampell, Millard: "´The Wall´: Its Message is Life." ADL Bul, vol.18 #6 (June, 1961): 4-6.

8194. Landes, Daniel: "Modesty and Self-Dignity in Holocaust Films." Grobman: Genocide, pp.11-13.

8195. Lanzmann, Claude: Shoah: An Oral History of the Holocaust [New York: Pantheon Books, 1985] * Text of Film

8196. Liebman, Robert: "´Our Hitler´: A Film from Germany." Mid, vol.26 #8 (Oct., 1980): 37-38.

8197. Lustig, Arnost and J. Lustig: "The Holocaust and the Film Arts." Sherwin: Encountering, pp.351-382.

8198. ___ et al: "The Esthetics and Public Relations of the Holocaust." NJM, vol.92 #10 (June, 1978): 12-14, 16, 18, 20.

8199. Martin, B.: "NBC´s ´Holocaust´: The Trivialization of the Tragic." JRJ, vol.25 #3 (Sum., 1978): 43-46.

8200. Matis, D.: "Films of the Holocaust." Yiddish, vol.1 #1 (Sum., 1973): 12-23.

8201. Milton, S.: "Sensitive Issues about Holocaust Films." Grobman: Genocide, pp.8-10.

8202. Platt, D.: "´Judgment at Nuremberg´: An Indictment. Powerful Anti-Nazi Film Challenges U.S. Policy on Germany." J Currents, vol.16 #1 (Jan., 1962): 9-11.

8203. Quigly, Isabel: "Whitewashing Nazism on the Screen." J Affairs, vol.13 #10 (Oct., 1958): 21-23.

8204. Rachleff, Owen S.: "Assessing ´Holocaust´." Mid, vol. 24 #6 (June/July, 1978): 50-54. <see #8190 and #8206>

8205. Rosen, Robert: "The Holocaust in Theater and Film." Yiddish, vol.3 #3 (Win., 1978): 84-88.

8206. Rosenfeld, Alvin: "The Holocaust as Entertainment." Mid, vol.25 #8 (Oct., 1979): 55-58.

8607. Rosensaft, Menachem Z.: "Distorting the Holocaust." Mid, vol.24 #6 (June/July, 1978): 54-56. <see #8190 and #8204>

8208. Sherwin, Byron L.: "The Holocaust Universe of Arnost Lustig." Mid, vol.25 #7 (Aug./Sept., 1979): 44-48.

8209. Shneiderman, S. L.: "A Film Epic of Polish Jewry." CBW, vol.32 #10 (May 24, 1965): 8-10.

8210. Soudet, Pierre: "Misuses of the Holocaust by the Film Industry." Centerpoint, vol.4 #3 (Fall, 1980): 151-152.

8211. Sterling, Eleonore: "´Das Dritte Reich´: A German TV Experiment and How it is Faring." J Affairs, vol.16 #4 (April, 1961): 4-7.

8212. Toeplitz, K. T.: "A Film on the Warsaw Uprising." Poland, #9/25 (1956): 25-27.

8213. "Watching ´Holocaust´." Moment, vol.3 #5 (April, 1978): 34-41.

8214. Wortsman, Peter: "The Holocaust and the Camera." J Sp vol.42 #1 (Spr., 1977): 22-24.

REVIEW AND CRITIQUE OF HOLOCAUST LITERATURE

8215. Aaron, Frieda W.: "Poetry in the Holocaust Dominion." Braham: Perspectives, pp.119-131.

8216 Alexander, Edward: "Abba Kovner: Poet of Holocaust and Rebirth." Mid, vol.23 #8 (Oct., 1977): 50-59.

8217. ___: "The Holocaust in American-Jewish Fiction: A Slow Awakening." Judaism, vol.25 #3 (Sum., 1976): 320-330.

8218. ___: "The Holocaust in Jewish Novels." JBA, vol.35 (1977): 25-46.

8219. ___: The Resonance of Dust: Essays on Holocaust Literature and Jewish Fate [Columbus: Ohio State Univ. Press, 1979]

8220. Bauke, J. B.: "Nelly Sachs: Poet of the Holocaust." JH, vol.10 #4 (Spr., 1968): 34-39.

8221. Berenbaum, Michael G.: "Elie Wiesel and Contemporary Jewish Theology." Con Jud, vol.30 #3 (Spr., 1976): 19-39.

8222. ___: The Vision and the Void: Theological Reflections on the Works of Elie Wiesel [Middletown, CT: Wesleyan Univ. Press, 1979]

8223. Berger, Alan L.: "Covenant and History: The Holocaust in the Fiction of Hugh Nissenson." JRJ, vol.31 #3 (Sum., 1984): 47-65.

8224. Bilik, Dorothy: Immigrant-Survivors: Post Holocaust Consciousness in Recent Jewish Fiction [Middletown, CT: Wesleyan Univ. Press, 1981]

8225. Dawidowicz, Lucy S.: "Pictures of the Jewish Past." J Digest, vol.21 #4 (Jan., 1976): 53-62.

8226. Dewey, B. R.: "The Elie Wiesel Phenomenon: Interpretation and Prediction." Con Jud, vol.25 #1 (Fall, 1970): 25-33. <see #8227>

8227. Dresner, Samuel: "The Elie Wiesel Phenomenon: Witness for Judaism." Con Jud, vol.25 #1 (Fall, 1970): 34-41. <see #8226>

8228. Edelman, Lily: "Kaddish for the Six Million: The Work of Elie Wiesel." JH, vol.8 #4 (Spr., 1966): 40-47.

8229. Ehrenburg, Ilya: "About Anne Frank: Introducing Her Diary to Russians and the Unfinished Business of Nazism." J Currents, vol.15 #1 (Jan., 1961): 18-21.

8230. Esrati, Stephen G.: "The Holocaust: The Myth and the Literature." Recon, vol.47 #3 (May, 1981): 7-14.

8231. Ezrahi, Sidra de Koven: By Words Alone: The Holocaust in Literature [Chicago: Univ. of Chicago Press, 1980]

8232. Fine, Ellen S.: "Elie Wiesel´s Literary Legacy." JBA, vol.41 (1983/1984): 57-69.

8233. ___: Legacy of Night: The Literary Universe of Elie Wiesel [Albany, NY: SUNY Press, 1982]

8234. ___: "The Surviving Voice: Literature of the Holocaust." Braham: Perspectives, pp.105-117.

8235. Friedlander, Albert H.: "In Memoriam to German Jewry: Nelly Sachs and the Nobel Prize." Recon, vol.32 #17 (Jan. 6, 1967): 7-19.

8236. ___: "Nelly Sachs: Poet of the Holocaust." JQ, vol.14 #4 (Win., 1966/1967): 6-9.

8237. Friedman, M.: "Elie Wiesel: The Job of Auschwitz." CCARJ, vol.21 #3 (Sum., 1974): 3-36.

8238. ___: "Witness and Rebellion: The Unresolved Tension in the Works of Elie Wiesel." Judaism, vol.28 #4 (Fall, 1979): 484-491.

8239. Friedman, Norman: "God Versus Man in the Twentieth Century." Recon, vol.32 #12 (Oct. 28, 1966): 21-28.

8240. Friedman, P.: "The Literature of the Catastrophe." Recon, vol.26 #4 (April 1, 1960): 11-16.

8241. Gamulka, Lawrence: "The Trauma of the Holocaust Survivor in American Literature." V CJQ, vol.9 #1 (May, 1975): 36-48.

8242. Garber, Frederick: "The Art of Elie Wiesel." Judaism, vol.22 #3 (Sum., 1973): 301-308.

8243. Gillon, Adam: "Here Too As in Jerusalem: Selected Poems from the Ghetto." Polish Rev, vol.10 #3 (Sum., 1965): 27-46.

8244. ___: "Martyrs' Testament." Ch J Forum, vol.20 #4 (Sum., 1962): 283-287.

8245. Glanz-Leyeless, A.: "Poems from the Warsaw Ghetto." CJR, vol.8 #2 (April, 1945): 129-136.

8246. Glicksman, Wm. M.: "New Beginnings." Recon, vol.43 #3 (April, 1977): 19-25.

8247. Grunberger, Richard: "The Literature of Remorse." JBA, vol.22 (1964/1965): 26-41.

8248. Grynberg, Henryk: "The Warsaw Ghetto in Polish Literature." SJA, vol.13 #2 (May, 1983): 33-48.

8249. Gutman, Israel: "Remarks on the Literature of the Holocaust." Dispersion, #7 (1967): 119-134.

8250. Halperin, I.: "From the Literature of the Holocaust." Pilch: Catastrophe, pp.143-202.

8251. ___: "Holocaust Writers and the Critics." Ortho J Life, vol.34 #5 (May/June, 1967): 19-22.

8252. ___: "Meaning and Despair in the Literature of the Survivors." JBA, vol.26 (1968/1969): 7-22.

8253. Hevesi, F.: "Recent Jewish Literature in Hungary." JBA, vol.6 (1947/1948): 71-75.

8254. Kahn, Lothar: "The Jew in Postwar German Literature." JBA, vol.24 (1966/1967): 14-22.

8255. Kalisch, Shoshana: Yes, We Sang! Songs of the Ghettos and Concentration Camps [New York: Harper & Row, 1985]

8256. Kaufman, S.: "Who Are the Living and Who Are the Dead? (The Poetry of Abba Kovner)." Eur Jud, vol.8 #1 (Win., 1973/1974): 23-28.

8257. Kimmel, Eric A.: "The Distant Smoke: Children's Literature and the Holocaust." Response, vol.9 #1 (Spr., 1975): 23-31.

8258. Kirschner, Robert: "Yitzhak Katznelson´s ´The Song of the Murdered Jewish People´." Response, vol.11 #3 (Sum., 1978): 73-86.

8259. Klirs, Tracy: "Holocaust and Faith: Aaron Zeitlin´s Poems." Sh´ma, vol.8 #141 (Nov. 11, 1977): 184-187.

8260. Knopp, Josephine Z.: "Elie Wiesel: Man, God, and the Holocaust." Mid, vol.27 #7 (Aug./Sept., 1981): 45-51.

8261. ___: "What are Writers Doing to the Holocaust?" Sh´ma, vol.7 #133 (April 29, 1977): 107-109.

8262. ___ and A. Lustig: "Holocaust Literature II: Novels and Short Stories." Sherwin: Encountering, pp.267-315. <see #8302>

8263. Kobrin, N. H.: "Holocaust Literature in Judeo-Spanish Portuguese and Spanish." Tradition, vol.18 #3 (Fall, 1980): 288-294.

8264. Kohn, Murray: "Holocaust Motives in Hebrew Poetry." JQ, vol.20 #4 (Win., 1973): 20-23.

8265. ___: The Voice of My Blood Cries Out: The Holocaust As Reflected in Hebrew Poetry [New York: Shengold, 1979]

8266. Lamont, R. C.: "Holocaust Imagery in Contemporary French Literature." Braham: Perspectives, pp.133-147.

8267. Langer, Lawrence L.: The Age of Atrocity: Death in Modern Literature [Boston: Beacon Press, 1978]

8268. ___: The Holocaust and the Literary Immagination [New Haven, CT: Yale Univ. Press, 1976]

Studies the imaginative literature that has grown up to explain the Holocaust. Uses literary critical techniques to dissect and understand the literature of atrocity. Points out new stylistic features of each author.

8269. ___: "Imagining Atrocity: The Writer and the Holocaust Experience." CM, vol.46 #4 (May, 1979): 10-14; #5 (June, 1979): 15-17.

8270. ___: "The Writer and the Holocaust Experience." Friedlander: Ideology, pp.309-322.

8271. ___ and Sondra Langer: "Children and the Literature of the Holocaust." Shoa, vol.1 #1 (1979): 2-5.

8272. ___ (ed.): Versions of Survival: The Holocaust and the Human Spirit [New York: SUNY Press, 1981]

8273. Leftwich, Joseph: "The Songs and Poems of the Death Camps." JM, vol.2 #6 (Sept., 1948): 344-359.

8274. ___: "Songs of the Death Camps: A Selection with Commentary." Com, vol.12 #3 (Sept., 1951): 269-274.

8275. Leiter, Robert: "Books: About the Holocaust." Commonweal, vol.108 #14 (July 31, 1981): 438-447.

8276. Lust, P.: "The Holocaust in German Post-War Literature." V CJQ, vol.2 #4 (Win., 1967): 23-31.

8277. Mesher, David R.: "Reading the Holocaust." Judaism, vol.31 #2 (Spr., 1982): 177-184.

8278. Mintz, A.: Hurban: Response to Catastrophe in Hebrew Literature [New York: Columbia Univ. Press, 1985]

8279. Mirsky, David: "Abuse of the Holocaust Literature." JBA, vol.37 (1979/1980): 39-48.

8280. Niger, S.: "Yiddish Poets of the Third Destruction." Recon, vol.13 #10 (June 27, 1947): 13-18.

8281. Orsten, Elizabeth: "Light in Darkness." Bridge, vol.3 (1958/1959): 325-339.

8282. Pawel, Ernst: "Fiction of the Holocaust." Mid, vol.16 #6 (June/July, 1970): 14-26.

8283. Pinsker, S.: "Fictionalizing the Holocaust." Judaism, vol.29 #4 (Fall, 1980): 489-494.

8284. Pommer, Henry F.: "The Legend and the Art of Anne Frank." Judaism, vol.9 #1 (Win., 1960): 37-46.

8285. Rosen, Norma: "The Holocaust and the American-Jewish Novelist." Mid, vol.20 #8 (Oct., 1974): 54-62.

8286. Rosenbloom, Noah: "The Threnodist of the Holocaust." Judaism, vol.26 #2 (Spr., 1977): 232-247.

8287. Rosenfeld, Alvin H.: A Double Dying: Reflections on Holocaust Literature [Bloomington, IN: Indiana Univ. Press, 1980]

Analysis of Holocaust literature. Divides literature into two types: "inauthentic responses", which use the Holocaust as a literary device, and "authentic responses" which use literary forms to give texture to an understanding of the Holocaust.

8288. ___: "The Holocaust in American Popular Culture." Mid, vol.29 #6 (June/July, 1983): 53-59.

8289. ___: Imagining Hitler [Bloomington, In: Indiana Univ. Press, 1985]

8290. ___ and Irving Greenberg (eds.): Confronting the Holocaust: The Impact of Elie Wiesel [Bloomington, IN: Indiana Univ. Press, 1978]

Anthology of Literary criticism assessing the impact Elie Wiesel has had in making the world aware of the Holocaust.

8291. Roskies, David G.: Against the Apocalypse: Responses to Catastrophe in Modern Jewish Culture [Cambridge, MA: Harvard Univ. Press, 1984]

8292. ___: "The Literature of Destruction." Recon, vol.46 #1 (March, 1980): 12-18.

8293. Roth, John K.: A Consuming Fire: Encounters With Elie Wiesel and the Holocaust [Atlanta, GA: John Knox Press, 1979]

8294. Rothchild, Sylvia: "Writing About the Holocaust." PT, vol.9 #3 (Spr., 1982): 52-55.

8295. Rubin, Ruth: "Yiddish Folksongs of World War II: A Record of Suffering and Struggle." JQ, vol.11 #2 (Sum., 1963): 12-17.

8296. Seidman, Hillel: "Voice from the Holocaust." Ortho J Life, vol.32 #3/4 (Spr., 1965): 72-76.

8297. Sharoni, Edna: "Abba Kovner´s Observations." J Sp, vol.44 #4 (Win., 1979): 17-20.

8298. Sherwin, Byron L.: "Elie Wiesel on Madness." CCARJ, vol.19 #3 (June, 1982): 24-32.

8299. Silberschlag, Eisig: "The Holocaust in Hebrew Literature." J Sp, vol.43 #4 (Win., 1978): 16-23.

8300. Steinbach, A. Alan: "Nelly Sachs - Nobel Laureate." JBA, vol.25 (1967/1968): 42-52.

8301. Steiner, G.: Language and Silence: Essays on Language Literature and the Inhuman [New York: Atheneum, 1966]

8302. Syrkin, Marie: "The Literature of the Holocaust: I. The Diaries." Mid, vol.12. #5 (May, 1966): 3-21. <see #8262>

8303. Szeintuch, Yechiel: "The Work of Yitzhak Katznelson in the Warsaw Ghetto." Jer Q, #26 (Win., 1983): 46-61.

8304. Waxman, R.: "O the Chimneys: On Reading Nelly Sachs." Con Jud, vol.22 #4 (Sum., 1968): 48-55.

8305. Weiss-Rosmarin, Trude: "The Heroic Element in Jewish Life and Literature." JBA, vol.4 (1945): 5-15.

8306. Wiesel, Elie: "Art and Culture after the Holocaust." C/C, vol.26 #3 (Fall, 1976): 258-269.

8307. ___: "Conversation with Nelly Sachs." JH, vol.10 #4 Spr., 1968): 30-33.

8308. Winegarten, Renee: "Italian Voices." Eur Jud, vol.2 #1 (Sum., 1967): 36-39.

8309. Wisse, Ruth R.: "Aharon Appelfeld, Survivor." Com, vol.76 #2 (Aug., 1983): 73-76.

8310. ___: "The Ghetto Poems of Abraham Sutzkever." JBA, vol.36 (1978/1979): 26-36.

8311. Yudkin, L. I.: "The Israeli Writer and the Holocaust." Eur Jud, vol.7 #2 (Sum., 1973): 41-46.

8312. Yuter, Alan J.: The Holocaust in Hebrew Literature: From Genocide to Rebirth [Port Washington, NY: Assoc. Press, 1984]

18

Yizkor Bicher—Memorial Volumes

Byelorussian S.S.R.

8313. Chinitz, N. and S. Nachmani (eds.): Slutsk and Vicinity Memorial Book [New York/Tel Aviv: Yizkor Book Committee, 1962]

Czechoslovakia

8314. Ben-Zeev, M. (ed.): The Book of Michalovce [Tel Aviv: Committee of Michalovce Emigrants in Israel, 1969]

8315. Werner, Alfred: "In Memoriam: Czechoslovak Jewry." Am Heb, vol.153 #12 (Jan. 21, 1944): 4-5, 10.

France

8316. Klarsfeld, Serge (ed): Memorial to the Jews Deported from France 1942-1944 [South Deerfield, MA: The Beate Klarsfeld Foundation, 1983]

Germany

8317. Aron, William: The Jews of Hamburg [New York: American Jewish Committee of Hamburg Jews, 1967]

8318. Carlebach, Alexander: Adas Yeschurun of Cologne: The Life and Death of A Kehilla [Belfast: Mullan, 1964]

8319. Dicker, Herman: Creativity, Holocaust, Reconstruction: Jewish Life in Wuerttemberg Past and Present [New York: Sepher-Hermon Press, 1984]

8320. In Commemoration of the Frankfurt Jewish Community on the Occasion of the Acquisition of the Frankfurt Memorbuch [Jerusalem: Jewish National and University Library, 1965]

8321. Schwab, Hermann: A World in Ruins: History, Life and Work of German Jewry [London: Edward Goldston, 1946]

8322. Weiss-Rosmarin, Trude: "Epitaph for German Jewry." Lib Jud, vol.13 #10 (Feb., 1946): 45-51.

8323. Werner, A.: "2000 Years of German Jewish History." CBW, vol.31 #4 (Feb. 24, 1964): 7-13.

Holland

8324. Van Praag, Siegfried E.: "The Passing of Dutch Jewry: An Elegy." Com, vol.6 #4 (Oct., 1948): 322-326.

Hungary

8325. Kleinwardein (Kisvarda) Memorial Book [Tel Aviv: The Kleinwardein Society, 1980]

8326. Lewy, A. (ed.): The Jewish Community of Maad, Hungary [Jerusalem: Maad Commemorative Committee, 1974]

Latvia

8327. Bobe, M. et al (eds.): The Jews in Latvia [Tel Aviv: Assoc. of Latvian and Estonian Jews in Israel, 1971]

Lithuania

8328. Alperovitz, Yitzhak (ed.): Gordz Book: A Memorial to the Jewish Community of Gordz [Tel Aviv: The Gordz Society in Israel, 1980]

8329. Chrust, Josef (ed.): Keidan Memorial Book [Tel Aviv: Keidan Assoc. in Israel, South Africa and USA, 1977]

8330. Hessayon, Arthur: "Kaddish for Kovno." J Digest, vol. 27 #5 (Jan., 1982): 64-66.

8331. Levite, Alter (ed.): Memorial Book: The Ritavas Community. A Tribute to the Memory of Our Town [Tel Aviv: Ritovo Society in Israel, 1977]

8332. Marcus, Pesach: "Let Us Mourn the Dead - and Remember the Living." Lith Jew, vol.2 #5/6 (March, 1945): 1.

8333. Noy, S. (ed.): Yizkor Book in Memory of the Jewish Community of Yanova [Tel Aviv: Irgun Yotzey Yanova, 1978]

8334. Rabinovitch, Jacob (ed.): Lithuanian Jews: A Memorial Book [Tel Aviv: Hamenora Pub. House, 1974]

8335. Ran, Leyzer (ed.): The Jerusalem of Lithuania: Illustrated and Documented 3 vols. [New York: The Vilna Album Committee, 1974]

Poland

8336. Alperovitz, Yitzhak (ed.): Jaroslav Book: A Memorial to the Jewish Community of Jaroslav [Tel Aviv: Jaroslav Societies in Israel, 1978]

8337. Amitai, Mordechai et al (eds.): The Jewish Community Rohatyn: A Town that Perished [Tel Aviv: Rohatyn Association of Israel, 1962]

8338. Austri-Dan, Yeshayau (ed.): Memorial Book of Czortkow [Haifa: Irgun Yotzye Czortkow, 1967]

8339. Ayalon, Ben-Zion H. (ed.): Antopol (Antepolie) Yizkor Book [Tel Aviv: The Antopoller Yizkor Book Committee in the USA, 1972]

8340. Bachrach, Sh. (ed.): Memorial Book to the Community of Proshnitz [Tel Aviv: Proshnitz Landsmanschaft in Israel, 1974]

8341. Baker, Julius L. et al (eds.): Jedwabne: History and Memorial Book [Jerusalem: Yedwabner Society in Israel and the USA, 1980]

8342. Beller, Ilex: Lest My Village be Forgotten: A Jewish Childhood in Poland [New York: Alpine Fine Arts Collection, 1981]

8343. Ben-Meir, J. et al (eds.): Our Hometown Goniondz [Tel Aviv: Committee of Goniondz Associations in the USA and in Israel, 1960]

8344. Biderman, I. M. (ed.): Kolbuszowa Memorial Book [New York: United Kolbushover Society, 1971]

8345. Blond, Shlomo et al (eds.): Memorial Book of Tlumacz: The Life and Destruction of a Jewish Community [Tel Aviv: The Tlumacz Society, 1976]

8346. Blumenthal, Nachman (ed.): A Memorial to the Jewish Community of Baranow [Jerusalem: Yad Vashem, 1964]

8347. ___: Mir [Jerusalem: Encyclopaedia of the Diaspora, 1962]

8348. ___: Rozwadow Memorial Book [Jerusalem: Yad Vashem, 1968]

8349. Borowski, Judah et al (eds.): Piesk and Most: A Memorial Book [Tel Aviv: Piesk/Most Societies in Israel and in the Diaspora, 1975]

8350. Buechler, Y. R.: The Story and Source of the Jewish Community of Topoltchany [Jerusalem: Committee for Comm. the Jewish Community of Topoltchany, 1976]

8351. Burstein, Aviezer and Dov Kosowski (eds.): Govrovo Memorial Book [Tel Aviv: Govrover Societies in the United States, Israel and Canada, 1966]

8352. Carmi, Israel (ed): Nadworna: Memorial and Records [Tel Aviv: Nadworna Landsmanschaften in Israel and America, 1975]

8353. Chrust, J. (ed.): Memorial Book of the Jews of Rudki and Vicinity [Tel Aviv: The Rudki Society, 1978]

8354. Danzig 1939: Treasures of a Destroyed Community [New York: The Jewish Museum, 1980]

8355. Diamond, Benjamin (ed.): Husiatin: Jewish Settlement Founded in 16th Century - Annihilated in 1942 [New York: Group of Husiatin Landsleit in America, 1968]

8356. Druck, Samuel: Swastika Over Jaworow: The Tragic Chronicle of the Jaworow Jewish Community [New York: First Jaworower Independent Association, 1950]

8357. Ehrlich, Elhanan (ed.): The Staszow Book [Tel Aviv: Irgun Yotzey Staszow in Israel, 1962]

8358. ___: The Zdunska-Wola Book [Tel Aviv: Zdunska-Wola Associations in Israel and in the Diaspora, 1968]

8359. Eisenberg, Eliyahu (ed.): Plotzk (Plock): A History of an Ancient Jewish Community in Poland [Tel Aviv: Hamenora Pub. House, 1967]

8360. Eisenstadt, Shmuel and M. Gelbart (eds.): Kamenetz Litowsk, Zastavye and Colonies Memorial Book [Tel Aviv: Kamieniec and Zastavye Committees in Israel and in the USA, 1970]

8361. Falstein, Louis (ed.): The Martyrdom of Jewish Physicians in Poland [New York: Exposition Press, 1963]

8362. Farber, Kalman and J. Se´evi (eds.): Memorial Book of the Community of Vileika [Tel Aviv: Vileika Society, 1972]

8363. Ganuz, Yitzhak (ed.): The Stepan Story [Tel Aviv: The Stepan Society, 1977]

8364. Gelbart, M. (ed.): Memorial Book Dobromil [Tel Aviv: Dobromiler Societies in New York and Israel, 1963]

8365. ___: Memorial Book Konin [Tel Aviv: Association of Konin Jews in Israel, 1968]

8366. ___: Oshmana Memorial Book [Tel Aviv: Irgun Yotzey Oshmana, 1969]

8367. Geshuri, M. S. (ed.): Sefer Podhajce: The Podhajce Memorial Volume [Tel Aviv: Book Committee of Sefer Podhajce in Israel, 1972]

8368. Goldwasser, P. (ed.): The Community of Trzebinia [Haifa: Com. of Trzebinians in Israel, 1969]

8369. Gorin, George (ed.): Grayevo Memorial Book [New York: United Grayever Relief Committee, 1950]

8370. Halevi, Benjamin (ed.): Rozhan Memorial Book [Tel Aviv: The Rozhan Organization and Sigalit Pub. House, 1977]

8371. Halpern, Henoch et al (eds.): The Tragic End of Our Gliniany [Brooklyn, NY: The Author, 1946]

8372. Harpaz, M. (ed.): My Town: In Memory of the Communities Dobrzyn-Gollob [Tel Aviv: Association of Former Residents of Dobrzyn-Gollob, 1969]

8373. Harshoshanim, H. et al (eds.): Radomysl Wielki and Neighbourhood: Memorial Book [Tel Aviv: Irgun Yotzey Radomishle, 1965]

8374. Hinitz, N. (ed.): Memorial Volume of Steibtz-Swerznie and the Neighbouring Villages [Tel Aviv: Irgun Yotzey Steibtz in Israel, 1964]

8375. Kagan, Berl (ed.): Yizkor Book of Luboml [Tel Aviv: Editorial Committee, n.d.]

8376. ___: Yizkor Book Szydlowicz [New York: Shidlovtser Benevolent Association, 1974]

8377. Kallay, S. (ed.): Boiberke Memorial Book [Jerusalem: Assoc. of Former Residents of Boiberke and Vicinity, 1964]

8378. Kanc, Shimon (ed.): Memorial Book Grabowitz [Tel Aviv: Irgun Yotzey Grabowiec, 1975]

8379. ___: Przedborz Memorial Book [Tel Aviv: Przedborz Societies in Israel and America, 1977]

8380. ___: Ripin: A Memorial to the Jewish Community of Ripin, Poland [Tel Aviv: Irgun Yotzey Ripin, 1962]

8381. ___: Yizkor-Book in Memory of Rozniatow, Perchinsko, Broszniow, Swaryczow and Environs [Tel Aviv: Irgun Yotzey Rozniatow in Israel and the USA, 1974]

8382. ___: Yizkor Book in Memory of Wlodawa and Region Sobibor [Tel Aviv: Irgun Yotzey Wlodawa, 1974]

8383. Kaplinsky, Baruch (ed.): Pinkas Hrubieshov: Memorial to a Jewish Community in Poland [Tel Aviv: Hrubieshov Assoc. in Israel and the USA, 1962]

8384. Katz, Menachem (ed.): Brzezany Memorial Book [Haifa: Brzezany-Narajow Societies in Israel and the United States, 1978]

8385. Kirshner, Sheldon: "Poland: The Graveyard of Our Heritage." HM, vol.59 #8 (April, 1978): 12-13, 42-46.

8386. Kriv, Yosef (ed.): Horchiv Memorial Book [Tel Aviv: Horchiv Committee in Israel, 1966]

8387. Kudish, N. et al (eds.): Seifer Stryj [Tel Aviv: J. L. Peretz Pub. House for Former Residents of Stryj, 1962]

8388. Kugelmass, Jack and J. Boyarin (eds. and transls.): From a Ruined Garden: The Memorial Books of Polish Jewry [New York: Schocken Books, 1983]

8389. Lask, I. M. (ed.): The Kalish Book [Tel Aviv: Kalish Societies in Israel and in the USA, 1968]

8390. Lazarowitz, Leopold and S. Malowist: "Martyred Physicians." Falstein: Martyrdom, pp.301-497.

8391. Leoni, E. (ed.): Ciechanoviec (Bialystock District): Memorial and Records [Tel Aviv: Ciechanovitzer Immigrant Association in Israel and the USA, 1964]

8392. ___: Wolozin: The Book of the City and of the Etz Hayyim Yeshiva [Tel Aviv: Wolozin Landsleit Association in Israel and the USA, 1970]

8393. Lewinsky, Yom-Tov (ed.): The Book of Zambrov [Tel Aviv: The Zambrover Society in Israel, the USA and Argentina, 1963]

8394. Lichtenstein, Kalman (ed.): Slonim: Memorial Book [Tel Aviv: Irgun Yotzey Slonim in Israel, 1979]

8395. Manor, A. et al (ed.): The Book of Sambor and Stari-Sambor [Tel Aviv: Sambor/Stari-Sambor Societies, 1980]

8396. ___: Sepher Lida: The Book of Lida [Tel Aviv: Irgun Yotzey Lida in Israel, 1970]

8397. Meiri, S. (ed.): The Jewish Community of Wieliczka: A Memorial Book [Tel Aviv: Wieliczka Assoc. in Israel, 1980]

8398. Mermelstein, Max et al (eds.): Skala [New York/Tel Aviv: Skala Benevolent Society, 1978]

8399. Meyerowitz, Aharon (ed.): Vlodimeretz Yizkor Volume [Tel Aviv: Irgun Yotzey Vlodimeretz in Israel, 1962]

8400. Mondry, Adele (Moshe Spiegel, transl.): Wyszkowo, a Shtetl on the Bug River [New York: Ktav, 1980]

8401. Nitzan, Shmuel (ed.): Rachov-Annopol: Testimony and Remembrance [Tel Aviv: OZ Commemoration Fund and Association of Rachov-Annopol, 1978]

8402. Perlov, Yitzhak and Alfred Lipson (eds.): Radom Book [Tel Aviv: Radom Society in Israel and the USA, 1961]

8403. Rabin, Haim (ed.): Bielsk-Podliask: Book in the Holy Memory of the Bielsk-Podliask Jews Whose Lives were Taken during the Holocaust between 1939 and 1944 [Tel Aviv: Bielsk Immigrants Assoc. of Israel and the USA, 1975]

8404. ___: Vishograd [Tel Aviv: Irgun Yotzey Vishograd, 1971]

8405. Rapoport, J. (ed.): Pinkas Zaglembye: Memorial Book [Tel Aviv: Hamenorah Pub. House, 1972]

8406. Remba, A. and B. Halevy (eds.): Kolno Memorial Book [Tel Aviv: Sifriat Poalim, 1971]

8407. Rimon, J. (ed.): The Jewish Community of Szrensk and Vicinity: A Memorial Volume [Jerusalem: Irgun Yotzey Szrensk in Israel, 1960]

8408. Rubin, I. Z. (ed.): Stavisk Yizkor Book [Tel Aviv: Irgun Yotzey Stavisk, 1973]

8409. ___: Visoka-Mozovietsk [Tel Aviv: Irgun Yotzey Wisoka Mozovietsk, 1975]

8410. Russak, Shmuel: "Our Village." J Sp, vol.31 #1 (Jan., 1966): 9-11. * Golub and Dobrzn.

8411. Schutzman, Mark (ed.): Wierzbnik-Starachowitz: A Memorial Book [Tel Aviv: Wierzbnik-Starachowitz Relief Society in Israel and the Diaspora, 1973]

8412. Segal, M. (ed.): Monasterzyska: A Memorial Book [Tel Aviv: Monasterzyska Association, 1974]

8413. Shaiak, G. (ed.): Lowicz: A Town in Mazovia, Memorial Book [Tel Aviv: Former Res. of Lowicz in Melbourne and Sydney, Australia, 1966]

8414. Shalit, Levi: "The Chelm That Once Was." J Affairs, vol.10 #4 (April, 1955): 19-21.

8415. Shamri, Aryeh and D. First (eds.): Pinkas Novy-Dvor [Tel Aviv: Former Residents of Novy Dvor in Israel, USA and Argentina, 1965]

8416. Shayari, Avraham (ed.): Busk: In Memory of Our Community [Haifa: Busk Organization in Israel, 1965]

8417. Shedletzky, Ephraim (ed.): Minsk-Mazowiecki Memorial Book [Jerusalem: Minsk-Mazowiecki Societies in Israel and Abroad, 1977]

8418. Shmulewitz, I. et al (eds.): The Bialystoker Memorial Book [New York: The Bialystoker Center, 1982]

8419. Shneiderman, S. L.: "The Dead Shtetlakh." J Sp, vol. 43 #3 (Fall, 1978): 41-47.

8420. ___: "Dead Shtetlakh on the Vistula." HM, vol.57 #5 (Jan., 1976): 14-16.

8421. ___: The River Remembers [New York: Horizon Press, 1978]

8422. Shtokfish, David (ed.): Druhitshin Memorial Volume [Tel Aviv: Druhitshin Society, 1969]

8423. ___: Gniewaszow Memorial Book [Tel Aviv: Irgun Yotzey Gniewaszow, 1971]

8424. Siegelman, J. (ed.): Sefer Budzanow [Tel Aviv/Haifa: Irgun Yotzey Budzanow in Israel, 1968]

8425. Sohn, David (ed.): Bialystok: Photo Album of a Renowned City and Its Jews the World Over [New York: Bialystoker Album Committee, 1951]

8426. Sokoler, Shlomo (ed.): Telekhan Memorial Book [Los Angeles: Telekhan Memorial Book Committee, 1963]

8427. Starkman, Moshe et al (eds.): Mosty-Wielki Memorial Book 2 vols. [Tel Aviv: Mosty-Wielki Societies in Israel and the USA, 1975]

8428. Strzegowo Yizkor Book [New York: United Strzegower Relief Committee, 1951]

8429. The Tragic End of Our Gliniany [New York: Emergency Relief Committee for Gliniany, 1946]

8430. Tsoref, Ephraim (ed.): Gal´ Ed: Memorial Book of the Community of Racionz [Tel Aviv: Irgun Yotzey Racionz in Israel, 1965]

8431. Tur-Shalom (Tash), Eliezer (ed.): The Community of Semiatych [Tel Aviv: Semiatyzer Societies in Israel and the USA, 1965]

8432. Tzurnamal, Zeev (ed.): Lask Izcor-Book [Tel Aviv: Irgun Yotzey Lask in Israel, 1968]

8433. Unger, Shabtai and Moshe Ettinger (eds.): Kalusz: The Life and Destruction of the Jewish Community [Tel Aviv: Kalusz Society, 1980]

8434. Vinecour, Earl and Chuck Fishman: Polish Jews: The Final Chapter [New York: New York Univ. Press, 1980]

Illustrated post-Holocaust survey. An elegy to a thousand-year old Jewish community, until the advent of nazism the biological core of the Jewish world.

8435. Walzer-Fass, Michael (ed.): Korelitz: The Life and Destruction of a Jewish Community [Tel Aviv: Korelitz Societies in Israel and the USA, 1973]

8436. ___: Remembrance Book Novy Targ and Vicinity [Tel Aviv: Townspeople Assoc. of Novy Targ and Vicinity, 1979]

8437. ___ and Moshe Kaplan (eds.): Book of Remembrance - Tooretz-Yeremitz [Tel Aviv: Tooretz-Yeremitz Soc. in Israel and the USA, 1978]

8438. ___ and N. Kudish (eds.): Lancut: Life and Destruction of a Jewish Community [Tel Aviv: Former Residents of Lancut Soc. in Israel and the USA, 1963]

8439. Wielun Memorial Book [Tel Aviv: Irgun Yotzey Wielun in Israel and in the USA, 1971]

8440. Yariwold, M. (ed.): Rzeszow Jews: Memorial Book [Tel Aviv: Committee of Rayshe Landsleite in Israel and America, 1967]

8441. Yasheev, Zvi (ed.): Apt: A Town Which Does Not Exist Any More [Tel Aviv: Apt Organizations in Israel, USA, Canada, and Brazil, 1966]

8442. Yassni, Wolf (ed.): The Book of Jadow [Jerusalem: The Encyclopaedia of the Diaspora, 1966]

8443. Yiddish Lodz: A Yiskor Book [Melbourne, Australia: The Lodz Center, 1974]

8444. Yizkor Book of the Jewish Community in Dzialoszyce and Surroundings [Tel Aviv: Hamenora, 1973]

8445. Youkelson, Florence et al (eds.): Strzegowo Yizkor-Book [New York: United Strzegowo Relief Com., 1951]

8446. Zicklin, Jack (ed.): Gombin: Life and Death of a Jewish Town in Poland [New York: The Gumbiner Society of America, 1969]

8447. Zik, Gershon (ed.): Rozyszcze My Old Home [Tel Aviv: Rozyszcze Societies, 1976]

8448. Zinkower Memorial Book [Tel Aviv: Joint Committee of Zinkower Landsleit, 1966]

8449. Zwolen Memorial Book [New York: Zwolen Society, 1982]

Rumania

8450. Abramovici, Moscu (ed.): Our Town Bivolari [Haifa: Bivolari Immigrants Organization in Israel, 1981]

8451. Carmilly-Weinberger, Moshe (ed.): Memorial Volume for the Jews of Cluj-Kolozsvar [New York: The Author, 1970]

8452. Guersen-Salzman, Ayse: The Last Jews of Radauti [New York: Dial Press, 1983] * Photographs by L. Salzman.

8453. Tamari, M. (ed.): Bendery and Her Holy Congregation [Tel Aviv: Bendery Society in Israel and the USA, 1975]

8454. Zwergbaum, Aaron: "Memorial to the Jews of Bukovina." CW, vol.30 #2 (Jan. 21, 1963): 13-14.

Ukrainian S.S.R.

8455. Ori, A. and M. Bone (eds.): Zhvil - Novo Gradvolinsk [Tel Aviv: Irgun Yotzey Zhvil and Environs, 1962]

Varia

8456. Abramowitch, Raphael (ed.): The Vanished World [New York: Forward Association, 1947]

8457. Bass, David (ed.): "Bibliographical List of Memorial Books Published in the Years 1943-1972." YVS, vol.9 (1973): 273-322.

8458. Bloch, Sam E. (ed.): Holocaust and Rebirth: Bergen-Belsen, 1945-1965 [New York: Bergen-Belsen Memorial Press/World Federation of B-B Assoc., 1965]

8459. Blumenthal, Nachman: "Memorial Books by Survivors of Communities." YVB, #3 (April, 1958): 24-27.

8460. Patai, Robert: The Vanished World of Jewry [New York: Macmillan, 1980]

Survey of Jewish Communities that no longer exist. Attempts to reconstruct their lives in both pictures and words. Each community is reviewed independently - from Eastern Europe to North Africa to the Middle East. Picture research by Eugene Rosow with Vivian Kleiman.

8461. Rosenthal, D.: "Remembering the Jews of the Ghettos and Camps." J Fr, vol.43 #4 (April, 1976): 8-12.

8462. Schulman, Elias: "A Survey and Evaluation of Yizkor Books." JBA, vol.25 (1967/1968): 184-191.

8463. Starkman, Moshe: "The Character of Our Yizkor Literature." JCA, vol.3 #1 (Jan., 1956): 1-3.

8464. Wein, A.: "´Memorial Books´ as a Source for Research into the History of Jewish Communities in Europe." YVS, vol.9 (1973): 255-272.

* All Yizkor Books cited above are in English and/or in combination with Hebrew, Yiddish, Polish, and Hungarian. All memorial volumes without English were not listed.

19

Distorting the Holocaust

WORKS ON DISTORTION

8465. Alexander, Edward: "Stealing the Holocaust." Mid, vol.26 #9 (Nov., 1980): 46-51.

8466. Alter, Robert: "Deformations of the Holocaust." Com, vol.71 #2 (Feb., 1981): 48-54.

8467. Ariel, Joseph: "The Eichmann Trial in the Neo-Nazi Press." YVB, #11 (April/May, 1962): 13-18.

8468. Arnsberg, Paul: "How Many Jews were Quislings." JOMER, vol.12 #6 (Feb. 8, 1963): 11-12.

8469. Aronsfeld, C. C.: "After the Murders - the Lies." J Fr, vol.46 #4 (April, 1979): 24-27.

8470. ___: "A Propos of a British Historical Review: Facts of the Holocaust." PoP, vol.8 #4 (July/Aug., 1974): 11-16.

8471. ___: "Debauchers of the Truth: How the Facts of the Holocaust are being Distorted." J Fr, vol.45 #6 (June/July, 1978): 9-13.

8472. ___: "The Extermination of Jews was no ´War Crime´." J Fr, vol.44 #7 (Aug./Sept., 1977): 18-19.

8473. ___: "The Hoax of the Century." J Digest, vol.22 #10 (June, 1977): 23-28. * On Arthur Butz.

8474. ___: "The Institute for Historical Review: Revisionists who Whitewash Nazism." IJA Res Rep, #4 (May, 1982): 1-8. * Includes 3 page bibliography.

8475. ___: "Whitewashing Hitler: Revisionist History Distorters at Work." PoP, vol.4 #1 (Jan., 1980): 16-23.

8476. Barnes, Ian R. and R. P. Vivienne: "A Revisionist Historian Manipulates Anne Frank´s Diary." PoP, vol. 15 #1 (Jan., 1981): 27-32.

8477. Bar-On, Zvi and Dov Levin: "Problems Relating to a Questionaire on the Holocaust." YVS, vol.3 (1959): 91-118.

8478. Bauer, Yehuda: "Antisemitism Today - A Fiction or a Fact?" Mid, vol.30 #8 (Oct., 1984): 24-31.

8479. ___: "Can Friends Obliterate Martyrdom of Holocaust?" J Digest, vol.26 #6 (Feb., 1981): 53-61.

8480. ___: "Whose Holocaust?" Mid, vol.26 #9 (Nov., 1980): 42-46.

8481. "Ben-Gurion, Golda Meir - Allies of Eichmann." JIEE, vol.4 #2 (July, 1969): 17-19.

8482. Berkovits, Eliezer: "Rewriting the History of the Holocaust. " Sh´ma, vol.10 #198 (Oct. 3, 1980): 139-142.

8483. Billig, J.: "The Launching of the Final Solution." Klarsfeld: Mythomania, pp.1-104a.

8484. "Blood Libel." JIEE, vol.2 #2 (May, 1963): 34-39.

8485. Bulawko, Henry: "Those who Deny the Holocaust." IH, vol.30 #7/8 (Sept./Oct., 1982): 24-25.

8486. Dawidowicz, Lucy S.: "Lies About the Holocaust." Com, vol.70 #6 (Dec., 1980): 31-37.

8487. Eban, Abba: "Arnold Toynbee and Jewish History." J Fr, vol.22 #2 (Feb., 1955): 25-30.

8488. "The Eichmann Case: Soviet Version." JIEE, vol.1 #8 (July, 1961): 14-19.

8489. "Fascism Under the Blue Star." JIEE, vol.5 #2 (Nov., 1972): 15-16.

8490. "The First Unabridged Publication of the Two ´Korherr Reports´." Klarsfeld: Mythomania, pp.165-210.

8491. Forster, Arnold: "The Campaign That Failed." ADL Bul, vol.25 #1 (Jan., 1968): 7-8.

8492. ___: "The Ultimate Cruelty." ADL Bul, vol.16 #6 (June, 1959): 1-2, 7-8.

8493. Fresco, Nadine and Nina Farhi: "How History is Being Revised." PoP, vol.15 #2 (April, 1981): 21-32.

8494. Friedlander, Albert H.: "Misuses of the Holocaust." J Digest, vol.29 #6 (Feb., 1984): 7-16.

8495. Gardner, Jigs: "The Keegstra Affair." Mid, vol.31 #9 (Nov., 1985): 7-9.

8496. Geffen, Mark: "The East European Press on the Warsaw Ghetto Revolt." Dispersion, #3 (Win., 1963/1964): 35-52. * Twenty Years after the Ghetto Revolts.

8497. Goldhagen, Erich: "The Soviet Treatment of the Holocaust." Mid, vol.25 #10 (Dec., 1979): 5-7.

8498. Grynberg, Henryk: "Appropriating the Holocaust." Com, vol.74 #5 (Nov., 1982): 54-57.

8499. Guri, J.: "The Jewish Holocaust in Soviet Writings." YVB, #18 (April, 1966): 4-11.

8500. Haft, C.: "Visiting My Family´s Grave - at Birkenau." Sh´ma, vol.3 #53 (April 27, 1973): 98-99.

8501. Harris, Sam: "The Underground Nazi Propagandist." J Fo, vol.31 #1 (Jan., 1948): 7-9; #2 (Feb., 1948): 29-31.

8502. "´Harwoods´s´ Distortion of Holocaust Facts." PoP, vol.9 #3 (May/June, 1975): 25-27. * On Richard E. Harwood´s Did 6 Million Really Die?

8503. Heiman, Leo: "How Moscow Falsifies History to Conceal the Identity of Hundreds of World War Heroes of the Soviet Union." NJM, vol.79 #3 (Nov., 1964): 16, 18.

8504. Himmelfarb, M.: "No Hitler, No Holocaust." J Digest, vol.29 #10 (June, 1984): 3-12.

8505. Ivy, I.: "The Conspiracy of Silence Surronding the Holocaust." J Fr, vol.43 #1 (Jan., 1976): 12-14.

8506. "Jews Accused of Ritual Blood Drinking." JIEE, vol.1 #6 (Dec., 1960): 3-5.

8507. "Jews and the War." JIEE, vol.3 #1 (Nov., 1964): 51-52.

8508. Klarsfeld, Serge (ed.): The Holocaust and the Neo-Nazi Mythomania [New York: The Beate Klarsfeld Foundation, 1978]

Two essays and a documentary study whose purpose is to ascertain the truth about the Holocaust and to expose neo-Nazi revisionist and antisemitic propaganda which deny the reality of the events. Billig´s essay is also a useful summary on the stages of Nazi policy which culminated in the Final Solution.

8509. Korey, William: "Down History´s Memory Hole." PT, vol.10 #2 (Win., 1983): 50-54.

8510. ___: "Eichmann and the Socialist Press." IH, vol.10 #3 (March, 1962): 8-12.

8511. ___: "In History´s Memory Hole: The Soviet Treatment of the Holocaust." Braham: Contemporary, pp.145-156.

8512. ___: Jews as Non-Persons: A Study of Soviet History Textbooks in Elementary and Secondary Schools [New York: B´nai Brith International Council, 1973]

8513. ___: "´Soldaten Zeitung´: Echoes of the Nazi Past." ADL Bul, vol.23 #3 (March, 1966): 1-2.

8514. ___: "Updating The Protocols of the Elders of Zion." Mid, vol.22 #5 (May, 1976): 5-17.

8515. Krakowski, Shmuel: "The Slaughter of Polish Jewry - A Polish Reassessment." WLB, vol.26 #3/4 (Sum./Aut., 1972): 13-20.

8516. Kulka, Erich (Lilli Kapecky, transl): The Holocaust is Being Denied! The Answer of Auschwitz Survivors [Tel Aviv: The Committee of Auschwitz Camp Survivors in Israel, 1977]

Review of the antisemitic and anti-Zionist usage of denial of the Holocaust. Covers all Holocaust denial literature from the United States, Europe, and the Third World. Gives numerous examples from the United States, Germany, and the Soviet Union. Includes copious notes.

8517. Kuznetsov, Anatoly: "The Guilt of Babi Yar." Atlas, vol.13 #2 (Feb., 1967): 10-14.

8518. "The La Rouche Network." ADL Bul, vol.39 #6 (June, 1982): 6-7.

8519. "Le Charivari." ADL Bul, vol.25 #3 (March, 1968): 3, 8.

8520. "Les Juifs: Fact-Fiction Without Facts." ADL Bul, vol. 22 #8 (Oct., 1965): 4-5.

8521. Levin, Dov: "Fact and Fiction." YVN, #4 (1973): 22-23, 26.

8522. Littell, Franklin H.: "Holocaust Revisionists Offer Recurring Themes." M&R, vol.9 #4 (March/April, 1983): 10-11.

8523. Lowe, David: "The Make Believe World of the I. H. R." ADL Bul, vol.40 #9 (Nov., 1983): 1, 5-6.

8524. Meisel, Nachman: "Allies ´Stopped´ Gas Warfare Except for Jews." IH, vol.13 #8 (Oct., 1965): 14-15.

8525. "Merchant of Hate." ADL Bul, vol.21 #3 (March, 1964): 1-2.

8526. Mermelstein, Mel: "The Revisionists." Littell: Education, pp.107-112.

8527. "The Most Vicious Anti-Jewish Book Since the Nazi Era." J Digest, vol.11 #4 (Jan., 1966): 75-78.

8528. "Neo-Nazi View of the Holocaust." PoP, vol.7 #5 (Sept./Oct., 1973): 19-21.

8529. "NPD and Rathenau Murderers." PoP, vol.2 #2 (March/April, 1968): 15-16, 20.

8530. Poupko, Bernard A.: "Protocols of the Elders of Zion: Soviet Version." Ortho J Life, vol.35 #4 (March/April, 1968): 29-34.

8531. "Pravda Equates Zionism with Fascism." IJA Res Rep, #2 (March, 1984): 1-7.

8532. Prinz, Joachim: "Misleading the German People." CBW, vol.35 #10 (Sept. 16, 1968): 8-10.

8533. Rosenfeld, Alvin H.: "Imagining Hitler." Mid, vol.31 #4 (April, 1985): 50-54.

8534. Rosenthal, Ludwig: The Final Solution to the Jewish Question: Mass-Murder or Hoax? [Los Angeles: Judah L. Magnes Memorial Museum, 1984]

8535. Roth, S. J.: "Making the Denial of the Holocaust a Crime in Law" IJA Res Rep, #1 (March, 1982): 1-12.

8536. Samuel, Maurice: The Professor and the Fossil: Some Observations on A. J. Toynbee's 'A Study of History' [New York: A. A. Knopf, 1956]

8537. Shneiderman, S. L.: "Distortions in Warsaw." CBW, vol. 30 #10 (May 27, 1963): 5-8.

8538. Silverberg, Mark: "The Holocaust and the Historical Revisionists." JJCS, vol.59 #1 (Fall, 1982): 16-25.

8539. Singer, Herman: "Antisemitism Without Jews." ADL Bul, vol.20 #7 (Sept., 1963): 4-5.

8540. Soviet Antisemitic Propaganda [London: IJA/WJC, 1978]

8541. "The Soviet Press on Eichmann." JIEE, vol.1 #5 (Aug., 1960): 3-7.

8542. Swigard, Kent: "An Ex-Nazi and an Auschwitz Survivor Join Forces." CM, vol.50 #1 (Jan., 1983): 12-13.

8543. Syrkin, Marie: "Mr. Toynbee and the Jews." J Fr, vol. 21 #12 (Dec., 1954): 5-8.

8544. ___: "Soviet Jewish Stooges: The Anti-Zionist Committee." Mid, vol.29 #7 (Aug./Sept., 1983): 50-52.

8545. Waite, R. G. L.: "The Hitler Whitewash." J Digest, vol.23 #2 (Oct., 1977): 5-8.

8546. Weiss-Rosmarin, Trude: "Toynbee and Jewish History." J Sp, vol.12 #12 (Oct., 1947): 7-10.

8547. Wellers, G.: "The Number of Victims and the ´Korherr Report´." Klarsfeld: Mythomania, pp.139-162.

8548. ___: "Reply to the Neo-Nazi Falsification of Historical Facts Concerning the Holocaust." Klarsfeld: Mythomania, pp.107-138.

8549. Werner, AAlfred: "Schacht´s Apologia." Ch J Forum, vol.9 #3 (Spr., 1951): 184-189.

8550. Whartman, E.: "Eichmann: Hero of the Arab Press." J Fr, vol.28 #10 (Oct., 1961): 16-18.

8551. Wiesel, Elie: "What Really Happened to Six Million." J Digest, vol.23 #8 (April, 1978): 36-38.

8552. Wistrich, Robert: "The Anti-Zionist Masquerade." Mid, vol.29 #7 (Aug./Sept., 1983): 8-18.

8553. Yaffe, Richard: "The Obscene Comparison." IH, vol.15 #6 (July/Aug., 1967): 16-20.

8554. "Zionists ´Encouraged´ Nazis in Persecution of Jews." JIEE, vol.4 #6 (Aug., 1970): 38-42.

8555. "Zionist Forgeries About Jewish Resistance." JIEE, vol.4 #1 (Jan., 1969): 35-36.

WORKS OF DISTORTION

8556. App, Austin J.: "Hitler-Himmler Order on Jews Uncovered." Liberty Bell, (Jan., 1978): 5 pp. pamphlet

8557. ___: The Hitler-Himmler Order on the Jews [Brooklyn, NY: The Revisionist Press, 1984]

8558. ___: The Holocaust Sneak Attack on Christianity [Brooklyn, NY: The Revisionist Press, 1984]

8559. ___: The Six Million Swindle [Takoma Park, MD: Boniface Press, 1973]

8560. Brown, S. E. D. (ed.): "Atrocity Propaganda: Reminder to Christian Leaders." South African Observer, vol.22 #11 (July, 1978): 35-49.

8561. Butz, Arthur R.: The Hoax of the Twentieth Century [Los Angeles, CA: Noontide Press, 1978]

8562. Christophersen, T.: Auschwitz: Truth or Lie [Toronto: Samisdat Pub., 1974]

8563. de Kayville, Victor: "Is the Orthodox Jew Harmless?" Liberty Bell, (Jan., 1978): 7 pp. pamphlet.

8564. Faurison, Robert: Is the Diary of Anne Frank Genuine? [Torrance, CA: Institute for Historical Review, 1985]

8565. ___: The Problem of the "Gas Chambers" or the Rumor of Auschwitz [Rochelle Park, NJ: Revisionist Press, 1979]

8566. Felderer, D.: Ann Frank´s Diary: A Hoax [Torrance, CA: Institute for Historical Review, 1979]

8567. ___: Auschwitz Exit [Taby, Sweden: Bible Researcher, 1980]

8568. Grimstad, Wm. N. (ed.): The Six Million Reconsidered: Is the ´Nazi Holocaust´ Story a Zionist Propaganda Ploy? [Torrance, CA: Committee for Truth in History, 1979]

8569. Harwood, Richard E.: Did Six Million Really Die?: The Truth at Last [Richmond, VA: Historical Review Press, 1974]

8570. ___: Nuremberg and Other War Crime Trials: A New Look [Torrance, CA: Noontide Press, 1978]

8571. ___: Six Million Lost and Found [Brighton, England: Historical Review Press, 1979]

8572. Heinz, A. Heinz: Germany´s Hitler [Torrance, CA: The Institute for Historical Review/Noontide Press, 1976]

8573. Hoggan, David L.: The Myth of the Six Million [Los Angeles, CA: Noontide Press, 1978]

8574. Morris, Warren B.: The Revisionist Historians and German War Guilt [Brooklyn, NY: The Revisionist Press, 1980]

8575. Rassinier, Paul: Debunking the Genocide Myth: A Study of the Nazi Concentration Camps and the Alleged Extermination of European Jewry [Los Angeles, CA: Noontide Press, 1978]

8576. ___: Drama of the European Jews [Silver Springs, MD: Steppingstones Press, 1976]

8577. ___: The Real Eichmann Trial: Or the Incorrigible Victors [Brighton, England: Historical Review Press, 1979]

8578. Rittenhouse, Stan: For Fear of the Jews [Vinna, VA: The Exhorters, 1982]

8579. Sanning, Walter N.: The Dissolution of Eastern European Jewry [Torrance, CA: Institute for Historical cal Review, 1983]

8580. Stimely, Keith (ed.): 1981 Revisionist Bibliography [Torrance, CA: Institute for Historical Review, 1981]

8581. Walendy, Udo: Forged War Crimes Malign the German Nation [Vlotho, W. Germany: Verlag fuer Volkstum und Zeitgeschichtsforschung, 1979]

8582. ___: The Methods of Re-Education [Vlotho, W. Germany: Verlag fuer Volkstum und Zeitgeschichtsforschung, 1979]

8583. ___: Truth for Germany: The Guilt Question of the Second World War [Torrance, CA: Institute for Historical Review, 1981]

8584. Weber, Charles E.: The "Holocaust": 120 Questions and Answers [Torrance, CA: The Institute for Historical Review, 1983]

8585. Yahya, Faris: Zionist Relations with Nazi Germany [Beirut, Lebanon: Palestine Research Center, 1978]

20

Historiography, Bibliographies and Guides

HISTORIOGRAPHY

Methods and Issues

8586. Ainsztein, Reuben: "Jewish Tragedy and Heroism in Soviet War Literature." JSS, vol.23 #2 (April, 1961): 67-84.

8587. Arendt, Hannah: "Social Science Techniques and the Study of Concentration Camps." JSS, vol.12 #1 (Jan., 1950): 49-64.

8588. Aronsfeld, C. C.: "Fifty Years After Hitler: Thoughts of a German Revolution." PoP, vol.17 #2 (April, 1983): 21-30.

8589. Ball-Kaduri, Kurt Y.: "Evidence of Witnesses, its Value and Limitations." YVS, vol.3 (1959): 79-90.

8590. ___: "The Role of Interviewing in the Research of the Holocaust Period - Three Papers." YVS, vol.3 (1959): 77-78.

8591. Bauer, Yehuda: "Against Mystification: The Holocaust as a Historical Phenomenon." Bauer: Perspective, pp. 30-49.

8592. ___: "Holocaust Questions." CM, vol.47 #4 (May, 1980): 8-9.

8593. ___: "Trends in Holocaust Research." Bauer: Hol History, pp.9-38.

8594. ___: "Whose Holocaust." Porter: Genocide, pp.35-45.

8595. ___ A. Margaliot and Y. Gutman: Essays in Holocaust History [Jerusalem: Division of Holocaust Studies, 1979]

8596. ___ and Nathan Rotenstreich (eds.): The Holocaust as Historical Experience: Essays and a Discussion [New York: Holmes & Meier, 1981]

8597. Benavie, Barbara S.: "The Holocaust: Something for Everybody." J Digest, vol.27 #5 (Jan., 1982): 3-6.

8598. Blumenkranz, Bernard: "How Holocaust History is (not) Taught: Shortcomings in French Textbooks." PoP, vol.9 #3 (May/June, 1975): 8-12.

8599. Blumenthal, David R.: "Scholarly Approaches to the Holocaust." Shoa, vol.1 #3 (Win., 1979): 21-27.

8600. Blumenthal, Nachman: "From the Nazi Vocabulary." YVS, vol.6 (1967): 69-82.

8601. ___: "On the Nazi Vocabulary." YVS, vol.1 (1957): 49-66.

8602. Braham, Randolph L.: "Researching the Catastrophe." NJM, vol.71 #7 (March, 1957): 10, 27-28.

8603. Conway, John S.: "The Holocaust and the Historians." Annals, #450 (July, 1980): 153-164.

8604. Dawidowicz, Lucy S.: The Holocaust and the Historians [Cambridge, MA: Harvard Univ. Press, 1981]

Investigation of the place that the Holocaust has attained in current historiography. Dawidowicz´ often excellent perceptions are, however, considerably weakened by her at times unfair and imprecise vendettas against some Israeli and Zionist historians.

8605. ___: "Toward a History of the Holocaust." Com, vol.47 #4 (April, 1969): 51-58.

8606. Dobkowski, Michael N.: "American Antisemitism and American Historians: A Critique." PoP, vol.14 #2 (April, 1980): 33-43.

8607. Dobmann, Franz: "Modern History Teaching in Current German Textbooks." PoP, vol.4 #6 (Nov./Dec., 1970): 15-17.

8608. Dorpalen, Andreas: "Weimar Republic and Nazi Era in East German Perspective." CEH, vol.11 #3 (Sept., 1978): 211-230.

8609. Eck, Nathan: "Observations on the Ringelblum Questionnaire." YVB, #1 (April, 1957): 12-15.

8610. Eckardt, A.: "Studying the Holocaust´s Impact Today: Some Dilemmas of Language and Method." Judaism, vol. 27 #2 ((Spr., 1978): 222-232.

8611. Eliach, Yaffa: "Defining the Holocaust: Perspectives of a Jewish Historian." Peck: Jews/Chr, pp.11-23.

8612. Esh, Shaul: "Words and their Meaning: 25 Examples of Nazi Idiom." YVS, vol.5 (1961): 133-168.

8613. Feingold, Henry L.: "Determining the Uniqueness of the Holocaust: The Factor of Historical Violence." Shoa, vol.2 #2 (Spr., 1981): 3-11, 30.

8614. Fox, John P.: "The Holocaust and Today´s Generation." PoP, vol.17 #1 (Jan., 1983): 3-24.

8615. Friedlander, A. H.: "The Misuses of the Holocaust." Eur Jud, vol.17 #1 (Sum., 1983): 3-11.

8616. Friedlander, Henry: "The Language of Nazi Totalitarianism." Shoa, vol.1 #2 (Fall, 1978): 16-19.

8617. ___: On the Holocaust: A Critique of the Treatment of the Holocaust in History Textbooks [New York: Anti-Defamation Leaque, 1972]

8618. Friedman, Mark: "American Scholarship on East European Jewry." Response, vol.12 #1 (Sum., 1979): 41-56.

8619. Friedman, Philip: "American Jewish Research and Literature on the Holocaust." Friedman: Roads, pp.525-538.

8620. ___: "European Jewish Research on the Holocaust." Friedman: Roads, pp.500-524.

8621. ___: "Outline of Program for Holocaust Research." Friedman: Roads, pp.571-576.

8622. ___: "Polish Jewish Historiography between the Two Wars (1918-1939)." JSS, vol.11 #4 (Oct., 1949): 373-409. Also in Friedman: Roads, pp. 467-499.

8623. ___: "Preliminary and Methodological Aspects of Research on the Judenrat." Friedman: Roads, pp.539-553.

8624. ___: "Preliminary and Methodological Problems of the Research on the Jewish Catastrophe in the Nazi Period." YVS, vol.2 (1958): 95-131.

8625. ___: "Problems of Research on the Holocaust: An Over-View." Friedman: Roads, pp.554-567.

8626. ___: "Problems of Research on the Jewish Catastrophe." YVS, vol.3 (1959): 25-40. Also in Gutman: Catastrophe, pp.633-650.

8627. ___: "Research and Literature on the Recent Jewish Tragedy." JSS, vol.12 #1 (Jan., 1950): 17-26.

8628. Gatzke, Hans W.: "Hitler and Psychohistory." AHR, vol.78 #2 (April, 1973): 394-401.

8629. Hamerow, Theodore S.: "Guilt, Redemption and Writing German History." AHR, vol.88 #1 (Feb., 1983): 53-72.

8630. Harris, Frederich: Encounters with Darkness: French and German Writers of World War II [New York: Oxford Univ. Press, 1985]

8631. Hertz, D.: "Signs of Oppression: Pre-Nazi Germany." Littell: Education, pp.47-52.

8632. Hiden, John and John Farquharson: Explaining Hitler´s Germany: Historians and the Third Reich [London: Batsford Academic and Educational, Ltd., 1983]

8633. Katz, Jacob: "Was the Holocaust Predictable?" Com, vol.59 #5 (May, 1975): 41-48.

8634. Kent, George O.: "Research Opportunities in West and East Germany Archives for the Weimar Period and the Third Reich." CEH, vol.12 #1 (March, 1979): 38-67.

8635. Kolinsky, Martin and Eva Kolinsky: "The Treatment of the Holocaust in West German Textbooks." YVS, vol.5 (1961): 149-216.

8636. Korman, Gerd: "The Holocaust in American Historical Writing." Societas, vol.2 #3 (Sum., 1974): 251-270.

8637. ___: "Warsaw Plus Thirty: Some Perception in the Sources and Written History of the Ghetto Uprising." YIVO Annual, vol.15 (1974): 280-296.

8638. Korzen, Meir: "Problems Arising Out of Research into the History of Jewish Refugees in the USSR during the Second World War." YVS, vol.3 (1959): 119-140.

8639. Kren, G. L. and L. Rappoport: "Failures of Thought in Holocaust Interpretation." Dobkowski: Toward, pp.377-401.

8640. Kwirt, Konrad: "Historians of the G. D. R. on Anti-semitism and Persecution." LBIYB, vol.21 (1976): 173-198.

8641. Laqueur, W. Z.: "Nazism and the Nazis: On the Difficulties of Discovering the Whole Truth." Encounter, vol.22 #4 (April, 1964): 39-46.

8642. Lavi, Theodore: "Jews in Rumanian Historiography of World War II." SJA, vol.4 #1 (May, 1974): 45-52.

8643. Locke, H. G.: "The Holocaust and Genocide: Some Problems in Interpretation and Understanding." Littell: Education, pp.23-28.

8644. Magurshok, Dan: "The Incomprehensibility of the Holocaust: Tightening up Some Loose Usage." Judaism, vol. 29 #2 (Spr., 1980): 233-242.

8645. Mau, Hermann and Helmut Krausnick: German History, 1933-1945: An Assessment of German Historians [London: Oswald Wolff, 1959]

8646. Michel, H.: "The Need for a History of the Nazi Concentration Camp System." YVB, #10 (Dec., 1965): 4-8.

8647. Ophir, Baruch: "Bibliographical Problems of the ´Pinkas Hakehilloth´." YVS, vol.1 (1957): 31-48.

8648. "´Pinkas Hakehilloth´ Series: An Encyclopaedia of Jewish Communities." YVN, #2 (June, 1969/June, 1970): 11-12.

8649. Poliakov, L.: "Changing Views in Holocaust Research." YVB, #20 (April, 1967): 3-5.

8650. ___: "Human Morality and the Nazi Terror: The Problem of the ´Useless Mouths´." Com, vol.10 #2 (Aug., 1950): 111-116.

8651. Rabinowitz, Dorothy: About the Holocaust: What We Know and How We Know It [New York: American Jewish Committee, 1979]

8652. Ranz, J.: "Misconceptions and Truth about the Holocaust." J Fr, vol.44 #4 (April, 1977): 11-14.

8653. Renn, Walter F.: "Confronting Genocide: The Depiction of the Persecution of the Jews and the Holocaust in West German History Textbooks." Braham: Contemporary, pp.157-180.

8654. ___: "The Holocaust in West German Textbooks." Shoa, vol.3 #2/3 (Fall/Win., 1982/1983): 26-30.

8655. Robinson, Jacob: "New Problems in Study and Research of the Holocaust." YVN, #3 (June, 1970/June, 1971): 3-4, 30-32.

8656. ___: Research on the Jewish Catastrophe." JJoS, vol.8 #2 (Dec., 1966): 192-203.

8657. ___: "Research on the Jewish Catastrophe: Where Does It Stand Today." 4 WCJS, vol.1 (1967): 15-20.

8658. Rosenberg, Bernard: "Balance Sheet of Madness." J Fr, vol.22 #6 (June, 1955): 6-10.

8659. Schickel, Alfred: "Treatment of the Nazi Crimes in New German History Textbooks." PoP, vol.8 #2 (March/April, 1974): 13-16, 21.

8660. Segal, Robert A.: "The Historical Inexplicability of Antisemitism." C/J, vol.5 #2 (Fall/Win., 1980): 66-73.

8661. Sherwin, Byron L.: "Ideological Antecedents of the Holocaust." Sherwin: Encountering, pp.23-51.

8662. Sonntag, Jacob: "The Ringelblum Archives." J Sp, vol. 18 #6 (June, 1953): 23-27.

8663. Spangenthal, Max: "New German Books on the Nature of Nazism." YVB, #21 (Nov., 1967): 38-40.

8664. Syrkin, Marie: "On Hebrewcide." J Fr, vol.12 #7 (July, 1945): 10-12.

8665. Szafar, Tadeusz: "Endecized Marxism: Polish Communist Historians on Recent Polish Jewish History." SJA, vol.8 #1 (May, 1978): 57-71.

8666. Tal, Uriel: "Excursus on the Term: Shoah." Shoa, vol. 1 #4 (1979): 10-11.

8667. ___: "On the Study of the Holocaust and Genocide." YVS, vol.13 (1979): 7-52.

8668. Tenenbaum, J.: "For the Sake of Historical Balance." YVB, #3 (July, 1958): 9-11, 14.

8669. Trefouse, H. L.: "German Historians´ Verdict on Hitler." Com, vol.16 #3 (Sept., 1953): 264-269.

8670. Waite, R. G. L.: "Hitler and the Nazi Years: A Historian Refutes Attempts to Whitewash the Holocaust." ADL Bul, vol.34 #6 (June, 1977): 7-8.

8671. Whitfield, S. J.: "The Imagination of Disaster: The Response of American Jewish Intellectuals to Totalitarianism." JSS, vol.42 #1 (Win., 1980): 1-20.

8672. Wilder-Okladek, F.: "A Note on Jewish Research in Tainted Countries." JSS, vol.30 #3 (July, 1968): 169-174.

8673. Yahil, Leni: "Historians of the Holocaust: A Plea for a New Approach." WLB, vol.22 #1 (Win., 1967/68): 2-5.

8674. ___: "The Holocaust in Jewish Historiography." YVS, vol.7 (1968): 57-74. Also in Gutman: Catastrophe, pp. 651-670.

8675. Zuroff, Efraim: "Conferences and Symposia on the Holocaust (1973-1974)." YVS, vol.10 (1974): 295-306.

Review Essays

8676. Ainsztein, Reuben: "New Documents on the History of the Warsaw Ghetto." JQ, vol.12 #3 (Aut., 1964): 33-36.

8677. Cohen, Arthur A.: "Silence and Laughter." JH, vol.8 #4 (Spr., 1966): 37-39.

8678. Cohn, Bernhard N.: "Germans and Jews." J Sp, vol.37 #4 (April, 1972): 24-25.

8679. Cole, Margaret: "Recognizing Genocide." Eur Jud, vol. 6 #1 (Win., 1971/1972): 29-31.

8680. Eulenberg, Julia N.: "Coming to Terms with the Holocaust." J Sp, vol.48 #4 (Win., 1983): 40-42.

8681. Fein, Helen: "Holocaust Chronicles." J Sp, vol.39 #3 (Fall, 1974): 52-54.

8682. Halivni-Weiss, Tzipora: "Holocaust and History." J Sp, vol.41 #1 (Spr., 1976): 47-50.

8683. Hoffman, Gerald H.: "How Not to Write about the Holocaust." Am Zionist, vol.69 #2 (Nov./Dec., 1978): 18-20.

8684. Kagan, R.: "Russians on German Concentration Camps." YVB, #4/5 (Oct., 1959): 17-20.

8685. Laurence, Alfred E.: "Non-Answers About Germany." J Sp, vol.36 #10 (Dec., 1971): 26-27.

8686. Mashberg, Michael: "Escape in a Frozen World." J Sp, vol.39 #4 (Win., 1974): 34-38.

8687. Milward, A.: "Fascists, Nazis and Historical Method." History, vol.67 #219 ((Feb., 1982): 47-62.

8688. Musmanno, Michael A.: "The Imperishable Record of an Infamy." Ch J Forum, vol.20 #2 (Win., 1961/1962): 110-112.

8689. Roditi, Edouard: "The Criminal as Public Servant: The Record of Some Recent Writing." Com, vol.28 #5 (Nov., 1959): 431-435.

8690. Rosenfeld, Alvin H.: "On Holocaust History." Shoa, vol.1 #1 (Sum., 1979): 19-20.

8691. Schappes, Morris U.: "Documenting the Holocaust." J Currents, vol.37 #4 (April, 1983): 18-21.

8692. Sereny, Gita: "Germany: The ´Rediscovery´ of Hitler." Atlantic, vol.242 #2 (Aug., 1978): 6-14.

8693. Stone, D.: "Surviving and Meaning." J Sp, vol.44 #4 (Win., 1979): 56-58.

8694. Wistrich, Robert S.: "An Old-New Pathology." Mid, vol. 31 #4 (April, 1985): 48-50.

Books and Authors

8695. Barnouw, D.: "The Secularity of Evil: Hannah Arendt and the Eichmann Controversy." MJ, vol.3 #1 (Feb., 1983): 75-94.

8696. Ben-Horin, Meir: "Hannah Arendt Reconsidered." J Sp, vol.47 #4 (Win., 1982): 15-19.

8697. Biale, David: "Arendt in Jerusalem." Response, vol.12 #3 (Sum., 1980): 33-44.

8698. Brand, E.: "The Soviet Writer V. Bielayev and his Works on the Holocaust in the Lvov District." YVB, #13 (Oct., 1963): 63-65.

8699. Broszat, Martin: "Hitler and the Genesis of the Final Solution: An Assessment of David Irving´s Thesis." YVS, vol.13 (1979): 73-125.

8700. Chworowsky, Karl M.: "Hitler´s Professors." J Fo, vol.29 #10 (Oct., 1946): 223, 225.

8701. Dawidowicz, Lucy S.: "In Hitler´s Service." Com, vol. 50 #5 (Nov., 1970): 85-89.

8702. Donat, A.: "Revisionist History of the Jewish Catastrophe: An Empiric Examination of Hannah Arendt." Judaism, vol.12 #4 (Fall, 1963): 416-435.

8703. Eck, Nathan: "Hannah Arendt´s Malicious Articles." YVB, #14 (March, 1964): 12-19.

8704. ___: "Historical Research or Slander?" YVS, vol.6 (1967): 385-430. * On Raul Hilberg.

8705. Eliav, Benjamin: "The Holocaust in the ´Encyclopaedia Judaica´." YVS, vol.9 (1973): 247-254.

8706. Ezorsky, Gertrude: "Hannah Arendt Answered." J Fr, vol.33 #2 (March, 1966): 7-12.

8707. Feingold, Henry L.: "Arendt Revisited." Judaism, vol. 29 #1 (Win., 1980): 122-128.

8708. ___: "The Bureaucrat as Mass Killer: Arendt on Eichmann." Response, vol.12 #3 (Sum., 1980): 45-51.

8709. Feldman, Ron (ed.): The Jew as Pariah: Hannah Arendt on the Modern Jewish Condition [New York: Grove Press, 1978]

8710. Friedlander, Albert H.: "Arendt Report on Eichmann and the Jewish Community." CCARJ, vol.11 #3 (Oct., 1963): 47-55.

8711. Goodman, Saul: "Sitting in Judgment on the Victims." Recon, vol.29 #2 (March 8, 1963): 27-31. * On Hilberg.

8712. Grossman, Frances G.: "Blaming the Victim: A Critique of Bruno Bettelheim´s Theories on the Holocaust." IH, vol.32 #5/6 (May/June, 1984): 19-25.

8713. Halperin, Irving: "Scrolls of Agony - and Praise." Judaism, vol.16 #1 (Win., 1967): 66-83. * On Kaplan.

8714. Hirsch, Valia: "The Black Book: An Indictment." Today, vol.1 #6 (April, 1945): 8-9.

8715. Kaufman, M.: "A Critique of Hannah Arendt´s Thesis on Totalitarianism and Modern Antisemitism." Gesher, vol. 5 #1 (1976): 60-74.

8716. Kellen, K.: "Reflection on ´Eichmann in Jerusalem´." Mid, vol.9 #3 (Sept., 1963): 25-35.

8717. Kermish, Joseph: "Emmanuel Ringelblum´s Notes Hitherto Unpublished." YVS, vol.7 (1968): 173-183.

8718. ___: "Mutilated Versions of Ringelblum's Notes." YIVO Annual, vol.8 (1953): 289-301.

8719. King, Joseph: "Where the Guilt Lies: A Fresh Analysis of Hecht's Controversial 'Perfidy'." J Currents, vol. 16 #7 (July/Aug., 1962): 8-13, 37-38.

8720. Laqueur, Walter Z.: "Hannah Arendt in Jerusalem: The Controversy Revisited." Legters: Western, pp.107-120. Comments: W. S. Allen, pp.121-124; D. Schoenbaum, pp. 125-129.

8721. Luck, David: "Use and Abuse of Holocaust Documents: Reitlinger and How Many?" JSS, vol.41 #2 (Spr., 1979): 95-122.

8722. Mamlack, Gershon: "The War Against the Jews, 1933-1945." Tradition, vol.17 #1 (Fall, 1977): 42-54.

8723. Mark, Ber: "A Dangerous Myth." JQ, vol.9 #4 (Win., 1962/1963): 7-12. * On Raul Hilberg.

8724. ___: "Falsifying the Jewish Resistance." J Currents, vol.17 #4 (April, 1963): 4-5, 7-17. * Refutes Hilberg's Thesis on Jewish Passivity.

8725. Muller, Sharon: "The Origins of Eichmann in Jerusalem: Hannah Arendt's Interpretation of Jewish History." JSS, vol.43 #3/4 (Sum./Fall, 1981): 237-254.

8726. ___: "The Pariah Syndrome." Response, vol.12 #3 (Sum, 1980): 52-57.

8727. Musmanno, M. A.: "Eichmann in Jerusalem: A Critique." Ch J Forum, vol.21 #4 (Sum., 1963): 282-285.

8728. Porter, Jack N.: "The Affirmation of Life After the Holocaust: The Contributions of Bettelheim, Lifton, and Frankl." Porter: Confronting, pp.122-129.

8729. Prinz, Joachim: "On the Banality of Hannah Arendt." CBW, vol.30 #11 (June 24, 1963): 7-10.

8730. Roback, A. A.: "Bettelheim's Theory of Escape." JQ, vol.9 #4 (Win., 1962/1963): 13-14.

8731. ___: "A Modern Balaam in Reverse: The Hilberg-Trevor-Roper Slur on Jewish Courage." JQ, vol.9 #3 (Aut., 1962): 6-8.

8732. Robinson, J.: And the Crooked Shall be Made Straight: The Eichmann Trial, the Jewish Catastrophe, and Hannah Arendt's Narrative [Philadelphia: J. P. S., 1965]

Line by line refutation of the charges made by Hannah Arendt in Eichmann in Jerusalem. Also includes new material, especially on the legal issues raised by the trial.

8733. ___: Psychoanalysis In a Vacuum: Bruno Bettelheim and the Holocaust [New York/Jerusalem: YIVO Institute/Yad Vashem Documentary Projects, 1970]

8734. Ruether, Rosemary R.: "The 'Faith and Fratricide' Discussion: Old Problems and New Dimensions." Davies: Foundations, pp.230-256.

8735. Schappes, Morris U.: "The Strange World of Hannah Arendt: An Examination of a Controversial Book on the Eichmann Case." J Currents, vol.17 #7 (July/Aug., 1963): 3-9, 32-34; #8 (Sept., 1963): 12-22; #9 (Oct., 1963): 14-23.

8736. Shneiderman, S. L.: "The Black Book of Soviet Jewry." Mid, vol.27 #10 (Dec., 1981): 49-52.

8737. Silver, Isidore: "The Totalitarian Man." JQ, vol.11 #4 (Win., 1963/1964): 23-26.

8738. Simon, E.: "Revisionist History of the Jewish Catastrophe: A Textual Examination of Hannah Arendt." Judaism, vol.12 #4 (Fall, 1963): 387-415.

8739. Suhl, Yuri: "Is This Responsible Scholarship, Dr. Hilberg? To Prove 'Jewish Passivity' and Ineffectiveness Dr. Hilberg Misrepresents his Own Sources." J Currents, vol.18 #6 (June, 1964): 16-18.

8740. Syrkin, Marie: "Miss Arendt Surveys the Holocaust." J Fr, vol.30 #4 (May, 1963): 7-14.

8741. ___: "Perfidy and Stale Venom." J Fr, vol.29 #1 (Jan., 1962): 13-17.

8742. Teich, Meir: "New Editions and Old Mistakes." YVS, vol.6 (1967): 373-384.

8743. Trevor-Roper, Hugh R.: "A. J. P. Taylor, Hitler, and the War." Encounter, vol.17 #1 (July, 1961): 88-96.

8744. Weiss, Yehuda: "The Perfidy of Ben Hecht." IH, vol.10 #5 (May, 1962): 14-19; #6 (June/July, 1962): 22-24.

THESES AND UNPUBLISHED WORKS

Jews in Prewar Europe

8745. Gitman, Joseph: "The Jews and Jewish Problems in the Polish Parliament, 1919-1939." New Haven, CT: Yale University, 1963.

8746. Glicksman, William M.: "The Economic Life of the Jews in Poland as Reflected in Yiddish Literature (1914-1939)." Philadelphia, PA: Dropsie University, 1957.

8747. Hagen, William: "Poles, Germans and Jews: The Nationality Conflict in Prussian Poland in the Nineteenth and Early Twentieth Century." Chicago: University of Chicago, 1971. <see #77>

8748. Pierson, Ruth L.: "German Jewish Identity in the Weimar Republic." New Haven, CT: Yale University, 1970.

8749. Rheins, Carl J.: "German Jewish Patriotism 1815-1935: A Study of the Attitudes and Actions of the ´Reichsbund Judischer Frontsoldaten´, the ´Verband Nationaldeutscher Juden´, the ´Schwarzes Fahnlein, Jungenschaft´, and the ´Deutscher Vortrupp, Gefolgschaft Deutscher Juden´." Stony Brook: State University of New York, 1978.

8750. Schwab, Georg D.: "German Jewish Thoughts on Vital Problems During the Years 1920-1933." [BA] New York: College of the City of New York, 1954.

8751. Thompson, Margaret R.: "The Jews and the Minorities Treaties, 1918-1929." Washington, DC: The Catholic University of America, 1966.

8752. Weinberg, David H.: "The Paris Jewish Community in the 1930s: A Case-Study of the Attitudes and Behavior of Pre-War European Jewry." Madison: The University of Wisconsin, 1971. <see #185>

Pre-Nazi Europe

8753. Creekmore, Marion V.: "The German Reichstag Election of 1928." New Orleans, LA: Tulane University, 1968.

8754. Dumin, Frederick: "Background of the Austro-German Anschluss Movement 1918-1919." Madison: University of Wisconsin, 1963.

8755. Gordon, Harold J. Jr.: "The Reichswehr and the German Republic, 1919-1925." New Haven, CT: Yale University, 1953.

8756. Greene, Fred: "French Military Leadership and Security Against Germany, 1919-1940." New Haven, CT: Yale University, 1950.

8757. Hertzman, Lewis: "The German National Peoples Party (DNVP), 1918-1924. Cambridge, MA: Harvard University, 1955.

8758. Ireland, Waltraud: "The Communist Party of Germany Between Social Democracy and National Socialism 1929-1931." Baltimore, MD: Johns Hopkins University, 1971.

8759. Kunkle, Wray, A.: "Gustav Stressmann, the German Peoples Party, and the German National Peoples Party, 1923 to 1929." Washington, DC: American University, 1969.

8760. Lentz, Jacob B.: "Weimar´s Hopeful Years: Studies in German Political History, 1925-1929." Cambridge, MA: Harvard University, 1972.

8761. Loewenberg, Peter J.: "Walter Rathenau and German Society." Berkeley: University of California, 1966.

8762. Myers, D. P.: "Germany and the Question of Austrian Anschluss, 1918-1922." New Haven: Yale University, 1968.

8763. Quinn, Pearle E.: "The National Socialist Attack on the Foreign Policies of the German Republic, 1919-1933." Stanford, CA: Stanford University, 1949.

8764. Ripper, M. Marcella: "The German Center Party from the November Revolution 1918 to the Adoption of the Weimar Constitution." Chicago: Loyola University of Chicago, 1967.

8765. Ruark, Lawrence B.: "Admiration for Mussolini Among German Intellectuals, 1922-1932." Boston, MA: Boston University, 1970.

8766. Sanford, Donald G.: "Walther Rathenau: Critic and Prophet of Imperial Germany." Ann Arbor: University of Michigan, 1971.

8767. Shepard, Carl E.: "Germany and The Hague Conferences, 1929-1930." Bloomington: Indiana University, 1964.

8768. Smith, Arthur L.: "General Hans von Seeckt and German Secret Rearmament 1919-1925." Los Angeles: University of Southern California, 1953.

8769. Steinberg, M. S.: "Sabres, Books, and Brown Shirts: The Radicalization of the German Student, 1918-1938." Baltimore, MD: Johns Hopkins University, 1971.

8770. Stern, Fritz R.: "Cultural Despair and the Politics of Discontent: A Study of the Rise of the Germanic Ideology." New York: Columbia University, 1953. <see #335>

8771. Welisch, Sophie A.: "The Sudeten German Question in the League of Nations." New York: Fordham University, 1968.

8772. Woolley, William J.: "Poland in the League of Nations 1932-1934." Bloomington: Indiana University, 1969.

Antisemitism

8773. Boxerman, Burton A.: "Reaction of the St. Louis Jewish Community to Antisemitism, 1933-1945." St. Louis, MO: St. Louis University, 1967.

8774. Clary, Norman J.: "French Antisemitism During the Years of Drumont and Dreyfus, 1886-1906." Columbus, Ohio State University, 1970.

8775. Engel, David J.: "Organized Jewish Responses to German Antisemitism during the First World War." Los Angeles, University of California, 1979.

8776. Levy, Richard S.: "Antisemitic Political Parties in the German Empire." New Haven, CT: Yale University, 1969. <see #667>

8777. Marrus, Michael R.: "The Politics of Assimilation: A Study of the French Jewish Community at the Time of the Dreyfus Affair." Berkeley, CA: University of California, 1968. <see #673>

8778. Niewyk, Donald L.: "German Social Democracy Confronts the Problem of Antisemitism, 1918-1933." New Orleans, LA: Tulane University, 1968. <see #534>

8779. Ragins, Sanford: "Jewish Responses to Antisemitism in Germany 1870-1914." Waltham, MA: Brandeis University, 1972. <see #676>

8780. Sable, Jacob M.: "Some American Jewish Organizational Efforts to Combat Antisemitism, 1906-1930." New York: Yeshiva University, 1964.

Fascism

8781. Micaud, Charles: "The French Right and Nazi Germany, 1933-1939: A Study of Public Opinion." New York: Columbia University, 1944.

8782. Proctor, Raymond L.: "The Blue Division: An Episode in German-Spanish Wartime Relations." Eugene: University of Oregon, 1966.

Nazi Germany

8783. Allen, Wm. S.: "Thalburg: The Nazi Seizure of Power in a Single German Town, 1930 to 1935." Minneapolis: University of Minnesota, 1962. <see #955>

8784. Baird, Jay W.: "German Home Propaganda, 1941-1945 and the Russian Front." New York: Columbia University, 1966.

8785. Becker, Peter W.: "The Basis of the German War Economy Under Albert Speer, 1942-1944." Stanford, CA: Stanford University, 1971.

8786. Bessel, Richard J.: "The SA in the Eastern Regions of Germany, 1925 to 1934." Oxford: Oxford University, 1980. <see #957>

8787. Buchsbaum, John H.: "German Psychological Warfare on the Eastern Front 1941-1945." Washington, DC: Georgetown University, 1960.

8788. Cronenberg, Allen T. Jr.: "The ´Volksbund fuer das Deutschtum im Ausland´. ´Voelkisch´ Ideology and German Foreign Policy 1881-1939." Stanford, CA: Stanford University, 1970.

8789. Dibner, Ursula R.: "The History of National Socialist German Student League." Ann Arbor: The University of Michigan, 1969.

8790. Domandi, Mario: "The German Youth Movement." New York: Columbia University, 1960.

8791. Fox, Barry C.: "German Relations with Rumania, 1933-1944." Cleveland, OH: Case Western Reserve University, 1964.

8792. Frank, Robert H.: "Hitler and the National Socialist Coalition, 1924-1932." Baltimore, MD: Johns Hopkins University, 1969.

8793. Gasman, Daniel E.: "Social Darwinism in Ernst Haeckel and the German Monist League: A Study of the Scientific Origins of National Socialism." Chicago: University of Chicago, 1969.

8794. Grill, Johnpeter H.: "The Nazi Party in Baden, 1920-1945." Ann Arbor: University of Michigan, 1975.

8795. Hackett, David A.: "The Nazi Party in the Reichstag Election of 1930." Madison: University of Wisconsin, 1971.

8796. Hartshorne, Edward Y.: "The German Universities and National Socialism." Chicago: University of Chicago, 1938. <see #1166>

8797. Held, Joseph: "Embattled Youth: The Independent German Youth Movements in the Twentieth Century." New Brunswick, NJ: Rutgers University, 1968.

8798. Heller, Karl H.: "The Reshaping and Political Conditioning of the German ´Ordnungspolizei´ 1933-1945: A Study of Techniques used in the Nazi State to Conform Local Police Units to National Socialist Theory and Practice." Cincinnati, OH: University of Cincinnati, 1970.

8799. Jelavich, Barbara B.: "The German Alliance System, 1939-1941." Berkeley: University of California, 1948.

8800. Kele, Max H.: "Nazi Appeals to the German Workers, 1919-1933." New Orleans, LA: Tulane University, 1969.

8801. Koehl, Robert L.: "RKFDV: German Resettlement and Population Policy in Poland, 1939-1945." Cambridge, MA: Harvard University, 1950. <see #1304>

8802. Koshar, Rudy J.: "Organisational Life and Nazism: A Study of Mobilization in Marburg an der Lahn, 1918-1935." Ann Arbor: University of Michigan, 1979.

8803. Kugler, Ruben F.: "Germanny´s Axis Policies in Europe 1933-1939." Los Angeles: University of Southern California, 1953.

8804. Mitchell, Otis C.: "An Institutional History of the National Socialist SA: A Study of the SA as a Functioning Organisation within the Party Structure 1931-1934." Lawrence: University of Kansas, 1964.

8805. Phelps, Reginald H.: "The Crisis of the German Republic 1930-1932: Its Background and Course." Cambridge, MA: Harvard University, 1947.

8806. Quinn, Charles M.: "Totalitarianism: Nazi Germany as a Case Study. A Curriculum Unit for Undergraduate Students." Pittsburgh, PA: Carnegie-Mellon University, 1979. [DA]

8807. Reiche, E.: "The Development of the SA in Nuremberg, 1922 to 1934." Wilmington: University of Delaware, 1972.

8808. Rempel, Gerhard: "The Misguided Generation: Hitler Youth and the SS, 1933-1945." Madison: University of Wisconsin, 1971.

8809. Shalka, Robert J.: "The General SS in Central Germany 1937-1939: A Social and Institutional Study of the SS Main Sector Fulda-Werra." Madison: University of Wisconsin, 1972.

8810. Stokes, Lawrence D.: "The Sicherheitsdienst (SD) of the Reichsfuehrer SS and German Public Opinion, September 1939-June 1941." Baltimore, MD: Johns Hopkins University, 1972.

8811. Weingartner, J. J.: "The Leibstandarte Adolf Hitler: 1933-1945." Madison: University of Wisconsin, 1967. <see #1244>

8812. Wernette, D. Richard: "Political Violence and German Elections: 1930 and July 1932." Ann Arbor: University of Michigan, 1974.

8813. Willertz, John R.: "National Socialism in a German City and County: Marsburg, 1933 to 1945." Ann Arbor: University of Michigan, 1970.

8814. Willis, J. R.: "The Wehrmacht Propaganda Branch: German Military Propaganda and Censorship during World War II." Charlottesville: University of Virginia, 1964.

8815. Wittgens, Herman J.: "The German Foreign Office Campaign against the Versailles Treaty: An Examination of the Activities of the ´Kriegsschuldreferat´ in the United States." Seattle: University of Washington, 1970.

8816. Ziemke, Earl F.: "The Ambassadors and the German Foreign Office in the Twentieth Century." Madison: University of Wisconsin, 1952.

The Nazis

8817. Addington, Larry H.: "General Franz Halder and the German Army and General Staff 1938-1941." Durham, NC: Duke University, 1962.

8818. Crowley, Christopher J.: "´Libertatem Delendam Est´: Franz Haiser Austro-Voelkisch Elitist (1871-1945)." New York: CUNY, 1978.

8819. Davis, J. W.: "Hitler and the Versailles Settlement." Madison: University of Wisconsin, 1964.

8820. Heineman, John L.: "Constantin Freiherr von Neurath as Foreign Minister, 1932-1935: A Study of a Conservative Civil Servant and Germany´s Foreign Policy." Ithaca, NY: Cornell University, 1965.

8821. Kestenberg, L.: "The Governing Ideology of Frederick II of Prussia and Hitler." Boulder, CO: University of Colorado, 1943.

8822. Leavey, William J.: "Hitler´s Envoy ´Extraordinary´ Franz Von Papen Ambassador to Austria, 1934-1938 and Turkey, 1939-1944." St. John´s University, 1968.

8823. Norton, Donald H.: "Karl Haushofer and His Influence on Nazi Ideology and German Foreign Policy 1919-1945. Worcester, MA: Clark University, 1965.

8824. Simpson, Amos E.: "The Position of Hjalmar Schacht in a Changing Germany, 1923-1939." Berkeley: University of California, 1955.

8825. Viereck, Peter R.: "Metapolitics from the Romantics to Hitler." Cambridge, MA: Harvard University, 1942. <see #1714>

8826. Wozniak, John S.: "Hermann Wagener´s Corporative Social Monarchy: German Conservatism at the Crossroads of the Social Question." Storrs, CT: University of Connecticut, 1969.

The Second World War

8827. Burdick, Charles: "German Military Planning for the War in the West, 1936-1940." Stanford, CA: Stanford University, 1955.

8828. Campbell, Fenton G. Jr.: "Czechoslovak-German Relations During the Weimar Republic." New Haven, CT: Yale University, 1967.

8829. Claphan, Noel P.: "Anglo-French Influence on Hitler´s Northern Policy, September 1939-April 1940." Lincoln: University of Nebraska, 1968.

8830. Horton, Albert C.: "Germany and the Spanish Civil War." New York: Columbia University, 1966.

8831. Leach, Barry A.: "German Strategic Planning for the Campaign in the East, 1939-1941." Vancouver, Canada: University of British Columbia, 1966.

8832. Mcrandle, James H.: "The Cities of Destruction: A Study of the Nature and Structure of the National Socialist Ideology and its Influence on the German War Effort, 1939 to 1945." Minneapolis: University of Minnesota, 1957.

8833. Miller, William J.: "European Reaction to Hitler´s First Moves Against Austria, January 1933-July 1934." Berkeley: University of California, 1968.

8834. Millikan, Gordon W.: "Soviet and Comintern Policy Toward Germany, 1928-1933: A Case Study of Strategy and Tactics." New York: Columbia University, 1970.

8835. Post, Gaines Jr.: "German Foreign Policy and Military Planning: The Polish Question, 1924-1929." Stanford, CA: Stanford University, 1969.

8836. Rusnak, Andrew J.: "Poland and the Molotov-Ribbentrop Pact: A Study of Selected Slavic-American Editorial Opinion, Mid-March Through September, 1939." Muncie, IN: Ball State University, 1970.

8837. Warren, Vernon C. Jr.: "Russo-German Relations, 1933-1936: The Years of Uncertainty." Lexington: University of Kentucky, 1965.

Europe Under the Nazis

8838. Anderson, Wm. D.: "The German Armed Forces in Denmark 1940-1943: A Study in Occupation Policy." Lawrence: University of Kansas, 1972.

8839. Barth, Werner: "Germany and the Anschluss." Austin: University of Texas, 1954.

8840. Dallin, Alexander: "German Policy and the Occupation of the Soviet Union, 1941-1944." New York: Columbia University, 1953. <see #2533>

8841. Fenyo, Mario D.: "Horthy, Hitler, and Hungary: A Contribution to the Study of German Hungarian Relations from June 1941 to the Fall of the Horthy Regime in October 1944." Washington, DC: American University, 1969. <see #2300>

8842. Heyl, John D.: "Economic Policy and Political Leadership in the German Depression, 1930-1936." Seattle: Washington University, 1971.

8843. Hondros, John L.: "The German Occupation of Greece, 1941-1944." Nashville, TN: Vanderbilt University, 1969.

8844. Jasperson, Michael: "Laval and the Nazis: A Study of Franco-German Relations." Washington, DC: Georgetown University, 1967.

8845. Jucovy, Jon: "The Bavarian Peasantry Under National Socialist Rule, 1933-1945." New York: CUNY, 1985.

8846. Karfunkel, Thomas: "A Critical Evaluation of Hungarian Governmental Policies, 1941-1944: The Role and Policies of Horthy with Regard to German Pressures on the Hungarian Regime." New York: New York University, 1968.

8847. Kitterman, David H.: "National Diary of German Civilian Life During 1940: The SD Reports." Seattle: University of Washington, 1972.

8848. Knight, Tommy Joe: "The Establishment of German Military Government in Belgium, 1940-1941." Austin: University of Texas, 1967.

8849. Lovin, Clifford R.: "German Agricultural Policy 1933-1936." Chapel Hill: University of North Carolina, 1965.

8850. Moyer, Laurence V.: "The ´Kraft Durch Freude´ Movement in Nazi Germany 1933-1939." Evanston, IL: Northwestern University, 1967.

8851. Pryce, Donald B.: "German Government Policy Towards the Radical Left, 1918-1923." Stanford: Stanford University, 1970.

8852. Pulliam, Wm. E.: "Political Propaganda in the Secondary School History Program of National Socialist Germany, 1933-1945." Urbana: University of Illinois, 1968.

8853. Ritter, H. R. Jr.: "Hermann Neubacher and the German Occupation of the Balkans, 1940-1945." Charlottesville: University of Virginia, 1969.

8854. Schindler, Alexander M.: "From Discrimination to Extermination: The Evolution of the Nazi Government´s Anti-Jewish Policy 1933-1945, Thesis." New York: City College of New York, 1949. [MA]

8855. Schleunes, Karl A.: "Nazi Policy Toward German Jews, 1933-1938." Minneapolis: University of Minnesota, 1966. <see #2097>

8856. Thompson, Larry V.: "Nazi Administrative Conflict: The Struggle for Executive Power in the General Government of Poland, 1939-1943." Madison: University of Wisconsin, 1967.

8857. Voorhis, Jerry L.: "A Study of Official Relations between the German and Danish Governments in the Period between 1940-1943." Evanston, IL: Northwestern University, 1968.

8858. Waite, Robert G.: "The German Free Corps Movement." Cambridge, MA: Harvard University, 1949. <see #1025>

8859. Warmbrunn, Werner: "The Netherlands Under German Occupation, 1940-1945." Stanford, CA: Stanford University, 1955. <see #2462>

8860. Winchester, Betty Jo: "Hungarian Relations with Germany 1936-1939." Bloomington: Indiana University, 1970.

8861. Wires, Richard: "The Anschluss: A Study in the Union of Austria and Germany 1936-1938." Cleveland, OH: The Case Western Reserve University, 1953.

The Holocaust

8862. Biderman, Israel M.: "Majer Balaban: The Historian of Polish Jewry." New York: New York University, 1963.

8863. Chary, Frederick: "Bulgaria and the Jews: The Final Solution 1940 to 1944." Pittsburgh, PA: University of Pittsburgh, 1968. <see #3564>

8864. Gordon, Sarah: "German Opposition to Nazi Antisemitic Measures between 1933 and 1945, with Particular Reference to the Rhine-Ruhr Area." Buffalo, NY: SUNY, 1979. <see #3584>

8865. Hatch, William M.: "The German Foreign Office and the Hungarian Jewish Question." Seattle: University of Washington, 1965. [MA]

8866. Hilberg, Raul: "Prologue to Annihilation: A Study of the Identification, Impoverishment and Isolation of the Jewish Victims of Nazi Policy." New York: Columbia University, 1955. <see #3427>

8867. Schindler, Peter: "Responses of Hasidic Leaders and Hasidim During the Holocaust." New York: New York University, 1972.

Resistance

8868. Copeland, H. J.: "The Resistance and Post-Liberation French politics, 1940-1946." Ithaca, NY: Cornell University, 1966.

8869. Delzell, Charles F.: "The Italian Anti-Fascist Resistance." Stanford, CA: Stanford University, 1951. <see #4832>

8870. Edelheit, Abraham J.: "Ideological Orientations in the Historiography of Jewish Resistance During the Holocaust." New York: Yeshiva University, 1981. [MA]

8871. Edinger, Lewis J.: "The History of the German Social Democratic Party Executive, 1933-1945: A Study of a Political Exile Group." New York: Columbia University, 1954.

8872. Gallin, M. Alice: "The Ethical and Religious Factors in the German Resistance to Hitler." Washington, DC: The Catholic University of America, 1955. <see #4775>

8873. Holland, Carol S.: "The Foreign Contacts Made by the German Opposition to Hitler." Philadelphia: University of Pennsylvania, 1967.

8874. Mastny, Vojtech: "The Czechs Under Nazi Rule, 1939-1942: A Study in a Failure of National Resistance." New York: Columbia University, 1969. <see #4724>

8875. Pronin, Alexander: "Guerrilla Warfare in the German Occupied Soviet Territories, 1941-1944." Washington, DC: Georgetown University, 1965.

8876. Sweets, John F.: "The Mouvements de la Resistance (MUR): A Study of Noncommunist Resistance in France, 1940-1944." Durham, NC: Duke University, 1972. <see #4758>

Churches, Nazis, and Jews

8877. Donohoe, James I.: "Hitler´s Conservative Opponents in Bavaria, 1930-1945: A Consideration of Catholic-Monarchist and Seperatist Anti-Nazi Activities." Cambridge, MA: Harvard University, 1956.

8878. Harrigan, William M.: "German Relations with the Holy See, March 1937 to September 1939." Ann Arbor: University of Michigan, 1955.

8879. Meinardus, Otto F. A.: "A Typology of Church Attitudes Towards the State with Special Reference to the German Church Controversy, 1933-1945. Boston: Boston University, 1955.

8880. Peters, Richard A.: "Nazi Germany and the Vatican, July 1933-January 1935." Norman: The University of Oklahoma, 1971.

8881. Riede, David Ch.: "The Official Attitude of the Roman Catholic Hierarchy in Germany Toward National Socialism, 1933-1945." Ames: The University of Iowa, 1957.

8882. Walker, L. D.: "Hitler Youth and Catholic Youth 1933-1935: A Study in Totalitarian Conquest." Berkeley: University of California, 1965. <see #5293>

8883. Wall, Donald Dale: "National Socialist Policy and Attitudes Toward the Churches in Germany, 1939-1945." Boulder: University of Colorado, 1969.

8884. Wright, J.: "The Political Attitudes of the Protestant Church Leadership, November 1918-July 1933." Oxford: Oxford University, 1969.

The Free World and the Holocaust

8885. Asch, Walter P.: "From Peaceful Change to Appeasement: A Study of Anglo-German Relations, 1933-1938." Chicago: University of Chicago, 1960.

8886. Bauer, Wolfred: "The Shipment of American Strategic Raw Materials to Nazi Germany: A Study in United States Economic Foreign Policy, 1933-1939." Seattle: University of Washington, 1964.

8887. Bell, Leland V.: "Anatomy of a Hate Movement: The German American Bund, 1936-1941. Morgantown, WV: West Virginia University, 1968.

8888. Bennett, Edward W.: "The Diplomacy of the Financial Crisis: The Relations of Germany with the Western Powers September 1930-September 1931." Cambridge, MA: Harvard University, 1960.

8889. Burke, Bernard V.: "American Diplomats and Hitler´s Rise to Power, 1930-1933: The Mission of Ambassador Sackett." Seattle: University of Washington, 1966.

8890. Camp, William D.: "Religion and Horror: The American Religious Press Views the Nazi Death Camps and Holocaust Survivors." Pittsburgh, PA: Carnegie Mellon University, 1981.

8891. Carden, R.: "From Potsdam to the London Conference: Britain´s Policy in Germany, 1945-1947." Chicago: University of Chicago, 1971.

8892. Couch, William J.: "General Sikorski, Poland, and the Soviet Union, 1939-1943." Chicago: University of Chicago, 1971.

8893. Cullen, Emma L.: "Chamberlain and Hitler, Failure of Appeasement." New York: St. John´s University, 1943.

8894. Day, David S.: "American Opinion of German National Socialism, 1933-1937." Los Angelels: UCLA, 1958.

8895. Diamond, Sandor A.: "Germany and the Bund Movement in the United States, 1923-1938." Binghamton, NY: SUNY, 1971. <see #6330>

8896. Donaldson, Robert C.: "British Policy Toward Germany, 1932-1933." Ann Arbor: University of Michigan, 1954.

8897. Etzold, Thomas H.: "Fair Play: American Principles and Practice in Relations with Germany, 1933-1939." New Haven: Yale University, 1970.

8898. Fagan, Ann: "Great Britain and Nazi Germany, 1933: The Origins of Appeasement." Bryn Mawr, PA: Bryn Mawr College, 1969.

8899. Friedman, Saul S.: "Official United States Policy Toward Jewish Refugees 1938-1945." Columbus: Ohio State University, 1969. <see #5589>

8900. Futch, Jefferson D.: "The United States and the Fall of the Weimar Republic: German - American Relations, 1930-1933." Baltimore, MD.: Johns Hopkins University, 1962.

8901. Gottlieb, Moshe: "The Anti-Nazi Boycott Movement in the American Jewish Community, 1933-1941." Waltham, MA: Brandeis University, 1967. <see #5970>

8902. Gottsacker, Mary H.: "German-American Relations 1938-1941 and the Influence of Hans Thomsen." Washington, DC: Georgetown University, 1966.

8903. Kacewicz, George V.: "The Polish Government-in-Exile and Great Britain, 1939-1945." Bloomington: Indiana University, 1969.

8904. Kranzler, David H.: "The History of the Jewish Refugee Community of Shanghai, 1938-1945." New York: Yeshiva University, 1971. <see #5738>

8905. Kuklick, Bruce R.: "American Foreign Economic Policy and Germany, 1939-1945." Philadelphia: University of Pennsylvania, 1968.

8906. Liebschutz, Thomas P.: "Rabbi Philip S. Bernstein and the Jewish Displaced Persons." New York: Hebrew Union College, Jewish Institute of Religion, 1965. [MA]

8907 Matthews, Roy T.: "The British Reaction to the Accession of the National Socialists to Power in Germany." Chapel Hill: University of North Carolina, 1966.

8908. Mertz, Richard R.: "The Diplomats and the Dictator: A Study of Western Diplomatic Reactions to the Rise of Hitler September 1930-November 1933." Washington, DC: Georgetown University, 1963.

8909. Murphy, Frederick I.: "The American Christian Press and Pre-War Hitler´s Germany 1933-1939." Gainesville: University of Florida, 1970.

8910. Neuringer, Sheldon M.: "American Jewry and United States Immigration Policy, 1881-1953." Madison: University of Wisconsin, 1969.

8911. Newman, Gemma M.: "Earl G. Harrison and the Displaced Persons Controversy: A Case Study in Social Action." Philadelphia: Temple University, 1973.

8912. Offner, Arnold A.: "American Diplomacy and Germany, 1933-1938." Bloomington: Indiana University, 1964.

8913. Papp, Nichols G.: "The Anglo-German Naval Agreement of 1935." Storrs: University of Connecticut, 1969.

8914. Pinsky, Edward D.: "Cooperation Among American Jewish Organizations in Their Efforts to Rescue European Jewry During the Holocaust." New York: New York University, 1980.

8915. Redlich, Shimon: "The Jews Under Soviet Rule During World War II." New York: New York University, 1968.

8916. Remak, Joachim: "Germany and the United States, 1933-1939." Stanford, CA: Stanford University, 1955.

8917. Reynolds, Warren H.: "Britain´s Relations with Poland 1919-1939." New York: Fordham University, 1959.

8918. Saide, Fred: "The Dynamics of Appeasement: Britain, Germany and North Central Europe, October 1938-May 1939." Durham, NC: Duke University, 1971.

8919. Schoenthal, K. F.: "American Attitudes Toward Germany 1918-1932." Athens: The Ohio State University, 1959.

8920. Shafir, Shlomo: "The Impact of the Jewish Crisis on American-German Relations 1933-1939." Washington, DC: Georgetown University, 1971.

8921. Smith, Glenn H.: "Senator William Langer: A Study in Isolationism." Ames: University of Iowa, 1968.

8922. Stein, Joshua B.: "Britain and the Jews of Europe." St. Louis, MO: Saint Louis University, 1972.

8923. Stern, Sheldon M.: "The American Perception of the Emergence of Adolf Hitler and the Nazis, 1923-1934." Cambridge, MA: Harvard University, 1970.

8924. Stiller, J. H.: "George S. Messersmith: A Diplomatic Biography." New York, CUNY, 1984.

8925. Trefousse, Hans L.: "Germany and American Neutrality, 1939-1941." New York: Columbia University, 1952.

8926. Van Everen, Brooks: "Franklin D. Roosevelt and the German Problem: 1914-1945." Boulder: University of Colorado, 1970.

Holocaust and Rebirth

8927. Ganin, Zvi: "The Diplomacy of the Weak: American Zionist Leadership During the Truman Era, 1945-1948." Waltham, MA: Brandeis University, 1975.

8928. Haron, Miriam J.: "Anglo-American Relations and the Question of Palestine, 1945-1947." New York: Fordham University, 1979.

8929. Lorimer, M. Madeline: "America´s Response to Europe´s Displaced Persons, 1948-1952: A Preliminary Report." St. Louis, MO: St. Louis University, 1964.

8930. Pritchard, Anton: "The Social System of a Displaced Persons Camp." Cambridge, MA: Harvard University, 1950

8931. Rich, Melina S.: "Children of Holocaust Survivors: A Concurrent Validity Study of a Survivor Family Typology." Berkeley: California School of Practical Psychology, 1982.

8832. Sage, Jerry M.: "The Evolution of U.S. Policy Toward Europe´s Displaced Persons: World War II to June 25, 1948." New York: Columbia University, 1952.

8933. Tripp, Eleanor: "Displaced Persons: The Legislative Controversy in the United States, 1945-1950." New York: Columbia University, 1966.

Occupation and Reconstruction

8934. Griffith, William E.: "The Denazification Program in the United States Zone of Germany." Cambridge, MA: Harvard University, 1950.

8935. Schwada, John: "Policy of the Western Allies Toward Postwar Germany: Development and Evolution 1941-1949." Austin: University of Texas, 1951.

8936. Willis, Frank R.: "The French Zone of Occupation in Germany, 1945-1949." Stanford, CA: Stanford University, 1959.

Historiography

8937. Gredel, Zdenka J. M.: "The Problem of Continuity in German History as seen by West German Historians between 1945 and 1953." Buffalo, NY: SUNY, 1969.

8938. Tobler, Douglas F.: "German Historians and the Weimar Republic." Lawrence: University of Kansas, 1967.

BIBLIOGRAPHIES AND RESEARCH GUIDES

Bibliographies

8939. Ball-Kaduri, K. Y. (comp.): "Testimonies and Recollections about Activities Organized by German Jewry During the Years, 1933-1945." YVS, vol.4 (1960): 317-340. * Catalogue of Ms. in Yad Vashem archives.

8940. Bass, David (ed.): Bibliography of Yiddish Books on the Catastrophe and Heroism vol.11 [1970] <see #8985>

8941. Bayme, S.: "Classified and Annotated Bibliography." Hirt: *Issues*, pp.109-115.

8942. Bernbaum, John A.: "The Captured German Records: A Bibliographical Survey." *The Historian*, vol.32 #4 (Aug., 1970): 564-575.

8943. Bloch, Joshua: "Nazi-Germany and the Jews: An Annotated Bibliography." *AJYB*, vol.38 (1936/37): 135-174.

8944. Braham, R. L. (ed.): *The Hungarian Jewish Catastrophe* vol.4 [1962] <see #8985>

8945. Brickman, S. H. (comp.): *On Teaching the Holocaust: Bibliography, Periodicals, Audio Visual Material and Unit Outline* [Perth Amboy, NJ: AZYF, 1972]

8946. Buse, Dieter and J. Doerr (eds.): *German Nationalism: A Bibliographic Approach* [New York: Garland, 1984]

8947. Canadian Jewish Congress: *The Holocaust: An Annotated Bibliography* [Montreal: National Holocaust Remembrance Committee, 1980]

8948. Cargas, Harry J.: *The Holocaust: An Annotated Bibliography* [Haverford, PA: Catholic Library Assn., 1977]

8949. Celnik, May: *A Bibliography on Judaism and Jewish-Christian Relations* [New York: ADL, 1965]

8950. Duker, Abraham G.: "A Bibliography of Publications on Jewish Post-War Problems." *JBA*, vol.2 (1943/1944): 16-22.

8951. Friedman, Philip: *Bibliography of Books in Hebrew on the Jewish Catastrophe and Heroism in Europe* vol.2 [1960] <see #8985>

8952. ___: "The Bibliography of the Warsaw Ghetto." *JBA*, vol.11 (1952/1953): 121-128.

8953. ___: "The Jews of Greece during the Second World War: A Bibliographical Survey." in *Joshua Starr Memorial Volume* [New York: Conference on Jewish Relations, 1953]

8954. ___ and Joseph Gar (eds.): Bibliography of Yiddish Books on the Jewish Catastrophe and Heroism vol.3 [1962] <see #8985>

8955. ___ and Kopel S. Pinson: "Some Books on the Jewish Catastrophe." JSS, vol.12 #1 (Jan., 1950): 83-95.

8956. Gar, Joseph (ed.): Bibliography of Articles on the Catastrophe and Heroism in Yiddish Periodicals vols. 9-10 [1966/1969] <see #8985>

8957. Hirshberg, Jeffrey: "The Holocaust in Literature, 1978-79: A Bibliography." Shoa, vol.2 #1 (Spr./Sum., 1980): 31-36.

8958. Kehr, Helen and Janet Langmaid (comps): The Nazi Era 1919-1945: A Select Bibliography of Published Works from the Early Roots to 1980 [Salem, NH: Mansell Pub., 1982]

8959. Krould, Harr. J.: The Displaced Persons Analytical Bibliography [Washington, DC: Library of Congress, 1950]

8960. Laska, Vera (ed.): Nazism, Resistance, and Holocaust in World War II: A Bibliography [Metuchen, NJ: Scarecrow Press, 1985]

8961. Low, Alfred D.: The Anschluss Movement, 1918-1938: An Annotated Bibliography of German and Austrian Nationalism [New York: Garland Pub., 1984]

8962. Lowenthal, E. G.: "In the Shadow of Doom: Post-War Publications on Jewish Communal History in Germany." LBIYB, vol.11 (1966): 306-335; vol.15 (1972): 223-242; vol.23 (1978): 283-308.

8963. Neuman, Inge S. (ed.): European War Crimes Trials: A Bibliography [New York: Carnegie Endowement for International Peace, 1951]

8964. Phillips, Leona: Hitler: An Annotated Bibliography [New York: Gordon Press, 1976]

8965. Piekarz, M. (ed.): The Holocaust and its Aftermath As Seen Through Hebrew Periodicals vol.15 [1978] <see #8985>

8966. ___ (ed.): The Holocaust and its Aftermath: Hebrew Books Published in the Years 1933-1972 vols. 13-14 [1974] <see #8985>

8967. ___ (ed.): The Jewish Holocaust and Heroism Through the Eyes of the Hebrew Press vols.5-8 [1966] <see #8985>

8968. Reiss, Asher: "A Quarter Century of Books on the Warsaw Ghetto Battle." JBA, vol.26 (1968/69): 23-33.

8969. Robinson, Jacob and Ada J. Friedman (eds.): The Holocaust and After: Sources and Documents in English vol.12 [1978] <see #8985>

8970. ___ and Philip Friedman (eds.): Guide to Jewish History Under Nazi Impact vol.1 [1960] <see #8985>

8971. Schneiderman, Harry: "Books of the War Years." JBA, vol.3 (1944/45): 45-51.

8972. Showalter, Dennis E.: German Military History, 1648-1942 [New York: Garland Pub., 1984]

8973. Singerman, R.: Antisemitic Propaganda: An Annotated Bibliography and Research Guide [New York: Garland Pub., 1982]

8974. Stachura, P. D.: The Weimar Era and Hitler 1918-1933: A Critical Bibliography [Oxford: Clio Press, 1977]

8975. Szonyi, David M. (ed.): The Holocaust: An Annotated Bibliography and Resource Guide [New York: National Jewish Resource Center, 1984]

8976. Weinberg, David: "The Holocaust in Historical Perspective." Sherwin: Encountering, pp.52-83.

8977-8983. Wolff, Ilse R. and Helen Kerr (eds.): The Wiener Library Catalogue Series 7 vols. [London: Valentine Mitchell for the Wiener Library, 1949-1978]

1. Persecution and Resistance Under the Nazis (1949)
2. From Weimar to Hitler: Germany, 1918-1933 (1958)
3. German Jewry (1958)
4. After Hitler: Germany, 1945-1966 (1963)
5. Prejudice: Racist, Religious, Nationalist (1971)
6. German Jewry Part II (1978)
7. Persecution and Resistance Under the Nazis (1978)

8984. Woodman, Gayle M.: "Bibliography of Periodicals: The Holocaust, 1939-1945." Ryan: Responses, pp.261-278.

8985. Yad Vashem-YIVO Joint Bibliographic Series 15 vols. [Jerusalem/New York: Yad Vashem/YIVO, 1960/1978] * See individual volumes under their editors.

8986. YIVO Institute of Jewish Research: Desiderata of Nazi Literature on the Jews [New York: YIVO, 1945]

Reference Works

8987. Aster, Sidney (ed.): British Foreign Policy 1918-1945 vol.4 <see #9000>

8988. Baer, George W. (ed.): International Organizations 1918-1945 vol.5 <see #9000>

8989. Bernstein, T.: "Documents in the Archives of Poland: A Basis for Historical Research Concerning the Jewish Population During the Nazi Occupation." YVS, vol.3 (1959): 67-76.

8990. Brugioni, Dino and R. G. Poirier: The Holocaust Revisited [Springfield, VA: CIA National Technical Information Service, 1979] * Photos on Auschwitz.

8991. Cassels, Alan (ed.): Italian Foreign Policy 1918-1945 vol.3 <see #9000>

8992. Catalogue of Camps and Prisoners in Germany and Ger- German-Occupied Territories 2 vols. [Arolsen, Ger.: International Tracing Service, 1949/1950] * Catalogue supplement published in 1951.

8993. Crowe, David M. Jr.: "The Holocaust: Documents in the National Archives of the United States." Am J His, vol.70 #3 (March, 1981): 362-378.

8994. Distel, B. and R. Jakusch (eds.) (J. Vernon, transl.): Concentration Camp Dachau 1933-1945 [Brussels: Comite International de Dachau, 1978] * Museum guide.

8995. Gilbert, M.: The Holocaust [London: Board of Deputies of British Jews, 1978]

8996. ___: The Macmillan Atlas of the Holocaust [New York: Macmillan, 1982]

Well researched and extensive cartographic history of the Holocaust. An important and useful reference, research, and teaching tool.

8997. Not Used.

8998. Guide to Unpublished Materials of the Holocaust Period J. Robinson, Y. Bauer and S. Krakowski (eds.) 6 vols. [Jerusalem: Hebrew University and Yad Vashem, 1970/1979]

8999. In Everlasting Remembrance: A Guide to Memorials and Monuments Honoring the Six Million [New York: American Jewish Committee, 1969]

9000. Kimmich, Christoph M. (general editor): The European Diplomatic History Series: Guides to Research and Research Materials 5 vols. [Wilmington, DE: Scholarly Resources, 1980] * See individual volumes under their editors.

9001. ___ (ed.): German Foreign Policy, 1918-1945 vol.1 <see #9000>

9002. Klibansky, B.: "The Archives of the Late Dr. Abraham Silberschein." YVB, #13 (Oct., 1963): 69-71.

9003. Levai, Eugene (Jeno): "Research Facilities in Hungary Concerning the Catastrophe Period." HJS, vol.1 (1966): 261-293.

9004. Mendelsohn, John: "The Holocaust: Rescue and Relief Documentation in the National Archives." Annals, #450 (July, 1980): 237-249.

9005. Scenes of Fighting and Martyrdom: Guide. War Years in Poland 1939-1945 [Warsaw: Sport i Turystyka, 1966]

9006. Smolen, Kazimierz (ed.): Auschwitz 1940-1945: Guide-Book Through the Museum [Oswiecim: Panstwowe Muzeum w Oswiecimiu, 1976]

9007. Struggle, Death, Memory: 1939-1945 [Warsaw: Art Pub., 1964]

9008. Szajkowski, Z.: An Illustrated Sourcebook of Russian Antisemitism 1881-1978 2 vols. [New York: Ktav, 1980]

Collection of visual materials that illustrate the status of Russian Jews in the last century. Evenly divided between the Czarist and Soviet suppression of Russian Jews, the main focus is on emigration.

9009. ___: An Illustrated Sourcebook on the Holocaust 3 vols. [New York: Ktav, 1977/1979]

Collection of visual materials illustrating the public nature of the Holocaust. Proves conclusively that information on the fate of European Jewry was widely, if not readily, available to all who might have been interested and shows the silent acceptance by Europeans in general, and Germans in particular, of the Final Solution.

9010. The Warsaw Ghetto in Pictures: Illustrated Catalogue Yiddish/Eng. [New York: YIVO Institute, 1970]

9011. Wigoder, Geoffrey (editor-in-chief): Encyclopaedia Judaica 16 vols. [Jerusalem: Keter Pub., 1971] * See individual articles under both geographic and topical headings.

9012. Yad Vashem: The Blackbook of Localities, Whose Jewish Polpulation was Exterminated by the Nazis [Jerusalem: Yad Vashem, 1965]

9013. Young, Robert (ed.): French Foreign Policy 1918-1945 vol.2 <see #9000>

9014. Yusim, Beverly: "Resources for the Study of the Holocaust." Sherwin: Encountering pp.473-500.

Index of Authors